EPIC MYTHOLOGY

GRUNDRISS DER INDO-ARISCHEN PHILOLOGIE UND ALTERTUMSKUNDE
(ENCYCLOPEDIA OF INDO-ARYAN RESEARCH)
BEGRUNDET VON G. BUHLER, FORTGESETZT VON F. KIELHORN,
HERAUSGEGEBEN VON H. LUDERS UND
J. WACKERNAGEL.

III. BAND, I HEFT B.

EPIC MYTHOLOGY

BY

E. WASHBURN HOPKINS

GYAN

Published by

GYAN

Gyan Publishing House
5, Ansari Road
Daryaganj, New Delhi-110002
Phone: 011-47034999, 9811692060
E-mail: books@gyanbooks.com

Distribution Network
gyanbooks.com
India, USA, Canada, UK, Australia, France

ISBN : 978-81-212-2496-3 (HB)
First Published, 1915

2nd Impression 2021

Printed at: Gyan Press, Delhi.

Epic Mythology
Author: E. Washburn Hopkins

GRUNDRISS DER INDO-ARISCHEN PHILOLOGIE UND ALTERTUMSKUNDE
(ENCYCLOPEDIA OF INDO-ARYAN RESEARCH)
BEGRÜNDET VON G. BÜHLER, FORTGESETZT VON F. KIELHORN,
HERAUSGEGEBEN VON H. LÜDERS UND J. WACKERNAGEL.

III. BAND, I. HEFT B.

EPIC MYTHOLOGY

BY

E. WASHBURN HOPKINS

STRASSBURG
VERLAG VON KARL J. TRÜBNER
1915

ENCYCLOPEDIA OF INDO-ARYAN RESEARCH

FOUNDED BY G. BÜHLER, CONTINUED BY F. KIELHORN,
EDITED BY H. LÜDERS AND J. WACKERNAGEL.

VOL. III, PART IB.

EPIC MYTHOLOGY

BY

E. WASHBURN HOPKINS.

I. INTRODUCTION.

§ 1. **Date of Epic Poetry.** — The mythology of the two epics of India represents in general the belief of the people of Northern India along the lower Ganges within a few centuries of the Christian era. For the Mahābhārata the time from 300 B. C. to 100 B. C. appears now to be the most probable date, though excellent authorities extend the limits from 400 B. C. to 400 A. D. The Mahābhārata as a whole is later than the Rāmāyaṇa; but R is metrically more advanced, the work of one author, a skilled metrician, who has improved the rougher epic form of the Mahābhārata, as his work represents a life less rude than that depicted in the great popular epic, this being the work of many hands and of different times. Both epics have received long additions. The germ of the Mahābhārata has been referred to the Vedic period and the Rāmāyaṇa has been assigned to pre-Buddhistic times (its germ also recognised as Vedic), but the data, in part negative, oppose the assumption that either epic poem existed before the fourth century B. C. Discussion is futile without a careful definition of the word "germ". That the Rāmāyaṇa was the norm, according to which the Mahābhārata was built, or that the Rāmāyaṇa was completed as it is to-day (barring the first and last books) before the Mahābhārata was begun, are theses impossible to establish. The Rāmāyaṇa has two flagrant additions, books one and seven. The Mahābhārata has been increased by the late addition of the Harivaṃśa (perhaps 200 A. D.), and much of the first book is late. By the fourth century this epic was recognised as a poem of one hundred thousand verses, and it has been argued[1]) that this implies the existence of the Harivaṃśa at that time. Such may be the case,

[1]) For example, by Professor Macdonell, Sanskrit Literature, p. 267. The reasons for assuming an earlier date for both epics than that accepted above are set forth in this chapter of Macdonell's work. In regard to the kernel of the great epic, referred to about 1000 B. C., it may be questioned whether the war between Kurus and Pañcālas is the historical germ of the epic at all. Professor Winternitz, Geschichte der Indischen Literatur, p. 396, arguing from the fact that the Tipiṭaka does not know either epic, though it shows acquaintance with the story of Rāma, assumes the termini 400 B. C. to 400 A. D. for the present Mahābhārata. The Rāmāyaṇa, he thinks, was "made by Vālmīki probably in the fourth or third century B. C." (p. 439), before the Mahābhārata had its present form. Professor Jacobi in his excellent work, Das Rāmāyaṇa, regarding the Mbh. as due to the influence of Vālmīki (p. 78), is inclined to assign a much greater age to the Rāmāyaṇa. The germ of the Mbh. appears, however, to be older than the Rām.; it represents a ruder age as well as a ruder art.

since the (corrected) Northern version contains 84,126 verses, which, with the 16,375(526) verses of the Harivaṃśa, make 100,501(651) verses. But, on the other hand, it might be said, from the off-hand way the Hindus have of assigning a round number of verses to a poem, that they would be quite likely to refer to an epic even approximating one hundred thousand verses as a poem of a lakh of verses. Now the Southern recension, in so far as the recently published text represents it, has twelve thousand more verses than the Northern recension and, without the Harivaṃśa, contains 96,578 verses (or prose equivalents)[1], not including the circa two hundred extra verses of single manuscripts. It is therefore doubtful whether the attribution of a lakh of verses necessarily implies the existence, as part of the lakh, of the Harivaṃśa. Yet on the whole this is probable, owing to the fact that the expansion in S appears for the most part to be due rather to the inclusion of new material than to the retention of old passages. Important is the fact for the mythologist that the Harivaṃśa is more closely in touch with Purāṇic than with epic mythology. It is in fact a Purāṇa, and "epic mythology" may properly exclude it, as it may exclude the Uttara in the Rāmāyaṇa, though both are valuable here and there to complement epic material. In no case, however, may passages from either of these additions be assumed to represent epic ideas, although of course epic ideas may be contained in them. It is most probable that Śānti and Anuśāsana were books (XII and XIII) added to the original epic, but equally clear that they were included in the Mahābhārata containing a lakh of verses. They may be looked upon in general as later though not modern additions[2], yet as we know that one portion of Śānti has been enlarged in quite modern times[3], there should be no hesitation in granting that passages may have been added at any time within the last few centuries. The palpable additions made in the interest of sectarian belief in the Southern recension are merely an indication of what has probably happened in both epics. — Geographically, the Mahābhārata represents the western and the Rāmāyaṇa the eastern districts of Northern India, but only in a limited sense (circa Delhi to Benares). In general it may be said that middle India between the Ganges and Nerbudda was the country most familiar to the poets of both epics. North and South are fabulous but travelled lands. The Punjab is better known but lies remote.

§ 2. **The Concept Deva.** — Epic mythology, however, is fairly consistent. There is no great discrepancy between the character of any one god in Mbh. and that of the same god in R. Nor is the character of gods very different in different parts of Mbh., save for the sectarian tendency to invert the positions of the three highest gods in favor of the sect. There are of course differences, but not such as to imply that we are dealing with totally diverse conceptions or traditions. In both epics the older gods

[1]) In reckoning the verses of the Northern recension, account must be taken of the egregious typographical errors in the Calcutta edition, which in Vana make eleven thousand odd into seventeen thousand odd verses, in Udyoga convert six thousand one hundred into seven thousand, etc. The Bombay Vana has 11,712 verses as contrasted with 12,082 in the Southern (S) recension. The total sum 84,126 is the number for C as corrected by B. As an indication of the difference between S and B-C, Ādi has 11,080 verses in S, 8479 in C.

[2]) Śānti in S has 15,050 and Anuśāsana 11,184 verses, as contrasted with 13,943 and 7,796 in the Northern recension. Holtzmann, Das Mahābhārata, I, 194, argued for a modern epic throughout, but this view has not been substantiated.

[3]) In Śānti, Parv. 342 to 353, S has many more sectarian additions in honor of the Nārāyaṇa lauded in these interpolated chapters.

are reduced in estate, in so far as they represent personifications of nature; in both, new gods are throned above the old. The conception Deva, god, embraces all spiritual characters, as it is said, "the gods beginning with Brahman and ending with Piśācas" (Brahmādayaḥ Piśācāntā 'yaṃ hi devā upāsate)[1]), but loosely, so that in the very clause thus specifying the host of gods, Śiva, as the greatest god, is set in antithesis to them all as the one being through devotion to whom even Kṛṣṇa-Viṣṇu pervades the universe. Nor is the world of men without close kinship with the gods, who descend to earth and are reborn as mortals. Not Viṣṇu alone but those who worship him become earthly Avatars. Kuśika is permeated with Indra, and Gādhi, son of Kuśika, is in reality son of Indra; in other words, for the purpose of having a son Gādhi, Indra becomes incorporate; Gādhi is Indra on earth (putratvam agamad rājaṃs tasya lokeśvareśvaraḥ, Gādhir nāmā 'bhavat putraḥ Kauśikaḥ Pākaśāsanaḥ, 12, 49, 6).

II. THE LOWER MYTHOLOGY.

§ 3. **Definition.** — It is obvious that a mythology which on the one hand touches upon that of the Purāṇas and on the other reaches back to the Vedic age may best be presented chronologically, and this would be the case were it not that there is an aspect of mythology which does not fit into this scheme. This will be referred to again under the head of General Characteristics. At present it will suffice to say that at all times in India there has been under the higher mythology of gods and great demons a lower mythology of spiritualised matter less remote than the gods of sun, storm, etc., and less remote even than the recognised spirits inhabiting yet not confined to such matter, spirits that receive their proper recognition in the pantheon. Though this lower mythology has various aspects which blend it with the higher, as in the case of the Corn-mother already absorbed into a title of a high goddess, yet in part it stands aloof and may be treated separately, at least in its broad divisions of river- and mountain-mythology, the lesser traits of divine trees and pools being more conveniently discussed under the head of the divinities into whose province the lower spirits have been drawn.

§ 4. **Divine Rivers.** — Water has always had a healing (hence supernatural or divine) power. The epic recognises this, but in conjunction with the act of a god. Thus a god revives the dead with a handful of water, though a divine fiat is sufficient for this purpose, or the use of a magical plant[2]). But as a self-conscious power, aiding the right, water also dries up before a sinful priest, who tries to escape by way of water (as a guard against evil influence; compare the popular notion that evil spirits cannot pass running water). Water is also a divine witness against wrong, for which reason one who curses or takes any oath touches water, as one does in accepting a gift. In fact in any solemn event a sort of bap-

[1]) This inclusion of Piśācas under Devas occurs in the exaltation of Śiva in 13, 14, 4 and verses added in S to 13, 45. Ordinarily the Devas exclude the demons; they are as light to darkness, but (as shown below) all spiritual beings are sons of the Father-god and so all are divine. It is rather the nature of the individual which determines whether he is "god" or "demon", than the class to which he is assigned.

[2]) See the writer's paper on Magic Observances in the Hindu Epic (Am. Philosophical Society, vol. XLIX). In 12, 153, 113, S has pāṇinā for cakṣuṣā. For the other examples, see 3, 136, 9f.; 1, 74, 30; 3, 110, 32; and the cases cited, loc. cit.

tism of water takes place, for water is one of the "three purities". As truth is another "purity", a speaker of the truth can walk over water without sinking[1]). The priestly influence predominant in the epics proclaims (3, 193, 36) the sin-expelling quality of water sprinkled by the hand of a priest, and this is the idea of the Tīrtha, that it has been made effective through an outer influence, priestly or divine, which imparts power to wash away ill-luck and sin or to bestow upon the bather "beauty and fortune" (3, 47, 29:82, 43 f.). But the cult of such powers, though constantly recommended by the less orthodox writers of the epic, is not in conformity with the sacred writings and is not infrequently depreciated, as a deśātithi or "cultivator of places" stands opposed to the view that "all rivers are Sarasvatīs" (12, 264, 40), that is, all rivers are holy in themselves; though certainly the modified view, for example that "rivers are hallowed if Rāma bathes in them" (R 2, 48, 9), is normal. This example also shows that rivers and ponds are regarded as living persons, to whom the predicate kṛtapuṇyāḥ (blessed or hallowed) can properly apply. Especially holiness attaches to the Payoṣṇī, because of its relics; to the Cauvery, because of its nymphs; to the Godāvarī, because of its saints and contact with Rāma; to the Ganges, because of Rāma's passage over it; and to any union of river with river or with ocean, because the sacred nature of each is doubled by contact with the other (3, 85, 22 f. and R 4, 41, 15). The Cauvery is "half the Ganges" but at the same time is wife of Jahnu and daughter of Yuvanāśva (H 1421 f.), as all rivers are wives of ocean, though not always so completely anthropomorphised[2]). Offerings are made to rivers and they are invoked for aid as divine beings (R 2, 55, 4 f.; ibid. 4, 40, 9), the offerings when made by Sītā being a thousand cows and a hundred jars of brandy, perhaps intended eventually for the priests. Although over a hundred and sixty divine rivers are mentioned by name (6, 9, 14 f.; ibid. 11, 31 f.; 3, 188, 102 f.; ibid. 222, 22 f.; 13, 166, 19 f.) and the Rāmāyaṇa says that five hundred rivers furnished water for Rāma's consecration (R 6, 131, 53), yet the time-honored designation Five Rivers is still used (Indus being the sixth) to designate a group sometimes also vaguely called the Seven Rivers, this latter group including the Ganges (see below). The Five are named as the (modern) Sutlej, Beas, Ravi, Chinab, and Jhelum (8, 44, 31 f.). As the rivers are recipients of offerings, so in turn they make to Indra an offering of praise but are overawed by the presence of Śiva and, like the birds, when he appears, cease to make a sound (3, 96, 6; 5, 17, 22). Their bestowal of purification may be unconscious, owing to their divine purity, but they consciously save as well. Thus the Beas and Samaṅgā (3, 139, 9 f.; 13, 3, 13) act consciously in saving a man from drowning. All these rivers used to bear gold, but now only Ganges has that bye-product of Śiva's seed (7, 56, 6, etc.). The mental state of rivers is often alluded to as a matter of course. They are troubled in mind, run backward in fear, or cease to flow in mental distress (8, 94, 49; R 5, 16, 4, etc.). Ganges converses with Ocean and explains why huge trees but not slender reeds are carried on her waves (the trees resisting are overwhelmed, the reeds by bending

[1]) Both Pṛthu Vainya and Dilīpa, as "speakers of truth" pass over water without sinking, even in a battle-car (7, 61, 9 f.; 69, 9).

[2]) For further references, see The Sacred Rivers of India in (the Toy volume) Studies in the History of Religions, p. 215. Few rivers are masculine, though male rivers, Indus, Oxus, Lohita, Śoṇa, etc., are representatives of the masculine form (but also Śoṇā, fem.) and Ocean is "lord of rivers male and rivers female" (R 3, 35, 7, etc.).

escape destruction, 12, 113, 2 f.); she also explains to Umā the habits of good women (13, 146, 17 f.). The river is sometimes a reborn saint, as the Cosy (Kauśikī) is an Avatar of Satyavatī, wife of Viśvāmitra (R 1, 34, 8), as in the Purāṇas Gaurī, wife of Prasenajit, became the river Bāhudā. On the other hand, the Nerbudda (Narmadā) became the wife of the king Purukutsa (15, 20, 13). This river fell in love with a Duryodhana, by whom she had a fair daughter, Sudarśanā, whose son in turn married Oghavatī and "half of her became a river" (13, 2, 18 f.). A crooked river, hence evil, may be in effect an evil woman reborn. Thus Ambā remained in life half as a human being and half as a crooked river (5, 186, 41). Sons of rivers are human heroes. Bhīṣma is son of Ganges; Śrutāyudha is son of the river Parṇāśā, by Varuṇa (cf. § 63; 7, 92, 44 f.); Duṣyanta is great-great-grandson of the Sarasvatī, whose son was Sārasvata. Śuktimatī was a river who became the mother of a son by a mountain (1, 63, 35 f.; ibid. 95, 27; 9, 51, 17 f.). As intimated apropos of Ambā, a river may represent sinful power, but the Vaitaraṇī is the only river leading to hell, under the name Puṣpodakā (Vaitaraṇī being a sacred stream of Kalinga as well as the river of hell, 3, 200, 58; 8, 77, 44). The Yamunā (Jumna) is called Kālindī from the mountain Kalinda, and its place of union with the Ganges is celebrated as holy (Bharadvāja's hermitage is there); but it is often omitted from lists where it might be expected to appear, as in 13, 146, 18 f., where Ganges is the glorious last of a list of sacred rivers: Vipāśā ca Vitastā ca Candrabhāgā Irāvatī, Śatadrur Devikā Sindhuḥ Kauśikī Gautamī tathā, tathā devanadī ce 'yaṃ sarvatīrthābhisaṃbhṛtā, gaganād gāṃ gatā devī Gaṅgā sarvasaridvarā. Ganges is here apparently derived from her "going" (cf. Sarasvatī and European parallels from roots meaning go or run). She is the most completely personified of all the holy rivers, not only as mother of Bhīṣma, Gāṅgeya, āpagāsuta, āpageya, nadīja, and of Kumāra (Kumārasū, H 1081) but as co-wife with Umā of Śiva, and as assuming human form, to become wife of Śāntanu (1, 98, 5). She is called "daughter of Jahnu" (ibid. 18), Jahnusutā and Jāhnavī, and "daughter of Bhagīratha", by adoption, though her true patronymic it not Bhāgīrathī but Haimavatī (6, 119, 97), as she is the daughter of the Himālaya mountain. Her title among the gods is Alakanandā, and as she is regarded as identified with other streams so she is identified with Puṣpodakā Vaitaraṇī (1, 170, 22). Usually she is spoken of as threefold, three-pathed, as in 6, 6, 28 f., where Sarasvatī, Ganges, is said to issue from the world of Brahman and to fall like milk from Mount Meru into the lake of the moon, which her own fall has created, after being upheld for one hundred thousand years on Śiva's head. She is said to be both visible and invisible and is represented as divided into seven streams, the names of which vary but appear in the Mahābhārata as (6, 6, 50) Vasvaukasārā, Nalinī, Pāvanī, Jambūnadī, Sītā, Gaṅgā, and Sindhu. In the Rāmāyaṇa (1, 43, 12) the Hlādinī and Sucakṣu take the place of the first and fourth. She appeared first at Bindusaras (6, 6, 44 f.; R 1, 43, 10), when Bhagīratha induced her to come to earth to baptise the bones of Sagara's sons, since till that was done these sons could not attain to heaven (3, 108, 18). The famous story of her descent is told in R 1, 43. As she sank when weary upon the lap of Bhagīratha, she is said to have chosen him for her father (cf. 3, 109, 18 f.; and 7, 60, 6 f.). The Southern recension says that she was angry at being forced to go to hell and got caught in Śiva's hair (cf. R 1, 43, 5). She is three-fold as the river of sky, earth, and the lower regions, tripathagā, trilokagā, etc., and her titles incorporated into Tīrthas called Tri-Gaṅga and Sapta-Gaṅga, Sapta-Sārasvata-Tīrtha (3, 84, 29; 13, 25, 6f.) preserve the double account. As the three-pathed Ganges she is called veṇīkṛtajalā (R 2, 50, 16, here "wife of Ocean"), but the post-epical Triveṇi refers to the mystic union of "three-stranded" Ganges with the Yamunā and (lesser) Sarasvatī at Prayāga (Allahābād). At this place the holiness of the river exceeds all bounds. A bath at Prayāga, "the lap of earth", imparts more virtue than do all the Vedas, and Ganges is here "the one Tīrtha of the (Kali) age" (3, 85, 75 and 90). Ganges and Yamunā are invoked together by Sītā (R 2, 52, 82 f.). At the entrance to the ocean (it is said, 1, 170, 19 f.), Ganges divides into seven streams (cf. 6, 119, 76 and 7, 36, 13) and "one is purified from sin who drinks the waters of Ganges, Yamunā, Sarasvatī (Plakṣajātā), Rathasthā, Sarayū, Gomatī, or Gaṇḍakī." According to R 1, 43, 12 f., there is a (later) division into the three Ganges of the East, namely the Hlādinī, Pāvanī, and Nalinī; those of the West, Sucakṣu (Oxus?), Sītā, and Sindhu; and, seventh, "she who became Bhagīratha's daughter". In this epic too the origin of Ganges's title Jāhnavī is explained. Jahnu swallows Ganges because he is disturbed by her flood but lets her out through his ears on condition that she be known as his issue. The same late book of R makes Manoramā (or Menā) the mother of Ganges (R 1, 35, 16). This nymph was daughter of Mount Meru, and wife of Himavat, and bore him two daughters, Gaṅgā and Umā (a Purāṇic legend). Ganges's place of origin (Gaṅgotri), the so-called Gate, Gaṅgādvāra (Hardwar), the place of her union with Yamunā, and, fourth, the place where she "unites with Ocean" (debouches into the gulf of Bengal), have always been the most sacred spots in her course. Gaṅgādvāra (13, 166, 26) and Prayāga are the most famous in the epic. The river has stairs (ghaṭs), gold in her bosom, etc. As a divine being she is "destroyer of sin", identical with Pṛśni ("mother of Viṣṇu") and with Vāc, and renowned as "daughter of Himavat, wife of Śiva, and mother of Skanda". She is also called Viṣṇupadī (coming from Viṣṇu's toe? See 13, 26, a chapter devoted to her, and R 2, 50, 26; VP. 4, 4, 15.) As above, she is also "wife of Ocean" as well as wife of Śiva (3, 99, 32; 187, 19; R 2, 50, 25). Mandākinī is a name she shares with earthly rivers (5, 111, 12, etc.). Ākāśagaṅgā ("of the air") is her heavenly name (3, 142, 11). On the special adoration paid by Skanda's form to Ganges, see Skanda (§ 161). Devanadī and Suranadī, "river of the gods", are common titles in both epics; Lokanadī, river of the world, is found S 1, 186, 2. She is so anthropomorphised that when her son is fighting she appears on his chariot, holding the reins for him and guarding his life, as she previously gives him advice (5, 178, 68; 182, 12 f.). There is no epic authority for the belief that children were flung into the Ganges as sacrifices, though jhaṣas abound there (1, 228, 32).

§ 5. **Divine Trees and Groves.** — Many trees are holy from association with the gods. Thus the Śamī is the birth-place of Agni (13, 85, 44) and the Aśvattha, representing the male element in the production of fire, is also tabu (only ascetics live on its fruit), while all the samidhas, wood for sacrificial fires, are sacrosanct, Palāśa as well as Pippala (Aśvattha), and Śamī, and perhaps the tabu-trees, pratiṣiddhānna, the "fruit of which is forbidden", have a previous religious use as the reason for the tabu. These include besides those just mentioned the Vaṭa (ficus indica), Śaṇa (cannabis sativa), Śāka (tectona grandis) and the Udumbara (ficus glomerata)[1]. The Aśvattha is the chief of trees (it represents the life-tree) and typifies that tree of life which is rooted in God above (6, 34, 26; 39, 1 f.). To revere this tree is to worship God. Viṣṇu is identified with the Nyagrodha and Udumbara and Aśvattha (13, 126, 5 and 149, 101). The famous Nyagrodha of Vṛndāvana (mentioned only in S 2, 53, 8 f.) is called Bhāṇḍīra. Otherwise no local tree except the Akṣaya-Vaṭa of Gaya is noticed in the texts. It is so called because it immortalises the offerings given there to the Manes, marking the spot where the Asura Gaya fell or made sacrifice. It is not interpreted to mean an undying tree[2]. A mound or sacred edifice makes holy the tree upon it and in a village the "one tree" which is conspicuous is said to be caitya arcanīyaḥ supūjitaḥ, that is, revered like a divinity (1, 151, 33, grāma-druma). An unholy tree is the Vibhītaka (entered by Kali; see 3, 66, 41). Trees are sentient beings, able to hear, move, see, feel, as philosophically proved in 12, 184, 10 f. The trees themselves wish to do this or that (S 7, 16, 14), as distinct from the dryads or spirits in the tree, "goddesses born in trees, to be worshipped by those desiring children" (S 3, 231, 16, has Vṛkṣikā as dryad; B Vṛddhikā). The ten Pracetas married a "tree-girl", Vārkṣī (1, 196, 15). Such spirits of trees are revered especially in the Karañja tree (3, 230, 55), where dwells the tree-mother. The "daughter of the Red Sea", Lohitāyanī, the nurse of Skanda, is worshipped under a Kadamba tree (3, 230, 41). Śiva himself is not only the "tree" par excellence (S 7, 203, 32); he is formally identified with the Bakula, sandal-wood, and Chada trees (13, 17, 110). Gods, saints, and demi-gods live in and resort to trees (1, 30, 2; 13, 58, 29). It is, however, not the spirits in trees but the trees themselves that beg boons, enjoy marriage (with human beings), talk (§ 12 c), grant wishes, and, in some favored localities, go about at will.[3] A lamp is offered to the Karañjaka tree itself, and to cut down trees on the day of the new moon is a sin equal to that of murdering a priest (13, 123, 8 and 127, 3). The moon is here the source of vegetal energy. The five trees of Paradise can be transplanted to earth, and Kṛṣṇa thus robs Indra of the Pārijāta tree (5, 130, 49). The Saṃtānaka tree is found also in the world of cows (13, 81, 23) and in the heavenly hills of the North (5, 111, 13); it is mentioned with the Pārijāta (3, 231, 23). The Pārijāta in H 7168 f., is identified with the Mandāra tree, another heavenly, divya, tree, the flowers of which are offered by the Vidyādharas to the sun (3, 3, 42; all the allusions are late). The trees that grant wishes, Kalpavṛkṣas (1, 219, 3), are either magical or heavenly, but on occasion are to be found on earth (1, 29, 40; cf. kappa-

[1]) See the account in 13, 104, 92, and cf. 12, 40, 11; 13, 14, 58; the Palāśa is butea frondosa and the Pippala is the ficus religiosa. One may not use Palāśa wood to make a seat nor Tindukawood for toothpicks, though sinners do so (7, 73, 38; omitted in C but found in B and S).

[2]) See the writer's Great Epic of India, p. 83, note 2, and the references 3, 84, 83; 87, 11; 95, 14; 7, 66, 20; 13, 88, 14; R 2, 107, 13. In general, all Caitya trees are homes of spirits (12, 69, 41 f.).

[3]) Compare 7, 69, 5 f.; 3, 115, 35 f. Tree-marriages are still practiced (JAOS. 22, pp. 228 and 328) to avoid the evil effect of a marriage with a third human bride (the tree is made to receive the threatened disaster). Trees going about at will (5, 100, 15, etc.) generally produce any kind of fruit or flower, i. e. they are magical trees belonging to some superior region. They are called kāmacārin and kāmapuṣpaphala in Hiraṇyapur (loc. cit.). The dryads are vegetal divinities that eat human flesh and have to be appeased with offerings, though the tree-mother is kind (3, 230, 35 f.), but the sentient trees are usually kindly, as all of them used to be (7, 69, 5 f.). On seeing golden trees, as a sign of death, cf. JAOS. 30, p. 351.

rukkho). The Kālāmra tree is a mango a league high east of Meru (6, 7, 14 f.). Its juice gives immortal youth. Sudarśana is the name of the Jambūvṛkṣa, which grants all desires. It is one thousand and one hundred leagues high, touching the sky, and like the preceding tree (of Bhadrāśva Dvīpa) is frequented by saints and heavenly beings. It bears red gold in its juice which makes a river flowing around Meru to the Uttara (Northern) Kurus (6, 7, 20 f.). The Ganges rises from the root of the great jujube tree on Kailāsa (3, 142, 4 f.; 145, 51).

These individual heavenly trees grow between earth and heaven and it is on the mountains that the divine groves are found. The grove of Deodars (13, 25, 27), the grove of Kadalīs on Mt. Gandhamādana (3, 146, 51 f.) are typical of the vanaṃ divyam or devāraṇyāni (5, 14, 6; 186, 27), which are sacred to the gods and in which the gods perform religious rites. Such a sacred grove is found by Yudhiṣṭhira on his journey (3, 118, 9 f.), where there are altars (shrines) of saints and gods, Vasus, Maruts, (Gaṇas), Aśvins, Yama, Āditya, Kubera, Indra, Viṣṇu, Savitṛ, Bhava, Candra, the maker of day (Sūrya), the lord of waters (Varuṇa), the troops of Sādhyas, Dhātṛ, the Pitṛs, Rudra with his troop, Sarasvatī, the troop of Siddhas, "and whatever immortals there be". These groves are the parallel to the nemus and lucus of the Roman, Teuton, etc.

§ 6. **Divine Mountains.** — Every mountain is a potential divinity, as well as a resort of the gods, Gandharvas, etc. The mountains north of India lend themselves especially well to the notion that snow-clad hills pierce heaven, but as these mountains are invisible from the lower habitat of the epic poets, most of the particular descriptions must have been generalised from hearsay. The range south of the Ganges is treated more familiarly. Here lies, for example, the mountain referred to above, who begot a son on a river (1, 63, 35 f.) and a daughter who became wife of Vasu, Girikā. This mountain, Kolāhala, is expressly "intelligent". Mountains speak (R 5, 1, 111, Maināka in human form; cf. 12, 333, 30 as echo, 334, 25); they revere Śiva and Indra (13, 14, 399; 5, 17, 22); and they are themselves revered (1, 220, 6; 13, 166, 31 f.; 14, 59, 4 f.), as is one in a mahas tasya mahāgireḥ or "feast in honor of the mountain", by the offerings of fruits, flowers, etc. In 2, 21, 20, a hill called Caityaka is revered as the place where a māṃsāda ṛṣabha (minotaur) was slain, the help of the mountain being perhaps implied. Hills bewail Sītā (R 3, 52, 39). The mountain Ariṣṭa wakes at dawn, opens his eyes of metal, stretches his arms of Deodars; yawns with peaks; speaks in waters (R 5, 56, 10 f.). The high place especially favored by the gods as their meeting-ground as well as dwelling-place, is always a hill, the higher the better; hence a preference for the northern mountains as tridaśānāṃ samāgamaḥ, "assembly of gods" (3, 39, 40), where, on the top of Himavat, they sacrificed of old (7, 54, 25), for this is the locality "beloved of gods" (3, 37, 39). "Seven Mountains" (like other sevens) designates the several ancient "doors of heaven", renowned as Kulaparvatas in 6, 9, 11. The Seven are the Orissa chain, the southern part of the Western Ghats, and the northern part (these three beeing called Mahendra, Malaya, and Sahya), the range called Śuktimat (in the east), the Gondwana range called Ṛkṣavat, the (Eastern) Vindhya, and the Northern and Western Vindhya called Pāriyātra; among which Mahendra (from which Hanumat leaps, R 4, 67, 43) is best known to the epic poets as a sacred place (R 5, 43, 5; Mbh. 1, 215, 13; 3, 85, 16, etc.; R 4, 42, 18 f., Pāriyātra as Western). In 14, 43, 3 f., seven trees and twelve mountains are called "kings", but in calling Arjuna the "eighth mountain" (S 4, 3, 36) the epic reverts to the old phraseology[1]). Legends abound in regard to the mountains as holy beings as well as holy places. Like saints and gods they perform sacrifice (12, 321, 182). "Wingless" (and winged) mountains refers to the legend (R 5, 1, 125) of Indra cutting off the wings (clouds) of mountains and making earth firm (RV. 2, 12, 2; MS. 1, 10, 13), as this expression is used e. g. in 7, 26, 65 and ib. 37; also 7, 103, 6 (at the present day mountains do not move as of old); R 3, 51, 4, etc. Himavat is Śailaguru (9, 51, 34) and his son is Mainâka, whose son in turn is Krauñca, who, however, is also called son of Himavat. Mainâka alone escaped when Indra cut off the wings of other mountains, and this mountain appears as type of stability (7, 3, 4f.; 9, 12f.), as it stood firm against Nagâri (Indra). It lies north of Kailâsa, beyond Krauñca (R 4, 43, 31); a barrier against Asuras (R 5, 1, 93) and in it Maya deposited, near Bindusaras, a mass of gems. It has a vinaśana (cleft), where Aditi cooked food for the sake of her son of old (3, 135, 3). It escaped Indra's design and Ocean gave it refuge (1, 21, 15). Mainâka's son, Krauñca (R 6, 67, 19), is the White Mountain of silver as contrasted with "golden Himavat" (3, 188, 112; 13, 166, 30f.), but also "golden" (R 6, 126, 14). Seven-headed dragons guard it and in it is a golden lake, where the mothers of (Skanda) Kumâra nursed him. Shot at by Skanda, Krauñca fled but returned and was pierced and "fell shrieking" and then again fled (3, 225, 10f.; 9, 46, 84). Though son of Himavat and Menakâ it is called "Rudra's seed" (3, 229, 28), that is, it consists in the seed of the god, elsewhere described as the seed of Agni-Rudra cast into Ganges (8, 90, 68; 9, 17, 51; 44, 9; 13, 85, 68). R 7, 104, 6, however, makes all mountains from the bones of Madhu and Kaiṭabha (creation of Râma-Viṣṇu). Mainâka leaps out of ocean to hinder Hanumat (R 5, 1, 92f.; "mountains under the sea", ib. 3, 33, 6). It lies "in the West" according to 3, 89, 11.

The Vindhya legend represents that home of plants and metals (13, 166, 31) as angry with the sun for refusing to walk the deasil around it (as men and gods should "walk the deasil" around a divine mountain, 1, 220, 6) and hence as growing to obstruct the sunlight despite the request of the gods to stop. Agastya persuaded it to let him pass over and not grow till he returned and the Vindhya still awaits the saint's return (3, 103, 16 and 104, 12f.). The belief in a totem-mountain obtains. Balâdhi, the saint, desired an immortal son; the gods granted a son whose life should not end till the object in which his life was bound up should perish. The life of the son Medhâvin was therefore bound up in an "indestructible" mountain, but being sinful he provoked Dhanuṣâkṣa, a saint who took the form of a buffalo and destroyed the mountain, and therewith Medhâvin also. Dhanuṣâkṣa in S transforms himself into the buffalo; other versions make the animals the means used by the saint (S 3, 135, 52f.). Other mountains sacred if not so personally conceived as is the case with Mandara, Krauñca, Mainâka, and Himavat, are the mount where the ark landed (3, 187, 50, Naubandhana); the hill Govardhana, upheld by Kṛṣṇa (5, 130,

[1]) The Seven Mountains, known as doors of heaven, appear in Vedic literature (TS. 3, 12, 2, 9; 6, 2, 4, 3). Viṣṇu is here the lord of hills, not Śiva (3, 4, 5, 1). In Śâkadvîpa the seven remain in epic descriptions (6, 11, 13). Bhṛgutuṅga, Agastyavaṭa and Mt. Kuñjara, "Vasiṣṭha's mountain", and other peaks show that saints as well as gods live on the hills, the sanctity of which destroys sin, as in the case of Hemakûṭa (Ṛṣabhakûṭa), the "divine grove of Brahman", where silence must be observed, tûṣṇîm âssva (3, 114, 16). Hariv. has Purâṇic additions (Meghagiri, 12846, etc.).

46, etc.); Mahendra, where Rāma lived after extirpating the warriors (7, 70, 21 f.); the beryl-mountain on the Narmadā where Kauśika drank Soma with the Aśvins and Cyavana paralysed Indra (3, 89, 13 and 121, 19); Mandara (R 3, 47, 39), used by the gods to churn the ocean (1, 18, 13; R 1, 45 = 46, 18 f.); Gandhamādana, home of medicinal plants and groves leading to heaven (7, 139, 86, etc.). Mandara lies east of Meru and Gandhamādana and is the home of Kubera and his Yakṣas, hurled to its place in the east by the hand of Viṣṇu (3, 139, 5; 163, 4; 101, 15). Although placed in the north and south as well as the east (5, 111, 12 and 109, 9) and even in the west (ib 110, 9), it is more regularly an eastern hill and is probably the modern Mandaragiri near Bhagalpur. Its "western" location implies that its roots extend to the western ocean, as Himavat does also. Gandhamādana is especially the abode of Kubera, though also of Indra; Kailāsa of Śiva; Meru of Brahman; but all the gods live on occasion on any of these. The gods seeking Śiva find him on Mandara (7, 94, 57), and Brahman receives audience on Gandhamādana (6, 65, 42). Certain mountains, however, are formally assigned to certain gods. The demons also live where gods live. Rākṣasas live on Himavat; Guhyakas on Kailāsa; serpents and Nāgas on Niṣadha; all the gods and Asuras on the White Mountain (Śveta); Gandharvas on Niṣadha; and Brahmarṣis on Nīla, "but the resort of gods is the peaked hill" (6, 6, 51 f.). As the hills are all peaked with three or a hundred peaks assigned to different hills, and only devī Śaṇḍilī, Agni's mother, is ascribed to Mt. Śṛṅgavat (like Meru it has three peaks), a special or general range of peaked hills may be meant.[1]) Mandara has two peaks, is shaped like a bow (R 4, 31, 11; R 5, 22, 27). Himavat is described as "a mine of gems of all sorts, cultivated by saints and singers, called the holy father-in-law of Śaṅkara" (Śiva, R 4, 11, 12 f.; 13, 25, 62). He is father of Ganges and Umā (above) and father of Mt. Abu (3, 82, 55). Kailāsa is the most famous range in Himavat and lies beside the upper Ganges near Mt. Maināka beyond the Northern Kurus (3, 145, 17 f.; S 1, 243, 31). Both Kailāsa and Gandhamādana have the monster jujube; Kṛṣṇa once lived on Kailāsa (3, 12, 43, not S). Later the two are different hills. In 6, 6, 1 f., Gandhamādana lies north of Mālyavat (the "flame-encircled" home of saints who precede Aruṇa, 6, 7, 28), which is north of Niṣadha, which in turn lies west of Kailāsa. Mt. Meru has three peaks, reaches higher than the sun, has rocks and red sides like other mountains (e. g. Citrakūṭa, R 2, 94, 4 f.), is self-luminous, the abode of gods, etc., and is thirty-three thousand leagues in extent and eighty-four thousand high. On its slopes and top sit saints and gods. It lies north of Gandhamādana and is especially the home of Prajāpati and the spiritual sons of Brahman, and there rise and set the seven divine seers. But above its peak is the home of Viṣṇu. The sun and stars revolve around it. Yet it is like other hills, "beaten by rain", and appears to be thought of as one among many northern hills, having a vinaśana like Maināka's (above). Sumeru in Mbh. is not an antithetic mountain but an epithet of Meru itself. Meru forms one of seven ranges running across Jambūdvīpa and is represented by the flag-staff in the gods's allegorical car. Only R Uttara knows Sumeru as the name of an independent mountain (R 7, 35, 19), the home of Kesarin. South and

[1]) Cf. 6, 8, 9 and 13, 123, 2 f. Śiva and Umā live by predilection in the Karṇikāra grove on Meru; Garuḍa lives on Hiraṇmaya; the Gandharvas on Mandara, Meru, etc. Harigiri is in Kuśadvīpa (6, 6, 24 f. to 12, 11).

east of Meru lie the ranges Niṣadha, Hemakūṭa (Kailāsa), and Himavat, the thousand leagues between each making a valley, varṣa; and north and west of it lie Nīla, Śveta, and Śṛṅgavat (on the sea). Kaśyapa (Caspian?) lies farther west and Nāgadvīpa (S, Śāka-) lies south of the whole group (6, 6, 56). The oceans are four or seven (several). The original conception is that of four seas around earth, into which run four rivers from the middle mountain, and round the flanks of Meru lie the four lands Bhadrāśva, Ketumāla, Jambūdvīpa, and the Northern Kurus (Hyperboreans), ib. 12. But the peak of Himavat joins that of Meru (they clash together like Symplegades, 12, 334, 9f.). The epic knows nothing of the seven planetary spheres as such (even 13, 16, 34 and 52 do not imply them), and nothing of Meru as axis of the world.[1]) The addition of Maharloka, Janaloka, Tapoloka, and Satyaloka to the epic three, Bhūrloka, Svarloka, and Bhuvarloka, is Purāṇic; it names the previously (Vedic-Epic) seven bhuvanas or worlds hitherto sufficiently understood as a group. Rām. treats Meru as if one of the mountains of earth (one flying looks down upon Himavat, Vindhya, and Meru from above, R 4, 61, 9), it is "a very big hill", a range "like a snake lying in water" (ib.). Its "three peaks" may be conventional (cf. R 6, 91, 34). Later epic poets (RG 4, 44, 46; H 12853) know a hill Triśṛṅga (perhaps Himavat, cf. R 6, 69, 24). Maināka has a hundred golden peaks (R 5, 1, 105). The Sunrise and Sunset Mountains appear to be unmythological; they are merely where the sun may set and rise (udyadgiri is unique, R 7, 36, 44), unless Parvata Udyanta = Udaya (3, 84, 93) whereon the "track of Sāvitrī" is found. Himavat's "three daughters" are known only in H 940f. Their mother was Menā, spiritual daughter, of the Ṛṣis. One, Aparṇā-Umā, married Śiva (q. v.), one, Ekaparṇā, married Asita Devala, and the last, Ekapāṭalā, married Jaigīṣavya.

§ 7. **Vegetal Divinities.** — The epic poets naturally ignore as separate divinities those of whom they disapprove and those whom they do not understand. Such divinities are sometimes found hidden away in the sacred watering-places and sometimes they remain as titles of gods who have absorbed them; for the process of absorbing divinities into the name and glory of greater divinities began before history and continues to this day. In this manner are concealed both vegetal and animal gods. Of the magic of the Tīrtha tales this is not the place to speak.[2]) They contain, however, traces of many deities lost or ignored. Thus with the Buddhist goddess Śaṅkhinī is to be compared the passage in 3, 83, 51, where a Tīrtha pilgrim is strongly advised to "go to the Śaṅkhinī Tīrtha and bathe in the Tīrtha of the goddess", in order to acquire a beautiful form. Although it is not expressly said that the Devī is Śaṅkhinī, yet the implication is that such is the case, not that Devī is one of the higher goddesses (in masculine form the epithet śaṅkhin is a title of Viṣṇu). Then there is the Tīrtha of the goddess Śākambharī (3, 84, 13), which must be the holy place of the local Corn-mother, utilised or adopted as a title of Durgā (6, 23, 9),

[1]) See for the details the references in JAOS. 30, 366f. Only S adds to 6, 6, 10 the words of VP. 2, 2, 8, to the effect than the apex of Meru is twice the size of its base. On plants and mountains as the fat and bones of ancient giant demons, see Rākṣasas, § 17. On gold and trees made by Agni, see § 49f. In R 6, 67, 67, Laṅkāmalaya is apparently the trikūṭa (a peak is broken off); ib. 3, 73, 32, Ṛṣyamūka is a mountain in the South where the dreams of the good come true; ib. 4, 37, 2f. has a list of southern hills.

[2]) Compare a paper on this subject in the Proc. Amer. Philosophical Society, vol. XLIX, 1910, p. 24f.

for Devī Śākambharī stands by herself as an independent[1]) goddess, though the narrator knows her only as a form of the great goddess into whom she was absorbed, and tells that the Tīrtha was so named because Durgā lived there on śāka or vegetable produce aud entertained her guests with vegetarian fare (3, 84, 16.) Sītā herself is a Corn-mother. She "rose in the field where the ploughshare brake it, rending the earth" (R 5, 16, 16 and ib. 2, 118, 28). She is represented by the ploughshare, which serves as Śalya's battle-sign and is likened to Sītā for its golden beauty sarvabījavirūḍhe 'va yathā Sītā śriyā 'vṛtā (7, 105, 20).[2]) To this category belongs also the youngest wife of the great fiend, whose son is Atikāya, the "giant" (R 6, 71, 30). She herself is called Dhānyamālinī, "corn-crowned", and appears in R 5, 22, 39f., as endeavoring to divert her lord from his attention to the Furrow (Sītā). These are but faint traces of a cult of vegetal deities who may be added to the divine trees and tree-spirits already discussed. No one of them quâ goddess is of epical importance, but that is not to be expected in a poem of warring men and higher gods. They are to be considered somewhat in the light of those animal gods who remain in the shadow of the great divinities. But there are no vegetal deities so important as are several independent animal gods. Compare also the bucolic god enshrined in Balarāma (q. v.). Perhaps the use of the tilaka sign may revert to the tila as holy (sesamum-oil is used for embalming the dead, R 2, 66, 14).

§ 8. **Animal Divinities.** — Animals are divinities partly by birth, partly because they are forms of demoniac or divine powers, and partly because they are the life-givers of any community. Human beings, especially saints or others potentially fearful, may also become incorporate as animals and thus make them divinely terrible. Even when no divinity is ascribed to an animal it is often looked upon as a supernatural being and as any man may be cursed to become an animal, this animal-man is looked upon with the reverence which is paid to any superhuman creature. Certain animals also have a quasi divinity or devilry in being potent to bring bad luck. As all animals talk, the gods appear as talking animals in many fables, but this is only one side of the belief that an animal anyway may incorporate a higher power. At the very beginning of the great epic two seers curse each other to become an elephant and a tortoise, respectively (1, 29, 15f.). The later Rāmāyaṇa relates that Saudāsa shot a tiger not knowing that it was a man-tiger, puruṣavyāghra, as Rākṣasa, and that its mate assumed in turn a human form to avenge it (R 7, 65, 10f., a later form of the legend; see Ṛṣis). This man-tiger is a spirit recognised in Vedic literature (a madman is offered to it, VS. 30, 8). All animals have divine creative powers assigned to them as their particular ancestors, but these are for the most part abstract creative energies regarded as daughters

[1]) Śākambharī is from śāka and bhar, "bearer of herbs" (vegetables), as the native commentators admit. There seems to be no reason for confounding this śāka with śaka in śakambhara (an epithet meaning "dung-bearer" obscurely applied to a people or clan in AV. 5, 22, 4), as is done in PW.

[2]) Sītā occasionally is recognised in her human role in Mbh. apart from the formal Rāmakathā. In S 3, 114, 24, an added verse cites her as an example of the faithful wife. In Vedic theology she was wife of Savitṛ or of Indra, TB. 2, 3, 10, 1, Sāvitrī; and Pār. G. 2, 17, 13 (or 9), Indrapatnī. The orthodox Sītāyajña, "sacrifice in honor of Sītā" is recognised in the Harivaṃśa as especially offered by ploughmen (H 3816) in contrast to the "sacrifice in honor of the hill" offerred by cowherds (though, characteristically, Kṛṣṇa became the hill, so that the sacrifice as described was made to him, ib. 3876).

or grand-daughters of Dakṣa and wives of Kaśyapa (see § 139, Creation). Some animals are sons of higher divinities (see Garuḍa) or forms of Viṣṇu (§ 143). Of the abstract generators only Surabhi, "mother of cows", has reality, evinced by dramatic scenes and dialogues in which she appears (see Indra). Independent actors in the epics are the semi-divine apes and bears, of whom only the chief in each class is of mythological importance, the others acting like ordinary demi-god heroes and being content with divine origin. As the bear was created before the ape, he may take precedence here. Jāmbavat or Jāmbava (R) is "king of bears", ṛkṣarāja, the son of Prajāpati Brahman, in appearance like a dark cloud (R 4, 39, 27, etc.). He was born of the yawn of Brahman and hence is called son of gadgada, "stammer" (R 1, 17, 6 and 6, 30, 21). On account of his wisdom he is chief of Vidyādharas (q. v.) and at the bidding of the gods he coursed over earth twenty-one times, collecting herbs from which ambrosia was made (R 4, 66, 31). He once helped Indra, and revered Viṣṇu (q. v.) by walking the deasil around him. His brother is Parjanya-like (R 6, 27, 9) and is called Dhūmra, "smoke-colored", which, however, is a common epithet of bears. Jāmbavat is not prominent as sage or warrior in the great epic, though he leads millions of black bears with white faces into battle (3, 280, 23; ib. 283, 8; ib. 284, 26), to help Rāma. He was brought up beside the Narmadā in the Ṛkṣavat (bear) mountain and is stronger than his brother, but by Rāma's time had become so feeble that he could jump only ninety leagues (R 4, 65, 13 f.). Dazed by Indrajit's blow he sends Hanumat for magic healing herbs (R 6, 74, 21 f.) as soon as he revives. He is the father of Jāmbavatī in Mbh., who was wife of Kṛṣṇa and mother of Sāmba (3, 16, 12; see Viṣṇu). It is curious that he appears as an ape as well as a bear (R 5, 60, 6, harisattama, etc.). Jāmbavatī is called Kapīndraputrī, yet with v. l. Narendraputrī (13, 629 in C = B 14, 41 and S 45, 25); but Kapīndra is also Viṣṇu in 13, 149, 66 (B). The Hariv. tells how Kṛṣṇa overcame Jāmbavat, king of bears, and took away his daughter and the syamantaka jewel (H 2073). In H 6701, Jāmbavatī may be called Rohiṇī, "taking any form" (doubtful). With Jāmbavat's origin from Brahman's yawn may be compared Kṣupa's origin from the same god's sneeze (12, 122, 16 f.), and that of Prajāpati Kardama, born of his shadow (Bh. P. 3, 12, 27; Kardama also as Nāga, 1, 35, 16).

§ 8 b. **Hanumat and the Divine Apes.** — The great epic recognises Hanumat as the ape perched on Arjuna's staff, who fights on the side of Kṛṣṇa-Viṣṇu. The Rām. in both versions makes him one of the efficient aiders of Rāma-Kṛṣṇa. Apart from the Rāmakathā, the Mbh. knows him as "foe of the groves of the lord of Laṅkā" (4, 39, 10, Laṅkeśavanāriketu = Arjuna). Sītā calls him her "son", but this is (conventional) only in showing her grace: "O my son, thy life shall be commensurate with Rāma's glory, and through my grace heavenly enjoyments shall be at thy command" (3, 148, 18 and ib. 291, 45). On Arjuna's standard the ape is no mere figure; it opens its mouth and roars (7, 88, 26). "As Hanumat lifted Gandhamādana", so Bhīma lifted an elephant (7, 129, 139, 86), though the brotherhood of the pair is not here suggested; but it is explained in 3, 146, 65 f., where the Rāma-story is known. He is described here as having a tail like Indra's banner and as making a noise like the bolt of Indra, Śakradhvaja, Indrāśani, with a short thick neck, small lips, red face and ears, sharp white fangs, a moon-like face, and a mane like aśoka-flowers. He is son of Vāyu, the "life of the world" (wind as breath), by the wife of Kesarin, his strength being so great that Bhīma cannot even move his tail (ib. 147, 24 f.). Subsequently he expands his size till he is larger than a mountain. His nature here is not that of a god but of a pious monster, "glorious as the sun" who worships Viṣṇu (as Rāma, 3, 151, 7). He is, however, also a philosopher, lecturing his brother on the character of the four ages, and present-day customs and duties. He says he is to live as long as the story of Rāma will endure (ib. 148, 17), and will roar on the Pāṇḍu's standard (ib. 151, 17). In the later Mbh. Rāma-story, Hanumat crosses the ocean by his father's aid and so burns Laṅkā (3, 282, 59 f.). His name appears as Hanūmat when metrically convenient. His mother in R is Añjanā (Puñjikasthalā, q. v.), unknown in Mbh. When new-born he sprang up to eat the rising sun supposing it to be edible. With one jump he can go a thousand times around Mt. Meru, etc. These and other extravagances of R 4, 66 and 67 seem to belong to the Nārāyaṇa period when Viṣṇu was All-god (ib. 67, 3). They are later traits than those of the Mbh., as are the statements that his death depends on his own wish (ib. 66, 28); that his left jaw was broken on a mountain-peak after he had leaped up three hundred leagues and then been prevented by Indra from seizing the sun (ib. 66, 21 f.); and that in leaping to Laṅkā he followed the "path of Svāti" (ib. 67, 29). The legend here is that Hanumat was begotten by Vāyu (Māruta) on the Apsaras who had been cursed to become the wife of the ape Kesarin after she was born on earth as daughter of the king-ape Kuñjara; while in R 1, 17, 15 Hanumat is simply one of a lot of monkeys begotten by various gods at Brahman's exhortation. The former account agrees with R 7, 35, which also makes his mother Añjanā wife of Kesarin who lived on Sumeru. As Rāhu alone is entitled to devour the sun, Vāyu here chases Hanumat and it is Rāhu who induces Indra to smite Hanumat (thus injuring his jaw). This latest account describes him as a sort of evil being, who having received a boon of safety acts like any Rākṣasa in like circumstances, till the seers curse him to lose the knowledge of his own power. He is called indifferently Vāyusuta, Māruti, Añjanāsuta, and, as a child touched by Brahman's healing hand, śiśuka, and śiśu, having in fact a resemblance to Śiśu in his leaping and roaring, and being formally likened to him, "roaring like Śiśu on his bed of reeds" (ib. 7, 35, 22; 36, 3 and 33). Owing to his ignorance, he failed to aid Sugrīva against Vālin, but when released from his curse he became a distinguished scholar, astrologer, and grammarian. In leaping from Laṅkā he dashes down Mt. Ariṣṭa on his way back, as Maināka rising from the ocean to give him place to rest was also crushed by him. He takes a human form, as do the other apes, on reaching Ayodhyā (R 6, 128, 19 f.; ib. 130, 42). In RG 6, 160, where Hanumat goes to Gandhamādana to collect herbs he releases Gandhakālī, after killing Tālajaṅgha. She had been cursed to be a grahī till Hanumat's arrival, a new phase, shared with Rāma etc., showing a growing cult. He is here called Gandhavahātmaja, Vāsavadūtasunu (son of the messenger-god, R 6, 74, 62 and 77). The other texts have merely the account of the collecting of four healing herbs at Jāmbavat's instance; but all accounts agree in saying that being unable to find the hidden plants he breaks off the hill-top and brings it with him. He is no god here, only a giant ape, under bond of friendship to execute his master's commands; and so in R 4, 41, 2 Sugrīva sends Nīla, Jāmbavat, and Hanumat together to search for Sītā under the command of Aṅgada, though he has particular faith in Anilātmaja, Pavanasuta

(Hanumat), so that Rāma entrusts to him the "recognition-ring"; but an ape he does not cease to be (haripuṅgava, mahākapi) and at most is equal to his father in gait and energy (ib. 44, 3 f.). His incidental exploits are to find the cave of Maya (ib. 51); to evade the mother of serpents by slipping into her mouth, after becoming the size of a thumb; to evade Siṃhikā's attempt to arrest his soul-shadow; and to set fire to Laṅkā (ib. 5, 1 to 57), after getting caught, by magic and having had blazing wool fastened to his tail. In his fighting he resembles Bhīma or Ghaṭotkaca who also smite legions with a club and also expand and reduce their forms. Hanumat thus slays 80,000 fiends at one stroke; kills Akṣa (Rāvaṇa's son), Dhūmrākṣa, Akampana, Nikumbha (R 4, 42 and 47; ib. 6, 52 and 57 and 77), and goes under any form, as he will (R 4, 3, 24) when appearing as an ambassador "learned in grammar". The recognition-ring "marked with the name of Rāma" is another late touch not found in the Mbh. version but found in R 4, 42, 12 and 5, 32, 44 (= C 44, 12 and 36, 2). Hanumat disappears from the scene in Uttara with a necklace given him by Rāma (R 7, 40, 24), as at the end of the real epic Sītā gave him a necklace from her own neck (R 6, 131, 76). Hanumat is likened to Garuda (R 4, 66, 4), but he is not distinguished for divinity. He is inviolable because he has received a boon of the gods. He is exhorted to leap as "hero-son of Kesarin and Vāyu, by grace of the seers and Gurus and consent of the elder apes" (R 4, 67, 34). He is like Garuḍa in swiftness, like wind in strength, like a bull, a Nāga, an elephant, the moon (R 4, 67, 28 and ib. 5, 1, 2 f.). He is huge as a mountain or small as a cat or as four fingers (ib. 196 and 2, 49). His father killed Śamba, a demon appearing as an elephant (hereditary antagonism, R 5, 35, 81; ib. 6, 27, 25). All the great apes boast a divine paternity. Suṣeṇa was son of Dharma; Sugrīva's uncle, Dadhimukha, of the Moon; Vālin and Sugrīva, of Ṛkṣarajas (son of Viṣṇu), or they were respectively sons of Indra and Sūrya; Nīla was son of Agni; Dvivida and Mainda, of the Aśvins, etc., though different writers give different fathers (Dharma or Varuṇa as father of Suṣeṇa). In all this there does not seem to be sufficient ground for the ingenious suggestion put forward by Professor Jacobi (Rāmāyaṇa, p. 132) that Hanumat was a village reduction of Indra śipravat. Hanumat has no peculiar Indra-traits, for such as he has he shares with other apes, giants, and fiends. No one knows certainly what śipravat means, but if hanumat means "big-jaw-beat" it is appropriate enough to the ape. Hanumat appears to be merely the typical strong and clever beast in demi-apotheosis standing in this regard with Jāmbavat, Sampāti, Śeṣa, etc. He is not descending but ascending the scale of epic religious beings and appears to have lost nothing. He is not particularly drunken, does not use a bolt, does not reflect Indra in any striking way. He simply skips and throttles (Akṣa) and throws things, and gradually becoming cleverer ends as a priestly grammarian (RS 7, 36, 46 adds: so 'yaṃ navavyākaraṇārthavettā brahmā bhaviṣyaty api). His intelligence is primarily craftiness and cunning, as belongs to an ape, and his village-popularity seems to point to his original habitat as bordering on the forest where apes live. The Mbh. recognises as the great ape (Kapi) Sūrya (q. v. and other sun-gods), which probably reverts to the Vedic Vṛṣākapi.[1])

---

[1]) In JRAS. April, 1913, p. 398, Mr. F. E. Pargiter proposes to derive Hanumat from āṇ-mandi (Dravidian) = Vṛṣākapi.

§ 9. **The Cow.** — The divinity of the cow rests on the element in totemism which consists in the deification of that class of animals which provides a livelihood. A pastoral people naturally recognises its herds as its means of life and hence as in the case of the classic troglodytes regards them as its "sacred parents", or, as in the case of the Todas, as its divinity. This is brought out very clearly in the speech of the herder who says (H 3808 f.): "We are herdsmen, living in the wood and living on wealth got from cows, we recognise as our divinity cows and hills and woods. The object of one's closest knowledge (with whatever knowledge one is united) that becomes his divinity, supreme, to be revered and worshipped, for that (skill) alone assists him. We herdsmen make sacrifice to the mountain, for it is worthy of sacrifice. We will sacrifice sanctified cattle at a tree or a hill on a holy altar . . the cows shall walk the deasil around this best of hills". Here the hill is an object of worship because the herdsmen live upon it, and the cows themselves are their divinity because the cow-herders life on the wealth which comes from their cattle (vayaṃ godhanajīvinaḥ, gāvo 'smaddaivataṃ viddhi). Thus as early as the Ṛgveda the cow (less often the bull) is aghnyā, "not to be killed". By the time of the epics to kill a cow was worse than murder, excusable only when to do so was to obey a higher law. Such a higher law, says Rāma, is filial obedience, and for this reason, because Kaṇḍu obeyed his father in killing a cow he did not sin (R 2, 21, 30). Doubtless the sage objected to killing a cow even for sacrificial purposes, as the vegetarian substitutes for animal sacrifice were already part of the Viṣṇu cult; for the universal orthodox rule is that cows may be slain only for sacrifice and the epic doubts even this (paśutvād vinirmuktā gāvaḥ, 13, 66, 43). No Brahman may eat beef, cow-flesh being usually implied, though a formal tabu specifies as forbidden food fish, swans, frogs, etc., and anaḍvān (mṛttikā cai 'va, 12, 36, 21 f.; S, anuṣṇā), or bull's flesh. Especially sanctity attaches to a "blue bull", nīlaṣaṇḍa, which is sacred to the Manes (13, 125, 73 f.), though also sacred to Śiva (q. v.). To set loose a nīla vṛṣabha and to sacrifice a horse are equally meritorious (3, 84, 97). Despite the compassion for the suffering of the mother of cows, Surabhi, no blame or remorse is expressed for killing thousands of cows in sacrifice, whose flesh presumably is eaten (only S speaks of the cow as "mother of the world", 3, 131, 6); but the offer of the arghya cow is purely conventional hospitality (3, 295, 6, etc.), and cows are said now to be only for giving (13, 66, 43) to priests. Surabhi lives under earth (earth as cow is a common synonym), but the goloka or world of cows is Viṣṇu's heaven above the three worlds (5, 102, 1 f.; 13, 83, 37). To slay a priest or a cow is equally sinful (12, 145, 9); they are avadhyāḥ, "not to be slain" (5, 36, 66). The later epic has a gomatī vidyā, inculcating the doctrine of giving cows to priests for the sake of certain worlds (see § 23) to be gained by the giver hereafter. Cows had at first no horns but got them from Brahman; Śiva clove the hoofs of the bull; the river Carmaṇvatī is made of the blood of sacrificed cows (8, 34, 104 f.; 13, 66, 38 f.; ib. 78, 22 and 80, 1 f.; ib. 81, 13 and 44). As goddesses, cows are a source of good luck and are not to be struck or kicked; but bullocks may be goaded, for gods use a goad. A sonless man is rescued from his evil state by the gift of three cows (13, 22, 30 f.; ib. 67, 7 f.). Such gifts are to be made especially on the holy eighth day of the moon, when wish-getting ceremonies are performed (Kāmyāṣṭamī, 13, 71, 49). In lieu of the real thing, one may give cow-cakes made of sesamum or even a water-cow (jala-dhenu, 13, 71, 41). Cow-dung is used to smear the house, but it is also to be worshipped as an emblem of the discus of Viṣṇu, as is the yellow pigment from the cow (ib. 146, 48 and ib. 126, 3 f.). Śiva has the bull-standard because he approves of cows, which are the root of prosperity, the food of gods, the support of sacrifice, revered in heaven (13, 51, 27 f.; ib. 126, 38 f.; cf. 3, 133, 6 and ib. 130, 31, on the gift of a kapilā cow).

Though severity is permitted in handling bulls (5, 4, 5), they are not to be castrated nor to have their nostrils pierced (12, 263, 37 and 45 f.). It is not regarded as cruel to kill animals for sacrifice, since it ensures their going to heaven (12, 34, 28). Even a worm is induced by Kṛṣṇa Dvaipāyana to die for the attainment of bliss (13, 117, 7 f.). Besides the mythical mother-cow, the kāmadhug dhenu Nandinī is extolled as the wonder-cow whose possession by Vasiṣṭha (§ 124) caused a war of caste resulting in Viśvāmitra becoming a priest. Anything desirable, from milk to militia, can be milked out of her. She has all the female beauties and "the six flavors of ambrosia"; her milk rejuvenates for ten thousand years (1, 99, 20 f.). On the magical effect of bull's urine, see Magic Observances in the Hindu epic (op. cit.). On Surabhi and the cow-guardians of space, see § 92, § 139. On cows as born of the Sun, see § 36.

§ 10. **The Elephant.** — There is no myth of a world-upholding elephant. Divine elephants are mythological guardians of the quarters. They were originally four, afterwards, when the quarters became subdivided, they too appear as eight, to embrace the districts between East and South, etc. They are called diggajas, diśāgajas (R 5, 37, 65), diṅnāgas, digvaraṇas; the word nāga, meaning also the serpent, causes confusion between the two sets of beings. The chief elephant is Airāvata, belonging to Indra (§ 66). The four chiefs are called (6, 64, 57 f.) Airāvata (Airāvaṇa), Vāmana, Añjana (cf. R 4, 37, 5 and 20), and Supratīka (also the name of Bhagadatta's elephant), or Sārvabhauma (R 4, 43, 36, etc., ridden by Kubera). But Mahāpadma is also named among these magical "three-fold rutting", four-tusked steeds, which are ridden by demons (6, 64, 57). Supratīka is mentioned in 6, 12, 34; he is especially known as the ancestor of "king Airāvaṇa and of Vāmana, Kumuda, and Añjana" (5, 99, 15). S 4, 3, 26 calls him best of gajendras or chief elephants (as elephant of the North, see Indra). In 7, 121, 25, Añjana, Vāmana, Supratīka, Mahāpadma, and Airāvata appear as progenitors of earthly elephants, though the theory of creation (1, 66, 60 f.) assigns them to Mātaṅgī, Śvetā, and similar powers, Śveta as son of Śvetā being particularly mentioned as guardian of the quarters. Elsewhere Śveta is a name of a Nāga, a demon, etc., but as appellative it describes the white elephant of Indra. Kumuda is known to the epic only as mentioned above; Añjana and his (western) progeny are praised in 7, 112, 23. The name of the elephant later kown as guardian of the North-West, namely Puṣpadanta, appears only as a title of Śiva (R 7, 23, pr. 4, 49) and as the name of one of that god's followers (Mbh. 7, 202, 73). Śiva is "elephant-eared" (12, 285, 77). Both this and Puṇḍarīka are Nāga names (5, 36, 29; cf. Airāvata). R recognises the usual four and Sārvabhauma; but also gives a later technical list (R 1, 6, 25, bhadrair mandrair mṛgaiś cai 'va), and another list, viz. Virūpākṣa in the East, Mahāpadma in the South, Saumanasa in the West, and Bhadra in the North (ib. 24 and 40, 12 f.). The late grouping of the eight is not recognised in either epic, but for convenience may be given here: East, Airāvata; SE., Puṇḍarīka;

South, Vāmana; SW., Kumuda; West, Añjana; NW., Puṣpadanta; North, Sārvabhauma. The space-elephants carry the (§ 91) Lokapālas and are divine; they blow the winds out of their trunks (7, 94, 47; 6, 12, 36); they are described as living in Samā(-land, Sumeria? 6, 12, 32), in Himavat (3, 108, 10), where they have rubbed the mountains bare with their tusks (ib.); and elsewhere on occasion. Morally the protective elephants are always good, fighting against evil demons. In 8, 82, 25, a battle is likened to one between the lord of Daityas and the lords of directions, Digīśvaras (may be gods). Demons take the form of elephants, such as the one whom Indra killed at Benares (3, 173, 50), and there are Dānavanāgas, "demoniac elephants" (8, 18, 6). Elephants weep in battle and show three temporal streams, but Airāvata and Bhagadatta's Supratīka show seven (6, 95, 24 and 33). Other than the divine elephants have four tusks, but they live in Laṅkā (R 5, 9, 5) or in the mythological North (3, 158, 90). Ordinary elephants spurt water in war, throw weapons with the hand (7, 26, 50; 1, 81, 13, but for dvipahastaiḥ S has dvipastaiḥ), and even sing verses (R 6, 16, 6). See also § 51, § 93.

§ 11. **Demoniac Animals.** — Animals "possessed" by demons are common and are to be distinguished from animals which are merely temporary forms of demons, though to make the distinction is not always possible. In 12, 114, 17, manuṣyasālāvṛka is a human jackal but apparently only in a metaphorical sense, a mean man. In 3, 269, 7 f., sālāvṛka = gomāyu, announcing disaster because appearing on the left; ib. 173, 48, sālāvṛkas are demoniac forms in battle, but as these include apes, elephants, and bears, as well as Śarabhas, Bhūruṇḍas, and ghosts, they may be animals. Only in 12, 33, 29 they appear as forms of Brāhmaṇas called Sālāvṛkas because they fought, eighty-eight thousand in number, against the gods. The demons killing Kaca in 1, 76, 29 "gave him to the sālāvṛkas", but here, as in the earlier tale of Indra giving the ascetics to the same beasts, there is no reason to suppose that the animals were other than those in 6, 59, 127; 7, 30, 19 (etc., etc.) or in 10, 9, 5, i. e. real jackals or jackal-forms of demons[1]).

The Śarabha: This animal is represented as one whose roar, garjita, frightens other animals in the forest. In similes, it appears as a fighter and combatants "fight like tigers, hawks, and śarabhas" (7, 127, 41 and 132, 11). The Rām. knows a monkey-chief of that name, easily overthrown by Kumbhakarṇa (R 6, 67). Śarabha is a proper name but also a monster in Mbh., with eight feet, and slays lions (aṣṭapādaḥ śarabhaḥ siṃhaghātī, 3, 134, 15; 7, 1, 28, etc.). Yet it is found on Mt. Krauñca (9, 46, 87), but not as a monster; and on Gandhamādana, with lions, tigers, etc. (5, 158, 40), as if one of the ordinary animals of the wood and mountain. The later epic increases its monstrosity; it has both eight legs and one eye above, ūrdhvanayanaḥ, and eats raw flesh (12, 117, 13 f.), where it has part in the fable of the dog turned into a śarabha. It is, however, listed among edible animals as belonging to mṛgajātis which a gentleman offers his guest for dinner (antelope, śarabha, hare, bear, ruru-deer,

---

[1]) On the conception of the sālāvṛka as wehrwolf, cf. RV. 10, 95, 15; Brunnhofer, Arische Urzeit, 284 f. (Hyrcanians); and Oertel, JAOS. 19, 123 f., on the Vedic legend concerning Indra and the ascetics. S ed. has s, the Bombay ed. ś. Demons may be born beasts as well as assume temporarily beast-forms. So Bali is reborn as the son of an ass (12, 224, 6). Conversely, horses and cows become gods (3, 181, 13). For the divine horse, see sub Indra (§ 68).

eṇi, pṛṣata, nyaṅku, śambara, gayal, boar, and buffalo meat, 3, 267, 13). Besides being a personal name of heroes (not uncommon), it is one of the names of Viṣṇu (§ 143 f.), as of honored apes, demons, and Nāgas (cf. śarabha as title of Buddha). As an Asura the name said to be equivalent to uṣṭra, also an Asura, may be dialectic for karabha, camel (which suggests Zarathustra). A camel's roar would frighten any beast and on first appearance so queer an animal would be apt to breed queer stories. H 2651 has Uṣṭra as Asura; Śarabha is a Dānava 1, 65, 26, and a Daiteya, reborn as Paurava, in 1, 67, 27. The intimate relation between man, beast, and gods, may be illustrated by the story of Sārameya, son of Saramā, the devaśunī, who herself has a place in Brahman's heaven (2, 11, 40). When the sons of Janamejaya beat Sārameya, he induces his mother to curse the seer and the latter chooses as priest to allay the pāpakṛtyā a young sage whose mother was a snake (sarpī = Nāgī? 1, 3, 1 f.). The mythology of other real animals, except as regards their creation (§ 139 f.) through mediate powers, has to do with them as omens and cause of good luck. To touch a bull brings good fortune. The skin and teeth of others avert demons, Pramathas, etc. The tortoise, cat, and goat, and the skin and teeth of a hyena guard from such evil ("smiting") influence. The color is of importance: "He (say the evil Pramathas) is free from our influence who harbors in his house as rakṣoghnāni a cat or goat, black or brown-yellow" (13, 131, 10 f.). The destruction of the crab by its young, the destruction of the silkworm by its own coils, the rising of the spider from its destroyed web to a new home (life), and the fresh growth of horns in deer and skin in snake, are all genuine or erroneous epic (and pre-epic) observations of natural history utilised for philosophical reflection rather than mythological data, and need not be illustrated here.

§ 12. **Divine and Demoniac Birds.** — a) Many birds can talk, but the effect on the parrot of the curse of Agni (§ 49 f.) introduces myth. Religiously and mythologically the goose, haṃsa, is the most exalted bird, its high flight, loneliness (above other birds), and white color making it an emblem of the pure soul and of God, the supreme bird of a thousand wings (5, 46, 14 f.); yet because of RV. 10, 123, 6 the soul-bird is golden-winged (12, 47, 17 and 45), so geese that talk, qua spiritual beings, are golden (3, 53, 19), but usually the haṃsa is white (3, 304, 17; 7, 132, 29 f.). The goose goes to Meru, lives at lake Mānasa; its form is assumed by Varuṇa (§ 59 f.), etc. It flies high (R 2, 9, 44) and represents the sun (hence golden). The haṃsa separates milk from water (1, 74, 91 and passim), but so do other birds (VS. 19, 73). Not every goose is godly; the kalahaṃsa lacks this distinction (it is grey not white). The haṃsa is the vehicle of Viṣṇu, but also of Kubera (§ 22); its flight is exceeded only by Garuḍa (R 4, 58, 28). Luck in omens is indicated by position and sex of the observer (right side lucky for men), yet in a house, turtle-doves, parrots, sārikās, and cockroaches bring luck; but vultures, pigeons, fire-flies, and bees are unlucky (13, 104, 114 f.). A red-brown owl with green eyes attacking crows (cf. R 6, 17, 26) portends misfortune (10, 1, 37). Yet unlucky birds are used as standard-figures, apparently without thought of danger. Some of Garuḍa's sons are birds (by name), Sārasa, Kapota (5, 101, 11 f.). The first is auspicious, the second inauspicious, for vultures, crows (v. l. cranes), hawks (and especially pigeons) are unlucky, while peacocks, geese, sārasas, cātakas, and jīvaṃjīvakas are very auspicious

(5, 143, 18f.); as are cāṣas, śatapatras, and krauñcas. Herons, hawks, vultures, cranes, crows, though inauspicious, are auspicious (nimittāni dhanyāni) if they precede a warrior into battle (8, 72, 11f.), as these affect not the warrior behind, but the enemy who are advancing against him from the opposite direction. When one starts into battle, the rear is the auspicious position as is the left side. Before starting, the right is the auspicious side; omens which in general are favorable (good birds and agreeable sounds) are better in the rear, because from there they urge the troops on to victory, while in front they obstruct success (12, 102, 10f.). Red-footed birds and pigeons are particularly inauspicious (5, 143, 18f. and R 7, 6, 56). In R 6, 108, 21, a gṛdhracakram circles over the doomed man and follows wherever he goes (also gṛdhrakulam, "flock of vultures"). The pigeon is most feared, which made Śibi especially courageous in harboring this (Vedic) death-messenger, for it is a "horrible portent" if a pigeon alights on one (ghoraṃ kapotasya nipātam āhuḥ, 3, 197, 5; cf. R 2, 12, 43; ib. 14, 4, etc.; the tale is told in four different forms in the epic). Other birds are typical rather than ominous, cātakas typifying thirst; cakravākas the longing of love; the peacock, shameless, dances in joy of rain, etc. There is a tabu against eating the flesh of goats, parrots, and peacocks (13, 104, 93; on the indecency of the peacock, see 5, 73, 10 and 12, 114, 10), but peacocks, deer, goats, and boars are provided as a feast for Rāma (which shocks the scholiast, R 2, 91, 69, who says that they were not for Rāma to eat personally, but for the low-caste men, Niṣādas). The later interpretation of the cakora as a betrayer of blood is not mentioned by epic writers, who regard it as a red-eyed but pleasant singing bird (7, 126, 40; cf. 3, 158, 86 and 13, 54, 11). The curlew inspires Vālmīki (R 1, 2, 29f.). See also bird-forms assumed by the gods (Indra, etc.), and on Viṣṇu as sun-bird see § 143.

b) Of quite different character is the Bhāruṇḍa bird. It is the function of this bird to bury the Hyperboreans, when these near-immortals die (like Rāma they live ten thousand and ten hundred years, 6, 7, 12). Bhāruṇḍas have strong beaks and bodies and take up the corpses of the Northern Kurus and "bury them in caves". But along with the sālāvṛkas, etc., which appear with ghosts and demons in the tumult of battle, are certain Bhuruṇḍas (3, 173, 48) and probably these are the same as the Bhāruṇḍas, as soul-seizers, sirens or harpies (cf. 3, 207, 36, bheruṇḍa). The ruṇḍa is a mangled headless corpse, a late equivalent of the epic kabandha, a torso which dances on the battle-field. Like sirens, the Bhāruṇḍas sing (in the western and northern wilds) and have human faces, their songs being described as "exceedingly pleasant". They are here associated with the Bhūliṅga-bird, which cries "beware" while picking the lion's teeth (2, 41, 18; ib. 44, 28; 12, 169, 10). S omits Bhūliṅgas (in Śānti), thus ascribing human traits and sweet song only to the Bhāruṇḍas. Birds that talk are not mythological, as parrots, crows, sārikās, jīvajīvakas, etc. are kept in cages and mimic all sounds and talk. Compare in Mbh. the story of Pūjanī (12, 139, 4f.), and in R the tale of the talking crow (R 2, 95, pra. 13), for late exaggerations of the theme (R 2, 35, 18). Demons take bird-forms (Śuka, etc.), to act as spies (R 6, 20, 35, etc.). The birds tell a saint all that is going on (vāyasī vidyā, 12, 92, 7f.). The talkative vulture who lived a thousand years belongs to fable rather than to myth (12, 153, 54).

c) The lord of the feathered race is the mythological "fair bird", called Garutmat Suparṇa, the form Garuḍa being, however, the common one in the epics. "Garutmat carries off the ambrosia" (R 3, 30, 5) and, at the conclusion of the same rape of ambrosia in Mbh. 1, 33, 16, taṃ vavre vāhanaṃ Viṣṇur Garutmantaṃ mahābalam. Compare 3, 12, 90, Vainateyo yathā pakṣī Garutmān patatāṃ varaḥ (also 5, 105, 19). In such passages Garuḍa is formally identified with the (Vedic) Garutmat. He is brother of Aruṇa, the foregoer of the Sun-god (§ 38), and may have been originally a form of the sun (as bird), but the epic shows no other distinguishing solar traits in the character of Garuḍa. He is the egg-born son of Vinatā, hatched after a thousand years, the younger brother of Aruṇa, created, according to a late tradition, because the Vālakhilya saints, angry with Indra for insulting them, wished a rival "king of birds" to humiliate the god. Garuḍa is always son of Kaśyapa, and an Āditya, though called Vainateya from his mother (1, 16, 24; R 3, 14, 31), swift as wind or thought (1, 31, 13f.; 3, 155, 19; R 6, 34, 4, etc.), and especially distinguished as a rending, tearing, snake-devouring monster (1, 102, 46, etc.). The fulsome hymn in Ādi, in which he is called the sun, tapanaḥ sūryaḥ (1, 23, 9f. and 16), calls him also creator, destroyer, fire, Dakṣa, Brahman, Viṣṇu, etc, and is no index of the usual epic conception, which it marvellously exaggerates. This conception is that of a giant bird, whose most persistent traits are those expressed by the epithets bhujagāri, pannagāśana, etc., and suparṇa, that is, "a bird of beautiful feathers that eats snakes" (2, 24, 24, Garutmān pannagāśanaḥ; 1, 16, 24, pannagabhojanaḥ). The peacock is the only bird recognised by the epic as bhujagāśana (12, 120, 4, yathā barhāṇi citrāṇi bibharti bhujagāśanaḥ; N. mayūraḥ), and sarpāśana (sarpabhuj) is a later name for peacock[1]). The peacock is Garuḍa's gift to Skanda, "his dear son, the fair-feathered peacock" (the fighting cock being Aruṇa's gift, 9, 46, 51). Garuḍa may mean "devourer". But the epic makes a typical roc out of him. He frightens all, as he falls out of the sky, with claws extended, and the rush of his "double wings", which are like double gates of a city (1, 207, 32; 22, 227, 21), beats down forests (8, 76, 37; R 3, 25, 28), and even the sea is stirred by him (Tārkṣya, 7, 14, 60). His shape gives a name to a weapon, an army-formation, a fire-altar, etc. (R 6, 193, 21; ib. 1, 14, 27; Mbh. 6, 25, 2f.). He is best of birds or "the bird" (2, 19, 8; 5, 113, 2; vihaṅgama, pataga, also the sun, 1, 173, 23; 6, 12, 45). The eyes of the race of Vinatā are remarked upon by Sampāti, who says he can see a hundred leagues because he comes from that stock (R 4, 58, 29). Epic etymology connects his name with guru, "load", because (1, 30, 7) he carries a branch of the talking tree, heavy as earth, and an elephant and tortoise as big as mountains. In H 10775f., he fights with Mayūra dīptatejas. His great feat was to carry off ambrosia, of which however he did not eat, so that he remains mortal, but he won Viṣṇu's favor, who made him his vehicle (1, 23, 5f.; R 3, 35, 27f.). He is here called Tārkṣya as well as Vainateya (Aruṇa also has the last title, R 4, 58, 28). The epic formally distinguishes as

---

[1]) On Garuḍa and Viṣṇu, see § 143. The peacock as sun-bird (cf. Johansson, Solfågeln i Indien, p. 77f., referring to Jāt. 2, 33 and 4, 332f.) is the connecting link between the sun-bird, reflected in Garutmat-Garuḍa, and the epic roc that devours (Nāgas and other) snakes. The theft of Soma by Garuḍa is thus the oldest epic trait, parallel to that of the eagle (sun) Viṣṇu (Johansson).

Vainateyas, "Tārkṣya, Ariṣṭanemi, Garuḍa, Aruṇa, Āruṇi, and Vāruṇi" (1, 65, 40; cf. 5, 71, 5; H 12468), yet distinction is lost when Garuḍa-dhvaja = Tārkṣya-ketana (2, 45, 61), and "Tārkṣya" is the vehicle of Viṣṇu-Kṛṣṇa (13, 14, 43), as is Garuḍa (2, 24, 23). "As the ass cannot equal the speed of the horse, so no bird can equal the speed of Tārkṣya" (R 2, 105, 6; S 12, 117, 24 says that gāruḍaṃ balam may be given to other birds by divine power). Also in 5, 105, 18f. Garutmat = Tārkṣya, and so generally. The tārkṣyas are birds (as a race "Tārkṣyas" in 2, 52, 15, with Persians, may be Turks; it is a late insertion, not in S). Only S has the proverb preserved in Pañc. 1, 474: "Men honor not Tārkṣya, who kills snakes, but the snakes" (S 3, 28, 16; see Ind. Spr. 39), that is, they honor those they fear; but it brings out the chief function of Garuḍa (Tārkṣya). Tārkṣya as "antidote to poison" (in later use) suggests garuḍa as for garāda = viṣād. The emerald is elsewhere a "foe of poison" and "stone of Garuḍa" (garalāri, garuḍāśman), the first reminding one of bhujagāri as Vainateya (S 5, 94, 16). Garuḍa becomes the vehicle of Viṣṇu only after a struggle, in which the greater god showed that the great bird could not even move his arm (5, 105, 10f.), though in Ādi this happens as the result of Garuḍa's complaisance (1, 33). Garuḍa helps Viṣṇu by carrying him and even by fighting for him (R 7, 8, 19f.). Garuḍa makes friends with Indra by respecting the bones of his bolt (1, 33, 17f.). He shares with Hanumat the glory of sitting on a flag-staff of Kṛṣṇa (2, 24, 23). In Rām. he is not active except as the "vehicle of Viṣṇu" and type of speed and robber of ambrosia, save that he frightens away the snake-arrows of Indrajit and cures Rāma and his brother (R 6, 50, 33f.). Brahman's shaft is feathered with his lovely feathers (R 6, 111, 12). The blessing at Mbh. 1, 28, 14 is referred to in R 2, 25, 33, and Vainateya is said to have told Sagara how his sons might be revived, as he was the brother of Sagara's second wife Sumati (R 1, 38, 14). The Mbh. gives a series of his adventures, on the journey with Gālava (5, 107, 16f.), in which Garuḍa loses his wings, owing to his evil designs on Śāṇḍilī (ib. 113, 1f.). In the later epic he brings Uparicara to heaven at Viṣṇu's command (12, 333, 32f.). Already in 7, 143, 48, Kṛṣṇa bids Bhūriśravas go to heaven on the back of Garuḍa, but the warrior does not seem to have availed himself of the bird as psychopomp. Viṣṇu having kicked on to Garuḍa's breast the Nāga Sumukha, whom Garuḍa was going to eat, "since then Garuḍa lives at peace with Sumukha" (5, 104—5). In 6, 6, 14, Sumukha is a son of Garuḍa, the eldest of six (5, 101, 2), sires of all snake-eating birds: Sumukha, Sunāman, Sunetra, Suvarcas, Suruc, and Subala; though in the line, vaṃśa, of Kapila, and family, kula, of Vinatā there are thousands, all with the śrīvatsa sign, and all worshippers of Viṣṇu; all are Kṣatriyas also, but, because they destroy their "kindred" (by eating snakes), they cannot become Brahmans. The names are partly sun-, fire-, and Viṣṇu-names with many others, Vālmīki, Niśākara, Divākara, etc. The plural Garuḍas and Garutmats are demoniac forms of battle (3, 173, 48), or birds of prey (R 6, 131, 51; ib. 105, 22). Garuḍī = Suparṇī = Svāhā (3, 225, 9f.; see § 161 f.). The Vainateyas live either in the sixth (upper) world (R 4, 58, 28) or, usually, in Pātāla (5, 101, 6f.) or south of the Niṣadhas in the Golden Valley (varṣa, 6, 8, 6), or on Himavat (12, 328, 7, "which Garuḍa regularly occupies"). In R 4, 40, 38, however, Viśvakarman builds "the house of Vainateya" beside the Red Sea. Both Mbh. 1, 66, 69; 3, 279, 1, and R 3, 14, 31 derive Jaṭāyus and Sampāti from

Aruṇa and Śyenī, which makes the two brothers solar birds, nephews of Garuḍa. Sampāti, the elder, protects the younger when flying to the sun, but the sun burns him and he falls wingless upon Malaya (3, 282, 47 f.) or Vindhya (R 4, 58, 1 f.). This happened "after Vṛtra's death". The two are "vultures" (R 4, 60, 19), but monstrous, changing shape at will. In R 7, 5, 44, Sampāti is a demon. Those fleeing with Vibhīṣaṇa include Sampāti, seven in all, appearing as men or birds in battle (R 3, 37, 7 f.). Sampāti's son, who brought him food, is Supārśva (R 4, 59, 8 f.). The wings of these monster birds, who are all like rocs, are red, and two or more in number (ib. 63, 8 f.). Jaṭāyus, who helps Sītā, converses learnedly on genealogy (R 3, 14), contends with Rāvaṇa (ib. 51), tells his own story and then dies (ib. 67 f.). The brothers, Sampāti and Jaṭāyus, seem like under-studies of Garuḍa and Aruṇa (next generation, sons of Aruṇa), but the generalised birds called "warriors", Garuḍas and Tārkṣyas may conceivably have been human chieftains of the western coast, though mythologically they are all ātmajas of Garuḍa and scarcely present as strong a claim to euhemeristic interpretation as do their natural foes the Nāgas. The remaining members of the direct family of Vinatā, Ariṣṭanemi, Vāruṇi, and Āruṇi, are reckoned conventionally as belonging to the same bird-race, but each of them is a well-known seer of the epic, or rather, a well-known seer is called Āruṇi, etc. Ariṣṭanemi alone, however, is (Vedic) Tārkṣya (3, 184, 3 f.; ib. 186, 1 f.; 12, 289, 2 f.) and may be equivalent to Garuḍa in RG 5, 2, 10; but the v. l. putro for bhrātā (R 4, 66, 4, and B) makes the exact bearing of this passage uncertain. In R 1, 38, 4 and 14, he is father of Sumati, "sister of Suparṇa", and appears also in Jaṭāyus' genealogy (R 3, 14) as a Prajāpati. He is the brother of Pṛthu in Hariv. 1921. Garuḍa is also name of a son of Kṛṣṇa by the same late authority (H 9196).

§ 13. **Serpents.** — All serpents are of divine extraction, since one of Kaśyapa's eight wives was Tāmrā, whose daughter Śukī was mother of Natā and thus grandmother of Vinatā, and Vinatā was mother of Surasā, who bore the Nāgas, and of Kadrū, who bore serpents (pannagas; R 3, 14, 28 f., Mbh. 1, 66, 70). The distinction between Nāgas and serpents here indicated is lost, however, when Kadrū herself, as sister of Vinatā, is called the mother of the Nāga or Nāgas and Vinatā is mother of Garuḍa and Aruṇa (§ 12). The general abode of these divine serpents is below earth; and here is usually to be found Śeṣa, the Nāga of a thousand mouths, who "supports earth from beneath" (5, 103, 2 f.; 7, 94, 48, adhastād dharaṇīm . . sadā dhārayate). He is here conceived as an inhabitant of Bhogavatī, where he is "best of serpents", pannagas, rather than as upholding or entwining Viṣṇu. It is the "endless serpent lying upon the waters" that gets the name Ananta (bhogavat) and is regarded by later writers (R 7, 104, 5) as a creation of Viṣṇu's illusion, udakeśaya, "lying on the water", like Viṣṇu himself as Nārāyaṇa. In R 3, 14, 7, he is said to be one of the Prajāpatis. But this Nāga Śeṣa is called also an inferior Deva, moon-faced, of a thousand heads, who encircles the world and eventually curls himself over Viṣṇu; one of his titles being dharaṇīdhara (R 4, 40, 49; H 3027). He is described also as lying in the eastern district of the northern world on the top of Mt. Jātarūpa (thirteen leagues from Jaloda, where the Vaḍavāmukha is found), beneath a three-headed golden palm-tree; he has eyes as large as a lotus-leaf and is worshipped by all beings. The name Ananta (endless) is explained in particular as anantabhoga (R 6, 14, 18, anantabhogena sahasramūrdhnā nāgena as Rāma-Viṣṇu). Nīl. interprets anantabhogo bhujagaḥ krīḍann iva mahārṇave, in 4, 55, 22, as an allusion to Śeṣa. In Bhogavatī, Śeṣa appears like the White Mountain adorned with gems, having a thousand heads and fiery tongues (5, 103, 3). The later epic identifies Śeṣa with Kṛṣṇa and Viṣṇu and (Hariv.) even says that he was born of Śiva (H 7595); it also represents him as hanging from a tree in ascetic fervor for a thousand years, distilling kālakūṭa poison from his mouth and thus "burning the world" (H 12076). He is usually represented as associated with Viṣṇu rather than with Śiva. He comes from Balarāma's mouth (snake as incorporating a soul) and enters earth, being welcomed home by the other serpents after his Avatar in Baladeva (1, 67, 152; 16, 4, 13; list of serpents, ib. 15; cf. 18, 5, 23). Viṣṇu is Śeṣātman, but Śeṣa appears as an independent cobra coiled over the god (12, 47, 48, phaṇāsahasra), though still upholding the world (ib. 75). In the laud of Śiva, the "chief Nāga called Śeṣa" serves as the axis of his divine car (Nāgendra, 7, 202, 72). According to 1, 65, 41, Śeṣa, Ananta, Vāsuki, and Takṣaka are separate sons of Kadrū, but this distinction is ignored and vāsuki = pannaga (R 6, 51, 17). Ananta is Śeṣa, as Ananta dwells under earth, adho bhūmau, alone supporting earth, at the order of Brahman and he is "Śeṣa by name" (1, 36, 24 and ib. 21 f.). He is bhujaṃgamottama, best of snakes, and, as sustainer, Dharma (dhārayate), and appears to have got his position and influence through ascetic practices as a travelling Muni (ib. 7), thus winning the favor of Brahman who appoints him to his office; after which Śeṣa crawls under the earth through a hole and from below upholds it. The chief serpents (given in the preceding section) are Śeṣa, oldest and best, then Vāsuki, Airāvata, Takṣaka, Karkoṭaka, Dhanaṃjaya (also Vāmana, Āryaka), etc. some of the names being those of elephants, some referring to color, some to their sustenance, but others being clan-names, names of Kurus, Kauravya, Padma, Dhṛtarāṣṭra; while still other names are those of saints or heroes, Dilīpa, Nahuṣa, Aśvatara, Kapila (3, 84, 32; 5, 103, 15, etc.). Śeṣa seems to be the saved remnant, as there was only one good serpent, a parallel to Vibhīṣaṇa among the Rākṣasas (§ 17), as if the god said jīvatu śeṣaḥ when the others were to perish, "let the remaining one live" (cf. 6, 121, 52). The name nowhere in the epic (as later) appears as that of the world-elephant, which would be analogous to the case of Airāvata and Vāmana. The Nāga-clans embrace human relations, but the epic indicates rather a belief in divine marriage-relations and introduces, e. g., as a prospective son-in-law of Mātali (§ 68), Sumukha, the son of Āryaka's son Cikura, who was of the family of Airāvata and daughter's son of Vāmana (5, 103, 23 f.). The names indicate, however, that the Kurus were regarded as a Nāga-clan, which raises the question whether their enemies' name Krivi, Kraivya (connected with *kipi, kipya, worm?) is not kri-vi = krimi, a worm and a Nāgarāja-name. Perhaps the Pañcālas are five snake-clans (āla "poisoner" = Eng. eel). Dhṛtarāṣṭra, Airāvata, and Dhanaṃjaya are Vedic Nāgas. Cikura may contain the same root (kri, kir, kur) as cikkira, etc., for it means hair as well as snake, from the twisting curling form or movement (cf. Grk. κίρκος and Lat. cirrus). But the account of the snake-sacrifice[1]) in 1, 37, 11 f., shows that any

[1]) Professor Winternitz, Das Schlangenopfer des Mahābhārata, connects the account of this sacrifice with that of other popular legends, describing the destruction of serpents by magic formulas compelling them to cast themselves into the fire. Otherwise

distinction between snakes and Nāga-clans was lost. The snakes are here called indifferently Nāgas, bhujaṃgamas, sarpas, and pannagas. They talk and debate (Vāsuki addresses them and others reply, Nāgāḥ paṇḍitamāninaḥ, and Elāpatra), and they are slain "white, black, and blue, a kos long or a league long". Some have three heads, some seven, some ten. Takṣaka bites the king and Vāsuki intrigues by giving his sister Jaratkārū to bear Āstīka (a confused account, 1, 38, 1 f; ib. 57, 4 f.). In 1, 123, 70, the chief Nāgas are named in a list of divine beings as Karkoṭaka (sarpa), Vāsuki (bhujaṃgama), Kacchapa, Kuṇḍa, Takṣaka (mahoragas). In 1, 171, 38, a bhogavatī = sarpī is linked with devī, asurī, etc., as a type of female beauty (Bhogavatī is also the name of a female devil in Skanda's train, 9, 46, 8); cf. nāgakanyopamā śubhā, 6, 104, 30 etc. Any name implies any snake (gandharvoragarakṣasām, 1, 67, 146, etc., cf. Nala, 1, 29), except for certain special amphisbaena, scorpions, etc., whose nature is doubtful. Thus the ḍuṇḍubha and eṇīpada are mentioned in omens as different from sarpas ("the king will perish if a frog swallows eṇīpadas, or sarpas, or ḍuṇḍubhas", S 2, 69, 35). In 1, 9, 21 f., the ḍuṇḍubha is a metamorphosed seer who had been cursed to become a bhujaga, but (he says), "Bhujagas that bite men are of other sort; do not hurt the ḍuṇḍubhas, they only smack of snakes" (ahigandhena, ib. 10, 2 f.). Kālasarpa is especially the cobra (S 3, 158, 48), a rare epic word, usually kṛṣṇasarpa or kṛṣṇoraga, whose breathing, panting, is often referred to, as well as its double tongue (3, 268, 8). The double tongue in 1, 34, 23, comes from tasting ambrosia. Rāma's kingdom was free of all pests, including snakes and all creeping things, adaṃśamaśakā deśā naṣṭavyālasarīsṛpāḥ (7, 59, 16). Mantras can control snakes and make them harmless (vyālādīni, 5, 61, 16). Snakes "controlled in a circle", or overcome, "by Mantras and drugs" are referred to in R 2, 12, 4 and ib. 3, 29, 28. In 8, 40, 33, hataṃ vṛścika te viṣam is a reference to AV. 10, 4, 9 and 5, 13, 4. The evil in the eye of (man or) a snake is called the poison, netraviṣa, dṛṣṭiviṣa (2, 64, 20; R 6, 101, 54); and in regard to this poison there is, as was to be expected, a mixture of fact and myth. Nārada curses Karkoṭaka to be immobile till raised by Nala, and the Nāga bites him for the hero's own good (3, 66, 44 f.); the poison here changes his form. The fact that Āryaka was the grandfather of Kuntī's father, dauhitradauhitra, made this Nāga give Bhīma, when the hero fell into the river, some of his own power by letting him drink "snake essence" (1, 128, 60 f.; the Pāṇḍu as Kuru is thus of Nāga stock). An offering eaten at Maṇināga Tīrtha is an antidote for snake-poison (3, 84, 107; cf. Maṇināga in Magadha, 2, 21, 9; Sarpadevī in 3, 83, 14 is another Nāga Tīrtha). The maṇi called saṃjīvana cures snake-bite and even revitalises dead snakes (14, 80, 42). The distinction between the poison-snake, āśīviṣa, as "best of sarpas" and Dhṛtarāṣṭra as "best of Nāgas" (4, 2, 15 f.) does not imply that the Nāga is of human clan, as might be thought (S here has dṛṣṭiviṣa ivā 'hīnām). The priest,

Professor Jacobi, who regards the story as the historical reflex of change of habitat, as a result of which serpents were slain by the monsoon (I S. 14, 149). On Kadrū and Vinatā (Suparṇī), see the Suparṇādhyāya (Hertel, WZKM, 23, 273 and 320 f.). The epic Suparṇī is Garuḍī (3, 225, 10) as a general name for bird, not as mother of Garuḍa. In JRAS. 1898, p. 147, Professor Winternitz gives an account of the Grantha version of the sacrifice, according to which "Brahman gave the power of destroying snake poison to Kaśyapa (sic), and Kārkoṭaka, troubled about Kadrū's curse, promises to do his mother's bidding and turn himself into black hair."

it is said in 13, 104, 78 f., is superior to the poison-snake inasmuch as the snake destroys only as far as it can see, while the priest destroys as far as he can think, as well as destroys as far as he can see (cf. also Magic Observances, p. 35). The seer Nahuṣa always has the poison-look (5, 16, 26 and 32), and it is he who, as the ajagara or boa in the tale of 3, 180, 4 f., seizes the Pāṇḍus and will not let them go till his conundrums are answered (cf. dṛṣṭiviṣa, ghoradṛṣṭi, and ghorarūpa of Nahuṣa in 5, 16, 30 and 17, 17). His ascendency and exaltation as the king who lowered Indra and the gods may reflect Nāga power along the Ganges. Serpents with seven heads and poison-looks guard the White Mountain (3, 225, 11), and the same mountain is noted as containing gūḍhapādas, which are viṣolbaṇa, "strongly poisonous" (as in 1, 52, 10). But gūḍhapāda is a late snake-word, and the scene is late. Incidentally, pīṭha-sarpa in 3, 35, 22 is another late word, applied to the immovable boa (cf. the ājagara-vrata of the immovable Muni, 12, 179, 2 f., and 25), not to a "crippled" snake (as in PW.; in R 6, 31, 29, panasa, serpent, as in Suśruta, is used with punning reference to Panasa). Poison of the snakes neutralising vegetable (?) poison (kālakūṭa) is referred to in 1, 128, 57. Other references to the snake's poison are chiefly proverbial: the serpent unnoticed in one's clothing; the folly of removing the fang of a poisonous snake; of kicking a cobra; of playing with snakes; of feeding or waking a snake, etc. Myth appears when it is said that snakes lose their poison when Garuḍa appears (R 3, 56, 6); that they live on air (12, 299, 29); and in the implication that snakes have invisible legs ("only a snake can see a snake's legs", 12, 203, 13 = R 5, 42, 9). They are hard to track (12, 132, 20) and they steal jewels left upon the ground (but Yakṣas steal them from the impure and gods from sleepers, 14, 57, 23; cf. 1, 3, 128 f.). An Airāvata Nāga stole the famous ear-rings (14, 58, 25 f.), when Indra clove a way underground to recover them with Agni's help as a steed. The casting of a snake's skin is often used in epic as, less freely, in Vedic literature, to illustrate how one may free himself from sin, from grief, or even from a girl (cf. 5, 40, 2 and ib. 175, 19). That "everybody kills snakes" shows no great dread of their divinity (5, 73, 27) or strained ahiṃsā feeling.

The Nāgas live underground where Sunda goes to slay them (1, 210, 8) and the Nāgaloka described when Mātali seeks a son-in-law is entered by "descending into earth", avagāhya bhūmim (5, 98, 6; cf. praviveśa mahītalam, ib. 97, 21). But it must be remembered that "under earth" is water, a part of Varuṇa's domain. "The navel of the Nāgaloka is called Pātāla because water falls there sufficiently" (pātāla from patanti alam), and water-creatures called timis live there on the light of the moon in the water; also the Mare's Head and creatures slain by sunlight and demons of darkness (ib. 99, 1 f.). This city must not be confounded with the Nāgāhvayaṃ puram (S Nāgahrado mahān) in the Naimiṣa forest, where a Nāga is good enough to drag the sun's car for a month (12, 356, 2 and 358, 8); it is said here that Nāgas are to be revered as givers of boons, vandanīyā varadāḥ (ib. 361, 4). The water-habitat of the Nāgas is indirectly indicated in many passages. Kardama is father of Varuṇa (§ 59). Ulūpī, the daughter-in-law of Airāvata, who subsequently gave her (as widow) to Arjuna, lives in the water, and, when all is over for her, enters the Ganges again. She is addressed as devī, but this is conventional. She is Nāgarājasnuṣā and daughter of Kauravya, also sister of Vāsuki and mother of the human hero Irāvat, who is tardily but fully explained and extolled in 6, 90, 7f. (cf. 1, 214, 18 and 14, 91, 22; it is she who fetches the reviving jewel). Nāgarāja is a common epithet and is used of Karkoṭaka, Vāsuki, Dhṛtarāṣṭra, etc., as well as of Airāvata. According to 4, 2, 14, Arjuna carried Ulūpī off, hṛtavān, but the scholiast, who remembers the tale of 1, 214, says that this means captivated, not captured. Ulūpī is evidently connected with ulupin = dolphin. She is called also the "mother" of Babhruvāhana, the son of Citrāṅgadā, and creeps out of the earth in 14, 79, 8f., as "offspring of the snake", pannagātmajā, uragātmajā, Citrāṅgadā being also Kauravyaduhitṛ, as Ulūpī is Kauravyakulanandinī, that is, daughter of Kauravya (14, 81, 1 and 23; cf. ib. 5, tam uvāco 'ragapater duhitā prahasann iva, i. e. Ulūpī; S prahasanty atha). The food of the Nāgas is sudhārasa, as ambrosia is only for the gods (svadhā for the seers), and this may be milk rather than nectar, as the passages where the statement occurs are late (R 7, 7, 35 and 13, 26, 49), when the word had this meaning, and milk, as is well known, is a favorite food of the cobra. The Nāgas, cursed by their mother, go to dwell samudrakukṣau (1, 20, 7 and 25, 4), that is, in the swampy lands at the mouth of the Ganges, though they are represented as carried to the island called Rāmaṇīyaka (1, 26, 8). If Citrāṅgadā is of Kauravya descent, Maṇipur must have been one of the strongholds of the Nāga clan or race. As mythological beings or as historical factors they are represented, however, as living not only along the Ganges (and in it) but as inhabitants of the Punjab and the northern mountains, while as purely mythological they appear on occasion in heaven and the sky. The "great serpents" are usually Nāgas and they live on Gandhamādana and other hills of the North along with other snakes (3, 159, 19; 6, 92, 4); but they are especially associated with a lake in the mountains, and yield themselves up there, when the Śatarudriya is recited (7, 81, 14f.), to form Śiva's pāśupatyaṃ divyam, snake-weapon, namely the bow and arrows of Śiva. The fact that arrows are likened to flying snakes leads to the conversion of serpents into arrows. So in R 6, 103, 18, when Rāma's arrows become birds, Rāvaṇa's become real snakes. The Nāga Aśvasena, son of Takṣaka, had a quarrel with Arjuna dating from Khāṇḍava and went underground, but when that hero fought with Karṇa, the Nāga "became an arrow" in Karṇa's quiver and swept off Arjuna's diadem (given him by Indra), yet, being cursed to be "without base", that is of no account (1, 227, 5), he did not succeed in killing the hero, who slew him (8, 90, 12f., and ib. 54). In 8, 89, 89f., serpents as arrows enter earth and then, having taken a bath, return to fight (needing contact with their native environment to strengthen themselves, like Antaeus). For gold-guarding serpents in the mountains (7, 93, 34, etc.), see Kubera (§ 83—90).

The king of "lovely Bhogavatī" (1, 207, 31; ib. 51; 3, 57, 5, etc.) is Vāsuki (5, 186, 27), who has a Tīrtha at Prayāga (3, 85, 86), called Bhogavatī, and, if the text is right, those who visit the Godāvarī obtain his world (ib. 34, Vāsuker lokam, v. l. Vāyulokaṃ ca). His abode in 9, 37, 30 is Nāgadhanvan on the Bhogavatī or the Sarasvatī (cf. 3, 24, 20), where Vāsuki appears as king of pannagas and "there is no fear of snakes there" (ib. 33). It was here he was consecrated king and at the Tīrtha there live 14,000 seers. Nāgadvīpa (6, 6, 55) is one "ear of the hare", whose other ear is Kāśyapa-land (see § 6). Like Dhanaṃjaya and Kumārī live Vāsuki and his wife Śataśīrṣā, ruling over Bhogavatī in the South, which he guards (5, 117, 17f.; ib. 103, 9; ib. 109, 19), and with him live Takṣaka, Airāvata, and other "sons of Surasā", Nāgas marked with gems, gourds, discus, and svastika (cf. H 3934), having three, seven, ten, one hundred, five hundred, or even a thousand heads (Śeṣa himself lives there), great bhogas, coils, and great bodies, and they are called in general "sons of Kaśyapa" (5, 103, 5 f.). Surasā is called Nāgamātṛ and lives in the ocean, whence she rose in demoniac shape (persuaded by the gods to interfere with Hanumat!); she is called Dākṣāyaṇī (R 5, 1, 145 f. and ib. 58, 21). Like Citrāṅgadā she has the name of an Apsaras. Vāsuki is especially associated with Śeṣa in the churning of the ocean, where he acts as cord of the churn, his mouth being held by the Asuras and his tail by the gods (1, 18, 7 f.; cf. R 1, 45, 18). He is himself revered like a god and has a shrine in the asylum of Agastya (§ 20).

Vālmīki speaks of "serpents having the form of gods", devakalpāḥ pannagāḥ (R 5, 1, 6), as associates of Yakṣas, etc., on Mt. Mahendra; and in Mbh. hero-praising hosts and rows, nāgavīthi, of serpents fill the cars of saints in heaven (13, 107, 57; cf. 7, 145, 78).

R recognises the same leading Nāgas as does Mbh. Vāsuki, Takṣaka, (R 3, 32, 13), Śaṅkha, and Jaṭin (new) are conquered by Rāvaṇa (R 6, 7, 9). Their power is admitted (R 3, 38, 1) and the beauty of their females (R 5, 12, 21, captured; R 7, 88, 14, na devīṣu na nāgīṣu . . dṛṣṭapūrvā). Vālmīki (R 4, 41, 37) also places Bhogavatī far to the south (near Agastya's hermitage!) and calls Vāsuki its sarparāja. Historically important is Nāgāhvaya city (above) as the place where the Dharmacakra started, on the banks of the Gomatī, and the same as a title of Buddha on the one hand and of the Kuru or Pāṇḍu city (Nāgāhva = Hāstinapura) on the other. Also the appearance in the great war of serpents, uragas as Nāgas, acting as chariot-warriors, just like human heroes, is remarkable. The form and ornaments of Nāgas are those of heroes idealised (5, 169, 17 and 2, 9, 11). The "many-headed" Nāgas start with the comparison of a snake with an arm. The arm ends in five fingers, and is first said to be like a fat, smooth snake, then like a five-headed (the fingers) snake. It is for this reason that the five heads (mouths) are commoner than three or any other number (cf. 3, 157, 67, saṃhṛtya muṣṭiṃ pañcaśīrṣam ivo 'ragam, where the fist is the five-headed snake). Apart from this notion, the Nāgas carry banners, etc. in battle and wear svastikas, particularly the Māgadha Nāgas; a Nāga called Svastika lives in that district. In the domain of mythology, the great snake of the deep of an older period appears to have become an idle name, Ahi Budhnya, except for his connection with the finding of treasure, where he appears as the archetype of "treasure keeping" serpents (§ 83), and his reappearance as a Rudra (§ 113) or name of Śiva, the god wreathed in serpents. The Nāgas are anyway bhūmiśaya (7, 201, 24) and living underground have naturally charge of its metallic wealth.

The superstition of snake-birth may also be mentioned as of mythological value. The seizer, grahī, Kadrū, takes a subtile form and enters a pregnant woman, who then gives birth to a snake (3, 230, 37). There seems to be no reason to separate this fiend from the daughter of Prajāpati and Vinatā (1, 16 and 21 f.). Historically the most important Nāga is undoubtedly Takṣaka. He takes the side of Arjuna in battle, as do Vāsuki, Citrasena, Maṇika, and all the Kādraveya serpents, as well as the Airāvatas, Saurabheyas, and Vaiśāleyas (bhoginaḥ, 8, 87, 43 f.). Here S has Takṣaka and Upatakṣaka. Vaiśāleya (AV. 8, 10, 29; Śāṅkh. GS. 4, 18, 1) is an old patronymic of Takṣaka and probably is to be taken so here. Takṣaka is still the venomous, viṣolbaṇa, Nāga (6, 107, 15), according to S 4, 3, 28, the foremost of serpents, but his name, the "builder", and his especial glory (8, 79, 94, "glorious as Takṣakabhoja") show or indicate an historical character. He does not live in Māgadha, as do Arbuda and Svastika, but in the West, as Khāṇḍava is represented to be the ālayaḥ pannagendrasya Takṣakasya mahātmanaḥ (S 1, 248, 23), or, "he used to live in Khāṇḍava and Kurukṣetra" (1, 3, 139; 223, 7), where he was the especial friend of Indra, to whose heaven he went, though suspended in air through Āstīka's crying to him (1, 53, 18; 58, 2). By slaying Janamejaya's father he caused the eventual overthrow of the Nāgas (1, 3, 141 f.), an act committed ostensibly because of the king's despite of Brahmanic priests (1, 41), but really in revenge. He is Nāgarāja as well as bhujagottama (1, 227, 4; 228, 16). When it is said that he lives in Kashmir, it must be remembered that the Kāśmīramaṇḍala extends to Kurukṣetra (3, 82, 90). Upatakṣaka is mentioned only above (v. l. S 8, 91, 45) and R 7, 23, pra. 5, 23 (with Karkoṭaka, Kambala, Aśvatara, Dhanaṃjaya, Airāvata, Śeṣa, and Vāsuki). It was Janamejaya who conquered Takṣaśilā (1, 3, 20). R distinguishes between Takṣaka, whose wife was carried off by Rāvaṇa (R 3, 32, 14; ib. 6, 7, 9) and Takṣa (R 7, 101, 11) as "son of Bharata" and founder of Takṣaśilā in Gandharva-land as opposed to Gāndhāra-land, the other side of the Indus. The fate of all lower animals is supposed to be like that of men. Even fishes go to heaven (13, 51, 39 f., "go to heaven with your fishes . . on this the Niṣādas went to heaven with the fishes", saha matsyair divaṃ yayuḥ); cf. also under horses, elephants, etc. The change of a nymph into a fish is not extraordinary (see Apsarasas, § 87). The Fish-Avatar is discussed in § 142. For other animal Avatars, see § 148. The Tortoise is not an Avatar in 1, 18, where it upholds the mountain Mandara at the churning of ocean, but it becomes an Avatar of Hari in R pra. 1, 45 (VP. 1, 9), originally of (Brahman) Prajāpati (ŚB. 7, 4, 3, 5), perhaps still earlier a totem of the Bharatas.

III. SPIRITS.

§ 14. **Pretas.** — Through all periods from the Vedic age onward spirits known as ghosts, beings, and Fathers have been the object of a pious regard, expressed by both fear and devotion. They may be said to be spirits indifferently good or bad. The Pretas are embryonic Pitṛs (Fathers). The newly dead is a Preta or Pareta ("departed") ghost; the one long dead is a Pitṛ (Father divinity). The Pitṛs are the divinities even of gods. Only Pitṛs are divided into formal classes. The Pretas, as they are simpler and logically precede, may be discussed first. In both epics Preta is the usual form, but R uses also Pareta (2, 63, 15; cf. paretakāle, "at the time of dying", R 3, 51, 31), and Paretarāj is later use for Pretarāj (Pretakalpa is like gatāyus, used of men almost dead, R 3, 41, 20; pretyabhāva is death, R 4, 22, 18, etc.). Yama is lord not only of the Pitṛs but of the Pretas; Pretarāḍviṣayaṃ gata = Yamalokagata (R 6, 79, 14). Pretaloka is the antithesis of jīvaloka (7, 39, 24, etc.), the world of dead and that of the living. But the Preta though not alive is lively enough, and even the long dead Pitṛ is an active element in the living world. After Daśaratha has been dead for years, he appears in the sight of man, raised by Maheśvara, and stands dressed in bright garments, devoid of dust, and says he will never forgive Kaikeyī. Then be changes his mind, forgives her, and blesses Rāma, whom he embraces, and finally goes back to Indra's heaven (R 6, 122, 10 f.). To return really from death to life is possible if a god permits, or one can give a part of one's life to another who is dead and so revive the dead. Indra gives back to life even the monkeys slain for Rāma (ib. 123, 10 f.) and all the Pretas rise not only in vision but in reality when divine power exerts itself (15, 33, 1 f.; see also § 4 on the saṃjīvana). But usually the Pretas appear in ghastly battle-scenes (3, 173, 48, etc.) as demoniac forms dancing with Piśācas and Bhūts (§ 16—17) amid carnage (7, 146, 36); nor are they silent. The noise of a tumult is "like that of shrieking ghosts", pretānāṃ krandatām iva (7, 171, 9). They are, however, described as senseless, though perhaps stupid is the real meaning: those suffering in battle cry to the heroes, "as the witless dead shriek to their king", Arjunaṃ krośanti pretarājapure yadvat pretarājaṃ vicetasaḥ (8, 64, 59; cf. 10, 5, 13, pretā iva vicetasaḥ, sc. svapanti, sleep "like the senseless dead"). The voices of the wounded are like those of the dead (Pretas): "dreadful voices of those who shriek in battle like those who are dead" (in hell? 6, 46, 19). Those who are killed are said to be "gone (led) into the power of the Pretas", gatā (nītā) pretavaśam (3, 313, 29; S 1, 171, 64), but probably the apparent implication of power in the ghosts is due to this being a shortened form of expression for the usual phrase, pretarājavaśam ("dead" is pretībhūta, pretaga, °gata, 7, 19, 37; 5, 40, 16; R 4, 30, 22, pretagataṃ Yamakṣaye; saṃpretya in 13, 1980 is not in B, 58, 11, nor S 93, 11, but parāṃ gatim asaṃpretya, 5, 65, 3, is "while still alive"). The Pretas are, in a word, not honored by the poets. In the course of time, if honored by their relations with burial of the corpse and offerings to the ghost, they become honored by all as divine Fathers, but till then they belong neither to gods nor men, and so are like outcasts, cyutā devamanuṣyebhyo yathā pretās tathai 'va te (sinners and outcasts are "cast out from gods and men like Pretas", 12, 109, 25). Hence they must be offered food, pretabhāvānugaṃ vasu (S pretyabhāva); food "reaching the dead" is given by a man for his sons (15, 8, 9). Compare pretyabhāvikam īhante aihalaukikam eva ca (14, 37, 17) as "after death and here", and in S 12, 32, 36, rakṣa svadharmaṃ, Kaunteya, śreyān yaḥ pretyabhāvikaḥ (B 33, 48, has pretya, Bhārata). The Pretas do not appear as individuals so much as hosts or troops. The identity of Pretas and Pitṛs (in the end) may be shown by such a remark as that of Bhīma (4, 22, 4), when he says that he will kill the Kīcaka and expresses himself thus: "I will cause him to see his grandsires dead of old" (pūrvapretān pitāmahān). Pretarājapuram as the city of Yama is a commonplace, as the bourne from which there is no return (7, 93, 19; durdarśam, ib. 132, 33; but ib. 135, 14, "one might return from that city but not from this antagonist", in extravagant laud). Yama's city is "full of ghosts" (1, 173, 43, abhavat Pretarājasya puraṃ pretair ivā 'vṛtam). To perform the Pretakṛtyāni (°kārya, °karman) or ceremonies for the dead, renders one impure (tabu). After the funeral one becomes pure again (7, 52, 30). As objects of worship the Pretas are low down in the religious scale, being classed with the Bhūts. The men of purest soul worship gods; those of middle sort (passionate) worship Yakṣas and Rākṣasas; those of the lowest sort, whose souls are in darkness, worship Pretas and bands of Bhūts (6, 41, 4). Together with Bhūts,

Pretas are often associated with Piśācas and other "wanderers by night". They are conjoined with the Pitṛs in the phrase pitṛrajanicarāḥ (7, 73, 48), where the group is opposed to gods and Asuras, etc.; but when the saint says that he sees in Viṣṇu's stomach "Guhyakas and Pitṛs", paśyāmi Guhyakān pitaras tathā (3, 188, 119), he makes a similar connection as loose as his grammar, for in fact the Pitṛs have about as little to do with the one as with the other. The Pretas dance with Bhūts and Piśācas not only on battle-fields but in burial-grounds; yet the burial-ground is not called theirs but the "grove of the Pitṛs". As the gods have their Devavana, so the Fathers have their Pitṛvana (pretavana is a later word), and it is said, sarve pitṛvanaṃ prāptāḥ svapanti vigatajvarāḥ, "after life's (fitful) fever they sleep well, who reach the Fathers' grove" (11, 3, 5; and C 119 = 4, 16; B and S have °tvacāḥ), to render it almost literally in Shakespeare's words. Certain inconsistencies in belief are to be found, as with all people who believe in both ghost and soul. Thus it is absurd to suppose that the Preta within a few days of death and before the funeral has already "gone to the third heaven", as is asserted in 11, 9, 17. Compare ib. 17, 32: "This hero has already gained the worlds won by prowess, if tradition and revelation are true" (āgamāḥ and śrutayaḥ). The supposition that a hero is instantly carried up to heaven is, however, if not orthodox, at least a common idea. So the wife, already jealous of her dead husband who still lies unburied, cries (11, 20, 25 f.): "Whom dost thou now speak to, as if to me, after going to the Pitṛ-world? Wilt thou now in heaven disturb the hearts of the nymphs (Apsarasas) with thy beauty, gaining the world of the nymphs and righteous and associating with nymphs?" (idānīm and nūnam). It is after this that the "priests with matted locks pile the mound and light the fires and sing the three Sāmans while they lament" (at the funeral, 11, 23, 38 f.). Yudhiṣṭhira says (ib. 26, 12): "Those who have sacrificed their bodies (in battle) have obtained worlds like those of Devarāj . . or have gone to the Gandharvas . . or, even if cowardly, have gone to the Guhyakas, or have gone to the Uttara Kurus" (Hyperboreans), that is, before the Pitṛmedhas (of 26, 39) were performed, when "the noise of Sāmans and Ṛcas and of women weeping caused consternation in all beings" (sarvabhūtānām, ib. 40), after which the kriyās were performed, that is, the water-ceremonies, which are called particularly the salilakriyāḥ (27, 4) or udakakarman (ib. 27), this last immediately preceding the Pretakṛtya (ib. 28) or Śrāddha (see below).

§ 15. **The Pitṛs.** — The Fathers are divided into separate classes, but the classes are not fixed. By analogy with other hebdomads there are seven Pitṛvaṃśas (13, 91, 28), described as associating with the All-gods (who in Vedic literature include them; viśve devāś ca ye nityaṃ Pitṛbhiḥ saha gocarāḥ, ib. 24). They are also regarded as Pitāmahas, the seven beginning with Brahman (in connection with the Śrāddha, 13, 92, 22; pitāmaha for pitṛ also 1, 214, 12, etc.). By means of the Śrāddha feast "the Pretas are released", that is the ghosts become raised to the rank of Pitṛs. The feast begins with an offering to Fire (Agni), who saves the Fathers from indigestion (13, 92, 11). When water is brought, one offering is made to the water-god Varuṇa, and at the same time one to Soma, as the god of the Fathers. This differs slightly from Manu, 3, 211, where the offerings are to Agni, Soma, and Yama (food-details as in the law-books). The Fathers are worshipped not only by men but even by gods, demons, serpents, Piśācas, Kiṃnaras, etc. (ib. 87, 5), not after but before the gods (monthly, before the new moon becomes visible, the gods after it becomes visible), the afternoon being the right time, to agree with the after-half of the month (dark half). But every day is appropriate in the light half of the month except the deadly fourteenth day (13, 87, 6, and 18f. and Manu 3, 123). Demons (Asuras) and the Asurendra get all the worshipper eats when facing south; Yātudhānas and Piśācas get the feast if no sesame is given, or if it is performed by a Krodhavaśa (ib. 90, 19f.; this is "Yama's rule"). Atri first taught Nimi to give a feast to the Fathers instead of offering it "to the soul of his son" (ib. 91, 20). The cakes are offered first to one's father, then to one's grandfather, then to one's great-grandfather, and the Sāvitrī verse should be recited over each cake. A verse is said also to Soma as to the Pitṛmat god (ib. 92, 15, Somāye 'ti ca vaktavyaṃ tathā pitṛmate 'ti ca). Monthly Śrāddhas and daily offerings are made to the Fathers, and whenever one is in danger, as when one crosses water in an ox-cart (13, 92, 16f.). In this case the offering may be a handful of water, presented first to one's ancestors and then to those of friends and relations (the aupahārikam offering is that of Manu 3, 273f., in 13, 126, 35). These offerings are known as Śrāddha, Pitṛyajña, Pitṛmedha, and Aupahārika. The special god of the Fathers is Yama Pitṛpati and Pitṛrāja or Soma Pitṛmat. Only an atheist would disregard the Fathers. Compare R 2, 108, 14f. Jābāli, in regard to the aṣṭakā- (Manu 4, 150) pitṛdaivatyam, says that the dead cannot eat, yet he is an unbeliever. But the Mokṣa doctrine also ignores the cult of the Fathers (12, 289, 22f.). Elsewhere the Fathers are regarded as objects of reverence and proper recipients of prayers and sacrifice. Their wish is law, even in details. One must not chew a tooth-pick on the new moon's day because the Fathers do not like one to do so, since it hurts the new moon (13, 127, 4f.). Most of the Śrāddha rules concern themselves, however, with the persons who may take part in the feast, not with the Fathers' wishes. These persons include the proper relations and proper people; excluded are diseased persons, "women with their ears cut off", etc., the rules being referred to the Fathers as authority (sermon by the Pitṛs, 13, 125, 18f.). Much is old legal material but no one need fear to admit that much of this is also new and foisted upon the Pitṛs, who serve as stalking-horses, like gods and demons, for the writers of the later epic to impress trite morality but also to bring in new rules. For example, in 13, 129, 2: "An adulterer and a thief are not conversible to the Pitṛs and neither they nor gods will accept the offerings of such sinners" (asaṃbhāṣyā bhavanty ete Pitṝṇām, etc.) is a perfectly good old rule in new form; but in 13, 125, 73f. the statement that the Pitṛs are so delighted with the freeing of a blue bull (cf. 3, 2, 57f.) and with offerings of water and sesame and with the lighting of lamps that one thereby frees himself of all debts to his ancestors, even startles Vṛddha Gārgya so that his hair rises on his head and he asks, "What is the use of setting free blue bulls?" and is only quieted by the direct statement on the part of the Pitṛs themselves that they rejoice for sixty thousand years if their descendant sets free a blue bull which urinates. The talk of the Pitṛs here begins with a question of connubial intercourse on Śrāddha days and is carried on with a messenger of the physician gods (the Aśvins). It also takes up the disposition of rice-cakes at a Śrāddha. The first cake is cast into water and goes to the moon; the second is given to the wife of the deceased; and the third is cast into fire (ib. 19f.). The rice-cake of the Moon pleases the god and then (so) pleases the Pitṛs; that eaten by the wife causes the Pitāmahas (= Pitṛs) to give a son to one who wishes offspring; that cast into fire makes the Pitṛs happy, so that they grant wishes, etc. The Ṛtvij of a sacrificer becomes his Pitṛ (pitṛtvam anugacchati) and hence he must avoid connubial intercourse on that day (etc., etc.; the S text adds a mass of matter on these "gods of gods" and their feast). Offerings of grain, etc., to the Pitṛs are purificatory and apart from special cases they are made to the Pitṛs on the eighth day (aṣṭakā) after the full moon; especially at the beginning of winter or "when autumn is over and men desire more, and clothe themselves in skins, and set out on expeditions, and Himavat is really the home of snow, the sun having lingered long in the southern declension" (R 3, 16, 6f., navāgra yaṇapūjābhir abhyarcya pitṛdevatāḥ, etc., sevamāne dṛḍhaṃ sūrye diśam Antaka-(v. l. Agastya-)sevitām). In the special case where the king's body has been burned, after being embalmed in oil, ten days of mourning pass and the funeral feast is offered on the twelfth, with rich gifts to the priests as an aurdhvadaihikam of the departed (to make him happy), and on the thirteenth day is performed the śodhana or collection of his bones (purification), as described in R 2, 77, 1—5 (see below). As to the food offered, the same general rule obtains (yadannāḥ) as is applied in the case of the gods: "What a man eats, his gods eat" (R 2, 102, 30, etc.).

Allusion has been made above to the seven families of Fathers, divided according to the seers. In 3, 3, 43, seven gaṇas or troops of Pitṛs probably refer to the distinction made between the kinds mentioned as living at the court of Brahman, where are to be found "Agniṣvāttas, Phenapas, Ūṣmapas, Sudhāvatas, Barhiṣadas, and others incorporate". Compare 2, 11, 44f.: "Fathers swift as thought, in seven gaṇas, four being mūrtimantas (embodied) and three aśarīriṇas" (having no body; but S with B, śarīriṇaḥ). The Agniṣvāttas and Somasadas in Manu are the Pitṛs of the gods and the Sādhyas, respectively, while the Barhiṣadas are the Pitṛs of the Daityas, Dānavas (etc., Manu 3, 195f.) and are here also declared to be the sons of the seers, Marīci, Atri, etc. The three epic aśarīriṇas are Vairājas, Agniṣvāttas, and Gārhapatyas (= Barhiṣadas), who are all nākacaras, i. e. "they wander in the vault of heaven", and worship Brahman. The four mūrtimantas are Somapas, Ekaśṛṅgas (Unicorns), Caturvedas, and Kalas, who are worshipped among the four castes and with the others form part of the court of Prajāpati: "when these are satisfied (filled), then divine Soma is also filled" (etair āpyāyitaiḥ pūrvaṃ Somaś cā 'pyāyyate punaḥ, ib. 48). This division is also recognised in H 936, where it is said that the gods revere the Vairāja Pitṛs; but otherwise no such formal division is recognised, only the various classes are mentioned on occasion as Somapas, etc. The gaṇas here described appear to belong to the later epic, the Unicorns, Four-Veda Pitṛs, and Kalas being known only from this passage, perhaps an extension of the older groups, called Somavantas, Barhiṣadas, and Agniṣvāttas, as they are in ŚB. 2, 6, 1, 4f., where the Pitṛs are identified with the seasons. The six seasons and seven families are then equated with groups of Pitṛs. But even in the ordered account of Manu there are different and confusing systems involved and in the epic it is quite impossible to get any consistent grouping. Thus in 12, 270, 15, Pitṛs who "approve of Mantras for the dead" are cited as Arciṣmantas, Barhiṣadas, and Kravyādas, by whom the Mokṣa doctrine is contradicted (inferentially). The Ūṣmapas appear to be one with the Somapas, but the latter title is also applied to any who drink Soma (thus kings are Somapas, 5, 152, 18). The Phenapas, "foam-drinkers" are said to be those "excellent Munis" who live on the froth of the Ocean of Milk and are feared by the gods (5, 102, 6); but in 13, 141, 97 f., the Phenapas are Ṛṣis who drink foam left over from ambrosia drunk by Brahman at sacrifices. One class often represents the Fathers in general, as when Ūṣmapas are grouped as worshippers of Viṣṇu with Rudras, Ādityas, Vasus, Sādhyas, All-gods, Aśvins, Maruts, Gandharvas, Yakṣas, Asuras, and Siddhas (6, 35, 22 f.). In 5, 109, 2, they are assigned to the South (the general region of the Pitṛs), as opposed to the Dhūmapas of the East, and are called Devas, the Dhūmapas being Munis (ib. 108, 14). With Ūṣmapas and Dhūmapas are grouped Kṣīrapas (13, 14, 56), but they are merely ascetic priests (see §§ 118—126). In the later epic any number of these "drinkers" (cf. Ghṛtapas, etc., below) are predicated as heavenly beings. The Pitṛs are called "divinities even of the gods" in 9, 44, 32 f., where the Pitṛs visit Skanda (cf. Yāmas and Dhāmas under Yama). Manu's Sukālins (M 3, 197) are the Sukālas of H 985 (ib. 932, the seven gaṇas are as above, four mūrtimantas and three amūrtimantas).

The Fathers, whose very existence depends upon descendants (1, 179, 14 f.), are naturally opposed to too much asceticism. They advise against suicide (ib.) and anxiously ask: "Will our son or grandson give us food?" (13, 63, 20). This of course refers to the ordinary Fathers, not those who "exist on froth", etc. One feeds them with svadhā, as gods with Soma (12, 29, 116). It is their main preoccupation to get something to eat, but they continue to show an interest in the affairs of their family and occasionally come to help their descendants. Thus eight Fathers in the shape of birds (souls in bird-shape) hold up the fainting Bhīṣma. On different occasions they resemble planets in glory, hold one up, give him water to drink; give Bhīṣma advice as to the best weapon to use, reconsider the matter and advise him not to do as they had advised, etc. Pitṛs appear in battle or as a vision at night, and are called svadhābhujas, Fathers, Munis, and Vipramukhyas. They are not only "like planets", grahas, they are stars; but the souls of saints appear as stars, falling stars when their merit is exhausted (5, 182, 14 f.; 6, 119, 97; 3, 42, 35, etc.). Their usual appearance is "in the form of mortals", martyamūrtidharāḥ (3, 41, 9), but glorified. A Pitṛgraha, however, is a "Father-demon" who attacks people and makes them go mad (3, 230, 48), as contrasted with similar fiends called Devagraha, Gāndharvagraha, etc.; here the Pitṛ is acting as a fiend. The Pitṛs of the South are associated with the All-gods, Pitṛlokarṣis, Devarṣis, and Rājarṣis (5, 109, 5). The "course pursued by Pitṛs, Paitāmahas, and Rājarṣis" is the course of moral conduct for man to follow. The "favorite district of the Fathers" is the South (pitṛjuṣṭā dik, 7, 17, 37); pitṛsādana = Yamasādana (8, 77, 44); cf. pitṛrājāśritā dik (2, 46, 15) and dik pitṝṇām aśivā (5, 66, 14). The chief Father is the eponymous hero Aryaman (6, 34, 29). The intimate relation existing between the Fathers and descendants may be shown by the fact that the Fathers become hysterical when a child is born, wondering if he will bring good or ill to the Fathers (3, 159, 13; "the Fathers in the world of Fathers grieve and laugh", that is become hysterical). Agastya sees his Fathers hanging upside down in a pit because he has given them no descendants, and converses with them (3, 96, 14). Similar is the tale of Jaratkāru (1, 13, 18). Mandapāla lacking children could not stay in Pitṛloka and became a bird (1, 229, 5 f.).

The Fathers are called lokabhāvanas, "world-creators" (3, 41, 9), as they are among the creative forces by virtue of being ancestors of the gods, pūrvadevas. The special path, as distinguished from that of the gods, followed by the Pitṛs (Pitṛyāna) is (morally) one attained by sacrifices and practical duties (3, 2, 75 f.; ib. 41, 9). All duties are arranged in two groups, sacrifice, study, liberality, austerity in one, and truth, forgiveness, self-restraint, and lack of greed in the other. The first group is said in 3, 2, 75 to be Pitṛyāne sthitaḥ (but elsewhere in the epic, as in Hit. 2, 1, 7, the first group is dambhārtham, 5, 35, 57). As 3, 2 = 12, 7 is late, this Pitṛyāna interpretation is probably secondary, though the general idea is old (cf. TS. 5, 7, 2, 3 and Chānd. Up. 5, 10, 1 f.). Physical interpretation of the "Path of the Fathers" is more common. This is the path leading to the Moon (13, 16, 45), but also the path to the South, as that is where the Fathers live; but this is interpreted as the sun's dakṣiṇāpatha or dakṣiṇāyana (southern course, summer-time to winter). The northern path is followed by those who live a life of renunciation or quietism; that by the South, dakṣiṇena, is for those who follow the life of active religion, moral but not philosophic. It is also a "glorious" course, leading to the Moon and aiding priests, all of whom are supported by men of action (12, 19, 13 f.). The South is the path of Aryaman, of acts, and ceremonies; the North is the path of Pūrvavids and Yogins (12, 26, 9 f.). Among the Pitṛs appear also the Ṛṣis (§ 118), and they cannot always be distinguished from Pitṛs. Thus the Vaikhānasas are Pitṛs and Ṛṣis, and "Father Ṛṣis who have gone to heaven by means of study" are the Ajas, Pṛśnis, Sikatas, Aruṇas, and Ketus, who belong to the Vaikhānasa school (12, 26, 7 f.). The Sikatas and Pṛśnis appear again with Somapas, Ghṛtapas, Vālakhilyas, Prabhāsas, Vaiśvānaras, and Marīcipas, as families of Ṛṣis (12, 166, 24; also in 7, 190, 34, as Maharṣis). See also Yama, "king of Pretas", "king of Pitṛs", etc., and Ṛṣis (§ 54 f.; § 118 f.).

It is in all likelihood owing to the old-time identification of the Pitṛs with the seasons that the Ṛbhus (in 12, 208, 22 mentioned with the Maruts, but otherwise well-nigh ignored in epic poetry) are in 3, 261, 19 f. exalted as the highest divinities. Their earlier names are lost to the epic, though Vāja appears as son of a Manu in the Hariv. 465, and even as a group they are conspicuously absent from epical groupings of gods. But in this passage of Vana they appear as inhabitants of Brahman's heaven and "even divinities revere them", for "they are the divinities even of the gods", devānām api devatāḥ, and their self-moving world, self-illuminated, is one of wholly supersensuous beings. In their heaven is no "woman-made woe", no greed of world-lordship, no hunger, thirst, grief, sweat of toil, evil smell or bad air, nor other disagreeable things. No dust is there, and their garlands, as of gods, never fade; for their heaven is above the heaven where "those who are about to fall perceive their flowers wither", in the pure region of Meru, and thirty-three thousand leagues in extent. The Ṛbhus are also thirty-three according to the B text, but this is impossible and the S text has for ime devāḥ, which should be the Ṛbhus (trayastriṃśad ime devā yeṣāṃ lokā manīṣibhir gamyante), trayastriṃśad ime lokāḥ śeṣā lokāḥ, etc. (that is, "the worlds are thirty-three; the remaining worlds are attainable by the wise"). These

Ṛbhus "have no oblation, drink no ambrosia, have heavenly bodies, and are invisible (vigrahamūrtayaḥ); they seek no joy in joy; they are the eternal gods of gods (devadevāḥ sanātanāḥ), who change not as the æons change, know neither age not death, weal nor woe, possessing a lot desired even of the gods; since it is unattainable to those subject to desire, but attainable to those who have cast off desire and are become truly wise". This extraordinary exaltation of the Ṛbhus treats them as a group of beings who, for no apparent reason, have become the highest exponents of spiritual life. The Hariv. 436f., makes the Ṛbhus one of five devagaṇas of the Cākṣuṣa Manu (in the sixth Manvantara), a list which, as the Lekhas show, is post-epical: Apyāḥ Prabhūtā Ṛbhavaḥ Pṛthukāś ca divaukasaḥ, Lekhā nāma. Every group here is handed down in other forms, but the Lekhas have a doubtful individuality as beings set beside Yakṣas and Apsarasas (forms of parts of the personal incorporate Viṣṇu, Hariv. 14269) and regarded as Father-gods or gods who are also Pitṛs (13, 18, 74, with Somapas and Ūṣmapas as a group of gods, but with v. l. lokā for Lekhā). In VP. 3, 1, 27, the Ṛbhus are replaced by Bhavyas (Ādyas, Prasṛtas, Bhavyas, Pṛthagas, Lekhas (sic B, for Prastutas and Pṛthugas; here numbered with eight members to the group). It appears as if the Ṛbhus thus exalted must be Pitṛs; in which case the old equation of Pitṛs and seasons must have been in the mind of the poet, for the Ṛbhus represent the (originally) three seasons as creative forces. At least there seems to be no other reason for this late and sudden eulogium on beings so epically inconspicuous as the Ṛbhus, and the expression "gods of gods" used of a group (for devadeva is singly applied to several gods) can apply only to Pitṛs (cf. above where Pitṛs are revered by gods, and Manu's group of Pitṛs as "Pitṛs of gods"). The complete identification, as ekībhūta, of gods (Devas) and Pitṛs is rather a late touch made by Agni (1, 7, 9), who himself distinguishes them as two classes worshipped respectively at the new and full moon.

§ 16. **The Bhūts.** — The Bhūtas (or Bhūtāni) are indistinct to the epic poets, who have not yet arranged the genealogy of spirits so as to make the Bhūts derive from Krodhā, as is done in H 11554; nor, as in VP. 1, 5, 44, from Brahman kruddha (ib. 1, 21, 25, they and Piśācas come from Krodhā). They are not yet clearly ghosts, but they lie between ghosts and other Piśitāśinas ("eaters of raw flesh"). Evil Bhūts are closely associated with ghosts in the epic and in modern times Bhūts are identified with Pretas, the concept including imps, ghosts, and goblins. In the epics, apart from such use as appears in Bhūtakṛt and Bhūtakarman (names of the creator), Bhūtadhāman (a son of Indra, 1, 197, 29), Bhūtadharā (as earth, RG 4, 44, 129, but with v. l.), the Bhūt as a spiritual being is not so much an imp as he is a great fiend. In general, Bhūt is any creature, Kālaḥ pacati bhūtāni (11, 2, 24 = Mait. Up. 6, 15), but as a malicious demon its nearest parallel is found in Sattva, "being" and spirit, good or bad, but with a tendency toward evil. Thus in R 2, 33, 8f., the people press about to see the exiles, "Sītā whom not even the Bhūts going in space have seen", and they exclaim, "Daśaratha speaks as if possessed by a Sattva" (sattvam āviśya, S; sattvenāviṣṭacetanaḥ, G; ib. 10 = Mbh. S 2, 101, 10, satyam! This whole section is stolen from R with required changes in names!). Compare R 2, 58, 34, Bhūtopahatacitte 'va, of a woman. Bhūts are ākāśaga, but especially are they night-wanderers, naiśāni, going with Yakṣas, Rākṣasas, etc., in troops, all described as raudrāḥ, piśitāśanāḥ (R 1, 34, 17 f.). People think a Bhūt or Rakṣas committed the "more than human" act of killing Dṛṣṭadyumna horribly at night (10, 8, 26 and 32). Man's mountain foes are hidden Bhūts and Rākṣasas (3, 140, 1 and 12). The Bhūts are "huge and very strong" and are countered by austerity and fire-lauds (see Agni). A traveller is apt to suffer from them (1, 143, 18). Sattvas and Bhūta-grāmas follow an army desiring blood (R 7, 100, 23). At home, they are the recipients of offerings, bali, coming regularly after gods and between guests and Pitṛs in the order of distribution (3, 193, 32; in 13, 93, 15, the saṃśritas, servants of the house, are fed first and Bhūts are omitted). In the wilds, Sītā begins with a bali to Bhūts (agram pradāya Bhūtebhyaḥ, R 2, 95, 36, Prakṣip.); cf. Manu, 3, 90, etc. Bhūtasaṅghas applaud heroes in battle (7, 122, 68) and Bhūtāni call bravo (R 3, 51, 21). Bhūts of the air may be any beings, as khecara, khacara, is applied to gods, Gandharvas, and Rākṣasas, as well as to Bhūts (1, 210, 7), and even Siddhas are Bhūtāni khacarāṇi (R 4, 59, 18—19). They are usually called naktaṃcaras, niśācaras, expressions applied, however, more often to their companion Rākṣasas (R 5, 5, 9, naktaṃcarāḥ "extraordinarily cruel", atyadbhuta-raudravṛttāḥ; cf. ib. 7, 37, Prak. 5, 28, kṣaṇadācaras, night-going fiends), as in 3, 155, 33, praseduḥ kṣaṇadācarāḥ, of the Krodhavaśa Rākṣasas. A wise man "bows his head to Pitṛs, gods, and night-wandering Bhūts", before going to bed (5, 183, 1 f.). Bhūts are thus of three categories, the indifferent (abhayaṃ yasya bhūtebhyaḥ sarveṣām abhayaṃ yataḥ . . sarvabhūtahito maitraḥ, 5, 63, 19 f., "[wise is he] who fears no beings and none fears him"), the hostile, and the kind. All the night-wandering demoniac Bhūts belong among the hostiles, and the groups under Śiva Bhūtapati (3, 38, 32), dangerous demons of the mountains (cf. 2, 3, 14 and R 6, 71, 13, arciṣmadbhir vṛto bhāti Bhūtair iva Maheśvaraḥ). Like the "play-ground of Rudra" appears a field of corpses filled with Bhūts, Piśācas, Rakṣas, and other flesh-eating night-wanderers (11, 6, 12, and often). Kindly Bhūts honor a hero (7, 37, 37) and guard him or lament his fall (R 3, 52, 41; ib. 6, 91, 62), and these are included when one offers a bali with that to the gods and Pitṛs, as beings potentially evil but probably disinclined to injure the householder who shows them respect (cf. VS. 1, 11). As such they are very likely confused with the Pretas or ghosts. The mahābhūtam as "element" may be replaced by bhūtam, and, conversely, both bhūtam mahat and mahābhūtam may mean no more than a big Bhūt. Thus in S 3, 313, 43, praharanto mahābhūtaṃ śaptās tenā 'tha te 'patan means "have they fallen because they were cursed by some big Bhūt whom they attacked?", and has a parallel in B ib. 21 (S 314, 19) bhūtaṃ mahad idaṃ manye bhrātaro yena me hatāḥ, "it must have been a big Bhūt that felled my brothers". The form is indifferently masculine and neuter, generally neuter, but with a tendency to regard the neuter as personified, so that a masculine adjective may agree with it, as in R 6, 79, 35, sādhu sādhv iti Bhūtāni vyāharanti nabhogatāḥ (ib. 71, 66, Bhūtā Devāḥ, "Bhūts and gods"). To sum up the epic Bhūtas, as mythologically restricted, they designate beings of a rather vicious disposition, small and great, and very likely included at first as subdivisions the particular groups known by special names as cannibalistic night-wanderers. But as ghosts are also by predilection malicious, the term Bhūt had a tendency to interchange with Preta, till the modern equivalence, Bhūta

= Preta, became thoroughly established. The tendency to restrict the broad general meaning to a certain class is seen in the literature immediately following the epic (Hariv. and Purāṇas), in which Bhūtas are assigned their proper parentage (that is are restricted to a class) in the divine genealogies.

§ 17. **Rākṣasas, Yātudhānas, and Piśācas.** — The close connection between the various classes of evil demons and spiritual powers not exactly evil yet not divine enough to be regarded as gods will often be a subject of special remark. This is sufficiently illustrated by the interchange of the same name among various groups. Thus in Mbh. the Rāksaṣa Maṇimat is a friend of Kubera (§ 83), and Maṇimat is also a name of a Yakṣa, of a Nāga, and of a king who is reborn as such after existing as Vṛtra, while Maṇimatī designates a Daitya-town (in both epics Maṇimat is a mountain). It seems that certain characters stood out more as individuals than as fixed members of a group and that such individuals are sometimes considered as belonging to one and sometimes to another group. But beyond this, the interrelation of different groups is so close that marriage connections constantly occur between these different social, if spiritual, groups, so that the offspring are, in terms of social life, half-breeds. No group, again, is wholly evil or wholly good. All that can be said is that each is prevailingly good or bad. The same in regard to appearance. Thus the following facts are applicable to individual or to limited groups of Rākṣasas, who are on the whole prevailingly evil. They help the gods; they fight against the gods. They are beautiful; they are hideous. They are weaker than gods or Gandharvas; they overcome the gods with ease. They protect; they injure. They are different from Yakṣas; but they are so much like Yakṣas that the same terms are applied to both. The facts as thus stated will be illustrated in the course of this paragraph with the exception of the last. It will suffice to say here that the Rākṣasas duplicate in part the qualities of Yakṣas because, according to one tradition, the two species are born of the same mother, Khaśā (H 234 and 11552; VP. 1, 21, 24, Khasā), who is a daughter of Dakṣa (H 169). Red eyes and dark bodies characterise the Yakṣas who guard Kubera; the Rākṣasas are always red-eyed and those guarding Kubera are like fiery smoke in color (H 13132). Here the function of the Rākṣasa is to guard. Whether, in India, the injurer became the guardian, or the "guardian" (of treasure) became the injurer, is still debated (rakṣ means injure and guard); but the application and growth of the words would favor the first interpretation. Rakṣas (Rākṣasa) was at first one of the many harmful spirits, a nocturnal power, a demon of darkness, and therefore evil. But as injurer of those opposing it, the Rakṣas is also protector of what it values, so that rakṣin, etc., become words exclusively indicating protector; yet the demon-group, when once formed as injurious, seldom passes over into the opposed conception. This happens most naturally when their own chieftain appoints them as guards, as above. So too in 3, 153, 11, it is said that "the Rākṣasas called Krodhavaśas, at command of their king, guard this (paradise and treasure) by thousands, with encircling weapons". But occasionally the Rakṣas becomes a more general guardian, as when one "guards the Sun" (§ 38), or, again, when the Sun-god appoints a Rākṣasa to "guard" Draupadī (4, 16, 11). This genesis is also what is to be expected from the point of view of other protecting spirits, like the Assyrian bulls representing powers of evil converted to good use. Native data strengthen this view further, inasmuch as the Rākṣasa is most closely connected with other powers of evil, so that he is often confounded with the Daitya, Dānava (or Asura), and is most intimate (even interchanging) with the Piśāca fiend. The Mbh. makes the Rākṣasas less human than does the Rām. Their king is here rich but not, as in R, beautiful; only his raiment is fine, but he himself, despite rich dress and adornment, is more "like a tree in a crematorium than a kalpa-tree" (3, 281, 5). The demons are here expressly of two classes, fierce and friendly, raudrā maitrāś ca (ib. 139, 10). They will cook and eat a man, after slaying him (3, 154, 16; 159, 25). They live in caves and in trees. Their presence portends blood, and when they are seen to "fall from space" (the sky), it is a sign of battle (5, 48, 104, and loc. cit. below). Even in the Rāma-tale of Mbh., Rāvaṇa, the chief Rākṣasa, is less royal-human than in Vālmīki's version, and apart from this episode the prominent Rākṣasas of the Mbh. are typical ogres, whereas in R of the chief fiends only Kumbhakarṇa is of this lower and popular type, the others being, so to speak, too gentlemanly for that class. The chief Mbh. Rākṣasas in independent tales are Jaṭāsura, i. e. Asura, and Baka, called Asurarāj (1, 160, 4), whose name and title again show the close connection between Rākṣasas and other evil spirits; also Alāyudha, Alambuṣa, and Kirmīra, relatives of these ogres, and Hiḍimba, father of the half-human Ghaṭotkaca; and later, the virtuous Virūpākṣa. Hiḍimbā is a female counterpart of her brother Hiḍimba. Bhīma kills the male and marries the female, who thus becomes mother of Ghaṭotkaca. The last is thus only half Rākṣasa, but he has the nature of his maternal kin and is accompanied into battle with the recognised classes of Rākṣasas, called Paulastyas and Yātudhānas, who ride indifferently on cars, horses, or elephants, and appear in any shape they choose, as elephants, tigers, etc., the whole troop of them having the name of "Nairṛti army" (7, 156, 113 f.; ib. 135 f.). They carry divine and human weapons, have long tongues, and in particular Ghaṭotkaca's chariot is drawn by gajanibhas, creatures "looking like elephants" (Piśācas, N; see below; ib. 156, 59). Hiḍimbā's son is described in a repetitive section (7, 175, 4 f.). He has pointed ears, stiff hair, sunken belly, red eyes, thick nose, a copper-colored face and long reddish tongue, four fangs, a mouth stretching from ear to ear, etc., etc.; he carries brass armor, a gold crown and earrings, and rides in an eight-wheel car. The strength of all these monsters increases greatly at or after midnight (ib. 175, 39). They shower stones, hurl trees, and are either mountainous in size or small as a thumb, as they momentarily choose (ib. 52 and 63). Their forte is illusion, which is "born with them" and they commence to grow stronger the moment the evening gloaming begins (6, 90, 65; 7, 156, 69 and 77): Ghaṭotkaca is at last (7, 179, 58) slain by the dart kept by Karṇa to kill Arjuna. His mother's brother Hiḍimba is like other Rākṣasas, a puruṣādin, narāśana, cannibal. He lives in a Śāla-tree and has eight fangs, pointed ears, red hair, is very strong and is much pleased with the smell of man (1, 152, 1 f.; 153, 1; 163, 7). His sister Hiḍimbā takes human form, can fly through the air, knows the past and future (S), and is accustomed to eat man and then dance with her brother to various measures after dinner (1, 152, 14). Her savagery is softened in S by the assertion that she is virtuous and wise although a Rākṣasī (S 167, 27 f.). Virūpākṣa is an ordinary epithet applied to Rākṣasas and other spirits in both epics, but as a name designates a "virtuous" demon of this class, called Rākṣasādhipati of Meruvraja. He is devout and gives liberally to priests at Kārttika days, etc., posing as friend of the holy crane in one of the moral dialogues of the later epic, another illustration of the tendency to convert the fiend into a guardian of virtue. The same epithet may be the name of Ghaṭotkaca's charioteer in 7, 175, 15; in RG 3, 7, 6 = 2, 5, it interchanges with gabhīrākṣa as epithet of Virādha. Baka, the Asurarāj Rākṣasa, lives in a cave; he too is red-haired and has pointed ears. He gets one human being daily to eat, from a village where Bhīma stays, who kills him (1, 163, 7 f.), and his relatives seek during the ensuing war to take revenge. Alāyudha is his brother (probably) and, as described, is an understudy of Ghaṭotkaca, but "lovelier"; and his "elephant-like" coursers bray like asses. Even the vultures on the car are imitated from the description of the greater demon (7, 176, 1 f. and 19). He too is a lord of Rākṣasas and a friend of Hiḍimba and Kirmīra. His steeds bray (are kharasvanāḥ), while those of Ghaṭotkaca have Piśāca-faces (7, 175, 93 and 176, 16). He is at last slain by Bhīma, after the two have fought "like Vālin and Sugrīva" (7, 178, 29 and 33, Bakajñāti). The fighting of all these ogres resembles, either with each other or with the epic heroes, that of Indrajit, Rāvaṇa, the Asuras and gods (6, 100, 51 f.; 7, 96, 23; ib. 108, 13). The first simile is stereotyped. Compare the fight of Bhīma and Jaṭāsura in 3, 157, 60, tad vṛkṣayuddham . . Vāli-Sugrīvayor bhrātroḥ purā strīkāṅkṣiṇor yathā. This Jaṭāsura is defied by Bhīma "by his good deeds and sacrifices", i. e. as Bhīma was good and Jaṭāsura evil, the victory was sure. Jaṭāsura had been a guest disguised as a priest and then, watching his opportunity, had tried to run away with the Pāṇḍus and Draupadī (ib. 1 f.). Jaṭāsura's son is Alambuṣa, brother of Baka, also called son or descendant of Ṛṣyaśṛṅga, Ārṣyaśṛṅgi (6, 90, 49 and 69; 7, 108, 24 and 176, 15), who as Rākṣasendra has the best chariot of the Rākṣasa army opposed to the Pāṇḍus (also drawn by "horse-faced Piśācas", 7, 167, 38). He is ranked as a Mahāratha, is called a descendant of kings (pārthivaputrapautra, 7, 140, 19; cf. 5, 167, 33), and fights because of his ancient grudge (pūrvavairam anusmaran, Udyog. ib.). Though apparently of human ancestry in part, he is a true Rākṣasa, descending into earth, rising into the air again, and having any form at will; he is eventually killed by Sātyaki (7, 108, 27 f.; ib. 140, 18). Alambuṣā is the name of an Apsaras and the wife of Ikṣvāku (9, 51, 5, etc.; R 1, 47, 11, as wife of Ikṣ. and mother of Viśāla). Kirmīra, the "brother of Baka", is less important. He is mentioned in 3, 10, 23 (cf. 7, 176, 4) with Hiḍimba and Baka as a foe of the gods, but though he is tall as a mountain and even has eight fangs and employs illusion, he is finally throttled by Bhīma ("as deer by lion slain"). His illusion (3, 11, 58) is dispelled by Mantras that kill Rākṣasas. Oddly enough, he carries a firebrand, ulmuka, the very thing (see § 49 f.) used to dispel such creatures (3, 11, 6). He appears however like a lightning-charged thunder-cloud. He lives by eating men and says that even after death Baka is still gratified with blood (3, 11, 34), probably as a libation, since Jaṭāsura also cries out to Bhīma, "I will make a libation of your blood to the Rākṣasas you have already killed", teṣām adya kariṣyāmi tavā 'sreṇo 'dakakriyām (3, 157, 49). He lives in the Kāmyaka woods; Baka in the Vaitrakīya forest. Whether "brother of Baka" is to be taken literally or only as indicating that Kirmīra like Alambuṣa is a brother fiend, is perhaps of no importance. The Rākṣasas of Mbh., apart from the war and the family-feud with Bhīma, appear as dwellers in mountain-wilds, rough places, disturbing holy places, by their "beauty" destroying the meditations of saints (3, 113, 1 f.). Yātudhānas are Rākṣasas formed by Ghaṭotkaca to fight, illusive forms (7, 179, 39). The female Rākṣasī bears as soon as she conceives and her children are born adult in power (1, 155, 35 f.). When attacked by Nāgas, a Rākṣasa turns into the form of Garuḍa and devours them (6, 90, 75). As an illustration of the possible transference of function in the nature of Rākṣasas may be taken the case of Jarā, a female Rākṣasī living on meat and blood, appointed, however, by Brahman to destroy evil Dānavas. Her image must be painted on the wall of a pious man's house to bring him good luck, that is to keep all evil from him. As such she then is known as the Gṛhadevī, "goddess of the house" (2, 17, 39; 18, 1 f.); yet she is still so much of a Rakṣas that she collects raw flesh at cross-roads at night (ib.). One of the common evil deeds of Rākṣasas is to carry off women. In 1, 6, 1 f., an unnamed Rākṣasa who has been promised a bride subsequently married to a human saint (Bhṛgu) carries her off, but he drops dead, burned to ashes, when the saint's son is born, apparently, however, because the son was sun-like, and the fiends are coerced by luminaries (taṃ dṛṣṭvā .. ādityavarcasam, tad Rakṣo bhasmasād bhūtaṃ papāta). Rāma slew Rakṣas (rakṣāṃsi) because they had destroyed the sacrifices, and he thus gave back to the Manes and gods their wonted offerings (7, 59, 18). Kṛṣṇa slew Ogha (5, 48, 83, associated with Naraka and Mura), a Rakṣas.

Rākṣasas are sons of Pulastya, fourth son of Brahman, so that even Rāvaṇa when described as "thief of sacrifice and robber of girls" is still Pāulastyanandana (R 3, 32, 23; ib. 6, 114, 53 f.). According to the great epic, all Rākṣasas are sons of Pulastya; but those called Nairṛtas are in particular sons of Nirṛti (Destruction), the wife of Adharma, and also the mother of Fear, Terror, and Death (1, 66, 7; ib. 54 f.). The sons of the wicked king in this epic are incarnations of these Rākṣasas and of other evil beings; as sons of Pulastya the Rākṣasas are brothers of the Yakṣas (ib. 67, 89). The later Rām. recognises this origin of Rākṣasas but proposes another, according to which Brahman himself created creatures to guard the waters he had previously created and some of these creatures cried rakṣāmaḥ, "let us guard", while others cried yakṣāmaḥ, "let us gobble" (S jakṣāmah, VP. khādāmaḥ), so guards and goblins they became (R 7, 4, 4 and 12; VP. 1, 5, 41). The genealogy of the family of Rāvaṇa is uncertain. In Mbh., the mother of Rāvaṇa and Kumbhakarṇa was Puṣpotkaṭā; the mother of Vibhīṣaṇa was Mālinī; and the mother of the twins was Rākā, sent to Viśravas by Vaiśravaṇa (3, 275, 5 f.). The Rām. derives Rāvaṇa, Kumbhakarṇa, Vibhīṣaṇa, and one of the twins, Śūrpaṇakhā, from Kaikasī, daughter of Sumālin and wife of Viśravas, Sumālin being son of Devavatī, the daughter of the Gandharva Grāmaṇī, by Sukeśa, grandson of Fear, Bhayā, who was the sister of Yama (Kāla), by Heti, the last together with the ascetic Praheti being original royal Rākṣasas. Sukeśa was a favorite of Śiva and received special boons from him and Umā (R 7, 4, 31; ib. 5, 1 f.; ib. 9, 19). This genealogy is valuable only as showing how close is the connection mythologically between Rakṣas and Gandharva and Yakṣa on the one hand and, religiously, between Śiva (called Kumbhakarṇa) and the Rākṣasa host. It is even closer, for the grandson of the Gandharva married Ketumatī, a Gandharvī, and his brothers Mālin and Mālyavat married her two sisters (Vasudhā and Sundarī). Incidentally it may be remarked that Khasā or Khaśā (above) may be confused (cf. Kaṣāputra) with the Nikaṣā of the scholiast at RG 7, 76, as explaining the "mother of Rākṣasas"; the name is not epic (see note to p. 46, below).

It is to be remembered that the Viśravas mentioned above is also father of Kubera by another wife, Devavarṇinī, daughter of Bharadvāja. His nature is contrasted with that of the pure Rākṣasas, but, in this family also, a saintly Rāksaṣa is known, Vibhīṣaṇa, whose family and councillors are all good. An attempt is made to derive badness from precedent goodness in the case of all the Rākṣasas by insinuating that Kaikasī came at an "evil" hour to her husband and so her sons became evil; but this is artificial and the Rām. itself distinguishes between prākṛta Rākṣasas (the common lot) and these aristocrats or princes of evil (R 3, 29, 16f.). It is impossible here to go into the further details of the marriages and genealogy of these royal Rākṣasas. Suffices to say that Rāvaṇa's wife is Maya's daughter; Kumbhakarṇa's wife is Vairocana's daughter: and Vibhīṣaṇa's wife is Saramā, daughter of the Gandharva Śailūṣa. Vibhīṣaṇa's virtue is reckoned as one part of a boon given him by Brahman! The tragedy of the Rāma epic begins with "the root of woe", Śūrpaṇakhā, whose husband is slain by her brother Rāvaṇa and who is sent with Khara, nephew or brother of Rāvaṇa, to rule over Daṇḍaka, where, met and scorned by Rāma, her miseries incite her royal brother to war. Khara is an Ass in name and in sound (R 3, 22, 26, kharasvanaḥ). As the ass is not a mythological animal, it has not been included in the list (§ 8), but its relation to evil may be worth noticing. Above it was shown that ass-like braying creatures drag Rākṣasas' chariots. The sound of the ass portends evil; Duryodhana brays, like Khara, when born, and asses, vultures, jackals, and crows echo the evil omen (1, 115, 28). In the ritual, the ass is chiefly employed as a means of expiating sexual sins, inchastity, violating a woman, etc., either as a sacrificial victim or as a vehicle of dishonor. Besides Vibhīṣaṇa, the epics present Avindhya as a moral Rākṣasa, who advises Rāvaṇa not to slay Sītā (3, 280, 56f.; 289, 28f.; R 5, 37, 11f.); his daughter Kalā is also kind, as is the Rākṣasī Trijaṭā. The northerners, in distinction from this whole southern group, are represented as obstructive creatures, bahūni vighnarūpāṇi kariṣyanti (RG, 6, 82, 57). Though Rāvaṇa has ten heads and ten or twenty arms (Daśagrīva, daśakandhara; the arms vary, R 7, 16 and 103, 34), he sometimes has but two arms and in other respects is beautiful (despite the snakes in his hair and his hanging tusks, preserved as the inherited signs of his race). Hanumat on seeing him exclaims: aho rūpam aho dhairyam aho sattvam aho dyutiḥ, aho Rākṣasarājasya sarvalakṣaṇayuktatā, ("O the beauty, firmness, goodness, glory, and union of all marks of distinction, in this king of Rākṣasas"), and adds, "If he were not lawless, he would be a rakṣitṛ (rather than Rākṣasa) of heaven". But as it is, he is lokarāvaṇa, bhūtavirāvin (R 5, 49, 17f.; ib. 50, 1). Yet Rāma calls him pious and learned in the Veda (R 6, 112, 24). His piety was so great that Brahman gave him the boon of immunity from all spirits but not from men, because Rāvaṇa despised men; yet being cursed by one of the women he had injured, he was destroyed through a woman (R 7, 24, 1f.). He was cursed by so many that it is doubtful whose curse effected his downfall, whether Rambhā, or Vedavatī (Sītā), Umā, or Puñjikasthalā. Nandīśvara also cursed Rāvaṇa because he called Nandīśvara a "monkey" (R 6, 60, 7f.). Rāvaṇa's car is drawn by asses (also horses). His chief exploits are to carry off Sītā and stop the sun; he conquered the gods, overran Bhogavatī; forced

Madhu the Dānava to marry his sister, and Maya to give him his daughter as wife; stole Soma; and conquered Jaṭāyus, who tore off his arms is vain as they grew again (R 6, 7 and ib. 7, 1—23, etc.). The latest addition to R makes Viṣṇu's laugh send Rāvaṇa back to the underworld (Prakṣipta, 7, 23). Rāvaṇa is finally slain by "Brahman's weapon". His son and the other lesser demons are not so strong, but have the other traits of Rāvaṇa. Indrajit, his second son, overcomes Indra (hence his name and titles, Vāsavanirjetṛ, Śakrajetṛ, etc.) and is carried by tigers, dowered with divine boons, dattavara (the weakness of the gods mentally continually leads to their giving boons to their cunning foes), and is described in terms used to signalise Yakṣas, namely "black, with red eyes". He is described also as a Dānava in H 199, where no difference is maintained between these classes. Another son, Triśiras, is killed twice over, like a Homeric combatant (R 3, 27 and 6, 70). The monstrosity of the fiends is not emphasised except in the few cases where the name demands it in the case of the royal family, but elsewhere Triśiras' three heads are matched by the four heads and eight eyes of Kālanemi. The figure of Kumbhakarṇa is more popular. He has enormous hunger and sleeps six months at a time. As soon as he was born he devoured a thousand creatures and swallowed his foes "as Garuḍa swallows snakes" (R 6, 60, 13f. and ib. 61 and 65). He really sleeps thirty or thirty-four months (ib. 6, 60, 16). The later epic makes him an ascetic living in a cave (R 7, 7 and 10), perhaps because in R 6, 60, 24 he sleeps in a cave. Like other Rākṣasas are the lesser demon-nobles, that is, they are deceitful fighters, devoted to injury, delighting in slaying saints and kings, and are all by predilection "wanderers by night", niśācaras, rātriṃcaras (R 3, 42, 1f.; ib. 43, 5; ib. 45, 19; kūṭayodhinaḥ, ib. 60, 53). When the Rākṣasas are themselves divided, the man-eaters and Piśācas side with Daśānana Rāvaṇa, while Gandharvas, Kiṃpuruṣas, and Rakṣāṃsi stand for Vibhīṣaṇa and Kubera (3, 275, 33 and 38); but this distinction is not maintained (3, 281, 11). As said above, man-eating demons begin to have power when the night comes, and they are incapable of defeat at night (3, 1, 45 and 11, 4), for which reason fires are lighted at night to keep them off; since they fly from light and fire (13, 92, 13). Just between midnight and dawn their power is strongest (1, 154, 22; 7, 173, 57). Meteorological origin of some of the Rākṣasas seems assured by the fact that the "man-eating Lavaṇa", who is an understudy of Rāvaṇa (l = r? ralasya na bhedaḥ) in many points, has to be killed by Rāma's brother (with the weapon that killed his father Madhu in Viṣṇu's hand), "at the time when summer's heat is withdrawn and the night of the rainy season has arrived" (R 7, 64, 10). He is here king of Madhurā and nephew of Rāvaṇa; in the later Mbh. he is utilised by Indra to slay Māndhātṛ (1, 27, 2; 13, 14, 268; R 7, 67, 13f.). But as men are always liable to be turned into Rākṣasas (see Saudāsa, etc.), and as diseases are Rākṣasas, it is clear that the meteorological explanation, which also seems to be favored by the frequent appearance of Rākṣasas as thunder-clouds wielding bolts, etc., is not sufficient. Mārīca is an artificial Rākṣasa, turned into a cannibal fiend, as was Tāḍakā, a Yakṣiṇī, his mother. Men who hate priests become Rākṣasas (9, 43, 22). The female monsters who plague Sītā are simply malformed Rākṣasa devils with faces of animals, resembling the female fiends in Skanda's train. Rākṣasas seem to consist, apart from Dānavas and men metamorphosed into Rākṣasas, in two kinds of spirits. One serves as cloud and bolt and mirage, as a type of beauty; the other, disgusting, represents disease personified and other mean evils attacking man. Here belong the "seizers", Siṃhikā (see Nāgamātṛ) Aṅgārakā, who draw out a man's soul (shadow) and fasten on men as incorporate diseases. The inward fire which causes digestion keeps away Rakṣasas (= indigestion, 13, 92, 10). In families where evil obtains in consequence of the violation of marriage-laws, or of the wickedness of the king, are born decrepit and idiot children and "evil Rakṣas", pāparakṣāṃsi (12,90,93), apparently "bewitched" (i.e. unhealthy) children. When a woman faints, "Rakṣas-slaying Mantras" are said over her; that is, the weakness is itself the disease-devil (3, 144, 16). Putrid matter coming from a sore is spoken of as "a Rākṣasa head" sticking to the sore place (9, 39, 10—13). The so-called Brahma-Rākṣasa "sins involuntarily" and the evil of this creature comes from "woman's evil and the evil produced by the womb" (9, 43, 21). These creatures drink Sarasvatī's blood but excuse themselves on the ground that absence of religious teaching, evil acts, and sexual faults have caused their nature. If fire be there, Brahma-Rākṣasas do not hurt the sacrifice (13, 92, 12; N. as "priests reborn as Rākṣasas"; cf. R 1, 8, and 12, 17). Another class of Rākṣasas is that of the Pramathas (cf. Pramāthin as name, sub Apsaras). They appear in connection with Citragupta, who is unknown to the early epic, but they are fully described in the later epic, as attendants of Śiva (who in 12, 285, 87 is Pramathanātha). As invisible spooks they plague at night such people as sleep at the foot of a tree, eat unholy food, lie in the wrong direction, pollute water, or do not purify themselves after sexual connection. Such people have apertures which give admission to these "smiters" (pramathas); but good people and those who carry about with them gorocanā or orris-root or keep at home the skin or claws of a hyena or a hill-tortoise or a cat or a black or tawny goat, or keep up the sacrificial fire, are not troubled by them, as all these things are counteractants, pratighātas (13, 131, 1f.; 125, 6; also 13, 14, 389 and H 8146). Diti was destroyed through neglecting one of these rules (but by Indra, who thus acted as a Pramatha), when she slept with her feet at her head (i. e. where her head should be; R 1, 46, 16).

Piśācas are smaller demons associated with Rākṣasas and occasionally identified with them, as are Yātudhānas (R 6, 67, 68, etc.). As sons of Yadu the Yātudhānas differ from other Rākṣasas (R 7, 58, 7f.), but Rāvaṇa is Yātudhānasya dauhitraḥ (R 6, 114, 81), i. e. they are identical; though the Rākṣasī Hiḍimbā protests that she is "not a Yātudhānī" (S 1, 167, 17). But again a Rākṣasī made by an incantation is called a Yātudhānī (13, 93, 78), and Yātudhānas guard Kubera's mountain with Rākṣasas and appear as demons in battle, being raised by fire-mantras to slay seers (3, 139, 9; ib. 173, 51; 13, 93, 56f.). They are grouped (5, 100, 5; cf. H 11785f.) with Nairṛtas, as "born from the foot of Brahman". Śiva is a Yātudhāna of two forms (see Śiva) and Yātudhānas and Rakṣāṃsi are interchangeable terms for the servants of the Rākṣasa king (12, 172, 14 = S 171, 15). Those travelling in the mountains have to protect themselves against the "many Rākṣasas huge as hills (which are) Yātudhānas" (3, 92, 7; possibly distinct, sc. "and"). One sort of Rākṣasas is called Mandehas, who hang upon rocks and fall into water at sunrise, dying daily in fighting the sun (R 4, 40, 39; VP. 2, 8, 49). As Siṃhikā is a Rākṣasī, her son Rāhu, who devours sun and moon (eclipse), should belong to this category; but he is regarded as an Asura or Dānava (āsuraṃ tamas is Rāhu, R 2, 63, 2), or strictly as a Kabandha (1, 19, 4f.) = Svarbhānu (5, 110, 11; 182, 22; 6, 101, 36). Kubera takes with him (to Laṅkā) Nairṛta Rākṣasas with others whom he "creates". They come, in this legend, from the North, but belong in the South (cf. 12, 165, 51 or R 3, 64, 22, where Nairṛtī diś is South). Kubera is lord of the Nairṛtas (9, 47, 31). Rāvaṇa himself is a Nairṛta Rākṣasa, Nairṛtarāja, etc. (R 4, 62, 6; 5, 18, 18). The Krodhavaśas are northern Rākṣasas (3, 154, 20; 5, 50, 24), slain by Bhīma, but also called Yakṣas (3, 155, 24 and 31). They take away the merit of those who own dogs (17, 3, 10). The feminine form, Krodhavaśā, designates a daughter of Dakṣa (§ 139). A Rākṣasa (born a Dānava and reborn a Rākṣasa) is called Kabandha (R 3, 69, 26f.; Mahāsura in G ib. 75, 7). Among deformed humans such as Karṇapravaraṇas and Puruṣādas are mentioned Kalamukhas or Lohamukhas or Ghoralohamukhas (RG 4, 40, 29 with v. l.), known to Mbh. as "monkeys" (3, 292, 12), or Asitamukhas = golāṅgulas (ib. RG 6, 3, 35), a curious confusion of men and monkeys, possibly involving Rākṣasas, though these are always kravyāda (13, 115, 27). Dancing and drinking of blood are traits connecting Rākṣasas and Piśācas, who are usually little demons of the same sort, only meaner (7, 50, 9f.; 167, 38; and above; cf. R 3, 35, 6). In 12, 262, 7, Jājali is "seen by Rākṣasas", who must be identical with the Piśācas of the preceding account. S has "he was seen by Rakṣas and they (Piśācas) addressed him", but in B an "invisible voice" takes the place of the Piśāca in reproving Jājali, ib. 42). In R 3, 54, 14 and 17 and Mbh. 3, 280, 47, Piśācī = Rākṣasī. The Piśāca marriage-form, however, is lower than the Rākṣasa marriage-form (1, 73, 12). The Piśāca is the Dasyu's god and typical of cruelty (12, 278, 33 and 268, 22 in S, v. l. dasyuḥ . . ādatte Piśācāṃś cai 'va daivatam). Piśācas come from the mundane egg but are not said to be born of Brahman (1, 1, 35). The only reputable Piśācas are those that have ceased to be piśitāśana (= Piśāca, R 6, 61, 10, etc.) and act as guards of the White Mountain, a troop devoted to Skanda (3, 225, 11). These become vegetarian and "abandoning their usual diet live on the fruit of the tree (called Mahāśaṅkha) which grows there", on the Sarasvatī (9, 37, 22). But as this is a wonder-tree, "tall as Meru", the fruit was probably unique. There is also a worthy female Piśācī who wore pestle ornaments and gave advice as to holy watering-places to the wife of a priest (3, 129, 8), whether as indicating that Piśācas are human or that Tīrthas are not of much account, may be questioned. Another Piśācī is the guardian of a Tīrtha, Tīrthapālikā, and prevents the impure who do not love Kṛṣṇa from approaching it. After the baptism of a Brahman woman in the name of Hari she turns into an Apsaras (S 12, 336, 34f.). The Kiṃkara Rākṣasas, "born of mind", who serve Rāvaṇa are "like him", but the name means only servants of Yama (q. v.), or of Rāma (here called Muditas, R 7, 37, 18), or of Śiva (14, 65, 6), or of Maya, whose wealth is guarded by Kiṃkara Rākṣasas (rakṣanti . . Kiṃkarā nāma Rākṣasāḥ, 2, 3, 28; cf. 19). When Rākṣasas are called good, it is often flattery (3, 157, 13f.), or the merit of "protecting Rākṣasas" is united with that of protecting gods and priests; as the true protecting ruler (here Nahuṣa) guards all his realm (1, 75, 27). This view is really logical enough. One of the arguments against excessive taxation is that, if too heavily taxed, merchants will leave the country, and on the wealth given by them (to priests) "gods . . and Rākṣasas support themselves" (12, 89, 25; cf. 3, 157, 16f., "if men prosper, the Rākṣasas prosper"). To feed the fiends is to protect oneself, for it satisfies them and prevents them from injuring. The share given to them is small and mean, but they get a share regularly on holy days (R 2, 43, 5). Gifts are made to them, as their bhāga (share), of remnants of food, food sneezed upon or stepped upon, food leaped over, mixed with hair, insects, or tears, food seen or licked by a dog, or food not consecrated with Mantras (9, 43, 26; 13, 23, 3 f., at Śrāddhas). In the later moral epic the Rākṣasa resembles the medieval devil, to be overcome by virtue, with book and bell, or the equivalent Mantras, though in the narrative portion Rākṣasas annoy and slay pious priests without fear of Mantras or of virtue. Kings (in the Mārkaṇḍeya addition and in the pseudo-epic) are exhorted to have no dread of them: "The cruel planets favor the pure priest . . and cruel piśitāśanas, though huge and horrible, cannot hurt him" (3, 200, 85 f.). "I am not afraid", says a king who has been possessed by a cruel Rakṣas, rakṣo dāruṇam, "for I protect my people and cows; all my priests are learned men, and I constantly strive for virtue". And the Rākṣasa replies: "Because you are virtuous I leave you in peace. Kings who protect cows and priests need fear naught from Rākṣasas" (12, 77, 8—30). In the main, these demons scorn gods and goodness and overcome all powers of men except the power of the epic heroes vaunted by the poets. A close resemblance may be observed between the three- (or more) headed gigantic ogres of the popular belief and the three-headed Norwegian trolls, who were also originally gigantic. On the whole, the type shown in the Mbh. reveals the Rākṣasas as brutal and stupid gluttons of the wilds, but the term includes also a set of kṣudrā Rākṣasāḥ, mean little devils, like Piśācas, often conceived as disease-devils; and almost all nocturnal terrors are embodied as Rākṣasas. In R, the royal Rākṣasas are nobler and more like Asuras, though the close connection with the Piśācas is still kept and one Rākṣasa even has the name "Piśāca" (R 5, 59, 18). The Hariv. finally incorporates Piśācas into Brahman's creation as sons of Krodhā (H 11 554), a Purāṇic addition (see also under Asuras). Traces remain (above, and see note) of the (historical) Piśāca people, whose finale as devils is comparable with that of the Dasyus of an olden time; while the Dasyu descent to "robbers" is paralleled by that of the Nāgas as respects treasure and that of the Rākṣasas as respects women, though the country Rākṣasas are not represented as thieves but rather as cruel boors. Yet "Dasyu" is also applied to Asuras (q. v.)[1]).

§ 18. **The Asuras.** — To the epic poets the Asuras were in general the a-suras, the "ungodly". They included accordingly all the sinful demons, both the sons of Diti (called Ditija, Daitya, or Daiteya) and of Danu (called Dānava or Dānaveya), who are the chief opponents of the A-daiteyas or gods (cf. a-sura), and various special groups, such as the Kāleyas (Kālakeyas, Kālakañjas) and other "children of darkness", who upheld the great serpent-demon Vṛtra in his battles with the children of light, and are regarded as corporations, gaṇas, of Dānavas and Daityas. The typical leaders of the Asuras are Hiraṇyakaśipu, Bali, Jambha, etc.,

[1]) The question whether the Piśācas were originally uncivilised tribes or whether the demoniac name has been transferred to cannibalistic tribes has been discussed by Sir George Grierson, ZDMG. 66, 67 f., who has collected the passages referring to the Piśācas as human beings, inhabiting the N. W. (for the names of the Beas Piśācakas, Bāhlīkā and Hīka, 8, 44 = S 37, see my Sacred Rivers, p. 217), and concludes that the Piśācas were a tribe of omophagoi closely connected with the Khaśas, Nāgas, and Yakṣas (see Khaśā p. 41—42). Noteworthy is the absence in the epics of the Vetāla demons. A Vetālajananī is named in 9, 46, 13 among the late "mothers" ascribed to Skanda and various kinds of Vetālas are known to the Harivaṃśa, but the genus is not otherwise recognised.

demons slaughtered by Indra, Agastya, etc., or by Viṣṇu (2, 100—102), together with other groups of demons slaughtered en masse by Arjuna and other heroes and known as Khalins, Kīcakas, and Nivātakavacas ("Daityas, haters of the gods" 1, 123, 45). The sire of all these demons was Kaśyapa, who by various wives, for the most part daughters of Dakṣa (§ 139), became father of the Paulomas, as they are called after his demoniac wife Pulomā (7, 51, 17). But among the Asuras are often included (as already observed in the preceding section) the giant fiends known as Rākṣasas (really a sort of Asura in Vedic times), who in turn are sometimes confused with Piśācas; so that, as Asura exchanges with Rākṣasa and Rākṣasa with Piśāca, there is no clear line of demarcation between the groups, though the Piśācas are too mean and low to be confused with demons of the highest type (cf. 3, 285, 1, Piśācakṣudrarakṣasas commingling as one group). An Asura called Daṃśa (12, 3, 15 f.) is cursed by a saint to be reborn in the hellish state of a blood-drinking octopod. On being released from the curse he appears not as an "Asura" but as a red Rākṣasa riding on a cloud (Alarka, as he is called when a "pig-shaped worm with eight feet", is the name of a mad king of Benares, 3, 25, 13; 14, 30, 2). The Nāgas, though distinct from Asuras, are as a group affiliated, living with them and fighting on their side. The "roaring Asuras" are thus found in battle beside the Rākṣasas and Nāgas as opposed to the orthodox side of Kṛṣṇa and the Fire-god at Khāṇḍava (1, 227, 24 f.; see also below), and generally the Asuras and Nāgas belong together, though numerous exceptions occur in the case of the Nāgas (§ 13). Between the groups of Asuras the poets did not distinguish very carefully. Thus Danur nāma Diteḥ putraḥ describes the Kabandha of R 4, 4, 15, who, again (ib. 3, 70, 5 and 10) is Rākṣasa as well as Asura. Whether, like the Nāgas mentioned as kings (2, 8, 24) and the Piśācas mentioned as a tribe, with Kaliṅgas, etc. (6, 87, 8), the Asuras are euhemerised native races, must be left, from epic evidence, undetermined (see below). To the poets they are great spirits. They do not roam about battle-fields gorging themselves with blood and fat, as do the Piśācas (and Rākṣasas, e. g. 6, 86, 45). They are "elder brothers of the Devas" (§ 19) and are sometimes as generous and valorous as the gods. They are invoked in benedictions with the gods (R 2, 25, 16, tavā 'dityāś ca Daityāś ca bhavantu sukhadāḥ sadā). The Dānava Asuras were originally pious and moral, according to epic legend (12, 229, 27 f.), though when it is said here that they "worshipped the gods", credulity is strained. Pride made them sinful and so they were driven out of their celestial abodes, losing Happiness (personified), who forsook them, as she does all sinners. The moral is too obvious to permit belief that this legend in detail reflects tradition. Nevertheless, Asuras are represented as associating with the gods, and, with the Nāgas, as worshipping Varuṇa in his own palace, probably because Varuṇa's place is their home (see below). Moreover some of the Daityas and Dānavas are "beautiful" and their names, Sumati, Sumanas, etc. mean "kind-hearted" (2, 9, 7 f.). On the whole the Dānavas are more god-like than the Daityas and of course than the Asura Rākṣasas. The Asuras Madhu and Kaiṭabha, who "never told a lie", are Dānavas, and the "Ārya Asuras" of the tale of Happiness (above) are called Dānavas by Śrī herself; only the stupid Indra, who is hearing the story for the first time (!), alludes to them interrogatively as Daityas. This may be the implication of the fact that only rarely does a Daitya-female serve as a typical beauty, as Dānava-females do constantly. The foremost Dānava is the "very clever" Vipracitti, who with the other Dānavas is born of Danu, in antithesis to the "Asuras all born of Diti" (a late distinction, 12, 207, 27 f.), as if the Dānavas were not Asuras at all. The later epic calls Vipracitti Daitya and Dānava indifferently (12, 98, 49 f.; H 13 884 and 13 894 f.). Both groups of Asuras are said to be strong, but poetic necessity disposes of them as if they were weaklings, when it is said that Dānavas fall from their cars and are eaten by fishes and Daityas are routed by the Wind (-god; 3, 20, 31, and under Vāyu § 47). They were driven from heaven at the end of the Kṛta age (1, 64, 28) and took refuge in the caves beside the sea, in mountains, in forests (the Dānavas and Rākṣasas together, 1, 228, 1), under earth, but chiefly in the ocean (1, 21, 7 f.). They appear, however, on occasion in the air and in the sky, as if belonging there, as of old. The combined hosts of Daityas and Dānavas, on losing the ambrosia got from the ocean and on being defeated by the gods, first appear as mountain-hurling gods and then flee into earth and sea (1, 18, 46; 29, 25). Instead of mountainous shapes they often appear like animals, but, as here, fall finally into sea or earth. They are incorporate in the shape of animals and kings of the great war, to which fate they were doomed in consequence of their desire for power. They are opposed to the caste-system, the seers, and the Brahmanic power (1, 64, 32 and 36; ib. 30, Kravyādas). To the demons enumerated in general as Dānavas, Rākṣasas, Gandharvas, and Serpents (pannagas), and cannibals (puruṣādāni sattvāni, 1, 65, 5) are opposed the incorporate gods. Thus Kaṃsa is Kālanemi and the kings of Kaliṅga are the Asuras called Krodhavaśas. Aśvapati Kaikeya, Bāṇa, et al., are Asuras, slain by gods or heroes (the later legend regarding Bāṇa, H 9910, etc., to the effect that his daughter Uṣā loved Aniruddha, is not given in the epic proper). A number of inconsistencies are found in the great epic. Hiraṇyakaśipu is the only son of Diti; Hiraṇyākṣa is a later addition. Kumbha and Nikumbha are Rākṣasas in R; sons of Prahlāda and grandsons of Hiraṇyakaśipu, Asuras, in Mbh. They are brothers of Virocana, father of Bali and grandson of the above-mentioned "great Asura" Bāṇa, who was slain by Kṛṣṇa-Viṣṇu in one tale and by Skanda in another (5, 62, 11; 9, 46, 82). So too Danu has "forty" sons and forty-four are mentioned by name (1, 65, 21 f.). This prolific demon's most famous offspring are Śambara, Namuci, Puloman, Keśin, Svarbhānu, Aśva (who is reborn as Aśoka), Virūpākṣa, Naraka, Vātāpin (but Ilvala is a "son of Diti", 3, 96, 5). The Asura called Mayūra is omitted from the genealogical list, and the Sun and Moon mentioned as Asuras are said to be other than the sun and moon of the gods; moreover, the descendants of Danu are "without number" (1, 65, 21—30). The great Asura Vṛtra is listed as son of Danāyus, along with Bala and Vīra. The sons of Kadrū are the Nāgas and the sons of Kalā, Kālakeyas, are "smiters", chiefly moral personifications, Wrath, Destruction, etc. As priest of the Asuras appear not only Śukra but his sons (see § 125, Atri). The Asuras are frequently identified with natural phenomena and get their names in part therefrom, especially cloud-phenomena, to which they are often compared. Opposition to light and goodness, love of and use of māyā, illusion or deception (tricks), a roaring voice, ability to assume any shape (they are three-headed, etc.), or to disappear, are their general characteristics; in which they differ from Rākṣasas not at all and except for the first element not from the gods. The common traits being excluded, there remains as their peculiarity dislike to goodness and light (as goodness).

Not unlike the relation of the Rākṣasas to the Great-Father (god) is that of the Asuras, who also are continually receiving boons from Brahman. So Brahman, for example, gives to Mahiṣa, a "Dānava Asura in the Daitya army", the very power through which he was enabled to defeat the gods in battle, till Skanda cut off his head and made impassable for future use the road leading to the Hyperboreans (3, 231, 105). What distinguishes the pure Asuras from the Asura Rākṣasas is their greater cleverness. Maya the builder is a type of this trait; but also the Khalins, otherwise an undistinguished lot of Asuras, outwit the gods by recuperating and even reviving themselves after being wounded or slain by the gods, whereas the gods know none of these tricks till Vasiṣṭha aids them (13, 156, 17f.). Brahman had given them a boon, but even without this help the Asuras were cleverer than the gods (see § 123 Bṛhaspati). Maya is an architect, builder of palaces combining all "divine, demoniac, and human" designs (2, 1, 13). His chief work is a palace of such beauty as to be "like a god-guarded māyā" (3, 23, 12). Compare the play on māyā as deception: "women are māyā Mayajāḥ" (13, 40, 4; and R 3, 54, 13). It was Maya who built the three cities of the Asuras (below). He is the brother of Namuci, and was spared by Agni; for which reason he made earthly palaces for the god's friends. He was slain by Indra (6, 101, 22; according to R 4, 51, 14, because he violated the Apsaras Hemā), and also by Viṣṇu (7, 174, 36, a later tale). Vālmīki knows him as the great magician architect Dānava who makes a magic cave, the Dānava palace (R 4, 51, 14f.; ib. 43, 31 and ib. 5, 57, 24), and also the fiend's weapons (R 6, 101, 2 and 30). Maya is to the demons what Viśvakarman, the All-maker, is to the gods (2, 1, 6). Hemā is his wife and his daughter Mandodarī is the fair and noble wife of Rāvaṇa and mother of Indrajit; Māyāvin and Dundubhi are his descendants (R 7, 12, 6 and 13f.). Dundubhi in R 4, 9, 4 is said to be the son of Māyāvin; ib. 10, 22 (the scholiast says that son means brother). They are both "Asuras", Dundubhi being a bull-shaped monster who challenges Ocean, the Himālaya, and Vālin (ib. 11, 4f.). His māhiṣaṃ rūpam (buffalo-shape) is said to be like a cloud roaring like a drum (dundubhi, ib. 11, 25f.). He is here also regarded as a Dānava Asura (ib. 46, 9), and his cloud and roar and attack on sea and mountain represent him as a storm, if anything. Weber suggested (IS. 2, 243) that Maya is due to Greek Ptolemaios. The question whether Greeks originated the architectural demon is not settled by such a subtile suggestion, but it is reasonable to suppose that the forms of Aśvapati Kaikeya (Asura) and the Kīcakas (Kāleya Daityas and also sons of Kekaya, the king of Sūtas, by the Apsaras Mālavī; S 4, 21, 22f.) represent races (tribes), although on the other hand the forms of Vṛtra and other Vedic Asuras were purely phenomenal and the later time keeps adding to this sort of Asura. For example, Dhundhu is an Asura son of Madhu and Kaiṭabha (called both Daityas and Dānavas), who were slain by Viṣṇu (3, 203, 17f.). Madhu is the older figure, whose name may lie in (modern) Mathurā. But Dhundhu lives in the earth, concealed in sand, and when he wakes and breathes, he shakes the earth, while the sky is obscured by his breath. When attacked by the intrepid Kuvalāśva (to whom Viṣṇu had promised his energy) for seven days, Dhundhu spits out flames (3, 202, 18f.; ib. 204, 2—40). He thus appears to be as much of a volcano as the Sicilian giant. The Vedic Asuras are chiefly renowned for their contests with Indra and will be discussed under Indra, etc. Śambara still has his thousand tricks, but is slain by Indra with the help of Daśaratha (R 2, 9, 13 and 45, etc.). New points appear of course. Śambara is Timidhvaja and still later his wife appears as Māyāvatī (H 9213 f., also Māyādevī; not epic), as the characteristic śacī of Indra becomes his wife Śacī at an earlier date (cf. Neria, heroic power, as wife of Mars, etc.). There are other inconsistencies to be expected and actually found. Brahman gives the Asuras all boons except immortality, for immortality is withheld from them; yet Hari, son of Tāraka, obtains a lake (as a boon from the same god) which perpetually restores life to anyone bathing in it (8, 33, 9 and 30). Although described as beautiful and generally noble in appearance, the Dānavas have, as fighting foes of the gods, three heads, four fangs, four arms, etc. (3, 173, 53). Arjuna takes the place of Indra as slayer of demons in the epic, destroying Nivātakavacas, Hiraṇyapur, etc., although in fights waged by the hero Indra appears still as their typical opponent. The Asuras have no father-god except Brahman, for Brahman remains also their "father" and gives them not only boons but good advice (14, 26, 10, etc.). They have no one king, for various Asuras are called Asurarāj and Asurādhipa. Their overlord, in moral harangues, is Pride, the āsura bhāva. Pride, Wrath, and Delusion were king-demons and the chief king, adhipati, was Pride (12, 295, 10 and 20). Another account names, however, as recognised "truest Asuras", those who refused to obey Brahman, owing to wrath and greed and pride, Hiraṇyakaśipu, Hiranyākṣa, Virocana, Śambara, Vipracitti, Prahlāda = Prahrāda, Namuci and Bali (Dānavendrāḥ 12, 166, 26; Asurasattamāḥ, 31). Mada, Intoxication, the most famous personified vice, is a mahāsura but not a regular Asura, being only a phantom born of Cyavana. He was a monster (one jaw on earth and one in the sky, etc.), but Indra dispersed him, so that his power was dissipated and distributed among drink, women, dice, and hunting (3, 124, 19 f.; 13, 157, 33; 14, 9, 33; later accounts make him a son of Danu or even a son of Brahman; cf. JAOS. 26, p. 67, for the Vedic version). Later lists unite Mada with Pramada (H 2289 and 14290). In 1, 66, 52, Surā is sister of Bala, both being children of Varuṇa by Śukra's daughter Devī. The jātis of fiends are united in their underground home in Pātāla. Tāraka is a demon whose name does not appear in the old genealogical lists, but in what may be called the middle period of the epic he appears as claiming a boon from Brahman, though, as elsewhere, the boon is neutralised by a trick, into the account of which is woven the ancient tale of the lost Fire-god, and finally Tāraka is killed by Skanda, by Kṛṣṇa, and by Indra, as accounts differ. This Tāraka got Maya to build for his three sons three cities, of gold, silver, and iron, on sky, air, and earth, which were destroyed by Śiva (7, 202, 64 f.; 8, 33, 16 f.). The city in Pātāla is Hiraṇyapur and was made by the All-maker, Viśvakarman, though invented by Maya (5, 100, 2, nirmitaṃ Viśvakarmaṇā Mayena manasā sṛṣṭam, Pātālatalam āśritam), or, it was made by Brahman himself for the use of the Kālakeyas or Kālakañjas and Paulomas (3, 173, 11). It is also located beyond the sea as the home of the Nivātakavacas (4, 61, 27 and 5, 49, 16). It floats about at will and was destroyed by Śiva's weapon in Arjuna's hands (3, 173, 41 f.). Śiva (§ 155) is thus known as Tripurahan, etc. The Kālakeyas occupy in particular the stone city (R 7, 23, 17). Another city of Asuras is Prāgjyotiṣa, where Naraka Bhauma kept the ear-rings stolen from Aditi by the Nāgas. Both the "stone city on earth", aśmanagara, of the Kālakeyas and this town Prāgjyotiṣa are probably poetic versions of a real city (or cities), as Arjuna slew six thousand Asuras, Mura, and many Rākṣasas after the gods had sent him to kill the robbers (Dasyus = Asuras), and on getting back the ear-rings he brings back the "Asura women" as wives. Another account represents all three cities as being in the sky (13, 161, 25). Prāgjyotiṣa in 2, 45, 7; 14, 75, 1, etc., is clearly a human city (cf. Uttarajyotiṣa, 2, 32, 11, a western town). Muru (sic) and Pīṭha (Dānava) are associated with Naraka in the downfall of Prāgjyotiṣa at 12, 340, 92 (cf. 7, 11, 5, where Pīṭha, mahāsura, and Muru are slain by Vāsudeva, as was Hayarāja or Keśin, who dwelt beside the Yamunā). The same section speaks of Kṛṣṇa (Pradyumna) as destroying Saubha, a city of Daityas, a kos away in the sky, belonging to king Śālva. This city is at times described as aerial, at times as a human town. Maṇimatī as a Daitya-town (of Ilvala) is mentioned in 3, 96, 4. Both a royal seer and an Asura bear the name Vṛṣaparvan. The "Daitya's" daughter Śarmiṣṭhā Daiteyī married Yayāti (1, 81, 11; 2, 1, 17); and Vṛṣaparvan the Asura (reborn as king Dīrghaprajña, 1, 67, 16; he is wealthy, 2, 3, 3) is thus ancestor of the Kurus and Pāṇḍus through the Asurendrasutā. There is no close family connection among most Asuras as among the great Rākṣasas of the Rām. The best developed family is that of Virocana. Bali is always Vairocana (as earlier). Hiraṇyakaśipu, Prahlāda, Virocana, Bali, and Bāṇa represent five generations of distinguished fiends. Uṣā, the daughter of Bāṇa, marks a sixth generation. Hiraṇyakaśipu, if not Prahlāda (= hrāda), is a later addition to the tale. Prahlāda is an ardent worshipper of Viṣṇu, while his father is an infidel. Sectarian interest centres about this family as if it were a real (human) line. Bali, whom Viṣṇu cheats in his dwarf Avatar, is the oldest member historically. Virocana has the usual unhappy fate of one whose son is more famous than his father and is known chiefly as "father of Bali". Prahlāda appears as deciding a dispute of Virocana with a Muni (Sudhanvan), both claiming superiority and eventually agreeing to refer the matter to Prahlāda, whose natural partiality is modified by some wise words respecting lying uttered by Kaśyapa, so that he admits the superiority of Sudhanvan because his mother is superior to Virocana's (2, 68, 65 f.; details in 5, 35, 5 f.). In S, Prahlāda seems less afraid of lying than of having his head split by Sudhanvan, who threatens him with this and sundry ills if the does not decide "truthfully" in his favor and a holy haṃsa (bird) lectures the Asura on lying (instead of Kaśyapa). Naraka Bhauma is literally "son of earth"; S adds that his father was Nārāyaṇa. This is a "secret" certainly unknown to the genealogist of Ādi (7, 29, 32; 12, 209, 7 as mahāsura). His bones are to be seen at Ganges' Gate (Viṣṇu slays him in his Boar form). Karṇa is Naraka reborn; as expressed in 3, 252, 29: "The soul of slaughtered Naraka was born in Karṇa's form". It is noticeable that the death of the great Asuras is effected by deceit. Viṣṇu in the form of a man-lion thus slays Hiraṇyakaśipu because he was an unbeliever (7, 191, 36; 197, 23). Hiraṇyakaśipu is reborn as Śiśupāla. In his family were born Sunda and Upasunda, mahāsurau, who were brought to destruction through jealousy by means of the nymph Tilottamā. These Asuras enslaved the Nāgas and killed the saints (1, 209, 2 f.).

Despite the many tales of Asuras, most of those named in the epic remain mere names, such as Kapaṭa, or are named only as undistinguished victims of distinguished beings (Indra, Kṛṣṇa, etc.), such as Vegavat and Vivindhya, who appear only to disappear in the battle with Sāmba (3, 16, 12 f.). They fight and die, but others, like Ghaṇābha or Ghaṭābha and Vikaṭābha (H 12698), are empty names, as is Gaviṣṭha, named in the early genealogy and again named in H, but unknown between. In the same list appears an Asura Ghaṭodara, who is known also as an attendant on Varuṇa and in R is a Rākṣasa. Others who are Nāgas appear as Asuras, e. g. Mūka, who is an Asura, a Rākṣasa, and a Nāga, (1, 57, 9; 3, 39, 7, here B has son of Danu and S son of Diti; ib. 16 and 27f.). An Asura Pāka is made out of Indra's epithet Pākaśāsana. Some Asuras known by name in Mbh. actually do something in R. Thus Anuhlāda, son of Hiraṇyakaśipu, appears in the divine genealogy (1, 65, 19) but only in R 4, 39, 6 does anything (seduces Śacī). In 12, 227, 51 f., the list of Daityas and Dānavas, including pūrvadaityendra, contains many names unknown before (Virūpaka, Pratirūpa, etc.), unless Virūpa = Virūpaka (2, 9, 14). Virūpākṣa, Asura and Rākṣasa, was, as a Rudra, made lord of Bhūts and Mothers (see Rudra) by Viṣṇu (12, 207, 34). Some have animal names, some fiery, some are named from deformity (Aśva, Vṛṣan, Ṛṣabha, Varāha; Vahni, Viśvajit; Saṃkoca, Varītākṣa, etc.). Later lists in H (12932f.; 14282f.), beginning with 2281f., separate Varāhāśva into Varāha and Aśva. Hara and Hari in these lists of demons perpetuate the principle of permitting names of gods (Wind, Fire, etc.) to serve as names of demons. Compare the sons of Diti slain by Garuḍa (5, 105, 14), among them Vivasvat as (sun) demon. Perhaps the earlier usage shows that no great difference was felt between gods and demons. When good, a god; when destructive, a demon. Soma rapes Tārā, as if he were a demon, though she is wife of Bṛhaspati (5, 117, 13), thus bringing on the war about Tārā, Tārakāmaya, known to all the epic writers and described in full at H 1340f., in which the heavenly host is divided against itself, as it is divided when Khāṇḍava is burned (another Tārā is raped by Sugrīva in the Rāma-story, 3, 280, 39, etc.). Despite the large number of classes of demons mentioned as such by the epic poets, there were probably others known but not mentioned. The Kumbhāṇḍas (demons) are not known as such, but a Kumbhāṇḍa is minister of the Asura Bāṇa in H 9844f., and Kumbhāṇḍas appear in other literature (for example in the Mahāvaṃśa) as a class of demons (Kuṣmāṇḍī is a name of Śiva's wife, H 10245, and Kuṣ-, or Kūśmāṇḍaka, is name of a Nāga, 1, 35, 11). For the priest of the demons see § 26 and § 118f.

IV. THE GODS.

§ 19. **Origin and General Characteristics of the Gods.** — The chief Hindu gods are phenomenal, Spencer's effort to prove that Indra and Dawn were originally ghosts being only the first of various attempts to distort translucent facts. The language of the early literature is too clear to be misunderstood in this regard. But by the time the epics were composed the phenomenal side was greatly obscured. Anthropomorphism had rendered even Sun and Moon quite human in dress, talk, and action, while Indra was as much of a family-man as Thor became elsewhere. But the base remained not wholly covered and even Viṣṇu and Śiva occasionally reveal their origin. Animism and naturism blend in the unification of spirits and objective matter marked by ancestors worshipped as animals, mountains, stars, etc. But in one regard this chaos of mythology inherited from an older age is augmented rather than decreased by the generalising process conspicuous in the epic. Namely, mythology has been affected by the star-cult, but to how great an extent is hard to say. All the stars were divine or saintly beings. Aldebaran was, as Rohiṇī (female), the favorite wife of the Moon-god; the Pleiades were the "mothers" of Skanda; the Great Bear was known as the Seven Seers and Arundhatī, the wife of one of them, waited nearby; the "steadfast" dhruva (Pole Star) being less often personified in anthropomorphic form. But Dhruva is son of Nahuṣa, who in turn was born of Svarbhānu's daughter, Svarbhānavī by Āyu(s), the son of Purūravas and Urvaśī. Hence all Nahuṣa's sons, Yati, Yayāti, Saṃyati, Āyāti, and Dhruva, meaning "going", like āyu, or "steadfast", may have been stars, the myth of Yayāti pointing in the same direction (1, 75, 25f.) So the Aśvins are born "in the mouth" of the mare-goddess (§ 110), as asterism (?). Amāvasu (cf. amāvasyā) is also son of Āyu or Purūravas (H 958, 1373). A parallel unconsciousness may be seen when "Vṛtra and Bala smite Indra and (= as) the heat- and rain-months smite the world" (7, 30, 9f.) without thought that nidāgha and Vṛtra are the same (Bala = rain-month, often alone as smitten by Indra, 7, 134, 8; cf. 6, 45, 45; ib. 100, 32); the gharmāṃśavaḥ of Vṛtra and Bala (so B and S) are not distinguished. But most of this is lost in nebulous nomenclature.

Another prolific source of gods is abstractions, constantly personified. There is no limit to a pantheon where hope, hell, and hunger, cows and corn, the west and wisdom, etc. are all called gods. Constantly new images invoke new personifications. Right and Wrong and Gain make an ancient triad regarded as divine beings, and the "wives" of these beings are registered, together with female attendants without number. Memory, Affection, Endurance, Victory, Effort are incorporate forms in the van of Skanda's army, nor can one dismiss them as poetic metaphor when on an equal footing with them stands Lakṣmī, Happiness, the well-known wife of Viṣṇu, and even Effort appears in both epics as an actual being. Some of these abstractions have been raised to high place in the pantheon of active and very real gods. Many of them are Vedic or even pre-Vedic (Anumati, etc.); others are apparently new, yet no one knows how ancient. Natural phenomena thus serve with mental and moral traits to make an endless list of Devas or Daivatas. Night and Light (as son of Day), Dawn, and Twilight go hand in hand with Love, Wrath, Fear, etc. The same word indicates different divinities (so transparent is still the meaning) when Sarasvatī, a "flowing", is the goddess Fluency or Eloquence ("mother of the Vedas") in one place and the Flowing (river goddess) in another. Such abstractions are seen perhaps at their best in the morality-play of the later epic, where ethical and physical elements appear. Thus, after Sāvitrī, also "mother of the Vedas", has formally announced a discussion between Time, Death, and Yama, and the characters have been properly introduced by Sir Right (quite dramatic), Heaven (Svarga), and Desire, and Wrath play their parts, making a formal entrance on the stage:

(Svarga): "Know me, O king, as Heaven, who here arrive
" In person: Come, ascend to heaven with me."

But the king, who has learned to despise the joy hereafter, says:

"For heaven I have no use; depart, O Heaven,
"Go away, Heaven" (gaccha, Svarga! 12, 199, 77).

In 12, 200, 11, among various personifications, such as rivers and mountains, appear, as deified forms, ascetic practices, Yoga-rule, lauds (tapāṃsi, stobhas, etc.) which, bizarre as they seem even here, are really only an extension of the principle that makes a great goddess of Sāvitrī, the laud par excellence, who as a divinity sends her worshippers to heaven or to hell, and says, for example: "Thou shalt not go to hell where the priests go, but thou shalt go to Brahman's place" (12, 199, 14). How far the personification is felt as real, can be judged from the fact that Wrath and Fear and Diseases are "children of Śiva" (13, 14, 413). All faults are personified demons, as much as disease is a demon, and this is a primitive lasting conception. Yet in the description of the Hall of the Gods, it may be questioned whether the abstractions attending as courtiers are not in part poetical, for in the list of attendants stand divisions of time as well as Time, and the "wheel of right", poems, dramas, the senses, etc., which seem to be personified for the occasion (in the Hall of Brahman, 2, 11, "dramas" a late addition[1]). Rām. has the same sort of personification, natural phenomena and especially abstractions such as appear in the passage where Rāvaṇa asks: "Art thou Hrī, Kīrti, Śrī, Śubhā, Lakṣmī, an Apsaras, Bhūti, or Rati?" (R 3, 46, 16). Neuter words are thus made masculine by implication, as when the personified weapons (neuter) appear to sight as masculines, tathā 'yudhāni te sarve yayuḥ puruṣavigrahāḥ (R 7, 109, 7). Worship is extended to these material things on occasion and the Sikh's pūjā of the sword is anticipated in 12, 166, 87, aseś ca pūjā kartavyā. Ancient too are the personifications as gods of nomina agentis, the Maker, the Creator, the Disposer (Vidhātṛ), etc. Often epithets of gods are particularised as separate divinities (Dhātṛ = Brahman?), or functioning forces become epithets (Savitṛ becomes Sūrya?). The epic does not solve the problem. Prajāpati is sometimes Brahman and sometimes a separate god, etc.

When, as frequently occurs, a list of gods is given, there is no unvarying precedence and often in such lists there are remarkable omissions. In short, they are made arbitrarily, not according to a scheme. Very few of the gods mentioned in the epic are of any importance. Many are grouped gods of the Vedic age existing as a necessary part of a list of gods who give homage to a great god or applaud a hero. For all they do individually, they might as well be non-existent. Others live in a tale or two. A mass consists in the abstractions already referred to. Groups are named as such along with some of the individuals belonging to the groups, as if they were separate entities, as when Skanda is consecrated; but the poet at the end in despair of completeness says that he does not name all the groups of divinities, devatāgaṇas, "because there are too many" (9, 45, 1 f.) But there is a tendency in less exhaustive summaries to embrace the gods under the caption "celestials", opposed to spirits of air and earth, as divine, angelic, and demoniac, the three constituting the trailokyacāriṇaḥ (R 3, 64, 60). So in S 12, 12, 38 sadevāsuragandharvam idaṃ jagat, "the world with gods, Asuras, and Gandharvas" (cf. 5, 57, 11, etc.). The gods and other spirits usually come together for a consultation or to see an exhibition of arms, mingling amicably with saints, and often the spirits, good and bad, consort without evidence of conflict. Thus in R 6, 79, 25, to see a fight, assemble in the space between earth and the sky "gods, Dānavas, Gandharvas, Kiṃnaras, and great serpents". The gods seldom interfere in human conflicts, but occasionally they confuse the forms of the fighters out of partiality (7, 138, 13) or wipe the sweat from a warrior's face, as do Śakra and Sūrya (8, 90, 18), the latter being peculiarly adapted for this office! Except for ancient wars referred to constantly as the "war about Tārā" or the "war of gods and

[1]) See Prof. Winternitz's note JRAS. 1903, p. 572.

demons", the epic gods do little *en masse*. In connection with the Asuras they get ambrosia from the ocean, out of which rise Dhanvantari, the divine physician, sixty crores of Apsarasas, Surā, Uccaiḥśravas (§ 68), the jewel Kaustubha, and last of all ambrosia. In R 1, 45 and 4, 58, 13 (*jānāmi amṛtasya manthanam*) the story is well known. In Mbh. (1, 18) the divine king of tortoises of his own consent upholds the mountain; the later Rām. identifies the tortoise with Viṣṇu. Here the moon rises first, followed by Śrī and Surā (Vāruṇī), and the divine physician comes after the others bearing the ambrosia (this too in RG). Mbh. S adds the Pārijāta tree and Surabhi. Śiva in Mbh. drinks the poison at the request of Brahman, and Viṣṇu deceives the Asuras by means of a deceptive female form. In R there are other variations. In 5, 102, Surabhi's birth is given in this form, but in 8, 60, 7, the honor of having stupified the Asuras is given wholly to Indra and Agni (in 5, 107, to Viṣṇu). R 4, 66, 32 ascribes ambrosia to a decoction of herbs collected by Jāmbavat.

§ 20. **The Number of Gods is cited as "Thirty-Three", but is incalculable for reasons already given.** — Eighty-eight thousand Gandharvas are on Mt. Mandara and seven times six thousand Deva-Gandharvas once met on the top of a sacrificial post to dance there (12, 29, 75). Eighty-eight (like eighty-four) is a stereotyped number. In 1, 1, 41, the Devas are counted as "thirty-three thousands, thirty-three hundreds, and thirty-three", a late but very moderate estimate in view of traditional numbers of gods. More important and perhaps indicative of the gods actually revered is the number of shrines in a holy hermitage. Thus when Rāma visits Agastya he finds in the hermitage shrines erected to eighteen gods (including a group as a unit) and these are really the gods most in evidence as active beings, Brahman, Agni, Viṣṇu, Mahendra, Vivasvat, Soma, Bhaga, Kubera, Dhātṛ and Vidhātr, Vāyu, Vāsuki, Ananta (v. l. Garuḍa), Gāyatrī, the Vasus, Varuṇa, Kārtikeya, and Dharma (R 3, 12, 17f.). Nārada, implying that they are the gods he himself worships, advises others to worship Varuṇa, Vāyu, Āditya, Parjanya, Agni, Sthāṇu, Skanda, Lakṣmī, Viṣṇu, Brahman, Vācaspati, Candramas, Water, Earth, and Sarasvatī (13, 31, 6). Probably the poet was right, however, who said that "Men fear and honor the killing gods, not Brahman, Dhātṛ, Pūṣan, but Rudra, Skanda, Śakra, Agni, Varuṇa, Yama, Kāla, Vāyu, Mṛtyu, Vaiśravaṇa, Ravi, the Vasus, Maruts, Sādhyas, and Viśve Devas" (12, 15, 16f.), the general principle being that "without fear no one sacrifices, no one gives" (*nā 'bhīto yajate*, etc. ib. 13). The conventional number of gods, however, remains fixed as three and thirty, divided into families. Apart from this number, families of gods are everywhere accepted, though the members of a family are not always the same, and again, as sons of one Father-god, an effort is made to include among "families of gods" even the vegetable kingdom. Thus plants and animals are included with the Aśvins as Guhyakas (1, 66, 40). The "Three and Thirty" are reckoned as 12 (Ādityas) + 8 (Vasus) + 11 (Rudras) + 2 (Aśvinau), or as (in place of the two) Prajāpati and Vaṣaṭkāra (so Nīl. at 1, 66, 37), but in truth the distribution is a later product. The poets inherited the Tridaśa group and used it of the greater gods without defining it, till R 3, 14, 14 gives the definition above (the two as Aśvins; versus the Vedic definition of the two, as Indra and Prajāpati, ŚB. 11, 6, 3, 5; Bṛh. Up. 3, 9, 3). Tridaśa also means thirty (1, 113, 21) and is used of gods in general, for example, in 3, 85, 20, where "Brahman with the Tridaśas" has this general meaning, as it has quite frequently (see usage in following sections).

§ 21. **Leaders of the Gods.** — If, as in 3, 186, 30, the gods go to sacrifice, they are led by Agni; if to battle, by Indra, and later by Kārttikeya. But Indra as the war-lord remains the Sureśa, Surapati, king of Devas (1, 86, 8, etc.), and he is even called "the only king of heaven" (5, 45, 6 and 10). But geographical and other factors modify this statement. In his own district each god is supreme, and it is not often that the gods leave their proper places. When they do, it may be that they are led by other gods than the titular leaders. Thus Yama and Kubera lead a host of gods and other spirits going to a Svayaṃvara (1, 187, 6f.). Brahman and Soma head the gods going to see a battle (7, 98, 33). Each group of gods has its natural leader, as when Sūrya is lord of Grahas; Candramas, lord of Nakṣatras; Yama, lord of Pitṛs; Soma, lord of plants; Ocean, of rivers; Varuṇa, of waters; the Maruts, kings of groups; and Indra, king of Maruts; till in descending scale Mahādevī is named as mistress of women devoted to Bhaga (14, 43, 6f.). Here the North is lord of directions, but immediately afterwards the East is first (ib. 44, 13). Despite variations, largely due to sectarian influence, the gods are in general partitioned off into little groups, each under the lordship of one who is called best, either as king or as leader (5, 156, 12f.). When Kumāra (as here) is called leader of the Devas, it must be remembered that in 7, 7, 6 the succession from an older leadership is indicated by the words, "Of old the Suras with Śakra at their head made Skanda their general or commander-in-chief" (compare the list 6, 34, 21f., where Vāsava is best of Devas).

Distinctions between gods rest on general differences, such as that already mentioned between gods that kill and others and between Pitṛs raised to divinity and natural gods. The functions of gods make a distinction between them which is not very marked, as almost any god does what any other can do. An older grouping by pairs prevails to a certain (not marked) extent. In R 6, 12, 36, the speaker thus groups as gods he would dare to contend with Śakra and Vivasvat, Pāvaka and Māruta, Kubera and Varuṇa, adding that his own prowess and power is like that of Sāgara and Māruta (ib. 13, 16). The simplest distinction rests on physical traits, "lord of heat" (Agni), "lord as to sowing seeds" (Earth), "lord as to illumination" (Sun, 1, 88, 13). The geographical distinction coincides in part with this. Yama as lord of the (deadly) South; Agni as lord of the East (full of sacrificial fires); but it extends beyond this. Thus in the war with Garuḍa (1, 32, 16) the defeated celestials fly, the Vasus and Rudras to the South, the Ādityas to the West, the Aśvins to the North, the Sādhyas and Gandharvas to the East. The rules for offerings show geographical and sacrificial distinctions. Earth says that a householder must make an offering of rice and water, or of milk, roots, and water to the Pitṛs, and boiled rice to the Viśve Devas. This is offerred in the open air at morn and eve. Daily offerings are to be made to Agni, Soma, Dhanvantari, and a separate one to the Creator. To Yama the bali must be cast southward; to Varuṇa, westward; to Soma, northward; to Indra, eastward; to Dhanvantari to the north-east (13, 97, 5f.). Physically, Indra is typical of strength, Vāyu of speed; Soma of beauty; Death of anger (3, 141, 21). But in 8, 92, 13 and elsewhere gods typical of strength, bravery, and prowess are Kubera, Yama, and Indra. Prowess is also the mark of Viṣṇu, as beauty is that of the Aśvins, patience that of Earth, etc. (R 7, 37, 4f.). Both Yama and Varuṇa are famed for "control", the first controlling his just wrath against the sinner, the second controlling the realm and sinner (2, 78, 18f.). Similarly, of the gods, who are all wealthy, four are selected to represent this trait by Vālmīki's follower, when he says "such wealth was never seen before, not of Śakra, of the lord of wealth (Kubera), of Yama, or of Varuṇa" (R 7, 92, 17).

Before the general characteristics of the gods are discussed, it is necessary to remark that the term Devatā is also applied to a gentle host of sylvan deities who do not share the characteristics of the supernal Devas (also called Devatās). There are divinities of house and home and also of the woods, who seem to belong to earth and stay there. The greater and rougher epic has little to do with them, but Rāma's wanderings through the woods give opportunity for the more sentimental poem to exploit them. On occasion, however, they are recognised, as when one says in 1, 154, 3, "Art thou the Devatā of this wood, O thou divinely fair?". The Yakṣas are usually gentle but sometimes unpleasant, and probably Vanadevatās and Yakṣas are regarded as of the same class. The Vanadevatās run away, easily frightened, when any fiend or god appears. On seeing Sītā weep they tremble in every limb (R 3, 52, 43). They are called Sattvas and Daivatāni, and Sītā invokes them (ib. 45, 31; ib. 49, 33f.). The Devatā nagarasya is another earth-goddess, the tutelary divinity of the city (4, 9, 15), i. e. the incorporate city as goddess, lovely as a Kiṃnarī or Vidyādharī (cf. R 5, 3, 27f.). Every home has also its Gṛhadevī (§ 17). In 13, 100, 10, the pious man is told to give pleasure to these gṛhyā devatāḥ with incense and lamps as offerings. They are invoked with other beings as witnesses (R 2, 11, 15). In short, every place has its genius loci, whether grove, mountain, stream, village, or house.

§ 22. **The Signs of the Gods.** — All divine beings are fair. A woman is sufficiently lauded when called devarūpiṇī (1, 153, 11; 3, 65, 73). The One God alone is vidharman, without qualities; other gods have qualities distinguishing them from man, who is first of all mortal and so endowed with mortal qualities, martyadharman. The gods have these conspicuous traits: they are immortal (1, 18, 27); they do not quite touch earth with the feet (opposed to the martya who is padā bhūmim upaspṛśan, 2, 70, 14); they have "divine" beauty, devarūpa; they do not sweat, and have no dust upon their limbs or garlands; they do not wink their eyes; they have no shadow (3, 57, 23f.). Some of these points may be uncertain, as contradicted by other accounts. Thus the garlands of the gods fade when they are frightened (1, 30, 37). Rāma "sees the huge shadows of gods, Gandharvas, and Rakṣas" at a place on the Sarasvatī called Subhūmika (9, 37, 9, chāyāś ca vipulā dṛṣṭvā devagandharvarakṣasām). But S has śayyāḥ (couches) for chāyāḥ. Hanumat asks if Sītā is a goddess and says he thinks she is not, because of her "touching earth", also from her excessive weeping (R 5, 33, 11). The shadow-sign is often ignored; so in R 3, 36, Prak. 17f., where, as signs, are mentioned not touching earth, winkless eyes, dustless garments, and unfaded flowers. Indra as typical of all the gods (R 3, 5, 5f.) has no dust upon his garments or jewels and does not touch earth with his feet. Indra's attendants are ever immortal and beautiful and "appear to be twenty-five years old, for such is ever the age of gods" (R 3, 5, 18, etad dhi kila devānāṃ vayo bhavati nityadā). The voice of the gods is loud (S 3, 105, 1, nirhrādinyā girā . . uvāca Brahmā). Those who are "like gods" are by implication intelligent to a high degree, as put in

1, 183, 11, "they were like gods (that is) endowed with intelligence, prowess and might", buddhi, vīrya, bala. The "immortals" are synonymous with "intelligent", vibudhas = Devas. That gods are not always wise is shown by tales where they are outwitted by the fiends, but the respectful epithet remains as one of their characteristics at all times. An exception in appearance occurs if a god goes disguised. Then, as man, he appears as man, for gods go gūḍharūpāḥ with their true form concealed (and its characteristics). Most of the gods win their best battles by "concealed" form (deceit) and boast of it. The gods turn into animals at will, as evinced by the tales of Dharma as a dog, or the tale of R 7, 18, 2f., where, in fear of Rāvaṇa, Dharma became a crow, Varuṇa a goose, Kubera a lizard, etc. The gods appear and "go as they will" (but so do any spirits).

The gods live in fear of man, partly because of physical reasons, partly on moral grounds. They are dependent on the offerings given by men, and should these fail, they would be in a wretched state. Also the divinity of an epic hero in alliance with the All-god renders the Devas afraid (R 3, 23, 26f. etc.). A god again, if in high station, lives in fear of some mortal gaining merit enough to oust him from his place (3, 193, 23; see § 66).

§ 23. **Habitations of Spiritual Beings.** — When not directly interested in human affairs to the point of descending to earth, either to partake of a sacrifice or to intervene in worldly matters, the gods reside in the sky, where they live in courts of their own "on top of the sky, in the third heaven", or gather at the halls of their colleagues. Brahman's court is the highest of these, except when sectarian influence lowers him below another "highest" god. These residences of the gods are called assembly-halls, parks, cloudlike "vehicles", cities, worlds, and palaces, and it is occasionally impossible to say whether the poet thinks of them as separate or as including one the other, as is true also of the demons, so that, for example, whether Rāvaṇa's "car" is coterminous with his residence is difficult to say. The court or "hall" of Indra is the rendezvous of the other gods and this is called Sudharmā, but most of the halls of the gods appear to have no special name; possibly only the highest gods were regarded as possessing a "hall" at all. Agni, Sun, Moon, Indra, Brahman, Kṛṣṇa, Yama, Varuṇa, and Kubera are particularly named as having renowned and beautiful palaces of this sort. Even Indra's hall is known by name only in Hariv., the Purāṇas, and Rām. and late additions; 2, 3, 27; S 12, 37, 18 (praviveśa sabhāṃ rājā Sudharmāṃ Vāsavo yathā); cf. R 2, 56, 36, sabhāṃ yathā devagaṇāḥ Sudharmām .. viviśuḥ)[1]).

The general heaven called Triviṣṭapa is a name of the sun, as is Svargadvāra (door of heaven, 3, 3, 26). It is synonymous with Amarāvatī and Indra-loka (1, 207, 36 and 210, 7). It is the general synagogue of the gods (2, 60, 4), but is especially Indra's (3, 24, 21, as lord of Triviṣṭapa) and is typical of any very beautiful place (3, 100, 18). Mortals who sin

[1]) This verse is found in both the Bombay and Kumbakonam (sic) texts, but it is not in G. Yet RB 2, 81, 10 and G 82, 9 both have Sudharmā as the hall where Bṛhaspati and Indra go with their troop (of gods), evidently the same Sabhā as that of Mbh. 2, 3, 27. As these are the only passages where Sudharmā occurs as a hall, common in Hariv. and the Purāṇas, it is probably an indication that the "Halls" are a late description, a supposition favored by other evidence of the same character regarding their inhabitants (perhaps a loan from the Jains, who have a heaven and gods called Saudharma). Sudharmā in Mbh. is the wife of Mātali (see under Indra). In H 6565f., Vāyu takes the hall Sudharmā to Dvārakā.

cannot see Indra's city (3, 43, 1 f.), sinners being defined as those who do not sacrifice nor bathe in Tīrthas, and who do eat meat and get drunk. Indra is lord of the whole world, and his "hall" Puṣkaramālinī (2, 7, 30) is the abode of other gods, half-gods, etc., as well as of the Seven Seers. There is no use in mentioning all the gods resident there; it suffices to point out that although Agni and the Sun are said to have their own halls, that of Indra seems often to be their abode. "Like clouds" describes the "home of the gods" (2, 3, 25) and, without exaggerating natural phenomena as a base, there is probably something in that. The massed clouds suggest palaces and every god like every rāj has his palace or "assembly-hall", but the smaller chiefs live mostly at the court of the emperor, and Indra is described here after the emperor-idea is naturalised. Human conditions are reflected in divine. So the gods have their "play-grounds" as well as palaces, generally on the summit of mountains, some of these earthly resorts being still "marked with their feet" (devānām ākrīḍaṃ caraṇāṅkitam, 3, 139, 4; cf. ib. 158, 83, devākrīḍas, masc. or neut.) The favorite play-grounds of the gods are the mountains Meru, Kailāsa, and Maināka (1, 120, 11), where "a man who is even a little rash" is set upon by Rākṣasas and killed for his daring, since (ib.) it is the vihāro devānām amānuṣagatis tu sā, "gods' sporting-ground where man is not admitted". To be noticed is the fact, here expressed, that Rākṣasas are employed by the gods to guard their privacy. Not angels but devils guard the celestial city. Moreover, Kailāsa (the especial udyāna or park of Śiva), where only gods and the highest saints and divine seers can come, is also the home of Dānavas. It is, however, as much the home of Kubera as of Śiva. Kubera sits at ease on Gandhamādana and listens to the music of Tumburu on holy days (3, 159, 28). The palaces of earth are compared with such homes of the gods (not temples) when one wishes to exalt the human display of marble, jewels, gold, etc. In these palaces the gods are represented as feasting and lying on couches, living a life of drunken ease. "Drunk as gods" describes the condition of Raukmiṇeya and Sāmba at a festival (1, 219, 9; cf. 8, 10, 7 for the "comfortable couches"). Beyond and over these mountains of the North goes the Devayāna, "beyond Kailāsa"; this is the Devalokasya mārgaḥ and divyo devapathaḥ found by the mortal who might not go upon it (3, 148, 22). The home of Kubera is on the top of the mountain and beyond it stretches the divine path leading to the heavenly world, a "terrible uneven path only wide enough for one" (like a bridge to paradise). The path of the gods, devapatha, is, however, often the path by which the gods go (apparently) from any starting point, leaving its trail in the sky to this day. For example, by this path ascended Rudra to heaven after abandoning the sacrificial animal, and "it appears visibly to whoso touches water and sings to Rudra a Gāthā (hymn, 3, 114, 6—10); the spot from which he ascended being in the Kaliṅga country north of the (earthly) Vaitaraṇī river. Metaphorically the path of the gods is virtue and bravery[1]). The visible road may be the Milky Way. The Devapur is literally a stronghold in the third heaven (diva interchanges with Tri-

[1]) The Devapathas of the city mentioned in R 2, 17, 16 may be roads to temples or royal roads, catuṣpathān devapathāṃś caityāny āyatanāni ca pradakṣiṇaṃ pariharañ jagāma (B caityān). Devamārga as apānadvāra (!) appears in R 5, 62, 15—16 (G 61, 4). For the metaphorical use mentioned above, cf. 5, 27, 27: mā gās tvaṃ vai devayānāt patho 'dya; and 9, 5, 39 (of bravery).

viṣṭapa). The "three worlds" are those of sky, atmosphere and earth (trināka = tridiva; nāka interchanges both with vyoman and with diva). Another term is vīraloka, where dead heroes go, equivalent to the world of the blest or the highest course (7, 77, 15; ib. 195, 7). The worlds of the blest are many, opposed to the bad worlds, kṛcchrā lokāḥ, of sinners. Both are variously interpreted. Those who sacrifice go to other worlds than those of saints or of philosophers, and according to Kāśyapa, the worlds of the patient are the highest; the bad worlds being hells or worlds in the sense of rebirth in low forms (7, 125, 76; 3, 29, 39 and ib. 181, 9). The "three worlds" is chiefly proverbial (3, 134, 10) and becomes a mere formula, "famous in the three worlds", etc., though probably at first intended to cover the worlds of gods, Asuras, and men (cf. 7, 62, 1; R 7, 5, 11, etc.). Trilokanātha and Trailoka are epithets of Indra as lord of these worlds, called loka and bhuvana (5, 10, 3 and 6; R 6, 114, 18). With this interchanges another antique phrase "seven worlds" (3, 3, 45 and 52; 1, 179, 12 and 22; RG 1, 14, 41, sapta lokāḥ). These worlds are supported on earth or on water (4, 50, 3 and 1, 180, 17). Śiva is identified with the seven worlds he creates (13, 16, 34) "beginning with earth" (ib. 52, bhuvanāḥ sapta). They are personified (12, 187, 26) as sentient and talking beings (R 6, 101, 56). But in R 6, 119, 31f. ("the three worlds see Sītā enter fire"), gods, Gandharvas, and Dānavas are meant (ib. 120, 24). The gods and their worlds are not kept strictly apart, nor men and their world, the material being sensible. So Rāma "can destroy worlds" and again create "people", the two being thought of as one (R 3, 31, 26). The Purāṇic worlds beyond worlds has scarcely affected the epic, which in this regard as in many others shows its priority (9, 47, 14; 13, 14, 211). But the later writers influenced by Buddhism are not content with a few worlds and proceed to pile worlds on worlds as homes of the blest and the gods, worlds which even Indra cannot see; visionary worlds (svapnabhūtā lokāḥ), beyond Time (13, 73, 2f.; ib. 81, 18f.). So, in this view, the Maruts live no longer with Indra but have a world of their own, as do other gods, where men live blessed with millions or billions of years. A peculiar description in R 7, 23, pr. 4, 1f. enumerates different worlds as wind-paths, the first being that of the goose, haṃsa, the second that of three kinds of clouds, the fourth that of sanctified saints and singers (Siddhas and Cāraṇas), the fourth of pious beings, the fifth of aerial Ganges and Nāgas and elephants (water here becomes snow), the sixth of Garuḍa and his relations (jñātis and bāndhavas), the seventh of the sun and planets and stars (a thousand leagues above the aerial Ganges, upheld by Wind), and finally the world of the Moon. In 13, 102, 14f., a round dozen of desirable worlds are enumerated, implicitly in the order of preference: the region of Yama, of the aerial Ganges, Mandākinī, and Kubera, of Meru, of Nārada, of the Uttara Kurus, of Soma, of Āditya, of Varuṇa, of Indra, of Prajāpati, of cows, and of Brahman (sadana interchanging with loka). The characteristics of these worlds are not unlike: in the world of the Moon live kind people and no sorrow is there; in the world of the Sun live those who keep their vows; in Indra's world live centenarians, heroes, and scholars, etc. The "shining world of heroes" is really one with Indra's world. When a hero dies in battle, thousands of nymphs and Gandharva-girls vie with each other for the honor of becoming his wife (12, 99, 4 and 98, 46). All the worlds have these nymphs; only later are they restricted to a "seventh" heaven. Theology also invents dauhitraja worlds, won by those who get the benefit of sons through daughters' sons (1, 157, 36). But in general the epic imagines tier on tier of worlds topped by that of Brahman, Viṣṇu, or Śiva, as sectaries decide. Similarly the worlds of sinners are imagined as separate hells. The later epic delights in placing certain virtuous people, as reward of their virtue, in certain worlds. One who takes his early morning bath and is well read in the Great Epic receives "the worlds of Viṣṇu and the Moon" as his reward (13, 76, 18). Twenty-six or twenty-seven worlds (Buddhistic) may be inferred from the aṣcent of Jaigīṣavya from earth to the point where he disappears in the world of Brahman; though these world are those of saints and ascetics for the most part (after Yama's world and Soma's world), till the worlds of Mitra and Varuṇa, the Ādityas, Rudra, Vasus, Bṛhaspati (Nos. 16 to 20) bring him to the world of cows, "three other worlds", and the world of faithful women (9, 50, 26f.). Descriptions of the assembly-halls of the four Lokapālas and of Brahman describe them in terms of earthly luxury with some strange restrictions of inhabitants. Varuṇa's Hall contains, as was to be expected, Nāgas and waters and Daityas; Kubera's, besides Rākṣasas, Yakṣas, and Guhyakas, contains Gandharvas, Apsarasas, and Śiva ("God of the Bull"); Yama's contains kings; Brahman's, saints and seers; Indra's, gods, Gandharvas, and great seers and Hariścandra, a king-seer (rājarṣi); yet all who die in battle go to Indra's heaven and live happily with him (2, 12, 21) as do all ascetic suicides (ib. 22). Other descriptions allude to worlds without end, flowing with milk and honey, in each of which a favored mortal lives seven days (1, 92, 10 and 15f.). Stars are not only saints but worlds that both live and mourn and serve as future stations for those who live holy lives (1, 210, 36; 3, 42, 32 and 34; 12, 271, 25; 14, 17, 38f.). Opposed to heavens are the hells into which one falls or sinks, i. e. below earth. Below earth are the delightful regions of Rasātala, the seventh layer under earth, where is Bhogavatī, and in several passages no difference is to be seen between this Rasātala and Pātāla, the depth of earth, later resolved into several Pātālas, of which an interpolated verse in S gives a premonition (4, 18, 22), pātāleṣu pataty eṣa vilapan vaḍavāmukhe, "he will fall lamenting into the Mare's mouth in the Pātālas" (implying the fire of the Vaḍavāmukha in the water-world under earth). This under-world is reddened with flames and guarded by demons (R 6, 75, 52 and 41, 34f.), and the inhabitants of Pātāla are in the southern ocean (R 4, 64, 4f.), so that probably, though hell is in Yama's domain in the South, the "falling" and "sinking" were used originally of descent under earth, i. e. into the region known to the epic as the under-world. Neither epic gives the Purāṇic seven (eight) Pātālas (of which one is Rasātala) ascribed to different classes of beings and regents, each region having a depth of ten thousand leagues. But 5, 102, 11 may imply a knowledge of this, as it speaks of the seventh layer under earth as Rasātala and cites the verse which says that no heaven is so blessed a place (cf. VP. 2, 5, 5, which alludes to this). Pātāla as Rasātala is a watery under-world where Vāsuki (§ 13) reigns, but being also the abode of demons and fiends and of underground fires it later became synonymous with hell (see Yama).

§ 24. **Children and Wives of the Gods.** — Umā cursed the gods to have no children, because they had persuaded Śiva to have no son by her, so excepting Agni, who was out of hearing and so out of range of the curse, all the gods became childless (13, 84, 76). Rām. 1, 36, 22 tells the same tale differently, limiting the curse to the wives of the gods. In fact, the gods have many sons by many mothers, nymphs, Nāga-girls, fairies, etc. (R 1, 17, 9f.). Mbh. says that bears and monkeys were born at Brahman's command as sons of gods, Gandharvas, etc. (3, 276, 6). According to the genealogy of heroes, "part" of a god was born on earth as a hero, or one hero is a unified portion of certain divine powers. Thus Droṇa was a part of Bṛhaspati, but Aśvatthāman was born as the unification of Mahādeva, Death, Desire, and Wrath (ekatvam upapannānāṃ jajñe, 1, 67, 69f.). Yudhiṣṭhira was "son" of Dharma as a part of Dharma (ib. 110 Dharmasyāṃśam . . viddhi Yudhiṣṭhiram). Apparently this does not hold good in the case of evil spirits. Śikhaṇḍin is not born by this sort of fission but is a whole fiend incarnate (ib. 126, Agner bhāgaṃ tu viddhi tvaṃ Dṛṣṭadyumnam . . Śikhaṇḍinam . . . viddhi Rākṣasam), the whole war being in theory a contest of "parts of gods" and complete Rākṣasas (only Duryodhana is "part of Kali") and other demons, such as Aśoka, who was the demon Aśva; Candravarman, king of Kamboja, who was the demon Candra (son of Diti); and Viśva, who was the Mahāsura Mayūra (etc., 1, 67, 14—35). In effect, the detailed description of the greatest heroes shows that the gods were imagined as real fathers, though by reason of their Yoga power they can reproduce themselves divinely, so that Sūrya, the Sun, being called by a Mantra of the Atharvaveda, comes to Pṛthā and "touches" her, whereat she conceives; but "the sun did not pollute her" (3, 307, 28, immaculate conception). The gods have sons in five different ways. They may propagate by thought alone (the "spiritual" sons of Brahman, etc.) or by word, sight, touch, or, finally, by congress (15, 30, 22). Vālin, Sugrīva, Tāra, Gandhamādana, Nala, Nīla, Mainda and Dvivida, Suṣeṇa, and Śarabha, in the story of Rāma, are the respective sons by female animals of Indra, Sūrya, Bṛhaspati, Kubera, Viśvakarman, Pāvaka (Agni), the Aśvins, Varuṇa, and Parjanya; but Hanumat is son of Māruta (Vāyu) by the wife of king Kesarin and she is a nymph reborn on earth (R 1, 17). Heroes are said to be "like sons of gods", Devaputrasamāḥ sarve (6, 103, 21f.) Sītā is "like the daughter of a god", surasutopamā (R 6, 5, 20). The male children of the gods make a special group of celestial beings, grouped with Gandharvas, Apsarasas, etc., as devānāṃ śiśavaḥ, "sons of gods", in the procession of gods honoring Śiva (3, 231, 44). When the nymphs sport on earth, they join in play with the Tridaśānām ātmajāḥ (3, 240, 22), "own sons of the gods" (Three and Thirty). Such sons are identified with the Gandharvas in 4, 14, 50, where they are called "sons of the gods who roam the skies, the smiters" (pramāthinaḥ). Devaśiśur yathā and Devagarbha applied to Abhimanyu (4, 72, 8, etc.) also imply the existence of sons of the gods of one sort or another, as the gods themselves are called Dakṣasutāḥ (R 5, 48, 16). Perhaps Devagandharva itself means son of the gods: Nārada, Kali, and other such Devagandharvas are in fact (1, 65, 44) Mauneyas, grandchildren of Brahman by Muni, daughter of Dakṣa, a metronymic of the Apsarasas also (H 12473). The nymphs themselves are "girls of the gods" (Devakanyās sporting with Gandharvas, 11, 19, 18, implies this). The Devakanyā turned into a doe by Brahman is an Apsaras (3, 110, 37). The term is used in the same way in the tale of Ṛṣyaśṛṅga and in 13, 14, 38 and RG 5, 15, 16 stands in contrast to Devapatnī and Devamātṛ (wife and mother of gods). Probably after the term became current, it bred a belief in the special existence of a group thus called, for it sometimes seems to stand in contrast also with the Apsarasas themselves, Gandharvā Devakanyāś ca sarve cā 'psarasāṃ gaṇāḥ (5, 17, 22; 13, 166, 14). But "girl" is ambiguous and in such instances seems rather to indicate a krīḍānārī (play-girl) than a daughter of gods. In many cases the bliss of heaven is augmented by Devakanyās (e. g. 13, 107, 35f.) = Apsarasas. The kanyās of various special gods are here mentioned (just as Devayoṣitas occurs elsewhere to designate dancing nymphs, crowned with lotuses and golden-hued) and described as black, brunette and blonde Deva- and Daivatakanyās. These Surayoṣitas play on vīṇās and vallakīs (lutes) and are adorned with nūpuras (anklets), having eyes of doe or of cat, fair waists, and brilliant smiles. The Devastriyaḥ may be seen climbing up Mt. Meru, but these are the gods' wives (1, 134, 16; 13, 79, 25f.). The wife is always sharer of the honor of her divine husband, although he is rarely faithful to her. The wives differ from these gay girls and women, kanyās, yoṣitas, and kumāryas, or concubines of the gods, in dignity and in being accepted everywhere as the one wife, each being hidden from the eyes of the world, as queens are hid on earth: "What man may behold the (one) wife of Soma, of Indra, of Viṣṇu, of Varuṇa, in his house (concealed)?" (1, 82, 12, kaḥ .. striyaṃ draṣṭum arhati). Such a wife is the patnī (queen) and devī (as queen, devī is used of an earthly king's wife). Even when physical phenomena require that the Moon-god recognise twenty-seven "wives" (lunar stations, stars of the lunar zodiac) and each is called patnī, Rohiṇī is really the queen among them (1, 66, 16). As typical of conjugal bliss, divine pairs are strung together by the poets, who thus give us the names of most of these queens of the gods, though they do not always agree. For example, one list ascribes Yama's wife to Mārkaṇḍeya (saints and their wives are often included in the lists). Some of the names are of Vedic type, Rudra and Rudrāṇī, Indra and Śacī, Purūravas and Urvaśī, etc.; others are new creations and not so firmly fixed. Śiva himself gives such a list at 13, 146, 4f.: Sāvitrī is the good wife, sādhvī, of Brahman; Śacī, of Kauśika (Indra); Dhūmorṇā of Mārkaṇḍeya; Ṛddhi, of Kubera (Vaiśravaṇa); Gaurī, of Varuṇa; Suvarcalā, of Sūrya; Rohiṇī, of Śaśin (Soma); Svāhā, of Agni (Vibhāvasu); and Aditi, of Kaśyapa. These wives are all patidevatāḥ, "hold their husbands as their god". Dhūmorṇā in 5, 117, 8f. (in S), also in S 13, 166, 11, is paired with Yama in a similar list, in which Prabhāvatī and Ravi represent Prabhā (§ 84) or Suvarcalā and Sūrya (etc.) with a few additions, Nārāyaṇa and Lakṣmī, Udadhi and Jāhnavī (Ocean and Ganges), Pitāmaha and Vedī; though Kauśika here is Viśvāmitra (and Haimavatī). Bṛhaspati here pairs with Tārā; Śukra with Śataparvā; Dharma with Dhṛti; Vāsuki with Śataśīrṣā; Janārdana (Kṛṣṇa) with Rukmiṇī, etc. Vedī cannot be Sāvitrī, another instance of discrepancy. Dhṛti is also an All-god (masculine). Devasenā is added in some lists as wife of Skanda (3, 224, 1f.; S 4, 22, 9f.: Lakṣmī is here wife of Damodara, Śacī of Indra, Rudrāṇī of Śaṅkara, Sāvitrī of Brahman, and Devasenā of Guha). R has a similar list (R 5, 24, 10f.), embracing heroes, Keśinī and Sagara, Nala and Damayantī, Sāvitrī and Satyavat. The social structure suggested is not carried to its logical conclusion. Some gods belong to one caste, some to another; yet the Aśvins, though they are Śūdras (12, 208, 24), are warrior-gods, and as such receive offerings and sacrifice (see § 110). Bṛhaspati is a priest (god). Indra is a warrior. But no god is representative of the third estate and Indra is no more a Vanir-like trading-god; still less are there outcaste gods. All that is permitted here is the almost exclusive devotion of Parjanya as rain-god to the agricultural caste and the practically outcaste (outcast) condition of the Dānavas, etc. There are too no Mleccha barbarian gods, though the episode of the White Island, common to the pseudo-epic of both poems, recognises a barbarian God. The "sacrifice-stealing" gods are not said to be foreign, though they may be so. The later epic is very catholic. Bṛhaspati, the priest-god, says: "A black man who acts white is recognised by the gods as a Brahman, even if he be of the lowest caste. A virtuous and pure Mleccha is better than a Brahman who does evil" (S 12, 118 after B ib. 6; cf. also on the Śūdra-nature of an evil priest, 3, 216, 14f.).

§ 25. **Men as Gods.** — The first men were devakalpa ("god-like") saints who never did wrong, pure vehicles of virtue (dharmatantrāṇi). They all had the true nature of Brahman, went to heaven and returned again as they liked along with the gods, and being god-like died only when they wished. These were those now called Siddhas and Siddhārthas, the blest ("they attained their aim", 2, 183, 63f.; 3, 135, 11). But after thousands of years men became less virtuous; then they lost their power of going to heaven and "walked only on earth and sank sinning to hell". The Karma doctrine sealed this theory and emplasised euhemerism: "The lights of heaven, the Three and Thirty (gods), Nāgas and Yakṣas, Moon and Sun and Wind (god), all got to godhead from the human state through manly action" (13, 6, 3f.). But the Fathers of old remain in memory as men who become so godlike that they are all, even the later Pitṛs, called a kind of god, and philosophy, identifying functions of man with gods and his soul as one with God, while his body is the home of gods, reduces the distinction still more. Yet apart from philosophy, certain men are gods on earth. Whether this honor came first to priest, king[1]), or husband, the epic recognises fully that the priest as well as the king is divine, and that to every wife her husband is or should be her divinity. A distinction is made in the terms describing the first two classes. A king or prince or a royal seer is called naradeva; a priest is bhūmideva, "earth-god". It is only as a god that a king may accept a gift (he is Indra, Varuṇa, Kubera, and Yama incorporate, R 7, 76, 31f.); it is as a divinity that the priest is entitled to his superior position. The king has the high title naradevadeva (5, 30, 1). He incorporates many gods, Dharma, Bṛhaspati, Prajāpati, and even Bhava and Babhru (Śiva and Viṣṇu, 3, 185, 28). He is the Creator in earthly form and in proverbial language represents regularly five divinities (R 3, 40, 12, etc.) His touch is divinely healing (15, 3, 68). Modifications are due to conduct. If not kingly, he is no king, therefore no god; and as such may be slain like a mad dog (R 2, 196, 11; ib. 3, 33, 16). Hence, as he has "something human", being only "one quarter Indra" (ib. 7, 59, pr. 3; ib. 3, 1, 18f.), he is said to "obtain divinity" on dying (i. e. complete divinity); whereas, no matter how evil a priest may be, he remains an "earth-god" (bhūsura, S 12, 141, 92), created god on earth by the Creator above (13, 141, 62). This differs from the philosophical speculation that merely recognises as anybody's "going" a manifestation of Viṣṇu, power as Śakra, Agni in digestion, and Sarasvatī in hearing (12, 240, 8), and even makes deva mean sense, "the gods in the senses"

[1]) E. Kuhn, Zu den Arischen Anschauungen vom Königtum, p. 216, cites R 2, 102 (101), 4, devatve saṃmato mama to illustrate king as deva (ib. kṣitidevatā of priests, 13, 141, 62) by consent (cf. Mahāsaṃmata). The vs. represents rather the usual view (king is human) offset by the new view of the speaker ("in my opinion, divine"). G limits to the individual case, devatvaṃ for devatve (111, 4).

(certain in 12, 314, 1 f. = 14, 42, 24; ib. 43, 30f.; uncertain in 12, 175, 25). The identification is rather implied also in the theory that when a man dies and his soul escapes through his feet, it gets to Viṣṇu, through the crown to Brahman, through the eyes to Agni (etc. 12, 302, 20f.; 314, 1 f.; 318, 1 f.). The theory that the husband is the wife's divinity is a parallel to that which makes the parents the child's divinity. Neither (so common are both) needs illustration; but the underlying sense is totemic in that it establishes as a "god" that power on which one is dependent (see above, § 9). Woman herself is (poetically) a divinity, Śrīḥ strī (13, 46, 15). The theory of the "gods of gods" (above, § 15) is illustrated by R 2, 34, 52, pitā hi daivataṃ tāta devatānām api smṛtam (for the others, see e. g. bhartā daivatam, ib. 24, 21; 12, 267, 39; of both parents, etau maddaivataṃ param, 3, 214, 19f.).

§ 26. **Religion and Morals of the Gods.** — The priest of the gods, Bṛhaspati, exercises the usual functions of a priest, that is, the gods are a religious body and have their own "divine service". Curiously enough, the priest himself is no more of an authority than the priest of the demons (12, 58, 1 f.). In sectarian chapters of the epics all the gods worship Viṣṇu or Śiva, but their priest was not for this purpose, rather to obtain and retain for them the magical powers obtained by the sacrifice. For the same reason the gods perform austerities. Yet their pūjā is not of great import; any hero or saint is "honored" by the civil deities. They even dance and sing in honor of a royal saint like Śibi, who was "besung and bedanced by the gods" in admiration (nṛttaś cai 'vo 'pagītaś ca pitāmaha iva prabhuḥ, by nymphs, angels, and gods, 13, 32, 32)[1]). The gods meditate, perform penances, offer sacrifices, etc., and the places where of old were the fires of their sacrifices are still shown on earth. All the gods took part in the building of the fires at Viśākhayūpa, for example, and Maruts, Aśvins, and Sādhyas also muttered their prayers, and saints and seers sang hymns at Gaṅgādvāra, where Śiva received the Ganges (āhnikaṃ japate and sāma sma gāyanti sāmagāḥ, 3, 142, 6f.; cf. 3, 90, 15; 12, 12, 3). The gods' festival, however, is not on earth, but at Indra's city. It is a pūjā but not religious, consisting in drinking, song and dance; in fact, it resembles a human festival, as divine religious exercises resemble their human models. The gods come and take their seats in "due order" as the spectators of the dance, which is an essential part of the feast of heaven, svargasya utsavaḥ. Mahendra, being host, dismisses his guests after they have enjoyed themselves sufficiently; the festival being a musical exhibition given by the Gandharvas and Apsarasas (3, 46, 27f.). The human utsava is a samāja in honor of a god (1, 143, 9), but the divine utsava is to do honor to a human heroic son of Indra. The Soma of the gods' sacrifice mingled with the river Payoṣṇī and is still mixed with it (3, 120, 32f.). That Indra drank Soma with the Aśvins on the Narmadā river is referred to elsewhere (§§ 4 and 110).

If ethics be part of religion, the divine religion is moral. All in all, as light to darkness, so is the religion approved of the gods as compared with that of the demons. The demons are false and eat meat; the gods

[1]) This use of nṛtta = upanṛtta is perhaps proleptic, as upagīta follows. The normal use occurs in 5, 123, 4, upagītopanṛttaś ca (of Yayāti on entering heaven). Dance is a common token of honor and worship, but "fore-dancing", pra-nart may indicate insult (= prati-nart) as well as honor; pranṛtta is used not of the recipient of the honor but of the dancing person (see s. v. P. W.).

are true and drink nectar. Apparently they eat flesh at sacrifices, but they do not eat bloody flesh, only the essence of sacrifice. Despite the many sins of the king of the gods, who is famous as an adulterer, deceiver, and drinker, the epic moralist attributes repentance to him. Dissent from the belief that the gods love truth appears only in the splenetic utterance of an impatient king who says that "now-a-days even the gods lie", Devā 'pi nūnam anṛtaṃ vadanti (8, 68, 15). Opposed is a mass of testimony: "Sun, Fire, Wind, all gods, all creation, depend on truth; truth is equal to a thousand horse-sacrifices; it pleases the gods and Pitṛs; it is man's highest duty" (13, 75, 29). Banal morality, however, is to be tempered by common sense. Not to injure animals is a moral law, but Balāka won heaven by killing a blind beast; and Kauśika went to hell for telling an inopportune truth (8, 69, 39f.; 12, 109, 7). To deceive one's friend is wrong; to deceive one's enemy is right, etc. All the greatest victories of the gods were won by deception of which they boast with pride. The gods cause the fall of the sinner (or slay him, devatāḥ pātayanti, v. l. ghātayanti, 12, 132, 18). So the gods are appealed to as arbiters: "To the Thirty-three thy act of violence is hateful" (3, 161, 11; S ib. 162, 13, v. l. "even to the gods"). The gods "seek wisdom and love purity; they will not accept an offering from a man without faith" (3, 186, 18f.). Faith means to "revere all the gods and obey all their laws" (12, 110, 18). But Indra as the god of valor demands of his worshippers virtue in the Roman sense; his warriors lacking bravery fail to go to his heaven and not lacking bravery but dying face to the foe they attain bliss, irrespective of their moral state otherwise. Those who desert their friends in battle are to be burned alive, for "Indra and the other gods whom he heads give over to misfortune (asvasti tebhyaḥ kurvanti) those who, deserting their friends, come home unwounded from war" (12, 97, 21). Such a deserter "sinks to the hell Raurava in a sea of woe without a boat" (S after 6, 77, 35). Indra is god of guests; so hospitality is another means of winning Indra's heaven; as Brahman's heaven is won by treating well the Brahman priest (as teacher), and Prajāpati's heaven is won by obedience to one's father. Hence the saying: "The guest has power over Indra's world". In other words, the appropriate god must be propitiated by observing his own way of morality. That is the reason why "the heaven of the All-gods is won by those who are kind to their maternal and paternal relations" (as they are Pitṛ-gods; all in 12, 244, 17f.; maternal and paternal probably represent the distinction in jāmis and jñātis). The order of the state is also regarded, as an ethical matter, by the gods. Marriages are made in heaven; "monogamy is the state decreed by the gods for women" (2, 68, 35). The wife is "given by the gods" (1, 157, 31). To see whether a man observe these laws, the gods spy upon him; conversely, they are invoked as witnesses (passim). The chief witnesses are (12, 322, 55) Fire, Sun and Wind; others are Moon, Earth, and Water (as divinities). Later comes the idea of "the inner man" (conscience) and of Dharma, Right or Justice, as witnesses (1, 74, 29f.). Yama, as god and judge of the dead, is also naturally invoked, and the Twilights, as complementary to Day and Night (as divine witnesses ib.). Fire is a witness of the world" (R 6, 119, 24f.; cf. 3, 291, 22f. S makes Yama the sākṣī lokasya karmaṇām)[1].

[1]) The thorough treatment of ethics "approved by the gods" would demand a volume, but mythologically it is unimportant, human terms being simply rendered as divine. Virtuous demons are known and sermons preached by them to the gods are given in the later epic with telling effect, the stupid and rather boorish Indra being here set against the urbane demon (see Indra). Compare above, pp. 39—40, on virtuous demons.

§ 27. **Relation between Gods and Men. Worship.** — As shown above (§§ 4 and 19) the gods help men in battle. When propitiated by penances or satiated with offerings, they bestow in return largesse after their kind, or by means of heavenly messengers they give good advice. One thing only they commonly refuse, immortality, but even this is given by special gods (see Brahman, etc.). The gods live in Agastya's hermitage and wait upon the saint, the spot being so sanctified by austerity that in it the gods, when properly propitiated, ārādhitāḥ, "bestow upon pure creatures spirithood and immortality and kingdoms various" (R 3, 11, 94: yakṣatvam amaratvaṃ ca .. atra devā prayacchanti; G 17, 32 has "wealth" also as one of the gifts, but the donor is here one god, narāṇām atra bhagavān vidadhe tapasā vibhuḥ). The free gift of yakṣatva as well as that of immortality, whether made by one or more gods, naturally sets aside the Karma doctrine, according to which "gods and saints get heaven by their acts" (12, 332, 45; cf. 13, 6, 14). Other gifts are regarded as due to merit and possibly immortality or the condition of a Yakṣa (spirit) might be roughly thought of as based on the same cause, but as expressed the two theories are incompatible. Otherwise the gods assist men by proxy. A demon (see Rākṣasas) is sent to interfere with a good woman's seducer; a woman (see Tilottamā) is created to help Viṣṇu and man, etc. The "bodiless voice", so often heard from the sky, is always the voice of gods or their proxy (messenger), uttered to warn or advise, even when it is not expressly stated to whom the voice belongs. In 3, 156, 13, a voice aśarīriṇī divyā ākāśāt, "incorporate, heavenly, from space", gives advice as to the royal pilgrim's route through the mountains. A messenger may be sent, taking any form, so that Hanumat is thought to be "sent either by Vāsava or by Vaiśravaṇa" as messenger (R 5, 42, 15; cf. ib. 50, 10, where he is thought to be sent by Viṣṇu as Rāma or as having assumed the "lovely form" of Kubera, etc.). Dhṛtarāṣṭra is supposed to have been born on earth as a Gandharva (messenger of Indra), to help the cause of right (15, 31, 8!), an involuntary Avatar, though he is perhaps only on a par with other spirits born for the purpose at the will of Brahman (in 1, 67, 3f. and 84 he is "Haṃsa, a lord of Gandharvas, son of Ariṣṭā"). As a voice the Devadūta informs Ruru that life may be restored in return for life if Yama wills, a "means provided by the gods" (1, 9, 7f.). In 3, 260, 30f., a Devadūtaka comes on a car in person to take Mudgala to heaven and tell him of the happiness there (ib. 261). Another, "of terrible form", commanded Yayāti to fall from heaven, saying thrice in a prolonged cry "fall thou" (plutena svareṇa, dhvaṃsa! 1, 89, 20). A voice in space, "of a certain divine messenger", prophecies that the eighth son of Devakī will slay Kaṃsa (S 2, 23, 11). A voice of this sort encourages Bhīṣma to keep on fighting, as this is the "time appointed by the Source of All (Viśvayoni as Brahman) for accomplishing his decrees" (6, 48, 98). Other signs are given for mortal assistance. When Rāvaṇa threatens Sītā, who does not know that he is practically impotent, the Devagandharva maidens, who know all about it, try to signal the truth to her by pouting and winking or averting their eyes (oṣṭhaprakārair aparā vaktrair netrais tathā 'parāḥ, R 5, 22, 11). In combats of men the pleased gods shower flowers (4, 64, 37f.; as is done also by Devayoṣās, 9, 46, 96, on Skanda's victory). Not content with this, the gods lend men their own weapons. The twin brothers of the righteous king thus carry the "bows of Viṣṇu and the Aśvins" (Vaiṣṇava and Aśvija, 7, 23, 92f.).

The gods in the night-battle themselves seize torches and lamps in the sky, when waked by the glare of the battle-field (7, 163, 13f.). Usually they are content to cry sādhu and svasty astu to the heroes (7, 170, 12, etc.). Conversely, the help of the gods is shown by opposition to the favorite's foe. Such opposition is a fatality, a "divine oppression", which may attack a whole city (blest is a city devatābādhavarjitam, "without divine oppression", 1, 207, 35). It is only the philosopher who says that gods give man no physical aid, but help him by making him intelligent. "Gods do not take a stick and guard men like a cowherd; him they wish to guard they gird with knowledge" (5, 35, 40). Another implicit contradiction of the Karma doctrine comes out in the statement that the grace of God is effective (yasya prasādaṃ kurute, etc. 12, 337, 20, Upan. verse and doctrine) and conversely, and materially, a man's personal defects, blindness etc. are not due to acts of a previous birth, but "the gods close the doors" of the deaf and blind (devair apihitadvārāḥ, 12, 263, 13), as it is the gods who give success (5, 191, 15, daivam; S 8, 80, 21, devāḥ sakalaṃ sādhayantu). The very life of a man depends on the grace of the gods (1, 151, 38). The gods help Uparicara because he argues on their side the important question whether seeds may be considered goats for sacrificial purposes (see Vasu). One form of the bestowal of grace is for the gods to give children, particularly sons. It is granted as a reward for austerity, and devatejyās, and laudation, and magical rites (in the list abhicāra comes last, 3, 205, 17f.). It is only the grace of the gods that makes every oblation fruitful (13, 22, 5; see § 31).

The formal worship of the gods consists in austerity, because that is a means of winning their good-will, as much as sacrifice itself, and laudation, vandana, etc. The Vedic cult passes as the usual accepted cult save for the (Viṣṇu) passages which inculcate simpler rites and less bloody offerings. But in the later theory all gifts to the gods are overpassed in value by gifts to the priests (13, 61, etc.), whether of cows, jewels, houses, or land. Lamps, flowers, gold, sandals, etc., every desirable thing, has its reward in heavenly worlds, divine favor, and sensual bliss hereafter. Incense and lights are given to priests and gods alike, the former being for this purpose particularly "gods of earth". The thanksgiving service to the gods, a rite almost lacking in the older cult, is represented as common. Thus on the report of a victory, the gods are worshipped with flowers as offerings (4, 68, 23). Sacrifice itself is divine and a divinity identical with the god Prajāpati. Most gods are sviṣṭakṛtaḥ, "they perfect sacrifice"; only the fifteen Mitra-gods, begotten by Tapas, "steal the sacrifice" (see Proc. Am. Philosoph. Soc. 1910, 24f.). At a hermitage, no attempt is made to please with elaborate rites. Vegetables and water are here the offerings (12, 9, 10, vanya and āpas). There is a difference in flower-offerings. Sharp-scented and thorny flowers and red flowers are for magic, abhicārārtham ("as explained in AV."). Other are the flowers offered to Gandharvas, Nāgas, and Yakṣas; they make glad the heart, hence they are called sumanasas, eumenides. To Bhūts are offered red or black flowers. Owing to their association with demons, one should not wear red flowers but white; yet a red flower may be worn on the head (except the kamala and kuvalaya, lotus and lily, 13, 104, 83f. and ib. 98, 15f.). The gods take the perfume of flowers, Rākṣasas accept their appearance with pleasure, and they please the Nāgas by serving as food (ib. 98, 35). The food of Yakṣas and Rākṣasas, however, must be a mixture of meat and brandy (any spirituous liquor); that of Bhūts, sesame, sugar, etc. The gods should be offered (by a householder) milk and flowers as a bali; then, being pleased with him, they make him prosper (ib. 60, the discourse of Uśanas with Bali, the Asurendra). The same passage discusses the forms of incense pleasing to the gods. Some are inauspicious, but all dhūpas except the perfume made from sallakī are delightful (to the gods) if of the first class. For there are three classes, niryāsa, sarin, and kṛtrima ("artificial", as opposed to the gum and burning stick-incense); the best of all is guggulu (of the first class) i. e. bdellium; aguru (of the second, sarin, class) is best for Yakṣas, Rākṣasas, and serpents (candana and aguru together, 9, 11, 52; as dhūpa, R 5, 9, 28, etc.). The sallakīya incense, hateful to the gods, is the favorite of the Daitya demons; but gods, Dānavas, and Bhūts are all pleased with the incense made of deodar pine and the vatica robusta (13, 98, 38f.). Women are particularly enjoined to make offerings of flowers, as they are excluded from the elaborate Vedic rites. What they have to do in reference to the gods is explained by Umā to Ganges: "Good women should rise early, clean the house with cow-dung, be devoted to the Fire-cult (Agnikārya), and always, with their husbands, offer flowers to the gods" (13, 146, 49). The conduct of good women, as here explained, touches the gods further in that a chaste woman may not look on Sun or Moon (because they are male), nor at "a tree with a masculine name" (na candrasūryau na taruṃ puṃnāmnā, ib. 43). All the gods should be worshipped by a man in the forenoon; and to get long life (hundred years) one should rise before the sun in the hour of Brahman, brāhme muhūrte, be pure, not break things (this is the sympathetic sum of "not bite's one's nails, nor cut grass, nor break sods"), and not look at the sun when he rises or sets nor at midday nor when eclipsed; but the seers, Ṛṣis, got long life simply by adoring the Twilights. When one worships the gods, one should put on clean clothes and not prepare for oneself the food for the gods (saṃyāva, kṛsara, śaṣkuli; 13, 104, 15f.; 87, 41 and 87). The flesh of goats, cows, gavya, and peacocks (ib. 93) is taboo anyway, whether or not on account of religious associations is not stated. To urinate against the sun, cows, priests, or the road, shortens life (ib. 75; cf. with all this, 12, 193, 13f.). According to 13, 104, 64, the rule against looking at sun, moon, and stars, nakṣatra, is for those sacrificially impure.

§ 28. **The Days of the Gods.** — These are mentioned adventitiously and incompletely in the epic poetry. Kārttikī, the full-moon day of the month Kārttika is spoken of as most holy (3, 182, 16), but Mārgaśīrṣa is the chief month (6, 34, 35). The twelfth of each month is sacred to Kṛṣṇa-Viṣṇu, and he should be adored under a different name every month on that day (13, 109, 3f.). Compared with ib. 106, 17f., this section appears to make the year begin with Mārgaśīrṣa, as the rules for fasting and observance through the year start in each case with Mārgaśīrṣa and end with Kārttika. The fifth and sixth lunar days are for sacrifices to the gods; the eighth and fourteenth of the dark half of the month are propitious for fasting. Rewards of the virtue of fasting once a day for each month are enumerated. Phālguna the spring month, is Bhagadaivata (marriage-month, under god Bhaga). The thirteenth lunar day of any month is lucky (praśastā, 3, 134, 20). The day of the new moon, amāvāsyā, is propitious for fighting, because sacred to Indra (Śakradevatā, 5, 142, 18). Auspicious days are those of the new and full moon, the eighth, and the thirteenth; also the lunar days (called divinities) represented by the first part of the day of the new and of the full moon and the latter part of the day of the new and full moon, Sinīvālī, Anumati, Kuhū, Rākā (lunar days as divinities, 8, 34, 32). In 3, 275, 5, Rākā is an evil demon. Sinīvālī and Kuhū (new moon) make a pair as opposed to Anumati and Rākā (full moon). Devasenā, Ṣaṣṭhī, Skanda's wife, is called Sinīvālī and Kuhū (see § 161). In 3, 218, 5, Sinīvālī is the third daughter of Brahman's third son, Aṅgiras (father of Bṛhaspati) and, "owing to her excessive thinness she is both visible and invisible". People call her Kapardin's daughter (Rudra = Śiva wears her on his forehead, the crescent moon). Kuhū is also a daughter of Aṅgiras (see Agni). The moon-month was virtually divided by holy days (when one must remain chaste) into weeks, the day of the new moon, that day week ("eighth day"), full-moon day, and the eighth day after the full moon. Kṛṣṇa and Skanda (v. s. v.) have special days in each month. Skanda has by preference the fifth or sixth of the crescent month (moon, Śrīpañcamī and ṣaṣṭhī). Kṛṣṇa has the twelfth, as already remarked, and the Janmāṣṭamī, eighth. The eighth day anyway is half way between new and full and so is a "joint" day (Parvan) and as such very holy and especially adapted for the fulfilment of desires, when offerings are made to the gods (Kāmyāṣṭamī). Sunday is the seventh day of the week, or, as an alternative, the sixth; better is the seventh because the Sun-god has seven steeds (3, 3, 63 and 64, saptamyām atha vā ṣaṣṭhyām). The year itself is a form of the creator-god, Prajāpati or Brahman (q. v.); in its northern course the Sun begins to take pity on man. The northern course belongs to the gods, the southern to the Fathers (passim). See also JAOS. 24, p. 24; and for the year's possible beginning (in spring), Tilak, Orion, p. 23f.

§ 29. **Shrines and Temples of the Gods.** — The usual word for a shrine is āyatana or devāyatana and these words are often translated as temple or chapel (e. g. PW. s. deva° and devatāyatana), probably without special consideration of the architectural value of a "temple". If buildings of any importance are meant by this translation, it must be said that it is inaccurate for most of the epic occurrence. The āyatana ("resting-place" or "support") is originally a mere place for the sacred fire, and a small shrine gives its architectural value for the Mbh. in all except a few doubtful cases. In Rām., where architecture is more modern than in Mbh., the case is different. It strikes the mind at once that in Mbh., although the homes of kings and lesser men are described in detail, with a full account of the palatial homes of the gods in heaven, and even the watering-places are described as having marble steps, no ornate description of a god's earthly home (temple) is to be found. On the contrary, in many descriptions of sylvan hermitages and impromptu settlements, the āyatanāni appear as hastily erected huts or mounds of earth sacred to a god. For example, in 13, 10, 20, a Śūdra leaves a hermitage in the mountains, and going farther into the wilds proceeds to make a little retreat for himself. There he builds himself a vedi, altar, a bhūmi, to sleep on, and devatāyatanāni, which are clearly not of architectural value. When Rāma in the woods builds himself also a hut, a vedi, caityas and "āyatanāni suitable for an asylum" (R 2, 56, 33, caityāny āyatanāni ca āśramasyā 'nurūpāṇi) he builds the same modest shrines, but the modifying expression shows that the writer recognises more ambitious āyatanāni which would not be suitable for an asylum. And, in fact, as far as Rām. is concerned, in the same book Rāma and Sītā are described as sleeping śrīmaty āyatane Viṣṇoḥ, R 2, 6, 4, which must be a temple large enough for a royal couch; but this is in the city. So too in the same book, R 2, 33, 20, when the "homes" are described as unswept, and "deserted by the divinities", the gods' homes, veśmāni, may be implied, and this would mean temples (doubtful). But at any rate the first case represents something different from the simple sthānaṃ Kauberam, Dharmasthānam, etc., enumerated in the asylums (R 3, 12, 17 f.). The Kaccit chapter, which is found in both epics, alludes to devasthāna in R 2, 100, 44, along with tanks, altars, wells, feasts of the gods, caityas (ib. 62), etc., but the expression is not found in the corresponding version of Mbh. (2, 5, 100 has caityā vṛkṣāḥ). But in the late passage where Mārkaṇḍeya describes the end of the age and the evils thereof, the devasthānas and devagṛhas ("god-houses", bethel) are brought into direct contrast with the reliquaries (of the Buddhists) known as eḍūkas (3, 190, 65 and 67; jālūka, v. l.), and in this case, as in many others, one is not able to say whether a god-house means a temple or not. So with the more frequently mentioned devāyatanāni, most of the occurrences in both epics might apply to a simple shrine or to a temple, if they stood by themselves. When, however, a determining factor shows what they mean, it is evident that in Mbh. they are not temples. Neutral in value, for example, are such cases as those in 5, 152, 2, where one is warned against disturbing śmaśānāni, hermitages of the great seers, Tīrthas, devatāyatanāni and āyatanāni, in pitching a camp; since the distinction may apply to shrines of seers, as in Agastya's hermitage, which had shrines to gods and to seers. The same warning is given in 3, 16, 3, to avoid, in pitching a camp, Caitya trees and devatāyatanāni. The devagṛhāṇi burned by Hanumat in RG 5, 49, 16, are not mentioned in the other text (Bomb. and S), but Rāvaṇa's palace is compared to a devagṛha in R 3, 55, 6, and this passage is found in both texts, the simile suggesting that a temple is meant. This must too be the meaning of devāgāra, as used in R 2, 71, 39, where it is said that at the king's death the devāgāras were empty (devāgārāṇi śūnyāni na cā 'bhānti yathāpuram). Here too (ib. 42) reference is made to devāyatana-caityas. In the addition to Rām., 7, 37, 13 f., a king is described as going to a temple favored by his family, devāgāraṃ jagāmā 'śu puṇyam Ikṣvākusevitam, after rising and making oblations to the Fire-god, hutahutāśanaḥ, and there honoring the gods, Fathers, and priests; and this devāgāra is described as having an outer court, bāhyakakṣyāntaram, where, after divine service, the king received his ministers. Perhaps the same interpretation may be put upon the word in R 7, 59, pra. 1, 20, where a virtuous dog lectures on propriety and says that dogs are not admitted into devāgāra, nṛpāgāra, dvijaveśma, for Fire, Indra, Sūrya, Vāyu, the divine king (= Dharma in person), and other gods in the person of the king (viz. Soma, Mṛtyu, Dhanada = Kubera, and Varuṇa) are in such places. Although the devāgāra is called puṇya, holy, it is not probable that puṇyagṛhāṇi, to be erected by kings, are temples. They are rather puṇyaśālas or dharmaśālas, rest-houses, giving merit, puṇya, to the erectors. The word occurs only in R 2, 67, 12 (devāgāra is not in Mbh.; devatāgāra, Manu, 9, 280). The negative cases in Mbh. may be illustrated by 6, 112, 11, devatāyatanasthā devatāḥ, images of gods "standing on their shrines". They are the object of pūjā (1, 70, 49;

R 1, 44, 14), but the āyatana of Kaśyapa is mentioned in the first passage (vs. 51) and this is not a temple. So when Bhīma is carried aloft and visits mountain-peaks and devatāyatanas, these are like the tāpasāyatanas of the same account (1, 155, 22 and 29). Such places are holy in either case. They are associated with Tīrthas, are objects of interest to travellers, and, as holy places, form a safe place for criminals to consort (1, 140, 64; ib. 215, 4; ib. 9; and 12, 218, 1, in the West and "beyond Kaliṅga"). All the devatāyatanas are adorned with flowers to show joy (3, 77, 8). Animals howling there are of course an evil omen (devatāyatanacaityeṣu; a common collocation, 2, 80, 30; devāyatanacaityeṣu, R 2, 3, 18). In R 2, 6, 11, "on devatāyatanas and . . . on turrets", aṭṭālakeṣu, refers to the city turrets (common to both epics). The Caitya itself is a temple in R 5, 15, 15 (ib. 43, 3), where it is described as having vedikās, terraces, coral stairs, a thousand pillars, and a high roof. No such Caitya is described in Mbh.; in R it is a palace, prāsāda caitya. Usually the Caitya is a sightly tree, holy as the abode of spirits, not to be cut down, or to be cut only as a tactical exploit in invasion (12, 59, 63). In R 5, 12, 18, vedikāś caityasaṃśrayāḥ, they are trees standing at four corners. They were perhaps originally only trees without buildings, hence caityā vṛkṣāḥ (above), and, when alone, masculine (seldom neuter: in R 4, 19, 24, caityam; but in R 2, 17, 16, Rāma makes pradakṣiṇa around catuṣpathān devapathāṃś caityāny āyatanāni ca, the v. l. is caityāṃś ca; in R 6, 130, 2f.: "Let pure men revere with perfumes and wreaths and music the daivatāni and caityāni of the city"), Mbh. 5, 192, 58, "revering with perfumes and wreaths the devatās, caityas (masc.), and four corners". The word tree, vṛkṣa, druma, is frequently added (3, 16, 3, etc.; R 3, 39, 4; RG 5, 20, 24 śmaśānacaityadrumavat) not as if the tree were not the Caitya; since the Caitya is the tree in other passages. In S 12, 69, 41 +, it is said, apropos of the Caityavṛkṣas: "One should avoid to cut them down, as not even the leaf of a Caitya may be destroyed, for Caityas are the resorts of gods, Yakṣas, Rākṣasas, Nāgas, Piśācas, serpents, Gandharvas, Apsarasas, and cruel Bhūts", where devānām āśrayāḥ must be interpreted by the preceding caityānāṃ sarvathā tyājyam api pātrasya pātanam. But the Caitya is a shrine or a temple when it is "erected", as in the description of Māṃdhātṛ who "got half of Indra's seat" because of his piety as citacaityaḥ, or when it is said that "earth had little room left because of the Caityas raised by Gaya" (3, 121, 13; ib. 126, 38). "Caityas of the Three and thirty" (gods) are mentioned in 3, 125, 17, and all these passages alike imply shrines. In 12, 193, 8, the "goṣṭha of gods" may be shrines or a temple (this vs. corresponds loosely with Manu 4, 39 but has not Manu's idols, daivata). In 12, 121 (see § 124) a Cāṇḍāla temple has images and bells (post-epical).

§ 30. **Idols of the Gods.** — Images of elephants and other animals and statues of men are frequently referred to in the epics, and in like manner images of the gods are found in the Tīrthas. "On seeing Viśveśvara of great glory with Devī at Jeṣṭhila one wins the worlds of Mitra and Varuṇa" (3, 84, 134) means seeing the image, as more clearly expressed in 13, 25, 61, Nandīśvarasya mūrtiṃ tu dṛṣṭvā mucyeta kilbiṣaiḥ ("the sight of Śiva's image frees from sins"). In Dharmaprastha at the Dharma-Tīrtha, where spiritual rewards equal those of a horse-sacrifice, "Dharma sits forever", and one must stroke him, that must be the image, Dharmaṃ tatrā 'bhisaṃspṛśya (perhaps washing the image, 3, 84, 102;

tatra Dharmo nityam āste). At another Tīrtha (3, 88, 8), "a mortal would reach Śiva's city on seeing the horn of the trident-bearer made by (the god Śiva) himself" beside the Payoṣṇī river (it is holy enough to destroy all sin; there Indra got drunk on Soma); but it is not clear what the horn represents; it is "high as heaven and spotless", svargād uttuṅgam amalam viṣāṇam, probably the crest on the head of the image (in this same section is another "visible Dharma", ib. 88, 24, sākṣād devo Dharmaḥ). A fetish-use of the teacher's image is mentioned in 1, 132, 33, where Ekalavya makes a clay image of his teacher and worships it to get instruction refused by the teacher himself. Perhaps the divine Tīrtha images are, like this, mahīmaya, of clay. Yet Bhīma makes an iron image of his pet foe and cudgels it (9, 33, 4; 11, 12, 15, etena hi kṛtā yogyā āyase puruṣe, "he practiced on the iron image"). The images used as battle-standards are of metal and some of these are images of the gods, pratimās of Dharma, Māruta, Śakra, and the Aśvins (7, 23, 88 and ib. 40, 18). So the pratikṛti or image of Hanumat stands on Arjuna's staff (5, 56, 9, etc.). Yet these are not idols in the sense that they were prayed to, but rather effigies (the first, of the heroes' celestial ancestors), carried for encouragement or even adornment, as ib. 105, passim, images of animals. Śalya's standard, ketu, is "a great silver elephant, and adorned with golden peacocks" (ib. 24f.). But the images, devatā-pratimās, tremble, laugh, and vomit blood, as well as sweat, dance, and weep, and fall down from the standards (6, 2, 26 and ib. 112, 11), just as the (temple-) images of Laṅkā in RG 6, 11, 28 tremble, sweat, and laugh, pratimāś ca prakampante svidyanti (khidyanti) ca hasanti ca. The "golden cows" made by Viśvakarman and given away to the priests by Gaya (3, 121, 12) are probably sacred images; compare the golden images of kings and elephants used for the same purpose (7, 69, 29f.). When the beauty of Sāvitrī is likened to "a living image of Śrī", it may be a statue of the goddess' vigrahavatī 'va Śrīḥ, for the people, seeing her, pratimāṃ kāñcanīm iva, "like a golden image", thought that she was a Devakanyā (3, 293, 25f.). Compare the "golden (image of the absent) queen" (in R 7, 91, 25; 99, 8, kāñcanī patnī). In the first tale Satyavat makes images of horses (3, 294, 13; cf. 6, 3, 9; and R 2, 15, 35). The Hariv. speaks of images of metal, clay, wood, butter, and salt (H 7810 and 7812), and shrieking images of all the gods (ib. 12801). Stone images are mentioned in H 7613 and 7813. The devalakas, or people who make or carry about images, are mentioned in Manu and Mbh. (Manu 3, 180, etc.; Mbh. 13, 90, 11, etc.). Manu punishes adultery with a red-hot image, but the epic with an iron bed (Manu 11, 104; Mbh. 12, 165, 65).

§ 31. **The Gods collectively as Fate.** — Out of the great mass of epic literature respecting destiny and free will it is possible here only to select a few passages serving the immediate purpose of this paragraph, which is to show that Fate or destiny is a power developed into individuality out of the general concept of divine power, until it merges with Time = God. Death is diṣṭānta or diṣṭā gatiḥ (R 2, 103, 8), i. e. the end or course "appointed". This diṣṭam, "appointed" is daivam, "the divine", and both are synonyms for Fate, as bhavitavyam, "that which is to be", is personified in bhavitṛ (masc.) in 7, 201, 77. Daivam is the highest power known, daivam eva paraṃ manye (R 1, 58, 23, and passim), and is recognised as such traditionally (daivam atra paraṃ smṛtam, 7, 152, 24). It is one with diṣṭam, for example, in 5, 77, 8f.

man's evil "opposed by Daiva", "inflicted by diṣṭa". This again is daivavidhi = vidhi, as that which is "disposed" (ordered) by the gods or by Vidhātṛ as representing the gods (3, 71, 31; 5, 82, 46). This vidhi is then regarded as personal, Vidhinā saṃpraṇuditaḥ (3, 10, 32), as a man is said to be "in the will (power) of Diṣṭa, because Vidhi is all-powerful" (cf. Diṣṭasya vaśam eṣyati, 5, 32, 19; Vidhiś ca balavān .. Diṣṭasyā 'smi vaśe sthitaḥ, 2, 59, 18). Vālmīki affects the use of Kṛtānta in the same sense (R 2, 24, 5, etc.). The identity of daiva = diṣṭa leads to v. l., daivam, v. l. diṣṭam eva paraṃ manye (2, 47, 38 and 5, 159, 4). This co-operates with Karma and ability (2, 16, 11 f.). Another equivalent of vidhi is niyati, "controlling power" (R 4, 25, 3 f.), personified as a goddess (2, 11, 42, along with Āśā, Saṃvṛtti, Hope and Fulfilment). Niyati operates till one reaches the highest philosophic knowledge (parapratyaya, 12, 217, 23). The relative power of Karma, the divine power (Daivam), and one's own nature is the subject of endless discussion; briefly put in 12, 233, 19, "Those who teach the Karma doctrine preach the efficiency of the act; priests say that the divine (Daiva) is efficient; natural philosophers say that one's own nature" (is the chief thing). That the divine power is sometimes analysed as the power of the stars may be suspected from the antithesis of "natural philosophers" (bhūtacintakāḥ) and daivacintakāḥ as astrologers (12, 121, 46). For a further discussion of the knotty point just stated, cf. above, R 4, 25. Fate again is expressed by bhāgya and bhāgadheya, the "portion" (9, 2, 30 f.) given by the gods (cf. bhaga; see Bhaga). It coincides with Greek moira, as in the refrain, kim anyad bhāgadheyataḥ, "what else than this moira is of avail?" (ib. 43; bhāgya as fate, ib. 47). Heroic characters object to the fatalism of Daiva, not generally because of impiety, but because the concept has already merged into a personal abstraction which stultifies action (R 2, 22, 21 f.; ib. 23, 7 f. and 16). But a consciousness remains of the origin, for pious Rāma yields to Fate as the divine will, while energetic Lakṣmaṇa adds to his repudiation of fatalism the defiant remark that even the gods shall not hinder him (ib. 23, 21). Kāla alone (Time) is weightier than Daiva in Rāma's opinion (R 3, 64, 74; ib. 69, 49 f.), but pure Daiva causes Devī Earth to shake and the sun and moon to be eclipsed (R 3, 66, 11). In 12, 28, 18 f., Daiva, bhavitavya, Kāla, diṣṭa, vidhi, and vidhāna are all synonymous. In R 4, 56, 4, Vidhi is the Fate pursuing a man. As such, "fate" may become death, as in Greek. Fate, Kṛtānta, like Yama, "binds one with a cord and drags one off" (R 5, 37, 3, kṛtānta interchanging with vidhi, as in 9, 65, 16 Kṛtānta is like Yama or Kāla). So the simile daivadaṇḍam ivodyatam (10, 6, 29) makes Daiva personified as Fate in evil sense. It is a mere v. l. whether Daivaṃ nindanti or devaṃ nindanti be read in 8, 91, 1: "Low people blame the god" or "the gods' will", as S has diṣṭam for daivam in the important statement: "This is Daivam (diṣṭam) or bhavyam (to be); as Dhātṛ made it of old, so must it be" (6, 76, 19). Here the fate of an army is "made by (the god) Dhātṛ" and is Daivam (ib. 26). In 1, 89, 9 occurs a proverb, "Fate is the stronger", diṣṭaṃ balīyaḥ, and in vs. 8 this is daivādhīnam. Compare too the supposition expressed in 3, 65, 41, "Perhaps this is owing to the offended divinities", with the preceding, na hy adaivakṛtaṃ kiṃcit, "there is nothing not accomplished by Daiva". Moreover, though what is to be is synonymous in many passages with Daiva, in clearer expression it is said to be not quite synonymous but conditioned by Daiva: bhavitavyaṃ hi yad bhāvi Daivaṃ ceṣṭayate hi tat, "the divine works out the fate to be" (B has ceṣṭayatī 'va ca); cf. R 6, 113, 23: Daivaṃ ceṣṭayate sarvaṃ, hataṃ Daivena hanyate. It is indeed this divine power, expressed by that "appointed" or that "provided", which is specifically personified as Vidhātṛ to companion Dhātṛ = Brahman. It is or may be considered as a form of Brahman (hence Brahman is both Creator and Disposer), so that victory is "appointed by fate" or "by Dhātṛ" (see Brahman). Hence vihita with Vidhātṛ as the divine: evaṃ Vidhātrā vihitam . . daivaṃ puruṣakāreṇa na śakyam ativartitum . . kṛtāntam anyathā kartuṃ ne 'cchet so 'yam (S 9, 62, 77, after B 61, 68), "So has it been disposed by the Disposer . . the divine cannot be overcome by man's act . . wish not to change Fate" (who can destroy past, present and future). A similar passage in 2, 56, 17 and 57, 4 explains Daivam (regarded as "the highest and hard to overcome") as the power which is expressed in what is appointed by Dhātṛ, Dhātrā diṣṭasya vaśe (sarvam ceṣṭati or tiṣṭhati, ib. 58, 14). Instead of diṣṭasya vaśe appear in 2, 58, 18 the words Dhātuś ca vaśam anveti pāśair iva naraḥ sitaḥ, "as if fastened with thongs a man comes under the will of Dhātṛ" (preceded by "as a falling luminary steals away the sight, so does the divine power, Daivam, steal away a man's intelligence"). Compare further, 3, 173, 15, the destruction of evil demons is nirdiṣṭo Brahmaṇā purā; and 5, 39, 1, anīśvaraḥ . . Dhātrā tu diṣṭasya vaśe kṛto 'yam, "man was made devoid of free will at the Creator's injunction". Here all is appointed by the god (asvatantro hi puruṣaḥ, 5, 159, 14f.). In another passage there is a diatribe against the haṭhadurbuddhi, who, as haṭhavādaka, ignores the fact that the "lord creator", Dhātṛ īśvara, appoints or disposes and apportions (vidhā and vibhajya) according to one's former acts; what a man does is done according to Karma but through Dhātṛ (3, 32, 12—21, and ib. 183, 86f., slightly modified, a man's course is determined in part by Daiva, in part by haṭha, in part by Karma). Haṭha is power, force, fate as necessity, impersonal necessity or accident. Haṭha as opposed to Īśvara appears again in 12, 32, 12f. (in 19, read haṭham for hatam). The personal Daiva is also expressed by Kāla, so that daiverita and Kālahata amount to the same thing (2, 71, 16; cf. daivayogāt, "fatally" and "by chance"). Opposition between the will of individual gods and Daiva may be observed in 3, 236, 23: "What is it save Daiva, if, when the field is sown and the god rains, deve varṣati, there is no crop?". So vidhi makes the gods (as well as men) suffer (5, 8, 52). Indra "recognises fate" (diṣṭam anupaśya) and renounces the attempt to save Khāṇḍava from the flames (1, 228, 22). Here the will of the gods has been converted into a power expressed by the Creator acting above the gods. Śiva takes the Creator's place in sectarian writings: mahādevena diṣṭam (3, 106, 23). Time, Kāla, is vaguely personified as son of Dhruva, the Pole star, a Vasu, who also acts as charioteer of Śiva (1, 66, 21 and s. Śiva), but as personified he is usually identified with Death or Yama, as representing him. But "Kāla, the all-compelling", appears as an old man to summon Rāma secretly to heaven in R 7, 103, 1f.; Kālajñapta, ib. 6, 53, is one with Mṛtyupāśāvapāśita, "fettered by Death's fetters" (ib. 58). As an entity, Time is then subdivided and the four ages, Yuga, emerge as divisions having separate names as the constituents of an aeon, or whatever it may be called, one of the ceaseless revolutions which bring the universe back to its beginning, the wheel of time conceived by ages. Of these only one is mythologically important. Kṛta, the perfect age, is no more personified than are other time-divisions, nor is the succeeding Tretā age of more mythological worth, while Dvāpara appears on the stage only with Kali, the last of the ages. The first theoretically lasts four thousand years and each succeeding age a thousand less, with the deified Twilight ages between reckoned in corresponding centuries, so that Kali is the bad present age of a thousand years duration (later as years of the gods).

§ 32. Kali thus embodied may well be the finale to the general subject of gods, for under him the gods are neglected in favor of Buddhistic teaching (as above, eḍūka), and again he may be added to the above remarks in regard to Kāla, for he is of like origin. There are two epic Kalis, however, one the musical demi-god son of Muni (1, 65, 44), whose only function is to appear as a chorister with other gods and Gandharvas, to whom he is closely related (1, 123, 57). This Kali (originally Kalí) derives from kal meaning noise (Śiva is the noisy god, Kalakala). But the time-spirit of evil is Káli, who like Kāla derives from kal, drive, press, oppress, so that an oppressive king is called a kali and "Kali catches careless kings" (12, 12, 29 and 31; ib. 91, 28). Any form of Time is personified, so that even Kālarātrī ("fatal night") appears not only "noose in hand", but as an old woman, a black and bloody housewife, kuṭumbinī, scantily clothed (10, 8, 70). She may be Durgā (9, 17, 43). The demon, Dānava, Kālanemi (in Rām. as Rākṣasa) incorporate as Kaṃsa (1, 67, 67), "whose diadem was cut off by Viṣṇu" (S 2, 51, 22), is nothing but the "wheel of time" as a form of fate. Kālī again is the "dark" wife of Śāntanu and mother of Vyāsa (5, 147, 19), but as name of Durgā (q. v.; cf. R 5, 27, 28) she unites the idea of fatal time and dark time (cf. kālāntakopama of Indrajit, etc. R 6, 88, 2). Kali is evil fate, a synonym of alakṣmī: "Lakṣmī came to the gods; alakṣmī to the Asurās", and with alakṣmī enters Kali and destroys them, "pervaded by alakṣmī and smitten by Kali" (3, 94, 9f.). So Kali is plain destruction: "In war there is ever kali and lives are lost" (5, 72, 49). Yet the conception is not that of a permanent being but rather of personified destruction, liable to spring into existence on occasion: "When virtue is destroyed, Kali is born", and Kali thus appears incorporate in all destructive kings, as Dhautamūlaka was the Kali of the Chinese (5, 74, 12f.); Duryodhana was a part of Kali (11, 8, 30); and Subhadrā "was born as Kali and for the destruction of the Vṛṣṇis" (S 1, 245, 19). Vidulā says to her pusillanimous boy: "You have been born my Kali" (5, 133, 30). Kali is the middle one of the triad "virtue, gain, and desire"; gaining is destructive strife (5, 124, 35). From destruction to bad luck is but a step; hence "they say that Kali (bad luck) is in broken vessels" (bhinnabhāṇḍe kaliṃ prāhuḥ; all broken beds and vessels are apraśastāni, inauspicious, as are cocks and dogs and trees in a house, 13, 127, 16). In 13, 23, 4, a kalipūrvam is a gift of food obtained by strife, and, like anything leaped over or licked or kālahīna, is impure and taken by fiends. As the sun represents Time (Kāla), Kali, like the sun, is called sarvamalāśraya (3, 3, 20) in his part as agent of all ills. As the fiend of the dice, Kali is then playing only one part of his general character. In the great gambling scene of the epic he plays no part at all. Only S has a maladroit interpolation stating that Yudhiṣṭhira was penetrated by the power of Fate, daivabalāviṣṭa, and "for a moment entered Kali, and, being entered by Kali, he said 'So be it', and played" (S 2, 98, 24f.); but this is only in the second game and the confusion between Kalim āviśat and āviṣṭaḥ Kalinā is not happy (probably copied from Nala). In 3, 174, 5, where Arjuna "remembers the kali produced by gambling", kali (as above) is strife or injury. In Nala, Kali enters the king along with Dvāpara (apparently), though the last scarcely appears except as subject to Kali and then disappears (3, 58, 1f.). Here Kali becomes a suitor of Damayantī, converses with Indra, and is cursed for his insolence (S ib. 56, 10 has devābhibhūta, Puṣkara overpowered by the god Kali, as is Nala by Fate, daivāviṣṭa, but B 59, 9 says "Nala entered by Kali"). Kali "went home", after vomiting the Nāga's poison and escaping the "curse-fire" (ib. 72, 43), after the Vibhītaka nut had been forever rendered infamous by his presence in it (ib. 41).

§ 33. After this brief résumé of the general aspects of epic divinities those divinities themselves must be discussed individually. Yet as several of these appear as forms of special gods, the concept rather than the names applied to the forms will best designate the divinities, as far as this is possible. Of all the innumerable gods counted as such only about a dozen have any reality as separate beings. The others are mere names or shadows of gods, and of the dozen not all are of first-rate importance. The older epic pantheon is presided over by Brahman as creator and beneficent ancestor of the other gods, among whom Agni, Yama, Varuṇa, Kubera, and Indra (not least) are the most energetic, most commonly referred to, and invoked. They are, in short, most real to the poets, who regard them as over-gods, guardians of the quarters, though they have not quite systematised the Four Guardians (see § 91). Sectarian influence, affecting this older pantheon, gradually raised Viṣṇu from an inferior position as form of the Sun-god to a predominant position, while the worshippers of Śiva elevated him in the same way to a point where he theoretically surpassed all other gods, till even his son was made to oust Indra. To present all this material it seems best to follow as well as may be (that is, rather roughly) the historical outline, beginning with the earlier Vedic divinities and ending with the Trimūrti or triad which remains till to-day as the three forms of one God. The order in which the gods are discussed will then be, in general, such that after Sky and Earth follow the eight great gods (later) recognised as Guardians of the World; then the minor gods or spirits recognised less as individuals than as hosts; then the divine seers, who are practically gods; and finally the three greatest gods of the trinity. When convenient, however, individuals will be discussed in their proper environment, Kāma immediately after the Apsarasas, and Skanda after Śiva, Parjanya under Indra, etc.

§ 34. **The Sky-god.** — The venerable Dyaus of the Rig-Veda is reduced in the epic period to a mere shadow of his former personality. In the formal scheme of creation he is regarded as a link in the chain of development (1, 1, 29f.) from the mundane egg, and the sons ascribed to him are epithets of the Sun: Bṛhadbhānu, Cakṣus, Ātman, Vibhāvasu, Savitṛ, Ṛcīka, Arka, Bhānu (cf. Bhānu also as son of Prādhā and form of Agni), Āśāvaha, and Ravi, one of whom, however, Ṛcīka, is father of Janamejaya with human descendants (S adds Manu). A Vasu is called Dyaus and Dyunāma (1, 99, 39 and 47), although the formal list of Vasus does not contain this name. He is represented as a thief, afterwards born on earth to expiate his crime. The original sense of Dyaus as "shining" (= vasu) may have led to the name. Dyaus is often feminine: "The (fem.)

Dyaus, sky, was embraced by his head, the earth by his feet" (3, 12, 55); "shone like Dyaus with the stars" (2, 36, 8); "like the autumnal sky, śāradī Dyaus, with the stars" (R 5, 9, 41); "Saramā (fem.) pleased Śītā as Dyaus with water pleases earth", and "Laṅkā with the hero like Dyaus with the sun" (R 6, 34, 1; ib. 73, 15, fem. implied; cf. dyaur iva magnatārakā, R 2, 9, 66). When Sky and Earth appear as witnesses, the former may be male (1, 74, 30), but when presented as a rain-giver (R 4, 28, 3), Dyaus is represented as a female pregnant for nine months and then bearing rain-water conceived of sun-beams. Compare 12, 229, 91: "In the home of the self-existent Great Father the gleaming (fem.) Dyaus poured forth ambrosia and Indra rained upon the crops" (in 2, 45, 29, "Dyaus poured rain", etc., the gender remains at least doubtful). Without personification, dyaus in the form divi, "in the sky", and in the phrase pated dyaus (nipated dyaur mahīm), is the sky conceived of as person no more than are the clouds which, to be sure, are liable to be personified but ordinarily are not (cf. with the simile above, "like nabhas, cloud-land, with the stars", R 5, 10, 34). Dyaus is not "heaven", though the cognates diva and tridiva are synonymous with svarga, the light-world heaven of the gods. Compare "fill dyaus with noise", or "fill tridiva" (mahīm āpūrayāmāsa ghoṣeṇa tridivaṃ tathā, 1, 69, 16). "The god rains", as a parallel to "Indra rains", might imply this god or Dyaus or Parjanya. The citations above show Dyaus in the only activities recognised as his or hers, as progenitor, rain-giver, and witness of wrong, in none of which does Dyaus play the part of a real god. He is a memory only.

§ 35. **Earth.** — Earth is the Great Mother, the Broad Goddess, mahī, pṛthivī, the "mother of all created things", the nursing mother, dhātrī, who is imaged as a divine cow giving milk to all her children (3, 200, 70; 7, 69, 20, as daughter of Pṛthu Vainya and as Virāj; cf. 1, 49, 9 and H 11829f., with H 12019). As the giver of all good, Earth is "father and brother and sons and sky and heaven", the "cow that milks wishes" (fulfills all desires, kāmadhuk, 6, 9, 71 and 76). It is a later idea that she will have no "joy of bearing sons", owing to the curse of Umā (cf. § 24; R 1, 36, 24). Earth is constantly personified, not only as drinking blood, but as approving of priests, and as typical of patient endurance, 1, 68, 14; 3, 26, 14; 51, 40; R 3, 30, 6; R 5, 35, 9; kṣamayā Pṛthivīsamaḥ, 1, 100, 14, etc.). But she is over-burdened; even one person of no account is a "burden upon earth" (3, 35, 7, bhūmivardhana), and a mass of evil creatures or even the normal growth of population renders patient earth very impatient; "I cannot endure these people", she cries (S 2, 51, 45f.), and she complains to Brahman, who creates Death to relieve her of her burden (7, 53, 4f.). Or Viṣṇu assures her that war will relieve her and bids her still "support the worlds" (lokān dhāraya, 11, 8, 25). The form of Death, a lovely woman, as here depicted is not old. Earth is bhārārtā, oppressed (7, 53, 4) and Death is created to relieve the strain, even gods being mortal, sarve devā martyasaṃjnāḥ (ib. 54, 48). The tears of Death seeking to avoid her task become diseases, which kill men, for "Death does not come with a club". H 2939, Earth's address to the gods, derives her from Madhu's marrow. As nurse of all, Earth is helper, medinī, provides wealth, being herself wealthy, vasumatī, and rejoices to give corn to a generous man (3, 200, 41; cf. R 5, 40, 2). In an Aeschylean image, though differently applied, Sītā says, "I shall rejoice to see his dear face even as Earth, the giver of good, vasundharā, rejoices, having the corn half grown, when she receives the rain" (R 5, 40, 2; cf. ib. 6, 33, 37). In another, when a hero sinks to death, "Earth like a dear mistress embraces him as he sinks upon her breast" (9, 17, 54f.; R 3, 30, 7; R 4, 20, 5 and 23; ib. 6, 32, 16; ib. 114, 85). In general, the dead śerate gāṃ (γῆν) samāśritāḥ (R 6, 54, 9, etc.). Though it is the weight of sinful demons that afflicts Earth (1, 64, 43), yet when Viṣṇu assumes the form of a boar and raises her, it is simply the weight of towns and peoples which sinks her. Here she is an overburdened goddess, "the divine bountiful producer of corn, whose ear-rings are the mountains", śivā devī mahābhāgā sarvasasyaprarohiṇī .. śailakuṇḍalā (3, 142, 45; cf. ib. 32 and 29). In poetic phrase, it is not the earth which holds the mountains, but the mountain which holds earth, jagatīdhara; cf. "he sustained grief as a mountain sustains earth" (1, 176, 43). "As long as earth endures" (R 6, 101, 57, etc.) is a proverbial phrase, but it is recognised that "Earth will come to an end" (12, 206, 30). As a hapless divinity she is adopted (Urvī from ūru) by Kaśyapa and so is called Kāśyapī (12, 49, 71f.); in 13, 155, 6, he pervades her by yoga, taking her post, another late tale. She tells him of new warriors and goes to heaven. To the same epoch belong the tales which utilise Earth as a moralist. Thus she advises Indra to employ priests for the removal of sin (13, 34, 21f., as mātā sarvabhūtānām); yet apart from acting as witness of innocence (R 6, 119, 27) and being invoked for victory with many other divine beings (7, 94, 47), she is not so important as a goddess as she is quâ land, object of the earth-hunger so conspicuous in the later epic. In this guise she sings her own song on the virtue of bhūmidāna, grants of land, and her secret name is Priyadattā (cf. 13, 62, 35, where Bhūmir bhūtir mahādevī is cited in Bṛhaspati's talk with Indra, the Bhūmigītā Gāthās). He who has her has all (yasya bhūmis tasya sarvam, 6, 4, 20), but one should renounce her for his own sake (5, 37, 17; 129, 49). Earth deserts the sinful and treacherous (5, 124, 28). For her son Naraka Bhauma (p. 50) she begs a boon and this is significant, since he is an evil demon, and earth is recognised as the goddess of demons and spirits, Bhūts, although one with Aditi as goddess of the gods. Thus in H 3281, where Aditi is identified with Durgā, it is said that the same goddess is "Aditi to the gods, Sītā to the ploughmen, and Earth, Dharaṇī, to the Bhūts" (on Sītā, cf. § 7). Yet land and earth are so inseparably one that it may be questioned whether even as land divinity does not still inhere in the Great Mother. Thus, as the divine Sun is afflicted by eclipse, so "divine Mother Earth" (jagatāṃ mātā devī lokanamaskṛtā bhūmiḥ, R 3, 66, 9) is afflicted by earthquakes, due to the same cause that produces untoward lightning or rain (some divine power apart from her, 2, 45, 28f.), or to the movement of a demon (see § 18, Dhundhu), or to the shaking of the world-elephant's head (R 1, 40, 14). Even when described as "four-cornered earth" (3, 126, 40; 5, 149, 9; R 5, 31, 5), the ground where Bhūts live and bodies are buried, the "home" below (avani, in 3, 310, 6, "house"; cf. avanīpāla as king, 12, 311, 8; avanīṃ gataḥ, R 6, 54, 33), she is still the goddess. So Śibi is described, ekacchatrāṃ mahīṃ cakre (12, 29, 41), "he put the great (mother) under one umbrella" (sceptre, cf. ib. 132 and 12, 321, 134). Four-cornered by the bye, is rather offset by the epithet samudranemi (3, 26, 14; 4, 8, 11, etc.), implying a round surface like the felly of a wheel, "whose circle is the sea". The conquest of earth includes "her mountains, forests, open spaces, ākāśa, seas, and valleys, niṣkuṭa, towns, cities, and islands" (3, 254, 31), as parts of her, also divine (see § 4f.). Metaphorically she is the chariot of gods or of a god-like hero, mountains being the pole, staff, etc. (3, 175, 4, etc.). Earth, vasumatī, is "clothed with seas" and at the same time a goddess, devī, "having mountains, forests, towns, etc." (1, 170, 63; 3, 237, 8f., forests, mountains, and rivers have no owners, but land otherwise is possessed; "a gift of land saves seven generations", 13, 66, 31 and 36). She has seven seas and islands in R 7, 37, pr. 1, 56 (v. § 6).

§ 36. The later epic regards the earth as belonging to Viṣṇu, and inferentially as born of him: "As gold is born of Fire and cows are born of the Sun (Sūryasutāś ca gāvaḥ), so Earth belongs to Viṣṇu (bhūr Vaiṣṇavī), so that he who gives these three gives the three worlds" (3, 200, 127f.). At times, mahī is opposed to the mountain, as if only the fruitful earth were the great mother. Thus mahīm āvasa means "descend (from the heavenly hill) to earth" (3, 176, 11). Jagatī is the earth of moving beings opposed to the adri or mountain rock (3, 237, 18; jagatīpāla, -pati is king; Jagatpati is a title of Kāma, Viṣṇu, and Śiva). When Sītā is carried away by the goddess Earth, called Mādhavī Devī and Dharaṇī Devī (as wife of Viṣṇu Mādhava, says the scholiast, R 7, 97, 15f.), she calls upon Earth three times to hide her, and the divine Earth rose on a seat supported by Nāgas and bore Sītā down to the depths (rasātalam). With this conception of the goddess Earth sinking into earth may be compared the scene where Earth declares that she will give up earthhood, bhūmitvam, and go to heaven, and is then restrained by Kaśyapa (13, 155, 2f.; cf. also 12, 49, 71f., where Earth again praviveśa rasātalam). The location of the "navel of earth" at a place in the Himālayas seen by Hanumat (R 6, 74, 60) introduces an old conception in more precise form. The witness of Earth may be implied when the deceived heroes march wrathfully off casting dust and sand about and over themselves, whilst lightnings flash and earth quakes (2, 30, 5f. and 28), though the act is explained as prognosticating the arrows they would shoot. When wrestlers prepare to contend, they rub earth on their hands (S 4, 15, 33) and when Bhūriśravas is about to die, he "touches earth with his head" (as if in protest against his unfair antagonist), yet both acts may be due to natural causes, for ease in wrestling and from weakness (7, 143, 44). To put to earth the head or grass into the mouth signifies defeat[1]), but there is no other invocation of earth except in the direct and formal phrase "earth may split, the sky fall, Himavat turn" (or "lose its snow"), and "ocean dry up" (e. g. 3, 249, 31f., with v. l. in S; ib. 278, 38, etc.), i. e. before this thing happen, the impossible will happen. Earth is honored with a laudation at Śrāddhas, after Fire, Moon, Varuṇa, and the Allgods. As such she is called Vaiṣṇavī, Kāśyapī, and akṣayā or eternal (13, 91, 25), as well as Pṛthivī and nivāpasya dhāriṇī or sustainer of crops. H 12076f. adds a new feature to the figure of earth in representing her first as ruined by the poison of the great serpent and then undergoing penance and sustained by Viṣṇu, whose right arm in upholding her makes a shadow reaching from earth to the moon. Earth

---

[1]) A man who says "I am thine" in battle is not to be attacked, nor one who proclaims defeat by having his mouth full of grass, tṛṇapūrṇamukha (12, 98, 49). Cf. the modern examples of this in the second edition of Colonel Jacob's Third Handful of Popular Maxims (1911). On prostration with head to earth, cf. 7, 80, 43, jagāma śirasā kṣitim, of Kṛṣṇa abject before Śiva.

is here without means of productivity, aliṅgā, till Viṣṇu supplies the deficiency and makes her fruitful (ib. 12095).

§ 37. **Aditi and the Ādityas.** — Aditi is the "mother of gods" (9, 45, 13) and as such heads the list of goddesses, Hrī, Śrī, etc., here differentiated from Pṛthivī, though elsewhere identified with Earth (p. 79). In particular she is mother of the Thirty-three (R 3, 14, 14); also of the winds, Mārutas (12, 329, 53, or Diti, cf. § 48). R regards Dhātṛ as her special son (R 2, 92, 21); Mbh. says, Indra is chief and best-beloved of her sons; when he is away, she yearns for his return, though equal mother of all the gods, called by her name Ādityas (1, 65, 11, etc.). As Revatī she appears as a disease-goddess (3, 230, 29) and R makes Aditi's womb a refuge for Rāvaṇa (R 4, 1, 120), but her usual aspect is that of beneficent mother-goddess renowned more for her motherhood than anything else, though known also as having cooked food for the gods' success and as having lost her ear-rings, which were subsequently recovered from Naraka and given to Sūrya (3, 135, 3; ib. 307, 21). She presides over Punarvasu (R 1, 18, 8). As mother of gods she is opposed to Diti, mother of demons; both were wives of Kaśyapa. She is blessed by Brahman for her asceticism (13, 83, 27, called Mahādevī as mother of Viṣṇu). Her sons, the Ādityas, are eleven, twelve, or thirteen in number, according to various lists, but "the wise say, there are twelve of them" (3, 134, 19). S 1, 132, 49 emends B 123, 66 so as to agree with H 12911 f., thus omitting the odd thirteenth, caused by a desire to get Viṣṇu into the list. Elsewhere the later epic and H include others (Jayanta, etc.) as Ādityas, and the genealogy calls Bṛhaspati by this title, but the last may be merely a parallel to 13, 62, 46, where good men are Ādityā iva tejasā bhuvi, that is "like gods" in general or "like suns". They are given by pairs (2, 11, 30) and the usual grouping is in conformity with this. Indra is the chief, and Viṣṇu, when mentioned, is "last but not least", ajaghanyo jaghanyajaḥ (H 594; 1, 65, 15 f.)[1]. They all come from the mundane egg in 1, 1, 34. They are all sons of Aditi Dākṣāyaṇī and Kaśyapa Prajāpati Mārīca; in H 11549, Indra heads the list and even Manu is an Āditya. In Śānti, they are said to be of warrior caste and Vivasvat Mārtaṇḍa is eighth (Vedic position) and father of the Aśvins (12, 208, 15 f.: cf. § 110). The names are chiefly those of sun-gods, Bhaga, Mitra, Savitṛ, Vivasvat, Pūṣan, Viṣṇu, together with the clan-god Aryaman, and the creator-god as Dhātṛ, Tvaṣṭṛ; the earliest grouping being: Dhātṛ and Aryaman, Mitra and Varuṇa, Aṃśa and Bhaga, Indra and Vivasvat, Pūṣan and Tvaṣṭṛ, Savitṛ (or Parjanya) and Viṣṇu. Aryaman's importance lies in his being chief of Pitṛs (6, 34, 29). Tvaṣṭṛ is artificer, yielding in dignity to Viśvakarman (with whom he is often confounded). He "made Sītā" and made Vṛtra (q. v. and 3, 274, 9), also Indra's bolt and Śiva's spear (see Indra and Śiva). A v. l. makes him adhirāja of Rudras (for rūpa, forms, 14, 43, 9). Nahuṣa sacrificed a cow to him (12, 269, 5 f.). Dhātṛ interchanges with Vidhātṛ and both with Brahman as creator. The two forms are as Viṣṇu under the titles kartā vikartā ca (3, 188, 19), Vidhātṛ also being treated as an independent Āditya (3, 125, 23). Dhātṛ establishes laws of life and of death, appoints good and ill, becomes Fate (§ 31), the disposer of disposition as of events ("Methinks I shall ever be as Dhātṛ may have disposed me", vidadhīta,

[1]) Here, however, the Ādityas are born direct from the flaming face of Vivasvat Prajāpati (H 593, as sun, Ādityā dvādaśai 've 'ha saṃbhūtā mukhasaṃbhavāḥ), Aditi being ignored altogether; as is the fact that they are thus born from one of themselves!

1, 89, 10). Dhātṛ makes and marks; for example, he makes a mole on a maiden's cheek as sign that she will be happy (3, 69, 7); all creatures are inscribed through their acts by Dhātṛ (abhilikhitāni, 11, 7, 12). In 1, 66, 50, Dhātṛ and Vidhātṛ are "sons of Brahman". Vidhātṛ tests in person a man's piety (see Śibi) and comes disguised to earth (3, 198, 25); generally a power rather than a person. Saṃvidhātṛ (vyadadhāt, 2, 67, 15) adds a new name equivalent to Vidhātṛ, meaning controller (as court-officer, comptroller). Lists of Ādityas will be found also in H 12911 and 14167f.; 13, 150, 14f. (H 12456 has only eleven; in H 11549, Viṣṇu has second place). Soma, śaśin, is Āditya, H 13143f., where "Parjanya" is paired with Mitra, and Tvaṣṭṛ = Viśvakarman. Jayanta in 13, 150, 15 may be Soma. Parjanya as "youngest of the Ādityas" (H 12498) might be Viṣṇu, but, as their "chief" also, is probably Indra. Compare H 175 and 593, and see below for Parjanya (§ 71), Sūrya (§ 38), and Viṣṇu (§ 143). The group of Ādityas crosses that of the Lokapālas (§ 91f.). This later group, as will be shown below, comprises the chief gods outside the triad of highest gods, but these chief gods are not yet recognised as the eight World-protectors of later mythology. In the following, however, they will be discussed in their later order. They differ from the group-gods to be discussed later in that they are individually important and only gradually form a group, whereas the group-gods (gaṇas) start as an organic group without individually important members and gradually develop members with special names and individuality. The Ādityas form the first division of the Thirty-three, whose other divisions will be noticed among the Gaṇa-gods (hosts of spirits by groups, §§ 111 and 112). Before taking up the first of the Lokapālas, who is the Āditya par excellence (the Sun), it will be necessary to say a few words in regard to synonymity in divine groups. Telang in his introduction to the Anugītā (SBE. 8, 219) thinks it doubtful whether, when Soma and Candramas are mentioned as presiding over tongue and mind respectively, they indicate the same god. As far as the epic is concerned, there can be no doubt that Soma = Candramas and Arka = Mitra. The fact that in the same passage Indra is differentiated from Maghavat in the same way shows that the author treats the same god as having different functions, not that he regards Maghavat as another god than Indra or Arka as another god from Mitra. Nor does it show (as the author also contends) that epic mythology is not far removed from Vedic "theogony", because the emancipated soul is identified with Viṣṇu, Mitra, Agni, Varuṇa, and Prajāpati, as gods "held in highest repute at that time". Such groups are casual; they are not carefully selected; they aim only at mentioning a few respectable high gods. The literary rather than scientific value of the phraseology is important. In one passage the first "lord" of lights is Indu; immediately after, the first "beginning" of lights (jyotiṣām in each case) is Āditya (14, 43, 6 and 44, 4). Candramas is here lord of Nakṣatras, but in many other passages this is Soma; while here again Soma is merely "lord of priests" (ib. 43, 10), just as the lord or chief of directions is the North and again is the East (ib. and 44, 13), and Soma again is lord of plants, while the lord of priests is Bṛhaspati. This does not mean that Soma = Bṛhaspati or that North = East, nor does divergence of functions in the same god as a type mean that the two names given represent different gods. All that can be maintained is that different aspects of a god are considered in one case and identical functions are ascribed to different gods in the other case. It is quite possible that Mitra, Arka, and Sūrya represented different sides of the same god without differentiation sufficient to make these aspects different individuals. So Indra as Puraṃdara may not be taken as a different god but as the same god under a different aspect than that presented by his title Maghavat Indra. A third point remains. Soma is "king Soma", as Varuṇa and Yama are "kings"; but such titles are inherited from a remote past and do not in the least affect the divinity of those to whom such titles are applied.

V. THE EIGHT GREAT DEVAS.

§ 38. **The Sun-God.** — Sūrya (Helios), the Sun, is, as god, known under other names, which are synonymous as far as the epics are concerned. Āditya alone is the sun and one of the commonest designations of the sun-god. To this metronymic the epithet "day-maker" is sometimes added; ādityapatha = Divākarapatha or Bhāskarādhvan. A qualifying "thousand-rayed" or "ray-wreathed" is used alone or added to Āditya (7, 187, 1 f.; R 4, 39, 2, etc.) to designate the luminary (having fewer rays than the moon, q. v.). Pūṣan is recognised as the god kicked by Śiva, who also knocked out his teeth when Pūṣan was eating cakes at Dakṣa's sacrifice (7, 202, 49; ib. 59; 13, 161, 19), and as elder brother of Parjanya, and the lover of Sandhyā (Twilight, RG 5, 25, 27) in distinction from Suvarcalā, wife of Sūrya (ib. 26); but this last passage is not in the alternate text (it also makes Kriyā the wife of Brahman instead of Dharma as in 1, 66, 14, and Dīkṣā wife of Soma). In the former passage, Śiva as Hara Virūpākṣa is also Bhaganetrahara (1, 221, 8) or Bhagaghna (7, 202, 47), that is, Pūṣan is distinguished from Bhaga, as in the formal lists of Ādityas (§ 37) and in maṅgalas (so in 10, 18, 16, Śiva "put out the two eyes of Bhaga and broke the two arms of Savitṛ"). In the extended maṅgalas particularly, Pūṣan, Bhaga, and the Ādityas, are all mentioned separately (e. g. R 2, 25, 8—23), and as the arms of the cosmic giant are Dhātṛ and Vidhātṛ, so are his hands Bhaga and Pūṣan (R 7, 23, pra. 5, 22). But the identity of Pūṣan with the Sun-god remains, for he is the god who "shone in the wars of the gods and Asuras of old" (7, 105, 22) and the god who "goes, having a thousand rays, after warming the earth, to the western mountain at the close of day" (5, 179, 39). Savitṛ "on rising takes away the glory of the stars" (9, 32, 18; R 6, 12, 20 and 24, 21) and "the day-maker on rising takes away the glory of the heavenly lights". Sūrya is gavāṃ pati, and Arka (sun) is united with tejomayair gobhiḥ (R 1, 7, 22; cf. H 2943, gavāṃ guruḥ, and 3, 3, 52, gobhir bhāsayase mahīm), as he is apāṃ pati (cf. gopati of Varuṇa), who is "attacked by Rudra" (babhau Rudrābhipannasya yathā rūpaṃ gavāṃ pateḥ, R 6, 76, 93). The disc of Savitṛ (7, 38, 18) leaves no doubt in regard to the identity of Savitṛ, who "sets in the west" etc. (5, 75, 12; 12, 58, 22). Savitṛ is sarvalokaprabhāvana and vibhāvasu; in the east Savitṛ rises and sings the Sāvitrī, bestowing, as Sūrya, the Yajus-formulas (12, 319, 2 f.). The rising Illuminator destroys the Asuras (of darkness, 5, 108, 3 f.). Vibhāvasu is a common name of the sun (1, 86, 8, etc.). Other synonyms are Vivasvat, Ravi, Tapana (1, 68, 13; 111, 18; 171, 20; 3, 133, 10f.; 6, 101, 51 f.; 8, 49, 42). Arka, Bhāskara, and Savitṛ are indeed sons of Dyaus (as if separate), but as the first two are epithets, the assertion simply shows how easily epithets become persons. Vivasvat (Savitṛ) is the husband of Tvāṣṭrī (daughter of Tvaṣṭṛ), who under the form of a mare bore him in mid-air the two Aśvins (1, 66, 35). Ravi, the sun, is guarded by Aṅgiras as Indra is guarded by Dadhīci (3, 92, 6). Śiva, Indra, and the Sun-god all bear the title Deveśvara, "lord of gods" (2, 50, 16, bhāsi divi deveśvaro yathā). These names are also applied to demons and inferior spirits; Sūrya is an evil spirit; Bhaga is a Rudra; Vivasvat and Mitravat are evil demons; Arka is a Dānava. They probably represent a time when evil and good spirits were not absolutely differentiated, as indeed they are not in the epics, otherwise the maṅgala would not entreat "safety from all (other) gods and those that lurk around the path" to harm travellers (R 2, 25, 22). Sūrya is lord of the Grahas or seizing spirits (Arka, of heats, 14, 43, 6 and 8; R 7, 23, pra. 5, 3). Karṇa, son of Sūrya, is Sāvitra (1, 136, 3 and 8). Though formally identified with Sūrya (3, 3, 16), Bhaga is the sun especially as procreative power and as such his constellation, uttarā Phalgunī, is suitable for weddings (1, 8, 16; R 1, 72, 13 and R 7, 5, 34); the means of securing a husband's love and obedience is called yaśasyaṃ Bhagadaivatam (3, 233, 8, v. l. vedanam and vetanam), or Bhagādhānam (H 7013). For Mitra, see below, p. 89.

§ 39. The sub-divided sun includes the myth of Aruṇa, appointed to go before the sun on his rising, thus protecting the world from excessive heat. Brahman thus appoints him, to reassure the seers, but Aruṇa is son of Kaśyapa; he acts as charioteer of the sun (1, 24, 3 f.). Hence Aruṇa and Garuḍa, who was brother of Aruṇa, are reckoned among the Ādityas. Aruṇa's wife is Śyenī (but Aruṇā is an Apsaras). Aruṇa is deformed. According to one tale, both brothers were born to avenge the Vālakhilya saints on Indra, who had insulted them (1, 31, 34; see § 12, Garuḍa). For 66000 years Aruṇa is preceded by 66000 saints, who, fallen from Brahman's heaven, go before Aruṇa to guard all creatures, until they enter the disc — of the moon! (6, 7, 30). Aruṇa is "like a red wheel", but the foregoer of the sun, at sight of whom all men begin to pray (7, 186, 3 f.). He is father of Jaṭāyus, younger brother of the roc Sampāti (R 1, 1, 52; ib. 3, 14, 31). He, like Garuḍa, is Vainateya (son of Vinatā). Other sub-divisions of the sun amount to multiple suns marking the end of the world. At the time of universal dissolution, the twelve Ādityas appear as twelve suns (the sun is "twelve-souled", 3, 3, 26), of whom only Viṣṇu is eternal (3, 3, 59; 5, 181, 8; 13, 140, 34); though in reality ekaḥ sūryaḥ (3, 134, 8; 12, 352, 10), "the sun is one". Passages (3, 188, 67; ib. 190, 78) colored by Buddhistic thought speak of seven such suns. When it is said that the sun rains (Ādityāj jāyate vṛṣṭiḥ, 12, 264, 11), the process of gathering up the water and letting it out again is meant. The usual function of the sun is to drive away darkness and demons (from the gods in the sky as well as on earth, 3, 185, 30). At sunset he absorbs into himself all the glory of earth, even the light of flashing swords, and then all evil demons appear (6, 48, 114; 7, 50, 3; also 6, 86, 42). Light is goodness and the sun is superlative goodness, as all sinners are darkness (7, 146, 144; 14, 39, 14, Ādityaḥ sattvam udriktaṃ kucarās tu tathā tamaḥ). But there is a "sun of the sun" which supports earth and sky (5, 46, 3), a "sun that eats the sun", sūryādaḥ sūryaḥ, or, aṇ "over-sun" without parts (God; 12, 319, 29; v. l. S 323, 29 and 42, atisūryas tu niṣkalaḥ). Yet this is not myth but philosophy. According to it, a bastard mythology makes sun and moon the eye (sic) of God (the sun lights, and the moon enlightens; as the mystic seems to say, 12, 343, 66). As "eyes of the world" the two suffer eclipse (R 3, 66, 10). The sun has, besides light, a black part, pāda, or foot (cf. Viṣṇu as ekapād), which is that which absorbs water during eight months: "Vivasvat draws up water"; "eight months he drinks and then pours forth for four" (8, 79, 78; 12, 363, 5f.). In Sūrya, Ravi, Vivasvat, live the saints (Śānti, ib. 9; cf. R 6, 74, 60, sūryanibandhana). Even God is established on some of his rays (yasya tejoviśeṣeṣu svayam ātmā pratiṣṭhitaḥ). Vivasvat extends his two arms when a saint approaches to enter his disc, and reaching out his right hand welcomes him; then the glory of the saint becomes one with the glory of the sun (Śānti, ib. 16). The tapas, heat, of the sun is identified with the ardor of the saint (tasmāt sūryo virājate, 5, 46, 1). But the sun also slays. The warrior kills with arrows, "like Savitṛ" and "like Āditya" (6, 48, 34f.; 106, 78; R 5, 47, 9, and 15f.). To see the sun kabandhāṅka (R 3, 23, 11) i. e. with the appearance of a headless trunk (masses of clouds), is a bad omen. Epithets of the sun are regularly sahasraraśmi ("of a thousand rays") and, less often, gabhastiśatasaṃvṛta (7, 13, 26), probably "having hundreds of hands" (rays), but he eats with these rays as well as protects with them (3, 33, 71). As the twelvefold sun (above), Sūrya has one hundred thousand rays (12, 313, 4). The rays make a wreath about his head, mandamarīcimaṇḍalaḥ (S for mantra-, at 5, 182, 29; cf. mandaraśmiḥ sahasrāṃśuḥ, 7, 148, 24). He drives a monocycle, ekacakram, dragged by seven horses, which grow weary after the day's work (5, 46, 5; 6, 120, 53; 7, 189, 54; R 3, 71, 30). A divine (Viṣṇu) Nāga replaces them on one occasion for a month (12, 358, 8; 363, 1). His steeds carry him ten thousand leagues in half an hour (R 4, 42, 41) or three hundred and sixty-four leagues in one wink (S 1, 189, 19f. after B 173, 17). The sun, even as measured disc, is still called the "exalted bird". The measure of the sun is in accordance with the fact that the eclipse demon (Rāhu) devours sun and moon, so he must be the largest (also as circle) of the three. The circle of the demon is 12,000 leagues (diameter) by 42,000 leagues (circumference); that of the moon (larger than the sun) is 11,000 by 38,900 leagues; and that of the sun is 10,000 by 35,800 leagues (but "to those coming near he seems as large as earth", 6, 12, 40f.; R 4, 61, 13). Both Rāhu and the Sun are Mahāgrahas; Sūrya seizes the light of the moon, etc. Thus he is attacked by "cruel Mahāgrahas" (6, 76, 11), while reckoned as one of these (grahāḥ sūryādayaḥ, 3, 200, 85; cf. 8, 87, 4) evil planets.

§ 40. In all these references to the sun, though disc or bird or horse (see Agni) or bull, he is ever the god, never inanimate. He drinks, goes home, possesses hands, hair, etc., bestows wisdom, makes speeches, acts as a witness, etc. He has quite a family. His wife Suvarcalā (see Sandhyā above, loved by Pūṣan) is mentioned in 13, 146, 5; R 2, 30, 30; R 5, 24, 9, as a type of conjugal affection, his "devoted follower". As Suvarcalā is a plant it may be a sun-flower (heliotropic) myth which she represents. Older is the story of his espousals with Tvāṣṭrī (above). She is called Sureṇu and Saṃjñā, and, according to H 545f., bore to Vivasvat Manu Vaivasvata, Yama and Yamunā, but unable to endure her husband longer created a similar self, her shadow (Savarṇā Chāyā) and commissioned her to act as wife (she bore Sāvarṇa Manu, etc.). This Chāyā of H and the Purāṇas is not known in the epic, but S 1, 203, 34 cites Uṣā as wife of Sūrya (Uṣeva Sūryam, etc.). That Vivasvat became a horse and begot by Tvāṣṭrī the Aśvins is referred to in the epic and told in extenso in H (601, see above). Śanaiścara is said to be his son by Chāyā in H (loc. cit.) and this legend with that of the future Manu is recognised in 12, 350, 55; cf. VP 3, 2, 4. Śanaiścara is the planet Saturn (the planets which appear to meet the Day-maker and Night-maker with especial pleasure are Śukra and Bṛhaspati, Venus and Jupiter, R 2, 99, 41). Sūrya's daughters are Suprajā, wife of Bhānu (3, 221, 9), and also (?) Śraddhā Vaivasvatī (12, 265, 8, perhaps identical with Sāvitrī, but N. says sāvitrī here is sā avitrī, "guardian and generatrix of pure birth"). The southern seer "Cakradhanus" is also called his son, "born of Sūrya" (5, 109, 17), the South being called the quarter given by Vivasvat as dakṣiṇā (ib. to his Guru, sc. Kaśyapa, ib. 1); the text says: vidur yaṃ Kapilaṃ devam, "whom (Cakradhanus) they know as the divine Kapila" (ib.). Kapila is a name of the sun (3, 3, 24), as well as of Viṣṇu (3, 47, 18), and the Kāpilas (Sāṅkhyas) are a sect especially favored by the sun (below). In R 1, 17, 9; ib. 5, 62, 36, etc., Sugrīva, uncle of Dadhimukha, who has the honey-grove, is "begotten of Tapana", "the son of him of a thousand rays", Sūryātman, "born of Sūrya's self" (R 4, 14, 22) and at death he enters the disc of the Sun (R 7, 110, 22). Other sons of the Sun, who return into their father at death, are the apes Śveta and Jyotirmukha (R 6, 30, 33).

§ 41. Sāvitrī, given in marriage by her father the Sun to Brahman (3, 110, 26; S 4, 22, 11; 13, 169, 9), is the "mother of the Vedas", the recitation of which divine being as verses purifies from sin (3, 200, 83 and 12, 35, 37), a thorough identification of the verse and goddess (japan devīṃ vedamātaram). As goddess she is attendant on Pārvatī (3, 231, 49). She appears to king Aśvapati (who, to get children, had worshipped her for eighteen years with Mantras and ten thousand fire-oblations daily, eating only at the sixth meal-time), and in person, rūpiṇī, promises him a daughter, "glorious Sāvitrī", whose story of devotion to her husband is known to both epics (1, 241, 48; 3, 293, 10f.; R 2, 30, 6 and ib. 118, 10). The goddess intercedes with her husband to have the boon granted; she has "divine ear-rings which she gave for a priest", and so got to heaven (12, 235, 24). She saves from difficulties, durgataraṇī, and as such abides in the palace of Brahman (2, 11, 34). She is both the mother of the Vedas (whom "she does not desert", 3, 81, 5) and the mother of the initiated regenerate (3, 100, 34; cf. Manu 2, 29 and 170). As a dramatic figure she blesses a Paippalādi priest, a Kauśika, and announces a discussion between Time, Death, and Yama, who as "son of the Sun" (12, 196, 6 and 199, 1 f.) is called Sūryaputra and Vaivasvata (the former being applied also to Saturn and the Aśvins). The mark of Sāvitrī's foot is still visible at the Udyanta mountain (where too is the yonidvāra, but the allusion is lost, 3, 84, 93 f.). Sāvitrī, as all knowledge, seems to be differentiated from Gāyatrī: "Sāvitrī is first of knowledges and is all (spoken), as Prajāpati is first of the gods, as Gāyatrī is first of metres" (14, 44, 5 f.).

§ 42. Several stories are told of Sūrya, whose southern limit was set for him by Manu Sāvarṇi and the son of Yavakrīta (5, 109, 11). When Mt. Vindhya is angry with him (see § 6), Sūrya says: "Not by my own will do I revere Meru. My path is laid out for me by those who made the universe" (3, 104, 5). The daughter of the saint Harimedhas, Dhvajavatī, was once estopped from further flight through the western sky by the command of Sūrya, who twice commanded her to "stand still", and she stood still (5, 110, 13). The sun burns Jaṭāyus' feathers (R 4, 58, 4), but it is not said that this is due to anger. In the Anuśāsana, however, Sūrya burns the wife of Jamadagni and being threatened by the saint disguises himself as a priest and reproaches Jamadagni for trying to shoot the Day-maker, who is a benefactor, providing food by "raining on the seven continents" (13, 95, 18f.). Jamadagni replies that at noon the sun stands still for half a wink and at that instant he is resolved to shoot. His anger is averted by supplication, however, and as a reward for his leniency Sūrya gives Jamadagni shoes and an umbrella, which first introduced this sun-guard to man (ib. 96, 6 and 14). In a late passage, R 7, 23, pra. 2, the sun declines to fight Rāvaṇa. His door-keepers are here (vs. 9) Piṅgala and Daṇḍin, and he is called Āditya, Sūrya, Ravi, Ādideva, lord, Mārtaṇḍa, "witness of the world", "he of the seven steeds", "maker of day" (and of light), and described as adorned with ear-rings and bracelets, smeared with sandal paste, with yawning mouth and a thousand gleaming rays. The reason he gives for not fighting is that he "cannot spare the time" (nā 'haṃ kālakṣipaṃ sahe). As "witness of the world" the Sun sees all that is done and "with his heavenly eye" watches the rape of Sītā, being so shocked that he loses light (R 3, 52, 13). Rāma calls on him to tell where Sītā is gone, addressing him (Āditya bho lokakṛtākṛtajña) as one who knows what is done and not done, witness of actions true and false (R 3, 63, 16). A very late passage called "the mystery of Citragupta" also makes the sun the witness of all man's acts, but as witness the god here recounts it all to the judge of the dead. At Parvan time what a man does goes to the sun, and if he has been generous and given lamps to priests, then, as he goes through hell's darkness, the gods of light, Moon, Sun, and Fire, lend him light to see. The "mystery" ends, not very apropos, with the hearer, who is Vibhāvasu himself, saying: "This is the mystery of Citragupta; the five worst sinners are he who kills a cow, or a priest; an adulterer; an unbeliever; and he who lives on his wife. These five are avoided by gods and Manes and will live in hell on pus" (13, 130, 17f.; see Yama). The sun will not hurt Rāma because he knows him (R 2, 44, 8). He upholds right but, as general benefactor, "Sūrya shines upon the good and the wicked" (12, 73, 24). Like Wind, Fire, and "the mothers of the worlds, the cows, who are deities among men", Sūrya is also said to be born of Brahman ("son of the Self-existent"), and as a divinity he must not be offended; one must not urinate against the sun nor look at him rising, etc. (as in the law-books, 13, 125, 64; cf. ib. 60 and 62, and 12, 193, 17 and 24, na meheta; 13, 104, 17). He who offends thus against Ravi, Bhānumat, lives eighty-six years in hell. In R 2, 75, 21, sūryaṃ ca pratimehatu is a curse, parallel (cf. AV. 13, 1, 56) to "may he kick a sleeping cow". Sūrya comes when called by a magic formula of Kuntī, yellow as honey, great-armed, wearing bracelets and diadem (3, 306, 10) and "making his body twofold, on earth and in the sky" begets Karṇa by mystic Yoga-power, who was born with radiant armor and ear-rings. He visits this son in a vision and gives him advice (3, 300, 6f.). He is here the beneficent god of a thousand rays, Bhānu, conqueror of Rāhu (Svarbhānusūdana, 3, 302, 18 and 20). When Karṇa dies, the sun, bhakta, devoted do him, bathes in the western ocean to purify himself (8, 94, 30). Aditi (§ 37) gives him the ear-rings (3, 307, 18f.). The story of Karṇa forms the basis of some of the strongest scenes in the epic and is often referred to (12, 6, 6 and 15, 30, 9). It is possible that Karṇa himself ("son of the bull") represents the sun. He is called Vaikartana from his cutting off the armor, and to distinguish him from the son of Dhṛtarāṣṭra (1, 67, 95). His death at the hands of (Indra as) Arjuna might point to a sun and storm myth. His family is the object of special regard on the part of the god, who gives Kuntī a copper dish of inexhaustible food (origin of the grail according to Prof. von Schroeder) and saves Kṛṣṇā from the amorous Kīcaka by giving her a demon guardian, Rakṣo rakṣārtham (3, 3, 72; ib. 262, 2; and 263, 21; 4, 15, 20). The ancestor of the Kurus called Saṃvaraṇa is a devout sun-worshipper, and his name is a personification of the veiling surrounding the sun, while his wife Tapatī is "daughter of Tapana". She is a younger sister of Sāvitrī and is born of Tapana Sūrya (1, 171, 6), and is formally bestowed upon Saṃvaraṇa by Vivasvat (1, 173, 18f.). According to 1, 1, 44f., the Kurus, Yadus, and Bharatas are descendants of the divine beings called (Daśajyoti, etc.) Ten-, Hundred-, and Thousand-light, sons of Subhrāj, son of Devabhrāj and grandson of Sahya (v. l. Manu), the youngest Vivasvat (Dyaus' son). Kuru is son of Tapatī Saurī, hence Tāpatyas as metronymic of the family. At 1, 189, 19, the priest Vasiṣṭha in S goes a niyuta of leagues upward to intercede for Saṃvaraṇa as suitor of Tapatī and here, in a brief hymn to Bhāskara Vivasvat, the god has the (Viṣṇu) epithets sahasracakṣus, trayīmaya, and Viriñcanārāyaṇaśaṅkarātman, a hymn approved by the sun, who said it should be muttered by all the faithful (ib. 24f., japyā bhaktānām). "Thousand-eyed" is an epithet of Viṣṇu and of Indra in other places; it here stands for the usual "Thousand-rayed". Haridaśva and Haryaśva are both sun-names (R 6, 107, 11f.).

§ 43. All the hymns to the sun are late, as shown by internal evidence. They may be due to a recrudescence, perhaps political in origin, of this cult. But even in the older texts mention is made of the ascetic Ūrdhvabāhus, who stand with arms up-stretched (R 2, 95, 7, beside the river Mandākinī), as does Saṃvaraṇa (1, 173, 12, ūrdhvamukhaḥ). The Pāñcarātras derive their doctrines from the sun himself (12, 340, 120), and they number 66,000 or (v. l.) 88,000 (but both numbers are conventional; the larger number in S). In the camp of the Pāṇḍus there were "a thousand and eight others who were Sauras" (7, 82, 16). That many worshipped the sun particularly, may be seen from the names of the Kurus' battle-friends, Sūryadhvaja, Rocamāna, Aṃśumat (etc., 1, 186, 10f.; Sūryadatta, 4, 31, 15). There was also a "secret Veda of the sun" taught to Arvāvasu (3, 138, 18f.). The Bhāgavatas identical with the Kāpilas have a doctrine taught Sarasvatī by the sun (12, 319, 6f.; ib. 302, 54 and 85; ib. 345, 14f.; 349, 3 and 57). R 6, 107 = Bomb. 105 (106) has one of these late hymns, introduced as a hoc signo vinces, but not found in the Bengal text. The sun is here identified with all the gods, including those of the Trimūrti; he is the bird, of a thousand flames, of seven steeds, saptasapti, the golden germ, twelve-souled, maker of all, witness of the world, devadeva, soul of all gods, destroyer and maker of the world. Compare yugāntasūrya for the usual yugāntāgni (R 5, 37, 65). The Mbh. describes the sun on the occasion of the gift of the food-vessel and then cites a hymn, first uttered by Brahman to Indra, and told to Nārada, who gives it to Dhaumya. He first gives the names of the sun, reckoned as one hundred and eight (3, 3, 5f.). In S, the names follow the hymn. The lists of names differ, and in neither text are there the stated numbers (nāmāṣṭaśatam). Here the Sun is Victory, Jaya, and especially the refuge of the Kāpilas (Sāṅkhyas); he illumines with his rays (gobhiḥ) the thirteen continents; he is lord of Manus and of Manvantaras; as twelve suns he dries the ocean; he is Indra, Rudra, Viṣṇu, Prajāpati, Agni,

Brahman, the goose (haṃsa), Vṛṣākapi, Vivasvat, and inter alios Mitra and Mihira. The last (Persian) name gives the approximate period to which the hymn belongs, evidently that of the Pāñcarātras also. The sun is also Bhūtātman (S) and is to be worshipped with loving devotion, bhakti, especially on the sixth or seventh day. His adorers, believing in his love (tvadbhāvabhaktāḥ), will live long. His followers, who clasp his feet, are Māṭhara (3, 3, 68; cf. 12, 293, 8, another late touch), Aruṇa, Daṇḍa (aśanikṣubha, as lightning?), the divine mothers (cf. the Saurā Mātṛs of 9, 46, 38), Maitrī and Kṣubh (Love and Harm?), and the mothers of the Bhūts. Among his noticeable epithets here are alolupa (epithet of Śiva, free from passion), the sacred fig-tree, Kapila, the divine physician Dhanvantari, "door of heaven", and different divisions of time and fire. S has Vaiśravaṇo, v. l. for vai Varuṇo (error for Vaiśvānara?), devakartā for dehakartā, etc. and adds as epithet, maṇiḥ suvarṇaḥ, which refers to the maṇiḥ śuddhaḥ or "pure gem", supposed to drink the rays of the sun (12, 299, 12). It is once referred to under its usual later name sūryakānta (12, 218, 29). Mitra has lost his individuality in the epics except in the late (Uttara) tale of his quarrel with Varuṇa (§ 59f.). The name is that of a Marut in H 11545. Mitrasena, Mitrabāhu, and other Mitra-names appear in Kṛṣṇa's family (H 9186, etc.). Many of the epic data are Vedic tradition, the sun as rain-giver, lord of cows, demon-dispeller, father of Yama, etc., but others are found only in the hymns, the pseudo-epic, Hariv., and Purāṇas. As philosophical adhidaivatam, Mitra and Arka appear differentiated from Sūrya (12, 314, 2 = 14, 42, 26, and 43, 7); also here as neuter, Mitram (14, 21, 4). The perfected saint of the same (perhaps antique) range of thought is identified severally with Viṣṇu, Mitra, Varuṇa, Agni, Prajāpati, Dhātṛ, and Vidhātṛ (ib. 42, 65). Sons "like Mitra and Varuṇa" (1, 105, 41, etc.) are promised a devotee, i. e. sons of special glory. On a group of "Mitra" gods see § 50. For Mitra as war-god, see Varuṇa, § 59.

§ 44. **The Moon-God.** — Never a god of much importance in India, save as it mystically represented the yellow Soma plant whose name it assumed, the epic Moon-god remains much more restricted than its rival luminary, though it is supposed as a heavenly body to be higher (in space), larger, and better endowed with rays (1, 18, 34; R 7, 23, pra. 4, 16). It belongs probably to a lower class than does the Āditya sun, for it is one of the group of eight Vasus (1, 66, 19), three of whom, Moon, Wind, and Fire, are retained in the epic list of these pre-epic deities. Only late lists (§ 37) of Ādityas include Soma. The moon is of course never aught than a god (husband of Dīkṣā, § 38), yet it is generally referred to rather as delighter of eyes and hearts, a gleaming luna candida, Candra, Candramas, than as a god; that is, its gentle beauty and cool light (1, 177, 40) are regarded. It is physical, as in the figures, "the child crying for the moon", (R 3, 47, 41), "hard to touch as the moon", the nocturnal phenomenal body, rajanīcara, rather than the divinity is implied (4, 14, 51; 5, 130, 37 f.). Compare 8, 39, 16, where candraṃ jighṛkṣuḥ is parallel to a "frog croaking at a rain-cloud". In this sense also śaśāṅka (marked with a hare) and śaśin is generally used. Thus Karṇa is śaśīva divi (3, 301, 12), "like the moon in a cloudless sky" (Viśākhayor madhyagataḥ), that is, the physical moon shining between two stars with which his ear-rings are compared (cf. 8, 20, 48), describes Karṇa. For Candra, cf. the use in 7, 16, 54, citre rathe . . babhāse nakṣatracitre viyatī 'va candraḥ. So Citrayā Candramā iva (R 3, 17, 4). It is

Candra that is "like a white goose in the blue lake of the sky" (R 5, 2, 58, etc.) When speaking of the sickle of the moon and of the moon increasing in the bright half of the month, this is the word usually employed (Candra, or Śaśin, not Soma), though there are exceptions, and when Somasuta is described, naturally sahasrasomapratimaḥ is preferred (7, 23, 29); also a saumya (gentle) king is likened to Soma (passim). Besides Candra, Śaśāṅka, and Soma, the moon is called Uḍurāj, Uḍupa(ti), "water-lord" (boat?), and Indu = Soma(drop), besides names which are periphrases, Night-wanderer, Water-born, King of Stars, Cool of Ray, etc. In R 5, 16, 31, naikasahasraraśmi is the moon. Soma as a fighting god is almost forgotten. Indeed it is said that though he once had a bow and a war-chariot he gave them away to Indra (1, 225, 4f.). His not very reputable exploit of raping Tārā, the star-wife of Bṛhaspati (Jupiter), brought on the Tārakāmaya war, which is frequently alluded to as an event of the long ago. The son born of this pair was Budha (Mercury). Soma stands here on the side of Uśanas (Venus), the star-priest of demons, of Rudra, and of the demons themselves. As far as the later epic story goes, Budha is son of Soma and Tārā (H 1340), not the son of Rohiṇī (R 3, 49, 16), the favorite wife of Soma. Dakṣa gave the twenty-seven stars of the lunar zodiac (his daughters) to Soma. The remaining twenty-six objected to Soma's partiality for Rohiṇī, and Dakṣa, after warning him three times, cursed him to have yakṣman, consumption, which still causes his monthly consumption, though by bathing in the Sarasvatī (where it joins ocean at Prabhāsa), and by worshipping Deveśa, Soma recovered. Yet he has to keep up the remedy, "drinking there the six essences of Varuṇa", to ensure health. As Soma is "lord of plants" and as the gods depend on vegetable offerings, his decline devastated the world and frightened the gods, so that they interceded for him (1, 66, 17; 9, 35, 43f.). The star-wives are here Yoginīs, engaged "in time and weather". He is called here Soma, Candra, Uḍupati (Uḍurāj in 5, 34, 55). This curse is alluded to in Manu 9, 314, as in the epic 12, 344, 57 ("consumption came upon King Soma through the curse of Dakṣa"). The Moon is lord of lotuses, kumudanātha, and his crescent, the boat (uḍupa), is the type of female loveliness, as the full moon ("the quiver of Love"; cf. the Jain Kalpa-Sūtra, 38) is the image of a beauty (smaraśarāsanapūrṇasamaprabhaḥ, 7, 184, 46f.). Urvaśī (e. g.) is candralekheva (3, 46, 15). The moon has a mark, lakṣman (7, 2, 5), which is jagat, the earth (shadow, see H, below), though "men see it without knowing it" (12, 203, 8). As lord of plants, the Moon restores to them the moisture taken from them by the sun (12, 52, 33). Soma also is the "king of priests" (5, 111, 8; 12, 79, 13), and delights the Fathers with ambrosia in the dark half, the gods in the bright half of the month (12, 47, 39). He is "water-born Soma, and grahagaṇeśvara; without him is nothing produced" (nīrajātena hi vinā na kiṃ cit saṃpravartate, 13, 67, 11f.). As benefactor of men he lives with cows in the world of Brahman (ib. 66, 38). In H 1330, he is ruler of waters.

§ 45. Soma is son of Atri, the seer who had power over the sun, not ineptly selected, though rather late, by the genealogists, who wished to assure equal dignity for the parvenu Moon-race with that long claimed by the solar dynasty. In 7, 144, 4f.; 12, 208, 9, and probably in 13, 155, 12 (by inference), Soma's father is thus made out to be Atri, the line being then confirmed in Hariv. and Purāṇas. But the early epic does not know this derivation, making Soma rise at the churning of the ocean (1, 18, 35) or appear as son of Prajāpati and Śvāsā (also later of Aditi). The anvavāya, however, is eventually established as Brahman-Atri-Soma-Budha-Aila, etc. In 9, 43, 47, Atri is the hotṛ (priest) of Soma at the god's Tīrtha (cf. his āśraya in 3, 84, 157, which Budha visits), but this may imply what the same expression has in expanded form at H 1311 and 1334: "Soma the Rājarāj (whose car is drawn by a thousand horses) was son of Atri, born of his tears, and Atri was his hotṛ". Yayāti is "sixth from Soma" and Soma alone is called the Prajāpati of the Kurus (5, 149, 3), as if the Atri legend were still unknown. Atri became the moon and sun (to rescue them and the other gods) in the legend of 13, 157, 7f., when they were afflicted by Rāhu. H 8811 has Budha as father of Purūravas and, ib. 629f., gives the story of Budha in relation to Ilā, related also R 7, 87, 3f. Ila was exposed to the female power and became female, but was permitted by Umā to be man one month and woman the next. Budha saw Ilā (as woman) and after turning her female companions into Kiṃpuruṣīs became by her the father of Purūravas (Ilā feminine is Manu's daughter and so of solar origin). Soma's daughter Bhadrā was given by Atri to Utathya and then stolen by Varuṇa (q. v.; 13, 155, 12). His daughter Jyotsnākālī married Varuṇa's son Puṣkara (5, 98, 12). In the Mbh. heroic genealogy, Varcas, part of Soma, becomes Abhimanyu (lives sixteen years, corresponding to the sixteen days of the bright moon); and in Rām. Dadhivaktra or Dadhimukha is begotten by Soma (1, 67, 114f.; 18, 5, 18; R 5, 61, 9f.; ib. 6, 30, 23, saumyaḥ Somātmajaḥ). Soma is identified with Agni (12, 342, 59). With Agni and Vāyu he receives the fruit of Rāma's merit (R 2, 109, 28). See also under Indra. He acts as witness with sun and wind and other gods (see Vāyu and Agni) and unites with Yama in fearing a saint (1, 71, 39), but apart from Yama (here and in Śrāddhas) he is an isolated god, though perfunctorily serving as giver of blessings and hence perhaps having a shrine in a hermitage (R 2, 91, 20; ib. 3, 12, 17f.), since his special business is to prepare food, being "lord of plants" (5, 156, 12; 13, 98, 17, "Soma's self in various ways produced on earth"); whence his peculiar province is taste, as the Sun's is sight and Wind's is touch (rasajñāne, 14, 43, 30; cf. above on the moon's making moisture in plants, and 1, 227, 2, Candramas makes fog). In 3, 57, 37, annarasa as a gift of Yama might revert to the lunar quality of the god. Like other gods the Moon has his earthly place (apart from Tīrthas, above), which appears as a mountain north of the Northern Kurus, "hard even for gods to reach" (Somagiri, R 4, 43, 57f.; perhaps in 13, 166, 33 the same "sunless land beside the northern sea" is meant; H 12413, Saumyagiri, is imitation of the description in R). In R 4, 42, 14, Somagiri (at the mouth of the Indus) has v. l. Hemagiri (S). Somā and Somadā are names of Apsaras and female Gandharvī (§ 93f.). For the moon as a gentle form and as diadem of Śiva, see § 155f. His asterism is Mṛgaśiras (13, 64, 7, gifts according to asterisms). The moon has sixteen parts, only one of which remains intact; the others increasing and decreasing (12, 305, 3, image of jīva, one sixteenth pure soul). All Parvan days are sacred; on days of new and full moon especially one must be chaste (13, 104, 89); the seventh day the moon is very bright (11, 19, 8) and almost consumed on the fourteenth (ib. 21, 13, saptamyām iva; caturdaśāhe, of the dark half, na prītikaraḥ śaśī).

§ 46. The moon disappears but is not lost, and so it is the same soul which reappears with a new body, as the moon reappears encompassed with stars (12, 203, 15f., amāvāsyām aliṅgatvān na dṛśyate). As a good god the moon is tamisrahan, and tamo nighnan, destroying darkness, "with the help of Budha and Śukra" (7, 84, 20). Candra Śaśāṅka destroys evil, rising like a horned bull with a hump, like an elephant with a gold-bound tusk, like a haṃsa in a silver cage, etc. (R 5, 5, 1f.). The effect on the ocean of the moon's power is a trite simile (e. g. 6, 58, 32; 7, 172, 35). Gifts at the full moon or on the twelfth day increase "Soma and ocean"; Soma grants all his wishes who gives ghee and grain to the priests (ib. 8); the same increase of Soma and ocean is produced by a bali of rice and honey offered to the rising full moon in a dish of udumbara wood (ib. 134, 6). The moon is lokakānta, beloved, though fading (R 2, 19, 32), but reviving on the day of the new moon after the fourteenth of the dark half (R 6, 93, 65). The moon-stone candrakānta is comparable to the sun-stone and as rarely mentioned (Rāma's face is fair as the candrakānta, R 2, 3, 28, atīvapriyadarśanam). In R 7, 102, 6f., a town is so named. This stone is made of moon-beams. In the bright half of the month Pauṣa, when Rohiṇī is in conjunction, one should bathe and lie in the open, half naked, and drink moon-beams (Somasya raśmayaḥ pītvā, 13, 126, 49). The next section gives rites and prohibitions for different phases of the moon (the rite of the lunar day is taithika, ib. 12). Not to cut a tree or chew a toothpick on the new moon's day benefits Candramas (Soma). The connection with the Pitṛs (§ 15) is here close; it is they who are afflicted by the chewing of the toothpick (ib. 4). The rule, however, is ascribed to the authority of the Sun-god (the Pauṣamāsa rite, to Brahman) and is actually found in the law-book of Viṣṇu (61, 17). The Candravrata or moon-vow (ascribed to Bhīṣma) is not the cāndrāyaṇa of the law-books. It should be undertaken in the month Mārgaśīrṣa, when the moon, candra, is joined with the asterism Mūla: "When his feet are joined with Mūla, Rohiṇī in his calf, his knees in Aśvinī, his thighs in the two Aṣāḍhās, when his rump is Phālgunī, his waist Kṛttikā, his navel in Bhādrapada, the eye-circle in Revatī, back and front in Dhaniṣṭhāḥ and Anurādhā, his arms the Viśākhāḥ, the hands in Hasta, when his fingers are Punarvasu, his nails in Āśleṣā, neck in Jyeṣṭhā, ears in Śravaṇa, mouth in Puṣya, lips (teeth) are Svāti, his laugh Śatabhiṣā, his nose Maghā, his eyes Mṛgaśiras, Mitra in his forehead, his head in Bharaṇī, and his hair is Ārdrā" (13, 110, 3f.). As the moon is full on the night of the full moon, so will he become full-limbed who performs this rite, which assures beauty and good fortune to the performer and also the "luck of knowledge" (ib. 10). The rite consists in gifts to the priest as well as in making the identifications, limb by limb (Mitra in vs. 8, lalāṭe mitram eva ca, is for Citrā). The chief reason for the Moon-god's importance is his influence over the Fathers (see the "Fathers' Path" and Pitṛs and Yama). As a god he has a vehicle drawn by sixteen (perhaps) or a thousand steeds (cf. H 1321, and 12, 37, 33, where a king drawn by sixteen horses is like god Soma mounting his ambrosial car, amṛtamayaṃ ratham . . tārakārājaḥ). R 7, 23, pra. 3 and 4, 29, says that the world of Candramas is above the seven worlds of wind, but the passage is late, describing how Rāvaṇa attacked the world till Brahman intervened, giving Rāvaṇa a Mantra for the hour of death, which he is to mutter as he grasps his rosary, akṣasūtra, yet it is interesting as distinguishing the Somaloka (where Rāvaṇa's father Parvata tells him of the local saints and the fiend fights Māṃdhātṛ) from the world of Candramas above the seven wind-worlds (Soma and Candramas here quite distinct). So 14, 43, 6f. Candramas is lord of Nakṣatras (as Sūrya is of planets) and Soma is lord of plants (Soma is the moon-plant). Soma as ambrosia raped by Garuḍa (§ 12) and as the divine sacrificial plant has its own position as usual. To sell Soma would not be wrong if one had the higher knowledge in reference to it, though usually it would be a sin (tattvaṃ jñātvā tu somasya vikrayaḥ syād adoṣavān, 12, 34, 31). The pūtikā-plant may be substituted for Soma, and so a month or day for a year (3, 35, 33 and 52, 23f.). Pressing of Soma and Soma-sacrifice are assumed as common meritorious actions. The Nakṣatras are both the wives of the god Soma (as Moon) and also the general stars of which he is Nakṣatrarāj (3, 237, 11), and Nakṣatramārga is Suravīthi, perhaps the Milky Way or path by which the dead go (7, 192, 72 and 3, 43, 12). Nakṣatranemi is both Moon and Viṣṇu (who is Nakṣatrin), and the best of Nakṣatras is Śaśin the moon (6, 34, 21). The Nakṣatras are personal attendants of higher beings (Śiva, etc.), suffering and enjoying Karma-fruit like other beings (5, 29, 15). Nakṣatradakṣiṇās offered by Gaya (nakṣatreṣu) were probable given to the special stars of the lunar zodiac (7, 66, 10). Asterisms unsuitable for Śrāddhas are Proṣṭhapadas, Āgneya, that of one's birth, any evil or hostile (dāruṇa, pratyari) asterism, and any forbidden in astrology (jyotiṣe, 13, 104, 127f.). Āgneya is Kṛttikāḥ. The list as given in 13, 64, 5f., is as follows: Kṛttikāḥ (Āgneya), Rohiṇī, Somadaivata (Mṛgaśiras, later the fifth), Ārdrā, Punarvasu, Puṣya (Tiṣya), Āśleṣā, Maghāḥ, Phalgunī (pūrvā, uttarā), Hasta, Citrā (as twelfth, earlier the fourteenth), Svāti, Viśākhā, Anurādhāḥ, Jyeṣṭhā, Mūla, Aṣāḍhāḥ (pūrvāḥ, uttarāḥ), Abhijit, Śravaṇa, Dhaniṣṭhāḥ (earlier Śraviṣṭhā), Śatabhiṣā, Bhādrapadāḥ (pūrvā, uttarāyoga), Revatī, Aśvinī, Bharaṇyaḥ (pl.), as twenty-eighth. Mṛgaśiras is called (ib. 89, 3) Mṛgottama; Śatabhiṣā is called Vāruṇa (ib. 12); Proṣṭha = Bhādrapadāḥ (pūrvāḥ, uttarāḥ, ib. 13); like Bharaṇyaḥ is Aśvinyaḥ (pl.) in vs. 14. One should not point out Nakṣatras nor tell the tithi pakṣasya (13, 104, 38). Excluded inter alios from Śrāddhas are kuśīlava, devalaka, and "he who lives by stars", nakṣatrair yaś ca jīvati (13, 90, 11, an astrologer). Lunar omens are rare. To see the full moon with broken light on the right is unlucky, but the same is true of a lamp, and the broken light is the important factor (portends death, 12, 318, 9). When Soma enters the sun (at the time of new moon), the gods are fighting Asuras (3, 224, 11f.). See Anumati, Rākā, etc., as phases of the moon under Agni (Aṅgiras). For the moon as representing mind, see § 37, Candramas. While the adventures of the Moon are few and unimportant in the real epic, the tale of his rape of Tārā and consumption being almost all told of him as a hero, the Purāṇas give more details of his equipment (ten steeds, three-wheeled car, not in epics) and even Harivaṃśa rather delights to exploit him as a warrior (as well as the calf of sacrifice, H 369, see Kubera), a fact probably not unconnected with the desire of the lunar dynasty to see its progenitor exalted, as Soma even becomes a name of Śiva and Viṣṇu (H 7581 and 2382). Here Soma is dvijeśvara; "his body is marked with the elephant's shadow", gajacchāyā (2476); he is first invoked to fight against the demons (2584f., has lokacchāyāmayaṃ lakṣma), and uses his "weapon of cold" (as Varuṇa aids him with water) against the fire of Maya; also fights against Śambara (13440f.), when Bhaga retires defeated, etc. The most elaborate description of the moon (R 5, 5) is also late, but this is poetical rather than mythological exaggeration. For Soma and Agni, see § 52. It is possible that Trita may represent the moon. He is cast into a pit and curses his brothers to become wolves, but is rescued by prayer (cf. for interpretation as the moon on the third day of conjunction, Siecke, Drachenkämpfe, p. 21); but the epic version does not reflect any such origin. The three brothers are here sages who report the monotheistic cult of the White Islanders (12, 336). They are "sun-like in glory" and called sons of Gautama (9, 36, 10).

§ 47. **The Wind-God.** — He is called Vāyu, Vāta, Māruta, Anila; or, as purifyer, Pavana; as forceful, Prabhañjana; as bearer of odors, Gandhavaha; as constantly in motion, Satataga and Sadāgati; he has too a venerable title of unknown meaning, Mātariśvan, and as messenger of Indra he is Vāsavadūta. As indicated by the last title, he is closely connected with Indra, whose messenger and servant he is, though in other respects he appears as a mighty independent divinity, associated especially with his friend (son) Agni (see Indra and Agni). Often the names are used as if no divine being were in mind but only the physical phenomenon (if this is ever true), and then vāyu or vāta are preferred, whereas for the god quâ god Māruta is the favorite name. Compare "horses swift as thought or wind" (vāyu, 1, 225, 11); "clouds mixed with wind" (miśravāta, 7, 95, 7); "like a rotten old tree felled by the wind" (vātarugṇa, 3, 16, 20); the whirlwind is viṣvagvāta (7, 46, 10). Yet all the names interchange rather freely. Māruti is in one epic Bhīma, "son of Vāyu" whose "power derives from Mātariśvan" (1, 1, 114; 2, 24, 4), "son of Prabhañjana" and "like Vāta" by nature (1, 67, 111, etc.); in the other, Vāyusuta Hanumat, Vātātmaja, (R 4, 37, 16; R 5, 9, 31 f.; R 6, 28, 10) and Gandhavahātmaja (R 6, 74, 70). Vāta teaches Arjuna the use of arms (1, 165, 12); to Vāta is addressed the wail of Rāma: vāhi Vāta yataḥ kāntā, tāṃ spṛṣṭvā mām api spṛśa (R 6, 5, 6). A sportive Vāyu or Māruta may raise the dust and plays with trees (R 3, 23, 12 and 14; ib. 4, 1, 12 f.). As a Marut, Vāyu is the only one to "have great fame" in the sky, the other Maruts being distributed, one in the world of Indra, one with Brahman, and four in the four directions as followers of Indra, probably those in the "army of Maruts surrounding Indra" (R 1, 47, 5 and R 4, 64, 14). As independent gods their blessing is sought with that of other gods (R 2, 25, 8). Vāyu (Vāta) is the friend of Agni and helps him (1, 223, 78; 227, 14; 228, 40). The hosts of Maruts in the story of Maṅkaṇaka, progenitors of the Maruts, are called Vāyuvega (cf. Vātavega, son of Garuḍa), Vāyubala, Vāyuhan, Vāyumaṇḍala, Vāyujvāla, Vāyuretas, and Vāyucakra (9, 38, 36 f.). The Māruta world or "world of the seven Maruts" (13, 107, 111; cf. ib. 80 f.; ib. 95 and 126 f.) and the allusion to the wind "pleasant, cool, and fragrant", which (or who) carries perfected saints to heaven, nabhasaḥ paramāṃ gatim, as the "best of seven Maruts" (12, 302, 75), show that the usual conception is that of seven winds. This agrees with the seven Prāṇas (ib. 27, etc.) in the metaphysical interpretation of breaths (winds), though they are distinguished from "mighty eight-souled Vāyu". This eightfold Vāyu, like the twelve-souled Sun, appears at the general dissolution of the world (12, 313, 10, aṣṭātmako balī), called yugāntavāta (7, 146, 2; cf. 1, 154, 24, balaṃ Vāyor jagataḥ kṣaye), and blows in every direction, so it probably represents the eight directions (cf. § 10, elephant-protectors of the eight directions, blowing out winds). The "paths of Vāyu are seven" (12, 47, 89 = 51, 6), as other sevens are for several, or to conform to the seven Maruts (which amounts to the same thing); but, as the Prāṇas are also five, so "Vāyu, who moves created beings as their soul, divides himself fivefold and enters the body" (12, 47, 65), namely as devadeva, or lord of the senses (12, 259, 49). Hence Pavana, wind as purifying power (pavanaḥ pavatām asmi, 6, 34, 31) and the deity of touch (12, 314, 10), becomes a numeral "five" in post-epical literature. In the epics, citing revelation, Pavana is the "lord of life" or, as Vāyu, the soul of all, and even is the all: Vāyuḥ sarvam idaṃ jagat (TB. 3, 11, 1, 9; Mbh. 3, 313, 66; R 7, 35, 61; cf. R ib. 55, "without Anila, Pavana, father of Hanumat, lord of life, the body becomes a mere log"). A great wind is the "breath of Viṣṇu", hence the Veda should not be read when a gale is blowing (12, 329, 26f., Vyāsa to Śuka; ib. 55f., Viṣṇor niḥśvāsavātaḥ). The path of gods leads to Viṣṇu, of Pitṛs the path leads downward. There are here seven paths of the winds, Vāyumārgas, and the Prāṇas are explained anthropomorphically. Samāna, son of the Devagaṇāḥ Sādhyāḥ, had a son Udāna, father of Vyāna, father of Apāna, father of Prāṇa, who had no child (ib. 32f.). Cosmically, Samāna is Pravaha, a wind of clouds and thunderstorms. Āvaha is a noisy wind; it makes the moon and other heavenly lights rise and is identical with Udāna (S, however, inverts the first and second names). Udvaha, the third wind, sucks up water for Parjanya to rain. Saṃvaha bears the gods' cars, roars in clouds and rends mountains. The fifth wind is dry, incorporate in the Valāhaka clouds, bringing portents of disaster (but in 6, 91, 13, Valāhaka clouds are rain-clouds, prāvṛṣi), and is called Vivaha. Parivaha, sixth, upholds the atmospheric waters (Ganges, etc.), obstructs the sun, and makes the moon wax. The seventh wind is the death-wind, followed by Death and Yama, which disperses the breath of all beings that breathe; it is called Parāvaha. The seven are then identified with the Mārutas, sons of Diti (or Aditi), which blow everywhere; probably the same as "the seven Vāyus", with whom, as with the seven Agnis, Śiva is, as All-god, also identified (ib. 53 and 13, 14, 410). As material power, Vāyu overthrows trees (agamas, R 6, 97, 19), blowing hardest "at winter's end" (7, 95, 7) and "at the end of the hot season" (4, 65, 1; ghoro mahānilaḥ, 7, 95, 11; cf. uṣṇaparyāye, 7, 98, 31). "At the end of the rains Māruta dispels the rain-clouds" (R 5, 46, 23). Vāyu gives testimony from the air when invoked as witness, with the Sun and Moon (3, 76, 36; R 6, 119, 27). Philosophically, like the Sun, Vāyu is the "life of the world" (jagadāyu, 3, 147, 27) and despite his many forms is but one (eko Vāyur bahudhā vāti loke, 12, 352, 10), the soul of all, on whom all depends (2, 19, 14). In the later epic, he holds windy discourses on castes and kings (12, 72, 2f., with Purūravas). In one of these he says that he is the "messenger of the gods" who speaks from the sky (13, 153, 26; cf. 3, 76, 36). In 13, 154, 3f., he tells how he retreated from Aṅgiras into the Agnihotra and lectures on privileges, Brahman's birth, etc. Usually Vāyu is the messenger not of any god but of Indra. Hanumat is Vāsavadūtasūnu (R 6, 74, 62). Indra treats Vāyu Māruta even as a servant, telling him to raise the dust, for "that is thy work", and Vāyu obeys (1, 32, 8). Indra again bids him help Menakā seduce Viśvāmitra (1, 71, 41 and 72, 1), here as Sadāgati. As Vāyu is a Vasu and Indra is the lord of Vasus (§ 112), this relation is natural from the epic point of view as well as traditional. His friend Agni is also a Vasu, and Vāyu drives Agni's chariot, and helps him burn the forest (12, 229, 86, etc.; cf. Agni as Anilasārathi, Vātasārathi, 1, 15, 1; 1,

228, 40). Agni is also called "son of Wind" (see § 49). Vāyu is typical of freedom, "cannot be bound" (R 3, 55, 24), and serves as type of the freed saint (na vaśe kasya cit tiṣṭhan sadharmā Mātariśvanaḥ, 1, 119, 19). He goes through air, the swiftest of beings; racing horses "drink the wind"; he is the strongest god (12, 154 to 157, stronger than Indra, Death, etc., ib. 155, 10). He has physical power; Indra has fighting ability (8, 31, 14). He alone put to sleep (in death) the demons of the West, though accompanied, as forms of himself, by mahāvātas (5, 110, 5). He is the "smasher" (R 4, 31, 13); hence Arjuna is called Prabhañjanasutānuja (7, 146, 116; but Indra is Vāyubhūta, takes his form if he will). Perhaps because of their freedom the Maruts first instituted the self-choice of a maiden (13, 44, 35). The "troop of Maruts" is said to have begotten several heroes, Sātyaki, Drupada, Kṛtavarman, and Virāṭa (1, 67, 79f.). In 6, 50, 51, B and S have Mārutāḥ as a people.

§ 48. The later epic, like the VP., may imply that the Maruts are seven times seven. In 9, 38, 37, the seven progenitors of the Maruts (above) are seven gaṇas, which may mean seven groups of seven, as the Hariv. and VP., in giving the tale of Indra dividing the embryo of Diti into seven parts and saying mā rudaḥ (H 249, mā rodīḥ, origin of the name, as in R 1, 46—47), also say that the Maruts were forty-nine (VP. 1, 21, 39); but the epic does not openly recognise this number (till H 252). The story of Diti is alluded to again in 5, 110, 8. Indra is Marutpati and king of the Maruts (1, 173, 48; 2, 62, 17; 14, 43, 7), with whom he is identified as their chief (13, 14, 324), and who as his sacivas, socii, laud ever their nāyaka, leader, and with moon and stars and planets add lustre to him (3, 157, 72; R 2, 3, 26; ib. 3, 32, 4; ib. 5, 51, 45; ib. 6, 12, 9). In 6, 34, 21, "Marīci am I among Maruts", the root and the fact that each is of a group of seven helps to put Marīci in this category. The mother of Maruts is Marutvatī (H 145, etc.) or Diti (below), as their father is Dharma (loc. cit.) or Kaśyapa (H 11 849). In 12, 328, 53, the cosmical winds described above are Aditeḥ putrā Mārutāḥ (and so S, but Diteḥ may be right). Speed, strength, and his attribute of "bearing perfumes" are the chief characteristics of Vāyu (Analasakha is iṣṭagandha, sukhasparśa, sarvendriyasukhāvaha, 12, 229, 86), till the later epic emphasises his moral eloquence (above). As the lover of Kuntī he comes riding upon a deer, mṛgārūḍhaḥ (1, 123, 12). The distribution of the special provinces of the winds, Vātaskandhas, is applied to the Mārutas as winds in general (R 1, 47, 5). Vātaskandha (H 13 894, v. l. Vāyuskandha) is the name given to regions of winds. In 3, 231, 55, the army-corps of Skanda, which is especially protected by him, is called the saptama Mārutaskandha, referring to its seven constituents. In H 2479, Vāyu supports the three worlds as saptaskandhagata. Vāyu and Agni together wave fans over Skanda (3, 231, 47) while Indra and Śrī march behind the new battle-god. In Rām., as father of Hanumat, Vāyu plays a very active rôle. He comes and speaks to Lakṣmaṇa, advising him to kill Atikāya with Brahman's weapon (R 6, 71, 98). He is Prabhu, Bhagavat, Sarvātman, and Satataga (R 6, 28, 11 and R 5, 13, 63). As Sarvātmaka he attempts to corrupt all the nymph-mothered daughters of Kuśanābha, cursing and deforming the girls who object to his amorous advances (R 1, 32, 10f.). When "penetrated by Love" (Manmatha, R 4, 66, 14f.), Māruta Pavana dallies with the nymph (Añjanā) Puñjikasthalā, and becomes father of Hanumat. Vāyu refused to move when Indra struck Hanumat (§ 86) on the jaw and so the earth dried up; but the gods soothed the irate father by bestowing gifts on the son (Indra gave him the privilege of dying when he chose and Brahman gave him invulnerability, R 4, 66, 25 f.). Hanumat is here called "son of Kesarin", but only as son of his mother's husband. Vāyu's later name Jalakānta is not known, nor is the Purāṇic exploit mentioned of his contest with Garuḍa, in the endeavour to convert the top of Meru into Laṅkā. In Hariv., Vāyu is a great warrior, fighting (H 13176) with Puloman in company with Sāvitra, here and elsewhere in H called "fifth of the Maruts" (ib. 12787, the seven are Āvaha, Pravaha, etc., as above). Vāyu (H 14288) is listed with Namuci, etc., as a Dānava (H 2285 = 14288); but in H 11540, Vāyu is one of the eight Vasus, born of Dharma and Sādhyā. He is lord of "the bodiless Bhūts", as well as of odors and sounds (ib. 265 and 12493). At the assembly of gods, to hear the complaint of Pṛthivī, Vāyu as Prabhañjana, "being urged by Brahman", went through the assembly, calling out Silentium! (mā śabda iti), thus acting as a "masher" among the rude gods (H 2911). His roar in battle terrifies the demons; he is the bhūtam uttamam ("highest being"), and bodiless; the charioteer of Agni (Agner yantṛ); and, as lord of sound, is born in the seven notes of music (H 2480). He joins Agni to subdue Maya, and becomes one with Agni (ib. 2617, so 'nilo 'nalasaṃyuktaḥ so 'nalaś cā 'nilākulaḥ). In 13, 25, 38, Marudgaṇa is the name of a Tīrtha. The host, gaṇa, comes to earth followed by Indra Marutvat and his spouse Śacī (3, 168, 11). Indra "Pākaśāsana conquers his foes with the help of the Maruts" (12, 23, 29). Any Māruta travels through space on a car (R 2, 71, 8), probably a cloud, as in 8, 19, 8, clouds cover Himavat in summer impelled by winds (Marudbhiḥ preritā meghāḥ). The list of (twenty-three) Marutvats or Maruts "born of Marutvatī" (H 11544 f.) is unique but noteworthy as including under the title the names of Ādityas and kings as well as names of fire (see § 111).

§ 49. **The Fire-God.** — Agni (ignis) is Anala, son of Anila, the Wind-god (2, 31, 48; RG 5, 50, 14); described as having seven red tongues (also seven red steeds), seven faces, a huge mouth, red neck, tawny eyes (honey-colored), bright gleaming hair, and golden seed, "the first dispeller of darkness created by Brahman". Most of the epithets given him occur passim, but a few, located below, are unique or almost so. For the formal description, cf. 1, 228, 37 and 232, 5 and 19 (saptajihva here = RV. 3, 6, 2; Muṇḍ. Up. 1, 2, 4), and with piṅgākṣa cf. piṅgeśa (2, 31, 44). His right to distinction and many of his attributes are conveyed by these epithets, which fall into three classes, as they describe his appearance, functions, and relations. Thus he is Dahana, burner, Plavaṃga, leaper, Śikhin, pointed, Arka, light, Vibhāvasu, Jvalana, Svargadvāraspṛśa, gleaming to heaven's door, Kṛṣṇavartman, Dhūmaketu, black-tracked and smoke-bannered, Citrabhānu, Timirāpaha (Tamonuda? 3, 217, 14), bright remover of darkness, Pāvaka, Pāvana, purifier, and Śuci, Śukra, pure; also, as all-devouring and especially as eater of oblations, he is Sarvabhuj (-bhakṣa), Havyavah, Havyavāha, -vāhana, Vahni, Hutabhuj, -vaha, Hutāśana, and mouth of the gods (mukhaṃ devānām). As the wise god, he is Kavi, Jātavedas, Pracetas; as maker and lord he is Loka- and Bhūtabhāvana, Dhātṛ, Kartṛ, Bhūtādi, Bhūtapati, Sureśa, Sureśvara; as child of the water he is Apāṃgarbha; as maker of gold, he is Hiraṇyakṛt, Hiraṇyaretas, Vasuretas; as universal, he is Vaiśvānara and Pāñcajanya; as springing from the fire-stick, he is Śamīgarbha and Araṇīsuta (R 5, 13, 41); and as father of Kumāra, he is Kumārasū (Rudragarbha); while as maker of paths and of Vedas, he is Pathikṛt (pontifex) and Vedakartṛ. On introducing himself to Śibi he says "I am Vaiśvānara Jvalana Dhūmaketu" (3, 197, 25), and to the Pāṇḍus he says "I am Pāvaka Agni" (17, 1, 36 f.). His common name, Anala, has already been mentioned under Vāyu, who acts as his charioteer (Anilasārathi, Agner yantṛ, etc.). "Hutāśana Jvalana, mouth of the gods, is ever present at Prabhāsa" (3, 82, 59; Vātasārathi, 12, 172, 1; cf. 1, 15, 1). Rāma and Lakṣmaṇa are Agnimārutakalpau, (R 5, 39, 53); "Lakṣmaṇa is as Anila to Rāma as Pāvaka" (R 3, 31, 17). Many of these epithets are shared with other gods: Varuṇa, the wise; Vāyu the purifyer; the Sun-god, pure and far-shining; Indra and others as creators. Oblations are poured into Agni's mouth (7, 102, 32), who himself is then "mouth of the gods". "Swift as Agni or as Wind" are Indra's horses, and Agni is manogatiḥ, swift as thought (S 3, 270, 6 Agnyanilogravegaiḥ for B atyanilo-). Like Sun and Wind, Fire is but one (1, 232, 13; 3, 134, 8), but his forms are many. He is trividha, threefold (in earth, air, and sky), in 1, 229, 24 = 5, 16, 2, and many in his functions (bahutvaṃ karmasu, 3, 217, 3). Always he has seven flames, Saptārcir Jvalanaḥ (1, 225, 35), tongues, or weapons (Saptajihvānana, -anala, -heti, 1, 232, 5 and 10; H 13956). The seven are also interpreted as seven distinct fires, the three sacrificial fires, agnitretā or tretāgnayaḥ (R 4, 13, 23), with which are identified the father with the Gārhapatya fire, the mother with the Dakṣiṇa, and the Guru with the Āhavanīya (12, 108, 7), together with the Sabhya, Āvasathya, Smārta, and Laukika (3, 221, 5 and 13, 14, 410 with N.'s explanation of the seven). Instead of seven flames, Agni has three points, Triśikha (H 12292), perhaps as fires. Metaphorically, five fires are "self and fire" added to the three one has to tend (father, mother, Guru). Other counts have to do with sacrificial fires: five, 3, 134, 12; six, 2, 35, 16; eightfold, 1, 229, 25 (cf. AV. 13, 3, 19); twenty-seven, in Indra's palace (2, 7, 21, yajñavāhāḥ pāvakāḥ, so, not asterisms); thirty (13, 103, 36). Agni divides himself into five as prāṇas (H 13938). The ordinary "five fires" refer to those about an ascetic (13, 90, 26 = Manu 3, 185; cf. 1, 86, 16, and Rāvaṇa as pañcāgni in 3, 275, 16).[1])

Among fires must be reckoned also those which to us are purely metaphorical, the audārya, "belly-fire" (of hunger, extinguished with food, 12, 17, 5), and the head- and navel-fires (3, 213, 3 f.; S adds nābhyām agniḥ pratiṣṭhitaḥ), as also the fires of love and wrath. That there may be no doubt as to these being real fires, the poet of 2, 71, 15; 72, 14, says that owing to the hero's "wrath-fire" krodhāgni (kopāgni, 4, 62, 14; 12, 139, 44, etc.) flames burst from his orifices, together with smoke, sparks, and fire, "as if from the holes of a burning tree". The "fire of battle" may be due to sparks from weapons, but "divine weapons" and even elephants' tusks add to this fire (7, 20, 39, etc.). Pure metaphor is "fire of grief, extinguished with water of wisdom" (11, 8, 49), and interesting only on account of the last expression. The "mental fire", mānaso 'gniḥ, is jīva (soul), "like pure fire, like fire of lightning" (12, 187, 31;

[1]) Fausbøll, Indian Mythology, p. 171, refers to "ten sorts of fires"; but the passage he cites gives not ten but seven (13, 1005 = 13, 14, 400, ye vāyavaḥ sapta tathai 'va cā 'gnayaḥ). He perhaps meant 14, 21, 4 f., where ten gods are called ten fires (with "ten oblations"), all metaphorical or philosophical, the gods of the senses receiving the fuel of the senses, etc.

ib. 241, 20). There are other fires, of knowledge, jñānāgni (6, 28, 37), of the curse (3, 72, 31), and above all of the eye, which can burn (evil eye). Even Gāndhārī, when she looks at Yudhiṣṭhira, raises a blister on his finger (11, 15, 30). But these and the "foe-fire", the "family-coal" (injurer, 12, 173, 24), must be passed over for the more important "fire of the demons" and the mystic forms of Agni. The normal fire is produced by twirling a fire-stick (araṇīm agnikāmo vā mathnāti 12, 81, 6) or "out-twirling fire" (nirmathiṣyāmi pāvakam, R 3, 68, 27), but the fire of demons comes from the oceanic fire in the underworld and will eventually destroy the world. It is the "water-fire in ocean" (toyāgniḥ sāgare, 12, 139, 44), or Pātālajvalanaḥ (1, 21, 7) and arises from the wrath of the Sun (3, 3, 57) or from the wrath of Aurva Bhārgava materialised (H 2149). It is commonly called Yugāntārka, Saṃvartaka Vahni (7, 32, 46f.; 3, 188, 69). In 6, 7, 28, it is located on the Mālyavat Mountain (Kālāgni), but in 5, 99, 3, it is in Nāgaloka. Apparently the same fire (5, 99, 17) is kept in a resplendent egg sunk in ocean. At the end of the æon the fire will hatch and consume the three worlds; no one knows the origin of this egg (ib. 18). From the ocean is taken the name "Fire of the Mare's mouth". One offers at Vāḍava Tīrtha a cake to Saptārcis, who appears morn and eve on Hemakūṭa, where Vāyu is ever to be seen (3, 82, 92; ib. 110, 5). The supreme deity, in the unitary conception of the universe, as Agni Vaḍavāvaktra, drinks the waters and lets them out again; as Saṃvartaka Vahni he is one with Saṃvartaka Sūrya and Anila; Fire, Sun, and Wind all being saṃvartaka as helping in the final overthrow (3, 189, 12). Thus the demoniac fire is interpreted as divine. Curiously, though fire is divine, no common fire, vṛthāgni, is sacred enough to burn the pious dead. The epic hero blames the Fire-god that he had not been hallowed when he consumed the hero's father (15, 38, 13f.; 39, 1 dhig Agnim, etc.). The crematory fire is a special form of fire; it is not much respected but is not impure (3, 222, 6; ib. 200, 89; R 3, 33, 3, na bahu manyante śmaśānāgnim). Fire is especially invoked at burial feasts (13, 91, 23f.). All good people worship fire. The king on rising goes to his bath-room, dresses, prays to the Sun, and then enters the Fire-chamber (agniśaraṇa), where he honors Agni with kindlings and oblations accompanied with Mantras (7, 82, 13). To discover signs of victory, Indrajit lights the fire of vibhītaka wood, and draws omens from the flame, with perfumes, grain, the sacrifice of a black goat, etc. (R 6, 73, 17f.; ib. 80, 5f.). The agniśālā or -agāra (-śaraṇa, -gṛha) is also found in the hermitages, and the fear of its igniting the forest, conjoined with the fear of its going out, probably resulted in the erection of these god-houses (cf. R 2, 91, 11, etc., and ib. 99, 12). Fires started by dry bamboos rubbing against each other were dreaded; only Indra could extinguish them. A phrase "igniting fire ignited" pradīpya pradīptāgnim (2, 64, 10) refers to camphor. Fire is the sire of gold (13, 84, 42 and 56) and tests gold (R 3, 29, 20), as Agni tests man's truth. He is the deity presiding over speech (12, 314, 5, etc.) and man's truth is tested by an appeal to Agni, the test consisting in walking through fire (below, Sītā), or in submitting to Agni's action, whether he burns the man's house, etc. So Jātavedas "spares the houses of the good" (3, 134, 27; cf. Manu 8, 108). Dull fires alarm augurs (4, 46, 25); smoking flame implies disaster (R 6, 10, 15). Suttee is recognised by both epics (1, 76, 46; ib. 125, 31; 12, 148, 9f.; R 2, 66, 12; R 5, 26, 7, the asatī does not die with her husband). In 15, 33, 21, "good women true to their husbands" perform suttee by drowning. Committing suicide on the pyre of a beloved object is not confined to wives (3, 137, 19).[1]) Agni is witness of the world and as such is invoked by conspirators, doubted wives, etc. (7, 17, 27; R 6, 119, 24f.). In H 13928f., Agni is the son of Śamī and of Śāṇḍilī (cf. H 992), and "witness of the world". In R 4, 5, 15 f., Hanumat "makes a fire", janayāmāsa pāvakam, as preliminary to forming a military alliance and the contracting parties then shake hands (hastaṃ pīḍayāmāsa pāṇinā) and circumambulate the fire as witness (R 4, 5, 13), which is placed between Rāma and Sugrīva and "revered with flowers" (cf. the expressions Agnisākṣikaṃ sakhyam, sāgnikam, etc., R 7, 33, 18; cf. ib. 5, 58, 138). Agni's so-called son Dṛṣṭadyumna is born from a sacrificial fire enkindled to injure the foe. The strength of the foe "is poured upon the fire" (5, 126, 2, medhāgni = saṃgrāmāgni). On the other hand, fire drives away demons (13, 92, 13). On entering a forest, Arjuna swings a torch for protection against evil spirits (1, 170, 4), and priests keep off evil from the king by making him mount an elephant and carrying fire around him (2, 21, 23). Real wifehood implies the presence of fire (ceremony); hence Agni evades the truth in acting as a witness (though he fears a saint's curse more than a lie, 1, 5, 27f.). It is on this occasion that Bhṛgu curses the god to be an "all-eater" (1, 6, 14), but the fulsome laudation of Agni here amounts only to the usual flattery of a god in a hymn or laudation (Brahman calls Agni "lord of the world" and "creator", etc.). Only the hinder rays are his "all-eating form" (1, 7, 20f.).

§ 50. The varied activities of the Fire-god led to the theory of the Adbhuta and other "various Agnis" exploited as historical, genealogical characters in 3, 217f. As descendants of mother rivers the different Agnis appear in the history of Agni hiding in water, Agni being created by Brahman and identified with Aṅgiras, third son of Brahman. Angiras' son by Subhā or Vasud(h)ā was the gods' Guru, Bṛhaspati; his eldest daughter was Bhānumatī (the fairest); next came Rāgā (best loved); next, Sinīvālī (so thin as to be visible only at times), called also "daughter of Kapardin" (Śiva); the fourth and fifth daughters were Arciṣmatī (as masculine, a name of Agni) and Haviṣmatī (S has Kuhū and Arciṣmatī as fourth and fifth); the sixth and seventh were Mahiṣmatī and Mahāmatī (seen at very grand sacrifices), and lastly (but see S above) "the blessed one, whom the people, as they see her, address with the exclamation kuhū! and say that she is without a portion (kuhukuhāyate ekā 'naṃśe 'ti; S, ekānekā). There are thus six or seven lunar days as female forms of Agni. The account continues with the names of seven holy fires as six sons and one daughter of Bṛhaspati by Cāndramasī, his lunar wife, who bore Śaṃyu, Niśayavana, Viśvajit, Viśvabhuj, Vaḍavāgni, Sviṣṭakṛt and the putrikā Manyatī, Svāhā (mother of Kāma, Amogha, and Uktha). Each of these fires has his restricted work. Śaṃyu is occupied with seasonal and horse-sacrifices; his wife Satyā, daughter of Dharma, is mother of Bharad-

[1]) Ascetics may die by fire, though the general epic rule forbids suicide. Compare Holtzmann, Mahābhārata, 1, 26 and 147; also JAOS. 21 (1900), 146f. The possibility of suicide on the part of a wife is recognised in both epics and is approved as the proper thing to do for a Satī; but it is not practised except in the later addition of Mbh. (1, 125), describing the suttee of Mādrī, the wife of Pāṇḍu. That a wife should die with her husband is so common a rule (found in Africa, South America, etc.) as to make it improbable that the idea of suttee is modern. What is (comparatively) modern is enforced suttee by fire.

vāja and Bharata (fire of full-moon sacrifice). Bharadvāja's wife, Vīrā, bore Vīra (Rathaprabhu, Rathādhvāna, Kumbharetas), father of Siddhi (Mithyā) by the Sarayū. Bharata had a son Bhārata and a daughter Bhāratī; he is called "lord of three maidens" (= Puṣṭimati in 221, 1!) The "league-making" fire comes from Niścyavana ("not budging"), and he also "makes good" or cures and hence is called Satya Niṣkṛti, whose son causes wounds and makes people cry, hence Svana Rujaskara. Viśvabhuj (no "children") is the digestive fire and he married Gomatī (this river appears as Gopatī in S). For Manyatī (Svāhā) Manu is also read. Her son Kāma (love-fire) is "more beautiful than any being in the sky", and Amogha is like his brother in that he has a bow and wreath of flowers; but he is the "fire of battle". So, as warrior, Agni has a bow and discus (7, 11, 21; 23, 94, given to the Pāṇḍus) and becomes Śiva's arrow (13, 161, 29). In describing the Pāñcajanya fire, who begot "the awful fire of the Pitṛs and the Bṛhat and Rathantara" (melodies), S makes Hari (Viṣṇu) his son, and both texts make him father ("from the navel") of Śiva (and "born of strength") of Indra, and of Vāyu (S omits the absurd "and of Agni"). He begot also the (two) Anudāttau and viśve bhūtāni (sic), also the five (B as twenty-five) sons of Pitṛs. Śiva as fire is devoted to Śakti (Śaktipūjāparaḥ, 3, 221, 2, S has Śaktipūjāyaniḥ!). Here too belong, as fires, strange groups of gods (§ 27) who "steal sacrifices", arranged in three pentads, one being Mitra gods. There are others, not less vague and mystic, sons of Tapa(s), Purandara, Uṣman, Prajāpati Manu, Śambhu, Āvasathya, the five Ūrjaskaras, "five gold-like sons of sacrifice", also the "exhausted sun", Gavāmpati Pari-(or Pra-)śrānta, who "created demons, Asuras, and mortals". Aṅgiras's son Bṛhadbhānu had as wife Suprajā, daughter of the Sun (Sūryajā, but S reads Bṛhadbhāsā ca Somajā), and this Bhānu had six (S, four) sons, Balada, Manyumat, Viṣṇu (Dhṛtimat), and Āgrayaṇa ("his oblation unites with that of Indra") and "Agraha and Stubha" (not in S). S adds the account of Niśā, wife of (Bhānu) Manu and her five sons, but omits from her sons "the two Agnīṣomau", and changes her daughter's name from Rohiṇī to Hariṇī (both texts unclear; apparently making this daughter of Manu the wife of Hiraṇyakaśipu). The five Pāvakas (sons of this wife of Manu) include Kapila, "author of the Sāṅkhya-Yoga"; the other four are Vaiśvānara ("honored with Parjanya"), Viśvapati, Saṃnihita (the "fire that evokes speech"), and Agraṇī ("who causes bodily activity"). The Gṛhapati (222, 4) fire is next derived from Saha Āpa, the "power in the water" (husband of Muditā), and is identified with Adbhuta, whose wife is Priyā and whose son is Bharata. This fire fears his descendant Niyata Kratu, the fire that burns the dead, and his history introduces the story of Atharvan (below), at the end of which all fires are said to be mothered by the rivers and to be essentially one; also as mental offspring to be derived through Atri from Brahman (3, 222, 28). Though reeking with mysticism, this account is fairly clear and very instructive, showing that as different distinct fires were conceived the fire of digestion, the fire of love, the fire that hurts and cures, the fire that guards leagues; and that the new-moon fire, etc., are special divinities apart from the moon. This last fire, daughter of Aṅgiras, called Sinīvālī (new moon, also birth-goddess) is differentiated not quite logically from Kuhū. The epic admits four such moon-phases (8, 34, 32), as fastenings of the heavenly car, Sinīvālī, Anumati, Kuhū, and Rākā, the first two being the prior (days of the) new and full moon respectively, and the last two being the succeeding parts (lunar days) of the new and full moon. But in 3, 229, 50, Devasenā, wife of Skanda, is called Aparājitā (also name of Durgā), the Unconquered, Giver of Good, Lakṣmī (also wife of Viṣṇu), Āsā, (read Āśā, Hope), Ṣaṣṭhī and Sinīvālī and Kuhū, that is, both moon-phases are one with the Ṣaṣṭhī (lucky sixth day after birth). Agni Pathikṛt is adored when one starts on a journey, either in this world or to the next world, with the remainder of the new- and full-moon sacrifices (3, 221, 30; 5, 83, 9; ib. 16, 43). A special service is necessary if sacred fires cross, in honor of the Śuci, Vīti, (cf. AB. 7, 6) and Davāgni (fires). The last is common as a forest-conflagration (da° or dā°). If a woman in her courses touch the oblation-fire, a rite must be performed in honor of the Vasumat fire. If the fire of a woman who is lying in touch the āgnihautrika fire, a rite is ordered (tabu of sūtikā). If cattle die, a rite is performed in honor of the Surabhimat fire, or if one alive is reported to be dead. This Purāṇic analysis of fires is comparable, but not the same, with the "forty-nine fires" recognised in VP. 1, 10, 17, ekonapañcāśad vahnayaḥ.

§ 51. Agni is an actor in several epic scenes. He was cursed by Bhṛgu (above) and disappeared, but was found in the Śamī wood (9, 47, 14 f.). The Saha fire, fearing the funeral fire, made Atharvan his proxy, gave up his body, and hid, but he was betrayed by fishes, whom (Vedic tale) he cursed to be eaters of everything; then (also Vedic) from water he fled into earth and made emeralds, metals, deodars from his bones, iron from his liver, etc. (3, 222, 7 f.). Agni was made sick by eating butter for twelve years and was advised by Brahman to try a change of diet. With Vāyu's help he devoured the Khāṇḍava forest (historical?), though the elephants formed a fire-brigade and seven times thwarted him, till Arjuna helped him (against Indra, 1, 223, 64 f.). Elsewhere Agni coops up elephants as fires surround them (7, 22, 14). Atharvan as a fire appears also in the demoniac ceremony to raise an apparition from fire in secret rites (aupaniṣadāḥ kriyāḥ), performed by means of the Mantras of Bṛhaspati and Uśanas as declared in the Atharvaveda (a karma vaitānasaṃbhavam, 3, 251, 21 f.). There is no doubt that the poets regarded this Veda as a work pertaining to evil magic and to a fire-cult for evil purpose. But the seers are Atharvabhūtāḥ, H 11520. Agni's disappearance in 1, 37, 9 is described as hiding in a cave. In 13, 85, 8 f., he retreats first to the sea, then to the trees, and is betrayed by frog, elephant, and parrot in turn, each of whom he curses. So the frog loses his taste, the elephant has his tongue turned back, and the parrot loses his voice. But the gods compensate each. Agni is here older than Śiva; he is creator of all, one with Love, father of gold and (by proxy) of Skanda. Other gods being sterile (see § 24), Agni alone is competent to raise a son capable of combating Tāraka. Agni is "father of Skanda" in 2, 31, 44, at which place the god is also exalted and a general prayer is addressed to him and other gods in these words: "May Agni give me energy, and Vāyu give me breath; may Earth bestow upon me power, and Water make me blest" (ib. 42, the "Vedas are born for Agni's sake" . Direct identification of Fire with lightning and Sun (q. v.) is common. Thus when Agni searches for Indra and fears to enter water, he is reminded (in another laud, 5, 16, 6) that he is "clouds and lightnings", and this is probably the threefold fire, namely Agni, Sūrya, and Vidyut, though explained as "maker, sustainer, and destroyer" (ib. 2 = 1, 229, 24; cf. 1, 7, 19 f.: tvaṃ kartā cā 'nta eva ca, tvaṃ dhārayasi lokāṃs trīn[1]), thus a first Trimūrti). He "whose light is from Brahman" carries the other gods and drags the car of Brahman (8, 46, 38), saptitāṃ gataḥ, perhaps a conscious assimilation to his seven steeds. His own golden car he gave to Arjuna (8, 31, 55). Perhaps this was the "horse-yoked car" (the horses are red, H 13936), which Prajāpati gave offhand to Indrajit to bribe him (R 7, 30, 15). Besides becoming a horse, when disguised, Agni appears as a goat or a pigeon (below); but when he hunts for Indra, he, for obvious reasons, "puts on the garb of a female" in the tale already narrated. He, like Indra, is fond of women and is an adulterer, and for these reasons he is presented as a goat. No maiden may offer libations to Agni; if she does, she goes to hell. He is chāgavaktra as Naigameya Agni (bahuprajaḥ) in which form he amuses Skanda (3, 226, 29; ib. 228, 3 and 5). An oblation poured on a goat's ear (or on gold) is virtually made to Agni. A goat, a ram, and a horse represent, respectively, Agni, Varuṇa, Sūrya (13, 75, 37; 84, 47 and 56; 85, 147 f.). Agni is unscrupulously voracious, burning up the hermitage af Āpava (12, 49, 38 f.), burning a child (3, 127, 2 f.), and accepting other human sacrifices, even accepting for an evil purpose the sacrifice of the ten heads of the fiend (3, 275, 20). The head of a horse is put on the fire-altar in the horse-sacrifice to work ill to one's foes (7, 143, 71), and this or any other fire of destruction is all good to him, is himself; for he is consecrated for progeny-getting and for suicide equally (1, 120, 40; 10, 7, 56). He is "the priest" and as a priest he appears disguised in the Khāṇḍava episode (1, 222, 30 f.; so chasing Maya, ib. 228, 41). In the story of Sudarśanā (daughter of a king Duryodhana and of the river Narmadā), his beloved, he appears as priest to woo her, and gives as śulka his continued presence as Agni in Māhiṣmatī (13, 2, 32)[2]). The son of the god and of the girl is called Sudarśana (name of Agni's discus) as a sort of metronymic (but also Pāvaki). He married Oghavatī, who was raped, in accordance with the guest-right, by a priest, who was Dharma in disguise! Agni supports the guest-right as he is "guest of all creatures" (3, 313, 66). The account in 2, 31, 23 f., says that Nīla, king of Māhiṣmatī, was attacked by Sahadeva after the hero had got tribute from Mainda and Dvivida, sons of the Aśvins (monkeys), who lived near the famous caves of Orissa, but Nīla could not be overcome because Agni helped the king. Sudarśana and his son Agnivarṇa appear in Daśaratha's genealogy (R 1, 70). Agni is represented as an adulterer, pāradārika, who gave a boon to all the women living in that place, that they should wander free and not be restrained (svairiṇyaḥ, aprativāraṇe, 2, 31, 38); but he is lauded by Sahadeva as father of Rudra and destroyer of sin, son of Wind, origin of water, and god of purity, who bestows happiness, and is invoked: "Cleanse me by thy truth and give me, O Agni, contentment, prosperity, learning, and joy" (ib. 50). As protector of the guest-right in another form, the right of the refugee, Agni tests Śibi, under the form of a pigeon. Despite the fact that the pigeon is ominous of death (§ 12), Śibi refuses to give up his unwelcome

---

[1]) Fausbøll, op. cit. p. 174, compares the three forms with the "explanation" of 1, 7, 19; but it should be said that this is not the explanation of the text. Agni is one of the three horrible forms of Śiva (q. v.) and is identical with sun and lightning also as forms of the same god. In H 7422, conversely, Śiva is lauded as Atharvan = Agni, yajñe hūtaḥ, etc.

[2]) The father of the bride gives a dowry and the bride-groom gives a śulka in this tale.

guest. According to 3, 208, 7, this tale shows that it is right to eat meat! In 1, 197, 29, both Śibi and Viśvabhuj appear as names of former Indras, but here he is son of Uśīnara and Mādhavī, daughter of Yayāti, with whom Śibi and his brothers sport in heaven (1, 86, 6), though also represented as son of Hiraṇyakaśipu (1, 65, 18; 5, 118, 2, 9, and 20). As Sauratheya, Śibi is son of Surathā (an Apsaras, H 14164) and father of Kapotaroman (3, 197, 25 and 28), the "bull of the Saurathas" (so S). A parallel story to the received version, according to which he weighs out his flesh to compensate the hawk (Indra) for the loss of the pigeon (Agni), is to this effect: that Śibi killed and cooked his own son for a priest to eat (3, 198, 2 f.; usual tale in 3, 131, 28), and would have eaten thereof himself, had not the priest, who was Vidhātṛ in disguise, resurrected the son. The same story of the pigeon is told of his son Vṛṣadarbha or Bṛhadgarbha (13, 32, 4 f.), but Agni does not here appear; only Indra with the gods come to see the great act (in this version Śibi actually dies). Agni is "more pleased with the feeding of guests than with offerings of food and flower and paste" (3, 200, 22).

§ 52. Agni's amorousness stops at violating the wives of the great seers. He fell in love with them when they slept, but, though glorious, they were cold and "pure as moon-beams". Becoming the Gārhapatya fire he "as it were, fondled them", but, being unable to rouse their passion, he went to the forest (of all places!) to commit suicide (3, 224, 29 f.; ib. 38). In the meantime Svāhā (1, 199, 5; 5, 104, 8; R 5, 24, 26, devī), daughter of Dakṣa, who loved Agni, assumed the forms of the wives (except that of Arundhatī) and through her instrumentality was born Skanda (Pāvaki, Svāheya), son of the supernatural Adbhuta Agni, who had been engaged in carrying oblations to the Sun's disc (3, 224, 14 and 28), till the sight of the seers' wives induced him to transform himself into the special Gārhapatya form of fire. Svāhā is recognised regularly as Agni's wife (13, 146, 5 and oft). The rest of his family is variously interpreted. A god who is his own father and has as many forms as there are sacrifices, with parents and sons in each form, who is born of Śāṇḍilī, or Araṇī, or water, whose father is Brahman, or Aṅgiras, and who is sire of all the gods as well as sprung from the mouth of Viṣṇu and appears as a form of Rudra and is listed among Pitṛs and among Viśve Devas (above, and 13, 91, 29) and Vasus, is not a god to be genealogically fixed. One recurrent phrase makes him chief of the Vasus (Holtzmann) and this is the only important item (Āpa Saha mentioned above as an Agni, husband of Muditā, is a Vasu in H 152. Cf. 6, 34, 23; 7, 6, 5, etc.). Śāṇḍilī (and Agni Śāṇḍilya) as mother is distinctly later than Araṇī. Besides the Sudarśana of the legend above, Dṛṣtadyumna is son, i. e. a bhāga or part of Agni; and Agniveśa was a saintly hero "born of Agni". He learned the use of "fire-arms" (āgneyam astram is used by gods and heroes) from Bharadvāja and taught them to Dṛṣtadyumna's father (1, 130, 39 f.). The north-eastern mountaineers in general are also born of Agni (7, 112, 31, Kirātā Agniyonayaḥ), perhaps because Agni's district is the East (cf. VS. 9, 35, Agninetrā Devāḥ are in the East), though as world-protector he has the South-east (4, 30, 25, his district is East), but his altar inclines to the North-east (R 2, 99, 24). As sons of Agni, the Rāmāyaṇa adds Nīla (the ape) and "fiery-mouth", Ulkāmukha, also Asaṅga (R 1, 17, 12; ib. 4, 41, 2 f.; ib. 6, 30, 25), and the "very glorious saint" Suprabha is also "son of Agni" (R 7, 96, 4). Agni himself is the ape-sun (3, 3, 61) Vṛṣākapi

(H 12292, etc.), but only as supreme Ātman (Śiva, 7, 202, 136). Agnikanyāpura is the city of the "girls of Agni", but they are the divine maidens of his harem (13, 25, 43). H 7738 assigns them to Umā's court, though H (73 and 83) also recognises, as real daughters of Agni, Āgneyī and Dhiṣaṇā. The saints called Agniṣvāttas and Agnidagdhas might be called connections of Agni, as they are regarded as Pitṛs, "without fire and with fire", according to VP., where they follow the enumeration of fires (VP. 1, 10, 18); but they are apparently connected only through having been burned by Agni (or eaten) at what the epic calls the Agnicaya or Agnirāśi (RG 4, 60, 17).

The relation between Agni and the other gods has already been shown in part. Kṛṣṇa (q. v.) overcomes him, but he is one with Kṛṣṇa-Viṣṇu, as he is one with Śiva, for whom he "removes difficulties" (12, 343, 23), and with the Sun. He is especial friend of Vāyu and fights against the demons (Asura Bali, 7, 25, 20) on Indra's side, but against Indra in his own interest, to aid the Vālakhilyas in creating Garuda, as also against Varuṇa and other gods (Khāṇḍava, 1, 225, 13 f.). The Agniṣṭut, because it praises Agni alone, is disliked by Indra (13, 12, 4 f., Indradviṣṭa). Vāyu is friend and soul of Agni (cf. Vāyu as father of Agni, § 49) and the friendship of the two is as proverbial as that of David and Jonathan (cf. 3, 147, 29, "the love of Agni and Anila"). "Pavana the friend of Anala" lives in the western district (5, 110, 19), but Agni's own district is in the East (above). Together they create the White Mountain and Śaravana, birth-place of Kārttikeya, through Śiva's seed, and with the seed Agni produces gold in the Ganges (R 1, 36, 19; ib. 37, 22); Agni as Vāyusamanvitaḥ; cf. 6, 86, 20, Agner Vāyusahāyasya yathā kakṣaṃ didhakṣataḥ, but whether personification as divinities be intended here may be doubted. Agni and Soma (united above in the late Mārkaṇḍeya episode as forms of fires, Agnīṣomau) are "born from the eyes of Brahman" in the hodge-podge of 12, 343, 9 f., sa Puruṣaḥ prajāḥ sisṛkṣamāṇo netrābhyām Agnīṣomau sasarja; cf. ib. 342, 68, Agniḥ Somena saṃyukta ekayonitvam āgataḥ. An attempt is made here to cast them as priestly and warrior-like into different orders, but it is confused, as Agni is a Brahman and Brahmans are Agnibhūtāḥ (ib. 343, 15), and Agni is also a Kṣatriya: yaḥ Somas tad Brahma yad Brahma te Brāhmaṇā, yo 'gnis tat Kṣatraṃ, Kṣatrād Brahma balavattaram (ib. 9). The Vedic distinction (ŚB. 10, 4, 1, 5) between Agni as the priestly caste and Indra as the warrior (so created) is here lost sight of (cf. Agnīṣomīyaṃ Brahma, 12, 343, 65 f.; the two gods uphold the priestly power). Agni will carry no oblations in a kingless land (12, 67, 5). Soma and Agni, combined in the East, appear as the "two eyes of Dharma", because it is the East which was first made the starting-point of oblations (so at least N. explains cakṣuṣī Dharmasya, 5, 108, 4). Agni is Kumārasū (Skanda is Āgneya, 3, 232, 3; Agnija, R 7, 4, 24), and is Śiva (and Brahman, 13, 85, 147), whose eye he is (13, 14, 324), and general lord of Pitṛs (ib. 313), whom he saves from indigestion, as he does the gods, by keeping off the indigestion devils (12, 92, 10 f.). He is himself in epical and Vedic literature "all the gods" (3, 224, 20, S has agniḥ sarvāś ca devatāḥ). That Agni is all the gods, is called a devasya śāsanam (14, 24, 10, read vedasya?). As father of Kumāra (S 7, 41, 28 calls Kumāra Vahnisuta), Agni gives him a goat, chāga, the vehicle of Agni, with which he is identified (13, 86, 24). The Kṛttikās and Agni constitute the "asterism and divinity of the sword", respectively (12, 166,

82). In 3, 231, 44, Skanda is Kṛttikāsuta and the Kṛttikās are a "seven-headed" asterism (3, 230, 11) of the personified Sword (as Dharma), and (1, 221, 85) they are the nakṣatraṃ Vahnidaivatam, that is, Agni is their divinity, which shows that the Kṛttikās means sword and also that Agni himself was understood as a war-god. He takes upon himself part of the sin of Indra, on condition that he may cast the sin off again upon those who do no not worship him with "seeds, plants, and flowers", but this is a sectarian insertion in favor of bloodless sacrifice (12, 283, 31 f.). Another slight indication of Agni's being a warrior (besides his actual battles) may be found in the comparison introduced when he searches for the lost Indra and fears water, "since fire arose from water as the kingly power arose from the priestly" (each is overcome by its source, 5, 15, 34 = 38, 13). Having found Indra, Agni agrees to help him on the understanding that he shall share in Indra's great ceremony, Mahākratu (Indrāgnyor bhāga ekaḥ, 5, 16, 32). Agni helps Indra's son particularly by giving him (Arjuna) his bow and ape-standard (1, 61, 47 f.). His insatiate greed (5, 26, 6) has the general redeeming feature that "he is unwearied in doing work for man" (5, 29, 10). Agni's beauty is often spoken of, especially at night, and when strengthened by prayer and butter, mantrahutārcimālī (6, 60, 25). The abhimantrita fire only a boaster pretends to defy (5, 61, 9). Fires as heroes defend Bāṇa's city (H 10458 f.).

§ 53. As the god of ritual, Agni is recognised as approached by the threefold circumambulation. The bird that sacrifices itself in fire "goes thrice around Agni" as a beginning (agniṃ triḥ parikramya, 12, 146, 23), and in the marriage-ceremony this is the rule (R 1, 73, 36, trir agniṃ te parikramya ūhur bhāryāḥ). As upholder of priests, his rule is their model: "the law of Fire is the law of priests" (12, 141, 64; here, in contrast to the aindro dharmaḥ of warriors, the āgniko dharmaḥ gives the right to eat all things: brahma vahnir, mama balam, says Viśvāmitra when hungry enough to eat a dog). As one ceremonially impure may not look at Sun, Moon, or stars, or touch a cow or priest, so he (the ucchiṣṭa, 13, 104, 63) may not touch Fire. Such a man is excommunicated, "Agni accepts not his oblation" (13, 126, 29 f.). Nor can any oblation be made without fire: naṣṭaṃ hutam anagnikam (5, 39, 42). Above it was shown that Agni as pāpahan burns sinners (cf. 12, 68, 42, pāpān dahati, of the king functioning as Agni). But Agni has the same rôle when acting as the Saṃvartaka fire. Compare 5, 48, 65: "Like Agni at the end of the age, introducing a new age, I shall burn all the hosts of robbers, destroying them" (N. yugānte śatrūṇāṃ saṃhāre jāte sati), though it may be forced to assume that here the simile implies Agni pāpahan. Elsewhere, however, the Fire of Destruction is expressly to bring to an end the Kali age and reissue goodness unsullied. As averter of obstacles (above) Agni precedes Gaṇeśa, (§ 145), who appears only as deus ex machina in Ādi, and in this rôle, as well as giver of boons, he is said to have blessed Gaya; he also introduces here the pernicious doctrine of the "grace of the Guru". Thus he grants Gaya the power to know the Vedas without study, simply, as Gaya begs, through "austerity, chastity, observances, vows, and the grace of the Gurus" (7, 66, 2 f.). Gaya concludes: avighnaṃ cā 'stu me nityaṃ dharmakāryeṣu, Pāvaka, "may there never be any obstacle in the performance of my duties", which request the god granted. To honor his own Guru, Bṛhaspati, and Indra, Agni, sent as a messenger by Indra, goes to Marutta and accepts hospitality, but when Marutta says that he will burn Agni with his (Marutta's) eyes, the Fire-god, "afraid of being burned", trembles and runs away (14, 9, 8 f.). In another section of the same book (58, 46), Agni burns fiercely to aid Utañka, after first appearing to him in the form of a black horse, and saying that he was his Guru's Guru. So by burning he frightened the Nāgas into giving Utañka the stolen ear-rings, as elsewhere (1, 3, 128 f.) the ancient Apāmgarbha Vaiśvānara is the horse of Indra (ib. 149; cf. yo 'śvaḥ so 'gniḥ, 167). Usually as horse he is white; his light has power and he is fearless; though like the light of the Sun his light cannot penetrate the "darkness of Death's realm" (in the South, 5, 109, 21, tamaḥ .. abhedyaṃ bhāskareṇā 'pi svayaṃ vā Kṛṣṇavartmanā). In H 13928 f., Agni is described as general Devadūta (messenger of the gods), whose soul is Wind, whose source is water, as he is the water's source, the red one clothed in blue, chief of gods (devāgryaḥ), the maker of the Vedas (Vedakartṛ, epithet of the Sun), the hara of oblations, and Hari; also Svadhādhipa, Svāhāpati, Devadeva, Rudrātman, etc., where, as warrior, he overthrows the Daityas. Otherwise, Devadūta is not applied to Agni, though it is not an uncommon expression and in 3, 55, 22 f. is used of Nala as messenger of Agni himself, inter alios (in 3, 260, 30 f., the "messenger of the gods" who converses with Maudgalya is not named). Agni's last appearance in the great epic is as a mountainous obstruction in the path of the heroes who are climbing up to heaven. He bids Arjuna cast into the ocean the bow the god had given him after receiving it himself from Varuṇa, and when the restitution was accomplished, "seven-flamed Pāvaka disappeared" (17, 1, 43). The epic does not ascribe to Agni the later epithets, Abjahasta, Tomaradhara, Rohitāśva, and Chāgaratha, though it suggests all save the first ("lotus in hand").[1] In H 11360 f., the sixteen priests of the fire-cult are enumerated, with many textual errors in C (= 3, 10, 6 f.), some of whom, like the Hotṛ, Śamitṛ, and Sāmaga (3, 100, 14) are common enough to be incidentally mentioned in the epic itself; others (Āgnīdhra, Neṣṭṛ, etc.) are too technical to find a place there, though all of course were well known, as were the Agnihotras (3, 82, 36, etc.) and Agniṣṭomas (ib. 83, 88 f.) incidentally referred to (with atirātras). Agnyāhitas and Anāhitāgnis (those wo do and do not keep up the sacred fires) are also mentioned in both epics, but these or equivalent terms are found everywhere. An Agni-Tīrtha is mentioned in 3, 84, 46 (Agnidhārāṃ samāsādya triṣu lokeṣu viśrutām, tatrā 'bhiṣekaṃ kurvāṇo hy Agniṣṭomam avāpnuyāt), as being so celebrated that a bath there brings the reward of an Agniṣṭoma. On "hell-fire", see § 54 f., and on Soma and Agni, § 45.

§ 54. **Yama.** — Yama is the son of Vivasvat (see Ādityas, § 32). According to 1, 75, 11 f., Yama Vaivasvata, son of Vivasvat Mārtāṇḍa, was born after Manu (also son of Vivasvat). Instead of the last statement, S has "and also Yamī was born as daughter of Mārtāṇḍa" (S 1, 69, 15). In H 552, the pair are called Yama and Yamunā. But the twin sister plays no part in the epic as such, being only a relic of the old Vedic myth. As Yama is sometimes identified with Kāla (Time, as the universal destroyer), the scholiast identifies with the sister of Yama the "sister of Kāla", Bhayā Kālabhaginī, who married Heti, the Rākṣasa king, father by her of Vidyutkeśa, who married the daughter of Sandhyā called Sālaka-

[1]) For a very complete monograph on Agni, in the Great Epic, cf. Adolph Holtzmann, Agni nach den Vorstellungen des Mahābhārata (1878).

ṭaṅkaṭā, mother of Sukeśa, whose three sons warred with the gods till, overcome by Viṣṇu and Garuḍa, they abandoned Laṅkā and fled under earth (R 7, 4, 16f., and 23; ib. 8, 49). According to Mbh., S 2, 23, 20f., the event described in VP. 5, 1, 70f., where it is said that the birth of Balarāma was transferred from Devakī to Rohiṇī through the agency of Viṣṇu's power, yoganidrā (cf. H 3306), took place through the activity of Yama by means of yāmyā māyā. The word here means "constraining", with which signification the epic always connects the god's name (6, 34, 29, Yamaḥ saṃyamatām aham, distinct from Kāla, ib. 30). The same notion underlies the raudrāṇi yāmyāni sāmāni, imprecative Mantras (2, 80, 8; or "addressed to Yama"?). Yamālaya is often a paraphrase for death itself (3, 313, 116). In Yamakṣaya there is a play on the double sense, "abode" or "destruction" of Yama (R 2, 60, 3; R 4, 53, 36 and often), and so Vaivasvatakṣaya (3, 96, 9; R 7, 73, 8), though the usual expression is Yamasādana (2, 77, 18; R 3, 22, 4, etc.), or equivalents (yiyāsur Yamalokāya, 7, 84, 28; Yamasya gehābhimukhaṃ hi pāpam [tvāṃ nayāmi], R 7, 68, 20), A vaguer term is viṣaya (9, 53, 20; R 2, 9, 63). Even a boar is addressed: nayāmi daṇḍadhārasya Yamasya sadanam prati (3, 39, 48; cf. ib. 10, netādya Yamasādanam, according to metre), for (see below) animals "go to Yama's abode". It is called the "city of the king of ghosts", Pretarājapura (1, 67, 122) and Dharmarājaniveśana (3, 240, 30, the objective of slain heroes in both cases). No distinction is made between this abode of the King of Justice and Naraka, hell (cf. R 2, 12, 89 and 92). Here "Death" leads one to Yama's abode, but usually the slayer leads (1, 41, 14; ib. 94, 21; ib. 151, 40; ib. 153, 29, gamiṣyāmi tvām adya Yamasādanam, for yātayiṣyāmi or gamayiṣyāmi). Heroes dying in battle are said to increase the realm of the god, Yamarāṣṭravivardhanāḥ (6, 79, 60 and oft); being "dedicated" thereto, Yamarāṣṭrāya mahate paralokāya dīkṣitāḥ (7, 153, 2; cf. pretaloka, ib. 155, 14). Paraloka appears as v. l. of Yamaloka (4, 16, 51 = S 20, 70). On the sacrificial aspect of battle, cf. 5, 58, 12; 12, 20, 12, etc. Yamasya netṛ is applied to Rāma (as Indra) "bringing to Yama" heroes slain (3, 25, 10). The son "leads his father up" out of hell (1, 74, 111). He who dies cannot escape the city of the king of ghosts (1, 118, 31f.); he "comes into the ghost-power" (Pretavaśaṃ gataḥ, S 1, 134, 71f., where Preta implies Pretarāj or Pitṛpati, 7, 50, 14, with v. l.). Besides being Pitṛpati, Yama is Dharmendra, acting as judge; as when he sentences Nṛga, who, after going to the Pitṛ-world of Yama and being ordered back, "falls headlong into a well", evidently from a confusion between the heavenly abode of Pitṛs and the lower home of ghosts (13, 70, 20f.). But the Pitṛs too in the epic live in the South: nayāmi vaḥ..diśam Pitṝṇām aśivām (S 5, 59, 13); "I saw Yama established in the South" (3, 168, 14); "Yama, righteous king and lord of all beings, presides over the South, the course of departed spirits" (3, 163, 8; yāmyā dik = South). The "sacred and marvellous palace of the Pretarāja" is called Saṃyamana (ib. 9). In 7, 142, 10 (not in S) it is called Saṃyamanī, as in 13, 102, 14: "Vaivasvatī saṃyamanī janānām" (the poets love to parody) = Vaivasvatasya sādanam, "where only truth is spoken, and the weak torment the strong" (ib. 16). In 7, 72, 44, Saṃyamanī sadā sukṛtināṃ gatiḥ is the abode of the dead, rendered glorious by the brightness of warrior slain, though Vaivasvata, Varuṇa, Śatakratu (Indra), and Dhaneśa (Kubera) are all represented as receiving him as guest (see Lokapālas). It is called the "royal residence", rājadhānī Yamasya (7, 83, 27). "Yama's rājadhānī, envelopped in darkness, (lies) beyond the end of earth" (in the South, R 4, 41, 45, as Pitṛloka). To be more exact, as is Mārkaṇḍeya, it lies eighty-six thousand leagues from the world of men (3, 200, 46). All human beings who die have to go to Yama's abode, but the inhabitants of Kurukṣetra do not have to "see the province of Yama", that is, on dying they will go direct to heaven (9, 53, 20, Yamasya viṣayaṃ te tu na drakṣyanti kadācana). Also there are tales of people and animals being taken direct to heaven. Thus in 13, 102, 62, Indra takes a priest and his pet elephant direct to heaven, and in the battle-scenes it is clear that heroes are thought of as being conveyed at once to abodes of bliss, their life-sacrifice exonerating them from all liabilities. Also animals "go to Yama"; he is prajāsaṃyamano Yamaḥ (3, 297, 66), constrainer of all creatures born. Compare 6, 77, 69: "With four arrows he dispatched the four war-horses to the horrible home of Yama (Vaivasvatakṣayaṃ ghoram) and with one arrow sent to death (mṛtyave) the charioteer" (cf. ib. 79, 11, aśvān anayad Yamasādanam). Even battle-cars are sent to the world of Death (Mṛtyulokāya, 7, 28, 30). But here they are conjoined with elephants and horses. Other passages show that not only human beings, but all "living beings" go to Yama's abode. Thus in 3, 200, 40f., the province and the road to it are described. It is as horrible as a dense jungle, but no trees give shade, as one goes to it. There is no water to drink, no place to rest. By the "messengers of Yama, who do his will" are dragged along the dead, men, women, and all other animate creatures of the earth (anye pṛthivyāṃ jīvasaṃjñitāḥ). But those who have been generous and ascetic find relief. Those who have given lamps have the way lighted; those who have fasted are carried by geese and peacocks. There is a river (§ 4) called Puṣpodakā, which is as pus to those who have done ill, but sweet water to those who have in life given water to others. In general, those who have been generous (to priests) "are free from Yama's words", which seems to be a repetition of what is said ib. vs. 24, namely that they who have been hospitable (to priests, bien entendu) do not go to Yama at all (no 'pasarpanti te Yamam), i. e. as judge. The further statement that one who gives saṃskṛtam annam (cooked food) to the priests (vipreṣu) obtains the world of Brahman, because Prajāpati is food (ib. 38 = Praś. Up. 1, 9, etc.) may also imply the direct ascent. Three persons "go the same", samaṃ yanti, the giver of food, speaker of truth, and he who gives without solicitation (ib. 42). Fear, Terror, and Death are sons of Wrong, Adharma, and Nirṛti Devī, mother of Nairṛtas, who keeps watch and ward over sinners (1, 66, 53f.; 12, 122, 46). Nirṛti is exit from life and so, as destruction ("he binds destruction, nirṛti, upon his mouth who speaks unkindly", 1, 87, 9) synonymous with niraya (cf. niryāṇa, death) and Naraka, the place of spirits below earth and place of those destroyed. Compare 5, 29, 45, ete vinaṣṭāḥ kṣayaṃ gatā narakaṃ dīrghakālam, like barren sesame seeds, ṣaṇḍhatilāḥ, "they have gone to destruction for the long time" (of thirteen years). They are not dead but banished and so gone to hell (destruction). In the same breath Kaikeyī is addressed as nirayagāmini and told to go to hell (destruction), narakaṃ gaccha, mā ca bhartuḥ salokatām (R 2, 74, 4 and 12); narakaṃ vrajet means "go to destruction". Those who look at Rāma with evil eye are smitten by Yama's rod and go at once to niraya (R 7, 82, 11). Narake and nidhane interchange as v. l.

when it is said that a priest-slayer's family fall to hell (destruction), in answer to a doubt as to whether hell exists, or, as expressed immediately after, "those sinners who do not sacrifice do not get to yonder world (heaven), but meet onslaughts (āpātān, N. narakān), just as savages do" (Pulindas and Śabaras). The explanation of this term (12, 151, 8) is elucidated by the concrete case: "Thou, who art guilty of priest-murder, shalt fall headlong for successive years; there shalt thou be tortured by vultures and peacocks having beaks of iron, and after that thou shalt be reborn on earth in a low form. Thou thinkest, dost thou, that the next world amounts to nothing? Let me tell you that Yama's messengers in Yama's home will remind you of the contrary" (pratismārayitāras tvām, 12, 150, 15f.). A sinner is "cooked by fire terribly in awful hell" (narake ghore, 3, 128, 12; as narakāgni). He finds woe in the river in Yamakṣaya (12, 302, 31). Dogs, ospreys, crows, with iron beaks, and vultures, all drinkers of blood, enter the body of one who disobeys his Gurus; and in man's destruction, narakadane, and going to hell, paramanirayaga, in hell, mahāniraye (Yāj. 3, 222), after he has sunk into the forest in the province of Pitṛs, Pitṛviṣayavipinam avagāhya, he is pierced with the wood's sharp axes and swords, plunged under hot Vaitaraṇī (§ 4) and comes for judgment before Yama, whose wind blows before him that is about to die (purā 'bhivāti māruto Yamasya yaḥ puraḥsaraḥ, etc., iambics, 12, 322, 29f.). Here Vaitaraṇī is mahānadī as if one with the Mahānadī river in Kaliṅga, two hundred and fifty miles south-west of Calcutta ("Byeturnee" in Cuttack), where "Dharma once sacrificed and Śiva once seized the sacrifice, upon whose northern bank lies the gods' way, the path to heaven" (3, 114, 4f.), a river holy enough to remove the sins of those that bathe in it (3, 85, 6). The river of Yama of the same name is also called Mahāvaitaraṇī (6, 59, 127) and is in Yama's southern district, "near the town of Yama", but it is horrible, raudrā ghorā (6, 103, 38; 7, 146, 37; ib. 171, 51), though also, as above, it is represented as in the home of Yama (12, 302, 31). Its heat, uṣṇā Vaitaraṇī, accords with its southern position. Vaitaraṇī is the river of passage filled with vaitaraṇas, passengers (5, 109, 14). The uncertainty as to whether the Vaitaraṇī is in Yama's realm or only leads to it and its double character as a holy river, Mahānadī, and as the river of torture in hell, makes it probable that it is the same river under two aspects. The heat is transcribed by "acid" (heat) below.

§ 55. In hell, cruel men with clubs, lances, and pots of fire torment sinners, who are also tortured by forests of swords, hot sands, thorny trees, and yātanās (torments) of various kinds, until, purified but not yet free, they are reborn as worms, etc. (13, 111, 92f.). Men slay again here those already slain; a field of carnage, where lie heaps of slain men, horses, and elephants, resembles the realm of Yama (8, 92, 10). Incorporate though the ghosts be, yet these Pretas feel the mutilations to which they are exposed and shriek aloud. Worms gnaw them; dogs (sārameyas) devour them; they are plunged into the river of blood, Vaitaraṇī; they are burned in hot sand, cut by sword-leaf trees, plunged into the hell of roaring, Raurava, and into the river of acids, kṣāranadī (Vaitaraṇī), and cut on razor-blades. They beg in vain for water; they hunger and thirst, and are pale and wretched, appearing, with loosened hair, muddy and rough (R 7, 21, 12f.). Both the river of acids and the river of pus (above) are elsewhere unknown to either epic, but Jain literature recognises the acid stream as Vaitaraṇī (Sūtrakṛtāṅga, 1, 5, 1, 8 and Uttarādhyayana 19, 59). In the Rām. scene, Rāvaṇa attacks Yama and sees these horrors as he approaches the realm, defended by Yama (and Vama's anucaras), Kāla, and Mṛtyu, conceived (as in 9, 45, 17) as distinct personalities, though, as already remarked, often identified (cf. 2, 56, 10: "Be happy while you can; neither disease nor Yama = death will wait for you to become happy"). Another passage introduces Yama and Death as one and is further remarkable for its reference to the tree of torture: "Didst not thou (Rāvaṇa) plunge beneath the ocean of Yama's army, whose monster is the rod of Death, (that ocean) adorned with Śālmalī trees, having as its mighty billows the noose of Kāla, and as its serpents the servant (club) of Yama, to win a great victory and repulse Death?" (R 6, 7, 13 f.). The Śālmalī (also -i) is the tree of torture in hell (as hell, cf. Manu 4, 90 and Yāj. 3, 222), known to later literature but not to the early epic. Sītā alludes to it in R 3, 53, 20: "The noose of Kāla noosed about thy neck I see; thou seest golden trees (art about to die); thou lookest upon the horrible Vaitaraṇī rolling down its flood of blood, and the fearful wood whose leaves are swords; and soon shalt thou see the Śālmalī tree, sharp, and loaded with thorns of iron, though its blossoms are of gold and its leaves of beryl". It belongs to the later epic and Purāṇas (cf. the kūṭaśālmali of the Red Sea, R 4, 40, 37; and as torture-tree, 13, 111, 93; 18, 2, 25; ib. 3, 4). As already indicated, Yama's hell is but temporary. A seller of Soma spends thirty (v. l. three hundred) years in the hell Raurava (13, 101, 13) and is then reborn in a low form, where (ib. 24) he may have a memory of former births. A murderer's years in hell equal the number of drops he sheds. Adulterers live in hell as many years as the body has pores (ib. 104, 22 etc.), etc. Hell is a watery place, a lake (3, 58, 2; 10, 5, 14), a muddy hole (R 5, 27, 27). Hells are spoken of as the "lowest worlds" (adhamā lokāḥ, 3, 199, 14) but how many there are is doubtful. Kālasūtra in 3, 157, 45 is not a hell but Fate's line baited for man. Manu and Yājñavalkya (loc. cit. above) recognise twenty-one hells. The Viṣṇu-Purāṇa, naming twenty-eight, adds that there are many others (VP. 2, 6, 28, "hundreds and thousands"), in fact a different hell for every kind of offence or at most for small groups of allied offences. These hells of the later eschatology are really compartments of the general "province of Yama" and are situated in VP. under the seven strata below earth's surface. Many of the later names are those used as descriptive epithets in the epic, such as "sword-leaf forest", somewhat as attributes of gods become special gods. Others are quite new and unknown to either epic, while a few attributives or descriptive terms, already names in the epic, are retained (Raurava, Kāla), although the sinners occupying them are not the same. But the chief interest from the epic point of view lies in the fact that the twenty-one or twenty-eight hells of the later period point to an original seven by first trebling and then quadrupling. As the epic has Rasātala as the seventh stratum (5, 102, 1) below earth's surface and places there the hell to which a liar goes (13, 6, 34), while the evil demons are punished by being confined in Pātāla, and as the worlds are seven (3, 3, 45), it is probable that this sacrosanct number operated to fix the hells, confused with strata, as seven (afterwards increased threefold). A survival of this primitive belief may perhaps be found in 13, 45, 19, which says that verses sung by Yama himself are to the effect that a man who sells his son or his daughter (by accepting a price, śulka, for her) "obtains as his portion urine and excrements in the hell called Kāla", niraye Kālasāhvaye, described as saptāvare mahāghore. Of course, saptāvare should be nominative plural. It usually introduces the statement that "seven earlier and seven later" (ancestors and descendants) suffer for a man's crime (as in 7, 198, 15; or in the form saptā 'varān sapta pūrvān punāti, 3, 186, 16; cf. 3, 85, 92 and 13, 26, 62, etc.); but here as the verb and subject are singular (mūḍhaḥ samaśnute) this in impossible and the author of the gāthā Yamodgītāḥ must have connected saptāvare with the following mahāghore niraye as a locative. A "hell on earth" (narako bhaumaḥ 1, 90, 4 f.) is rebirth (also as nom. prop.) and the tormenters here are Rākṣasas (vs. 8), but this is metaphor. To be reborn is hell, and earthly interests are the fiends that plague the soul, preventing it from entering the "seven doors of heaven" (ib. 22, seven moral qualities; N. says the fiends are wives!). That the hells actually are seven in number is asserted by several later authors (Rām. Ved. Sūtra, 3, 1, 15, etc.), both Brahmanic and sectarian, probably first Brahmanic. If in the (Jain) Uttarādhyayana 31, 12, the "fifteen", rather doubtfully recorded by Professor Jacobi according to names, could be fourteen (?), it would be a link between the seven and others (above).

§ 56. Yama as a god of war carries a bow (yāmyaṃ dhanuḥ, 7, 23, 94), which he gives to a mortal hero, and arrows given by him are also mentioned (R 6, 91, 46, Indrajit shoots a Yamadatta against Vibhīṣaṇa, the arrow of the god of justice being used by the fiend against virtue!). Usually Yama carries a rod (of justice) and noose (to catch souls). The battle-club or rod inspires that "fear of the other world" which alone makes men virtuous (12, 15, 5 f.; cf. 3, 56, 10). The rod itself is then personified and becomes Daṇḍa, a form of Yama himself (only a Śūdra is nirdaṇḍa, 12, 15, 9 f.). Yama and Antaka, "end-maker" (Death), are each daṇḍapāṇi (cf. daṇḍapāṇir ivā 'ntakaḥ or iva kruddhaḥ, standing phrases). Yama is higher. Yama wins the battle and Antaka cuts off the heads (3, 139, 14). He is classed with Kubera, Varuṇa, and Rudra as a warrior (5, 162, 27; 6, 83, 41). Yama uses also the Kāladaṇḍa, while Death and Kāla admire him (R 7, 22, 23 f.). The arrows of heroes are like Yama's daṇḍa, as is also Bhīma's great club (3, 154, 17; 6, 85, 33). The image is so conventionalised that one can say (3, 11, 43): "like Indra he let fall his club like Yama's". An unusual image compares an arrow to Yama's tongue or Antaka's tongue (7, 179, 54; 9, 11, 52). One who "has entered Yama's fangs" is virtually dead (7, 110, 19). "The door of Death" (Mṛtyu) opens upon Yama's home (R 4, 6, 25 f.). Both Kāla and Mṛtyu bear nooses and on occasion are felt as poetical equivalents of Yama, though, when analysed, Kāla is to Yama as Yama is to Mṛtyu, the superior power. Death's noose, rod, world, place, "the fangs of Death", etc., are all used as of Yama. Even Mṛtyuḥ kiṃkaradaṇḍabhṛt occurs (8, 56, 120) and an arrow is "like Mṛtyu's tongue" (v. l. sister, svasām for jihvām, 6, 116, 3; cf. 7, 116, 54). The servants of Yama are messengers or kiṃkaras, who live in the North as well as elsewhere (R 6, 74, 59). The club is the god's servant, so that a warrior is described as "like Yama with his servant (club) in hand" (9, 32, 42; cf. 50). Kiṃkaras are also a class of Rākṣasas (p. 45). In 13, 62, 27, Mṛtyur Vaikiṃkaraḥ is taken by the scholiast to be a derivative of Vikiṃkara (Kāla), "son of Time" (viparītaṃ karoti); but vai must be a separate word, Kiṃkara being the club of Yama. In 3, 298, 38, since Yama here comes alone and carries no club, there is a purely conventional force in sakiṃkaraḥ. The messengers, Yamadūtāḥ, are (like) Rākṣasas, having pointed ears, huge mouths, and reddish hair, and being deformed but massive (12, 138, 117). They fetch the dead (3, 297, 14) with exceeding speed (5, 151, 26). Rudras are also attendants on Yama, as Maruts are on Vāsava (3, 237, 11), and a hero is said to be appear like Antaka, rod in hand, like Rudra, and like Yama with the Rudras (6, 102, 36f.). Either Yama or his messengers noose the soul of the dying (11, 4, 11 and 3, 297, 17). In the last passage Yama does the work of his men, puruṣas, and is described as king of Pitṛs, Lord (Bhagavat, Deveśa, Īśvara, etc.), appearing with a diadem and red clothes, shapely, dark, with red eyes, glorious as his father the sun, and bearing a noose in hand. Philosophy sees in failure of the senses the messengers of Yama (R 2, 64, 66) and forms of Time (Kāla), while man's body is Yama's car (11, 7, 12, read vidhayaḥ with S; ib. 19, yāmyam āhū ratham). The tales treat the messengers more mythologically. Yama once said to a certain man clothed in black, who had red eyes and hair and the legs, eyes, and nose of a crow (the bird of death): "Do thou go to Brahman-town and fetch hither a man of the Agastya clan whose name is Śarmin. Don't make a mistake and fetch the wrong man". But Yama's messenger made the mistake and got another man named Śarmin, who on arriving wished to stay. But Yama told him that this was impossible; he did not understand Kāla's orders or he would not ask such a thing. So he was exchanged for the right Śarmin after a lecture from Yama (13, 68, 5 f.). The god also lectures Nāciketa (13, 71, 7f.), when this boy, cursed by his father to "see Yama" (die), fell as if thunderstruck and went to Yama. His father's tears, however, caused life to sprout in him and he returned to consciousness and told his father what he had seen. He said he had found the Vaivasvatā Sabhā or Hall of Yama a very charming place and had seen the worlds of the good where rivers ran milk and mountains were made of butter. In H 4924, Kṛṣṇa makes Ocean and Yama restore the drowned son of Sāṃdīpani.

§ 57. The Sabhā here mentioned is more fully described in 2, 8; it was made by Viśvakarman (All-maker), is more than a hundred leagues in extent, golden and sunny, where wishes are granted, and there is no cold, hunger, sorrow, old age, etc.; but all good things "to lick and chew" are there (all is tasty, rasavat; cf. Yama's gift to Nala, 3, 57, 37, annarasa). This palace contains royal and priestly seers (some found again in the palace of Indra), kings, saints, and heroes (Nala, the two Rāmas, etc.); also Kāla and Mṛtyu, Pitṛs, those who die during the southern course of the sun, etc. They are cheered with dance and song. Besides those mentioned there are also the Wheel of Time and "Yama's men appointed to lead time", that is, to reckon men's lives, as well as many trees and other incorporate objects. The Fire-god is in the Sabhā too, and all revere Dharmarāja (Yama). Late as is this passage, comparatively, it fails to mention at the court of Yama his scribe Citragupta, who belongs in fact entirely to the post-epical period of the pseudo-epic (13, 125, 6 and ib. 130, 14f.). At 5, 109, 6, Nīlakaṇṭha understands Citragupta to be implied by nigadyate (in the South, "Dharma, truth and Karman are reported there, and there is the fruit of action for the dead"), but there is no such implication. Even when Citragupta is mentioned, the Sun, as witness of acts, "reports" them when one dies (13, 130, 17). The late passage 1, 74, 30f., which speaks of Yama punishing sinners, says only that the witnesses of the evil act are the gods, Sun, Moon, Wind, Fire, Sky, Earth, Water, the heart, and Yama himself. Noticeable also but not unexpected is the fact that Yama's abode is one of bliss. As a god he lives happily and his residence is a heaven of saints and heroes like those of other gods. The antithesis is brought out clearly in several passages. Though he goes with "death and diseases" in a parade (3, 231, 36; Antaka's charioteer is Roga, disease, 12, 322, 42), yet he is master of the diseases, etc., and so can give Hanumat immunity from disease (R 7, 36, 17). As Dhamarāja, king of justice and right, he may even allow an exchange, whereby, if an equitable substitute be offered, one's death may be deferred. Thus Ruru by permission of Dharmarāja gives up half of what remains of his life to restore Pramadvarā to life (1, 9, 31 f.). The parents of the boy killed by Daśaratha will ask Yama as Dharmarāja to take them instead of the boy (R 2, 64, 28 f.). As god of right he is good to the good and bad to the bad (he also has goods, and is renowned as having wealth and happiness, a Plutos as well as a Pluto, R 5, 9, 9; ib. 6, 114, 33). He chastises, but as instructor: anuśāsti .. śivaḥ śivānām aśivo 'śivānām, but as death at his command comes to man as vices and "there is no death but this, though some call Yama death" (5, 42, 6 f.), so, to the pious, death is only a tiger made of grass, having no terrors for the good (ib. 15). There is much of this higher teaching and also allusions to hell as merely low births, as on the other hand there are allusions to hell eternal (3, 183, 70; 5, 132, 20, etc.); but one is a denial of a popular belief and the other is due to extravagance, for no one believes in eternal hell, and few believe in a hell merely mental, or expressed in terms of low birth. But the principle that Yama is not evil to the good leads back to the belief that good people who go to him enjoy themselves. Only the evil mourn in Yama's sādanam (13, 102, 14 f.). He is śubhakarman, "whose acts are noble" (8, 45, 31 f.). The viṣaya or province of Yama contains frightful regions, but also regions worthy of the gods, so that his abode is like that of Brahman (13, 111, 41 f.) On Rāvaṇa's inroad he saw the good rejoicing in song and music; those who had given houses during life now lived in beautiful houses and had gold and gems and radiated glory as they went. Rāvaṇa released the wretched sinners and for a moment they too enjoyed themselves; but then the Pretagopas (ghost-guards) and other Yamayodhas attacked the fiend and being assisted by Yama, Mṛtyu, and Kāla would have overthrown him had not Brahman intervened. Apparently on the appearance of their guards the sinful ghosts return to torment (R 7, 21, 10 f.). Only here is Yama's rod described as having nooses at its sides (Kālapāśas on Kāladaṇḍa, used by Yama). Yama helps that female death whose tears become diseases (R 7, 22, 24 f.; Mbh. 7, 54, 40 = 12, 259, 34 f., a late conception), an awful but beneficent power. In old days, Viṣṇu once assumed the part of Yama, Yamatvaṃ kārayāmāsa, and no one died (3, 142, 35). Then the population of the earth increased to such an extent that earth sank down under the weight and Viṣṇu had to raise her (see Viṣṇu). Possibly this may reflect the view of the Indo-Iranian Yama-Yima.[1]) The tale appears in various forms. In 1, 197, 1 f., Yama becomes Śamitṛ, or cook of the gods, preparing their sacrifice (see above on the rasa), and so men ceased to die. Again it is said that of old there was no fear of Yama as death,

[1]) Compare Jackson JAOS. 17, p. 185. On Yama as cook, cf. § 45 (moon?).

but when they became wicked Viṣṇu made Samavartin (Yama) regulator of sinners and of Pitṛs (12, 207, 35; cf. 122, 27), just as he made Śiva overseer of Bhūts and Mātṛs. The origin of the name is not explained. It may be for samāvartin (cf. Viṣṇu as Samāvarta, 13, 149, 96), but perhaps is better taken as it stands in the sense of "equal-acting", i. e. as a fair judge and punisher (even "of secret sins", 5, 35, 71).

Yama's name has demoniac associations in the name of Yamaśatru, a Rākṣasa (R 6, 44, 20, v. l. Yajñaśatru) and in the names of Rākṣasas in 12, 98, after 13, where S adds Saṃyama, Viyama, Suyama, as sons of Śataśṛṅga (perhaps taken here from Purāṇic sources). The Yāmas and Dhāmas who guard the road to heaven seem to be a sort of Pitṛs, but the text itself says that they are of unknown form (9, 44, 33); they are heavenly beings (3, 261, 6). The followers of Skanda given by Vāyu are called Atiyama and Yama (9, 44, 45), constraining (yam) powers; and so perhaps the Yāmas. Cf. the Yamaratha vow of Yama's wife, H 7941.

§ 58. The family of Yama is more restricted than that of most gods. He is absent from the group of gods who, in R 1, 17, are commissioned to become sires of monkeys and other opponents of Rāvaṇa. Later on this defect is rectified and in the expedition of Śatabali to the North he is accompanied with "the sons of Vaivasvata" (R 4, 43, 3). Still later (R 6, 30, 27), the five sons of Vaivasvata, all "like Kālāntaka", are Gaja, Gavākṣa, Gaveya, Śarabha, and Gandhamādana, of whom in the first book Gandhamādana is sired by Kubera and Śarabha by Parjanya (R 1, 17, 11 and 14). Not Yama, but Dharma is father of Yudhiṣṭhira: "From Dharma was born Yudhiṣṭhira; from Māruta was born Vṛkodara; from Indra was born Arjuna; and from the Aśvins came the yamau (twins) Nakula and Sahadeva" (1, 63, 116). The epic scarcely knows Yama as Dharma, but always calls him Dharmarāja or Dharmendra (7, 6, 6), except in one tale where (1, 108, 8) Aṇīmāṇḍavya, a discontented saint, goes to "the sadana of Dharma" and reproves him for a false judgment and punishment, cursing the god to be reborn (because of that punishment) as Vidura, a scene repeated in 1, 63, 93, but without this complete identification. Dharma in post-epical literature is constantly used for Yama. So in the stage-directions at 3, 128, 13f., only the extra-metrum title Dharma is applied to Yama. Here a priest is being cooked in hell fire, narakāgni, and his king, also in hell, speaks to "Dharmarāja" in behalf of his Guru. So when Mandapāla goes to the Pitṛ-world he asks the "gods near Dharmarāja" why he gets no reward (1, 229, 8); but when Bhīma is "bound by the noose of Dharma", he is not bound by Yama but only by restrictions imposed by right (2, 70, 16). In 5, 128, 45 and 47, the "nooses of Dharma" may be these, but might be Yama's. Dharmarāja is a title applied both to Yama and to Yudhiṣṭhira, and Yama seems to be on his way to identification with Dharma, but it is as well to observe the distinction (3, 84, 1 Dharmatīrtha, etc.) usually preserved in the text, especially as 1, 108 appears to be later than 1, 63, where "Dharma" is cursed to be born as Vidura, but is not called Dharmarāja and has no sadana, or in other words is not quite Yama. The difference is plain, if one thinks of Yama as father of Yudhiṣṭhira or as husband of the ten daughters of Dakṣa (1, 65, 14), one of whom, Lakṣmī, but only as identical with Śrī, is patnī Dharmasya par excellence (12, 59, 132), while Yama's wife (§ 24) is Dhūmorṇā (5, 117, 9 = 13, 166, 11). "Yama's mother" is mentioned in a simile comparing an arrow to the "night of Fate (Kālarātri), noose in hand",

and to "Yama's mother (or nurse) of horrible form", tāṃ . . Yamasya dhātrīm iva co 'grarūpām (9, 17, 43). In R 7, 20, 31, Yama is identified with Vidhātṛ and Dhātṛ (he is here preceded into battle by Agni, ib. 21, 2). As Dharmarāja he has seven priests, ṛtvijas, in the South, of whom the only prominent one is Agastya (Unmucu, Pramucu, Svastyātreya, Dṛḍhavya, Ūrdhvabāhu, Tṛṇasomāṅgiras, and Agastya), a late attempt to expand the "seven seers" of the North and apply the same groups in other quarters (13, 150, 34). One fifth of the divine energies which make Aśvatthāman is supplied by Yama (in conjunction with Śiva, Antaka, Kāma, and Krodha, ekatvam upapannānāṃ jajñe, 1, 67, 72). Later mythologies give as names of his wife Suśīlā, Vijayā, Hemamālā, which are not epic (in 3, 265, 3, it is intimated that his wife may be wandering about on earth as a beautiful woman). Nothing is made of Yama's relationship with Manu Vaivasvata, and indeed except as Vaivasvata nothing is made of his own relationship with the Sun-god. In the epic, Yama rides on a car or goes afoot; the buffalo (as his vehicle) appears first in H 14826. Yama is said in 13, 89, 1 f. to have taught the Śrāddha observances to king Śaśabindu in accordance with the lunar zodiac (what virtue lies in every star), though ib. 91, 7, the originator of the Śrāddha was Nimi. The usual verba ipsissima of the later morality-plays are ascribed to Yama (one has already been cited). "Yama said that an angry king consumes root and all like fire; but if pleased, he bestows wealth like a divinity" (12, 82, 31). "I cut short his life and deprive of children him who runs, studies, etc., while impure" (13, 104, 72 f.). These gāthā Yamagītāḥ perhaps extend into the following verses, but they are not edifying enough to cite. It is possible that Kṛtānta may mean Yama when it is said that Vasiṣṭha could "bring back his sons from Yama's abode but did not transgress Kṛtānta" (1, 174, 9). Kṛtānta appears "frowning and fiery" (yugāntakāle, 2, 72, 15), but is probably Fate as (pace Nīl.) he is in 3, 183, 79; so he is Fate in 12, 33, 15 and 47; 153, 13, and 50 (also a common name for Fate in Rām).[1] "Fourfold Death" (Mṛtyu), of whom Viṣṇu made Time the lord, includes according to the scholiast deaths by sword, foe, Yama, and acts, Karman (12, 122, 33). See § 31.

§ 59. **Varuṇa and Ocean.** — Vestiges of his ancient glory and position remain to "king Varuṇa" (16, 4, 16), who is armed with noose and thunderbolt (aśani, 1, 227, 32; cf. ib. 31, mahāśani as Indra's weapon), and once had a conch-shell (see below; 2, 53, 15 is doubtful, cf. ib. 49, 26, kāṃsyam or śaṅkhaṃ Vāruṇam, made of a thousand niṣkas of gold). A warrior in action is "like Varuṇa" (9, 55, 29) and warriors are "children of Varuṇa" or "like sons of Varuṇa" (7, 155, 45; ib. 36; Ambupati and Mitra are here leaders in battle). Varuṇa (Ambupati; Ambupa in R 7, 3, 18) and Mitra accompany Indra in the Tārakā war (7, 84, 21), as subordinate leaders (cf. R 6, 26, 18, "fighting like Varuṇa for Indra"). He performs the Rājasūya sacrifice as victorious king at the Yamunā-Tīrtha, after conquering in war men and gods. He is here "Aditi's very fortunate son, white Varuṇa" (9, 49, 12, sitaprabhaḥ). As a successful warrior, he is linked with Indra (warriors are "like Indra and Varuṇa", 3, 45, 12; in R a stereotyped phrase, e. g. R 3, 37, 3; R 3, 50, 4; R 4, 12, 10; ib. 52, 4), or with Yama (R 5, 40, 6; R 6, 66, 3); successful warriors defy "the bolt of Indra and noose of Salilarāja" (R 6, 71, 34). But only Rāma (Viṣṇu) breaks the bow of "immeasurable Varuṇa" (because this was really Viṣṇu's bow,

[1]) Compare also Kālāntaka-Yama and similar epithets of Fate in the form of Yama.

R 1, 77, 1; R 2, 118, 39f.). Janaka (ib.), however, received bows from him and perhaps other arms (R 2, 31, 27). As one of the "killing gods" he is to be honored (12, 15, 16f.). He inspires kingly control (vāruṇa saṃyama 2, 78, 19). The list of gods of power in 8, 92, 13, Kubera, Vaivasvata, Vāsava, is in S (ib. 99, 14) increased by the addition of Varuṇa. The conch-shell, belonging to Varuṇa because born in ocean, is given, in 3, 174, 5, to Arjuna by Indra, though in 2, 3, 9f., it is brought from Bindusaras (with Bhima's club) by Maya, who carried off the wealth there (where Bhagīratha dwelt and Indra had made sacrifice), originally hidden by Vṛṣaparvan, and it is here called (Vāruṇa śaṅkha) Devadatta. The bow and arrows (got originally from Soma), Varuṇa, at Agni's bidding, gives to Arjuna (Khāṇḍava scene), as also the club Kaumodakī and the war-car once used by Soma. In the subsequent story Varuṇa devadeva opposes Agni and, armed with his noose, is defeated by the pair he had thus befriended (1, 225, 1 f.; cf. 5, 60, 12). In H 10933, he has shell and bow.

§ 60. All this, however, is no indication of Varuṇa's real epic position. He is no longer a heavenly god, no longer a god rivalling Indra, or having stars as eyes. He is lord of water, Apāmpati, Salilendra, Jalādhipa, Jaleśvara, ambhasāṃ rājā, Vāripa, Udakapati, Ambupati, river-lord, Saritāmpati, and lord of the monsters of the deep (Yādasāmpati and -bhartṛ, 3, 41, 6, as Jaleśvara "with rivers male and female"), hence he is beryl-colored, vaidūryavarṇa (ib.) as well as white (above) and also (ib. 27) "cloud-dark" (jaladharaśyāmo Varuṇo Yādasāmpatiḥ). The waters are medicinal, curative; hence Varuṇa is lord of the "constellation having a hundred medicines", and "the physician who performs the rite in honor of his ancestors under the asterism of Varuṇa would obtain success" (13, 89, 12, nakṣatre Vāruṇe [= śatabhiṣaji; śrāddham] kurvan bhiṣak siddhim avāpnuyāt). He is also pracetas, the "wise" god (water and wisdom are ever united), and perhaps as such is reckoned the father of the epic poet. Varuṇa is formally consecrated by the gods as lord of rivers and waters (9, 45, 22; 46, 105) and told that his home shall be in ocean, the home of makaras; that Ocean, the Lord of Rivers, shall be under his will, and that his own decline and growth shall agree with the waning and waxing of Soma. There seems to be actually no difference felt here (though expressed) between Ocean and Varuṇa. Varuṇa is Saritāmpati; Ocean is nadīpati; the home of Varuṇa is to be "always (sadā) in ocean"; and the final words can refer only to the tides of ocean, though addressed to Varuṇa (9, 47, 8). A different account (5, 110, 3) makes Kaśyapa appoint Varuṇa to "rule the monsters of the deep and guard the waters", and adds that the moon becomes renewed through drinking the "six flavors of Varuṇa Gopati" (lord of cows as waters, perhaps originally stars). Still another passage identifies Varuṇa and Ocean (3, 102, 1: samudraṃ te [Kāleyāḥ] samāśritya Varuṇaṃ nidhim ambhasaḥ; ib. 101, 23, Varuṇasyālayam). The later epic lets Varuṇa receive office as nātha, refuge, of monsters and owner of water, jaleśvara, from Viṣṇu (12, 207, 36). "All the gods" give him this office in 9, 47, 6. The Vedic identity of wit and water (ŚB. 7, 5, 2, 52) is expressed philosophically by saying that Varuṇa represents knowledge as Prakṛti, while Mitra represents spirit (12, 319, 39: Mitraṃ puruṣam, Varuṇaṃ prakṛtiṃ tathā, jñānaṃ tu prakṛtiṃ prāhuḥ). As Varuṇa lives below and Kubera above (on the mountains), the two are often placed in rhetorical antithesis (e. g. R 5, 21, 34), though joined together as (also rhetorical) a fighting pair of gods whom a vainglorious warrior would defy (e. g. R 6, 63, 43).

§ 61. As remarked above (§ 43), little is said of Mitra except as Āditya and form (name) of the Sun-god, and as paired with Varuṇa, with whom, however, in one case he appears as a rival. The nymph Urvaśī "belonged to Mitra but loved Varuṇa". Thus, owing to a family jar (so to speak), Mitra having cursed Urvaśī, Varuṇa became father of Vasiṣṭha (retaḥ kumbhe hy apāsṛjat). Yet Mitra claimed to be his father (same tale of Agastya, 12, 343, 51 and 3, 103, 13 f.), whence Vasiṣṭha was called Maitrāvaruṇi (R 7, 56, 4 f.; ib. 21; ib. 57, 6 f.; 9, 42, 29; 12, 303, 10, etc.). Maitrāvaruṇi (3, 104, 17) designates Agastya, as does Vāruṇi alone, and Vasiṣṭha is indifferently Vāruṇi (1, 99, 7) and Maitrāvaruṇi (above and 1, 178, 10). A stereotyped phrase speaks of (giving) "sons like Mitra and Varuṇa" (1, 105, 41; cf. Mitrāvaruṇayoḥ putraḥ = Agastya, 13, 166, 40), meaning heavenly or glorious. Mitra once held Varuṇa's office (because he performed the Rājasūya, R 7, 83, 6 f.) and is sundered from Varuṇa as spectator of battle (R 6, 73, 7, so S, but B has Rudra) and as divinity of utsarga (12, 314, 2; cf. 12, 318, 1 f.); also in 14, 21, 4, Mitram (sic) along with Pṛthvī, Agni, Viṣṇu, appears as one of the agnayo daśa of physiological metaphysics (cf. 14, 42, 26 and above § 43, perhaps Buddhistic), where Varuṇa is not mentioned. Varuṇa has a special world called the "abode of king Varuṇa", to which go those who perform the cāturmāsya sacrifices and the "one hundred and ten sacrifices", which ought to be the eighth upper world (9, 50, 32), but this is distinct from the "worlds of Mitra and Varuṇa" (Maitrāvaruṇayoḥ, ib. 39 and 13, 102, 35 f.).

§ 62. The heavenly world of Varuṇa is another reminiscence of his origin, but it does not offset the universal epic belief that his home is under the western waters, or in the waters under the earth, thought of as reaching westward rather than eastward, in contrast to Ocean whose wife is the Ganges (3, 99, 33 and 187, 19 f.). The Rām. places the home of Varuṇa on the very peak of the western mountains (R 4, 42, 43 and 45) in the general "district guarded by Varuṇa, who has a noose in hand" (as Lokapāla, § 91). Elsewhere he is represented as living in ocean or as occupying both ocean and the mountains (3, 163, 11). Both epics agree that his palace was made by Viśvakarman, the gods' artificer, and is bright or sunlike and white. As Lokapāla his general province is the West (2, 14, 14; 5, 102, 9; R 4, 45, 6, etc.); more narrowly, the land of Yavanas and Barbaras (3, 254, 18). This district is called Varuṇālaya or Varuṇāvāsa, his home, niketana, bhavana, sabhā, etc., being a hall or palace, where the white god sits in white glory, surrounded by reverent Ādityas. It is "undecaying", an epithet of ocean (R 3, 54, 8), and has walls, gateways, etc., being surrounded by trees bearing jewels, where sing beautiful birds; it is neither too hot nor too cold. Varuṇa, dressed in divine garments and gems sits there with Vāruṇī (S says she is Gaurī) and about him are garlanded and perfumed Ādityas, hosts of Daityas, Dānavas, and Nāgas, and the four oceans in person, rivers, lakes, 'tanks', the four personified directions, Diśas, mountains (who converse), aquatic animals, timi, timiṅgila, makara, jhaṣa, kūrma, grāha (these are presented to Skanda by Varuṇa with elephants, probably because gaja = nāga, 13, 86, 25),[1]), all vāruṇāni bhūtāni (not necessarily fishes, cf. 1, 18, 21; 22, 12;

[1]) For other animals, cf. 1, 21, 3 f.; 22, 6 f.; 25, 15. The gift to Skanda (9, 46, 52, a Nāga) appears in S as a chāga, goat.

6, 34, 29, etc.), as Varuṇa is Yādasām amburāj (7, 6, 6). Apsarasas and Gandharvas also revere Varuṇa (Jaleśvara pāśahasta), as does his minister Sunābha (R 7, 23, 51 calls him Prabhāsa), besides "sons and grandsons, Go(-nāman) and Puṣkara" (his son). This account (2, 9, 1 f.) is amplified in S, which adds a few more courtiers, Artha, Dharma, Kāma, Vasu, Kapila, Ananta, Vāsuki, and Garuḍa. Elsewhere it is said (5, 98, 6 f.) that the home of Varuṇa (Udakapati, Gopati) contains a lake of fire and an umbrella-house. From the umbrella (not here a cobra-hood, ābhoga), which is carried by the god's sons, drips cool but invisible water, pure as Soma yet "enclosed in darkness" (cf. H 6920). Here too appears Varuṇa's son Puṣkara and the abode of Vāruṇī (the intoxicating essence churned from water), also many arms made of old by the gods and taken from the demons, and the great bow made to destroy the world, from which bow that of Arjuna was named (Gāṇḍīva). The noose called dharmapāśa is the one carried by Varuṇa, who resembles Yama also in his saṃyama (above) or controlling power, both being gods of punishment, though Yama controls men, and Varuṇa the demons (dharmapāśadhara Deva is Varuṇa, 2, 9, 17). It is perhaps owing to this white color that Varuṇa becomes a white goose when Rāvaṇa scares the gods (R 7, 18, 5), and is sacrificially represented by a (white) sheep (12, 78, 6; 263, 41), or this last is but priestly tradition (VS. 13, 50). The Sabhā account (above) does not locate the palace, and one passage even says that Varuṇa "obtained happiness by entering the under-world, Pātāla, in the East" ("this place", atra, 5, 108, 12). The exact place is defined here as the "gate of day", where the Sun-god gave forth the Yajurveda and "the hundred paths of Om" were born, the pūrvā dik (East). But if Varuṇa started in the East to go to Pātāla, he soon turned West, to which quarter are thrown offerings made to him (13, 97, 11; see also § 91 f.). The demons seen at his court were at first his captives. They were bound by his noose as well as with the "noose of Right" and were kept under guard in ocean. Compare 5, 128, 45 and 47: "Varuṇa the lord of waters, having bound them with his own nooses as well as with the nooses of Dharma, guards them ever intently in ocean" (cf. 1, 21, 7 where "the home of Varuṇa and Nāgas", ocean, is called Asurāṇāṃ bandhanam, v. l. bāndhavam). Vāruṇī (above) is also daughter of Varuṇa, equivalent to Surā, personified intoxicant of the Suras (gods, R 1, 45, 23 f.; on the difference between surā and agryasauvīraka, kāñjika, see ib. 3, 47, 45). Vāruṇī as wife (4, 9, 16) is the older Varuṇānī. Suṣeṇa, son of Varuṇa and father of Tārā (R 4, 22, 12), leads the host of the West (R 4, 42, 2 f.). R 7, 23 tells how Rāvaṇa invades Rasātala, guarded by Varuṇa below earth, and full of serpents and Daityas. After overcoming Vāsuki's Nāga city of Bhogavatī, he conquers two demon-cities, Jeweltown and Rocktown, and then reaches Varuṇa's lofty city, "like Kailasa white with clouds", where is Surabhi flowing with the Milk-sea juices (ib. 23, 21; in Mbh. 5, 102, 2, this milk has the six flavors), and, challenging Varuṇa, destroys his family of sons and grandsons led by Go and Puṣkara. Varuṇa's minister, Prabhāsa, says that the god himself is not at home, having gone to Brahman's place to hear a concert, so that Varuṇa is not defeated in person by Rāvaṇa (as he was by Kṛṣṇa, 5, 130, 49; cf. H 9145; 10903 f.). A dead or defeated demon goes to Varuṇālaya as naturally as a dead man goes to Yamasādana (cf. R 7, 61, 20, where the Asura Daitya Madhu on dying, "abandoning this world went to Varuṇa's home"). The "worlds of Varuṇa" known to Sampāti (R 4, 58, 13) are interpreted as hells even for men. Thus Kaśyapa is asked what "other worlds" are the punishment for a recalcitrant or perjured witness and says in reply that such a sinner fastens upon himself a thousand nooses of Varuṇa, and it takes a year to loosen each (though nothing is said of hell). The later Rām. (7, 59, pra. 3, 36) has the same explanation. Varuṇa is satyasaṃgara (9, 45, 46), upholder of truth. So Bāṇa's cows are held by Varuṇa, H 10970.

§ 63. The descendants of Varuṇa are indefinitely multiplied through the practice of calling all descendants of Bhṛgu (and Aṅgiras and Kavi[1]) Bhārgavas or Vāruṇas, Bhṛgu having been born of Varuṇa's sacrifical fire (1, 5, 7), so that Bhṛgu is a form of Varuṇa as Varuṇa to the later writers is a form of Rudra-Śiva (13, 85, 88 and 125 f.). Agastya and Vasiṣṭha also claim (above) Varuṇa as their sire. Vālmīki is son of "Pracetas", who "guards the western half of the world" (R 6, 24, 19; 7, 111, 11; the Prācetasas are ten sons of Prācīnabarhis, 1, 196, 15; 12, 208, 6 and may revert to the same origin, though Pracetas is also a Prajāpati). R adds (the apes) Suṣeṇa, Hemakūṭa, and the Nāgas (in general) to the "sons of Varuṇa" (R 1, 17, 14; R 6, 7, 12; ib. 30, 33). Puñjikasthalā, the Apsaras mother of Hanumat (p. 14), was his kanyakā (R 6, 60, 11). A passage of S, cited p. 118, calls his wife Gaurī, as explicitly stated in 5, 117, 9. In 12, 301, 59, she is Devī Siddhi; in 13, 146, 5 and 166, 11, she is again Gaurī. The early epic says that Devī, the "eldest wife" of the god is the daughter of Śukra and she bore him a son Bala (also son of Danāyu; Vala?) and a daughter called Surā and Vāruṇī (in Brahman's palace, 2, 11, 42), through whom the gods got joy (intoxication) and godhead (pun on sura, 1, 66, 52; 5, 98, 14). His son Puṣkara, who lives in the palace called Puṣkaramālinī (2, 8, 41) and is "lotus-eyed", is called "son of Gopati" (Varuṇa 5, 98, 11), which calls to mind the connection of "Gopati and Varuṇa", enlisted among the inferior Devagandharvas (cf. Varuṇa as name of a Nāga), as descendants of Muni, the daughter of Dakṣa (1, 65, 42). Another son of Varuṇa was the sage Vandin, who, owing to his paternity, had no fear of drowning and even raised to life another man who had been drowned (3, 134, 31). Finally Śrutāyudha (§ 4), a valiant hero, was son of Varuṇa and of the river Parṇāśā. Parṇāśā, his mother, begged Varuṇa to give him immortality, but the god would only make him invulnerable, avadhya, by means of a divine weapon, not immortal, since "there is no immortality for man" and "who is born must die". This weapon was a "club with a charm said over it", which might not be hurled against a man unless he was fighting, since otherwise it became a boomerang and would return and kill the thrower. Śrutāyudha forgot, threw it at a noncombatant, and was slain, for it returned and smote him "like badly used magic" (7, 92, 44 f.). Similarly, Varuṇa limits the gift of life bestowed upon Hanumat (as grandson?): "He shall not meet death in a million years withal, from my noose (or) even from water", where perhaps water (sickness) is the noose (R 7, 36, 15). Here also may be mentioned the list of Varuṇa's seven seers, acting as sacrificial priests: Dṛḍheyu, Ṛteyu, Parivyādha, Ekata, Dvita, Trita, and Atri's son Sārasvata, "whose soul was virtue" (13, 151, 36 f.). They "belong to the West" (the first two are mentioned only here).

§ 64. Varuṇa's activities, apart from records of fighting and noosing, are not numerous. He was robbed of his "cows" (he is here Ambupati

[1]) Kavi is son of Bhṛgu (son of Brahman in the pseudo-epic) and father of Śukra Uśanas, 1, 66, 42 (13, 85, 106 f.).

as well as Gopati) by Kaśyapa. The cows are Kāmadughās, "giving all desires" (H 3148 f.; Kaśyapa's two wives, Aditi and Surabhi, are here born on earth as Devakī and Rohiṇī). Varuṇa also (§ 45) steals Soma's daughter, Bhadrā, from Utathya (so Dyaus, § 34, becomes a thief). When Nārada reproves him, he tries to throttle the saint (13, 155, 22). Utathya Aṅgiras then drinks up the god's domain and causes a drought, till Sarasvatī loses herself in the desert and earth is nearly dried up, when the god sees his error and restores Bhadrā. As a generous god he gives arms (above) and control of water and fresh garlands to Nala (3, 57, 38), and gives to Ṛcīka, son of Bhṛgu, a thousand "white horses" (each with a black ear), to enable that saint to marry, since such was the dowry demanded (3, 115, 26 f.). The horses came from Aśvatīrtha, a place reached "by going first to the residence of Varuṇa" (cf. H 2463). Four hundred of the horses were seized by the Vitastā river while being led across it (saṃtāre hṛtāny āsan Vitastayā, 5, 119, 8; but S has āsann itas tataḥ). Beauty distinguishes all Varuṇa's children and Varuṇātmajā is typical of female loveliness (S 1, 241, 17). Varuṇa himself is typical of prosperity (2, 35, 16). The white horses may be a literal interpretation of white billows ("Neptune's chargers") and the noose of the god may still be interpreted as illness. When a king is addressed, "Let not Varuṇa slay thee with his horrible nooses" (for wronging a priest, 3, 192, 48), it means repent in time, and the implication may be that he will die of disease if he does not repent. This is practically the only weapon Varuṇa uses; with it he marches even in processions (ugrapāśa, 3, 231, 38; 8, 42, 36). A proverb and parody of the holy text seems also to imply dropsy as the noose: "though bound with Varuṇa's nooses one thinks himself immortal; like a puffed out skin", etc. (mahādṛtir ivā 'dhmātaḥ, 12, 95, 20; cf. RV. 7, 89, 2). But for false witnesses the fetters are not loosed with death (above). Varuṇa himself appears as a witness for Sītā (3, 291, 29). In H 13138, three-headed snakes draw his car. See also § 143 f.

§ 65. Ocean, Sāgara (Samudra), is personified (above) as subservient to Varuṇa. He is husband of Ganges (above), and is called Aikṣvāka Sāgara (H 2989 f. makes him son of Brahman; Śāntanu is his name when born as father of Bhīṣma). As son of Ikṣvāku he grants the boon asked by Rāma (3, 283, 35; R 6, 19, 21 f.), and is described as wearing gems, a lotus-wreath, and the Kaustubha jewel (§ 19; cf. H 12161 f., date of churning). He persuades Rāma to shoot the Brahmāstra at the Dasyus and Abhīras, who had polluted his streams (R 6, 22, 17—31). Agastya, son of Varuṇa, drinks up ocean, to discover the Kāleyas (3, 104, 22 f.). King Sagara excavated Ocean's bed (the king's mother is Kālindī, the Jumna river, R 1, 70, 31; R 2, 110, 18), hence Ocean is called Sāgara (R 1, 38 f.). Sāgara exhorted a mountain to rise and help Hanumat (R 5, 1, 89 f.). He injured his mother and apparently (scholiast) went to hell for this impiety (R 2, 21, 27). Dundubhi challenged him to fight but he was afraid (R 4, 11, 9 f.). Kārtavīrya (q. v.) attacked Ocean (Samudra). Utathya also drank up ocean (above). He was cursed several times, to have sharks, by Bṛhaspati, because his water was unfit for rinsing the god's mouth (12, 343, 27); and by Vaḍavāmukha, the Mare's Mouth, to become salt, because he would not come to Mt. Meru when bidden to do so. Till the divine Mare's Mouth drinks him up he will remain salty (but cf. H 8323!), the sweat of the divine being having given him his salt (12, 343, 60). Hence

(3, 206, 26) it is said that a seer's wrath made ocean salty. Ocean is lord of rivers (above). His resolution not to pass his bounds is often referred to (R 2, 12, 44, etc.). He appears in R as four (R 5, 15, 12) or seven (R 3, 74, 25, etc.); in Mbh., only as four seas, as when he attends the court of Varuṇa (2, 9, 18; 3, 83, 156, etc.). The legend of Sagara, "born in the Ikṣvāku family" (3, 106, 7) implies that there was originally no ocean, nor place for it. He and his sons hollowed out a basin afterwards filled by Ganges. In 12, 289, 2 f., Sagara discusses philosophy with Ariṣṭanemi. Ocean is "lord of rivers"; Varuṇa is "king of waters" (also of rivers), according to 14, 43, 7. Aṃśumat, son of Asamañjas, son of Sagara, recovered the lost horse of Sagara. His grandson brought down the Ganges (3, 107, 39 f.; cf. R 2, 36, 19; Mbh. 12, 57, 9). Keśinī and Sumatī are the two wives of Sagara, the former mother of Asamañjas, the latter sister of Garuḍa and mother of the sixty thousand Sāgaras born in a gourd and preserved in oil till adult (R 1, 38, 3 f.; Ikṣvāku as gourd). Keśinī is in Mbh. the mother of Jahnu (1, 94, 32). H recognises both (797; 1416).

§ 66. **Indra.** — Indra, the favorite son of Aditi, was originally (a priestly) "son of Brahman", but became a warrior through his slaughter of nine nineties of his evil kin, thereby obtaining Indraship (lordship) of the gods (12, 22, 11). He slew them with the bolt made of Dadhīca's bones, whom the god tempted to lose his virtue through sight of Alambuṣā (9, 51, 7). Indra made all kinds of weapons of the sainted monster's bones; whence it is said that "Dadhīca guards Indra as Aṅgiras guards the sun" (3, 92, 6). Another story makes Brahman the originator of the plot to get the bones and has only the thunderbolt made from them (12, 343, 36). In 3, 100, 24 f., the bolt is made by Tvaṣṭṛ. Indra heads the gods in battle (R 3, 59, 15, etc.); hence Indraship as headship (13, 18, 64, etc.). He has yellow eyes and beard, rides in a yellow car with yellow steeds, wears golden chains, red clothes, and has two nymphs to fan him when at peace. A hundred youths surround him, singers chant to him, a white umbrella is over his head, and his garlands are ever free from dust; he is always twenty-five years old in appearance (see § 22; 3, 57, 24; R 3, 5, 5). In his palace, "he sits in beauty indescribable, having a diadem, red bracelets, white robes, and variegated garlands, lord of all the world" (2, 7, 4 f.). The diadem he gives to his son Arjuna kirīṭin (3, 168, 74), as he gives him his conch and car (ib. 85). He is the lord who pierces forts, īśaḥ puraṃdaraḥ (R 4, 51, 14). His district is the East (daśaśatākṣakakubh, 7, 184, 47). His constant epithets are "he of a hundred powers" and "he of a thousand eyes" (also assumed by Viṣṇu), Vāsava (Arjuna is Vāsavi), "lord of the third heaven" (Tridiveśvara), "lord of the thirty(-three) gods" (Tridaśesvara, 1, 34, 10 and 15). He is called also Devādhipa (5, 10, 7), Trilokanātha (R 6, 15, 5), Vṛtraśatru (paravīrahan, 3, 43, 21 f.), and by equivalent titles. Śakra and Maghavat are used like names; so is Pākaśāsana (passim). The last means "ruler of crops" (vegetables) but is understood as ruler or slayer of Pāka (demon); cf. Śambara-Pākahan, Śambara-Vṛtrahan. As equivalent terms to the above are used Devarāja, Sureśvara, Deveśa, Amareśvara, Amareśa, Maheśvara, Surārihan, Asurasūdana, Devendra, Prahlādahan, Vṛtrahantṛ, Valabhid, -han, Namucihan, Mahendra, Vajrin, Harihaya, Harivāhana (having yellow steeds). A favorite epithet is Vala-Vṛtranisūdana or Daitya-Dānavasūdana, -han. The popular epithet "thousand-eyed" appears in several forms, Sahasra-dṛk, -nayana,

-netra, -cakṣus, as well as the usual Sahasrākṣa. This and Hari and Ākhaṇḍala, and Sureśa are also applied to Viṣṇu, as Amareśa and Sarvadeveśa are shared with Śiva. The epithets Tridaśādhipati, Tribhuvaneśvara, Trilokeśa, Devadeveśa add nothing to the sense of those above. Pratāpavat is an epithet Indra shares with Agni. In 9, 49, 1 f., where Indra is Amararāja, it is explained that Śatakratuḥ ("of a hundred powers") means "having sacrificed a hundred times" (ib. 2, īje kratuśatena). Puruhūtapurī is the name of Indra's city Amarāvatī. Less common epithets are Devagaṇeśvara, "lord of hosts of gods" (1, 123, 31), Kauśika (3, 9, 9 and 135, 20), Nagāri "foe of mountains" (4, 39, 10; cf. § 6), Ākhaṇḍala (S 2, 47, 3; 12, 337, 4), Dānavāri (RG 2, 111, 9). In formal hymns, which always exaggerate, Indra is extolled as the final destruction-cloud, as Vāyu, Agni, Viṣṇu, Soma, earth, sky, ocean, etc., as well as Śacīpati, Namucighna, Valasūdana, and "our salvation, as the ship of safety" (1, 25, 7 f.; cf. with plavo bhava and trāṇaṃ the jñānaplava of 12, 238, 1). On hearing these epithets, Indra, as requested, gives rain. He said to the clouds, "rain pure ambrosia" and the clouds "let loose the water". As maker or recreator, by thus raining, Indra is known as Bhūtabhāvana and Bhūtakṛt (1, 67, 144; 3, 310, 15). He actually "creates" the being Ghaṭotkaca (1, 155, 46), but only by imparting a share of his own energy (as the other gods did) to Bhīma's son. Indra's business is to "bestow strength, energy, children, and happiness" (3, 229, 8 f.). He also frustrates the designs of the wicked and instructs (anuśāsti) all men in their duties (ib.). Indra is Vāsava as chief of the Vasus; Marutpati and Marutvat as lord of the Maruts (R 4, 31, 44); Śacīpati and Śacīsahāya as husband of Śacī (his personified power, 3, 168, 12); but the epics do not yet know him by his (later) titles, Pulomajit and Pulomāri. He kills Puloman in H 1174.

§ 67. Indra as a grāmaṇī, leading the gods, is armed with the bolt and a net; he also uses stones in fighting and his bow is often referred to, but is not used (the rainbow, Indracāpa, Śakradhanuḥ). The bolt implies both thunder and lightning, as it roars and kills; when the god is anthropomorphised, it becomes a javelin, returning to the hand (3, 310, 24). The vajra bolt is imagined as a six-sided club (3, 100, 11 f.; 7, 134, 10); also as having a hundred joints (R 3, 71, 10, śataparvan, Vedic); it is a "splitter", sphoṭana, and mahāraudra, "very terrible" (H 13997), and as already explained, it is made of the bones of the (Śivaite) saint Dadhīca (12, 285, 11 f.), whence perhaps it has these Śiva-epithets. It is hard as a diamond and surpassing swift, and is called (interchangeably) vajra, aśani, and vajrāśani (R 6, 59, 103). Indra seizes the aśani and hurls (it), the vajram astram (1, 227, 30), in rather a late scene in which he also hurls stones and rides a white elephant in battle. [As sundry gods are fighting, their weapons as here described may be mentioned together: Yama uses kāladaṇḍa; Kubera, a gadā club; Skanda, a javelin (boomerang in 9, 46, 92); the Aśvins, "gleaming plants"; Dhātṛ, a bow; Jaya (Sūrya?), a musala club; Tvaṣṭṛ, a mountain (so Indra hurls a peak); Aṃśa, a javelin; Death (Mṛtyu) an axe; Aryaman, a parigha club; Mitra, a discus sharp as a razor; Pūṣan, Bhaga, and Savitṛ use bows and swords, and the other gods, "various weapons"] [1]). Indra teaches Arjuna to use his conch Devadatta (3, 168, 85) and both his own weapons and those of other gods; he can use any weapon (3, 37, 14), but prefers the bolt to

[1]) The other fighting gods are Rudras, Vasus, Maruts, Viśve Devas, Sādhyas. Jaya is not explained; it may be abstract (Victory), but probably as solar epithet (§ 43) is Sūrya.

smite, and noose to snare (Bali, etc.). He invented sword and armor (5, 29, 30) for use against demons. He addressed his bolt, "Go thou and kill, becoming a tiger", when he would slay a child, and the leopard-bolt slew the child (tiger = leopard, 12, 31, 27 f.). When the weapon, āyudha, of Indra is referred to, however, it is usually his bow that is meant (R 3, 42, 18; cf. 8, 24, 47; Mahendracāpa, 7, 145, 97); but any weapon, particularly arrows, can be converted into the aindram astram by magic. The amoghā śakti or "unfailing javelin" of Indra, made by Tvaṣṭṛ, is kept by the Pāṇḍus and "worshipped with perfumes, garlands, and a seat, drink, and food", a real fetish, evidently a javelin inspired by Mantras into an Indra-astram (9, 17, 44). Another aindram astram is called viśoṣana, the "dryer", another is saṃmoha, "confuser", etc. (all gods give similar names to magic weapons, āgneya, kaubera, vāruṇa, etc.). In R 6, 91, 68, tad aindram astram is actually "the very arrow with which Śakra slew demons", a reversion to an older view according to which the Śakracāpa was a real bow of offence, not merely the beauty of the rainbow (as usual). The case differs from the Mantra-endowed arrow with which, for example, Arjuna shoots down horses galloping a kos ahead (3, 271, 54). A recollection of the battle-bow lies also in the legend of the three divine bows (Śiva's omitted), one made by Brahman and belonging to Soma (moon's crescent?), but given by him to Varuṇa (the Gāṇḍīva, made of gāṇḍī, 5, 98, 19); one called Vijaya, Indra's dhanuḥ; and one of horn belonging to Viṣṇu (śārṅgaṃ vaiṣṇavam, acquired by Arjuna). Of these it is said that Indra's was not used (5, 158, 5 f.), as Rukmin who owned it would not fight. Mahendra is the name of Yudhiṣṭhira's bow (7, 23, 91; but here all the Pāṇḍus have bows called after gods). On the other hand, when the Sun-god envelops his son Karṇa with his rays during the combat with Arjuna (all the gods "take sides"), Indra Harihaya looks lovingly at his son Arjuna and, as he does so, suddenly the Indrāyudha (rainbow) appears in the sky (a sign of good fortune; 1, 136, 24 f.; the weapon is here differentiated from "lightning and thunder" and must as usual be the bow). The "net" of Indra is deceit, a mere term for magical trickery, used by any warrior (3, 245, 17; 5, 160, 55; though ib. 118 in contrast to māyā: na māyā hī 'ndrajālaṃ vā kuhakā vā 'pi bhīṣaṇā, illusion, deception, and jugglery). The remark in 5, 37, 2 (dānavendrasya dhanur anāmyam) on fools who try to bend Indra's bow or smite the air, etc., also shows that the bow is the rainbow (dānava as "clouds", N.; but S has v. l. tān eve 'ndrasya).

§ 68. The car and charioteer of Indra: the car is called jaitra ratha, car of victory, and Mahendravāha, and is like lightning or a meteor; it descends to earth with the noise of thunder; it is decorated with gold, is sunlike, and is drawn by steeds described as golden and peacock-colored, one thousand or ten thousand in number (5, 104, 3; cf. 3, 168, 73; 170, 9); ten thousand peacock-like steeds drag his sunlike car (ib. 172, 23). The car is stored with all arms (including Nāgas), and above it on a yellow pole waves a dark-blue standard called "Victorious" (vaijayanta, 3, 42, 8 and 30). Indra and his queen and son Arjuna and the Aśvins ride in it, but very few can do so; even gods and demons cannot in general, nor can one who is not an adept in asceticism (ib. 17; cf. 7, 84, 18, for the Aśvins). Vaijayanta or -tī is not an uncommon name and is applied to elephant-banners (6, 112, 27); perhaps (so N.) to Indra's palace (2, 22, 19, "death in battle is aindro vaijayantaḥ). On this chariot the slayer of Namuci slew Bali Vairocana, Śambara, Namuci, Vala and Vṛtra (dual), Prahlāda and Naraka (dual), besides the seven hosts of the sons of Diti (3, 165, 7; ib. 166, 5). Heavenly musicians attend the car, so when it appears music is heard; and Maruts accompany it. On seeing it the wives of the demons of darkness flee wailing like ospreys. Nothing in the epic (but later Śakrāśva = Uccaiḥśravas) suggests that the steed of Indra ("of the yellow steeds") is Uccaiḥśravas (ib. 168, 9f.; ib. 62). On the contrary, Uccaiḥśravas (§ 19) is born from the sea with Indra's elephants but is not taken by Indra, as is the elephant (1, 18 = R 1, 45). He is the divine ever-youthful horse, produced at the churning of ocean, and famous only as the white roaring charger of the sea. What can that be save the roaring breakers? (1, 20, 1 f.; cf. 1, 17, 3 and 18, 35 f.; as roaring, 7, 196, 30; king of steeds, etc., 5, 102, 12; 6, 34, 27). In 12, 235, 15, "U. should be given to the good", S has "Prahlāda gave U. to Kāśyapa". Even VP. 1, 22, 6, merely says that Uccaiḥśravas is "best of horses". Indra never uses him in either epic. Only his offspring are in the sky and are given away by Indra, in H 8220; 8924. Mātali, the charioteer of Indra, Śakrasārathi, is recognised as the best charioteer in the world, though when he starts the car it lurches so that Indra cannot keep his position, and when the knight occupant fights, the charioteer drops his goad, lets the horses turn around, and gets confused and blinded (3, 168, 41, atiśakram idam; ib. 171, 15 f.). In R 7, 28, 23 f., Mātali first baffles the demons by his skill in driving and Indra then smites them. Mātali is councillor as well as charioteer (the office is very honorable; Śalya acts for Karṇa, etc.). The Sūta (charioteer) is a minister of the king and so Mātali is "Indra's friend, minister, and car-driver" (5, 104, 2 f.). Mātali's wife is Sudharmā, his son Gomukha, his daughter Guṇakeśī, his son-in-law Sumukha, a Nāga. He also acts as adviser of Rāma in battle, after serving him (R 6, 111, 1 f.). On Indra's car he takes Arjuna to heaven and back, guiding the ten thousand horses easily (3, 165, 1 f.; 170, 9 f.). He journeys around the world with Nārada, seeking a son-in-law (5, 97, 11 f.; 104, 22 f.). The car he drives is "like the sun" (originally the Sun?) when he helps Rāma in battle (3, 290, 12), and so in R 6, 103, 6 f., both car and horses are sun-like (here Mātali is wounded and the horses are slain). The combined efforts of Indra, Mātali, and his son Gomukha are sometimes unequal to the task of subduing the demons of Hiraṇyapur (5, 100, 8). Jayanta (H 7470 f.), son of Indra, and Gomukha, son of Mātali, attack the son of Rāvaṇa, till Puloman carries off his grandson (R 7, 28, 10). Indra tells Mātali of what sort are the people he likes (S 13, 153, 7 f.). Mātali's son serves Gada, H 8872.

§ 69. Indra's dhvaja (ketu) is the chief object in the "feast of Indra" (maha or utsava). Sometimes two are mentioned, weakened by rain and heat (R 2, 77, 25; ib. 9, and R 6, 45, 17). Earth is beautified with these poles (9, 9, 21; cf. ib. 12, 23), which were instituted as the "Indra-poles" (festival) by Uparicara, whom Indra persuaded to give up asceticism and become an aviator, "going through the air like a god" in an aeroplane (ākāśagaṃ vimānam, 1, 63, 13), and gave to him a victor's crown, vaijayantī mālā, of lotus-flowers, which protected him in battle and was called the "Indra-wreath", Uparicara's peculiar sign. Indra gave him a bamboo pole, protective of its worshippers, wherewith to worship him as slayer of Vṛtra. Indra's day comes when the rains are over and the roads are fit for war, and is the new moon's day of Saumya māsa (probably the end of Sept.; amāvāsyā Śakradevatā, 5, 142, 18). The pole is pulled down earlier than this, on the full moon of Āśvina (Āśvayuksamaye māsi, R 4, 16, 36). But if it is impossible to bring "Indra's day" into connection with Indra's festival, it is at least clear that the festival occurred after the rains had ceased and when New Year's was celebrated, for in its installation it is especially said that the feast takes place at the end of the year (gate saṃvatsare). The banner is only part of the decoration of the pole, which is scented and bedecked with gold cloth, garlands, and ornaments (streamers, etc.). Indra, as īśvara, or lord of the feast, is worshipped under the form of a goose (haṃsarūpeṇa). This festival of Indra Maghavat ("generous one") was afterwards generally adopted by other kings, who followed the example set by Uparicara and celebrated the occasion by royal gifts of jewels, land, etc. (1, 63, 27). The height and gaudiness of the pole are remarked upon in 1, 70, 14f., and elsewhere. Later this feast is shared with Kṛṣṇa, H 3787—4008.

§ 70. Indra's elephant (a cloud) is used as alternative to the vehicle drawn by fallow steeds or geese (the last is implied in S 5, 15, 23: Nahuṣa, to outdo Indra, dismisses the elephants Supratīka and Airāvata, the haṃsayukta vimāna and the hariyukta ratha, and yokes saints instead). The elephant Airāvata, which rose at the churning of the ocean, was seized by Indra (1, 18, 40). The peers of this first and "king" elephant are Añjana (cf. the āñjanaka breed, 7, 112, 17), Vāmana, and Mahāpadma, progenitors of Ayodhyā's stud (R 1, 6, 24). These four guard the cardinal points, as do the gods who mount them (see § 10 and § 91). Indra's elephant guards the East, as that is Indra's direction, or the North, as that is the Airāvatapatha (3, 162, 34, perhaps North-East; see Lokapālas). In many passages Airāvata and Airāvaṇa (e. g. 2, 9, 8) exchange, each form being applied to elephant and Nāga (serpent). In 4, 2, 17, Dhṛtarāṣṭra is best of Nāgas and among elephants Airāvaṇa is the best, but S has Airāvata (ib. 30). Airāvata is imagined as accompanied with two females (1, 114, 9f.). He is called Pauraṃdara (Indra's), as Añjana is the western elephant ridden by Varuṇa, Varuṇopavāhya, and Sārvabhauma, that of the North, by Kubera (R 6, 4, 20); he is Indravāhya: "As Jambha in battle attacked Śakra on Airāvaṇa Indravāhya" (9, 20, 12; ib. 6, Vajradhara Airāvaṇastha; S has both forms ib. 4 = 5 and 12). In 7, 112, 35, B and S both have Airāvaṇa. In 6, 64, 54—6, Airāvaṇa in B; Airāvata in S (S 5, 99, 8 has Airāvata after Airāvaṇa in 7 = 15). Like all the world-elephants, Airāvata has four tusks and three temporal streams; he is large and white (1, 227, 29; 7, 105, 26; S 2, 97, 26 and 38; cf. 5, 143, 37; 6, 64, 61). Indra mounts the king of elephants, gajarājavāhana, on back or shoulder or head, usually on the shoulder (12, 227, 10f.; ib. 117; ib. 223, 12; cf. R 5, 36, 40; ib. 37, 25). The two vaijayantīs, "bells of victory", Indra gave to Skanda and Viśākha (3, 231, 18f.). The epic recognises the elephant as a fighting vehicle, but in the earlier scenes Indra fights from a chariot and uses the elephant more for a quiet journey, as when he peacefully ascends to heaven on the elephant after his trouble with the demons is over (5, 18, 1), or takes a trip round the world (3, 193, 9; 12, 227, 10f.). Seated on his elephant he pours down rain (6, 95, 34). The god and his elephant appear disguised in a magic scene, the latter as a bull (1, 3, 167, Nāgarāj). According to 1, 66, 60 and 63, Airāvata is Devanāga and son of Bhadramanas, one of the nine creative powers, and less fighter than guardian. But in some late scenes, 1, 227, 29, etc., and especially in the

Rām., Airāvata acts as battle-steed. In the Uttara, Indra, "abandoning his car", mounts his elephant to fight (R 7, 29, 27). In H 2453f., he fights on the elephant and travels in his car. The later phrase "like Airāvata in battle" also shows the war-use of the elephants (in 7, 26, 20, a hero fights on an elephant descended from the one on which Indra fought, omitted in C): Airāvatasamā yudhi (7, 112, 35; R 5, 6, 32; R 6, 4, 19, etc.). In R 6, 67, 107 (late), Indra fights on the elephant, all the gods aiding; and R 6, 15, 6, Indrajit hurls Airāvata to the ground and tears out two tusks, frightening Indra; also ib. 61, 17, Kumbhakarṇa tears out a tusk and smites Indra with it; and Mahodara, another demon, mounts the elephant Sudarśana, "born in the family of Airāvata"; and Aṅgada (son of Vālin) tears out a tusk and fights with it (R 6, 69, 20; ib. 70, 15). Airāvata gouges Rāvaṇa and leaves on his body the marks of his tusks (R 3, 23, 24; ib. 3, 32, 7; ib. 6, 40, 5). Airāvaṇa draws up water from the under-world for Indra to rain (5, 99, 7), evidently from irāvat as the nourishing rain-cloud and its lightning-stroke; whence airāvatas are lightning-clouds, mahāghanāḥ sairāvatāḥ sāśanayaḥ (3, 3, 58); sairāvataśatahradāḥ (7, 98, 31); vidyudairāvatārciṣmad .dvitīyendradhanur yathā (R 6, 76, 39; ib. 5, 1, 165, personified; not "rainbow", as in PW.). Cf. H 3894f. "Airāvata elephants" (R 2, 70, 22) may mean from mount Irāvata. The four tusks of Airāvata are not peculiar to world-elephants. Laṅkā's guarding elephants have three or four tusks and are white (R 5, 9, 5 and R 5, 4, 27) in demoniac imitation of Airāvata, who stands guard at Indra's city, and also is "white, śubhra, with four tusks, huge as Kailāsa, victorious" (3, 42, 39f., vijayinam as in S, not vaijayinam). In H 8870f., he is guided by Pravara.

§ 71. **Indra as Benefactor and Rain-God.**—Indra gives his favorites, as already shown, gifts of arms and, even to a chance acquaintance (Nala), imparts the gait of a king and the knowledge how to worship. He is fond of giving jewels, to his son (3, 165, 10, with arms); to the father of Sītā (the cūḍāmaṇi, R 5, 66, 5), when pleased by sacrifice, etc. The god vies with Kubera in wealth, but his gifts go beyond gems and arms; he makes the dead live (R 6, 123, 1f.) as a favor to the living, and makes things grow out of season for Bharadvāja (R 2, 91, 13). His chief gift consists in the rain he gives to all. He is Ambudeśvara, owning rain. There may be growth "without the bolt-holder raining" (R 2, 12, 107), but artificial irrigation, āseka, is not of much use (5, 79, 2f.); the land depends on rain and Indra rains, first as slayer of Vṛtra (but the epic has almost forgotten this), then to "protect the people" (1, 64, 16). In return men give the "earthly rain" of soma, which he shares with all the other gods, even at last with the Aśvins (3, 121, 9; cf. § 110). That he is the regular rain-giver is attested by the fact that the phrase "when the god rains" is synonymous with "when Vāsava rains" (cf. S 1, 238, 9, vṛṣṭiṃ varṣati Vāsave, repeated ib. 18), though occasionally others usurp his function, as the Sun (q. v.) and Parjanya (below) also rain and Māṃdhātṛ (cf. Ṛṣyaśṛṅga) once, during a drought, "made rain while Indra was looking on" (miṣato vajrapāṇinaḥ, 3, 126, 42; cf. 123, 23). Indra "drives the clouds together and sends down water" (1, 227, 18f.), or he "rains stones" (hail, ib. 45). He also rains at any great event (12, 334, 7), and in all blessed places he rains regularly (4, 47, 26); otherwise (in the unblessed, kingless land) come famine, plague and the ītis (distresses) of the farmer (5, 10, 48; ib. 147, 25). "The crop-controller (Pākaśāsana) did not rain", introduces the story of such a famine and how Ṛṣyaśṛṅga forced Indra to rain and become yathartuvarṣin, "duly raining". Cessation of this activity introduces the final destruction (3, 188, 50 and 65), when even grain planted by a river, sarittīrtheṣu, will not grow (ib. 190, 23). This is the nadīmukhaiḥ-grown grain, in antithesis to Indrakṛṣṭa (grain raised by Indra, 2, 51, 11; cf. devamātṛka, 2, 5, 77 and R 2, 100, 46). Constantly the arrows of a hero are shot "like the rain shot by Puraṃdara" (etc. 3, 16, 12; 9, 16, 33; 14, 77, 27; R 6, 56, 11; R 6, 91, 22). Indra "enters the cloud with a mass of water and fills earth with it" (12, 143, 20). So Indra is called Vāsava bhūrivarṣa (7, 30, 36) and is thought of as the god who rains par excellence, whether water or blood be sent (varṣati devaḥ, 3, 110, 4; 12, 73, 15; vavarṣa rudhiraṃ devaḥ, R 6, 96, 35 and ib. 108, 20); he may "rain dust" and so destroy a realm (R 7, 81, 8), as he, Indra Maghavat, rains gold upon a favorite king (12, 29, 25). His rain the gods claim as "our rain" in antithesis to soma: "Our rain goes down and men rain up" (narās tū 'rdhvapravarṣiṇaḥ 12, 59, 26). If the gods are pleased with men, they speak in their behalf to Indra, who then sends rain and so gives food (annaṃ dadāti Śakraś ca, 12, 121, 38), for with this rain he "makes the rice grow in the fields" (R 4, 14, 15), though the same god's "stone rain" beats down the crops (R 3, 34, 8). Why Indra "unweariedly rains" is explained (1, 124, 11 f.) on the principle that actuates priests who keep on studying though they know the Mantras and that actuates saints to practise ever more austerities, viz., the yearning for glory! Work gives glory, hence the Sun toils ever, and ever blows the Wind, and ever Indra rains, to get glory, to become supreme (5, 29, 8 f.). As rain-god, Indra is identified with Parjanya, from whom he is formally differentiated. Parjanya rains on hill and ploughland (10, 2, 5); Vāsava rains upon the crops in the fields in due time (R 7, 70, 10); Parjanya is vṛṣṭimat, "rainful" (7, 89, 4; 9, 12, 59; R 2, 1, 37; so, significantly, are clouds, R 5, 45, 7); as such, Parjanya too shoots rain-arrows, like Indra (above and R 6, 80, 21). Parjanya is, in short, the rain-form of Indra, though given a distinct personality ("son of Pūṣan", 8, 20, 29, is doubtful; Puṣānuja is v. l. for Pūṣātmaja) as worshipper in parades, etc.; and in R 1, 17, 14, Parjanya is regarded as progenitor of the śarabha. Thus Indra ṛtuvarṣin and kālavarṣin (3, 190, 79) appears as kālavarṣin Parjanya (1, 68, 10; 3, 190, 91; 12, 29, 53 and ib. 91, 1); kāle varṣati Vāsavaḥ (above) stands beside kāle varṣati Parjanyaḥ in the same book (R 7, 99, 13). In 12, 29, 53, P. makes the crops grow and gives enough to eat, like Indra; and so, like Indra, under a good king Parjanya is nikāmavarṣin, "rains as is desirable" and the farmer's six ītis are not known (5, 61, 17). The roar, nāda, of Indra on his car (17, 3, 1 f.; R 6, 99, 25) is the roar, ninada, of thunder or of Parjanya (3, 12, 31; 5, 22, 11). Rāma is like Parjanya, it is said, his car also is like that of Indra ("noisy in the air", R 2, 16, 31). Parjanya is the best of roarers or rainers (4, 2, 16, varṣatāṃ, v. l. nardatāṃ). The same phrases are used of each, gharmānte Maghavān iva (9, 11, 23), Parjanya iva gharmānte nādayan vai diśo daśa (7, 162, 54) and 12, 37, 22 (idem) where "people long for and live on Parjanya" (often; cf. 12, 97, 15). Parjanya is the savior, nātha, of cattle (5, 34, 38). The "people" are especially those mentioned in R 2, 112, 12, "as the ploughmen long for Parjanya" (cf. R 2, 3, 29; ib. 31, 12; ib. 67, 9). In short, Parjanya is the bucolic Indra, chief god of ploughmen; but the greater province remains Indra's. "Created beings live on Parjanya;

on Indra live the gods" (2, 45, 65 f.; 3, 34, 21; 5, 133, 42; 12, 75, 13; 13, 61, 37).[1]) Parjanya (the cloud) is rain itself, being to the crops what ambrosia is to the gods; he brings the crops to completeness (3, 32, 47 and S 1, 77, 3: Parjanya iva sasyānāṃ, devānām amṛtaṃ yathā). Indra also "starts the crops and then ceases to rain" (R 4, 30, 22), but it is only one of his capacities; whereas Parjanya only rains; yet he rains as the thunderer, so that the normal position of the two gods is almost reversed when it is said that "Arjuna shot arrows as Maghavat shoots rain, and as Parjanya hurls lightning" (aśani, 7, 10, 15 f.). In the later epic there is no distinction between Indra quâ rain-giver and Parjanya. Thus in 12, 141, 5 and 15, the story begins avarṣati Parjanye and continues na vavarṣa Sahasrākṣaḥ. So in 3, 110, 43 f., "since the thousand-eyed (Indra) failed to rain . . the king inquired of his priests in regard to Surendra (Indra) raining as to how Parjanya might (be got to) rain". Parjanya "roars mightily in windy confusion", hurling hail (7, 21, 33); he is citravarṣin (= akāle, H 11145) at the aeon's end (cf. 12, 69, 96, kvacid varṣati Parjanyaḥ), but when all is well he sends food (6, 27, 14) and (as Indra, above) "rains gold", "rains all desires", on his favorite (kāmān varṣati Parjanyaḥ, 7, 56, 5). See also Ādityas (§ 37), where Parjanya is perhaps Indra, as in H 10257 (as seer, H 431).

§ 72. **Indra's Battles.** — In 12, 33, 26, the wars between gods and demons are said to have lasted 32000 years. The one greatest (not repeated) battle of the war-god was with Vṛtra who "because of his conduct became the foe of Indra" in the South (5, 109, 13), after the demon had covered the worlds twain (āvṛtya rodasī 3, 101, 1; under protection of the Kālakeya demons), and enveloped the whole movable world (vyāptam, 5, 10, 1). The epic confuses the story of Vṛtra with that of Namuci (below) and has two different accounts of the battle and its origin. Belonging to the pseudo-epic is the account of Vṛtra's conversion to the Viṣṇuites, his experiences after defeat and attainment of Yoginhood, together with the gītam or song composed by the "Daitya Vṛtra"; it astonished even the late pietist (12, 282, 1). Vṛtra is described as five hundred leagues high and three hundred round (ib. 282, 8; as yogin, ib. 281, 59) and as having stupified Indra; the battle between the two becomes typical of all remarkable duels, Vṛtravāsavayor iva (2, 23, 25; R 6, 58, 48; ib. 100, 31, etc.). Vṛtra is one of the four sons of Danāyus (Daitya above, and elsewhere, with the later indifference), Vikṣara, Vala, Vīra, and Vṛtra "the great Asura" (1, 65, 33). The first is incorporated as king Vasumitra (1, 67, 41) but is not known otherwise (except as a title of Kṛṣṇa-Viṣṇu), and even in H merely appears among other Dānavas and Asuras. Vala (written Bala) is the personified fortress or hole which gives Indra his title Valabhid (-sūdana, -hantṛ). Vīra is known otherwise only as an Asura killed by lightning. These appear as kings in the war (7, 25, 53), as does Vṛtra himself, as Maṇimat (ib.), not the Yakṣa of that name (see Kubera) but an earthly king. As Vṛtra is of Brahmanic family, his slaughter is regarded as "priest-murder", and the personification of the crime came out of his dead body wearing a garland of skulls and stuck to Indra "like a spell" (kṛtyā, 12, 283, 13), just as fire came from his mouth and his memory also came out of him in the shape of a jackal (ib. 2). Both Viṣṇu's power

[1]) Fausbøll, Indian Mythology, p. 97, takes Parjanyam as neuter (cloud) in the first passage, but the pāda is connected with the following upajīvanti, not with the preceding pāhi.

and Śiva's feverish energy assisted Indra, the former entering the bolt, the latter making Vṛtra yawn (282, 30; 283, 8), so that Indra could cast the bolt into his open mouth (variant below). Here he is said to have practised Yoga for 60000 years and to have received boons of Brahman, making him strong. He was "made by Tvaṣṭṛ" (like Triśiras) and hence Indra could not overcome him. Śiva gave permission to Tvaṣṭṛ to fashion him (7, 94, 49f.); the Maruts honor Indra on slaying Vṛtra (7, 179, 64) as being the only slayer; the sectarian view is late. Indra is the only foe of the demons (2, 65, 24), but (6, 83, 57, etc.) Viṣṇu is associated with him at an early stage (Indropendrau) before the power enters the bolt, as coequal antagonist "rushing the Daitya host", as Agni also assists him. After Indra had taken off the head of Vṛtra (śiro jahāra, 8, 91, 50), he was disgusted with the demon's foul smells. The later epic says that Indra struck him several times; after each wound Vṛtra retreated into water, light, and air, successively; taking away their qualities (taste, color, sound), and finally into Indra himself, who had to be roused with Vasiṣṭha's melody (rathantara) to kill him (14, 11, 8f.). The story goes back to the combat with Triśiras and begins with the Vedic words: Viśvarūpo hi vai Tvāṣṭraḥ purohito devānām āsit svasrīyo 'surāṇām, "Viśvarūpa, the son of Tvaṣṭṛ, was the family-priest of the gods, a sister's son of the Asuras" (TS. 2, 5, 1, 1; Mbh. 12, 343, 28f.), but instead of continuing with the original ("and had three heads"), the epic proceeds to say that Viśvarūpa gave part of the sacrifice in secret to the Asuras, while in public he served the gods. Then the Asuras, whose chief was Hiraṇyakaśipu, went to the Asura mother of Viśvarūpa and complained that her son, Viśvarūpa Triśiras, was the gods' priest, so that the Asuras grew weak. His mother found him in Nandana (grove) and persuaded him to side with Hiraṇyakaśipu, who made him chaplain after discharging Vasiṣṭha. Vasiṣṭha cursed Hiraṇyakaśipu (who in due time was slain by Viṣṇu as man-lion). Meantime Indra became alarmed at Triśiras's ascetic power and tried to seduce him through a nymph. Triśiras enjoyed the nymph but kept his power and began to drink the gods' soma with one mouth, eat the sacrifice with another, and consume the gods' power with the third mouth. On the advice of Brahman the distracted gods got Dadhīca to give up his bones, wherewith Dhātṛ made a bolt, which Indra shot at Triśiras and decapitated him (the bolt was infused with Viṣṇu-energy). But out of the mangled remains rose another (form of) Triśiras (Vṛtra), and Indra smote that, making two cases of Brahman-cide, which frightened Indra so that he fled and hid in a lotus-stalk. Then the gods made Nahuṣa their chief and with five hundred lights on his brow Nahuṣa guarded the third heaven, but tried to seduce Śacī, who, consulting with Bṛhaspati, had recourse to "boon-granting Rumor" (Upaśruti, an evil spirit in Sūtras). On being prayed to, Upaśruti revealed where Indra lay hid (in lake Mānasa). Indra agreed to return, after advising Śacī how to ruin Nahuṣa by getting him to yoke the saints and so fall under the curse of Agastya, who changed him into a snake. Indra performed a horse-sacrifice in honor of Viṣṇu and was reinstated as king of gods, dividing his sin of Brahman-cide between women, vanitās, fire, trees, and cows. But a black antelope was really used for the horse; Bṛhaspati officiated (ib. 48 and 52f.). Cf. R 4, 24, 14, Indra's sin taken by earth, water, trees, and women (see below). That Triśiras was a holy being is implied when it is said that Indra would not have made sacrifice after slaying "the Muni", if right had been the same as wrong (R 6, 83, 29). In 12, 283, 28 f., where also a sacrifice frees Indra at the end, the sin is cast upon Agni (created to receive it), who may pass it on to any one that does not make fire-oblations; upon trees and plants (transferred to one who cuts grass or trees on holy days); upon Apsarasas (who may turn it over to men lacking in restraint); and upon water, this last quarter of the sin passing into any defiler of water. In the account in Udyoga, where it is described as a purāvṛtta itihāsa purātana, "an ancient story of an old event" (5, 9, 2 f.), Tvaṣṭṛ created his son expressly to injure Indra, and the son's mouths (faces) were like sun, moon and fire (cf. Śiva's eyes), with which he respectively absorbed soma and Vedas, surā, and space. Indra slew him because he could not be seduced, but was scorched by his radiance, for Triśiras, "though stricken was glorious, and though dead lay as one alive". So Indra bade a carpenter cut off the heads of Brāhmaṇa Triśiras (cf. 5, 9, 34, Brahmahatyā; and on the carpenter, a Vedic trait, see WZKM. 26, 123, with Kāṭhaka ref.), telling the man that he should receive the head of sacrifice thereafter, Indra promising to free himself from sin by asceticism. From the head thus cut off flew out partridges, quails, sparrows, and hawks, as out of Vṛtra's blood came cocks (unclean for food, 12, 283, 60). Then Tvaṣṭṛ, "sipping water, cursed Indra as an ill-souled evil-minded" person, and "making an oblation in fire, produced Vṛtra", and bade him grow great as Indra's foe. So Vṛtra fought and succeeded in whirling Indra into his mouth, but the gods created (the yawn) Jṛmbhikā, as a great being, to destroy Vṛtra, and, Vṛtra yawning, out leaped Indra (but "Jṛmbhikā thereafter became part of breathing"). Indra and the gods retreating to Mandara-peak thought of Viṣṇu, "subduer of Bali, god of gods, who made three strides" (etc.), and Viṣṇu entered the bolt. Thus reinforced, Indra attacked Vṛtra again, after gods and seers had made a contract with Vṛtra, to the effect that he should not be killed with "dry or wet, stone or wood", etc. But Viṣṇu entered foam and Indra smote Vṛtra with it ("dry and wet" thunderbolts are recognised among magic arms, R 1, 27, 9). So Vṛtra was slain by a lie, and Indra, having committed Brahman-cide and being oppressed by the lie as well, feared and hid in water. Earth, losing Indra's rain, suffered; Nahuṣa was made king of gods (etc., as above; 5, 10, 15 f.; 29 f.). The Southern version adds that Śiva's Bhūts also oppressed Indra, yelling "Brahman-murderer" at him. Here (5, 13, 19) the sin is divided fivefold, between rivers, trees, mountains, earth, and women. Bṛhaspati is more prominent than above and a real horse-sacrifice takes place. Upaśruti is introduced after Śacī proposes to invoke "divine Night" (the passage is marked by verbal equivalence with R 7, 85, 18 = 5, 13, 12, rakṣārthaṃ sarvabhūtānāṃ Viṣṇutvam upajagmivān; cf. too ib. 23 = R ib. 86, 4, etc.). This murder of Triśiras appears to be alluded to in 1, 76, 52: "Whom, even Indra, would not Brahman-murder burn?" (Traiśīrṣā Brahmahatyā it is called, 5, 10, 44). Of the new characters in this version, Jṛmbhikā belongs to a class of inferior spirits called Jṛmbhakas accompanying Śiva (3, 231, 34; cf. Jambhakas). Nahuṣa was originally a pious king, son of Āyus, son of Purūravas (1, 75, 26 f.); he kicked Agastya because the latter was heterodox! (5, 17, 1 f.). His own sin of killing a cow was divided into 101 parts and became diseases (12, 263, 48 f.). His evil eye absorbed power from all he saw (13, 99, 17). Gifts to priests gave him power (13, 100, 11 f.). He lauds wealth as a means of such piety (12, 8, 11 f.). His usurpation of

Indra's rank and his fall, with memory of his past, in serpent-form is often an epic theme (3, 179, 13 f.; 3, 103, 14; H 8813, etc). Hiraṇyakaśipu was the only son of Diti (1, 65, 17; but see p. 48); he interchanges with Vṛtra-Namuci in the story of the compact (above) but with Kṛṣṇa as the god (H 12622; S 2, 46, 13), as he was the greatest opponent of Viṣṇu (so as Rāvaṇa, R 7, 37, pra. 5, 85 f.). The Rām., in its version of this greatest deed of Indra, when the "lord of the immortals slew the great Asura Vṛtra" (R 6, 67, 167), also represents smoke and fire as coming from the dragon's mouth (ib. 93, 19), when struck by the bolt (ib. 111, 22). Sampāti says, "long ago, after the slaughter of Vṛtra" (R 4, 58, 4), removing the action to an indefinite past.

§ 73. The account in R 7, 84, 3 f., agrees in general with that of Udyoga. Vṛtra is here so pious that earth thrives under him till he leaves his son to rule in Madhurā and began to torment gods with asceticism. Viṣṇu, appealed to, refuses to kill him on the score of auld lang syne, but agrees to enter (inspire) Indra, the bolt, and earth (divides himself threefold). Indra's sin was removed by a horse-sacrifice, and the sin was divided among rivers for four rain-months, earth, women during three days, and fourth among those who kill harmless priests with a lie (R 7, 86, 16). Another late passage makes Indra's evil (mala, filth) and hunger, after killing Vṛtra, give names to the Maladas and Karūśas (R 1, 24, 17 f.). Namuci, son of Danu, also fell beneath Indra (Namucer hantā, 3, 25, 10), who, "bolt in hand and combining with the Maruts slew Vṛtra and Namuci, hard to attack, and the Rākṣasī Dīrghajihvā" (3, 292, 4). Here, as in R 2, 106, 27, the Maruts help ("union is strength" is the expressed moral); or Indra alone is mentioned (8, 26, 21; R 6, 56, 17, etc.). The compact of Indra is here made with Namuci and its breaking is said to be good polity (2, 55, 13 abhimatā ripau vṛttiḥ). The head followed the god crying out at him, but Indra bathed at the confluence of the Aruṇā and Sarasvatī and became pure; the demoniac head fell into the river and the demon, who had first escaped into a sunbeam, went to a world of delight (9, 43, 33 f.), while Indra went to heaven. "Foam used on a foggy day" evades the agreement not to kill "with wet or dry by day or night" (ib.). Another version is that Indra was wounded (8, 85, 26 f.) when Namuci rushed at him (R 3, 28, 3), and Indra even ran away (6, 83, 40). A simile in 6, 88, 17 would imply that he was shot nine times, but such phrases as Vāsavo Namuciṃ yathā and Maghavān iva Śambaram are used by the poets without much regard to details (9, 7, 35 and 38; ib. 16, 33; ib. 17, 22, etc.). Rāma could slay Namuci or Bali (R 3, 39, 18). Namuci sermonises to Indra in the pseudo-epic, video meliora deteriora sequor (jānāmi śreyo na tu tat karomi, 12, 226, 9, with v. l. of S). His name is like that of the seer Pramuca or Pramucu, associated (§ 58) with Unmuca and Vimuca (also 12, 208, 29), but nothing suggests that it implies "not-freeing" (except the pertinacity of the head). He is son of Vipracitti and brother of Maya (below). The Rām. distinguishes the manner of death of Vṛtra and Namuci: "As Vṛtra (fell smitten) by the vajra (bolt); as Namuci by foam; as Vala by lightning" (R 3, 30, 28).

§ 74. Indra's other battles can be more briefly narrated. He confronted Bali in the great war of gods and Asuras and then worshipped Viṣṇu who defeated Bali (after helping Indra in the combat, 7, 142, 8; 8, 20, 51; ib. 93, 47; Agni assists, 7, 25, 20; cf. R 6, 73, 7). This demon (Mahābali, R 4, 65, 14, v. l.) was only son of Vairocana (hence Vairocana or -ni), and grandson of Prahlāda, whom Indra slew. Bali himself was father of Bāṇa (R 5, 50, 3 as Mahākāla); "like Indra and Vairocana" is a standard simile of rival fighters (1, 138, 46; R 7, 32, 58; etc., Bali-Vāsavayor iva, 3, 17, 11). He is best of Dānavas, as Indra is best of gods (S 4, 3, 25). His combat with Indra took place in the second age, Tretâyuga (S 2, 47, 1). Bali won wealth and bliss through favoring priests and was lost (for injuring them, 3, 26, 12), since Viṣṇu in dwarf-form bound him (3, 102, 23; 5, 10, 7; H 14312f.) as Balivīryaharo Hariḥ (R 5, 1, 197). The Vedic tale, how Viṣṇu asked for three paces and then cast out and slew the giver of the world, is known (R 1, 29, 5f.). Indra noosed him (R 2, 14, 11); Viṣṇu kept him in a fire in a cave (R 7, 23, pra. 1, 6f.); he was cast out of the three worlds (5, 38, 47). Cited as authoritative (5, 32, 24), he becomes a learned ass in the pseudo-epic (12, 223, 2f.) and instructs Indra in patience and humility after the latter had found him, who had (by magic) been Wind, Varuṇa, Agni, and Water. When Indra insults him, he replies: "You will see me there again when my time comes" (ib. 27 and 225, 30f.; 227, 7f.). His grandfather Prahlāda also (12, 124, 28f.) philosophises (as a saint, ib. 222, 3f.) in the same way, as "Indra of Daityas" (3, 28, 1f.; 6, 34, 30). He was killed by Indra (3, 286, 12; 289, 18; 12, 98, 49f.), though a devotee of Viṣṇu (R 4, 65, 14). Śakra and Prahlāda were rivals for the three worlds (7, 123, 65; 9, 57, 3). He cannot move Skanda's spear (12, 328, 17f.). Verses of his are cited on the "cat's way" (hypocrisy, 5, 160, 13; cf. ib. 33, 103f.). His sons Kumbha and Nikumbha (§ 18) are not important (1, 65, 19), though the latter is a "Daitya-chief" (1, 209, 2f.), father of Sunda and Upasunda and gaṇeśa of Śiva's host, when he slaughtered Saudāsa's army at Benares (S 12, 68, 46). The two in Rām. are fighting fiends, but their father is barely recognised except for the extraordinary allocution (vocative) when Nikumbha distinguishes himself (cf. R 6, 9 and 75) Prahlāda-Bali-Vṛtraghna-Kubera-Varuṇopama! (R 6, 76, 73). It may be remarked that Indra kills another member of this family, Mantharā, daughter of Virocana, "because she tried to destroy earth", an unknightly act (to kill a woman), excused on the score that "Viṣṇu also slew Kāvya's mother, the wife of Bhṛgu, because she sought to deprive the world of sleep" (or of Indra; anindram, v. l. for anidram lokam, R 1, 25, 20f.). Viṣṇu's victim should be Pulomā (1, 5, 13f.), but some other druh anindrā (RV. 4, 23, 7) may be meant. Amid all these victories, the poets admit that "even Indra suffered defeat" (7, 139, 107). Besides the victory of Skanda (3, 226, 17f.), and apart from Śiva himself and Viṣṇu (q. v.), Kumbhakarṇa defeats him (R 6, 61, 9f.) and Indrajit receives his cognomen as conqueror of Indra (3, 288, 2f.; R 6, 45, 22, etc.). Even Atikāya arrests his bolt (R 6, 71, 34), not to speak of the saints who withstand him. He is a great blustering vainglorious boy, as Bali says (12, 224, 28, "childish ever is thy mind, to-day as of old"). But like Bali and the rest, Indra too becomes a preacher, as in 12, 11, 2f., where out of pity "for beardless young fools" he takes the form of a "golden bird" and teaches them how to get to heaven by the "way of the gods", i. e. by rites, not by renunciation (ib. 12, 6). Whether Indra killed Maya is doubtful in Mbh., but not in R. The great epic says that "Maya, Namuci's brother", was guarded by Indra's son from the onslaughts of Kṛṣṇa and Agni (1, 228, 41f.), but that Indra and Maya had a terrible encounter in which Maya was defeated (6, 100, 20; 101, 22; 110, 31; 9, 55, 28); Rām. (4, 51, 14) says that Indra smote the Dānava Maya with his bolt because the demon was fond of the Apsaras Hemā.

§ 75. Indra also slew the demon of a hundred illusions, Śambara (Daśaratha aided the god, R 2, 9, 13; R 5, 16, 8); mashed Danu, son of Śrī, leaving him a headless trunk (kabandha, R 3, 71, 10); and broke Hanumat's jaw, but then gave him "death at will" (R 4, 66, 22 and 27; cf. § 8 f.), his opposition to Hanumat being based on the fact that the ape-god was encroaching on Rāhu's province (R 7, 35, 47 f.; the enemy of the gods defended by their king!). He slew the unborn fruit of Diti's womb, leaving enough alive to make the seven Maruts (R 1, 46 and 47; § 48). Indra is called son of Diti here (46, 21; and 47, 9; see § 37), Indra used to live at the town of Viśāla (son of Ikṣvāku and Alambuṣā) of the same name (ib. 47, 10). Jambha, as "disturber of sacrifice", was slain by Indra (8, 77, 3), later by Kṛṣṇa-Viṣṇu (3, 102, 24; 5, 48, 77; 5, 49, 15, "Nara decapitated Jambha about to swallow him"; 7, 11, 5). Still later, "Indra and Viṣṇu together by permission of Bhava (Śiva) sought to kill Jambha" (7, 81, 25). In the later Rām. he is associated with Vṛtra as typical leader, and father of Sunda (R 1, 25, 7; R 7, 6, 45). But Indra was first mentioned as the slayer: "In the struggle of gods and Asuras of old Indra slew Jambha" (7, 102, 17); "like Jambha deprived of prowess by Vṛtrahan" (9, 12, 63); "as Śakra and Jambha fought of old" (7, 96, 20 and 8, 13, 30). Kṛṣṇa slew a demon named Jambhaka (or king?, 2, 31, 7); cf. Jṛmbhikā, § 72, and the arms and magic powers called by the same names (R 1, 28, 9; RG 1, 31, 4 and 10). Śukra warned the Asuras that Jambha would prove their destruction (2, 62, 12). According to different passages the same transference of glory seems to have taken place in the case of the great demon Vipracitti (reincarnated as Jarāsandha 1, 67, 4), eldest son of Danu and Kaśyapa (1, 65, 22) and (H 213 f.) father by Siṃhikā of Namuci and Rāhu and other great demons. In 6, 94, 39 f., Indra is said to have wounded Vipracitti; in 9, 31, 12 Vāsudeva Kṛṣṇa says, "I slew Tāraka and Vipracitti by tricky means". S 6, 94, 32, gives still a third account: "He was conquered by Rudra after being smitten by Mātariśvan" (sa Rudreṇa jitaḥ pūrvaṃ nihato Mātariśvanā). Vipracitti here is described as a demon causing the three worlds to quake and very hard to assail. He is leader of the Vidyādharas (§ 116) as well as an occupant of Varuṇa's home (2, 9, 12), but a fiend once regarded by the immortals as if he were Death himself (6, 108, 39). Indra himself states that he slew most of the demons (as is generally admitted), in explaining that he became chief of the gods through prowess: "He who kills the commander-in-chief of the hostile army does an act equal to the prowess of Viṣṇu; he is equal to Bṛhaspati (as "lord of strength"); if he capture the commander, he will, on dying, come to my world, for my worlds shall be his (tasya lokā yathā mama). Hence they do not mourn, they do not bathe, for one slain in battle; for he is blessed already, and thousands of nymphs receive him into heaven when he falls. I too, even Indra, slew the sons of Diti and Danu, my foes (and so was blessed), Jambha, Vṛtra, Vala, Pāka, Virocana of the hundred illusions, Namuci, Śambara of many illusions, Vipracitti, and Prahlāda" (12, 98, 43—49). S conscientiously omits Jambha and characterises Virocana not as illusive but as monstrous ("having a huge body"). Later pious tradition ignores Prahlāda's death.

§ 76. Indra's victories are depicted in the later epic not as due to power of arm but as resting on character. Thus Śambara, disguised as an ascetic, tells Indra (13, 36, 1 f.) that he owes his position to piety toward priests. Similarly, Prahlāda gets Indra's power from him by character.

Indra then consults with Bṛhaspati, his Guru, and is told that Uśanas knows more; so he goes to him, but Uśanas sends him direct to Prahlāda. Then Indra disguises himself as a pupil and by adroit questions finds that Prahlāda's prosperity is based on character. Winning a boon from Prahlāda, he chooses his character, which at once issues from Prahlāda's mouth like a flame, and after his character, śīla, followed his virtue, dharma, his truth, conduct (acts), power and happiness (12, 124, 19f.). Namuci (who repudiates Karman) reminds Indra of his sins (12, 226, 1f.). Bali teaches him humility: as Time has bound Bali, so will Time bind Indra (in "the noose of Time and noose of Varuṇa", 12, 227, 82 and 111). Śrī herself instructs Indra (12, 228, 2f.) that only character insures success; she used to live with the Dānavas because they were virtuous, but she deserted them when they became immoral. Indra (3, 9, 7f.; R 2, 78, 18) listens respectfully to Surabhi's lament (plea for kindness to cattle). The god's sins are many, besides his acts of violence, murder of a Brahman, lying to Namuci (Vṛtra), and theft (R 1, 61, 6, Indra steals the sacrificial beast of Ambarīṣa, but this is to punish the king, the Śunaḥśepa episode). His adulteries lead to his punishment, especially his violation of Gautama's wife Ahalyā (5, 12, 6f.; ib. 13, 9). By Agni's advice, when, discovered by Gautama, he is unmanned, he is provided with a ram's vṛṣaṇa (R 1, 48, 16f.; ib. 49, 1f.); but according to R 7, 30, 33, he is punished by being defeated by Indrajit. The curse of Gautama turns Indra's beard yellow (12, 343, 23). He is called an habitual adulterer, parastrīkāmacārin. The story of how he tried to seduce Ruci, wife of Devaśarman, exposes only one of his many amours (13, 40, 18f.). In this case the pupil Vipula puts Ruci into a hypnotic state, which prevents her from responding to Indra's advances (under the young priest's influence she speaks Sanskrit, ib. 41, 15). Vipula reproaches Indra with having been cursed by Gautama with a thousand sex-marks which became eyes (ib. 41, 21). In 13, 34, 27, this is cited as proof of priestly power, since Kauśika Gautama was a priest; priests also cured Indra: "Behold, a mark was made on the moon (by a priest); the sea was made salt (by a priest); and great Indra was marked by a thousand sex-signs, who yet by the might of Brāhmaṇas became thousand-eyed" (so that he became sahasranayana, as he is now called). A different account of the origin of the eyes appears in the tale of Tilottamā (§ 100), an Apsaras so beautiful that when Indra looked at her, "large red-edged eyes, a thousand in number, appeared all over his body, before, behind, and on his sides, whence he was called sahasranetra" (1, 211, 27f.; sahasranayana also in R 7, 72, 8). The equivalent (sahasrākṣa) epithet is as old as the Ṛg-Veda, where it probably refers to Indra's flaming bolt, which has a thousand flames, while the same epithet is applied to fire (RV. 1, 23, 3; 79, 12; in PW., explained as stars, Indra's eyes). Indra was paralysed several times, twice at least because of his sins. Cyavana paralysed him when he struck the saint because of the Aśvins' being permitted to drink soma (3, 121, 22; 124, 17; 12, 343, 24f.). On another occasion Śiva, as a child on Umā's lap, paralysed Indra because of his jealous discontent (13, 161, 33). Śiva again paralysed him by a look so that "he stood like a post", as the greater god scoffed at him and finally cast him into a cave, to show him that Śiva was the real lord of the world (1, 197, 16). Indra's sin here is pride and his humiliation is his punishment. His "bolt was stayed", that is, he was practically paralysed by another saint (§ 79); cf. other cases, H 11940f.; 12555f.

§ 77. Owing to Indra's sin, Garuḍa undertook to carry off the soma, as Bṛhaspati says to Indra: "Through thy fault, aparādha, through thy wantonness" is this thing come upon the gods. For Indra, as a giant god, had insulted the thumbkin saints called Vālakhilyas, who were helping him collect wood for Prajāpati's sacrifice (1, 30, 40 f.). Indra's inability to hurt Garuḍa is a late feature of the epic (1, 33, 20). Oddly enough, especially in view of Indra as praiser of Śibi (§ 51), no reproach is cast upon the god for his cowardly abandonment of Takṣaka. Although Indra had been friendly with him, and even promised him immunity from fire if he should take refuge with Indra, yet when danger threatened and the frightened serpent was actually "hiding in Indra's upper clothes", the god, afraid that the priests' incantations would draw him into the fire, threw off the suppliant refugee and escaped, leaving Takṣaka to perish (1, 56, 10—14). But it is satisfactory to record that it is only the later epic which makes of Indra a coward and still worse a cad; as when he triumphs brutally over his fallen foe "with vulgar mind" (prākṛtyā buddhyā, 12, 223, 28 f.), till the wise ass (Bali) rebukes him: "This is not worthy of thy fame and family" and reminds him that, as Devarāja, he is only one of a long series of Indras, who reign but for a thousand years apiece (ib. 224, 55; 227, 70). In the earlier scene he sees a vision of "other Indras" who have preceded him and are now helpless (1, 197, 20, Viśvabhuj, Bhūtadhāman, Śibi, Śānti, and Tejasvin are the "five earlier Indras", ib. 29). Among Indra's nobler sins may be counted his heterodoxy as to the glory of cows (13, 83, 15 f.), an indication of sectarian prejudice in favor of Goloka (Viṣṇu's abode). A more venerable sin is Indra's objection to the Agniṣṭut, a praise offered only to Agni. King (rājarṣi) Bhaṅgāsvana offered it, to get children, and Indra stupified him and made him enter a lake which changed him into a woman. Then Indra made the children got by lauding Agni quarrel, "as the gods and demons of old, children of one Kaśyapa, quarrelled"; so they killed each other. But he restored them to life, when he was himself lauded and so pacified (the king preferred to remain a woman, as a woman has more pleasure in love than a man, 13, 12, 4 f.; ib. 20 and 51). Agni's praise is said to be Indra-dviṣṭa (ib. 4). The story is old; or at least it is as old as the late Sūtras.[1]) Indra's loud ridicule of the holiness of Kurukṣetra is only for dramatic effect, as he ends by singing a Gāthā in honor of this holy land (9, 53, 7 f.; ib. 21; cf. the Indragītā Gāthāḥ lauding Sahadeva's sacrifice, 3, 90, 6). Indra is not an object of much devotion himself and is naively delighted when the jujube-girl shows Śakrabhakti by intense devotion to him. She was the daughter of Bharadvāja and Ghṛtācī, a nymph, who seduced him. As the girl grew up and was called something of a scholar Śrutāvatī (by name), she preferred the love of god Indra, as Tridaśādhipati, Tribhuvaneśvara. Indra came to her in the disguise of Vasiṣṭha, first testing her hospitality by asking for jujubes, which she cooked for him, using her feet as fuel (being short of wood), and then he made her his wife (bhāryā, 9, 48, 1 f.; ib. 62).

§ 78. Disguise is commonly assumed when the god visits men. As above, Indra assumes the form of a saint, but his illusions are manifold and he can appear in any shape of form. His favorite form is that of a priest or seer (so Sūrya disguises himself, 3, 300, 5 f.), in which shape he seduces Ahalyā (as her husband) and Ruci (above). Sometimes (says Ruci's husband) Indra appears with bolt or bow or as a Cāṇḍāla or ascetic, of

[1]) Caland, Über das rituelle Sūtra des Baudhāyana.

any shape, of any color or caste, or as a bird or animal or Daitya, even as a fly or gnat, so that "even the All-maker, who made the universe, cannot penetrate his disguise, who (Indra) may be quite invisible or may seem wind" (vāyubhūtaḥ, below and 13, 40, 28 f.). It is as priest that Indra begs Karṇa for his armor (3, 310, 1 f.); so he converses with the good parrot, who was faithful to his blasted tree (13, 5, 12 f.), though both the bird and Karṇa recognise him at once. Indra revives the dead tree with the ambrosia which he seems to have handy at all times, though he would not give it to Utaṅka till Govinda bade him do so, when disguised as a dirty ascetic he offerred it as urine (digvāsas, mātaṅga), that Kṛṣṇa's devotee might reject it, which he did; but Kṛṣṇa in lieu of ambrosia gave Utaṅka the power to call up rain-clouds in the desert, and these clouds are still called "Utaṅka clouds" (14, 55, 15 f.) The dirty naked hunter with his pack of dogs appears to assimilate Indra (here opposed to Govinda) to Śiva, of whom it is said: digvāsāḥ kīrtyate ko 'nyo loke (13, 14, 217). In 1, 3, 131 f., Indra helps Utaṅka chase Takṣaka and is hymned by him; the god being here mystically represented as a man with a horse (ib. 167). With a dog too Indra appears disguised as a beggar, Śunaḥsakhasakhi, in the story of the theft of the lotus-stalks (13, 93, 142; as a dog Dharma tests the hero in 18, 3, 34). Disguised as a priestly pupil, Indra deceives Prahlāda (above, 12, 124, 28 f.); as a priest, he tries to overthrow the power of Viśvāmitra (R 1, 65, 5), after first trying to do so by becoming a cuckoo and conspiring with Rambhā and Kāma (ib. 64, 1 f.). Being tormented by the ascetic torments of Yavakrīta, Indra becomes an old priest and tries to undermine the saint's devotion (3, 135, 16 f.) by showing that one cannot learn Veda by asceticism. In 13, 102, 3 f., Indra discusses hells, disguised as a king, with a saint whose elephant he steals. As wind (vāyubhūtaḥ) he mixes up the clothes of girls who are bathing (1, 78, 4); but as he stopped on his way to war to do this, it is to be laid not to levity but to polity, since he knows in advance the ensuing quarrel and its dire result. As a soldier, bhaṭa, Indra tries to dissuade a saint from becoming too virtuous by enchanting him with the glitter of arms. When the holy man's intelligence "becomes rude" from too much contemplation of the sword, he looses his virtue and Indra has the satisfaction of seeing him go to hell (R 3, 9, 16 f.). According to R 1, 39, 7, Indra takes the shape of a Rākṣasa to drive away the horse of Sagara. The Mbh. says merely that the Sāgaras thought it had been stolen, not that the frightened gods had aught to do with the theft (3, 107, 13). Other disguises assumed by Indra are that of a goose (his goose-form is revered at his festival, above), probably the "golden bird" (above); of a jackal, to inculcate patience and instruct Kāśyapa (12, 180, 4 f.); and of a hawk in the tale of Śibi (omitted in 13, 32, 4 f.; see above, § 51). He also changes the shape of others. When Mataṅga, at Indra's advice, renounces the hope of becoming a priest, the god at the request of the saintly but lowborn man, changes him into a lovely bird honored of women and called "song (his) god"; for such seems to be the meaning of chandodeva (after Mataṅga has requested that he should become a "lovely bird", 13, 29, 22 f.); but the "song" is that of the Vedic verses to the would-be priest.

§ 79. The strength of Indra manifests itself in prowess, mentally and morally; Śakratulyaparākrama, "having Indra-like prowess", is applied to any strong creature, a stereotyped phrase (R 4, 32, 11, etc.). Indra is "the one hero amid gods" (1, 113, 32); to say "even Indra" could not conquer one, is a tribute to the god (1, 100, 78; 2, 67, 36, etc.), when not pure braggadocio (4, 49, 12). Indra is power: "To Indra he bows who bows to a stronger person" (12, 67, 11). Hence the king is divine power (Indram eva pravṛṇute yad rājānam, 12, 67, 4). A great king is "another Indra" (1, 85, 5, etc.); so "a weak realm with no Indra" (anindram abalam, 12, 67, 2). Hence, too, nṛbījam Indradaivatyam and indriyam, Indra is the divinity of procreative power (12, 214, 23, v. l. tribījam). But Indra is strengthened by the Maruts and by the Vasus (6, 96, 16, they surround him in battle), in fact by all the gods (12, 78, 15). Mental power is his as a seer. He recognises the future greatness of Kurukṣetra (above); he advises the rebuilding of Benares, with a view to the prosperity of Divodāsa Saudeva, whose son Pratardana (born of a sacrifice performed by Bharadvāja, and adult as soon as born) defeated Vītahavya, king of the Haihayas. According to S 1, 95, 12, Indra prophesies the greatness of Cakravartin Duṣyanta (cf. B, Kaṇva, in, 1, 73, 30f.). Though Indra is weakened by intoxication (his foe is Mada, 14, 9, 33), and delights always in soma (12, 71, 33; he revels in the seven kinds of Soma-sacrifice, 3, 88, 6; 12, 29, 36f.), yet he is a strict upholder of morality which appeals to him. This is "warrior morality", aindro dharmaḥ (12, 141, 64), and as the king has his physical power, so Indra as a moral power is incorporate in the king (12, 72, 25). Bṛhaspati guides his councils (R 4, 54, 4) and the later epic gives him seven "Seers of the East", modelled after those of the North (13, 150, 29f.), viz., Yavakrīta, Raibhya, Arvāvasu, Parāvasu, Auśija Kakṣīvat, Bala the son of Aṅgiras, and Kaṇva the son of Medhātithi (Barhiṣada is added; but the seers are seven in seven groups). Indra reveres only moral people (a list of them at S 13, 153, 7f.). With his bolt he splits into a hundred pieces the head of a false or recalcitrant witness (2, 68, 70); he casts his bolt upon him that gives up a refugee (5, 12, 21). Above all he delights in hospitality; he is himself the guest, a seat for the guest is a seat for Indra (3, 200, 62 and 68; also ib. 123, Parjanyo 'nnānusaṃcaran, in the sense of the scholiast, "who comes as a guest is Indra himself"). Who dies in battle is Indra's guest (also the priyātithi of Yama, Varuṇa, and Kubera, 7, 72, 46, as Lokapālas). Slain warriors are not called dead, but "guests of Indra" (7, 19, 36, Śakrasyā 'tithitāṃ gatāḥ) or "dear guests of Vala's slayer" (7, 27, 8). Those who die facing the foe are his dear guests and enjoy his world of delight (teṣāṃ kāmadughān lokān Indraḥ saṃkalpayiṣyati, 11, 2, 15; cf. 3, 54, 18, etc.), for they rejoice with him and he leads a joyous life (2, 7; 2, 12, 26; R 6, 54, 38). But Indra has his ups and downs (R 3, 66, 12) and it is part of his sagacity rather than an indication of cowardice that he is ever afraid of too much formal virtue. He recognises that merit stored up by the ascetic may become equal to or greater than his own, in which case he may be dethroned. Hence he always seeks to overthrow the asceticism of a too ascetic saint, generally by seducing him. Thus, according to Rām. and Mbh., respectively, he sends Rambhā or Menakā (1, 71, 20f.) to seduce Viśvāmitra, fearing "lest this man of sunlike glory shake me from my station". Rarely is this sagacious fear united with bodily fear, yet Indra sends Jānapadī (devakanyā) to seduce Śaradvat Gautama, because this great seer "mightily distressed the king of the gods by his skill in archery, dhanurveda, and asceticism" (1, 130, 5). Two men, one an ascetic and one a king, had power to control Indra. The first was Ṛṣyaśṛṅga, "through fear of whom the slayer of Vala and Vṛtra did rain" (3, 110, 24). The king was Māṃdhātṛ, of the race of Ikṣvāku, who, born by cleaving his father's side, became twelve years old in twelve days, and from being a suckling of Indra whose thumb he sucked, attained to such power that when he died "he got half of Indra's throne" (Śakrasyā 'rdhāsanam, 3, 126, 38) and "half his realm" (R 7, 67, 8). He actually "conquered Indra on the Gomatī at a Nāga-named town" (12, 356, 3) and was father of Mucukunda, being himself born of Saudyumni Yuvanāśva without a mother, conquering the whole earth and possessing Ājagava (Śiva's bow) and other special arms. Indra had to stand and look on while Māṃdhātṛ made rain (3, 126, 42, above, § 71). The Rām. says that when this "lord of the seven Dvīpas" reached heaven and was about to oust Indra from his seat, the wily god persuaded him that he was not a real world-conqueror and sent him back to earth to conquer Lavaṇa, the one foe left unconquered; but Lavaṇa slew him with Rudra's trident (boomerang, R 7, 67, 5 f.; ib. 23, pra. 3, 23 f.). Māṃdhātṛ once slew a sinful ascetic (R 4, 18, 35, here as Rāma's ancestor) and he conquered earth in one night, whereas Janamejaya took three and Nābhāga even seven nights to perform the same feat (12, 29, 81 f.; ib. 124, 16). Kings are sometimes said to have surpassed Indra, but this is usually mere panegyric; it does not mean that the god was actually overcome. It is said, for example, of Marutta (yaḥ spardhayā 'jayac Chakraṃ devarājaṃ puraṃdaram, 12, 29, 20), yet in 14, 10, 11, this Marutta says that a floating cloud shows Indra to be near and escapes as fast as he can. In Buddhistic narrations, the excellence of a very virtuous person "makes hot the throne of Indra", so that the god grows uncomfortable as if sitting upon a hot stove. The epics have no such absurd figure. The saints disturb Indra and shake his throne, but they heat, i. e. torment, only Indra, the gods, or the worlds (tāpayati is not applied to the throne but to the sitter, who is heated, disturbed, "all het up").

§ 80. With other gods except Tvaṣṭṛ (above) Indra's relations are in general those of friendly superiority. As was shown above, he objects to Agni's exclusive praise, and he takes part against him in the matter of the serpents' sacrifice (1, 26) and at Khāṇḍava, to save Takṣaka (1, 223, 7 f.); yet the two are grouped as "the two friends, Indrāgnī" (3, 134, 9), and Agni assists Indra against Bali (7, 25, 20). Indra promises Agni a share in the sacrifice (5, 16, 32) and Agni acts as Indra's messenger (14, 9, 8 f.). Anala (Agni) always conveys the oblation to Indra (R 5, 37, 21). With the Aśvins he was at first in enmity and then makes friends (see Aśvins, § 110). With the Sun-god (§ 38 f.) he is at enmity on account of their respective sons (Arjuna and Karṇa), but "Wind, Indra, and Sun" are allies (1, 1, 187, v. l. Śakrasūryau). With Kubera (§ 83 f.) Indra shares the North(-east) district, so that they have one sadman there (3, 163, 6 f.), and rivals him in wealth (R 1, 6, 3). Both gods possess the grove Nandana (below). With Yama and Varuṇa, Indra is associated as types of power, the former rarely (R 2, 1, 38, "like Yama or Śakra in power"), the latter in a stereotyped phrase, "like great Indra and Varuṇa" (e. g. R 6, 41, 6), a reminiscence of the old fighting power of Varuṇa (cf. a hero "like Indra or Varuṇa", R 6, 64, 18). With Brahman (§ 131 f.) Indra stands in the position of a favored son or is like a younger brother (R 6, 60, 96, by implication). Indra and Prajāpati are both saviors, nātha, to the other gods, though the latter is a father (R 7, 83, 11 f.). With Bṛhaspati Indra acts as any pupil to a Guru ("takes his feet", etc., R 2, 103, 28 and 30). With the growth of sectarian gods, Indra grows less. But with Viṣṇu (§ 143 f.) Indra is still on equal terms in many passages. Viṣṇu "assists" Indra (6, 59, 80). Arjuna Aindri is "like the younger brother of Indra and like Mahendra" (in power, 6, 49, 16). Śunaḥśepa lauds "Indra and his younger brother" (Viṣṇu, R 1, 62, 25 f.). In the rise of Viṣṇu, however, he as greater god makes Indra the gods' protector (5, 10, 7). Kṛṣṇa as Viṣṇu uses Indra as demiurge and is Indrakarman, that is "works through Indra" (13, 149, 97). But he robs Indra of the Pārijāta tree and opposes him by means of Govardhana (see Kṛṣṇa). Indra and the Maruts say their prayers on Mt. Mandara and here, for Indra, Viṣṇu slew Naraka, son of Diti, when Indra was in mortal fear of the demon and begged abjectly for Viṣṇu's help (3, 142, 7 and 20 f.). On the other hand, Indra begs vainly for Viṣṇu's aid against the fiends (R 7, 27, 14 f.), for the great god has other plans and Indra is made captive by the fiend Meghanāda (Indrajit, ib. ch. 29). Before Śiva too, Indra (as above) is powerless (1, 197), and Indra seeks advice and takes refuge here with Brahman, as usual, when in doubt. For Indra's blazing Śiva with the bolt, see Śiva. With saints and heroes of the epics, Indra is on familiar terms, a humanised god. He visits Śarabhaṅga (R 3, 30, 30) to get Rāma to slay Khara, "as he himself slew Vala", and so he visits other asylums (R 3, 5 and 7) near Nagpur (Rāmagiri). Indra stands beside the lad Daśaratha kills, as the youth goes to heaven in heavenly form (the boy himself goes to heaven but his soul remains in his body for a while, R 2, 64, 19, 48). He takes Lakṣmaṇa to heaven (R 7, 106, 17); gives special trees to the semi-divine monkeys (ib. 4, 33, 15), one of whom is Indrajānu (ib. 39, 32); and grants a boon to Hanumat after breaking his jaw (R 4, 66, 27). Worth noting is Indra's inferiority to the Rākṣasas in Rām., on a par with the despite of the later epic (as noticed above). This is due not so much to a new cult of special Rākṣasas as to the lowered position of Indra, which permits the poet to play with the idea of fiends capable of defeating the king of the gods but defeated by Rāma, an indication of later age or of a place where Indra's cult was much reduced. In general the Rām. Devas are not so authoritative or important as the early Mbh. Devas.

§ 81. The home of Indra as a palace or hall is described at length in the "account of the palaces of the world-protectors". Indra won his as "lord of the universe". It is adorned with lotuses, Puṣkaramālinī, a movable structure "going at will" (of Indra), five leagues high and one hundred and fifty by one hundred leagues in extent; fitted out with divine trees and thrones, where sit Indra and Śacī and Śrī and Lakṣmī with the Maruts as gṛhamedhinaḥ (house-keepers), waiting on him. He is waited upon also by nymphs and other fair women. In 2, 49, 26, the "immortal women" appear (to the scholiast) as plants (Soma, giving Indra to drink). Siddhas, seers, saints, ascetics, sacrifices, heroes, Faith, Fluency (Sarasvatī), Duty, Gain, Pleasure, etc., clouds, winds, the twenty-seven sacrificial fires, Ādityas, planets, stars, Apsarasas, Gandharvas, royal seers, Hariścandra, Marutta (et al.) — all these persons or personifications are to be found perpetually or temporarily in Indra's palace, as also Vālmīki, and (S text) Ekata, Dvita, and Trita (2, 7). Though only one "royal seer" is especially named, yet all kings who perform the Rājasūya live with Indra (2, 12, 6 f.). Indra's city is typical of any marvellous city, Indrapuraprakāśā (R 2, 71, 45, etc.). It is called Amarāvatī and contains a hundred palaces (3,

43, 7). The "residence", bhavana, 3, 15, 18, etc., is either the pura of Mahendra (1, 82, 1) or the city, situated in the third heaven (18, 1, 3). Arjuna visits it and it is described (3, 42, 42f.) as full of lovely flowers, trees, perfumes, saints, and singers; there is the grove Nandana (1, 85, 9; 3, 79, 3), where gods and saints dwell; but the city (like his car) is invisible to the sinful. The list of occupants is longer than that of the palace and includes many kings (in 7, 54, 53 of S text the grove Nandana is ascribed to Nārada). The road to Amarāvatī is the "path of stars" (Milky Way?), nakṣatramārga, suravīthi (3, 43, 12). Indra's son is received by Indra with a kiss and great love (premṇā, ib. 19f.), as the god sits under a white umbrella with a gold handle. To "enter Amarāvatī" is euphemistic for dying (7, 77, 19). The later epic speaks more of Indra's world(s) as goal of ascetics: one who dies by fasting, for example, might come to Vāsava-loka after a million years, going there on a car with "Indra's fair girls"; and such an one "might see even the sports of the gods' king" (13, 107, 21f.). Each god has his own world or place, sthāna, so that Indra's is distinct from that of the Maruts, as it is from that of Varuṇa, etc. (ib. 79f.). Indrakīla (6, 59, 122?) is a northern mountain sacred to Indra, perhaps Mt. Mandara, Indra's peculiar mountain (3, 37, 42). A "city fair as Indrakīla" (R 2, 80, 18; cf. ib. 20) treats it as if it were Amarāvatī; but Indra's home has various names, Śakrālaya, Vajrālaya, etc. (R 6, 74, 59), Mahendradhāman (R 2, 14, 29, etc.). Indra was consecrated on Mt. Meghavat in the West (R 4, 42, 33). Indra also loves to visit Mahendra mountain (R 4, 37, 2). His palace has too the name Sudarśana (S 4, 43, 1). In 3, 54, 18, Kāmadhuk may be the wish-cow Nandinī, daughter of Surabhi and Kaśyapa, or Indra's world called by the same general name. Indraprastha (Indrapat), also called Śakraprastha (cf. for the formation, 3, 84, 99, Dharmaprastha, "where the god Dharma abides ever"), is the Plain of Indra, as city of the Pāṇḍus, especially of Arjuna = Indra('s son).

§ 82. Indra's wife is called Śacī, sometimes Paulomī, also Indrāṇī (Mahendrāṇyā, C 3, 1677, is in B and S sahe 'ndrāṇyā). Indrasenā (S 1, 241, 17) as elsewhere (4, 21, 11, etc.) is probably Mudgala's wife. As type of conjugal felicity stands "Indrāṇī with Harihaya" (1, 199, 5). Nahuṣa's attempt to seduce her (Indrāṇī, Śacī, 12, 343, 46—50) has already been referred to (§ 72); it is the only story about her except for her escape from the demons prior to her marriage, as "Puloman's daughter" (10, 11, 26; R 3, 40, 22). She is not Śrī (R 6, 50, 25), though Lakṣmī = Śrī appears seated with Indra (12, 228, 89). But Śrī says she is Lakṣmī only (12, 225, 8, Lakṣmī 'ti mām āhuḥ), and as she is divided (ib. 19) and "deserts Bali for Indra" (12, 225, 1f.; ib. 90, 23), she is best regarded as personified Happiness (not as Śacī). "Like Indra (Mahendra, Maghavat) with Paulomī" is a stereotyped phrase (1, 112, 10; 3, 291, 40; type of loveliness, S 1, 242, 39). Śacī bore Jayanta (1, 114, 4), a son barely mentioned in the epic itself but known later (H 7481, etc.; R 7, 28, 11; Jayantī Indraputrī is a still later growth, not epic). Jayanta as Rudra (q. v.) is known in Śānti. The wifehood of Śrutāvatī (§ 77) is not mentioned again. Indra's son Arjuna fills the great epic; the Rām. makes Indra the father of Vālin, so grandfather of Aṅgada, Indra's naptṛ (R 1, 17, etc.). Aṅgada is Vajrahastātmajātmaja, "son of the son of Indra" (R 6, 67, 43). Both Arjuna and Vālin are called Vāsavi (5, 50, 46, etc.).[1]

[1] Compare for Indra in the Great Epic, the treatise of Adolf Holtzmann, Indra nach den Vorstellungen des Mahābhārata, ZDMG. 32, p. 290f. For the Maruts, see § 111. For Indra and mountains, see p. 9; for Sudharmā, p. 58.

§ 83. **Kubera.** — Kubera is called Vaiśravaṇa, as son of Viśravas, a Muni, and of Devavarṇinī, daughter of Bharadvāja (§ 17). He was so austere that Brahman granted him boons. Kubera chose the guardianship of the North and lordship over all treasure (vittarakṣaṇa, nidhīśatva), to which Brahman added the boon of an aerial car called Puṣpaka and also "equality with gods" (R 7, 3, 1 f.). By another wife Viśravas was father of the fiends, Rāvaṇa, etc., all of whom except Vibhīṣaṇa were enemies of the gods. They took from Kubera the car given by Brahman and destroyed Caitraratha, Nalinī, and Nandana. Caitraratha is the grove of Kubera, made for him by Citraratha (according to R 2, 91, 19, it should be in the land of the Northern Kurus). The leaves of this grove are jewels and the fruit are girls of heaven, some twenty thousand of whom Kubera sent to grace his grandfather's magic feast (ib. 43 f.). Kubera lived first at Laṅkā, afterwards in the North; his riches are proverbial, as is his happiness (R 5, 2, 24; ib. 20, 33). He had a gatekeeper Sūryabhānu (slain by Rāvaṇa, R 7, 14, 25 f.). He is represented in the later Rām. as deformed in one eye (ekapiṅga, RG 4, 44, 4, is not in Bomb. or S), which became yellow when he indiscreetly looked at Śiva and Umā (R 7, 13, 31), so that he was called Ekākṣipiṅgala (ib. 36, 17). He is also called (R 3, 32, 14) Naravāhana, "drawn by spirits" (naras, cf. Kiṃnaras;[1]) or, as interpreted by native authority, "drawn by men") and explained by the fact that when Kubera fares anywhere, he is carried by spirits called Guhyakas (also Gandharvas), described as half horse and half bird, though he also, as World-protector, rides an elephant called Sārvabhauma (R 4, 43, 36). Kubera, like Śiva, is called Bhūteśa (R 6, 4, 20). One of his usual titles is "king of kings" (which he shares with his half-brother Rāvaṇa) or "king of the whole world" (R 5, 34, 28), as lord of wealth; his city being Alakā = Viṭapā, type of luxury (ib. 2, 15, 36; ib. 16, 8, etc.).[2]) Among his councillors are Padma and Śaṅkha, personified treasures (R 7, 15, 17).

§ 84. In Mbh., Kubera is called Ailavila (9, 47, 25 f.), Dhanādhipati, and he is represented as gaining his lordship over treasure at the Kaubera Tīrtha. He is Yakṣarājan and in this version obtains several boons of Brahman, lordship over wealth, friendship with Śiva (Rudra), godship, suratvam, the post of world-protector, a son Nalakūbara (ib. 29), the Puṣpaka car (yoked with geese, swift as thought), and finally lordship over the Nairṛta demons. When Indra and Kubera are associated, they "guard the East" (3, 163, 5 f.), but Kubera alone belongs to the North (see §§ 91—92). His residence is Kailāsa (12, 44, 13), where Caitraratha (§ 83) is usually said to be and where he was consecrated as Dhanada, giver of wealth (5, 111, 11; 3, 80, 6). Nandana and the fair retreat called Vasvaukasārā (R 2, 94, 26) belong to both these gods of the North and East. Like Indra too he has as constant resorts Mandara and Gandhamādana, as well as Kailāsa (3, 139, 5 f.), and his udyānāni, or parks, are on Himavat (1, 120, 11), as is his "charming lotus-lake" (Nalinī ramyā Kuberakāntā, 3, 177, 9), guarded by Rākṣasas and Yakṣas, Kiṃnaras (etc., when assaulted by Bhīma). It is the playground of the gods or particurlarly of the Rājarāja (Kubera, 3, 153, 1 f.). Even men may see

[1]) See JAOS. 33, p. 60 f.

[2]) Viṭapā or Viṭapāvatī seems to stand for Alakā in R 5, 3, 4 and R 6, 77, 8. There is no distinction between Kubera and Vaiśravaṇa. The kauberaṃ paramāsanam is a car made by Viśvakarman for Vaiśravaṇa, etc. (R 6, 124, 10 f.).

Vaiśravaṇa sitting on Kailāsa on holy days; he is golden, like a sun (3, 159, 26 f.), and united with prosperity (Ṛddhi), which (who) then becomes his wife (cf. 3, 139, 8); as Prabhā to the Sun, Vedī to Brahman (§ 24), so is Ṛddhi to Kubera (5, 117, 9; 13, 146, 4; 166, 11). Kubera is also "united to Lakṣmī" (3, 168, 13), but she is not yet (as later) his wife. In 1, 199, 6, Vaiśravaṇa's consort is Bhadrā (Lakṣmī with Nalakūbara is in Kubera's court, 2, 10, 19). As already stated, and as said in 3, 274, 15, Pitāmaha gave godship, suratvam, amaratvam, to Vaiśravaṇa, because he deserted his father and clove to his grandfather. Pulastya, son of Brahman, had a son born of a (the) cow (not unique, cf. 1, 50, 2, ṛṣeḥ putro gavi jātaḥ), called Vaiśravaṇa, who deserted his father; whereat to revenge himself the father begot of himself another son, Viśravas, "half of himself", born as a priest. Pulastya's son Viśravas (a Muni) disliked Vaiśravaṇa Kubera, lord of Rākṣasas, who was then king of kings in Laṅkā. The latter, to win his favor, sent Viśravas three women, who (§ 17) became mothers of the brother fiends, Rāvaṇa, born of Puṣpotkaṭā (also mother of Kumbhakarṇa); Vibhīṣaṇa, born of Mālinī; Khara and Śūrpanakhā, born of Rākā. They all lived on Gandhamādana till, jealous of Kubera, they defeated him and took away his car; but Rāvaṇa was cursed never to ride in it because he had assaulted his Guru (uncle). Vibhīṣaṇa, pious like Kubera, took sides with Kubera and was made general of his Yakṣa and Rākṣasa armies; but "the cannibalistic Rākṣasas" and Piśācas sided with Rāvaṇa (3, 275, 35 f.). In 2, 10, 31, Kubera is half-brother of the fiends (as in Rām.), instead of being the uncle. The metronymic Ailavila makes Ilavilā the mother of Kubera (5, 139, 14), a later view, scarcely found represented before the Purāṇas. Nalakūbara (above) appears in the later parts of the epic and in Harivaṃśa. The description of Kubera's hall mentions him and he is said to have cursed Rāvaṇa because the fiend outraged his wife Rambhā (3, 280, 59; 291, 33). The story is dramatised at H 8695 f. In R 7, 26, 32 and 53, Rambhā is represented as wife of Nalakūbara and "daughter-in-law" of Rāvaṇa. Both epics know Rambhā as wife of Virādha or Tumburu (5, 117, 16) or as loved by him and cursed by Kubera (R 3, 4, 16) or as cursed by Viśvāmitra (R 1, 64, 12; though in R 4, 35, 8 it is Ghṛtācī whom he curses) and so in 13, 3, 11 (cf. R 6, 60, 11; ib. 7, 26, 14). The allusion to the "son of Dhaneśvara" (7, 46, 12) probably refers to Nalakūbara. Kubera becomes a lizard (as a hiding spirit), when frightened by Rāvaṇa (R 7, 18, 5).

§ 85. Kubera's attendants are chiefly "horrible Yakṣas" (3, 161, 49 f.), though he is overlord of Yakṣas, Rākṣasas, and Gandharvas (5, 111, 11). His floating palace is carried by Guhyakas (2, 10, 3), where he sits clothed in jewels and surrounded by many women. He wears bright ear-rings, is very wealthy, has a heavenly seat and footstool and is refreshed by breezes from Nandana and from (here a lotus-lake) Alakā Nalinī (2, 10, 8). In R 2, 98, 12, Nandana belongs to Kubera (otherwise Indra's grove, or belongs to both). With Kubera at his court are Śiva and Umā, the Vidyādharas with their chief (Cakradharman), Kiṃnaras and Druma, chief of Kiṃpuruṣas, Mahendra, Gandhamādana (Kubera's simian son, R 1, 17, 11), Vibhīṣaṇa, and other Rākṣasas and Piśācas; also Nandīśvara and the "roaring white bull" of Śiva whom Paulastya (Kubera) adored of old and who "became the friend of the wealth-giver". Śaṅkha and Padma, the "lords of wealth", are also there (cf. H 2467, as persons; there are eight of these Nidhis, ib. 6004). Kubera leads Yakṣas to battle; he is the refuge of Rākṣasas

(5, 156, 12; 13, 61, 38). Manibhadra or Maṇivara, a Yakṣarāj (Yakṣendra) like Kubera (5, 192, 44 f.), is Kubera's chief attendant. He is called lord of wealth and of treasure (Yakṣapati, -adhipa, Nidhīśa, Dhanapati, Draviṇādhipati, Dhanada; his name also appears as Māṇicāra) and is invoked as patron of merchants with Kubera. The Yakṣa attendants of Kubera (2, 10, 14 f. names some of them) are armed with clubs and this is Kubera's weapon (6, 48, 93); but Śiva's former "sleep-making" weapon he gave to Arjuna (3, 41, 35 f.). As generous giver he is proverbial (8, 39, 2). He (jāmbūnada ib.) has a body made of gold. Like all world-protectors, Kubera has seven seers (5, 111, 14; 13, 151, 38 f.); those of the North are his ṛtvijs or Gurus, Atri, Vasiṣṭha, Kaśyapa, Gautama, Bharadvāja, Viśvāmitra (Kauśika), and Jamadagni. His other attendants are noticeable only in part, from the fact that their names are his own or convey his attributes, Dhanada, Hemanetra, Piṅgala (all as Guhyaka-Yakṣas, 2, 10, 15 f.). Bibhīṣaṇa here is distinguished from Vibhīṣaṇa (S). Amogha, one of them, is a name of Skanda (3, 232, 5) and the Yakṣa Piṅgala is friend of Rudra (ib. 231, 51). The demoniac trees, Yamala and Arjuna, mentioned in R 7, 6, 35, destroyed by Kṛṣṇa, when later identified with Nalakūbara and Maṇibhadra, are called Guhyakas (Bhāg. P. 10, 10, 23 f.), but of this legend the epic has no trace till H 14741. In H, Kubera is fully god, he fights with Keśin (13189) but especially with Anuhrāda (13192 and 13808 f.). He is here Piṅgalākṣa, Dhaneśvara, Vaiśravaṇa (scene copied from R 6, 58).

§ 86. Bhīma's invasion of the North and slaughter of Maṇimat with the consequent defeat of Kubera in battle are regarded as expiation for an insult offered Agastya by Maṇimat, who spat on the head of the saint when he was once accompanying Kubera to a convention of gods at Kuśasthalī with a great host of Yakṣas. The home of Kubera described in this account represents it (sadana, ālaya, āvāsa, pura) as a high-walled town with towers, flags, garlands, girls, sweet breezes, fair trees, gold and crystal houses, inhabited by Kiṃnaras, Nāgas, Munis, Gandharvas, and Rākṣasas; the name Alakā appears to be that of Kubera's city as well as of his lake (3, 160, 36 f.). Another visit to the North implies the explanation of the title "king of kings". Dharmarāja Yudhiṣṭhira visited Ailavila, "under whose command stand all kings as servants" (5, 139, 14) and "received many jewels". Yakṣas and Rākṣasas in the account of the battle (above) are exchangeable terms and the attendants of Kubera are chiefly Yakṣas and Guhyakas rather than the fiercer Rākṣasas of Rāvaṇa's host. He is, however, called indifferently Yaksādhipati, Rākṣasādhipati, Yakṣarakṣodhipati, Rākṣaseśvara, and Guhyādhipa, the last epithet recalling the fact that he is himself a god of hiding (AV. 8, 10, 28) as well as lord of Rākṣasas (ŚB. 13, 4, 3, 10). His most intimate associates are the Guhyakas, with whom he lives on Kailāsa (6, 6, 41), these being here his only comrades. From Kailāsa he sends by a Guhyaka a magic eye-wash to Rāma, which enables him to see what is hidden (3, 289, 9 f.). Even when he is said to consort on Gandhamādana with Rākṣasas and Gandharvas he is still called Guhyakādhipa (6, 6, 34). Among his "dear friends" he numbers the Rākṣasa Maṇimat and the Gandharva Aṅgāraparṇa (formerly Citraratha), who boasts that he is the very particular friend of Kubera and reproves Arjuna for attacking one who is the "turban" (crown) upon the head of Kubera (1, 170, 13 f.; S 186, 15, v. l.). It is probable that Guhyaka was a general name for all the spirits of concealment, though sometimes made a special class. Thus when Kubera gives advice to Yudhiṣṭhira, he is called

Guhyakādhipa, though accompanied only by Yakṣas and Rākṣasas (in "cars full of cushions", 3, 162, 32 f.). Kubera's own car is the swiftest known, swifter than that of the Sun or of Rudra (7, 99, 11), and is drawn by bird-like steeds which gold-wreathed Gandharvas yoke. They "alight like birds" and "neigh at each other". This is the vimāna made by Viśvakarman for Yakṣādhipati Vaiśravaṇa (called Puṣpaka, 3, 161, 15 f.; cf. 159, 26 and vājinaḥ in 162, 35). The steeds, which fly, are expressly "horses" (ib. 161, 24 hayottamāḥ; also vimalākṣāḥ, which N. says means "having the ten whorls"!), but are also birds (haṃsayukta, "goose-yoked", describes his car in 9, 47, 31). It is just when he rides on this car that (3, 161, 42, etc.) he is described as Naravāhana, and as he is never described as being carried by men, it is clear that naras are spirits. Thus Arjuna tells how the world-protectors came to him and gave him gifts and says that he saw Indra and the others on cars, among them Naravāhana Kubera (3, 168, 13) and the scene thus described from memory, when actually presented (3, 41, 7), also describes Kubera as on a car. On another occasion a Yakṣa has exchanged his sex and become a female, so that he is ashamed to meet Kubera, who flies over earth above him in a car and is called Naravāhana even as he calls out to "stop the car" (5, 192, 42; the Yakṣa is Sthūṇa or Sthūṇakarṇa; K is called in this passage almost exclusively lord of Yakṣas, Yakṣādhipati, Yakṣapati, Yakṣendra, Deva Yakṣarāja, Kubera Naravāhana, Vaiśravaṇa, Bhagavat, as also Dhanada, Dhanādhigoptṛ). In 3, 231, 33, Bhagavat Dhaneśa with his Guhyakas leads the host of Śiva and is called Naravāhana even as he is stepping into his car, Puṣpaka, which is never dragged by men but always by the bird-horses described above. The Naras are called a special kind of Gandharvas, narā nāma (2, 10, 14), and so in VP. 1, 5, 57, Nara-Kiṃnara-Rakṣāṃsi (cf. Naraka as "place of spirits"; Nārāyaṇa, the place of water or spirits). The word then means a water-spirit particularly (water and vigor uniting in the idea of activity and strength). So the "lord of Gandharvas" is properly Varuṇa, the lord of water. There is no trace in the epic of the belief that Kubera was carried by aught save birds on Yakṣas or his thousand horses (H 13130). Another explanation is possible but not plausible, namely that a "king of kings" ought to be carried in a palanquin, and is therefore given this epithet of "man-carried". The strongest point in favor of this is that the epithet is rare in Rām. but common in Mbh., especially in the later passages (Nalakūbara may belong to the same later period, cf. where he is thus described, in 3, 274, 16, the late word rājadhānī for royal residence), as in later literature (H 2468 has Naravāhana climbing into his battle-car to fight).

§ 87. Kubera's (northern) district is called the "wealthiest" (5, 109, 16). Kubera possesses one quarter of the wealth of the golden mountain Meru and of that quarter gives one sixteenth to men (6, 6, 23). Even his two ministers are called dhaneśvarau (the two jewels). He, his followers, as well as one of Skanda's, are called dhanada (5, 111, 11; 9, 46, 13, etc.). There is a close connection between these followers of Kubera and Skanda. Another of Skanda's is called Vasudā (wealth-giver), another even has Kubera's name, Piṅgākṣī (ib. 5 and 18; cf. Vasudhā, R 7, 5, 41 = S 42; H 4362, Vasuda = Kubera). The Mothers in general are in part Kauberyaḥ and one is called Vittadā (9, 46, 28 and 36), as Kubera, possessed of vaittapālya, is called Vittapāla and Vitteśa (6, 34, 23; R 7, 11, 23 and 26; Manu 5, 96; ib. 7, 4 and 42) or Vittapati (7, 185, 25). These epithets meaning guardian of wealth fit in with his title as king, so that he is described as "best of kings" in antithesis to Indra, "best of gods" (8, 8, 24f.). This leads to the later belief that Kubera was a man. In H 259, "Varuṇa lord of water, Vaiśravaṇa lord of kings" (was made), suggests the manuṣyaprakṛti gods accepted as part of the pantheon (cf. GDH., 16, 34 and Āp. 1, 3, 11, 3, with scholiast, Kubera and Nandīśvara as human). The Gṛhya-Sūtras reckon him a god (Hiraṇ. GS. 2, 8, 19, 1). As lord of wealth Kubera shares the rôle of Indra (Dhanadā, Dhanapati, RV. 1, 33, 2f.; AV. 5, 23, 2), with whom he shares the northern district. In 14, 65, 11, the explorer before digging for treasure in the northern hills "reveres Dhanādhyakṣa and all the Nidhipālas and Śaṅkha and other treasures" as well as the Yakṣendra Kubera and Maṇibhadra, to whom and to the other Yakṣas and "lords of Bhūts" are made offerings (cf. ŚGS. 1, 11, 6) of meat and sesamum seeds, also flowers (partly to Kubera and partly to Rudra-Śiva and their attendants). The treasure is guarded by savage Kiṃnaras (ib. 63, 15). Nidhipa and -pati are titles of Kubera (cf. H 6277, 6922, 12495; and 12, 207, 35, asṛjat Sarvabhūtātmā nidhipaṃ ca Dhaneśvaram). Indra still rains gold in the epic (12, 29, 25f.) and his wealth is proverbial; he is sometimes especially grouped with Kubera Dhaneśvara as contrasted with other divinities (3, 19, 21). Kubera has śrī, which is material prosperity (a man is said to "become śreyān" or "reach śreyas" not morally but materially, "gets richer"); his son is "brought up in superlative ease" (atyantasukhasaṃvṛddha, 7, 46, 12); "as rich as Croesus" is expressed by śriyā Vaiśravaṇopamaḥ (2, 17, 15). Wealth (śrī) even greater than that of Guhyakādhipati (2, 49, 35) is the last of a series of inferior fortunes belonging to Indra, Yama, and Varuṇa. In short, though others rival him, Kubera has become the norm of exhaustless wealth (2, 58, 3; 12, 124, 13, etc.), as his town gives the standing phrase (e. g. R 1, 77, 15) Kuberabhavanopamam, "like Kubera's residence", in wealth. This wealth is gold, for gold is wealth. It is dug out of the ground with the help of Wind (purified by Vāyu) and Fire (Śukra) and it is given to men when the Fire-god is revered under the double constellation Proṣṭhapādau, for gold in earth is guarded by the regents of this constellation, namely, Ajaikapād and the Serpent of the Depth, Ahi Budhnya (5, 114, 1f.; Ajaikapād is also a name of Śiva, 13, 17, 103). The scholiast takes the handing over of the gold to Fire to mean "on Friday" (Śukre), but allows Agni to give the gold to Kubera. But in either case, gold (the son of Fire, 3, 200, 128 and passim) is here guarded by the Serpent of the Depth and is dug out and purified and handed over to man through the medium of fire, wind, and Kubera, suggesting a forge, bellows, and guhera (smith), which was very likely a function of the guhya (Kubera). All the gold comes from the North. The gods take that of the Jambū-tree (6, 7, 26) and men get that of the upper Ganges and of the mountains, either by digging, or through the medium of the mountaineers, who bring it down from the hills, after getting it from the ants. There is also a lake at Uśīrabīja (in the North which produces gold and there too are (Jīmūta's) gold-mines of the Himālayas (2, 52, 4; 5, 111, 23; cf. 5, 34, 32). The serpents who steal gold are familiar, as are those who carry off jewels (1, 3, 128; cf. 7, 93, 34). It is the Guhyakas who guard Hāṭaka, north of Druma's land of Kiṃpuruṣas, the source of hāṭaka gold (2, 28, 1f.). When Soma is the world-protector instead of Kubera, he too guards gold, so that Soma and Agni are reckoned as joint fathers of gold (Agnīṣomātmakam idaṃ suvarṇaṃ, 13, 84, 46), probably because of the difference between red gold and the whitish gold called mahārajatam (6, 7, 29; jāmbūnada gold is reddish, indragopakasaṃkāśa, ib. 26). This gold may be the "beloved thing of Kubera", which "gives immortality to mortals, makes the blind see, and restores youth to the old" (5, 64, 18). It is kept in a jar, guarded by dragons, like the Golden Fleece, or like the soma stolen by Garuḍa, and it is found in a cave, so hard to reach that those who attempt the climb usually lose life (ib. 22). The application of the famous proverb "he sees the honey but ignores the fall" (5, 51, 26; 11, 1, 37; 12, 310, 7; cf. 7, 51, 11 and ib. 133, 10), is in this case probably to gold, as it is mystically interpreted by Jambhasādhakas. It is "loved by Kubera", and described as madhu pītakamākṣikam.

§ 88. The epic has moral tales about Kubera. Vaiśravaṇa Alakādhipa holds converse with Mucukunda and offers him the earth (5, 132, 8 f.). Mucukunda fights with Kubera and is defeated by Nairṛtas "made by Kubera", after which he teaches Kubera that priest and warrior ought to unite, proving his point by having his priest Vasiṣṭha demolish Kubera's Rakṣas (12, 74, 3 f.). In the last passage, Kubera creates Rākṣasas and is "lord of good and ill"; but only as a subordinate, for Kubera says that he disposes of kingdoms only as he is instructed to do so by a superior power. Kubera is also overpowered by the priest of the demons (12, 290, 8 f.). Uśanas here through Yoga-power enters Kubera and steals his wealth, whereupon Kubera runs to Śiva for help, who tries to pierce Uśanas with his javelin; but Uśanas sits on its point and then jumps down Śiva's throat. Kubera is here king and god and "master of treasure" (N. as "treasurer of Indra", not necessary). Another late story tells how Kubera had a visit from Aṣṭāvakra, received him well, and entertained him with music and dance, a performance carried out by his Gandharvas and Apsarasas for a "divine year", without the guest noticing the lapse of time (13, 19, 33 f.). Kubera admits that "music is captivating", and lets him go. Then the guest departs, saying vṛddhimān ṛddhimān bhava (53), which looks as if Kubera's wife were not yet Ṛddhi. Other late traits of the god are not known to either epic, such as Mīnākṣī as his daughter, his three legs, and deformities of teeth, etc. Negative evidence is strong here, as in the case of other gods. Even in Hariv., he is not three-headed three-legged, or four-armed, as now. There is quite a gap between the epics and Purāṇas, though here and there the Purāṇa may conserve earlier traits than those of the epics.

§ 89. The Guhyakas are generally on earth or in the hills (1, 146, 12 and above). Like the gods and other spirits they did not exist in the first age (3, 149, 13 f.). They appear as luminous forms in heaven (3, 42, 36) and as demoniac forms in battle (3, 173, 50), but such aerial flights do not represent their normal condition, which is that of earth-gnomes, though they are sent on messages or visit battle-fields as spectators (R 6, 67, 163, etc.), being grouped with Suparṇas and other supernatural beings (ib. 71, 66). They "disappear like fata morgana" (1, 126, 34). They are associated with Pitṛs (3, 3, 43) as Sun-worshippers (cf. AV. 8, 8, 15) and may be ghosts but seem rather to be the half-gods such as fairies, gnomes, etc., for which reason, as not being Devas, though of divine origin, the Aśvins and plants and animals are grouped as Guhyakas (1, 66, 40). The character of the chief Guhyaka, Kubera, in being one of productivity, is similar to that of Śiva, whose phallic tendency may be paralleled in the invocation of Kubera "for the man" at the time Śiva Īśāna is invoked at weddings; the latter's son too is Guha and described as sarvaguhyamaya (1, 137, 13), of unknown origin or hidden. Like Kubera Guhya, this Guha lives on the mountains (R 6, 69, 30, etc.). The world of Guhyakas is for those who die by the sword, not ignobly but not bravely, and is next to the lowest earth-world of Yama (11, 26, 12 f.; 13, 102, 14 f.). This accords with the fact that Vasudharā is both "earth" and the name of Kubera (Jambhala)'s wife and city in Buddhistic lore[1]). His later title Kāmeśvara has to do with his rôle as marriage-divinity (hence three-legged, as Priapos). Hence too his close connection with the amorous Gandharvas; perhaps also with the (androgynous?[2]) Kiṃpuruṣas (Ailavila may be connected with the androgynous Ila). Kubera's haṃsas are fitting messengers for lovers (3, 53, 19f.).

§ 90. A few words in conclusion regarding Kubera's attendants. The Yakṣas assume any shape (3, 139, 7) and the female, Yakṣī and Yakṣiṇī, may appear as a beautiful woman, so that an unknown beauty is asked if she be goddess of the district or a Yakṣī, and a handsome man is said to look like a Yakṣa or Gandharva (3, 53, 13; 55, 17; 64, 120) or a Guhyaka (3, 147, 24). These females are usually invisible; they sit beside their lords unseen and peep at Bhīma longingly (3, 146, 30). They descend from Pulastya and Pulaha (1, 66, 7 f.) or come from the world-egg (1, 1, 35, a later view). Individuals are seldom named (1, 63, 125, Sthūṇa, and above the names of a few at Kubera's court); the nine spirits slain by Garuḍa (1, 32, 19) may be Yakṣas; they are "like clouds". The pretended Yakṣa who asks riddles is really Dharma (3, 314, 1 f.). The individual may be kindly (5, 191, 23), but as guardians with Rākṣasas they can fight (7, 94, 36). They are grouped with Nāgas (1. 1, 255), but more often form part of a general group of gods, Gandharvas, Nāgas, etc., as in 1, 212, 2 (robbed by Asuras). They are known as "good people", Puṇyajana, whose peculiar attribute is "disappearance", their mystic "milker" being Kubera, and their "calf" Śiva (7, 69, 24 = H 385, with v. l.), or "Kuberaka" is the calf and their milk is received from mother earth (Virāj). Puṇyajana is also applied to the former sons of Pracetas, who burned away the mighty jungle before man's ancestor was born (1, 75, 4). A Yakṣiṇī at Rājagṛha has a daily service and cult (3, 84, 105). Another Yakṣiṇī shrine is mentioned in 3, 83, 23 as "world-renowned". The number of Yakṣas guarding the northern mountains is three hundred and fifty-two thousand (3, 139, 6), unless the expression caturguṇā Yakṣāḥ means the four classes mentioned as Gandharvas, Kiṃpuruṣas, Yātudhānas, and Rākṣasas "savage and mild". Rajatanābha is the father of Maṇivara (H 382 f.; cf. AV. 8, 10, 28). A comparison of the AV. and epic passages shows that the "other people" are identical with the "good people", that is, spirits, perhaps including ghosts; but there is no other indication that epic Yakṣas are (as later) ghosts. Maṇibhadra is apparently meant when Maṇimat is mentioned (1, 2, 179 f.), but this is not certain and the name is also applied to a Nāga and a Rākṣasa (2, 9, 9, and above). The connection with the

---

[1]) Compare A. Foucher, Étude sur l'Iconographie bouddhique de l'Inde.

[2]) Compare the note below on p. 159. Kubera is chthonic in character and home (cf. Mahāvaṃsa, 10, 89, "the banyan-tree of Vessavaṇa" Kubera), and this may be indicated by his especial imps, the Nairṛtas, as gnomes or sons of the underground power Nirṛti (Hell as place or power of destruction).

Nāgas as treasure-hiders appears in the description of the gate-keepers of the Nāga-Tīrtha at Kurukṣetra, viz., Arantuka and Tarantuka on one side and Macakruka (v. l. Macakraka and Maṅkaṇaka) on the other; these are Yakṣa gate-keepers, as well as places bounding the holy land (3, 83, 9 and 52 and 208; S 81, 9).

§ 91. **The World-Protectors.** The eight gods discussed above (§ 38—§ 90) are grouped in later literature as guardians of the four chief and four subsidiary directions, the Sun-god of the South-West, the Moon-god of the North-East, the Wind-god of the North-West, the Fire-god of the South-East, and for cardinal points, Yama of the South, Varuṇa of the West, Kubera of the North, and Indra of the East. The exact district assigned to each is not specified so early as are the names. Thus the eight are found as Lokapālas in Manu 5, 96 (with ib. 7, 4 cf. 12, 68, 41), but without indication of the localities assigned to the individuals. On the other hand some late authorities make Nirṛti the guardian of the South-West, instead of the Sun; and Pṛthivī or Śiva Īśāna the guardian of the North-East, instead of the Moon-god. In the epic, which knows no such group of eight, the world-protectors are counted as four and only the cardinal points are represented. Sometimes the four appear as a group without express mention of the fact that they are regarded as Lokapālas, as in 7, 72, 45, where Vaivasvata, Varuṇa, Śatakratu, and Dhaneśa are represented as welcoming a dead hero. The fixed positions in the epics are those of Yama and Varuṇa, in the South and West, respectively. The four, however, are not always the same. In 3, 55, 6f., they appear as Indra (Śakra), Agni, Varuṇa, Yama. In 3, 41, 9f., Yama, Indra, Kubera, and Varuṇa, as Lokapālas, give gifts to Arjuna, and Yama stands in the South. Yama, as a form of Fate, is the only one who survives the ages (3, 313, 1 and 27), for here four stricken brothers look "like Lokapālas at the end of the Yuga" and the survivor exclaims: ko 'nyaḥ (imān) pratisamāseta Kālāntakayamād ṛte. The gifts made to Arjuna are alluded to in 3, 91, 13 and 168, 14f., where Yama is in the South and has of course the same coadjutors (Kubera, Varuṇa, and Indra) in their own quarters; only the intervening 3, 161, 8, hints that they belong in heaven as Devavaras, but this is not in the same connection and is only by way of a simile. The fact that Rāvaṇa calls himself the "fifth of world-protectors" shows that four was the regular number (3, 281, 14). They are said to be not only best of gods but swift as thought (3, 41, 48), and they are all war-gods. When they are said to be unable to kill a hero, it is a boast modified by an accompanying "even" into a compliment (9, 61, 65), much as when it is said that "even Yama and Soma" fear Viśvāmitra (1, 71, 39), who conquers all gods, even the strongest. In 8, 45, 31 f. it is said: "The gods living in the East have Agni as their leader; Yama of noble deeds guards the Pitṛs living in the South; the West is guarded by Varuṇa, who also guards other gods; the North is guarded by Bhagavat Soma and the priests". Here, though not expressly called Lokapālas, the protecting gods are evidently thought of as such (diśaṃ dakṣiṇāṃ guptāṃ Yamena . . pratīcīṃ Varuṇaḥ pāti pālayānaḥ surān balī; udīcīṃ bhagavān Somo brāhmaṇaiḥ saha rakṣati). The grouping of Agni, Yama, Varuṇa, and Indra seems older than when Kubera is substituted for Agni (as above). This substitution occurs, and Mahendra (though this is not very significant) stands for Indra, in the list of Lokapālas to whose homes Śakuntalā says she can go if she will (1, 74, 85). Of these

Lokapālas, though Yama is a constant member, only Varuṇa has his numerical position defined as "fourth of the Lokapālas" (1, 225, 3), as if the list began in the North. They are also called Lokapas, as when Yayāti says that the Lokapā Brahmaṇaḥ urge him to fall (1, 92, 7). The fact that Kubera is one of the four whose Sabhās are described (besides Brahman's) rather ranges that section in time with the period indicated by the passages cited above to the same effect. The four Lokapālas who "live on Himavat" (12, 328, 7), like the Diśāṃpālas of the North, who cry out morning and evening, "What can we do for anybody?" (kasya kāryaṃ kim, 5, 111, 26), may be the later Purāṇic four saints as Lokapālas (VP. 1, 22, 9f.; ib. 2, 8, 82f.); or, as they are grouped with Garuḍa, may be, like him, temporary visitors. Though each Lokapāla has his Sabhā, they all are found in that of Brahman (2, 11, 28). Inferentially Yama appears in the North as well as in the South (as sacrificing at Bindusaras, etc. 2, 3, 15). But in 13, 159, 31, there are only three Lokapālas. Now as there are three worlds (lokāḥ, ib.), one would expect three Lokapālas, if the protectors bore any relation to the worlds. Despite their title, however, the "world-protectors" are, in reality, Diśāṃpālas, guarding the earth and perhaps the regions above and below to East, South, West, and North. Conspicuously so are the two fixtures, Yama in the South but underground rather than above, and Varuṇa in the West and under water (gopati, salilarāja; cf. 5, 110, 3). It may be supposed, however, that originally there were three real world-protectors, in the sense that they protected not the diśaḥ, directions, but the worlds, earth and the worlds below and above. The sophisticated later age, which no longer traces the relation, may think of the four world-protectors and at the same time of the three worlds (R 6, 93, 10 and 42 f.). Vālmīki recognises four Lokapālas by inference (R 1, 72, 25) or expressly, as when (R 2, 16, 24) Indra, Yama, Varuṇa, and Kubera guard East, South, West, and North, and these four respectively impart greatness, restraint, beauty, and wealth to the ideal first king (R 7, 76, 41, the king exercises his Yāmya bhāga as punisher, śāsti; cf. Manu 7, 4 f.). Four world-protectors appear also in R 6, 131, 64. But in R 2, 91, 13, āhvaye lokapālāṃs trīn devān Śakramukhāṃs tathā, the natural meaning is "I invoke the three world-protecting gods with Indra at their head", not, as the scholiast says, the three and Indra besides. The variability of the fourth member especially may point to the same conclusion. In the great epic there is a confused account telling how Indra was conversing with Bṛhaspati in regard to getting rid of Nahuṣa, whose evil eye they feared, when there came along "the world-protector Kubera, and Yama Vaivasvata, the ancient, and god Soma, and Varuṇa". Then "great Indra addressed these world-protectors", saying that Varuṇa, Yama, and Kubera should be rewarded for their help, and "Indra gave Agni a share in the sacrifice, and Bhagavat made Kubera overlord of Yakṣas, and of wealth; Yama, overlord of Pitṛs; and Varuṇa, overlord of waters". Here Soma comes in first, and is then displaced by Agni, when the time for rewards comes, and Indra is certainly outside of the group he addresses as "world-protectors" (5, 16, 27 f.). In the same way Indra is not in the group when it is suggested that it would be a good thing for Arjuna to receive divine gifts from "Indra, Rudra, and also from the world-protectors", after the same idea has been expressed in the words "Indra, Rudra, Varuṇa, Kubera, Yama" (will give; 3, 36, 32 and 34). In Nala, the group Indra, Agni, Varuṇa, Yama (3, 55, 6) excludes

Kubera; and lokapālāś ca sāgnikāḥ (ib. 54, 24) should logically exclude Indra, since here "the world-protectors with Agni came to Indra's presence". But one may not be too logical, and the conclusion of this tale shows that Indra is at once recognised as Lokapāla. In 12, 166, 67, however, "Indra gave Asi to the Lokapālas", he is apart from them. There remains the explicit correlation of three protectors of worlds with three worlds, to point to an earlier group of guardians of the three. Soma still lingers in the epic as one of these; later he rules "above". Yama and Varuṇa may have been the other two. What remains also, however, is the later addition of Kubera, who was not a world-protector or even a god at first, so that when the four were established as guardians of directions rather than of worlds, the first grouping was probably Agni, Yama, Varuṇa, and Soma, the first and last then yielding to Indra and Kubera. Finally, the ejected ones (Soma and Agni, cf. 4, 30, 25) came back as guards of the intermediate points, North-East and South-East, respectively, Indra settling into the East (7, 184, 47), after Kubera had got the North. As a matter of fact, Indra belongs in the North-East, at least according to epic ideas, and epic tradition still recognises that Kubera was raised late to the position of world-protector and added to the group of Yama, Indra, and Varuṇa (R 7, 3, 17 f.). In 3, 163, 3 f., Dhaumya "takes Yudhiṣṭhira by the right hand, looks at the East", and says: "Here is to be seen Mt. Mandara which covers earth to the ocean. It is the district which Indra and Vaiśravaṇa (Kubera) together guard and the seers call it the seat of Mahendra and Vaiśravaṇa; it is where the sun rises. Yama the Dharmajña Rājan, lord of all breathing creatures, occupies the southern district, where dead beings go (pretasattvagati, Saṃyamana; above). Varuṇa protects the Asta (sunset) mountain and the sea. This northern district great Meru illuminates, the auspicious, where go those who know Brahman (Brahmavidāṃ gati); on it is the seat, sadman, of Brahman, and there abides the soul of beings (bhūtātman), Prajāpati, creator of all that moves and is immovable". The northern Lokapāla is not named here; on the contrary, only three "protected" districts are named as such, and Indra and Kubera together are assigned distinctly to the East, where the sun rises. But there is a good reason for this. The interview takes place in the North, so that what is here described as East is North-East from the plains, and that is really the position of Mt. Mandara. Thus Kubera and Indra are strictly guardians of the North and East together, meeting in the North-East. The interview with Kubera, just before this conversation, makes it plain that he is especially in the North (Gandhamādana mountain), where his minions (ib. 162, 12) "protect" the guest, as they have previously protected the country from the foe. Prajāpati is probably not thought of as the guardian of the North here, though Brahman, in the "Sabhākhyāna of Lokapālas", follows Indra, Yama, Varuṇa, and Kubera (2, 11) as if he were Lokapāla. The Vana passage really amounts to describing the Lokapālas in the way they are mentioned in other passages, with Yama and Varuṇa to South and West, respectively, and Kubera and Indra in the North and East, respectively; but it points out that the districts of the two merge in the North-East.

§ 92. In the Harivaṃśa there is a chapter beginning 12487 (= 3, 37, 1), which describes how the Creator distributed power among the gods. He first made Indra the king of the three worlds and then appointed kings over different departments, who were promptly "consecrated by

Indra": Viratha (?) in the East; Yama Dharmarāja in the South; the son of Kaśyapa, the god in the waters, salilāntargata, called amburāja (water-king, Varuṇa), in the West; Pulastya's son, the glorious lord equal to Indra, the one-eyed one, called Piṅgala (Kubera), in the North (saumyāyāṃ diśi). Here the absence of Indra from the group is necessary, as he is already king of the three worlds and consecrates the others to their office. The king of the East in 12509 may be Aruṇa (Langlois), but he is called Viratha: putro 'sya Viratho nāma Kaśyapasya Prajāpateḥ, rājā prācyāṃ diśi tathā Vāsavenā 'bhiṣecitaḥ.

There are then the following groups of epic Lokapālas:

East,	Agni	Kubera	Agni	Kubera	Indra
South,	Yama	Yama	Yama	Yama	Yama
West,	Varuṇa	Varuṇa	Varuṇa	Varuṇa	Varuṇa
North,	Indra	Indra	Soma	Soma	Kubera.

The representatives of South and West are constant. Agni and Kubera and Indra are assigned to the East; Indra, Kubera, and Soma to the North.

The last column to the right represents the Rām. view; in content (not distribution) it is one with the Mbh. view of the second column and period. Neither epic knows of the Purāṇic saints (above) as world-protectors. Both epics recognise elephants ridden by four world-protectors (see § 10). While neither epic has yet settled upon the four gods, both recognise only the group of four; but H 6042, Manu, later law-books, and the Purāṇas have a group of eight Lokapāla gods whose members are fixed.[1]) H 14337 adds Śeṣa below and Soma above to the four.

VI. THE HOSTS OF SPIRITS.

§ 93. **Gandharvas.** — Under Kubera it has been shown that he is lord of Gandharvas and that Gandharvas include Naras and Kiṃnaras. The name is derived from gandha, vapor. The poets take this in the sense of exhalation, or scent; Gandharvas and Apsarasas share the "scent" of the earth-mother in AV. 12, 1, 23. It has been shown also that AV. 8, 10, 27 is copied in the epic and again in the Hariv., and in the first of these passages the epic writer says that Gandharvas and Apsarasas got, in the milking of earth, puṇyagandha as their milk (7, 69, 25). It is probably from association with this idea of being possessed of pure odor that they are derived from the Creator's nose (H 11787), though Kaśyapa is also said to be their sire (ib. 11850). Their mothers are daughters of Dakṣa, Muni, Prādhā, Kapilā, and Ariṣṭā (1, 65, 42f., H 234 and 11553). They have several chiefs or kings. Thus Viśvāvasu is a Gandharvarāja (1, 8, 6), both ascetic and skilled in the dance and instrumental music and song; he has a Tīrtha on the Sarasvatī (9, 37, 10f.). The Gītā authoritatively makes Citraratha foremost of the Gandharvas (6,

[1]) It may be added that the four Mahārājas of the Buddhists combine the Lokapāla gods and the elephants of the directions (Vessavaṇa and Dhataraṭṭha) with other un-Brahmanic features (Virūḷhaka and Virūpakkha). The late passage above in the Hariv., which speaks of the guardians as Rājans may reflect this view. Compare Viṣṇu's epithet, cāturmahārājika (§ 155). The idea of space-protectors gives rise even to a theory of holy cows as guardians of the four quarters, but this does not appear to have become popular; it is probably a theoretical extension of the notion of a wonder-cow, one of the four being, in fact, called Sarvakāmadughā, "granter of every desire" (cf. § 139). On the sublimated forms of Lokapālas known as Nara, Nārāyaṇa, Hari, and Kṛṣṇa, see § 152.

34, 26) but refers to Nārada as a devarṣi (not a Gandharva as below). All Gandharvas have sweet voices, valguvādinaḥ, and are radiant as the sun, sūryavarcasaḥ; they sing on Meru, Mandara, Gandhamādana, or other mountains (1, 17, 6; 5, 109, 9; 7, 60, 7), though they are heard in the sky and frequent the woods (below). The lists of the Gandharvas do not give prominence to their various "kings"; probably out of the countless hosts of these beings (in Gandhamādana alone there are three millions of fighting Gandharvas under the kings Hāhā-Hūhū, RB 6, 82, 50), only kings are mentioned, though many of the names are of unimportant members apparently, some of them being of uncertain form (due to varied readings of the same list and metrical change). Sūryavarcas (above) is both epithet of all and name of one (in AV., as son of Citraratha). Deva-Gandharvas and Gandharvas are not as spirits differentiated; but as gandharvas are also human minstrels (1, 219, 7 f.; 7, 82, 28), the distinction may be merely between the minstrels of gods and of men. Gāndharva is music (2, 5, 9, yuddhagāndharvam "music of battle"; cf. R 1, 4, 10; R 6, 52, 24), and a gāndharvaśāstram, studied by kings, is known (13, 104, 149; cf. Gāndharva-Veda, 3, 91, 15; the word for musician is either gandharva or gāndharva, 2, 5, 1; 7, 57, 4; R 7, 94, 6). This is already indicated in the earlier distinction between "divine" and "human" Gandharvas (TUp. 2, 8, 1). Though lists of Gandharvas are obviously not meant to be complete, several formal lists are found (1, 65, 42 f.; ib. 123, 55 f.; 2, 10, 25; H 14156; R 2, 91, 16; ib. 45; R 4, 22, 27 f.; R 4, 41, 43), which, combined with occasional references (below), furnish the following catalogue (those found only in H are so marked): (Aṅgāraparṇa), Atibāhu, Anagha, Arkaparṇa, Alambuṣa, Ugrasena, Umbara (H, or Ḍ-), Ūrṇāyu, Ṛtvan (or Satvan), Karāla, Kali, Kārṣṇi, Gopa, Gopati, Golabha, Gomāyu (H), Grāmaṇī, Citrāṅgada, Citraratha, Citraśiras (H), Citrasena, Ḍumbara, Tamburu or Tum-, Tṛṇapa, Dhṛtarāṣṭra, Nandi, Nārada, Parjanya, Parvata, Pūrṇa, Pūrṇāyu, Prayuta, Babhru, Barhi, Bahuguṇa, Bṛhaka, Bṛhatvan, Brahmacārin, Bharaṇya (?), Bhānu, Bhīma, Bhīmasena, Bhumanyu (Su-), Mahāśruti (H), Yugapa, Ratiguṇa (Rā-), Varuṇa, Viśvāvasu, Śaru, Śāliśiras, Śikṣa (or Śighru or Sindhu), Śuka (or Śubhra or Sthāna), Śailūṣa, Satyavāc, Satvan (or Ṛtvan), Siddha, Sucandra, Sutanu, Suparṇa, Sumanyu (Bhu-), Suvarṇa, Sūryavarcas, Somavarcas (H), Haṃsa (H), Hahā (Hāhā), Huhū (Hūhū). Of these, Citraratha (originally called Aṅgāraparṇa), Viśvāvasu, and Sūryavarcas are the most important in legend and prestige as Gandharvas, though Nārada becomes more important as the later epic treats him as a god-seer. Probably Viśvaruci, the lord in the earth-milking, should be added (7, 69, 25); cf. Suruci, in H 388. Somavarcas is both Gandharva (H 14157) and a member of the Viśve Devas (13, 91, 33); Haṃsa is also a Dānava (H 9141) and a son of Ariṣṭā (1, 67, 83), who is mother of Gandharvas (H 234). Gopati is doubtless Gopa; he also is a Dānava (H ib.), a fact not unimportant, since the Gandharvas warred with gods (compare Asurā as name of an Apsaras). Alambuṣa and Ugrasena in 4, 56, 12 are probably Gandharvas (so Nīl.). Ūrṇāyu is the husband of Menakā and perhaps father of Somadā (cf. 5, 117, 16 and below). There are several Gandharvīs (below); the chief of these is the abstract Gandharvī or ancestress of all horses, which marks the centaur character of these spirits: "Rohiṇī produced cows; and Gandharvī, horses" (vājinaḥ, 1, 66, 68; R 3, 14, 28). Under Kubera it was shown that his steeds were Gandharvas or Guhyakas of half bird-like half horse-like appearance. As the number of

Gandharvas in Vedic times was reckoned as twenty-seven, so a verse in the epic, 2, 4, 37, "Twenty-seven sit about him, Tumburu and Citrasena with his ministers, Gandharvas and Apsarasas", seems to reflect this, but as if the author spoke with conscious uncertainty as to the real explanation of the twenty-seven; as how could he help doing when the epic mind held the doctrine that Gandharvas were everywhere and reckoned by millions? (S keeps the number twenty-seven; C omits it). Tumburu is here the special friend of the king and leads the Gandharvas in music and singing, which is performed by Gandharvas and Kiṃnaras, "skilled in song and in instrumental music, and in keeping time" (sāmyatālaviśāradāḥ, pramāṇe 'tha laye sthāne, etc., ib. 38 f.). At Kubera's court the "lords of the Gandharvas" (2, 10, 25 f.) are Viśvāvasu, Hahā-Huhū, Tumburu, Parvata, Śailūṣa, Citrasena (gītajña) and Citraratha. Such groups of kings are often found. In 15, 29, 9, for example, Viśvāvasu, Tumburu, and Citrasena come with Nārada, Parvata, and Devala (the last three also in 15, 20, 1) to visit the exiled king; but here the later view has prevailed which regards them only as Munis. They are not spoken of as Gandharvas, and in the later epic Nārada and Parvata appear almost entirely as Munis rather than as Gandharvas, as they do often in the early epic (Devala is never a Gandharva). The chief Gandharvas are Viśvāvasu, Nārada, and Parvata in 1, 187, 7 (cf. 5, 11, 15, where the first two are mentioned as heading the music-makers at Nahuṣa's court). Tumburu and Citrasena are mentioned as being in Indra's court (2, 7, 14; 3, 45, 2), and Citraratha is called "Indra's follower", Vāsavānuga (2, 52, 23). The grove he made, called Caitraratha, is Indra's special pleasaunce (R 6, 128, 28; but see below). The Gandharvas as Deva-Gandharvas playing at the court of the Northern king seem to be mythologically connected with the fact that the Buddhistic Gandharvas are chiefly at the court of Dhṛtarāṣṭra (the Northern Mahārāja). Bhāri of H 7220 may be the Barhi above.

§ 94. Viśvāvasu, whose name is also an epithet of Viṣṇu (6, 65, 47), is the most venerable of the Gandharvas (RV. 10, 139, 4 f.). He worships Brahman (5, 49, 3) and plays the lute so delicately that each who hears thinks he is playing for him alone (12, 29, 76). He sits as he plays in the midst of seven times six thousand dancing Gandharvas (cf. ib. with 12, 223, 22, where the same formula designates the number of dancing Deva-Gandharvas, in addition to the same number of dancing Devayoṣitas, ib. 19); the same phrase occurs at 7, 61, 7. Nīl. wrongly connects saptadhā with the lute-strings: he plays on seven strings while six thousand dance. Noteworthy is it that here and often the Gandharvas dance as well as sing. The Apsarasas are unnecessary as complement. Viśvāvasu, Citrasena, Nārada, Tumburu "and others" are gītakovidāḥ among Gandharvas, all of whom, however, are gītakuśalā nṛtyeṣu ca viśāradāḥ, "good at singing and skilled in dancing" (14, 88, 40). Usually the Gandharvas sing and play the lute (3, 46, 27) and the nymphs dance (R 2, 91, 26; R 6, 131, 68). On Mt. Mandara eighty-eight thousand Gandharvas serve Kubera and Māṇivara (3, 139, 6); they are called "swift-going". Viśvāvasu as the elderly friend of Arjuna and father of Citrasena (3, 168, 57) is old enough to preach a sermon on the duties of husbands and sing a religious śloka (3, 90, 18; H 11248; ib. 12474, he is son of Muni with "Bharaṇya", perhaps another Gandharva, but v. l. āraṇyāḥ). Yet he is cursed to become a Rākṣasa (3, 279, 42, slain by Rāma), and his daughter is a Rākṣasī (q. v.). He has another daughter by Menakā, viz. Pramadvarā (1, 8, 6). He teaches

Aṅgāraparṇa, who changed his name to Citraratha and whose wife Kumbhīnasī pleaded for his life (1, 170, 34f. and 43). Gandharvas are grouped in this passage with Rakṣas and Yakṣas as beings that injure men at the evening gloaming (ib. 9). This power increases at night (1, 170, 69), but in the case of the Gandharva with his wife it may be questioned whether the power is not peculiarly due to his dislike to being disturbed in conjugal amity at that time. However, the Gandharvas are warriors, armed with bows. Citraratha imparts to Arjuna, after he has changed his name and become his friend, the "science of seeing", cākṣuṣī vidyā (1, 170, 43; repeated S 1, 199, 5), which he had himself got from Viśvāvasu (through penance), who again had been taught it by the Moon-god, the only connection between Gandharvas and the Moon (cf. ŚB. 9, 4, 1, 9, the Moon as Gandharva); but here the Moon is only a link, for the Moon learned it of Manu. Citraratha then promises Arjuna one hundred horses of the Gandharva breed (Gandharvajāḥ, 1, 170, 54), which assume any form, fulfill all wishes, and go at will (cf. a reference to these "wind-swift" steeds in 5, 56, 13). Citraratha also tells the history of Tapatī and Saṃvarana and his desire for a Gandharva-wedding, the birth of Kuru, etc. (1, 171—182). Viśvāvasu in Rām. is invoked with Hahā-Huhū and Tumburu to make magic gardens for Bharadvāja (R 2, 91, 16f.). In the Uttara he is father by Analā of Kumbhīnasī (mother of Lavaṇa and wife of Lola's son Madhu, R 7, 61, 17). He shares the "path of the air" (R 5, 1, 169). Citraratha gives a name to Rāma's sūta (R 2, 32, 17). His park, which (above) is Indra's, is usually Kubera's; it is a typical spot of beauty (R 2, 71, 4; ib. 91, 47, etc., etc.). The Mbh. assigns it to Kubera only (3, 80, 6), which is proper, as it is on Kailāsa "where Kubera was made overlord" (5, 111, 11). Pilgrims visit it (1, 119, 48) and in this epic also it serves as the non plus ultra of beauty in landscape (1, 63, 45; 70, 30; 75, 48, etc.). Citraratha is all-wise and self-controlled (as son of Muni, 1, 65, 43). Besides the steeds mentioned above, Citraratha gives as tribute speckled (tittirikalmāṣa) Gandharva horses (2, 61, 22, here aśvān Gāndharvān). Citrasena is called Gandharvarāja by Indra, to whose court he belongs (3, 45, 2). He teaches Arjuna in Amarāvatī "song, instrumental music, and dancing" (ib. 44, 6f.; 168, 56f.). He is called son of Viśvāvasu (3, 91, 14; 168, 57) and appears with his family along with Nārada, Parvata, Viśvāvasu and the Hahā-Huhūs (parivāragaṇāḥ, 12, 200, 12). His encounter with the Kurus is an imitation of that of Citraratha with Arjuna (3, 240 and 241, 18f.). Arjuna defeats him and then converses amicably with his "friend" (ib. 245, 28; 246, 1). The slaughtered Gandharvas are revived by Indra, who sprinkles ambrosia over them (ib. 246, 18). The combat is alluded to again in 4, 49, 9. Another "Citra" Gandharva is known only from 1, 101, 6f., where Citrāṅgada challenges and slays a mortal king of the same name, after calling upon him (so S) either to "take another name" or fight. The fight lasts three years at Kurukṣetra on the Sarasvatī (S Hiraṇvatī), and "being stronger in magic", the Gandharva kills the man; who, however, is afterwards better known than his celestial conqueror (5, 172, 18, etc.). An Apsaras has the same name.

§ 95. Besides this group, the most popular Gandharva is Tumburu or Tumbaru, or Tamburu (as if he were the tambour personified). He leads the Gandharvas to watch men's battles (4, 56, 12, etc.). He gives Arjuna his Gāndharva weapon (7, 45, 22). Śikhaṇḍin's war-steeds are his gift (7, 23, 20, not in C; the horses are divyāḥ, heavenly, B and S). He goes to Meru with Nārada and other Gandharvas but only to worship (6, 6, 20). He is the "friend of Arjuna" and with Citrasena and others stays at Yudhiṣṭhira's court (above, 2, 4, 36). He leads the band that makes music when Arjuna is born (1, 123, 54). As "best of Gandharvas" he sings "with lovely song" in Amarāvatī and before Nahuṣa (3, 43, 28; 5, 11, 15). He plays to Kubera (q. v.), brings tribute to Dhṛtarāṣṭra (2, 52, 24), and is reckoned one of the best four (1, 65, 51, the Hāhā-Hūhū and Atibāhu also), but perhaps only as sons of Prādhā. He is set beside Nārada and Gopa as kings of song (R 2, 91, 45). A follower of Kubera has a similar plant (cf. Umbara) name, Kustumbaru (2, 10, 16). Tumburu was cursed to be born as a Rākṣasa, being too fond of Rambhā (see under Kubera). He is the martial hero of the group, yet one of the few yielding to love. In 5, 117, 16, he is described as wedded to Rambhā. Perhaps owing to their proclivity (as lovers of the Apsarasas) to this passion they are represented as having especially power over any love-lorn wight, kāmavṛtta, "though even a man in love can conquer a Gandharva if he is holy and guarded by a priest" (perhaps a pious afterthought, 1, 170, 73). The Gandharvas are tīkṣnakāmāḥ, "sharp in love" (as snakes are "sharp" in anger and vultures are "sharp" in hunger, R 4, 59, 9), which sufficiently indicates their specialty. The list of active Gandharvas is thus short. Only one more is of note. This was Golabha, who according to Rām. (R 4, 22, 27 f.) was slain after fighting fifteen years with Vālin. The same epic names as chiefs of the Gandharvas called Rohitas, Śailūṣa, Grāmaṇī, Śighru (v. l. Sindhu and Śikṣa), Śubhra (or Sthāna or Śuka) and Babhru (R 4, 41, 43). The Rohitas guard the extreme South and are "awful fighters" (other awful fighters guard the Western Vindhya, R 4, 42, 19). Such earthly Gandharvas seem to be permanent residents of the earth (cf. Nāgas as people). It is curious that the noteworthy Buddhistic Gandharva Pañcaśikha is not known as such in the epics. He has perhaps been naradised, as the name is pseudo-epic only, as that of a scholar-saint, Kāpileyo mahāmuniḥ (12, 218, 6). Tumburu (Timburu), however, is well-known in both circles. Nārada keeps enough of his unsaintly nature to be the "delighter in strife" (see § 130). He is a Devagandharva (H 9633) "beloved of Indra", apparently because he is saṃgrāmakalahapriya "fond of strife and quarrel" (ib.) He acts as messenger (H 7231, meghadūta?).

§ 96. The females of this group are worthy of notice. Mantharā is a sister of Bali and daughter of Virocana and was killed by Indra for seeking to destroy earth (R 1, 25, 20); but again she is a former Gandharvī by the name of Dundubhī (the "drum"), incarnated as fomenter of hate at Brahman's behest (3, 276, 16). Kumbhīnasī (above) seems to be demoniac as well as Gandharvan. The females as types of beauty are often named (e. g. 1, 171, 8) as distinct from Apsarasas and Yakṣīs; they are known as kāntās of kāminas, that is, as "the beloved of lovers" (cf. 3, 158, 96 with 159, 17), i. e. the Gandharvas, who are the lovers par excellence. All are graceful and tuneful; they dress in silk and wear garlands. All Gandharvas, male or female, are graceful, yaśasvinaḥ (R 6, 114, 4). Somadā is daughter of Urmilā (v. l. Ūrṇāyu), the servant of Cūlin the ascetic, who granted her the boon of a son, Brahmadatta, founder of Kāmpilyā (city); his touch healed the deformed daughters of Kuśanābha (R 1, 33, 11 f.; see Vāyu), who were born of Ghṛtācī (Ūrmilā is also the name of Lakṣmaṇa's wife). See also Devavatī, Narmadā, and Vasudhā, as Gandharva women-names (daughter of Grāmaṇī, etc., R 7, 5, 2 f.). Compare also R 7, 12, 24 (above pp. 41—42).

§ 97. Although the Gandharvas may be found in forests and caves (guhās, where live beasts and Kiṃnaras, R 3, 67, 5 f.; R 4, 38, 30 f.), yet their natural abode is in the air (1, 63, 34), the realm of fog and rain (R 3, 65, 14; R 5, 1, 165 and 169 f.), and such is the meaning of the fact that fata morgana are called "Gandharva cities", with which evanescent phenomena are (passim) compared. The sceptic says that virtue is like Gandharvanagara and disappears on examination, that is, has no substantial basis (12, 261, 13). Guhyakas disappear in air like Gandharvanagara, or a fiend suddenly disappears and the same simile is employed (1, 126, 35; 7, 175, 103). Sometimes the bright color is the tertium. Thus cars light as air are like Gandharvanagaras (vātāyamānāḥ, 6, 103, 20), or cars are bright as the cities of Gandharvas (8, 81, 18; R 6, 108, 1); or the bright deer that tempted Sītā is "bright as the sun and Gandharvapurasaṃnibhaḥ (R 3, 43, 6). The appearance of such a mirage is ominous of ill (5, 143, 22). The epic distinction between gods and Gandharvas shows that the latter are now more specialised (Agni and Vāyu were once Gandharvas), but though this distinction is constantly maintained (1, 88, 2; 9, 42, 40, etc.), yet the tradition that the three fires stolen by Purūravas were taken from the Gandharva-world (1, 75, 23) shows that they are still thought of as heavenly bodies. Again, they have a tendency to become earthly seers and act like saints. Citraratha (above) boasts of his asceticism; Yayāti instances them as renowned for the same trait (1, 88, 2); Nārada is a Muni. On the other hand, the "Gandharva king" is a model of beauty (R 2, 3, 27; ib. 37, 11); and as a class they give their name to the free-love union called the "fifth form" of marriage (1, 172, 19; S 1, 242, 5); their weapons are also famous (Gāndharvāstra, R 3, 25, 36, etc.), and though incarnated in human forms at Brahman's command (1, 64, 41), they are grouped with Dānavas and Rākṣasas as old foes of the gods (1, 65, 5). Their world is distinct from that of Brahman and the gods (3, 24, 7), but, as shown above, they live at the courts of the gods, and Indra is followed by their troop on sunlike cars (3, 166, 4). In 1, 225, 9, where Varuṇa gives Arjuna a bow which gods revere and also Dānavas and Gandharvas, the steeds of the hero are Gāndharvāḥ (ib. 10), which may point to a confusion between Gāndhāras and Gandharvas. In R 7, 100, 10, Gandharva-land is definitely located on both sides of the Indus, a fair district, rich in fruits and roots, guarded by Gandharvas skilled in fighting, the sons of Śailūṣa. The Gandharvanagara is here a real town, which Rāma is exhorted to destroy. He sends Takṣa and Puṣkala (Bharata's sons) with Bharata, who besiege the city and overcome it. Then Bharata fonnds two cities and settles his sons over them, Takṣa over Takṣaśilā and Puṣkala over Puṣkalāvata, in Gandharva-deśa and Gāndhāra-deśa, respectively (ib. 101, 11). In RG 6, 83, 13, Gandharvas admit the service of Hāhā-Hūhū alone as compatible with their dignity as free mountaineers, acknowledging no master. Some texts (as above) have iambic Hahā-Huhū, for metre.

§ 98. Whatever be the etymological discrepancy between Centaur and Gandharva, the likeness is close. Centaurs are nubigenae; Gandharvas are cloud-forms; the town of Gandharvas is cloud-land. Both are sensual (kāminaḥ; paiderastai); both have equine forms; both are musical. The Viṣṇu-Purāṇa (1, 5, 44) even derives Gandharva from gam-dhara, "song-maker", obviously forcing the etymology to give the sense felt to be necessary. Both become teachers. Nārada means the "water-giver" (cloud) and is at first a Gandharva and then becomes an expositor (Parvata, his companion, is cloud). Compare further Varuṇa as a Gandharva and the "sky-going horses", recognised as "mind-born sons" of Lakṣmī, sister of Dhātṛ and Vidhātṛ (1, 66, 51). Native authorities give gandh as "injure", perhaps as seizing (habeo); Gandharvas as grahas or robbers. The Vedic Gandharva thus seizes the bridle (rays) of the Sun and the bride of men. Gandhakālī (-ikā, as mother of Vyāsa) was an Apsaras who became a Grāhī, or seizing monster; "she took the lives of all she seized and even devoured gods and Gandharvas", till the sight of Hanumat put an end to the curse of the Muni Yakṣa (RG 6, 82, 74 and 160 f.). The connection with gandha as vapor seems more natural. Perhaps Śiva as gandhadhārin and gandhapālin is so to be interpreted. The Vedic (and Avestan) myths rather imply an origin from one "Gandarewa"; but the same view might be taken of the Apsarasas. More probably both groups are water-phenomena (clouds or stars), sometimes regarded as a unit phenomenon.

§ 99. **Kiṃnaras and Kiṃpuruṣas.** — These spirits are not formally distinguished in the epics, though named separately and ascribed to different progenitors, Kiṃnaras being decended from Pulastya and Kiṃpuruṣas from Pulaha (1, 66, 7). The Kiṃnaras are a kind of Gandharvas, distinguished from Naras (2, 10, 14), at Kubera's court; in the worship of Nārāyaṇa (1, 228, 21); and as subjects of Śiva, "lord of Naras, Kiṃnaras, and Yakṣas" (14, 44, 15). They are raudradarśinaḥ, rude of appearance (14, 63, 15; as separate spirits, ib. 88, 37). Kiṃpuruṣas accompany gods, seers, serpents, Gandharvas and Yakṣas, to see the ocean drunk up (3, 104, 21). Their lord is Druma (2, 10, 29), ācārya in an assembly of kings (2, 37, 13), a teacher, also renowned for prowess (2, 44, 16); as if he were king of a northern people (Gaṅgādvāra is the home of Kiṃnaras, 3, 90, 20; cf. H 5014, Kiṃpuruṣa Druma Parvatīya). Drumaputra is a fighting lord of the Kiṃpuruṣas in the northern White Mountain (2, 28, 1). Gandhamādana is the abode of Druma, the "lion of the Kiṃpuruṣas" (5, 158, 3 and 7); from him Rukmin got his bow and knowledge of arms. Like Gandharvas, the Kiṃpuruṣas are "wise in song", gītakovidāḥ (S has Kāpuruṣas for Kiṃpuruṣas here, v. l. to 12, 169, 5; cf. S 2, 71, 39). Kiṃpuruṣas wander in the forests with friendly Yakṣas, making it as charming as Nandana (with song, 12, 169, 7; with vānaras, 1, 70, 15). They fight (7, 111, 31) and Rāvaṇa says they cannot be around a hermitage (but he errs, R 3, 43, 11; cf. ib. 46, 28 and 67, 6); and they group themselves with frightened gods on fearful occasions (5, 12, 2; R 5, 56, 31). In 7, 199, 2, aśvakiṃpuruṣa, the battle-field is likened to a mountain "having horses as its Kiṃpuruṣas", possibly in reference to the horse-form of the spirits, who live chiefly in the mountains (3, 136, 2; 139, 6, etc.), where they go "in pairs", male and female (R 2, 54, 39; R ib. 93, 11; ib. 94, 11), wearing swords and fine garments (ib.). Royal praisers are likened to "skilled Kiṃnaras with lovely voices" (R 7, 37, 3). The females serve as type of loveliness (R 3, 46, 22; R 5, 33, 5 f.), and often as type of desertion on the part of fickle lovers (R 2, 12, 74). This is the meaning of the "fallen Kiṃnarī" simile (R 2, 9, 65; ib. 10, 24, etc.). A woman with a sweet voice is addressed Kiṃnarodgītabhāṣiṇi (1, 172, 10). They dance as well as sing but are not individualised like the Apsarasas (R 7, 23, pra. 3, 12). There is not the slightest allusion in either epic to the distinction (now become classic) made by the scholiast to VP. 1, 5, 57: "Naras have a human body except for an equine rump and Kiṃnaras have an equine head on a human body". There is little to indicate that any of the three classes was of equine form at all and only the mention of Kiṃnaras and Kiṃpuruṣas to support the (late) difference genealogically. Kiṃnaras here go with Rākṣasas, Yakṣas and monkeys to make one group, as opposed to Kiṃpuruṣas and fierce wild animals (śarabhas, lions, tigers, bears, and wolves; S has ṛkṣā for Yakṣā īhāmṛgāḥ in 1, 66, 8). Savagery can scarcely be the cause of differentiation, for in 3, 153, 9, Kiṃnaras go with Rākṣasas and Kiṃpuruṣas with the milder Yakṣas. According to the late genesis of H 11794, Naras and Kiṃnaras were born from the feet of Brahman (VP 1, 5, 47, confines this origin to animals). In R 7, 88, 22, Kiṃpuruṣīs are equivalent to Kiṃnarīs and they were created by Budha, who changed Ilā's companions into these mountain spirits (perhaps androgynous).[1]

§ 100. **The Apsarasas.** — According to a late tradition, sundry Apsarasas were born of Brahman's fancy (saṃkalpa, H 12476); others, of Dakṣa's daughters. The first make a group of ten plus one, beginning with Menakā, and are called Vaidikīs, sacrosanct, recognised by revelation, and as such distinguished from those born from Dakṣa's daughters. This group may be considered, therefore, as that of the most revered nymphs: Menakā, Sahajanyā, Parṇinī, Puñjikasthalā, Ghṛtasthalā, Ghṛtācī, Viśvācī, Urvaśī, Anumlocā, Pramlocā, and Manovatī. Eighteen are ascribed to Muni (sired by Kaśyapa), of whom the best known are Tilottamā, Rambhā, and Miśrakeśī. Six (names of) nymphs are ascribed to Prādhā (apparently should be eight); but H 11554 makes Prādhā mother of Apsarasas in general, as Muni is mother of Gandharvas; though, ib. 274, all Apsarasas come from Muni (so VP. 1, 21, 24). In the list below are included the group ascribed, in 1, 65, 45 f., to Kapilā and Prādhā (it takes in some of "Muni's daughters" in H), since Anavadyā and Subhagā appear in that group, who in H are apparently Apsarasas. Bhāsī in this group is different from the Bhāsī who is "mother of birds" (daughter of Tāmrā, 1, 66, 56 = R 3, 14, 17). Seven gaṇas of Apsarasas are mentioned (H 6798). Ten unnamed Apsarasas of the North are called Vidyutprabhās (5, 111, 21) "by name" ("lightning-glorious"). A group of eleven appears in the list of 1, 123, 61 f., where there are two well-defined divisions of twenty-eight and of ten plus one (compare above the twenty-seven Gandharvas). The Ādi group is only in part coincident with that of Hariv., but the half-agreement shows that the chief nymphs were thus grouped. The ten plus one may cast a light on the way the group of ten gods was made eleven and then trebled (the Three-tens were then reckoned as Thirty-three). Several names appear to be variants of the same word (e. g. Karṇikā = Parṇikā = Parṇinī), but as it is doubtful how far this is applicable, all have been enlisted. In 4, 9, 15 f., the S text does not have Indrāṇī immediately after Mālinī, who may, therefore, be a nymph (otherwise Durgā or even Draupadī, ib. 21). Urvaśī is the extra eleventh in Ādi (later she is taken out of the Vaidikīs

[1] According to Hertel, WZKM. 25, 160, Ilā is herself typical of these androgynous Kiṃpuruṣas, whose name ("what a man") indicates their double-sexed nature. Yakṣas change their sex, however, as easily as did Ilā's companions, and the epic itself gives no further hint on the subject. The Kiṃpuruṣas are usually not differentiated individually. They and the Kiṃnaras go with Vidyādharas (§ 116) and are found on Mandara, Citrakūṭa, etc., and in forests (Pampā, etc.; cf. R 5, 56, 31 and R 4, 1, 61; ib. 4, 40, 44; Mbh. 1, 18, 2; 3, 108, 10 f.; ib. 158, 39 and 96; ib. 159, 17). For criticism of Hertel's view see Keith in JRAS. April, 1913. Perhaps nara and puruṣa both refer to water rather than "man"; as Gandharva species they may be poor water-givers (clouds or stars), but the epic consistently regards them as spirits.

altogether). One Apsaras in particular is "dear to Kubera", viz. Vargā (1, 216, 16). Menakā is the very best of the "best six Apsarasas" (1, 74, 68 f.), and it is said in the same (late) passage that she is "born of Brahman". In epic tales the most prominent Apsarasas are Menakā, Urvaśī, Ghṛtācī, Miśrakeśī, and Rambhā. Several names coincide with those of their brother-lovers (1, 65, 48), the Gandharvas, Gopālī, Citrāṅgadā, Citrasenā; cf. Sugandhā. Urvaśī and Pūrvacitti (one of the "best six") live regularly on the Malaya mountains (12, 333, 19), though with them, as they watch the flight of Śuka, is Pañcacūḍā. All the northern mountains contain them. Other special localities mentioned as resorts of the nymphs are Mahendra, Subhūmika, on the Sarasvatī, the Kāverī, Yamunā and Gaṅgā, Nandana, Mandara, Muñjavat, etc., that is, they live chiefly on earth around rivers or on mountains, as in the courts of all the gods. The word Apsaras is explained as apsu rasa, the essence of the ocean-water produced at the churning, when Apsarasas and the physician god Dhanvantari first rose from it. There were sixty crores of them, not to speak of their "countless attendants" (R 1, 45, 20). In Mbh. this origin is attributed to Dhanvantari but not to the nymphs, and Nārāyaṇa himself in māyā form plays the part of the seductive woman (1, 18, 38 and 45), who induced the Asuras to give up the ambrosia. Seven times six thousand (S, thirteen thousand) Apsarasas dance on the point of Dilīpa's sacrificial post to the music of Viśvāvasu (7, 61, 7). The list of epic Apsarasas is as follows: Adrikā, Adrikṛtasthalī, Anavadyā, Anugā (H), Anūkā, Anūcānā, Anūnā (H), Anumlocā (H), Ambikā, Aruṇā, Aruṇapriyā (H), Arūpā, Alambuṣā, Asitā, Asurā, Irā, Umlocā, Urvarā, Urvaśī, Ṛtusthalā, Karṇikā, Kāmyā, Kumbhayoni, Keśinī, Kṣemā, Gandhakālī, Guṇamukhyā, Guṇāvarā, Gopālī, Ghṛtasthalā (H), Ghṛtācī, Cārunetrā, Cārumadhyā (H), Citrā or Mitrā, Citrāṅgadā, Citralekhā, Citrasenā, Jānapadī, Jāmī (see Yāmī), Tilottamā, Daṇḍagaurī, Dāntā, Devī, Nāgadantā (or -dattā), Pañcacūḍā, Parṇikā (H), Parṇinī, Puñjikasthalā, Puṇḍarīkā, Pūrvacitti, Prajāgarā, Prabhā, Pramāthinī, Pramlocā, Praśamī, Priyamukhyā (H), Budbudā (or Vudvudā), Bhāsī, Bhīmā, Madhurasvarā (-nā), Manu, Manoramā, Manovatī, Manoharā, Marīci, Mārgaṇapriyā, Mālavī, Mālinī (?), Mitrā, Miśrakeśī, Menakā, Yāmī, Rakṣitā, Rati, Rambhā, Ruci, Lakṣaṇā, Lakṣmaṇā (H), Latā, Vaṃśā, Vapus, Varananā (H), Varūthinī, Vargā, Vāmanā, Vidyutā, Vidyutparṇā, Vidyotā, Vipracitti, Viśvācī, (Vu. see Bu.), Śāradvatī, Śucikā, Śucismitā, Śraviṣṭhā (H), Samīcī, Sahajanyā, Sahā, Sukeśī, Sugandhā, Sugrīvī (H), Supriyā, Subāhu, Subhagā, Sumadhyā (H), Sumukhī, Surajā, Suratā, Surathā (H), Suramā (H), Surasā, Surūpā (H), Sulocanā (H), Suvṛttā (H), Somā, Saurabheyī (-seyī), Svayamprabhā, Hāsinī, Himā (R; v. l. Somā), Hemadantā (H), Hemā (R and H). Rām. alone has Adrikṛtasthalī, Nāgadattā (or -dantā), Vāmanā, and Himā (or Somā). Nandā, v. l. H 14165. All come from Brahman's eye, ib. 11787.[1])

§ 101. These nymphs dance and sing. They are called "gods' girls" (1, 130, 6). Their female companions are the Devapatnīs, proper wives of the gods. Like all Hindu celestials they are depicted as overloaded with gems and garlands (3, 43, 31; R 3, 35, 16 f.). They also wear necklaces, golden girdles, and anklets, which tinkle as they welcome saints to heaven. Saints or warriors ride to heaven on musical cars drawn by geese, lions, or tigers (13, 106, 49 and 56 f.) and are greeted by the music of vīṇā, vallaki, muraja and bells, while the nūpura of the waiting nymphs

[1]) Compare on the Mbh. Apsarasas, Adolf Holtzmann, ZDMG. 33, p. 631 f. (a few names omitted). Irā is properly wife of Kaśyapa; Pañcacūḍā may be Rambhā (ib. p. 632).

delight their ears as well (ib. 49 and 63). The nymphs wear their locks in five braids (pañcacūḍāpsaras; also as proper name, 3, 134, 12, etc.). Their fine clothes they lay aside when they bathe in the heavenly Mandākinī, but are much ashamed when seen naked by Vyāsa; only Śuka they do not mind, because he is all soul and no body (12, 334, 18 and 28 f.). Ordinarily they are not so shy. The best of them is described as lewd and pitiless (1, 8, 8). Rāvaṇa denies that they have husbands (R 7, 26, 41), and says they are free to all; but he makes this remark to Rambhā, a domestic Apsaras, wife of Kubera's son, and snuṣā (!) of her ravisher (see Kubera). Yet the nymphs are free in love (3, 46, 42) and ordinarily care only for love and play. When a hero dies in battle, thousands of them hover above him, each one seeking his soul and saying to herself: "May he be my lord" (12, 98, 46 f.). They also dance at human weddings (R 1, 73, 35), while Gandharvas sing finely, kalam; but the Apsarasas themselves sing sweetly with "song beautified by elocution" (the sounds made in three places; R 5, 4, 10, tristhānasvarabhūṣitam). At the magic entertainment prepared for Bharadvāja, the Gandharvas sang and the Apsarasas danced, who had come from the courts of Indra and Kubera and Brahman, Kubera sending twenty thousand of them (R 2, 91, 16 f.; ib. 26 and 44); though the names may be confused here with those of the Gandharvīs, who also come to the feast (Himā here interchanges with Somā, cf. 3, 43, 29). As personification of sexual pleasure one Apsaras is called Rati and all of them are the deities of love-lorn women: ratīnāṃ vasumatyas tu strīṇām Apsarasas (sc. jānīdhvam, 14, 43, 16; in 15, Umā is the mistress of all bhagadevānuyātās, i. e. a Venus). Subhūmika is a Tīrtha of the Sarasvatī, which is the playground of the Apsarasas, where gods, Apsarasas, Gandharvas, and seers go regularly once a month to enjoy themselves with divine sports (9, 37, 3). In no early passage do the Apsarasas do more than seduce saints or please gods by jingling their ornaments, revealing their beauties, singing and dancing. The kind of song or dance, still less the dramatic entertainments, with which they are credited in the Hariv., are unknown in the epics proper. The chief dance of this sort goes by the name of Hallīṣaka and the song is called Chālikya (H 8449 f.; cf. 9900). On the Rambhā-drama see Kubera (§ 84). Śibi "was danced and besung by gods, Gandharvas, and Apsarasas" (nṛttaś cai 'vo 'pagītaś ca (13, 32, 32). In 3, 148, 20, the Apsarasas sing the carita of Rāma, perhaps the beginning of a change in their conception, though to sing a hero and sing his deeds may be the same thing.

§ 102. Menakā was wife of Ūrṇāyu (5, 117, 16) and mother of Pramadvarā by the Gandharva Viśvāvasu. Being pitiless, she abandoned the child at birth, who grew up and married the son of the Apsaras Ghṛtācī by Pramati, son of Cyavana, whose son was Śunaka (1, 5, 9 f.; ib. 8, 8). Menakā also deserted her child Śakuntalā in the same way, except that here she was sent by Indra to seduce the father Viśvāmitra, which she does aided by Māruta and Manmatha, Wind and Love. She is "most distinguished in the divine qualities of the Apsarasas" and is "born of Brahman", best of Apsarasas, lewd and pitiless (1, 74, 69 f.). Her daughter says that Menakā is "among the Thirty-three gods and superior to them" (ib. 74, 83). Indra also sends Jānapadī (devakanyā) to tempt the saint Śāradvata Gautama, and she easily succeeds in doing so, though she is not one of the Vaidikīs, who are usually entrusted with such missions

(1, 130, 6). Indra too sends Alambuṣā to tempt Dadhīca (9, 51, 7f.), and the result is the birth of Sārasvata (celebration of Sarasvatī by nymphs, ib. 17). Ghṛtācī pṛthulocanā, "wide-eyed", shows herself accidentally to Bharadvāja and the saint is so moved as to beget Śrutāvatī (9, 48, 65). On another occasion, she meets the same saint with a like result and Droṇa is born (1, 130, 35; ib. 166, 1). The nymph in these cases only excites the saint, the child being born not of her but in an incubator. Ṛṣyaśṛṅga, the "horned" saint, was born of a doe by Vibhāṇḍaka when Urvaśī excited his passions by showing herself to him (3, 110, 35). This Urvaśī once "kicked Purūravas aud repented of it" (R 3, 48, 18). She was cursed to become his wife by Brahman (H 1375) or Mitra (q. v. R. 7, 56, 20f.); and she accompanied Purūravas when he fetched fire from the home of the Gandharvas (q. v.). She had by him six sons, Āyus, Vanāyus, Śatāyus, Dṛḍhāyus, Dhīmat, and Amāvasu (1, 75, 20f.; H 1363f. v. l.). Purūravas loses his wits and, though intelligent, is cursed for his contempt of the priestly power in this story. Compare H 1363 f. for the whole history. He lived near Ganges' Gate on Mt. Puru beside the golden-sanded Urvaśī = Ganges (2, 78, 17; 3, 90, 22f,; 12, 29, 68; in H ib. at Prayāga). With the Wind-god and Kaśyapa he holds learned conversations (12, 72, 2f.; ib. 73, 7f.). The son of Āyus, Nahuṣa, also, as Indra, enjoys the Apsarasas in Nandana (5, 11, 13), here distinguished from Devakanyās. Urvaśī is also the name of a Tīrtha (3, 84, 157; 13, 25, 46, Lauhitye). She is known as "mother of the race of Pauravas" (3, 46, 40). Despite her affection for Purūravas (1, 44, 10; son of Budha, king of Kāśī, and son of Ilā, R 7, 19, 5; ib. 87, 3 f.), she is in love with her descendant Arjuna, whom Indra commanded her to teach good behavior. To seduce him (for she loved him) she drank a little rum and when partially intoxicated, after bathing herself and smearing sandal-paste on her bosom, decorated with gold ornaments, she put flowers in her long curly hair and came to him "in the face of night" (evening) by moonlight, her body as slender as the digit of the moon and her countenance like the full moon. As she came swift as thought, she excited her imagination with sensual thoughts and arched her eyebrows as she walked, bending slightly forward with the weight of her deep breasts. Three folds showed in her waist; her hips were round and high; her feet were arched like a tortoise's back; her soles were flat; her toes were straight and copper-colored; on her ankles were little bells; her only garment was an upper cloth as thin and white as a cloud. This description lays weight on the vilāsana of the Apsaras, her beguiling and not too modest gestures. Arjuna said he would look on her as a mother and was promptly cursed by the slighted nymph (3, 46, 47). Tilottamā (daughter of Prādhā in the genealogy of 1, 65, 49) is loaded with gems as she seeks to seduce the demons; her beauty causing Indra and Śiva (q. v.) to become respectively thousand-eyed and four-faced. She is said to have been made of all loveliness by Viśvakarman or by Brahman expressly to tempt the demons Sunda and Upasunda (1, 211, 28; in 13, 141, 1f. she tries to tempt Śiva but fails). She is made of jewels or loaded with them, according to the poet's fancy. It is Indra who usually, afraid and trembling for his throne, sends a nymph to seduce a too pious saint. In 5, 9, 11f., he thus summons several of them (Devastriyaḥ) to seduce Triśiras but their names are not given. They employ hāva and bhāva, decent and indecent inducements (śṛṅgāraveṣa, jewelled attire), here in vain; but not so in 12, 343, 32. Coquettish looks and laughter are also theirs (2, 7, 24; 3, 43, 32).

§ 103. The mass of these nymphs appear only as dancing-girls, pranṛttāpsarasas, and are innocently enough employed to amuse a guest of the gods (13, 19, 44f.), or to dance before the gods. Troops of them are in Indra's train (1, 56, 9, etc.; at 2, 7, 24, S inserts the names of the best known as being at Indra's court). As the entourage of Vāsudeva, at Indra's command, sixteen thousand of them were born on earth (parigraha, as his wives, 1, 67, 155; but Rukmiṇī was a part of Lakṣmī herself). The Apsarasas are not infrequently cursed to be thus born on earth, often in low forms. Adrikā became a fish in the Yamunā river through Brahman's curse, and thus became mother of Matsya and Satyavatī by king Vasu (1, 63, 58f.); after which, released from the curse, she reassumed her heavenly form. The son of this nymph-mothered Satyavatī, viz. Vyāsa, on seeing Ghṛtācī, although she took a parrot-form (cf. kāmarūpiṇī, H 10002), was excited to beget Śuka, the pure soul alluded to above (12, 325, 2); at whose birth "Gandharvas sang and hosts of Apsarasas danced" (Apsarogaṇāḥ), while the drums of the gods sounded and Viśvāvasu and the (two pairs) Tumbaru-Nāradau and Hāhā-Hūhū (sic) sang praises (16). Such salutations greet Yayāti, especially favored by Viśvācī (1, 75, 48 and 85, 9), when he returns to heaven under a shower of flowers, sung and bedanced by groups of Gandharvas and Apsarasas (upagīto 'panṛttaś ca Gandharvāpsarasāṃ gaṇaiḥ) and praised by gods and Cāraṇas (5, 122, 2; 123, 4). At the birth of heroes, e. g. Duṣyanta (S 1, 95, 11), the same drums and songs and dances appear. The flowers are dropped by the Apsarasas, as at Bhīṣma's vow of celibacy, a curious time for them to show joy (1, 100, 98). A woman "like an Apsaras" is of course like in beauty, sometimes added (1, 102, 3; 106, 24; 3, 96, 29, rūpeṇā 'psaraso 'py ati). The Apsarasas do not wait to be sent on seductive errands. Five of them (Vargā, Saurabheyī, Samīcī, Budbudā, Latā) try to seduce a saint of their own accord and are cursed to become crocodiles for a hundred years (1, 216, 16f.; 217, 8), that is for an indefinitely long period, until they are redeemed by Arjuna. A similar story (or the same) is told of the "tank of the five Apsarasas" (R 3, 11, 12f.), who were ordered to seduce the aged Māṇḍakarṇi, and succeeded so well that he built a house and kept them all. They rejuvenated him, and the sound one hears of running water there is the music of their instruments (ib. 20), one of the rare instances where the Apsarasas' music is explained physically. A late passage describes the Apsarasas swarming by thousands around a divine car (R 7, 77, 13): "Some sing heavenly songs, others play on instruments, vādayanti, others hum, kṣveḍayanti, others dance, and others fan the face of the god". They shout sādhu (bravo) to heroes in battle or when a hero dies, and they place dead heroes on divine cars with loud sounds of song and instruments, played in the sky "but heard on earth", thus encouraging others (8, 49, 76f.; 57, 13f.; 9, 5, 35f.). They are thus peculiarly "Indra's girls", Indrakanyās (13, 107, 21), though they are found at home with all the fighting gods, Kubera (passim), Varuṇa (2, 9, 26; 13, 155, 15), and Yama (2, 8, 38); as they also adorn the courts of the highest (see under Brahman, etc.). The later priestly epic sees in their beauty, as in that of their brother Gandharvas, the reward for former merit (asceticism, etc.) and promises the possession of them, with all their sensual joys, as the reward of asceticism to-day (5, 44, 21; 13, 107, 18, etc.). It also regards them (not women in general) as inheritors of Indra's sin (12, 283, 43; cf. above, p. 131).

§ 104. Other Apsarasas than those mentioned have little activity. Some accounts confuse the same story. Viśvāmitra is seduced by Menakā (1, 71, 22; R 1, 63, 5) or by Ghṛtācī (R 4, 35, 7). He also curses Rambhā, to become a stone, for attempting to seduce him (R 1, 64, 12; 13, 3, 11). Ghṛtācī is the mother of Raudrāśva's ten sons, descendants of Pūru, in H 1658; but their mother is Miśrakeśī in 1, 94, 8. Ghṛtācī is also the mother of Kuśanābha's daughters (R 1, 32, 10). Of Hemā is related that she got a magic cave guarded by her friend Svayaṃprabhā, who was the daughter of Merusāvarṇi. Maya, Hemā's lover, was slain by Indra, and she meets Rāvaṇa after being thus "abandoned by Maya" (R 4, 50, 39; ib. 51, 10f.; ib. 16; ib. 7, 12, 6f.). Svayaṃprabhā is called dharmacāriṇī, and only the fact that she was the "dear friend" of Hemā indicates here that she is an Apsaras. Yet her name appears as that of an Apsaras in 3, 43, 29, and the later epic, as indicated even by some of the names above (Anūcānā is "learned"; Suvṛttā is "well-behaved") regards the Apsarasas as not altogether sinful, though it is apt to stigmatise them collectively and individually as wantons. Another Apsaras, who plays a part in Rām., is Puñjikasthalā, cursed to be born on earth as Añjanā, daughter of Kuñjara and wife of Kesarin, monkey-chieftains, and mother, by Māruta, of Hanumat (R 4, 66, 8f.). She is a Varuṇakanyakā and curses Rāvaṇa (R 6, 13, 11; ib. 60, 11), apparently at first an Apsaras (not daughter) in Varuṇa's realm. The ancient idea that an Apsaras was a harmful creature, injuring man otherwise than by shattering his mind by love, is retained in the tradition that the (unnamed) "mother of Apsarasas" is an infant-stealing fiend (3, 230, 39). The Hariv. has a few late touches: Apsarasas here are born from Brahman's eyes (H 11787). Urvaśī "rends the thigh" of (is born direct from) Nārāyaṇa (Viṣṇu, H 4601). The old story of Purūravas and Urvaśī is found in H 1363f. Menakā here becomes mother of Divodāsa and of Ahalyā; and Gopālī, mother of Kālayavana (H 1783 and 1960). Citralekhā, the "painter", who is described as kāmarūpiṇī, "assuming any form at will", is represented as painting the portraits of all the celestials for Uṣā, till Uṣā recognises her beloved among them (Aniruddha as lover of Uṣā, H 9994). Indra as lover of Rambhā appears in H 11250f.

§ 105. **Kāma.** — Kāma, Love (desire), belongs properly with the gaṇas of Gandharvas and Apsarasas, of whom the Hariv. (270 and 12499) recognises him as the "lord" (Kāmadeva as prabhuḥ). Kāma is the word by which philosophers designate Kandarpa, who is also called Anaṅga because Śiva consumed him, when Kāma dared to attack him (R 1, 23, 10f.). Yet also as Kandarpa he appears as cause of creation (6, 34, 28 and 31, 11). Kāma is general "desire", and as such, apart from mythology, appears in the triad, kāma, artha, dharma, though better than the other two elements (virtue and gain), because it is the sustaining power (12, 167, 33f.); unless indeed another view prevails, to the effect that all desire is evil (kāmaḥ saṃsārahetuḥ, 3, 313, 98). Philosophy and mythology mingle in the identification of Pradyumna with Kāma (1, 67, 152, Sanatkumāra), and in making Aniruddha, son of Pradyumna, "son of Rati" (H 10064). With Krodha, Wrath, Kāma enters into the composition of Aśvatthāman (1, 67, 72), but is not otherwise incarnate. The son of Kṛṣṇa and Rukmiṇī "exists in the nature of all and enters both demons and gods" (13, 148, 20). He himself says in his Kāmagītā Gāthās (14, 13, 12f.): "None can destroy me . . I am the one immortal and indestructible"; though Yoga power may overcome this pervasive power. It is this philosophically conceived Kāma Jagatpati that is "older than Rudra" and is regarded (cf. AV. 3, 21, 4; TS. 2, 2, 3, 1, etc.) as a fire, lord of the world, the eternal energising power, interpreted mythologically as a fire-form of Rudra (saṃkalpābhirucih Kāmaḥ sanātanatamaḥ . . sanātano hi saṃkalpaḥ Kāma ity abhidhīyate . . sarvabhāvanaḥ hṛcchayaḥ, 13, 85, 11, 16 and 17). With this tenuous mythological character the usual Love-god has little to do; only it is important to know that he is thus philosophically identified with the hṛcchaya "heart-love".

§ 106. Kāma has many names as Love-god, but they do not indicate separate personalities, only different ways of regarding the same being, as "longing", Smara, as "mind-disturber", Manmatha, as "intoxicator", Madana, as "insolent" (? Kandarpa), as "limbless", Anaṅga. Darpa, Insolence, is himself personified as son of Sin and Bliss, "through whom many gods and Asuras have been led to destruction" (12, 90, 26); Rāvaṇa is called Devadānavadarpahan (RG 6, 79, 2), with the personification in abeyance. In VP. 1, 7, 25, however, Darpa is son of Dharma, not of Adharma, as Kāma is son of Dharma and Faith (1, 66, 33). Kāma's wife is Rati (ib.), probably the Apsaras of that name (13, 19, 45). His two sons are Harṣa and Yaśas, Joy and Grace (H 12482), by Rati; and Kāma himself in this passage is son of Dharma and (Śrī) Lakṣmī (in VP. 1, 7, 29, Rati as Nandī bears to Kāma only one son, Harṣa). The identity of the different forms (names) of Kāma is made clear by the fact that Rati is wife of Manmatha (3, 68, 12 = RG 3, 4, 9), and of Madana (S 1, 203, 34, "Śacī chose for her lover Indra, Svāhā chose Agnideva, Lakṣmī chose Mukunda, Uṣā chose Sūrya, Ratī (sic) chose Madana, and Parvatarājaputrī chose Maheśvara"). Rati appears as an abstract deity without reference to Kāma in 2, 11, 43, and as a common noun in kāmarati, a man stultified by desire (R 4, 33, 54 f.). It is recognised that Kāma stultifies as well as burns, but it is not always certain whether personification is intended (kāmamohita, 1, 172, 1; kāmenā 'loḍyate manaḥ, 1, 219, 16). Ratiguṇa is son of Prādhā (1, 65, 47), a Gandharva, otherwise Rātiguṇa (Ratā is mother of one of the Vasus, who include Agni). In 4, 14, 24, the peculiar word Agnimadana, "fire-madness" (of love), is identical with Madanāgni in R 6, 5, 8 (perhaps personified here).

§ 107. Love is armed with arrows, Kāmabāṇa (1, 171, 34; 3, 46, 49; R 3, 55, 2); Manmathaśara (R 2, 11, 1); Kandarpabāṇa (1, 187, 5 and 12); so Puṣpaketuśarāhata; Kāmabāṇārta almost passim, but Smaraśarāsanapūrṇasamaprabhaḥ (7, 184, 48) is unique. Love's sign is a flower; so his arrow. The effect of the shot stupifies, Kandarpeṇābhimūrcchita, Anaṅgaglapitā (of Urvaśī, 1, 214, 19 f.); or maddens, Apsarasaḥ Kandarpeṇa darpitāḥ (ib. 217, 2); Kāmābhihatacetas, Kāmopahatacetana (1, 172, 3; R 3, 62, 1). The effect on the man is like that on a woman when "penetrated by Love" (or Love's dart, Manmathāviṣṭa, 1, 173, 28; R 4, 66, 15; Manmathaśarāviṣṭa, R 3, 46, 13 and ib. 48, 17); cf. Rāma as Kāmavaśaṃgata, nityaṃ dhyānaparo Rāmo nityaṃ śokaparāyaṇaḥ, etc., R 5, 36, 41 f., just like Damayantī in this sentimental epic (vaśa is will and power, cf. kāmavaśya, kāmabāṇavaśaṃgata = Kāmasya vaśam īyivan, 3, 46, 49). Only once (in S) is the hook used for the arrow; this is the hook employed to direct the elephant, S 1, 241, 19, Kāmāṅkuśanivāritaḥ. As arrows are poetically serpents, the victim of Kāma complains that he has been "bitten by the great serpent of Kāma" in 1, 172, 9 (Kāmamahāhi; he is also "burned with Love's fire"). In 13, 107, 26, the arrows of Kāma are first reckoned as five in number (śarāgni = pañcatriṃśat). In H 4607 (cf. v. l. 10882) the arrows are also five.

§ 108. Kāma is a form of fire, whence Kāmabāṇaprapīḍita, 4, 14, 5, is followowd by Kāmāgni and in vs. 25 by Manmathānala. Here too the disease induced by Love, Kāmavyādhi, is spoken of (vs. 23), which suggests the fate of the lustful "son of Death" (Mṛtyu), called Vena (connected with Venus?), a king who destroyed himself by passion and hate (rāgadveṣavaśaṃgata), son of the "sensual" Atibala, the son of Anaṅga, though Anaṅga is here son of the Prajāpati Kardama (son of Kīrtimat, son of Virajas, son of Viṣṇu). From Vena's thigh came all the Niṣādas and Mlecchas, but from his arm the virtuous Pṛthu, a form of Viṣṇu (whence kings are a form of Viṣṇu), whose chaplain was Śukra and councillors the Vālakhilyas and the "Sārasvatyo gaṇaḥ" (12, 59, 91 f.). According to 1, 75, 15, Vena was son of Manu. Hariv. makes his father Aṅga and says that Vena deified himself (294 f.), his pride and not his lust causing his fall. Manu, 9, 66, ascribes to him the origin of Niyoga (levirate marriage), but (ib. 7, 41) ascribes his fall to pride (the seers cut him up with kuśa-grass). Love as Death, māra, is a late identification (Buddhistic) of Hariv. 14912 f. (māra = smara = Pradyumna). As words meaning Love are constantly used for love, desire (jātamanmathaḥ, 3, 45, 16; Arjunasya kandarpaḥ, 1, 219, 15, etc.), it is possible that another word, manobhava, may be a name of Love, as in 1, 191, 13, saṃpramathye 'ndriyagrāmaṃ prādur āsīn manobhavaḥ (cf. S. 1, 241, 15, idem). The destruction of the members of Love by Śiva (R 1, 23, 12 f.; R 3, 56, 10 in Bomb. yathā Rudreṇa is not in S or G) does not prevent the "limbless god" from possessing limbs, perhaps only as a poetical phrase, Anaṅgāṅgavihāriṇī (4, 14, 17), and Anaṅga has power and arrows (Anaṅgavaśam āgatā, 3, 46, 35; Anaṅgaśarapīḍitā, 5, 175, 10; R 7, 80, 5, of Daṇḍa). Kāma is located with Umā and Śaila (Himavat) in the North, but this is in conjunction with Roṣa (Wrath) at the birth of Skanda (5, 111, 10). Love as Manmatha (1, 71, 41) or Kandarpa (R 1, 64, 6 and 16) helps Menakā (Rambhā) seduce Viśvāmitra. His name (māṃ mathnātī 'va Manmathaḥ, 1, 171, 35 and 40) is explained as disturbing by burning "with sharp fire" (ib. 172, 7 f. and 16, "wounds me with sharp arrows", cf. R 3, 34, 21); cf. the metaphor, 1, 172, 17, "extinguish with the water of thy affection, prīti, the conflagration produced by the fire of Manmatha, whose weapon is of flowers, whose arrows are terrible" (puṣpāyudha, pracaṇḍaśarakārmuka). So in 4, 14, 25 f., the lover begs his mistress to "extinguish the fire of his love with the rain of self-surrender" (her breasts are Kāmapratodau, "two goads of Love"). The state of Urvaśī is thus described as "inflamed by Manmatha", her mind being "wounded by his arrows" (3, 46, 2 f.). Manmathavat is a lover (R 4, 28, 13, manmathavatāṃ hitāḥ . . diśaḥ; cf. kāmavat, ib. G 29, 2). Rati as wife of Manmatha (R 5, 15, 29) is the expression of physical desire (cf. R 7, 23, pra. 5, 18, manmathaḥ śiśnam āsthitaḥ). Both as Kandarpa and Manmatha, Love is beautiful (3, 54, 28; ib. 53, 15 and 28). Rāma, like Nala, is Kandarpa iva mūrtimān (R 3, 17, 9; ib. 34, 5, -sadṛśaprabha, -samarūpa); cf. R 5, 18, 23, samakṣam iva Kandarpam apaviddhaśarāsanam; ib. 5, 34, 29.

§ 109. The ensign of Love is the makara (3, 281, 27); as an auspicious sign it appears on the hand of Śrī, mātā makaradhvajasya (13, 11, 3). It is also the ensign of Pradyumna as Kāma (3, 17, 2 and 7, 111, 25, Kārṣṇi). Between love and fish there is perhaps an aphrodisiacal connection (cf. Adrikā the Apsaras as fish), but Mīnākṣī is not recognised in the epic (she is afterwards daughter of Kubera and to-day she is "wife" of Śiva), and Mīnākṣa is only a Daitya (H 12933, v. l. = 3, 49, 4, vyāghrākṣa). Possibly it is the disturbing element in the makara, a huge beast (3, 270, 19) frightening other fishes (3, 17, 7) and always leaping into or splashing in the sea. No early passage recognises the makara as sign of Kāma (makaraketu H 10882 and -ketumat ib. 10639 and 3, 18, 11 refer to Pradyumna). Another emblem of love is the peacock, but it is found as such only in an allusion in the later Rām. 4, 1, 37, where Rāma says that the dancing peacocks rouse in him the thought of love, mama manmathavardhanāḥ. In Mbh. even this allusion is absent. In 3, 158, 65, plants, sindhuvāra and kurubaka, are (described as) like the darts, tomara, of Manmatha, and arrows of Kāma which "cause desire in those overcome by love" (ib. 67, kāmavaśyautsukyakarān kāmasye 'va śarotkarān), and buds of mangoes with bees are like Anaṅga's arrows (ib. 68); but the peacocks dancing appear only as a beauty of the landscape (ib. 62), though the amorous nature of the dance is clearly depicted. Among the mass of Kāma's later names (unknown in the epics), Dīpaka in the epic is son of Garuḍa (5, 101, 11). Offerings to Kāma (as in Āpast. DhS. 2, 2, 4, 1) are not mentioned, nor is his armor; but this is put on by the cosmic power of AV. 9, 2, 16 and appears to be only a spell. The Kāmaśāstram of 1, 2, 383 is merely part of the triad, artha-, dharma-, and kāmaśāstram, which Vyāsa declared as the great epic. Only Kāma and Smara seem to be pre-epical names for Love; who in AV. 6, 130 is associated with the Apsarasas; as Kāma himself, "sweet yearning love", is a Gandharva as early as TS. 3, 4, 7, 3.[1])

§ 110. **The Aśvins.** — Logically this pair of gods belongs to the Gaṇas because, though there are but two of them, they have the Gaṇa characteristic of being treated as one, till in H 13591 one alone, ekas tu . . aśvī, attacks Vṛtra. They are a Vedic survival. Almost nothing is said of them which has not already been said in the sacred tradition, their names, office, restoration of youth, and unity of existence are Vedic-epic traits, simply handed down without important alteration. In both epics they are incorporated in part as sons of heroes, and as such they are severed from their Vedic unity. But even then they are presented in such a way that they form a sort of unit over against other heroes. They lack the individuality of other humanised gods in these hero-forms. At most the difference between Sahadeva and Nakula, the incarnations of the Mbh. as "sons of the Aśvins", is like that popularly established between Seraphim and Cherubim ("one love more and one know more"). Sahadeva is always good, and Nakula is always clever; but Nakula is never bad, and Sahadeva is never stupid. Yet one feels that "good" Sahadeva is the appropriate epithet, as it is the one usually given to him. Only when fighting is done in different places are the two inseparables parted, to perform their allotted tasks and then coalesce again, as the blameless pair of heroes who reflect the blameless pair of gods. The parents are not differentiated (1, 124, 16,

[1]) On Kāma see IS. 5, 225; 17, 290; Muir, OST. 5, 402. Brunnhofer, Arische Urzeit, p. 183, regards kandarpa = gandharva.

tāv āgamya sutau tasyāṃ janayāmāsatur yamau), but Nakula was older than Sahadeva (ib. 21), apparently by a year, for anusaṃvatsaraṃ jātāḥ (ib. 22) includes the twins.[1])

In Rām., the Aśvins are reborn as Mainda and Dvivida (conquered in Mbh. by Sahadeva!). They are "fair and rich" and are grouped with Ādityas, Vasus, and Rudras as sons of Aditi (R 1, 17, 13; ib. 3, 14, 14; ib. 4, 39, 25); R 1, 22, 7; ib. 48, 3; ib. 50, 18 refer to them as beautiful followers of Pitāmaha; R 2, 58, 10, as coming to Indra's home in Mandara; and R 4, 12, 19 speaks of them as resembling each other and as hero gods, vīrau devau. As already shown (§ 40), they are the "fair pair, strong and beautiful", sons of Sarasvatī and of the Sun (H 11550), or Marutvatī and Dharma (v. l.). Mbh. has more to say about their names and history and cult, points completely ignored in the Rām. Individually the Aśvins are called Nāsatya and Dasra. They are fathers of (reborn as) the twins Nakula and Sahadeva (1, 3, 58, Nāsatya-Dasrau sunasau; 12, 208, 17, "Nāsatya and Dasra are called the two Aśvins, sons of Mārtaṇḍa, the eighth Āditya"; H 602, idem but "eighth Prajāpati"). Allusions to their beauty are found constantly (e. g. 1, 102, 69; 3, 53, 27). They are born on earth as sons of the (western) Mādrī, "unequalled in beauty", that is the earthly heroes are parts of the gods, who were in one account born with the Ādityas of the mundane egg, but according to the usual tradition were "Guhyakas" born in mid-air of Savitṛ and the mare-form of Tvaṣṭṛ's daughter (1, 1, 34; 32, 17; 66, 35 and 40; 67, 111; 124, 16; cf. 1, 1, 114). They live in bliss and glory in the sky (nākapṛṣṭhe, 1, 222, 30) and are generally called devau, though as Śūdras, physicians of the gods, devabhiṣajau, they had (at first) no social rank. Their right to drink Soma was contested by Indra, till Cyavana secured it for them by throwing water on Indra and frightening him with Mada, the demon of intoxication, who had a thousand teeth. Indra says devair na saṃmitāv etau, "they are not the equals of gods"; to which Cyavana replies that they are gods quâ Sūryaputrau, as sons of the Sun (13, 157, 17f.). The status of gods is usually accorded without question; "like the two gods, the Aśvins" appear Arjuna and Kṛṣṇa, and more, "like these two gods receiving offerings at a sacrifice" (8, 56, 94). As physicians (and dentists) they receive the laudation of the blind Upamanyu, who in imitative verses calls them "primeval gods, eternal, two fair-nosed beings, birds divine, weavers of light, creating the wheel of time (which has seven hundred and twenty spokes; or nave of six seasons with twelve spokes; also the year as calf of three hundred and sixty cows), supreme Brahman, powers creating space (the ten directions) and sky, who set sun and moon in the sky; makers of three-colored light, parents of all, and child of each". On hearing this ridiculous laudation "in Vedic verses", vāgbhir ṛgbhiḥ, the divine physicians cured him with a cake, apūpa, and gave him gold teeth (1, 3, 56; abridged translation). This hymn is not only a poor

[1]) The text gives the time of birth only in the case of Yudhiṣṭhira, son of Dharma by yogamūrti, who was born at the eighth muhūrta (Abhijit), when the star of Indra (Aindra = Jyeṣṭhā) was ascendant, on the (fifth) day of the moon, at noon (divā madhyagate sūrye tithau pūrṇe 'tipūjite; N. ayaṃ yogaḥ prāyeṇā 'śvinaśuklapañcamyāṃ bhavati (1, 123, 6). In 2, 31, 10, Āśvineya is Sahadeva (conquers Orissa, Mainda, Dvivida, and the South; Nakula, the West, ib. 32). In 2, 65, 12f. Nakula is staked before Sahadeva, as if the younger (so Arjuna before Bhīma), but probably in the order of merit, as Nakula is physically mighty but Sahadeva is a teacher and wise. Yudhiṣṭhira prefers Bhīma to Arjuna, and so reserves the former to be the last.

imitation of Vedic verse but it answers to no epic conception of the Aśvins, who are not so great as here depicted in the late Book of Beginnings, though the text shows well how little weight can be laid on any fulsome hymn as index of a divinity's real worth. A late pseudo-epic passage explains the meaning of the name Nāsatya (connected with "nose"). One frees oneself from fever, roga, by praising the Aśvins, sons of Mārtaṇḍa, born by exodus through the nostrils of his spouse Saṃjñā and hence called Nāsatya and Dasra (13, 150, 17; H 601). The sunasau above ("with good noses") states also their claim to belong to a good caste, as a good nose indicates good family. In 13, 85, 109, they are born of tears of Agni (late fancy; cf. also § 145). They are associated with Bhṛgu, Vasiṣṭha, and Raghu as helpers and curers of praisers according to the "epic Sāvitrī" (above, 13, 150, 81, syād Aśvinau ca parikīrtayato na rogaḥ). One Aśvin is mentioned in a simile: "he was lofty as Yayāti, lovely to see as Soma, in beauty (as) one of the Aśvins" (rūpeṇā 'nyatamo 'śvibhyām, 3, 294, 18). The two "best physicians, who have all desirable attributes" send a khecara, aerial messenger, to Indra to ask about the theory of the Śrāddha (above, p. 32) in 13, 125, 18 f. They "drew out of his father's womb" the embryo Māṃdhātṛ, conceived through the drinking of some (magical) sacrificial butter (here devau, Aśvinau, 7, 62, 2 f.). Indra above is represented as no friend of the Aśvins, but in 7, 84, 18 two heroes are "like the two Aśvins mounting the car after Indra, as he goes to Śaryāti's sacrifice", and this accords with the traditional friendship of Indra for the twin gods. In 4, 56, 3, Indra mounts to Sudarśana with the All-gods, Aśvins, and Maruts, to see a battle (Sudarśana is here the palace, S 4, 53, 1, not "the car of Indra" nor the Dvīpa). In 8, 65, 18 f., the Aśvins are delighted at the sight of Vāsava (Indra), and the king felicitates Arjuna and Kṛṣṇa, "as Vivasvat felicitated the Aśvins and the Guru (Bṛhaspati) felicitated Indra and Viṣṇu on the death of the great Asura Jambha". The last clause is not explained; it probably refers to the father's joy in the heroic ability of his sons. As for the trip to Śaryāti's sacrifice, Agni elsewhere reproaches Indra (14, 9, 31) for interfering "when Cyavana took the Soma alone as he was going to sacrifice for Śaryāti along with the Aśvins". The full account of the event is given in 3, 122, 24 f., where Nāsatyau is applied to both Aśvins, who restored Cyavana's youth after they had tried to seduce his young wife Sukanyā. As a reward they were made sharers in the benefits of Soma-drinking. Indra, objecting, calls them "menial physicians" and "earth-wanderers" (3, 124, 12). In memory of this event the Aśvins have a sacred watering-place (near Kurukṣetra), where "one becomes beautiful" by bathing in the pool, as did Cyavana (3, 83, 17). The name Nāsatyau (dual) is their earliest common designation, probably meaning "healers" (Dasra is "wonder-maker"). On the "nāsatya birth" (12, 348, 42), see Brahman (§ 137). See also § 68 (Indra and Aśvins). For the Aśvins' birth from Viṣṇu's ears, see § 145.

§ 111. **The Maruts.** — The Gaṇa-gods really begin with the Maruts, though the Aśvins are sometimes grouped with other Gaṇas. But one can scarcely call a pair a group and it is admitted that "the Maruts are kings of the Gaṇas" (14, 43, 6), though they usually stand (3, 62, 24; R 5, 13, 56) in close conjunction with the Aśvins at the end of the list ("Ādityas, Vasus, Rudras and Aśvins with Marut-host", in maṅgalas), or are even omitted altogether as being adjuncts of Indra. All the Gaṇas or groups of gods of this class are individually developed later. This can be seen even in the case of those groups which properly speaking are not Gaṇas. Thus the Ādityas, though composed of clearly defined individuals, are not always made up of the same individuals (§ 37), and it has just been shown that the Lokapālas (§ 91) are also somewhat ill-defined. These are the only groups of which the constituents were recognised as individuals, till a later age (post-epic) evolved individuality for the different members, since the Trimūrti can scarcely be called an epic group at all. The Maruts as a Gaṇa are known from remotest antiquity (RV. 10, 137, 5, etc.). They make a group of seven (13, 107, 111). In 6, 34, 21, Marīci is named as best of Maruts, clearly because of the radical similarity of names and the inclusion of Maruts as Prajāpatis. They are always attendants of Indra, as fighting youths or winds (see § 66, § 80f.). As seven Gaṇas instead of seven individuals, they should number forty-nine (as perhaps 9, 38, 37), but even Hariv. knows by name only twenty-three or -four: Agni, Cakṣus, Havis, Jyotis, Sāvitra, Mitra, Amara, Śaravṛṣṭi (or -dṛṣṭi), Saṃkṣaya, Viraja, Śukra, Viśvāvasu, Vibhāvasu, Aśmanta, Citraraśmi, (nṛpa) Niṣkuṣita (or -karṣin), Nahuṣa, Āhuti, Cāritra, Brahma- (or Bahu-)pannaga, Bṛhat, Bṛhadrūpa, Paratāpana, and Mahābāhu (? H 11544f.). The mother of this late Marutāṃ gaṇaḥ is Marutvatī (Marutvanto devān [Marutāṃ gaṇaṃ] ajanayat); the father is apparently Dharma. Sāvitra is known as a Marut fighter (ib. 13174) and as a Vasu (below, § 112); Cāritra and the rest are new inventions or old characters in a new rôle. For the birth of the "sons of Diti" (5, 110, 8) and etymology (mā rudas), and for their number, see under Vāyu (§ 48). The real epic knows no individual Marut.

§ 112. **The Vasus.** — The Vasus, Rudras, and Aśvins, as constituent parts of the Thirty-three gods, never vary in number. There are eight Vasus, though also many other beings, such as earthly kings, are so named, and the masculine and feminine forms designate Viṣṇu and the Ganges, respectively (13, 149, 87; 13, 80, 5; Viṣṇu, as Rāma, as Prajāpati of Vasus, R 6, 120, 8). Their father is Dharma (12, 207, 23), as he is father here of Rudras, Maruts, Viśve Devas, and Sādhyas; but another account makes their father a Prajāpati son of Manu or of Muni (1, 66, 18f.), or Manu Prajāpati (12, 208, 21); another account derives them from the mundane egg (1, 1, 34). The passage in Ādi gives the names of each Vasu and that of each mother (in H 145, 12449, 12479, the daughter of Dakṣa and wife of Dharma or of Manu is mother of Vasus and is called Vasu: Vasos tu Vasavaḥ) as follows: Dhara and Dhruva, sons of Dhūmrā; Soma (Candramas) and Śvasana (Anila), sons of Śvāsā; Ahar, son of Ratā; Anala (Hutāśana), son of Śāṇḍilī; Pratyūṣa and Prabhāsa, sons of Prabhātā. H 11538 gives (with v. l.) the eight Vasus (sons of Sādhyā and Dharma) as Dhara or Maru, Dhruva, Viśvāvasu or Vivasvat, Soma, Parvata, Yogendra, Vāyu and Nikṛti or Nirṛti (it names here also as Sādhyas Cyavana, Īśāna, Viśvāvasu, etc.). The descendants of the Vasus in the former list are also given. Sons of Dhara are Draviṇa and Hutahavyavaha; Kāla is son of Dhruva; Varcas is son of Soma, and Śiśira, Prāṇa, and Ramaṇa are sons of this Varcas. Ahar's sons are Jyotis, Śama (though also son of Dharma), Śānta, and Muni. Anala's son is Kumāra Kārttikeya (§ 161). The wife of the Vasu Anila (son of Śvāsā) is Śivā, who bore him Manojava and Avijñātagati. Pratyūṣa was father of Devala, and Prabhāsa was father of Viśvakarman by the sister of Bṛhaspati. In 13, 150, 16f., the list of Vasus is: Dhara, Dhruva, Soma, Sāvitra, Anila, Anala, Pratyūṣa, and Prabhāsa. In H 152: Āpa, Dhruva, Soma, Dhara, Anila, Anala, Pratyūṣa,

Prabhāsa. In the last passage the sons are given as above with minor differences (Āpasya putro Vaitaṇḍyaḥ Śramaḥ Śānto Munis tathā), which reflect the Purāṇic genealogy (VP. 1, 15, 112 has the same sons of Āpa except Dhvani for Muni). R 3, 14, 14 makes Aditi mother of Vasus (as of all the Thirty-three gods). Both epics regard Indra as the lord of eight Vasus, though Agni is chief among them (6, 34, 23). Vāsava as name of Indra implies that Indra was lord or first of Vasus, and the standing phrase (e. g. 5, 146, 12) "as Vasus revere Vāsava", retains the idea that Indra was their lord, though none of the texts has his name, which, considering that Fire, Moon, and Wind are enrolled as Vasus, shows that Indra was already fixed in the Āditya group. The phrase above is common to both epics (R 4, 26, 35, "they consecrated him with water as the Vasus did Vāsava of a thousand eyes"). Indra, however, sanctions the curse put upon them (below) and shows no especial intimacy with them, though they always follow him as "mighty" fighters (12, 284, 7). Like the Maruts and Viśve, they worship the sun at evening on Meru (R 4, 42, 39) as Divaukasas, "celestials". They are invoked with Rudras, Ādityas, Aśvins, and Maruts (R 5, 13, 56). They are always the bright gods; whose cars are light, whose forms are "like gleaming fire", jvalitāgnikalpāḥ, as they wait in air to convey the incorporate eighth Vasu (Bhīṣma) to the worlds "whence the wise return not" (12, 51, 14 f.). Their number (eight) never varies (1, 123, 70; 3, 134, 15, etc.). They were cursed by Vasiṣṭha to be born in human form. The Vasus, "Pṛthu and rest", came to the seer's hermitage and the wife of one of them, called Dyaus, desired Nandinī, the cow whose milk gives youth for ten thousand years. So Dyaus, Pṛthu, and the other Vasus stole the cow. Vasiṣṭha cursed them all except Dyaus to be born on earth as men for only a year, but the guilty Dyaus had to remain longer in human form and childless. Ganges, also in human form, bore them to Śāntanu, but drowned seven at birth, the eighth being preserved (Bhīṣma, Gāṅgeya, Devavrata) to be the "eighth Vasu" (1, 99, 1 f.). Another story says that the Vasus flew above Vasiṣṭha as he was "seated at twilight" (in prayer), wherefore he cursed them, "for a little fault", alpe 'parādhe, so that they lost their beauty and were born of Ganges, to whom each imparted one eighth of his power to be incarnate as Bhīṣma (1, 96, 21). This is a different interpretation as well as a different legend. Not one Vasu but one eighth of each Vasu becomes Bhīṣma. It is this curse which Indra sanctions (1, 67, 74 f.), niyogād Vāsavasya. Of the names given above, besides those of gods of light (Moon and Fire and Wind) and the star Dhruva and abstractions or forms of fire, the name Sāvitra attracts attention as it is that of a Rudra (12, 208, 20), though the vague text regards both classes here as Pitṛs. In R 7, 27, 34, the eighth Vasu is Sāvitra and, distinguished from the others, fights as a hero with Sumālin. As a son of Nṛga is a Vasu and also a son of Kuśa (R 1, 32, 7; R 7, 54, 8), and the Mbh. recognises Uparicara as Vasu (1, 62, 29 f., etc.), and sons of Manus (H 415 and 465) are Vasus (cf. 1, 94, 18 and 2, 33, 35, Vasu as brother of Duṣyanta and as father of Paila), it is clear that the word still retained its vague value of "good" without specific application to the celestials. The Vasus curse Arjuna, Indra's son, for killing Bhīṣma, but mitigate the curse to his defeat at the hands of his son (14, 81, 15 and 18). The death-scene of Bhīṣma records that he "enters his own body and gets to the Vasus, so that eight Vasus are visible" (18, 5, 11), which shows that the "eighth Vasu" was imagined as one complete Vasu. In 13, 169, 31, Bhīṣma is thus recognised as one Vasu who has now gone to heaven. He is called "one of the Vasus, a Vasu of great beauty" (5, 185, 18); though, according to 1, 96, 12, when cursed they were all naṣṭarūpāḥ, as when born again they were all "like immortals (1, 98, 12). The Vasus anyway are typical of beauty (1, 55, 15). Bhīṣma is even called the ninth Vasu, as one outside of the eight (12, 50, 26, Vasūnāṃ Vāsavopamaḥ . . navamo 'navamo guṇaiḥ). Vasuvega as epithet of Śiva the scholiast interprets as if Vasu were Wind (13, 17, 68; cf. C 205 Śiva Vasurūpa); but Vasuretas of Agni (etc.) shows that vasu often has the sense of bright = good = goods, i. e. wealth. Compare Vasumanas, who was vasupradaḥ and Vasubhyo vasumattaraḥ, "wealth-giver" and "wealthier than the Vasus" (5, 116, 17). A review of the places cited above shows that till the time represented by Uttara and Ādi and the pseudo-epic and Hariv., there are no individual Vasus, but that the number is unchangeable and that the Vasus retain their old association with Agni (Vasu) in the real epic, even while regarded as followers of Vāsava (Indra), who is treated as their chief. The "ten Vasus with Indra as the eleventh" (discussed IS. 5, 241) are of no more significance than are the ten Rudras and ten Ādityas, each with Indra as eleventh, in the same Vedic passage (Kāṭh. 28, 3); nor do the three hundred and thirty-three Vasus (TS. 5, 5, 2, 5) appear to have epic imitation. On the other hand, the definition of Vasus in ŚB. 11, 6, 3, 6, as the eight gods causing the world to abide (vas), however foolish the etymology, is retained, at least in part; for the Vedic eight are Fire, Earth, Wind, Air, Sun, Sky, Moon, and Stars, and the pseudo-epical (and Purāṇic) list is Fire, Earth, Wind, Day or Water or Sāvitra (see above), Dawn-light, Glory (brightness), Moon, and Pole-star, a list which shows that in a vague way the Vasus were thought of as the bright gods, even cutting across the Āditya-list with which it had to combine in making the Thirty-three. But the Vasus belong more to earth, the Ādityas more to heaven, and Dyaus is not in the regular lists of Vasus, though he appears with Pṛthu (above), as if he were a recognised leader of the group. The VP. also (1, 15, 110) calls them Āpa, Dhruva, Soma, Dhara, Anila, Anala, Pratyūṣa, and Prabhāsa, and says that they are jyotiḥpurogamāḥ, "light-led" as well as "powerful gods". No doubt the priests who composed Ādi and Anuśāsana simply copied roughly what they had got from ŚB., for this Brāhmaṇa is the Brāhmaṇa to the epic priests (who seem to be Yajurvedins). This would explain why such a list comes up again in the later epic, Hariv., etc., while unknown in the real epic. In R 6, 120, 8, Ṛtadhāman may be a Vasu-name (or epithet of Prajāpati? late passage).

§ 113. **The Rudras.** — A characteristic Gaṇa is that of the Rudras, originally forms of Rudra, who in the Ṛg-Veda is father of the Maruts. They are closely associated both early and late with Vasus, Viśve, and Ādityas, and, as already said, make eleven of the Thirty-three gods. The epic makes them subject to Sthāṇu, who in 1, 211, 24f., is Śiva (the passage explains how four-faced Sthāṇu Mahādeva and thousand-eyed Indra received these characteristics). Sthāṇu is son of Brahman in 1, 66, 1, which mentions the "eleven sons of Sthāṇu" and gives their names. Sthāṇu is son of Brahman here only by inference, but this is correct (N. "seventh son of Brahman"), as it is confirmed by 12, 166, 16. Though Sthāṇu as Śiva appears not infrequently (3, 38, 3; 125, 14, Sthāṇor mantrāṇi, etc.), it is not to be assumed that Sthāṇu (the immovable post, sthāṇubhūta, ascetic) always means Śiva (S has more passages, e. g. 7, 9, 41, where such is the meaning). Sthāṇu and Marīci are ordinary Prajāpatis (R 3, 14, 8) and Sthāṇu is a Rudra, as the list of the eleven is given in 1, 66, 1 f. and 1, 123, 68 f.: Mṛgavyādha, Sarpa, Nirṛti, Ajaikapād, Ahi Budhnya, Pinākin, Dahana, Īśvara, Kapālin, Sthāṇu, and Bhaga. In philosophy, Rudra makes "ten others", as vikāras of himself: Rudro roṣātmako jāto daśā 'nyān so 'sṛjat svayam, ekādaśai 'te Rudrās tu vikārapuruṣāḥ smṛtāḥ (12, 341, 37). The native explanation of the word (H 11530; cf. rudrapradhānān aparān viddhi yogān, 12, 317, 5) has a respectable antiquity (Chānd. Up. 3, 16, 3); it makes the Rudras howlers (and runners) rather than ruddy gods (rudra is used for "breath"), but the application is perhaps not so much to the howling of wind-gods as to the shrieking of the bolt (hrādinī, lightning, is the "shrieker", 9, 11, 25). Kāpālin (sic) is of the Rudras the foremost (S 4, 3, 27), which is perhaps equivalent to the expression (6, 34, 23) of Kṛṣṇa, "Of Rudras I am Śaṅkara; of Vasus, Pāvaka", as both Kapālin and Śaṅkara mean Śiva. In 12, 208, 21 f., the Rudras are eleven sons of Tvaṣṭṛ (so S) and are called: Viśvarūpa, Ajaikapād, Ahi Budhnya, Virūpākṣa, Raivata, Hara, Bahurūpa, Tryambaka (lord of gods), Sāvitra, Jayanta, and Pinākin (the "invincible"). In 13, 150, 12 f., there are other names, eleven, but known as a hundred, thus: Ajaikapād, Ahi Budhnya, Pinākin, Ṛta, Pitṛrūpa, Tryambaka, Maheśvara, Vṛṣākapi, Śambhu, Havana, and Īśvara, (ekādaśai 'te prathitā Rudrās tribhuvaneśvarāḥ, śatam etat samāmnātaṃ Śatarudre mahātmanām). In 13, 14, 390, the eleven are "eleven hundred Rudras", surrounding Śiva. In 4, 2, 21, Arjuna as the twelfth Rudra, thirteenth Āditya, and ninth Vasu shows that the number is fixed. The Rāmāyaṇa makes Aditi the mother of Rudras (R 3, 14, 14), while H 11530 and 12477 makes their mother Surabhi, "mother of ambrosia, Brāhmaṇas, cows, and Rudras"; the father, Brahman or Kaśyapa; while 12, 207, 23 makes Dharma (as Yama? see below) father of Vasus, Rudras (mighty), Viśve Devas, Sādhyas, and Maruts (Marutvantaḥ). Hariv. 165 and 11531 makes a list of eleven, mainly by combining those given above from the Ādi and Anuśāsana (Senānī is new). For still later Purāṇic lists, see Wilson's note to VP. p. 121. The epic knows the Rudras as companions of Indra, servants of Śiva and of his son, and also as the escort of Yama who appears surrounded by them (3, 237, 11). They are described as of immeasurable strength and fiery (H 16273), with golden necklaces and "like lightning-illumined clouds". On the Śatarudriya, see my Great Epic of India, p. 368. On the "eighth Rudra" (implying seven?) see § 115.

§ 114. **The Viśve Devas.** — In 4, 58, 71 f., Indra comes to see a battle; the gods come with him, arranged in groups, nikāyas; his personal attendants are especially the All-gods, Aśvins, and Maruts, all in one Gaṇa (Viśvāśvimarutāṃ gaṇaḥ). The words have united (Viśvedevān, Viśvedevaiḥ, 9, 45, 6, differentiated from Pitṛs) into one title of gods who accompany Indra and with the other groups especially accompany the Pitṛs (earlier, e. g. AB. 3, 31, they include the Pitṛs). They belong (it is said) geographically to the South with the Pitṛs, and "there they rest revered and sharing the fortunes (oblations) of the Fathers" (5, 109, 3, atra Viśve sadā devāḥ Pitṛbhiḥ sārdham āsate, etc.). In 3, 43, 13, Arjuna on his way to heaven meets Sādhyas, Viśve, Maruts, Aśvins, Ādityas, Rudras, and Vasus (similar grouping, 1, 123, 70). With Sādhyas and Vālakhilyas they fear Viśvāmitra (1, 71, 39), but they are here associates also of Soma and Yama, greater gods. Their origin from the mundane egg is especially mentioned (1, 1, 34). The five sons of Draupadī are their incarnations (1, 67, 127): Viśvān devagaṇān viddhi saṃjātān, as if that number represented them. Along with the hosts of Fathers, Saints, Death, and Time, they see and bear witness to the acts of men and give rewards accordingly; also as "lords of hosts", Gaṇeśvaras, they are associated with Saumyas, Raudras, Yogabhūtagaṇas, and other followers of Śiva Nandīśvara (13, 150, 18f. and 24f.). Yet this specific occupation of the pseudo-epic does not interfere with the purely epic character of the Viśve as "gocaras or constant associates with the Pitṛs" (13, 91, 24); but this post-epical passage elaborates them into a list apparently of sixty-four who receive Śrāddha offerings, though the texts vary in regard to some of the names, and it is possible that after the name Varin in this list the original Viśve-group ended, for the verse ends "the eternal Viśve Devas are these" (whose mouth is Agni). In that case there would be twenty-nine Viśve-names; but this would leave an unexplained supplementary group, called, as receivers of Śrāddha-offerings, the "gatigocaras of Kāla". In either case, two Somavarcas appear in both texts, and two Kṛtis in the Southern text. Paramakrodhin is probably one name, though the natural number of sixty-four would then become one less, an unusual number for any group. Finally it may be said that it is of little importance whether one list or the other is right, as the names are mere epithets, some of them the epithets of the great gods, Indra, All-maker, etc. The S text (13, 138, 39f.) substitutes Saha, Kṛti, Grāmya, and Śrīmat for the Northern names Bala (balam!), Dhṛti, Pārṣṇi, and Hrīmat. The names follow: Bala or Saha, Kṛti or Dhṛti, Vipāpman, Puṇyakṛt, Pāvana, Pārṣṇi or Grāmya, Kṣema (Kṣemya), Samūha, Divyasānu, Vivasvat, Vīryavat, Hrīmat or Śrīmat, Kīrtimat, Kṛta, Jitātman, Munivīrya, Dīptaroman, Bhayaṃkara, Anukarman, Pratīta, Pradātṛ, Aṃśumat, Śailābha, Paramakrodhin, Dhīroṣṇin, Bhūpati, Sraja, Vajrin, and Varin; and also (Viśve or heavenly beings like them): Vidyudvarcas, Somavarcas, Sūryaśrī, Somapa, Sūryasāvitra, Dattātman, Puṇḍarīyaka, Uṣṇīnābha, Nabhoda, Viśvāyu, Dīpti, Camūhara, Sureśa, Vyomāri, Śaṅkara, Bhava, Īśa, Kartṛ, Kṛti, Dakṣa, Bhuvana, Divyakarmakṛt, Gaṇita, Pañcavīrya, Āditya, Raśmivat, Saptakṛt, Somavarcas, Viśvakṛt, Kavi, Anugoptṛ, Sugoptṛ, Naptṛ, Īśvara. The list in H 11541f. of the Viśve Devā viśveśāḥ, sons of Dharma and Viśvā, is shorter: Sudharman, Śaṅkhapad, Uktha (or Dakṣa), Vapuṣmat, Ananta, and Mahīraṇa, as "of Cākṣuṣa Manu" and also Viśvāvasu, Suparvan, Nikumbha ("Viṣkumbha"), and Ruru ("Rudra"), the last being "ṛṣiputra and sunlike in glory". Viśvāvasu, here one of the All-gods, is also a Gandharva, a Marut and a Sādhya (in H). In H 11849, the Viśve and other groups are sired by Kaśyapa; in H 12479, by Manu. The last list agrees with that of the Purāṇas in number (nine or ten). That these gods were originally forms of Manes may be surmised from their constant association with the Pitṛs at the funeral feast. They are also placated when a new house is built. So when Lakṣmaṇa builds a hut for Rāma, the latter "makes an offering to the All-gods", as he does to Rudra and Viṣṇu, to avert evil and bring luck (R 2, 56, 32, Vaiśvadevabaliṃ kṛtvā.. vāstusaṃśamanīyāni maṅgalāni pravartayan.. pāpasaṃśamanaṃ balim), before he bathes. The Vaiśvadeva offering is thrown upon the ground, like that to the lower spirits, and it is eaten only by dogs and birds and men who eat dog-meat. It is offered regularly morn and eve. (3, 2, 59). The same rule is repeated (13, 97, 23) with an addition, specifying that the offering should be made out of doors in connection with offerings to the dead. The Viśve are somewhat perfunctorily invoked for protection with other groups, "Ādityas, Vasus, Rudras, Sādhyas, Viśve ca Devatāḥ (sic), the Maruts with Indra, the Diśas, and Digīśvaras" (3, 308, 11 f.) — for the benefit of a traveller; after a more formal invocation of King Varuṇa ("guard thee on the water") and Tapana Tamonuda, the "darkness-smiting Sun". They are all invoked to save the traveller from the Bhūts of air, earth, and sky.

§ 115. **The Sādhyas.** — These "perfected" (successful) ones are militant gods who accompany and fight for the Devas of celestial origin. They have no individual members till the Harivaṃśa period, when a nominal mother Sādhyā begets Sādhyas called Prabhava, Cyavana, Īśāna, Surabhi, Araṇya, Maruta, Viśvāvasu, Baladhruva, Mahiṣa, Tanūja, Vidhana, Anagha, Vatsara, Vibhūti, Suparvata, Vṛṣa, and Nāga, among whom Vibhūti receives the imposing epithet sarvāsuranisūdana, "slayer of all the Asuras" (H 11536). The real epic knows none of these as a Sādhya, (rather as Ṛṣi, god, and other spiritual forms). Except for this passage the Sādhyas are an indeterminate host, often mentioned but nowhere defined except explicitly as gods invoked as witnesses and born of the mundane egg (1, 1, 35; R 7, 97, 9). In 5, 36, 3, they say Sādhyā devā vayam, "we are gods" (cf. RV. 10, 90, 16), and they are addressed as "eaters of ambrosia" by the Golden Goose (i. e. God, 12, 300, 4 and 7). The mother Sādhyā appears in H 147, etc. As fighting gods they even precede the Maruts (7, 35, 30). They appear usually grouped with other gods of smaller importance, as in 1, 71, 39 and 87, 1: "honored by the Thirty-three, the Sādhyas, Maruts, and Vasus, in the house of gods "(devaveśman). In R 6, 120, 8, Viṣṇu is "fifth of Sādhyas", as he is "eighth of Rudras" and "Prajāpati of Vasus".

§ 116. **The Vidyādharas.** — These wizards (wisdom-holders) are spirits who have become like fairies or sylphs. They have a leader but it is uncertain who he is (below). They gaze with astonishment at human prowess (7, 98, 34): "The gods leaned over the edge of their cars to stare (admire), led by Brahman and Soma, and crowds of Siddhas, Cāraṇas, Vidyādharas, and Mahoragas wondered at the duel". As they watch a combat, "they strew flowers" (7, 139, 55; S 6, 69, 71). They flee from danger with their wives (R 4, 67, 46 and R 5, 1, 26); rejoice with music and loud laughter (R 4, 43, 52 f.); are crowned with wreaths and are "fair of aspect"; possessing the "great wisdom", which is explained as the Yoga-trick of diminishing their size, etc., as Yogins can (mahāvidyā, R 5, 1, 27). With Gandharvas, Kiṃnaras, Siddhas, and Nāgas they share the epithets "doers of good and devoted to joy" (R 4, 43, 53). They are essentially spirits of the air, vihagas (12, 334, 15; R 5, 1, 171; R 5, 54, 51 and ib. 56, 31, etc.). In R 5, 1, 171, they go in Gaṇas and ib. 165, where the path of the wind is described as traversed by Airāvata and by kaiśikācāryas, the "teachers of singing and dancing "are explained (by the commentators) either as Gandharvas or as the Vidyādhara king. In R 6, 69, 71, as in R 5, 1, 27, Vidyādharamaharṣayaḥ seem to be great seers among them. It may be remarked that vidyāgaṇas are themselves animate "troops of sciences", accompanying Śiva's consort, animate though "made by sages" (kavibhiḥ kṛtāḥ); as Vidyā (Sophia) is herself an attendant on Pārvatī (3, 231, 48 f.). Any vidyā may be given away, imparted as a kind of magic. Thus the vidyā called pratismṛti is secretly imparted by Vyāsa to Yudhiṣṭhira (3, 36, 30), just as the secret teaching of teachers is imparted to a son or devoted pupil, without study (7, 194, 6). In 2, 10, 27, the leader of the Vidyādharas is Cakradharman (who appears to have sons) in Kubera's palace, for these sylphs are found especially in Gandhamādana and other northern mountains with Kiṃnaras (3, 108, 11; ib. 158, 33; ib, 159, 19, "wreathed and fair"). A second leader mentioned is Vipracitti (-purogamāḥ, in Indra's palace, S 2, 7, 24). This may show Jain influence, since the Jains regard the Vidyādharas as evil, and Vipracitti is an evil Dānava. Thirdly, the wise bear Jāmbavat is called Vidyādharendra, "chief of Vidyādharas" (13, 14, 28 and 42: Jāmbavaty abravīd dhi mām . . yad abravīn mām Vidyādharendrasya sutā. See Jāmbavat, § 8). The Vidyādharī is a female of great beauty (4, 9, 15, etc.). There is a terrible mahāstraṃ vaidyādharam (R 1, 56, 11) or weapon used by these sylphs, though they are not warlike (1, 228, 33, etc.). When a magic sacrifice forces Indra to come to earth with Takṣaka, they come with him, but not to help (1, 56, 9), only as companions of nymphs and the (sentient) clouds (cf. vāridhāras in R 5, 1, 165). Rāvaṇa conquered the Gandharvas and Kiṃnaras and Vidyādharas and carried off their women, the "fair women of the Vidyādharas" being held captive in his court (R 5, 12, 20; R 6, 61, 10). The Rām. locates their home among the Hyperboreans in the mountains beyond the Vaikhānasas (saints) and the "land of horse-faced women" (Piśācīs? R 4, 43, 32 and 52). They are also on Kubera's Gandhamādana (above) and on the Krauñca mountain (9, 46, 88); and Rāma finds the "playground of Vidyādhara women" on Citrakūṭa (R 2, 94, 12); as too they are seen on the hills of Malabar (R 6, 74, 44) and even in the forest of Khāṇḍava (1, 228, 33).

§ 117. **The Kapas.** — These are beings illustrating the gradual formation of new groups. They are not really epic but are described for the first and only time in 13, 158, 4f., where they are said to have been so powerful that they evicted the gods from heaven. Their leader was Dhanin. Though evilly disposed toward the gods, they were exceedingly religious in other regards, so that they resembled the great seers. But the priests of the gods, when they took up the strife, overcame them, for the Kapas could not withstand the fires and Mantras of the priests. They are regarded as a class of Dānavas (ib. 19), virtuous but godless; perhaps historically a sect or clan opposed to the orthodox cult. If they are Pitṛs (?), their opposition to the gods recalls the similar Vedic Pitṛs, who have gods as foes, deváśatravaḥ (RV. 6, 59, 1), an epic epithet of Asuras and Rākṣasas, as foes of gods.

VII. THE DIVINE SEERS AS STAR-GODS.

§ 118. The Ṛṣis interchange with Pitṛs on the one hand and gods on the other. They are the singers of old, seers glorified as forms of (fire and) stars and yet recognised as ancestors of mortal men. They are intermediaries. Brahman created Asi, the Sword, as a divine being to protect men, and gave it to Rudra, who gave it to Viṣṇu, who gave it to Marīci. Marīci passed it over to the Seers, and it was they who gave it to (Indra) Vāsava; he bestowed it upon the Lokapālas, and they gave it to the law-giver Manu (12, 166, 66). The seers here are the Maharṣis, who had accepted the law of Brahman, viz. (ib 22 f.), Bhṛgu, Atri, Aṅgiras, the Siddhas, Kāśyapas, Vasiṣṭha, Gautama, Agastya, Nārada, Parvata, the Vālakhilyas, Prabhāsas, Sikatas, Ghṛtapās, Somavāyavyas, Vaiśvānaras, Marīcipas, Akṛṣṭas, Haṃsas, Agniyonis, Vānaprasthas, and Pṛśnis. The seers are Mahīdevas, gods of earth (RS 6, 114, 4), not because they are all of the priestly caste (priests being kṣitidevatāḥ, 13, 141, 62), but because they are as gods, though of mortal nature of old. Thus it is said indifferently that the rules for funerals were made by Pitṛs or by Ṛṣis (R 6, 114, 108). Among Ṛṣis, some are Devarṣis and Dānavarṣis; some are Maharṣis, some are Paramarṣis (the arciṣmantaḥ or very bright stars about the polar star); others, like Triśaṅku, are Rājarṣis, of kingly extraction; or Brahmarṣis (Viprarṣis), of priestly origin. The most famous group is that of the Seven Seers of the North. Lists of the other groups, of seven some, in the East, West, and South are given (R 7, 1, 2 f.), though the "seven" are elsewhere not so clearly defined. (In the North): Vasiṣṭha, Kaśyapa, Atri, Viśvāmitra, Gautama, Jamadagni, Bharadvāja; (East): Kauśika, Yavakrīta, Gārgya, Gālava, Kaṇva, son of Medhātithi; (South): Svastyātreya, Namuci, Pramuci, Agastya, Atri, Sumukha, Vimukha; (West): Nṛṣadgu (-ḍgu), Kavaṣa (-ṣin), Dhaumya, Raudreya (mahān ṛṣiḥ) or Kauṣeya. Other seers functioning at Rāma's court are Vāmadeva, Jābāli, Kātyāyana, Suyajña, Vijaya, (R 6, 131, 60 f.; cf. ib. 1, 7, 5; ib. S 1, 8, 6). Kutsa appears in a later passage (R 59, pra. 2, 31). The Mbh. also has its distributed lists of seers, but it is confused with kings and Rājarṣis and does not agree except here and there with that of R (13, 166, 37 f.). In 13, 150, 40, besides the geographical sevens of the Lokapālas (§ 92), there is a fifth heptad of "world-making Munis" (seers), who, "when lauded, cause men to become praised and blessed". This is followed by another seven called dharaṇīdharas (Dharma, Kāma, Kāla, Vasu, Vāsuki, Ananta, and Kapila), and then a seventh seven-group, which, owing to the interposition of four others (Rāma, Vyāsa, Aśvatthāman, and Lomaśa), does not become apparent till vs. 44, where seven seers renowned on account of their austerity are listed: Saṃvarta, Merusāvarṇa, Mārkaṇḍeya, Sāṅkhya, Yoga, Nārada, and Durvāsas! In this bizarre combination all that is apparent is that the author is trying to make a seven times seven table of venerable seers and sages (cf. a similar list in 12, 208, 26 f.). The Southerners here are called Brahmarṣis and the Westerners Maharṣis. The "seven wind-seers" born of a saint and father of the Maruts (9, 38, 35) show the same tendency to make heptads. Many of the seers in the list first given above (12, 166, 24 f., cf. 7, 190, 34 f.) are families and sects of devotees like the Ūṣmapas, Phenapas, etc., mentioned as Pitṛs (for Akṛṣṭas and Vānaprasthas, v. l. are Karūṣas and Māṣaprasthas; cf. 3, 64, 62 and 13, 14, 57). Such seers en masse float through the air with gods (3, 36, 42; 7, 124, 40, etc.), and appear on holy days at certain points (3, 159, 16; on Parvan days, i. e. once a week). Among them are Vātikas and Cāraṇas (9, 55, 14) and they are described as vāyubhakṣas, abbhakṣas, dantolūkhalikas, etc. (ib. 37, 48 f.). The seer is called a Muni (1, 107, 15 f.; seers appear as birds at Bhīṣma's death), though there are special lists of Munis, important mainly in showing that class-names tend to become individuals. Thus Vāyubhakṣa and Parṇāda and Adhaḥśiras are kinds of Munis but are treated as names of individuals (2, 4, 9 f.; S 5, 83, 29 f.). The Saptajanā (nāma) Munis of R 4, 13, 18, eat only on the seventh night, then eat only air, and go to heaven in seven hundred years (calendar-saints).

§ 119. But the formal distinction between Brahmarṣis and Devarṣis is as little observed as that between Ṛṣis and Maharṣis; only the Rājarṣis stand out, on account of their royal origin. A Brahmarṣi of one passage is a Viprarṣi in another (13, 6, 37 compared with 3, 281, 14; 5, 176, 46), but the new name indicates that he who was first regarded as "seer of Brahman" has become a "Brahmanic (priestly) seer". Examples of Brahmarṣis are Atri and Aṅgiras; of Devarṣis, Nārada and Vasiṣṭha; of Rājarṣis, Vainya and other kings. Uśanas is a demons' Devarṣi (R 7, 81, 1), for there are also seers of the demons, Dānavarṣis (3, 169, 23). Utaṅka is a Viprarṣi (1, 3, 143). The Ṛsis in general are countless. Eighty-eight thousand without offspring and fifty thousand with offspring are in Brahman's court (2, 11, 54, stereotyped figure). There are Brāhmalaukikas (R 7, 98, 24), belonging to Brahman's sphere, also Pārameṣṭhya Ṛṣis. Pitṛlokarṣis (in the South) live with Devarṣis and Rājarṣis there (5, 109, 5; ib. 9, Viprarṣis). Surarṣi = Devarṣi (R 6, 129, 53), of Nārada. These seers, of course, appear constantly anywhere. For example, when Kṛṣṇa goes along a road, he meets Devarṣis and Rājarṣis on either side of the way, both with brāhmī śrī or holy beauty, but acting like mortals (Rāma Jāmadagnya is their spokesman, 5, 83, 65). When the gods visit Indra with the seers, the latter lead (1, 226, 15); but the seers themselves, even the great Seven, follow Indra (2, 53, 12). They come with the gods to visit men at peace or in battle, cry Bravo to the brave and murmur blessings on the worlds (R 6, 90, 37, etc.). In 14, 77, 17 f., the Saptarṣis, Devarṣis, and Brahmarṣis "murmur victory to Arjuna"; all but the last group being frightened. As priests utter maṅgalyas before kings, so the Ṛṣis before Indra (5, 83, 8); their best wealth is truth (12, 56, 18). They may have children by nymphs, or by the grace of Śiva, or without woman's aid (Ālambāyana in 13, 18, 5 f., but see below). Their form of marriage is not interfered with by the gods (R 3, 55, 34). It is the seers who made the worlds and even the Deity reveres them (13, 31, 25; see also Brahman and Creation).

§ 120. The families of Ṛṣis lead to jealousy and arrogance: "the best Ṛṣis in the world" are Bhṛgus, Aṅgirasas, Vāsiṣṭhas, Kāśyapas, Āgastyas, Ātreyas (3, 26, 7, i. e. priests of these classes). The plural is used as patronymic (as here), Bhṛgavaḥ, "sons of Bhṛgu"; so Gargas are "sons of Garga" = Gārgyas (1, 178, 15; 7, 190, 34, etc.). A later theory has it that Bhṛgu is a Vāruṇa, the Prajāpatis of all peoples on earth being Bhṛgu, Aṅgiras, and Kavi, of whom Bhṛgu had seven sons, and the others eight each. Bhrgu's sons were Cyavana, Vajraśīrṣa, Śuci, Aurva, Śukra, Vareṇya, and Savana; called Bhārgavas, and Vāruṇas because Śiva, as Varuṇa, adopted them (13, 85, 125 f.). The sons of the other two ancestors of the human race vary. Aṅgiras, to whom the genealogy of 1, 66, 5 gives but three sons, here has eight, Bṛhaspati, etc. to Sudhanvan (who is "even better than Virocana", with whom he converses, 5, 35, 5 f.). These are called also sons of Agni (Aṅgiras is son of Agni and of Brahman). Kavi's sons vary most (v. l.), one text having Bhṛgu, Virajas, Kāśi, and Ugra, against S, Varuṇa, Kāśyapa, Agni (S 13, 132, 42 f. = 85, 130 f.). Other seers are renowned as sectarian diadochi, the Phenapas handing down the tenets of Nārada to the Vaikhānasas, who gave the teaching to Soma in Brahman's first birth. In his second birth Brahman, receiving it, gave it to Rudra, and Rudra to the Vālakhilyas (in Kṛtayuga, 12, 349, 14 f.). In Brahman's third birth (as Logos, 349, 19 f.), Nārada imparted it to the Ṛṣi

Suparṇa (trisauparṇa), whence it came to Vāyu, and from him to the Ṛṣis called Vighasāśins. Barhiṣada and Jyeṣṭha (Sāmavedāntaga, 349, 45 f.) received it later. The Bhṛgu-Aṅgirasa-vaṃśajas, "not very angry", unite in cursing Hanumat, perhaps recognising in him the future scientist and grammarian, navavyākaraṇārthavettṛ (R 7, 36, 34 and 48). Most of this is later than the real epic.

§ 121. Bhṛgu is the greatest Maharṣi (6, 34, 25). He heads the list of Bhṛgus, Aṅgirasas, Vāsiṣṭhas, and Kāśyapas (3, 115, 2); and composes a Śāstra which differs philosophically from the one ascribed to Manu (12, 182 to 192), deriving fire and wind from water, while Manu derives water from light and light from wind. Bhṛgu teaches here that the earth is water solidified by the action of wind, which came from water. Wind here is not a god, but sun and moon are limited gods who can "see no farther than their own light". Bhṛgu was born from Fire, Pāvaka, at Varuṇa's sacrifice, though fathered by Brahman, whose breast he cleaves. He is father of Śukra Kavi (whose son he is in 13, 85, 133) and of Cyavana (by Pulomā), and thus grandfather of Pramati and ancestor of Aurva (named ūruṃ bhittvā, 1, 179, 8), the son of Āruṣī, daughter of Manu (1, 5, 13 f.; ib. 8, 1 f.; 66, 41). Aurva burned the sight of those descendants of Kṛtavīrya who stole the Bhṛgus' hoarded wealth (1, 178, 15 f.). He was father of Ṛcīka, the father of Jamadagni, and destroyed Tālajaṅgha (1, 66, 46 and 49; 13, 154, 11). Bhṛgu cursed Agni to "eat all things" (9, 47, 21); he cursed Himavat to lose its gems, because H. gave Umā to Rudra (12, 340, 62); and he cursed Viṣṇu, for beheading his wife Pulomā, who favored the demons, to be born as man and lose his wife (R 1, 25, 21; ib. 7, 51, 2, told by "Durvāsas, son of Atri"). When Vasiṣṭha cursed Nimi to lose his body, Bhṛgu kept him alive as nimeṣa (wink), Nimi being of Atri's race, son of Dattātreya (13, 91, 7 f.; he was king of Mithilā: āsīd rājā Nimir nāma, R 7, 55, 4 f.). A different genealogy is found in the story of Vītahavya, who attacked Divodāsa and changed his caste (tyājito jātim, 13, 30, 56 and 66). He became priest through Bhṛgu's lying statement that "only priests" were in his asylum (cf. AV. 5, 18, 10). Vītahavya's son is the Viprarṣi Gṛtsamada, about whom "there is a revelation in the Ṛg-Veda" (see AB. 5, 2, 4). He was fair as Indra and was attacked by the fiends in consequence. Gṛtsamada was first of his line born in the priesthood, vipratvam, as his father was a Kṣattriya who "got priesthood" (13, 30, 61 f.). Though a friend of Indra, Gṛtsamada worshipped Mahādeva; he was turned into a deer (13, 18, 19 f.). Bhṛgutuṅga preserves the name of the ancestral abode (1, 75, 57, etc.). He is ancestor of Ruru and Śunaka.

§ 122. The Bhārgavas' most famous member is Uśanas, the Kavi called Śukra, preceptor of Asuras, renowned no less for wealth than for intelligence (R 3, 43, 32; ib. 4, 51, 12). His daughter Arajā was violated by Manu's son Daṇḍa, whom Uśanas cursed, resulting in ashes destroying Janasthāna (Daṇḍaka-forest, R 7, 79, 18 f.), when he was Daṇḍa's Purohita. As Purohita of the Asuras he also favors the Rākṣasas and advises Meghanāda how to sacrifice, which he refuses to do as it "honors his foes" (R 7, 25, 6 f.). Uśanas is here quite anthropomorphic in distinction from R 6, 4, 48, where he is the planet Śukra whose "favorable rays" presage weal, like the aspect of Paramarṣis. Mbh. 1, 65, 36 f.; 66, 41 f., presents him as half planet (Venus) and half preceptor of Asuras, having four sons called "Asura-sacrificers", Asurayājakas, Tvaṣṭādhara, Atri, Raudra, and

Karmin. Kavi Uśanas is here son of Kavi (Bhṛgu), interpreted as controller of rain and also as uniting with Bṛhaspati in being Guru of gods as well as of Asuras through Yoga (refers to the inverted legend of Mait. Up., that Bṛhaspati as Uśanas mistaught the Asuras). He is called best of Bhṛgus (1, 80, 1) and Bhārgava usually implies him (3, 4, 2; cf. 9, 6, 10), especially as Nītiśāstra-kartṛ (so N. at 5, 39, 30; cf. 8, 8, 4). Uśanas' wife is Śataparvan (sic, 5, 117, 13); his daughter Devī is wife of Varuṇa. Devayānī (1, 76, 1), also his daughter, revives Kaca, when reduced to paste, a son of Bṛhaspati, and marries Yayāti, whom Śukra curses (1, 83, 37). For her sake he quarrels with Vṛṣaparvan, inducing this Asura king to make his own daughter the slave of Devayānī. Even here Śukra Kāvya is the power that "sends rain and makes plants grow" and so is "lord of all in earth and heaven" (1, 78, 38 f.; S adds sarvalokaguruḥ Kāvyaḥ). As military epigrammatist he is often cited (12, 138, 134; cf. ib. 56, 28 and 9, 58, 14 f.), but the same utterance ascribed to him and to Bṛhaspati shows uncertainty of origin. He appears here as Maharṣi Uśanas and as Lord Uśanas (12, 57, 2 and 40). Uśanas sided with the Asuras as natural heir of his father, whose wife's head Viṣṇu cut off (12, 290, 1 f.). His name Śukra is interpreted as Śiva's "seed", because the god swallowed him and then let him out, though he deserved punishment for stealing the wealth of Kubera, Śiva's friend. Umā interceded for him, so he became her son (ib. 32 and 34). He and Śiva thus oppose Viṣṇu and other gods (ib. 293, 17). He invented his system of Nīti at Kapālamocana Tīrtha, where the head of the demon hurled by Rāma fell off from the thigh of Mahodara (3, 83, 135; 9, 39, 8 f.). He teaches Prahlāda and other Daityas (12, 37, 10; ib. 139, 70 f.; ib. 142, 22; ib. 280—281; his Śāstra and Gāthās). The divyā kathā of the virtuous pigeon is his (12, 143, 8 f., ascribed to Bhārgava Muni; S says Uśanas). His Śāstra includes military matters (15, 7, 15). He found out "Indra's secret" (potency of fasts, 13, 103, 39); his place in heaven is distinct from those of Māruta and Brahman (ib. 107, 80, 94, 100); he makes his locks snakes and turns Rudra's throat blue (see Śiva). S adds new verses as "ślokas sung by Uśanas" (after B 12, 69, 73 and after 12, 73, 5, glorification of AV.; cf. also S 12, 94, 9 f.). H 12200 makes Śukra priest of Hiraṇyakaśipu. Other Bhārgavas of importance are Atri (see below); Cyavana, whose aim in life was to kill Kuśikas, till he delegated the vendetta to Aurva; and Aurva, who became the Aurva Fire or Mare's Mouth or Horse's Head, Hayaśiras, which will consume ocean (7, 135, 22; cf. 1, 170, 53; 180, 22). This fire in 12, 343, 60, is interpreted as Viṣṇu's energy. On Cyavana, see p. 168 (Aśvins). He healed with his hands, restored youth, created magic grounds, lived like a sunk log in water, and was sold for a cow (13, 50, 2 f.; to 56, 4). He lived in the West, where men become saints "with little trouble", near Mt. Maināka (3, 89, 13). See § 125 for other Bhārgavas.

§ 123. Bṛhaspati (1, 104, 10) is the most famous Āṅgirasa, though "best" of this family is applied even to Droṇa (grandson of Bṛhaspati). Aṅgiras himself is of no moment; he married the daughter of Marutta (12, 235, 28); he guards the sun (3, 92, 6); teaches rules of fasting (13, 106, 71); and is a form of fire, aṅgāra meaning coal (13, 85, 105; here too "Bhṛgu from burn"). The story of Aṅgiras taking the place of Agni and of his daughters, moon's phases, has been told under Agni. Aṅgiras is third son of Brahman in the list of Prajāpatis (1, 65 and 66; not R 3, 14); verses cited as his occur (12, 69, 71). But the glory is his son's. Bṛhaspati (the planet Jupiter) is preceptor of the gods and gives them instruction orally, as well as composes a Śāstra for them and others, but otherwise he is remarkably inactive. His wife Tārā, raped by Soma (p. 90), was the cause of the great "war about Tārā" (5, 117, 13, etc.). He restores dead heroes to life by plants treated with Mantras (R 6, 50, 28). He comes stammering into the presence of Indra (R 6, 92, 4), but otherwise is treated as revered Guru. He is regent of Puṣya (R 2, 26, 9), is invoked with or without Śukra for blessings (ib. 25, 11 and 99, 41), the instruction of the two upādhyāyas being the same (9, 61, 48), the pair being past masters of polity (8, 37, 20); Bṛhaspatisamo matau is a standing phrase. This best of Aṅgirasas (5, 16, 27) operates with fire (9, 41, 29) to aid the gods, making a sacrifice to protect Śacī from Nahuṣa, and sending fire as a messenger (5, 15, 25 f.; 12, 343, 48). As a reward he receives the Atharvāṅgiras Veda (5, 18, 5 f.), whence his name Atharvāṅgiras. He heads the Devarṣis and Siddhas when they visit Skanda; he is called both Devarṣi (1, 67, 69) and Maharṣi (5, 18, 2; 9, 44, 21 f., he consecrates Skanda). Whatever is for a Guru or Purohita to do, falls to Bṛhaspati; hence he is "lord of priests" (14, 43, 8). He violates his elder brother's wife (Utathya's Mamatā) and becomes father of Dīrghatamas; also, by a Śūdrā, of Kakṣīvat (etc., 1, 104, 10 f.). He befriends Trita (p. 94) in the pit (9, 36, 36 f.). For his Naya and Śāstra, see 2, 50, 9; 3, 150, 29; 4, 58, 6; 12, 58, 1 f.; 13, 111, 11. He is pupil of Manu (12, 201, 3), and after Manu he and Uśanas promulgate their treatises (12, 336, 45 f.). He appears as a god (12, 322, 61), with Pūṣan, Bhaga, Aśvins, and Agni (pleased with butter-oblation, 13, 65, 7). The later epic adds many details; of his cursing ocean (12, 343, 27) because it was not clear; of his weeping with anger and flinging his spoon at the sky (ib. 337, 14), etc.; and S has a long interpolation (12, 73) exalting the Atharva-Veda, and Bṛhaspati with this Veda. His pupils were Uparicara and Śuka (ib. 337, 2 f.; 325, 23). The Ādi reckons him among the Ādityas and makes his sister the wife of the eighth Vasu, Prabhāsa (1, 66, 20, 27, 39), and the mother of Viśvakarman. There is a distinction made between the Bārhaspatī Bhāratī or treatise on theology (divine cows, 13, 76, 28) and the Bārhaspatam Jñānam or Śāstram, his legal code, declared by Indra (12, 142, 17). He lectures to Asuras as well as to gods (as Devaguru and on sin washed out by good acts, ib. 152, 32 f.). Bṛhaspati's quarrel with Saṃvarta is mentioned in 12, 29, 21 and told in 14, 5, 4 f.[1]) Bharadvāja is eldest son of Bṛhaspati (§ 125). Saṃvarta is his brother, a Śiva-worshipper (14, 5—6), opposed to Indra and Bṛhaspati.[2])

§ 124. Vasiṣṭha and Viśvāmitra. — The Seven Seers are the most important group of Devarṣis. Like the Devas they have their maids, Devarṣikanyās, nymphs who welcome the Devarṣis to heaven (13, 107, 130; the general rule, but see above, is that seers cannot have children without women, 1, 74, 52). As the Brahmarṣis are headed by Aṅgiras and the Paramarṣis by the son of Brahman called Sanatkumāra, so Bṛhaspati heads the general group of Devarṣis (3, 85, 71; 12, 37, 9); but the Seven Devarṣis are headed by Vasiṣṭha, and these are they that have their rising

[1]) On Bṛhaspati, see remarks on Uśanas and Bṛhaspati in my Ruling Caste. p. 202; and on his epic connection with Atharvan, Atharvā sa Bṛhaspatiḥ (13, 14, 397), see Proc. Amer. Philosophical So., vol. 49, p. 39 f.

[2]) Compare Leumann, Die Bharata-Sage, p. 68 f., on the Saṃvarta-Maruttīya Itihāsa. According to H 1833 f., Marutta's daughter became Saṃvarta's wife, not the wife of Aṅgiras (as in 13, 137, 16). On Bṛhaspati's impious treatise, see H 1505 f.

and setting as stars on Meru in the North, in contrast to the Brahmarṣis and Maharṣis. Historical treatment of the two chief seers is here ignored. These Seven are sometimes implied by the word Devarṣis. Thus in the tale of Nahuṣa, "the Seven Seers and the Brahmarṣis will drag him", followed by "the Devarṣis and Brahmarṣis dragged him" (5, 15, 20; 17, 8). Compare too sapta saptarṣayaḥ Siddhā Vasiṣṭhapramukhaiḥ saha (14, 27, 18), where, as often, the later epic unites other blessed ones in heptads with the Seven Seers. Vasiṣtha stands so much at the head that the Vāsiṣṭhī kāṣṭhā is the "Northern course" of the sun (= dhāniṣṭhī, or Kuberan, 5, 109, 16). No difficulty is experienced in treating the seven as at once persons and stars: "The Seven Seers shine in the sky because they honor the law of the Creator" (3, 25, 14). Washed free of stains they shine like fires in Indra's heaven; they were with Manu in the ark (2, 7, 9f.; 3, 187, 31). Near the "field of Kapila" they have a Tīrtha (3, 83, 72). But as a group they have little action in common. They are occasionally identified with the seven Prajāpatis (12, 336, 27f.), but when enlisted are more often separated, as in 1, 123, 50f. (cf. H 14148), "all the Prajāpatis and the Seven Maharṣis, Bharadvāja, Kaśyapa, Gautama, Viśvāmitra, Jamadagni, Vasiṣṭha, and Atri, who rose when the sun was extinguished". Atri usually stands next to Vasiṣṭha or Kaśyapa, and like the latter, belongs to both groups. The Seven Seers are in the North with Arundhatī, wife of Vasiṣṭha (later of Dharma, H 145) or of all the seers (? 5, 111, 14). In the story of Svāhā (see Agni), each wife is personated by Agni's love. To be unable to see Arundhatī presages death (RG 3, 59, 16); to see her and the pole-star intermittently presages death in a year (12, 318, 9). In the Theft of the Lotus, the virtuous Arundhatī is accompanied by a maid-of-all-work, Gaṇḍā. Vṛṣādarbhi (Śaibya), angered at the rejection of his offering, produced a Yātudhānī and bade her kill the Seers, which she could do only by knowing the meaning of their names. Indra, disguised as a hunter, tested their virtue, and the Seven went to heaven with him — a tale immediately retold with variants, Indra being undisguised and Agastya the chief seer in action, as he and others in the second version take part in this tale (13, 93, 20f.). The Seven also unite in composing a code. They are called here the Citraśikhaṇḍinas, an epithet also of Viṣṇu (12, 336, 27f.). Arundhatī, though a model of faithfulness, yet suspected Vasiṣṭha and became "smoky-red" (1, 233, 28f.). She is a spotless adherent of Śiva, as is Viśvāmitra of Skanda (3, 225 and 9, 48); she may be the Jaṭilā of 1, 196, 14, "wife of seven Ṛṣis as said in the Purāṇa" (as in 12, 38, 5, called Gautamī). Vasiṣṭha is the "best" (etc., etymology, 1, 174, 6); born of Mitra-Varuṇa (see p. 118) or "owing to Kṛṣṇa's power and wish born in a jar" (13, 159, 19). As son of Varuṇa he is Vāruṇi, also called Āpava (1, 99, 5); he was born, bred, and died in the East (5, 108, 13). His special Tīrtha is Ujjālaka (3, 130, 17, or Ujjānaka). For the theft of his cow, see Vasus (§ 112). The cow, Nandinī, was also desired by Viśvāmitra, son of Kuśika's son Gādhi, who tried to steal it in a well-known tale (1, 174, 5f., as Brahmarṣi, here son of Brahman). His eldest son, Śakti, quarrelled with Mitrasaha Kalmāṣapāda, patron of Viśvāmitra, who had a Rākṣasa devour Śakti and the rest of Vasiṣṭha's hundred sons (1, 176, 6f.; R 3, 66, 8). Vasiṣṭha tried to drown himself, but the rivers Vipāś and Śatadru refused to drown him; afterwards he freed the king Kalmāṣapāda Saudāsa from possession by a Rākṣasa, and the king caused the Seer to beget by his wife, Madayantī, a son Aśmaka (1, 177, 47; Saudāsa also in 13, 6, 32; 14, 57, 19 f.). Another tale connects Vasiṣṭha and Viśvāmitra, the Apavāha, which relates how the two seers, living on opposite sides of the Sarasvatī, quarrelled. Viśvāmitra commanded the river to bring him his rival to kill. Afraid to disobey yet also afraid of the curse of Vasiṣṭha, the Sarasvatī carried him off to the other bank but brought him back before Viśvāmitra could kill Vasiṣṭha, who won over the river by fulsome praise. The Sarasvatī ran with blood for a year owing to the curse of Viśvāmitra (9, 42, 1 f.), and hence became the Aruṇā ("Red River", name of a branch of the Ganges). Vasiṣṭha is credited with several other deeds. He cursed Kārtavīrya (q. v.); he revived Indra, when the god was stupified (12, 282, 21); he slew the Khalin Asuras as priest of the gods, by bringing the Ganges, as Sarayū, to the lake in which they recovered life (13, 156, 17 f.). He exterminated, but with some difficulty, the demons of Vaiśravaṇa attacked by Mucukunda (12, 74, 6 f.). Kings gained merit by providing him with water, wealth, and a wife (12, 235, 17 and 30; 13, 137, 6; 15; 18). Both chapters say that he produced rain in drought; he is called Bhūtakṛt and Devarāj (13, 137, 13), "king of (priests as) gods". The pseudo-epic also employs Vasiṣṭha as sermoniser (12, 303, 7 f., etc.). His rival Viśvāmitra became a priest because he lacked the ability to be a king (9, 40, 16 f.); but as a priest he slew Vasiṣṭha's sons (R 1, 59, 18), created the Kauśikī (Pārā) river, served as priest of Mataṅga and elevated Triśaṅku, "made another world", became father of Śakuntalā, and is noted for his pitiless disposition (1, 71, 20 f.). He is called Bhūsura as a priestly god, and his guest Indra as Vasiṣṭha made him wait a hundred years serving him food (5, 106, 17 f.). Gālava waited on the seer and in the pseudo-epic is called his son (13, 4, 52). He also ate dog's meat in a famine (12, 141, 26 f.) occurring between Tretā and Dvāpara, which fixes his date. The village where he accepted meat from a Cāṇḍāla was adorned with temples decorated with images of birds and had iron bells. He enunciates the doctrine that a seer cannot commit a deadly sin (ib. 75). In 12, 293, 13 and 13, 3, 1 f., he is said to have created Yātudhānas and fiends, founded the race of Kuśika, delivered Śunaḥśepa, become father of Hariścandra, hung Triśaṅku head downward in the southern sky (cf. H 730 f.), changed Rambhā into a rock, and, as a star, is said to shine in the middle of the Seven Seers of the North and Dhruva Auttānapāda. Gādhi married his daughter to Ṛcīka, son of Cyavana, and by this Ṛcīka's advice mother and daughter, embracing two trees, became mothers of Viśvāmitra and Jamadagni. As his descendants are named Yājñavalkya, Nārada, Āśvalāyana, etc. (ib. 13, 18, 52 f.). According to R 1, 34, 3 f., it is his older sister Satyavatī who descended to earth as the Kauśikī river (ib. 1, 51 f., the story of Triśaṅku). His son Kapila is called Deva (3, 108, 18).

§ 125. The other members of the group of Seven Seers are not so important. Ahalyā lends interest to Gautama, who is argued down by Atri, serves as priest of Nimi, and is called Medhātithi, his son being Cirakārin, who objected to matricide enjoined by Gautama (12, 267, 2 f.). As sons are named Śatānanda, Kṛpa, Śarabhaṅga, Ekata, Dvita, Trita (§ 46), Vāmadeva. The last has "wonderful" swift steeds and appears beside Medhātithi in Śakra's court (2, 7, 17; 3, 192, 40 f.). Bharadvāja, eldest son of Bṛhaspati and priest of Divodāsa (13, 30, 24), provides Vītahavya with a son (by a sacrifice, ib.) and supplies Rāma Dāśarathi with a magic garden (R 2, 91, 11 f.). He is said to reside at Prayāga but is not an important figure in either epic, though father of Droṇa by Ghṛtācī (1, 166, 1 f.). The pseudo-epic says that he flung water at Viṣṇu and thus made the Śrīvatsa sign on his breast (12, 343, 54); but the same chapter (vs. 132) ascribes this sign to Rudra's trident.[1]) His son Bhumanyu (1, 94, 22; H 1730) is Bharata's by "legal transfer". Yavakrīta, another son, is resurrected with Bharadvāja after entering fire (3, 138, 22). Jamadagni is famous mainly as father of Bhārgava Rāma (R 1, 75, 3), though he is extolled as a great sacrificer (3, 90, 16). Rāma's fame rests on his being Haihayeśapramāthin, or slayer of Arjuna and the other Haihayas (5, 181, 12). Of warriors he slew 64000, cutting off their ears and noses and breaking their teeth, besides stifling 7000 Haihayas in smoke and torturing them, and butchering 10000 with his own axe. Altogether he cleared earth of warriors twenty-one times and then gave earth to Kaśyapa (1, 66, 48, etc). He contends with Bhīṣma (5, 179, 14), etc. The five lakes he filled with blood are known (3, 83, 27 f.) and he is often mentioned, in his rôle of destroyer, as "the most glorious increaser of the fame of the Bhṛgus" (7, 70, 23 f., as Bhārgava). He killed his mother Reṇukā to oblige his father (3, 116, 14; R 2, 21, 32), an act highly extolled, though she was a good wife (R 1, 51, 11); but her husband accused her in re Citraratha (3, 116, 6 f.). Rāma, however, restored her to life and received invulnerability and long life as his reward. He is a direct descendant of Indra, incarnate as Gādhi (12, 49, 6; a Śivaite, ib. 33). Rāma cut off the arms of Arjuna Kārtavīrya (whose followers killed Jamadagni), through the curse of Vasiṣṭha, as originally the hero got his thousand arms through grace of Dattātreya (a form of Viṣṇu). Vāyu argues with him on the folly of opposing seers (12, 49, 35; 13, 153, 7). See also § 150. The seer Kaśyapa is a Prajāpati (q. v.), but also priest of Paraśu-Rāma (3, 117, 12 f.). His son, the crane, is older than the Himalayan owl (3, 199, 7; 12, 169, 18 f.). Atri also is a kulapati and a seer, whose wife is Anasūyā (R 7, 1, 5). She was so vigorous an ascetic that she irrigated earth with the Ganges in drought and on another occasion "made ten nights one" (R 2, 117, 11), because her friend was cursed to "become a widow to-morrow". "Morrow shall not be", said Anasūyā, and extinguished it by making ten nights one. At least, so the scholiast explains the phrase daśarātram kṛtā rātriḥ; but it is more likely that, being a clever woman, Anasūyā shifted the calendar. Atri had many sons (1, 66, 6); he is son of Brahman and son of Uśanas as well (contradictions of the sort are common of course), also father of Durvāsas. Atri was the first to deify a king, so that Gautama called him a sycophant, but Sanatkumāra upheld the deification, and Atri got ten crores of gold and ten loads of jewels (3, 185, 35). The point of the story is that the king is god on earth, as is the priest, and they must combine to keep the lower orders in subjection. The king here is the Rājarṣi Pṛthu Vainya, whose astronomer was Garga. This king's father had been dethroned and executed for his sins, in accordance with the principle that a wicked king "should be killed like a mad dog", so that his son was naturally pleased to be made divine. Atri saved the gods, when Rāhu's arrows had pierced sun and moon, by becoming sun and moon and giving equal light (13, 157, 8 f.). Noteworthy in this version of the ancient tale is the attribute of arrows. Atri (originally an epithet of fire, like the names of all the Seven) "burns" the demon and then

[1]) On Bharadvāja as philosopher (12, 182—189), see Pizzagalli, La Cosmogonia di Bhṛgu (Memorie del R. Instituto Lombardo, 1910).

"illumines" the world with his own glory (tejas). According to 1, 21, 13, Atri tried for a century to get to the bottom of the ocean. He is mythologically important only as demon-expeller and father of Soma (q. v.). He is son of Brahman (13, 65, 1), well versed in physiology (12, 214, 23), and is cited for the dictum, "those who give gold grant all wishes" (13, 65, 1).

§ 126. Agastya is the chief seer outside the charmed circles of Bhṛgus, Aṅgirasas, and the Seven.[1]) He is still called Agasti in the epic and is famous for having become the Seer of the South (as star he is Canopus). He was a sort of half-brother, kumbhayoni, of Vasiṣṭha, son of Mitra-Varuṇa (3, 103, 13f.), hence called Kumbhasaṃbhava. He was told by his ancestors, whom he saw hanging in a pit upside down, to get offspring. He then made and married the perfect woman Lopāmudrā (3, 130, 6), for whose sake he sought jewels, but got from the Asura Ilvala the latter's well cooked brother Vātāpi to eat (3, 11, 37; R 3, 11, 57). Merely saying hum, Agastya reduced the Asura to ashes. In Śalya this is told as a clever trick (9, 31, 13; cf. 3, 96, 4,f.; 206, 28, etc.). As lokabhāvana he drank up ocean to free earth from the Kāleya Asuras or from Hiraṇyākṣa (1, 188, 15; 3, 103, 13 f.; 104, 15 f.; S 12, 208, 13 f.). He cursed Nahuṣa for insolence and Kubera (3, 179, 13 f.; 161, 58 f.). He tricked the Vindhya to stop growing till his return as he went South (conquered the South, R 6, 118, 14). His wife accompanied him (type of devotion, 3, 113, 23). He legalised hunting by dedicating deer to gods (1, 118, 14). He gave rain when Indra failed to do so (14, 92, 4 f.). He is expressly mentioned with the Seven Seers as examples of those who became hermits, "mighty in their own Sūtras and Śāstras", and eventually rose to heaven "not as Nakṣatras but as clusters of lights" (12, 245, 16f.; anakṣatrāḥ . . jyotiṣāṃ gaṇāḥ, ib. 22 f.). Such star-seers are still affected by earthly struggles (5, 51, 54). Agastya turns Mārīca and his mother into fiends (R 1, 25, 11); is visited by Rāma and aids him (cf. R 3, 11, 33 f.; ib. 7, 76, 23 f., etc.). He causes Mahendra to be set in the sea, gives Indra's spear to Rāma, and frees Śveta from the curse of eating his own body (R 4, 41, 20; R 6, 111, 4; R 7, 78, 19). His brother is Śarabhaṅga (R 3, 11, 39 f.). Agastya refused to be son of Mitra (R 7, 57, 5 f.). His pupil is Agniveśa, Guru of Droṇa (1, 139, 9 f.). His mother is not epic, but VP. 1, 10, 9 makes him an incarnation of Pulastya and Prīti, formerly called Dambholi (here also other later views regarding the birth of other seers). H 12845 agrees with R 4, 41, 35 in locating his abode on Kuñjara, but R places his asylum five leagues from Rāmagiri, on the Godāvarī, and on Malaya (ib. 3, 11, 39 and 81; ib. 4, 41, 16; ib. 6, 126, 41). Elements of the Agastya story appear in connection with other saints. His feat of drinking up ocean he shares with Utathya; but it is what any (§ 65) Yogin can do (12, 237, 24, kāmāt pibati cā 'śayān). The story of his eating Vātāpi, the brother of Ilvala, is like that (p. 180) of Kaca, son of Bṛhaspati, who was reduced to paste and eaten. The tale of the inverted ancestors and their advice is to be found in connection with Jaratkāru and others. These good stories exist, and are fitted on to various figures, like the beloved tale of the "wisest youngest" (yo 'nūcānaḥ sa no mahān, 3, 133, 12 = 9, 51, 50, and 12, 324, 6), a general apophthegm of the seers fitted on to Sārasvata, who was Vyāsa Apāntaratamas.

[1]) For details of the Agastya-story, see Adolf Holtzmann in ZDMG. 34, 589 f.

VIII. EARTHLY ṚṢIS.

§ 127. Other groups less definite than those above and a few more single seers are prominent. Among the groups are the Vālakhilyas, who sometimes appear on earth and sometimes are assigned to the sun, where they appear as Marīcipas, drinking the rays of the sun, or in the sun's disc or on Himavat (1, 30, 7; R 3, 35, 14f.). Garuḍa was born through their penance to rival Indra; their father may be Kratu (ib.; N. to 1, 66, 8). They belong to the class of Siddhas, who include saints of both worlds (R 3, 1, 23; ib. 2, 70, 30), and have attained their state through asceticism (siddhagati, 3, 145, 9; 146, 93; 158, 84), though the Siddhas also include star-saints (R 5, 54, 24). The Vālakhilyas worship beside Ganges (3, 142, 5) and make sacrifice (3, 90, 10). In the former passage they may be called Vaihāyasas, or these "spirits of air" may be a separate class (as later). They are often associated with Vaikhānasas (as at Mt. Arcīka, 3, 125, 17), also a class of supernatural saints (3, 114, 15). In 13, 141, 99f., the Vālakhilyas live, thumb-size, in the sun's disc, keeping the uñcha vow and having the power of gods (cf. H 11811 and VP. 2, 10, 21). They live 1000 ages. The Rām. identifies them with Vaikhānasas (R 4, 40, 58), but not always (R 3, 6, 2 and ib. 35, 14f.). The Sārasvatya gaṇa of 60000 saints mentioned with Gārgya may be identified with these saints of the Sarasvatī (9, 51, 51 and 3, 90, 10). Rudra teaches them (12, 249, 18).

§ 128. The Uttara Kurus are another class of Northern saints and seers, living beyond the gate barred by the head of the monster Mahiṣa, south of Nīla and on the flank of Meru (3, 145, 17; 231, 97f.; 6, 7, 2). They live ten thousand and ten hundred years and are buried by birds (cf. p. 20). They have heavenly felicity in food and freedom; their clothes are grown by trees; their women are not restrained (1, 122, 7f.; 13, 54, 16). They associate with spirits born of water and fire and mountain, and where they live, Indra "rains wishes", and jealousy is unknown (13, 102, 25, lokaḥ as modern log, people).

§ 129. a) Cāraṇas and Caras. — Other collective and indeterminate bodies called seers and Munis are the Cāraṇas, raised from the condition of earthly "wandering" minstrels to a heavenly state. The "path of Cāraṇas "is that of seers, yet they are found at the courts of kings as well as gods, as also in hermitages (1, 63, 66; 5, 123, 5, etc.; cf. R 4, 40, 30). They speak as heavenly prophets and are reckoned as Ṛṣis (R 5, 55, 30 and 34). A similar heavenly group is that of the heavenly Cyclists, a sort of Siddha (R 5, 48, 24), who accompany Nāgas, Siddhas, Gandharvas, etc., as in 3, 85, 72. The scholiast calls them the cycling heavenly bodies (sun and moon), but in 13, 141, 103, a distinction is drawn between these pure souls, called Cakracaras, the Somacaras, and the Vālakhilyas, as if all were sainted seers, with whom are the Pitṛ Seers called Aśmakuṭṭas, Samprakṣālas, etc. The Saumyas and Raudras of 13, 150, 26 are apparently groups of Pitṛ Seers (as in Manu 3, 199); but the Śvetas and Yatis who support the Pāñcarātra Sāṅkhya religion (of 12, 349 and 350) are earthly sectarians.

b) Finally, the Tuṣita spirits or gods also illustrate the negligible distinction between gods and spirits. They are created by Śiva, who (in the pseudo-epic) creates and upholds the seven Munis and groups of gods, the drinkers of heat and of Soma, the Lekhas, and Suyāmas and Tuṣitas and Brahmakāyas and Ābhāsuras, the smoke-drinkers and Gandhapas, the eaters by touch (Sparśāśanas), drinkers by (or of) sight, the butter-drinkers, thought-gleamers (Cintyadyotas), and groups more familiar (Suparṇa-Gandharva-Piśāca-Dānavā Yakṣās tathā Cāraṇa-pannagāś ca), some being seers and some gods (13, 18, 73 f.). The Tuṣitas are Buddhistic and are found only here and in H (171, 418, 1346), being as unknown to the real epic as are the Ābhāsuras and Lekhas (v. l. lokas).

§ 130. Several individual seers, sometimes without family, sometimes assigned to a well-known group, exist for the purpose of a story or moral. The seer Tanu is such a Ṛṣi, an allegory of hope. He was eight times as long as other men and as thin as one's little finger, and he talked with a hopeless king around whom sat the Munis "as round Dhruva sit the Seven Seers" (12, 127, 6f.; ib. 25). Mataṅga, famous in R, where the trees are said to have grown in his hermitage from the sweat of his pupils (R 3, 73, 23 f.; ib. 74, 21 f.), and owing to whose curse Vālin's followers turn to stone if they intrude on him (R 4, 11, 52; ib. 46, 22), appears in Mbh. as authority for the rule, "break rather than bend" (as Mātaṅga, metri causā, 5, 127, 19). He was of low birth and was reproved by his ass for beating her, which caused him to exercise austerities till his accumulation of merit exercised the gods, and Indra in self-defence taught him that it was vain for a man of low caste to try to attain Brahmanhood and turned him into a bird (see p. 137). Dadhīci, or-ca, who took Indra's place for a thousand years and took sides with Śiva at Dakṣa's sacrifice, is known chiefly as giver of his bones to make Indra's bolt (12, 285, 11 f.; ib. 343, 28 f.). Many of this order are famous Rājarṣis, that is seers who had been kings, like Dilīpa (5, 109, 5, of the South), Yayāti, Mahābhiṣak, etc., who won and lost worlds (1, 102, 3, S has °bhiṣak). Mahābhiṣak, being cursed, apadhyātah, by Brahman to be born on earth, was born as the son of Pratīpa (Śaṃtanu, 1, 96, 3 f.). Yayāti Nāhuṣya is known as ancestor of the epic heroes and as one who attained to heaven and fell through pride but subsequently regained his heavenly place; the Yayātipatana on the Narmadā being still a holy spot (3, 82, 48; cf. ib. 129, 3 f., his place on the Yamunā). His son Yadu born of Devayānī, daughter of Śukra Kāvya, was cursed by his father, while Puru was made heir (5, 149, 2 f.). His love for Viśvācī, his Gāthās on desire, death by starvation, but otherwise his felicity are well-known themes (later is the tale of his daughter Mādhavī, 5, 115, 6 f.; ib. 121, 1 f.; cf. 1, 75, 32 f.; 83, 37; 85, 9; and 12, 26, 13; 327, 31 the Gāthā, na bibheti paro yasmāt, etc.). He has a Rājopaniṣad or secret of royal policy, which is to kill every foe (12, 93, 39). His last words were nālam ekasya tat sarvam, "the universe is not enough for one man" (7, 63, 9). The Rāmāyaṇa tells the story of his wives (7, 58, 7 f.), besides referring often to his felicity and misfortune (R 3, 66, 7; R 4, 17, 10, etc.). Yadu's sons became Rākṣasas and Yātudhānas (R 7, 59, 15); his other disinherited sons became ancestors of wild tribes, Druhyu, Turvasu, Anu. R 1, 70, 40 makes Yayāti the thirty-sixth descendant from Brahman as first; Mbh. (1, 76, 1) makes him tenth. Less general are the tales of Ṛṣis like Gṛtsamada, cursed to become a mṛgaḥ krūraḥ, wild beast, because he made a mistake in recitation (Variṣṭha cursed him, but Maheśvara freed him and made him "immortal and free from sorrow", 13, 18, 20). Niśākara was a southern Ṛṣi who practiced penance for eight thousand years and could reconstruct the wings of Sampati when burned by the sun (R 4, 60, 8 f.). Suvarṇaśiras is the golden-haired ever young Muni who sings in the ocean, unseen, immeasurable, "whose song is the roar" of ocean

(5, 110, 12: not an "epithet of Svarbhānu", PW). The same passage (ib. 109, 11) says that Yavakrīta's son helped Sāvarṇi Manu establish the southern boundary of the sun. A Ṛṣi Maṅkaṇaka had vegetable juice for blood and danced till all the world danced with him. He was son of Wind and Sukanyā and begot seven sons with wind-names. Śiva converted him by turning his blood to ashes (3, 83, 116f.; 9, 38, 36f.). The later epic tells of Likhita's hands growing out after being cut off (12, 23, 18f.; 115, 22; 130, 29f.; 13, 137, 19), and of the Devarṣi called Bhūrbhuva, a son of Brahman, whom one sees in heaven (13, 107, 81; H 11509)! Occasionally a saint is split in two and makes a pair. Thus in 3, 26, 5f., Vaka or Baka Dālbhya (=Dārbhya); but in 3, 193, 4f., Baka and Dālbhya appear as "two long-lived seers". It is thus that Nārada Parvata (water-giving cloud) becomes N. and P. Whether history or myth underlies some of the tales of the Ṛṣis is doubtful. Aṇīmāṇḍavya, who was not a thief and yet was impaled as a thief (13, 18, 46), and opposed the Law, Dharma (§ 58), may reflect Christian tradition. Jīmūta the Ṛṣi who discovered a gold-mine in the mountains and gave his name to Jaimūta gold may also have been an historical character. He is named with Marutta of auriferous memory, a Rājarṣi (5, 111, 23; 178, 47; 7, 55, 37f.). So with the founders of schools such as Śāṇḍilya and his wise daughter Pañcaśikhā, befriended by Śiva, who paralysed Indra as he tried to kill the saint, "long-suffering Kāpileya", first pupil of Āsuri, born in the family of Parāśara (7, 202, 84; 9, 54, 6; 12, 218, 6f.; 254, 14; 321, 24; 13, 65, 19). Yet these characters are involved in mythology and even Mārkaṇḍeya lived to a mythical age, though this son of Mṛkaṇḍu (S 3, 130 interpolated after B 128) is but an ancient story-telling Ṛṣi (3, 25, 4f.; 183, 42f.; 199, 1, quest of an elder), of whom we know naught except his tales, save that he was opposed to meat-eating (13, 115, 38; perhaps ib. 125, 35) and was husband of Dhūmorṇā (ib. 146, 4). Other Ṛṣis, Yājñavalkya, who converses with Janaka Daivarāti on the eight principles and sixteen modifications known to metaphysics (12, 311, 3f.), Kātyāyana, Garga, Gārgya, etc. are really historical characters. Durvāsas, "son of Atri", and Nārada, "son of Viśvāmitra", are not dissimilar in their love of mischief. They both wander over the worlds, human and divine, and both make trouble. Durvāsas was a human form of Śiva, as Nārada was of Viṣṇu. Durvāsas's blessing provided Kṛṣṇa with 16000 wives (13, 160, 47; 161, 37)! The early epic merely makes him a disagreeable guest, a bald ascetic of ferocious temper (3, 260, 3f.). Nārada as Gandharva is a cloud-spirit, hence a rumbler and grumbler, finally a saint fond of strife. So Viśvāvasu, though a Gandharva, discourses philosophy (12, 319, 27f.). Nārada recited the epic to the gods, as did Asita Devala to the Pitṛs (Devalāsita teaches Nārada, 12, 276, 1f.). Of all these, Nārada is most transparent. His name means "water-giver"; he is at first the cloud, *parvata*, then Nārada Parvata, and finally Parvata becomes a shadowy second, till they even quarrel (7, 55, 14f.) and curse Nṛga to become a lizard (R 7, 53, 7f. cf. 13, 70, 1f., a different version of the popular tale of the curse attached to stealing a priest's cow). In 12, 30, 4f., as uncle and nephew, they curse each other to become a monkey and to lose heaven, because Nārada loves Sukumārī. Nārada is Maharṣi, especially Devarṣi, but he appears "on a cloud" (R 7, 21, 3). So Kuṇḍadhāra is a cloud (*jaladhara*) yet a Maharṣi who speaks, etc. (12, 272, 6 and 18f.). Nārada as *samarapriya* and *kelikara* sends Rāvaṇa to the White Island to be mocked (R 7, 20, 18; ib. 37, pra. 5, 13). One who dies is not at once reborn but wanders as a spirit like a great cloud through the sky (12, 298, 18). Nārada is lokacara, and as a cloud, with Śvasana (wind), goes as (cf. meghadūta) messenger (3, 19, 21 f.). Examples of his desire to foment trouble will be found at 9, 52, 11 f.; ib. 50, 66; 13, 155, 17; 158, 20, etc. Mātali tells him that he has a soul hiṃsātmakamana, or -la, "stained with love of strife" (5, 100, 19); but he does many good acts (3, 175, 18; 5, 185, 2; 7, 163, 15, etc.). Otherwise he is a fable-monger, philosopher, and sectarian teacher (5, 160, 15; 14, 24, 1 f.; 12, 339, 4 f.). Nārada's mother was Vīriṇī; but this is in a second birth (H 120 f.). See § 93 f.

IX. THE THREE SUPREME GODS.

§ 131. **Brahman.** — Brahman lacks the hold of the nature-gods upon popular imagination. He is vaguer and tends to pass back into the universal world-power out of which he emerged, the neuter brahmam.. param (R 7, 109, 4, sic) or brahman. Yet the personifying power invests even It with figurative anthropomorphism; "the city of Brahman" = brahman (brahmapuraṃ prāpya, brahma mahat, 12, 177, 50 f.). The brahman is philosophical; Brahman is mythological, the husband of Kriyā (§ 38) or of Sāvitrī (13, 146, 4; cf. § 41).

Brahman is ātmabhū, svayaṃbhū, "self-existent", and as such is generally identified with Prajāpati or the Great Father of the World, Pitāmaha, and with the other personified abstractions, Dhātṛ, Vidhātṛ (Maker, Disposer), and Viśvakarman, panurgos in a good sense, All-maker. He is Lokapitāmaha, imperishable, undeteriorating (5, 97, 2); "ageless, eternal, unborn" are his standing epithets. He is at once creator, preserver, and destroyer, combining in himself, in the earlier epic, the functions later appropriated by other gods. As Creator, Brahman created the worlds and all that moves and does not move; he is Bhūtapati (2, 3, 14), "lord of existent things"; he assigned also to all their occupations (9, 39, 35; 10, 3, 18). "Maker and lord of the world" he is called, by various terms (sṛṣṭikṛd deva, sarvasya dhātṛ, lokakartṛ, lokadhātṛ, sarvalokakṛt, jagatsraṣṭṛ, lokapati, jagatpati, etc). He is pūrvaja, "firstborn" as first being, and so aja, "unborn". His creation is through demiurges. He produces spiritually "mental sons" and they beget all creatures. Brahman's own birth from the mundane egg or from the lotus (below) is ignored in the earliest versions of his creation. Thus R 2, 110, 3 f., in substantial agreement with 12, 166, 12 f., makes Brahman born in the primordial waters, which, unintelligent, enveloped the world. R says in boar-form (RG as "Viṣṇu" is late), but Mbh. ignores the "form" and says that "Brahman created air, fire, sun, earth, space, clouds" (etc. divisions of time), "and then the Great Father, assuming a corporeal body, śarīraṃ lokastham, begot sons of great energy. Dakṣa, son of Pracetas (one of these), then begot sixty daughters, and the Brahmarṣis begot offspring by them, who bore all creatures, gods, Pitṛs (etc., down to the beings born of sweat and eggs). Then the Great Father of all the worlds declared to them the law as uttered in the Vedas". The first of these mental sons was Marīci; from him came Kaśyapa, from whom again came gods and men. The numbers and names of the sons differ in different accounts. In the S text of the tale above, Bharadvāja takes the place of Rudra, and Bhṛgu (as is right, cf. 1, 5, 7) appears between Marīci and Atri; also Prajāpati (Dakṣa) takes the place of Prācetasa. The list of sons is then Marīci,

(Bhṛgu), Atri, Pulastya, Pulaha, Kratu, Vasiṣṭha and Aṅgiras (dual), Bharadvāja (or Rudra); followed by "and Dakṣa Prācetasa (or Prajāpati) begot sixty daughters". The S text endeavors to remove Rudra (Śiva) from the stigma of inferiority, but it has one advantage, that of making the mental sons nine in number (as in some other passages). The genealogists (1, 66, 4 and 65, 10) call these sons "mental", but know only six, omitting Bhṛgu, Vasiṣṭha, and Bharadvāja or Rudra; yet they add Bhṛgu later. Nine sons beginning with Marīci are recognised in 3, 272, 45 (without further names); the scholiast here adds to the six the names of Vasiṣṭha, Nārada, and Bhṛgu (cf. 12, 340, 18; 346, 6). Manu adds all these together and so makes ten (Manu 1, 35). Rudra may also be got into the list by 1, 66, 1: "Six are the great seers known as Brahman's mental sons; eleven are the sons of Sthāṇu (called, the eleven Rudras"). The genealogist derives "Dakṣa and Dakṣa's wife", respectively, from the right and left thumbs of Brahman; gives Brahman another son, Manu (father of the Prajāpati whose sons were the eight Vasus), and says that Bhṛgu was born from the left breast (heart) of Brahman (to become father of Śukra and Cyavana), as Dharma was born "cleaving the right breast" of the Father-god. Dhātṛ and Vidhātṛ are here "set with Manu" (also a son of Brahman in 1, 73, 9 and 12, 341, 34); their sister is Lakṣmī, to whom also are ascribed cloud horses as "mental sons" (1, 66, 41 and 51). Six seem to be the traditional number. Eight bring the sons in accord with the eight prakṛtayaḥ of philosophy (so Manu and Vasiṣṭha are added in 12, 341, 34). As seven the sons are confused with the Seven Seers (§ 118). Thus in 12, 208, 3, the seven are patayaḥ prajānām or Prajāpatis (including Vasiṣṭha here) and also "seven Brahmans" (also H 42). In this chapter, Dakṣa is the only son of the ten Prācetasas (sons of Prācīnabarhis in the family of Atri) and is called Ka (Brahman's name), though in the preceding section Dakṣa is "seventh of the mental sons of Brahman" and the eldest, "born from the thumb of Brahman previous to the birth of Marīci" (12, 207, 17 and 19). As seventh son, Dakṣa is recognised also in 3, 163, 14. In R 1, 70, 17, a genealogy, Marīci is chief because he fathers Kaśyapa, ancestor of gods and men, and so elsewhere in genealogies. Dakṣa again is born in later accounts from the mundane egg or from the All-Soul and has his own "seven sons" (1, 1, 33) and twenty-one Prajāpatis, though called Prācetasa. In 1, 75, 4f., Prācetasa Dakṣa is Lokapitāmaha, since he married Vīriṇī, (daughter of Vīriṇa), called Asiknī (Night; cf. H 120) and begot fifty daughters, who were commissioned to bear him sons. They wed Dharma, Kaśyapa, and Soma, and to Kaśyapa thirteen of them bore the Sun and other gods; the Sun being in turn father of Yama and of Manu, who begot all men! If one believes in the unity of the epic one has a pretty task here, for elsewhere Dakṣa has sixty daughters and Manu is the direct son of Brahman and weds the extra ten (12, 343, 57; H 12450); and in 1, 65, 11 there are only thirteen daughters, Aditi being the first. Another tale, 10, 17, 10, makes Brahman appoint Rudra Bhava (Śiva) to be demiurge and create all beings, but Śiva runs and hides in water (like Agni), and when he, Sthāṇu, has disappeared, Brahman "created another creator to create beings", and this proxy "created beings and seven Prajāpatis, with Dakṣa first" (the S text has, "Dakṣa Prajāpati created seven"). Brahman here at least is higher than Śiva, and so he is in 8, 35, 2f., where Pitāmaha is abhyadhika, "superior" to Rudra. The special demiurge of the second creation is Dakṣa also in H 116, though in the deluge-story

Brahman creates the universe through Manu, who is the father not only of men but of gods and demons (3, 187, 53). In 2, 11, 18f., where the perfect hall of Brahman is described, the prajānāṃ patayaḥ include Dakṣa, Pracetas, etc., Gautama, Aṅgiras, Kratu, till the list runs into names that cannot be considered, but it suggests that when the "twenty-one" prajānāṃ patayaḥ of 1, 1, 33 are mentioned as twenty-one Prajāpatis (12, 335, 35) and only twenty are named, the name Prahlāda may have been left out as incongruous, the space being filled out by the inept yaḥ proktaḥ actually found. Brahman here himself heads the list of Prajāpatis as first of the twenty(-one). Perhaps the stated "six" (above) originally included Brahman, thus agreeing with the "seven creators" in number. R 3, 14, 6f. has a similar list including Kardama, Vikrīta and others mentioned here (12, 335, 35), but also others not in this list, Ariṣṭanemi, etc., and it omits Brahman. Kratu is son of Brahman and father of the Vālakhilyas (1, 66, 9). The mystic equivalents of the mental seven are Sana, Sanatsujāta, Sanaka, Sanandana, Sanatkumāra, Kapila, and Sanātana (12, 340, 72). Of the demiurges, Pulastya, the "beloved son" (3, 274, 12), begot Rakṣasas, Yakṣas, Apes, and Kinnaras; he is renowned as father of Viśravas (hence Vaiśravaṇa and Rāvaṇa), who was half of himself (3, 274, 12f.). The tale of Jaṭāyus in R 3, 14 assigns only eight daughters to Kaśyapa (among them Tāmrā) and is from the source of Mbh. 1, 66, though it upholds the later view that Dakṣa had sixty daughters. Ādi 65 and 66 were originally not parts of one creation myth but have been patched together. Many other beings are especially "sons of Brahman", Jāmbavat, Kavi (adopted son, 13, 85, 125), Death (7, 53, 17, born of Brahman's wrath), Rudra (idem, H 43), Taṇḍi (13, 14, 19); and Surabhi is (different to the account in 1, 66) born from Brahman's vomit of ambrosia, a disgusting tale (5, 102, 3). Earth and Jarā and Sarasvatī are also "daughters of Brahman" (2, 18, 2; 12, 343, 75; 13, 155, 2). Nārada and Sanatkumāra are first "great seers" only, and then become "sons of Brahman". Vācaspati and some other abstractions are not sired at all. The cosmic myth derives even Brahman from the golden egg and philosophy has him born of Ātman (1, 1, 32; 12, 312, 3), a theory united with that of the birth from Viṣṇu's navel (R 7, 56, 7). Vasiṣṭha adresses Brahman as "born of the egg, born of the lotus, god of gods, savior of the world" (cf. H 35f. and 7962f.). The egg-theory is repudiated in a speech ascribed to the Wind god: "How can he who is unborn be born of an egg? The egg means space; thence only was the Great Father born. There is no (cosmic) egg; but Brahman is; he is the king, the enlivener (creator) of the world" (13, 154, 19). Though "lotus-born", abjaja, is not an unusual epithet, it or its equivalent padmayoni, kamalāsana, etc., is found chiefly in late chapters of books seven and thirteen, in 1, 54, 11 and 3, 82, 25, a Tīrtha-praise of Puṣkara, also in the Mārkaṇḍeya episode. The birth from the lotus is formally recounted in 3, 272, 44; 12, 207, 13; and referred to occasionally, as in 3, 12, 38, nābhipadmād ajāyata Brahmā. The androgynous Brahman is found in H 50, where he divides himself to make male and female.

§ 132. Brahman's titles, and those the most magnificent, are given to him without regard to belief in what the titles imply. In the late passage where he is subject to Viṣṇu and this god produces him from his navel and curtly orders Brahman to attend to his "creative business" (prājāpatyaṃ karma, R 7, 104, 7), probably as late a passage as any in R, Brahman is "mighty lord of the world". In the same book he is described as tribhuvaneśvara, devadeva, "lord of the three worlds", "god of gods"; though the Uttara is intent on making not Brahman but Viṣṇu fit these titles (R 7, 98, 15 f., 23 f.). In R 7, 69, 22, Brahman is "god of gods and lord of gods and great forefather" (devadeva, deveśa, prapitāmaha); in R 7, 76, 38 f., he is devadeveśa, "lord of god of gods", an epithet usually applied to Śiva. The same thing occurs in H, devoted to Viṣṇu, but willing to give titular honors to Brahman, in Oriental style. Titles mean something historically, but they are no gauge of belief or of the estimation in which a god is really held. They are often mere survivals. Brahman's titles, Great Father (grandfather of the world), Lord of all, Creator, Owner of all, Guru of worlds and gods, Pitāmaha, Prajāpati, Viśveśa, Sraṣṭṛ, Dhātṛ, Lokaguru, Lokavṛddha, Suraguru (3, 274, 11; 5, 49, 4; cf. 1, 6, 5; 64, 39), are amplified more for grandiloquence than for added meaning by the epithets Sarvalokapitāmaha, Sarvabhūtapitāmaha, Lokabhāvana, Lokeśvareśvara, Lokādinidhaneśvara, Ādideva (7, 53, 13 and 20), Bhūtātman (3, 87, 19), Lokādi, Hiraṇyagarbha, and a few expressions of doubtful meaning, Viriñci (1, 38, 17), Niruktaga (12, 340, 50; cf. niruktam abhijagmivān, 12, 343, 73, of Yāska finding the lost Veda). Dhātṛ, often independent, is Brahman, e. g. in 3, 20, 27 f.; 3, 173, 8 (cf. 3, 19, 24; 5, 163, 44). Viṣṇu and Śiva eventually assume Brahman's titles Jagannātha, Vasudhādhipa, Śambhū, Sthāṇu, Parameṣṭhin, and even Pitāmaha (3, 231, 53). Agni and Indra as well as Brahman are called Bhagavat, Lokabhāvana, Īśa, Deveśa, and Brahman is Sarvabhuj (like Agni), when destroyer (12, 141, 55). Brahman is also "witness of the world", Lokasākṣin (Deveśa, of Brahman, 3, 142, 51). In a few places Īśāna and Īśvara are clearly used of Brahman (1, 188, 18; 3, 30, 22; 32, 1). Brahman is personified Fate (3, 30, 26 and 36). R 2, 14, 49 calls him Ātmabhū, Prapitāmaha, and has also the titles of the other epic, Lokapati, Varada, Sarvalokapitāmaha (R 6, 61, 23 f.).[1]

§ 133. The view that Brahman was the Ādideva or original god is modified only in the later epic by his superiority being set aside in favor of Viṣṇu or Śiva, with one exception. This exception indeed implies that the god is "lotus-born" and so comes under the head of Viṣṇu's general superiority. It is complicated, however, by the intrusion of another element, which recognises as coeval with Brahman the demon of darkness. The account in general resembles those already given. Brahman is born from the lotus; Dakṣa is the seventh son, and has fifty daughters. Dhātṛ Brahman is commissioned by Govinda to be "overseer of all beings" (12, 207, 17 f.; ib. 38). But immediately on Brahman's birth occurs that of the demon Asura Madhu, whose only origin is "darkness" and who is eventually slain by Kṛṣṇa-Viṣṇu, "to avenge Brahman", as the demon of darkness was endeavoring to kill the creator. Madhu, like Brahman, is pūrvaja, first-born, and from darkness (tamasā or, with S, tamasaḥ). His origin antedates creation and is due to the principle of darkness alone.

---

[1]) For other titles, expressing the idea of those above, add Aja, Pūrvaja, Abjaja, etc. already noted. Adolph Holtzmann, Brahman im Mahābhārata, has given, as indicated in the title, a conspectus of statements concerning Brahman for the Great Epic (ZDMG. 38, 167 f.). There too will be found a few more titles, synonymous with those registered above, such as Trilokeśa, Bhūmipati, Lokakṛt. The moral side of Brahman is emphasised in the titles Devasattama, Suraśreṣṭha (etc., e. g. 7, 94, 51), "best of the gods". On his epithet "four-faced" see below.

He is described as attacking Brahman to steal the Vedas (in 12, 348, 27 f.; earlier, without the title Pūrvaja, in 3, 12 and 202). Brahman as the principle of light thus creates also in a living being the soul which goes to his heaven as light. In R 3, 5, 44, he greets such a soul with a mere welcoming word, susvāgataṁ (Śarabhaṅga, the sainted suicide; but heroes also go to the world of Brahman, 7, 142, 29; 143, 34 and 47). But in 12, 200, 25, Brahman cries "welcome" and then "made conscious the flame (soul) and it entered his mouth".

The old Vedic tradition that the Creator was exhausted on completing the creative act finds a faint reflection in the epic statement that when Brahman had created, he rested under a certain Śālmali tree (12, 156, 7). He "created the worlds" at Pṛthūdaka on the Sarasvatī (9, 39, 35)!

§ 134. **Brahman as Preserver.** — The usual view that Brahman having created remains inactive, is true only in part. He appoints in the beginning the functions of his children, the gods (1, 31, 18); especially to Indra he hands over the kingship of the gods (1, 212, 25), and entrusts to him the combat with demons. But he himself is no idle observer. He continues to create (thus he creates death, 7, 52 = 12, 258), and, though usually found in Brahmaloka, often wanders about to various resorts (Prayāga, 1, 55, 1), the Mahendra Hills (favorite resort of Bhūtātman Brahman, 3, 87, 19 and 22), the Himavat (9, 38, 5, 11, 29) and Puṣkara, where Brahman made sacrifice, and the Brahma-lake, where Brahman himself erected the sacrificial post (3, 84, 86). Brahmaloka itself is no place for meditation. Both it and the Hall of Brahman are gay resorts. Saints and heroes and singers and dancers, one of whom is Brahman's own daughter (Menakā, 1, 74, 69), enliven Brahman's home (2, 11 passim and 1, 96, 3; 211, 3; 3, 82, 25), whether it be on high or on the earth. Brahman lives at Tīrthas and especially in Kurukṣetra, which is "heaven on earth" (triviṣṭapa, 3, 83, 4); for once every month "Brahman and the gods assemble there" (ib. 191). Probably the dawn-hymns give rise to the belief that the Vedas daily awaken Brahman: "The Vedas and Aṅgas and Vidyās awaken to-day, adya, the self-existent lord Brahman" (R 2, 14, 49). So day by day he makes the sun rise (3, 313, 46) and keeps daily guard over individuals as well as over the course of nature. He provides food in general, but in particular provides wives and husband (3, 224, 23; 229, 45). He determines the sex of the new creature (6, 98, 22) and imparts to it folly or cleverness (5, 31, 2). After "repeatedly calling to mind whatever was best", Brahman (Dhātṛ) created Aśvatthāman (9, 6, 12), a late creation. He constantly directs the course of events. As the embittered heroine says (3, 30, 21 f.): "Brahman, the Creator and Great-grandsire, Maker and Lord (Dhātṛ, Īśvara, Īśāna) gives weal and woe to every creature, and plays with man as a boy does with a bird bound to a string, or as a man with a marionette; sending this one to hell and that one to heaven". This is no drowsy god sitting apart from his creation. It is an active god, ruler and disposer, though more or less confused with the idea of Fate. Brahman's activities are remarkably varied for a god theoretically having nothing to do after creating. He constantly gives advice when the gods fear danger, tells them what to do, informs them that he has forseen, and provided against, the untoward event (1, 197, 5; 3, 100, 6; 106, 1, here he tells the gods how ocean, drained by Agastya, will be filled). He comforts "men and gods" in time of trouble (3, 107, 7; loka as modern log = men). Or a lone petitioner (3, 293, 16) seeks aid in behalf of another and "through the grace of the Self-existent" obtains the boon.

Long after creation, when men, who had been all Brahmans before (sarvaṃ brāhmam), were divided into castes, and sin flourished, Brahman created laws and punishment. He makes castes through the help of the good demon Bali, according to H 1688; but of his own initiative in 12, 188, 4 f. As "half of Viṣṇu", Brahman sleeps a thousand times four Yugas (3, 189, 39—42); but when he wakes he remains active till the end of his day. Thus he curses the sinner who shocks modest Ganges (1, 96, 6); curses a nymph to be born as a fish (1, 63, 58); curses another to be born as a doe (3, 110, 36) and become mother of the horned saint Ṛṣyaśṛṅga; and even curses the gods (but this is late) because they do not sacrifice to him (H 907). Yet all the curses in the real epic are for the good of the world, and so he curses Kumbhakarṇa to sleep half the year, because this demon (grandchild of Brahman) harries gods and men (R 7, 23); and so, though he permits Indra to be overcome, he instigates his release (ib. 61, 23). He gives immortality to Vibhīṣaṇa because, like Prahlāda, he is a good demon (3, 275, 31 = R 7, 10, 35). To sinful demons he refuses immortality (1, 209, 21). He allows the Asuras to grasp the shadow, not the substance (R 4, 40, 35). His recognition of Rāma as Viṣṇu is based on moral grounds (R 6, 120, 13 f.). From his mouth came the priests as utterers of truth (12, 72, 4, etc.) As Sarvalokaprabhu and Bhūtabhartṛ, he blesses the undertaking of the good (R 2, 25, 25). Even the victim of his rather inconsiderate boon yields with an expression of confidence in the self-existent Lokaguru (Hanumat, R 5, 48, 41 f.). He grants the boon of invulnerability not only to the Aśvins but to the more modern Hanumat (R 5, 59, 19). He takes from Uśanas and bestows his wealth on Maya, because one is evil and the other good (R 4, 51, 12 and 15). Both epics thus recognise him as an ever-active god. The gods sit round him and serve him as courtiers do a king (2, 4, 41). He sits in his "holy world-revered home" and advises Agni how to escape dyspepsia (1, 223, 68), when appealed to by that god; and without appeal comforts his daughter-in-law Pulomā (wife of Bhṛgu) and "names her tears" the river Vadhūsarā (1, 6, 5). A late tale makes him send Indra to comfort Sītā (after R 3, 50). He watches battles on earth and comes to earth to advise Vyāsa and Vālmīki (1, 1, 59 f.; R 1, 2, 23 f.). He had a war-chariot, which he shared with other gods (Indra, Varuṇa, and Īśāna, 7, 127, 1), but let it come into the possession of mortals. He journeys on a vehicle drawn by geese, the gods and seers being his escort (3, 291, 17 f.). He is called here Padmayoni, Caturmukha, Jagatsraṣṭṛ. He gives away weapons (R 2, 44, 11, etc.) and even makes them himself (1, 225, 19; R 3, 44, 14); as Dhātṛ he makes the bolt of Indra (12, 343, 41). The brāhmam astram was made by him to counteract other weapons (7, 201, 37), apparently distinct from "Brahman's rod" (R 6, 22, 5). He made (it is implied) defensive armor (7, 103, 20). He made Hiraṇyapura (3, 173, 11), or it was "made by Viśvakarman" (5, 100, 2), who is a secondary Prajāpati (1, 66, 28) as "maker of arts". Probably the two were sometimes identified, as "Viśvakṛt made the universe" (13, 40, 37). But usually Brahman does the thinking and Viśvakarman does the work. Thus it is both as creator and preserver that Brahman commands Viśvakarman to make Tilottamā, to tempt Sunda and Upasunda to their ruin (1, 211, 10). So (above) Brahman makes the bolt, but in 3, 100, 23, Tvaṣṭṛ, the artifex, actually converts the bones of Dadhīca into the bolt. As warrior-god, Brahman and Prajāpati taught Arjuna how to use weapons (4, 61, 26), Brahman in particular teaching him how to shoot. Here Prajāpati is not Brahman. So in 14, 35, 25, "spotless Brahman" is consulted by the seers including Prajāpati, a distinct personality; though ib. 34, "Prajāpati who is truth" is not the seer, and in 3, 183, 63, Prajāpati who "created men like gods" and is pūrvotpanna (= pūrvaja) is Brahman. After "creating the Vedas, men, gods, demons, worlds, times, other Prajāpatis, truth, law, austerities, usage, purity, and the castes" (12, 188, 11 f., asṛjat, vidadhe, nirmame for "create"), he helps the Seers find the Vedas stolen by the demons (12, 210, 19; 348, 28); he first "sang them in the East" (5, 108, 10). He fashions the warrior's heart (5, 134, 37), perhaps in the beginning, but it is late when he composes a law-treatise called the Trivarga, abridged by Bṛhaspati (and Indra, 12, 59, 30). His Gāthā Brahmagītāḥ are "songs composed by Brahman" (not "sung in the Veda"), for the synonymous expression is "sung by Prajāpati" (12, 265, 10 and 12; cf. ib. 136, 1). Other (all unimportant) sayings ascribed to Prajāpati, Dhātṛ, Svayaṃbhū, etc. are given in 13, 35, 4—12; 13, 20, 14; 1, 113, 12; 3, 31, 39 (cf. R 4, 34, 11, gīto'yaṃ Brahmaṇā ślokaḥ kruddhena, on ingratitude). Prajāpati (as year, etc. 3, 200, 37 f., 68) is pleased with food, as Indra and Agni are with a seat and a welcome, respectively. The Vedic mogham annaṃ vindate, etc. is a gītaṃ Brahmaṇā (5, 12, 18 f.). He arbitrates between the quarrelling breaths (14, 23, 7 f.); decides that aum is the best Veda for gods and demons (14, 26, 8); and instructs the Seers (ib. 35, 26 f.). In fact, in the later epic he is too active, personally manufacturing the diadem of Manu and Rāma (pra. R 6, 131, 65), etc., as he becomes a lay-figure for uttering discourses.

§ 135. Brahman's activity and impartiality lead to the fundamental weakness of his character. He is a god of asceticicsm, he is father of gods and demons. Therefore, to win his favor, gods and demons practice asceticism, and because he is an impartial father he grants invulnerability, etc., to either god or demon indifferently. As the demons always take advantage of this weakness, Brahman is ever engaged in preserving the world from the result of his own folly. One cannot call it ignorance, for he is prescient. He is "equable to all", that is his boast and glory (1, 49, 10; 13, 85, 3; R 1, 1, 13), but he is also well-disposed, suhṛd, toward both demons and gods (5, 78, 7), as being equally his children. He created them as an ascetic (mahātapāḥ, 3, 189, 47) and "the place of the Great Father" is obtained by like asceticism (12, 160, 32, 161, 2). So Sunda and Upasunda win their evil might (1, 209, 21); so Bali becomes a favorite (12, 223, 11 f.; Indra is forbidden to kill him). The whole drama of the Rām. is based on the criminal folly of Brahman in giving Rāvaṇa his power (3, 275, 20; 276, 1 f.; R 6, 41, 63, "Rāvaṇa's insolence is due to Brahman's boon"). Virādha (Tumburu) boasts of the same thing (R 3, 3, 6). The Kabandha exults in being able to attack Indra because Brahman was so pleased with his tapas that he gave him immunity (R 3, 71, 8). As Brahman is the priests' darling god (brāhmaṇavatsala, R 7, 5, 16); so Rāvaṇa's son is vallabhaḥ Svayaṃbhuvaḥ, to whom Brahman gives the very brahmāstra which ensnares Rāma and the means to conquer Brahman's own son Jāmbavat (R 6, 73, 64 f.; 74, 12 and 14). Restriction of Rāvaṇa's power is due only to Brahman becoming offended at the rape of Puñjikasthalā. Other examples might be cited. They show that

Brahman is constantly active, even if as preserver he preserves in great part from the consequence of his own acts. Yet he has taken a vow that "sinners must be slain" (8, 33, 43) and waits the issue calmly, confident that virtue will win (5, 128, 41; right makes might, 6, 21, 9f.). But his lack of initiative in slaying leads eventually to his dishonor: "One does not honor very much the gods that do not kill", and those cited as thus without very much honor are Brahman and Dhātṛ as well as the god of innocuous desuetude, Pūṣan (12, 15, 16). This is put less baldly in R 3, 64, 55: "If the heroic maker of the world were merciful, all would dishonor him". But he is not altogether disregarded. He is invoked for a blessing, karotu svasti te Brahmā (S 7, 94, 41; B has brahma); his favor is requested at the beginning of a tale (1, 64, 3). In his honor is performed a celebration, mahotsava, like that of Śiva, at the autumn harvest festival, in which wrestling and gladiatorial games are performed, perhaps at the time of the new moon, when seers visit the god in Brahmaloka (12, 192, 20 and 1, 96, 3f.), as if the Father God were still a god delighting in destruction (4, 13, 14 and 40; the contest of men and wild animals is held in the inner court of the palace so that ladies may look on).

§ 136. **Brahman as Destroyer.** — He created Death (above), that the world might be preserved, but he is also known as the god "whose anger burned the world" (12, 257, 16), and this anger seems to be ever in the mind of the unsectarian believer. "Surely", cries Mātali, "this must be the destruction of the world which is caused by Brahman" (Pitāmahena saṃhāraḥ prajānāṃ vihito dhruvam = jagataḥ kṣayaḥ, 3, 171, 21). He is "Lord of the World's Destruction", Lokādinidhaneśvara (see above, § 132), and the destruction of earth is caused by his wrath, who is Sarvapitāmahaḥ sarvasya Dhātā caturānanaḥ (R 5, 54, 37 and 43). This is not the destruction caused by his sleep, but by his wrath, Svayaṃbhukopena. The world-destruction caused by Brahman's falling asleep is but a phase of eternal life. How long it lasts is doubtful, as the epic authorities cannot agree even on so vital a point as this. A Yuga lasts 12000 years and a thousand Yugas measure the duration of Brahman's sleep and of his day, or, as expressed in terms of the means of destruction, "at the end of a thousand Yugas, Fire (Vibhāvasu) destroys all", and Brahman, whose sons are here mystically interpreted as the "Fathers of Fathers" (Mind, Intelligence, etc.), begins to sleep (12, 47, 56; cf. 3, 3, 55; 3, 188, 28; 6, 32, 17). But in 12, 312, 1f., where also the gods are "sons of the Pitṛs", and Brahman is produced by the All-soul (Avyakta as God), the day of Brahman is "one quarter less" than a day of God, and a day of God is ten thousand times forty-eight thousand years; that is, Brahman's day is seventy-five thousand Kalpas, or 360000000 years. A "day of the elements" lasts 144000000 years according to this system, which, however, is quite unknown to the real epic. But even the pseudo-epic does not have such calculations as are found in the Harivaṃśa and Purāṇas, in which one period of a Manu is seventy-one times the four ages or a period of 4320000 human years and fourteen Manvantaras make one day of Brahman (H 531). The earlier calculation is that of 12000 years making one day of Brahman (3, 188, 22f.). An insert at S 2, 51, 41 says that 3600000 years pass while Viṣṇu sleeps (jagmus tasya . . varṣāṇi . ṣaṭtriṃśacchatasāhasram mānuṣeṇe 'ha saṅkhyayā). Unless specially restricted the years are to be calculated as human years, and probably till the period of the later epic, which is represented by 3, 3 and 3, 188 (above) as well as by the pseudo-epic, the only period known was the Yuga-complex of twelve thousand years. Then a thousand such were made a day of Brahman, and with the introduction of Manvantaras in the later epic speculation, this was replaced by astronomical calculations based on the knowledge of the precession of Āryabhaṭa or Hipparchus.[1])

§ 137. Brahman is caturmukha (passim), caturānana (R 5, 54, 37), caturvaktra (12, 351, 11; R 7, 5, 12), not as having four faces and so four heads, and as bearing a Veda on each head, but as being omniscient, seeing in all directions. Except for an allusion to his "Veda-knowing hand" (R 7, 36, 3) this is almost the only descriptive epithet of his form. He is, as also said, sarvajña, "all-knowing", and as such he is also caturmūrti as he is caturveda, embracing four forms or divisions of law and Veda (3, 203, 15; S adds caturvarga); or, again, he is amitadhīḥ, "of unmeasured wisdom" (2, 11, 57), more particularly, "he knows the past, the present, and the future", bhūtabhavyabhaviṣyavid (7, 54, 32). He is as Īśa and Śambhu (later epithets of Śiva) aware of what will happen, and as such a Suraguru, most venerable of gods, he commands Viṣṇu to be born on earth, and Viṣṇu receives the command carried to him by Indra, says "it is well", and obeys. Useless to conceal the fact of Viṣṇu's inferiority in the defiant addition that Viṣṇu himself is Prajāpatipati (1, 64, 43 f.). So in 3, 276, 5, Brahman says "the four-armed god has been sent to earth by my orders" to overcome Rāvaṇa. It is he who makes Soma lord of plants and Dhruva lord of stars and protects from the fire below (H 64, 1330, 2557). The boar-incarnation is not Viṣṇu's in the older Rāmāyaṇa but Brahman's (R 2, 110, 3), and the gods do not at first recognise the boar-form of Viṣṇu at all (3, 142, 50). It is Brahman who fears no one (R 2, 30, 27); it is he whom Viṣṇu and Indra revere as Deveśa, Lord of gods (9, 34, 18). Viṣṇu as the "one eternal son of Aditi" is, to exalt him, said to be "like Brahman" (5, 97, 3). Brahman outranks Viṣṇu, leading the gods (3, 85, 70 and 73); and "all the gods along with Viṣṇu" come in fear to him (3, 105, 19). These passages are not sectarian; but it is even more surprising that Kṛṣṇa-Viṣṇu is unknown to the gods and has to be explained by Brahman (6, 66, 4). At first, Brahman is a "pure-souled" (1, 212, 22) and "eternal, immeasurable" being, higher than all the Devas. But the later epic, and long before the gross additions of the pseudo-epic, inverted this relation. Viṣṇu now creates Brahman as male demiurge, for at best Brahman from brahman is a form of Viṣṇu as pure soul (3, 272, 44; 6, 65, 59). Brahman binds upon Viṣṇu his armor (binds it with a brahmasūtra or mantra, 7, 94, 70). He becomes the demiurge of Viṣṇu, as Manu was once his demiurge (6, 65, 71 f.); he worships the horse-head form of Viṣṇu and receives the law from him (12, 341, 91 f.); he is the sixth form of Viṣṇu Nārāyaṇa (12, 350, 4); he becomes the "general agent" of Viṣṇu (12, 340, 50: Hiraṇyagarbho lokādiś caturvaktro niruktagaḥ, Brahmā sanātano devo mama bahvarthacintakaḥ). Brahman's birth is from the lotus of Viṣṇu's navel; yet this is but the seventh of a succession of such births. "First", says Brahman, "I was born from thy will; second, from thy eyes; third, from

[1]) Compare on this point the conclusive reckoning in the Book of Indian Eras (Cunningham, 1883), p. 4, where it is shown that the estimate of 4320000 years must have been based on astronomical calculations. For the Purāṇic reckoning, compare Wilson's note to the Viṣṇu-Purāṇa, p. 24.

thy speech; fourth, from thy ears; fifth, from thy nose; sixth, as egg from thee; and this is my seventh birth, from the lotus" (12, 348, 43). The sectarian passages are sometimes naively expressive of Brahman's attitude toward the new rôle of Viṣṇu. Thus in R 7, 110, 3 f., Brahman comes in a car to greet Rāma (Viṣṇu), and hails him as Viṣṇu Lokagati, adding, "savior of the world, though some do not acknowledge thee".

§ 138. Śiva, like Viṣṇu, seeks advice from Brahman (1, 211, 4). Brahman calls Śiva "sonny", putraka, sets him a task, and tells him not to kill (7, 52, 45; 54, 13). Brahman begets Śiva (12, 352, 20; 166, 16; H 43) in Viṣṇuite passages; Śiva springs from his forehead (lalāṭaprabhavaḥ putraḥ Śivaḥ, 12, 351, 11); yet this is more to depreciate Śiva than to honor Brahman. It is only through Brahman's boon that Śiva's son Skanda can conquer the demons (3, 231, 105). In 1, 18, 42 and 10, 17, 10, Brahman apparently orders Śiva to drink poison for the good of the world. On the other hand, in late passages, Brahman makes obeisance to Skanda (7, 202, 90 f.; 9, 44, 30 f.), and "Śiva creates the Creator". In Droṇa and Karṇa (in part) and in Anuśāsana, Śiva is superior (Brahman acts as his charioteer, 8, 34, 120 f.), and as Prajāpati and Devadeva creates Brahman (Brahmāṇam asṛjat, 7, 201, 74; 13, 14, 4). Brahman eulogises Śiva and confesses his superior power (7, 202, 90 f.). Brahman is made the revealer to Indra of Śiva's power (13, 17, 175). Brahman is a form of Śiva (8, 33, 58, i. e. "Brahman" is a title of Śiva). At this period the great pair take over Brahman's epithets. Brahman and Śiva are both caturmukha; Brahman and Kṛṣṇa-Viṣṇu are both trikakud and tridhāman (12, 43, 10; 343, 93; R 7, 36, 7, etc.). In 12, 121, 57 f., a contest of cults results in an inextricable confusion of text, whereby Brahman becomes father (by sneezing) of Kṣupa (cf. R 7, 76, 38), who was born from the sneeze, kṣup, of the god, and had entrusted to him the system of punishment. Brahman adored Viṣṇu (S has Śiva), who made part of himself Punishment, which passes into various hands (through Kṣupa again to Manu), the passage ending with the glorification of Śiva (ib. 122, 53; cf. ib. 166, 68 f., where Manu receives the Sword invented by Brahman and gives it to his own "son Kṣupa").

As the true god, Brahman is god of troth; any oath taken "in front of Brahman" is to be fulfilled (1, 37, 5). He even directs fate and can modify a curse (1, 16, 5; 20, 16), but he cannot alter entirely such an oath. On such recognition of Brahman as still the highest god rests the statement that only those who die during the northern course of the sun go to Brahman (6, 32, 24; 13, 169, 9 f. etc.), as if he were the supreme representative of the divine power. It is only surprising in epics infected by later views to find so much that still recalls the glory that was Brahman's before the rise of unorthodox sects.

§ 139. **Creation.** — Brahman's creation, given above in outline, is best considered in detail with other schemes of creation. R 3, 14, 6 f. and Mbh. 1, 65, 10 f. differ in detail and in some important points but agree in general. Both differ from the creation-scheme of the mundane egg (cf. Ch. Up. 3, 19, 2), according to which Brahman, Viṣṇu, Śiva, the twenty-one Prajāpatis, sky, earth, "the 33000, 3300, and 33" gods, etc., come out of the golden (cosmic) egg; and, in particular, the human race, as represented by the family of Yayāti, derives from Dyaus, the Sky, through Vivasvat, the Sun. The late passage (R 7, 23, pra. 5, 36) puts the number of gods (suras, S, for svaras B) seen within Nārāyaṇa Deva (Viṣṇu as

Kapila) at three crores. The genealogy of 1, 65 starts with Brahman, gives him six mental sons (already named § 131), says that Marīci, the first of these, had a son Kaśyapa, father of all creatures by daughters of Dakṣa, thirteen in number (elsewhere fifty, of whom twenty-seven married Soma, ten married Dharma), mothers of all created beings, as follows: Aditi became mother of the Ādityas; Diti, of Hiraṇyakaśipu, the father of Prahlāda, Saṃhrāda, Anuhrāda, Śibi, and Bāṣkala; Danu, of the (forty!) Dānavas, Vipracitti, Śambara, Namuci, Puloman, Asiloman, Keśin, Virūpākṣa, Nikumbha, Vṛṣaparvan, etc., among them several aśva-names (as Westerners?); Kalā, of "sons of wrath"; Danāyu, of Vṛtra, Vala, and Vīra; Siṃhikā, of Rāhu, Candrahantṛ (and other eclipse-demons); Krodhā, of "wrath-conquered" demons; Prādhā, of several female spirits and nymphs, a few gods and Gandharvas; Vinatā, of Garuḍa, Ariṣṭanemi, etc.; Kadrū, of Śesa and other serpents; Kapilā, of cows, Gandharvas, Apsarasas, Brahmans, and ambrosia; Muni, of some gods and Gandharvas (Varuṇa, Parjanya, Kali, Nārada, etc.). Viśvā (omitted here!) is in H 146f. mother of Viśvadevas (but wife of Dharma). As already remarked, the daughters are fifty in 9, 35, 45, or sixty; in this case Manu (§ 142) marries ten; cf. R 3, 14 and H 142. Vasus and Rudras, All-gods, Sādhyas, and Maruts are born of the ten daughters who married Dharma (12, 207, 20); Prahlāda, above, was father of Virocana, Kumbha, and Nikumbha (!), the first of whom was father of Bali (the father of Bāṇa, a Śivaite, Rudrasyā 'nucaraḥ, 1, 65, 18f.). The sun and moon are assigned to Danu but they are here demons! Reverting now to Brahman's other sons the genealogist says that Atri's sons were numerous seers and saints; Aṅgiras' were Bṛhaspati, Utathya, Saṃvarta; Pulastya's, Rākṣasas, Kiṃnaras, apes, Yakṣas, etc.; Pulaha's, fabled animals, lions, tigers, Kiṃpuruṣas; Kratu's, the sun-guarding seers. Dakṣa (cf. 12, 207, 19) came from Brahman's right toe and his wife (Vīriṇī) from the left toe. Dakṣa made her mother of the fifty daughters aforesaid. The ten marrying Dharma are abstractions (virtues, etc.), Kīrti, Lakṣmī, Dhṛti, Medhā, Puṣṭi, Śraddhā, Kriyā, Buddhi, Lajjā, Mati. Dharma, born of Brahman's heart, had as sons Śama, Kāma, Harṣa (Peace, Love, Joy), whose wives were Prāpti, Rati, Nanda (Possession, Passion, Delight), "on whom rest the worlds". Rati as wife of Kāma is recognised elsewhere (e. g. R 5, 15, 29). A v. l. makes it uncertain whether Manu or Muni (1, 66, 17) is meant as origin of Vasus. Prabhātā is mother of Prabhāsa, whose wife is Bṛhaspati's sister and mother of Viśvakarman. The last is not identified here with Tvaṣṭṛ, whose daughter, wife of Savitṛ in mare-form, bore the Aśvins (ib. 27f.). This pair of gods and animals and plants are "Guhyakas"; but Bṛhaspati is here called an Āditya. Bhṛgu is father of Śukra; and Dhātṛ (already son of Aditi) and Vidhātṛ are sons of Brahman ("staying with Manu"), brothers of Lakṣmī, whose "mental sons are the sky-going steeds". Śukra's daughter Devī is wife of Varuṇa and mother of Bala and Surā (suranandinī), "the intoxicating drink which delights gods". Suggested perhaps by Surā, Sin (Adharma) is then said to be born of Destruction, his wife being Nirṛti and his sons Bhaya, Mahābhaya, and Mṛtyu (Fear, Terror, and Death). Nirṛti gives her name to the Nairṛta Rākṣasas; and "Death has neither wife nor son" (but in 12, 59, 93, "Death's daughter" is Sunīthā, mother of Vena). Next comes the genealogy of animals. Tāmrā had five daughters, Kākī, Śyenī, Bhāsī, Dhṛtarāṣṭrī, Śukī (Crow, Hawk, Vulture, Duck, Parrot), who became mothers of these creatures and their like. Krodhavaśā had nine daughters of wrathful nature like herself, mothers of deer, bears, elephants, steeds, apes, etc., especially prominent being Surabhi as mother of Rohiṇī and of Gandharvī, mothers, in turn, of cows and horses, respectively, and also mother of Vimalā and Analā; of whom the latter became mother of the seven piṇḍaphala trees (dates, palms, cocoanuts) and of Śukī! One of the nine was Surasā, mother of cranes and Nāgas (so 5, 103, 4). Śyenī was wife of Aruṇa and bore him Saṃpāti and Jaṭāyus (Aruṇā and Garuḍa are sons of Vinatā). Kadrū bore pannagas, in antithesis to Surasā's brood of Nāgas. This defective and self-contradictory list is eked out by the statement in R 3, 14 and H 170, that Tāmrā was one of the eight daughters of Dakṣa whom Kaśyapa married, given here as Aditi, Diti, Danu, Kālikā, Tāmrā, Krodhavaśā, Manu, and Analā, of whom the first four (S omits Danu) became willingly the mothers of gods, Daityas, Aśvagrīva (also in Mbh. as representative Dānava), and Nāraka and Kālaka; while Tāmrā became mother of the birds (krauñcī, etc., v. l. kākī). Airāvata is here son of Irāvatī, daughter of Bhadramada (sic) instead of son of Bhadramanas, one of the nine daughters of Krodhavaśā (above). Śvetā is mother of world-elephants, Manu is mother of men (R 3, 14, 29). The chief variation is in the assumption of various Prajāpatis not in Mbh., altogether seventeen original progenitors, Kardama (known in Mbh. 12, 59, 91), Vikrīta, Śeṣa, Suvrata or Saṃśraya, Bahuputra, Sthāṇu, Marīci, Atri, Kratu, Pulastya, Aṅgiras, Pracetas, Pulaha, Dakṣa, Vivasvat, Ariṣṭanemi, and "last of all Kaśyapa" (some v. l. in G). Kaśyapa's wives are Balā and Atibalā or (v. l.) Manu and Analā; Siṃhikā is introduced among mothers of animals, and there are other minor variations. The incongruous finale of Mbh. is due to the R model; RB having been copied by Mbh., which in turn has influenced RG. Two other Rām. genealogies, 1, 70 and 2, 110, derive the human race from Manu, son of Vivasvat, son of Kaśyapa, son of Marīci, son of Brahman. For the incongruous accounts concerning Surabhi, see further 1, 99, 8; 2, 11, 40 f.; 3, 9, 4 f.; ib. 230, 33 (appears with the fiend Śakuni and Saramā, mother of dogs); 5, 102, 2 f.; 12, 173, 3, Dākṣāyaṇī Devī, below earth, her milk the Milky Sea, mother of the four cows of space, divine animals that guard the quarters, diśāṃ pālyaḥ, Surūpā, Haṃsikā, Subhadrā, Sarvakāmadugdhā; 5, 110, 10, she is in the West. She teaches Indra pity for her children (3, 9, 4 f.; R 2, 74, 18). Her milk, united with ocean, was churned and brought out Surā, Lakṣmī, ambrosia, Uccaiḥśravas, and the kaustubha (5, 110, 11). H makes her mother of Rudras by Kaśyapa, mother of Vasus, of various plants, and rūpārdhamayī patnī Brahmaṇaḥ (H 11527 f.).

§ 140. Philosophy speaks of nine creations, the first being that of the personal soul as Brahman; the second, consciousness; the third, mind; the fourth, the elements, etc., or, with a mixture of myth and philosophy, makes Brahman create earth and sky after his creator made the vegetable world (12, 182-192; ib. 311, 16 f.). Brahman then becomes the "mental son" of the superior Viṣṇu (as God) and is born of "the thought of God desiring to create"; the nāsatyaṃ janma or "nasal birth" of Brahman being the one in which he has a son Sanatkumāra, who teaches the Prajāpati Vīriṇa, who in turn teaches the diśāṃ pāla Kukṣi, even before the āṇḍajaṃ janma (egg-birth) of Brahman (12, 349, 27.). No one scheme obtains. The Kaśyapa as creative power may once have been the tortoise as earth-power (cf. ŚB. 7, 5, 1, 5) upholding Mandara (1, 18, 11), later (cf. VP. 1, 9, 86) interpreted, kāmaṭhaṃ rūpam, as a form of Viṣṇu (R 1, 45, pra. 11). Kamaṭha and Varāha are both epic proper names, but do not help to establish totemism, though Kamaṭhaka and Kūrma as Nāga names may suggest such an explanation. An Asura in shape of a tortoise was once killed by Viṣṇu (kūrmarūpeṇa, 3, 84, 121).

§ 141. Secondary creators are Viśvakarman and Tvaṣṭṛ (above). The former makes Soma's car (acquired by Arjuna) and is identified with the latter as Bhauvana, bhuvanaprabhu (Bhaumana in S; cf. 1, 32, 3, as guard of Soma). He is a Prajāpati, who is "house-maker" of the gods and a vardhaki, carpenter, best of artists (1, 66, 28 f.; 225, 12 f.; 4, 46, 3; 5, 56, 7; 6, 50, 43 f.; cf. S 5, 94, 15 and 19 and R 7, 5, 19). For Indra's sake, Viśvakarman made the bow Victory (vijaya), given by Indra to Rāma Bhārgava and by him to Karṇa (8, 31, 43 f.). He made Śiva's car, in which he overcame the triple city of demons (8, 34, 17 f.); Śiva's bow and ornaments given by Agastya to Rāma (R 1, 75, 11); and the golden wreath worn by Skanda (3, 229, 25); he also made Laṅkā (3, 279, 12; R 4, 58, 20; ib. 5, 2, 20, and often). But it is said also of Arjuna's car that "the gods made it", though doubtless this merely generalises (5, 57, 62). In 3, 114, 17 (cf. RG. 4, 44, 49 as Rudra) Viśvakarman seems to be a name of Brahman. He is not the only worker, as Brahman made and owned Arjuna's bow (4, 43, 1 f.), but under Brahman he made Tilottamā (above) and for Kubera he made the car Puṣpaka (R 5, 8, 2; ib. 6, 124, 29); for Prajāpati to give to Indra he made the conch got by Yudhiṣṭhira, etc., etc. Viśvakarman thus made the golden cows (images) given at sacrifices by Gaya (3, 121, 12); but his most famous work was the Śārṅgadhanvan, Viṣṇu's bow (3, 3, 48; R 3, 12, 33; R 4, 42, 25). In R 5, 20, 13, rūpakartā sa Viśvakṛt must be Viśvakarman. In R 2, 91, 11 f., he is differentiated from Tvaṣṭṛ as joint makers of a magical feast. Vālin's wonderful bier is made by Viśvakarman in R 4, 25, 24 (but "by artisans" in the Bombay text). R also ascribes to him the making of the homes of Kubera and of Garuḍa and of Agastya (R 4, 41, 35; ib. 43, 22). He was father of Nala, who built the bridge to Laṅkā (R 1, 17, 11; ib. 6, 22, 44). The Tvāṣṭram astram may be his work (R 1, 27, 19). Another secondary creator is Maya, who is to the demons what Viśvakarman is to the gods (R 4, 51, 11). He married Hemā (R 4, 51, 10 f.; ib. 7, 12, 3), is son of Diti, and builds palaces for the Pāṇḍus (2, 1, 1 f.). See p. 49.

§ 142. Manu Vaivasvata or Sūryaputra, brother of Yama, was a Prajāpati and mānavendra or first king, who founded the race of Ikṣvāku, the first king and bearer of the rod in the Kṛta age (R 1, 5, 6, etc.). More generally: "Vivasvat's son was Yama Vaivasvata; wise Manu was a younger son of the Sun. From Manu men were born" (1, 75, 11 f.). His wife is Sarasvatī (5, 117, 14, a daughter of Brahman, elsewhere daughter of Dakṣa and wife of Dharma, H 11525, v. l. Marutvatī; 12, 343, 75 has Sarasvatī as daughter of Brahman) and his daughter is Āruṣī (wife of Cyavana and mother of Aurva, 1, 66, 46). Ten wives are given him in later works (12, 343, 57), which give him ten of Dakṣa's daughters (above). He had ten sons named and fifty unnamed, who perished by mutual strife. Among the ten (13, 137, 19) are Vena, Ikṣvāku, Śaryāti, Ilā = Sudyumna, Nābhāga, and others less well known. Manu disposes as well as creates, determining how much cloudy weather Magadha is to have (2, 21, 10). As son of the Sun, he gives Soma the "seeing science" (1, 170, 43, cākṣuṣī vidyā). He was, as "oldest man", rescued during the deluge by a fish-form of Brahman (3, 187, 19 f.), perhaps like the tortoise a totem. H 51 first interposes a Virāj between his father and Brahman. With him in the ark were the Seven Seers, and after the deluge Brahman says: "I am Brahman the creator; naught is higher than I . . . Manu shall now create all beings, gods, Asuras, men, the whole movable and immovable world" (3, 187, 52 f.), but he adds "by my grace", i. e. Manu is demiurge. This Manu receives the law from Brahman (12, 349, 51), as he receives the system of punishment, but it is not he whose verba ipsissima are so often cited. He is born of the cosmic egg (1, 1, 32) and is a Rājarṣi or royal seer. The earliest passage to differentiate Manus is 6, 34, 6 (Gītā 10, 6), which speaks of Seven Seers and four Manus producing the world through Kṛṣṇa's thought. These are not the four Sāvarṇas but Vaivasvata, Svāyaṃbhuva, Cākṣuṣa, and Svārociṣa. The split began with distinguishing the son of the Sun from the son of Brahman (= grandson). Svārociṣa is a synonym of Vaivasvata, an epithet become a person. He also is a legal light. His son Śaṅkhapada and his grandson Sudharman or Suvarṇābha are mentioned in 12, 349, 37. Cākṣuṣa also had a son Variṣṭha (13, 18, 20). Then from misunderstood Vedic passages (RV. 8, 51, 1; 10, 62, 11) were fashioned new Manus, Sāvarṇa (cf. Merusāvarṇi, 2, 78, 14), known as the eighth Manu (12, 225, 30 f.; 13, 18, 48), etc. The aeons of these Manus occur in about the same order, the first mentioned by name being those of Vaivasvata and Svāyaṃbhuva (12, 335, 9; 337, 56), Sūryaputra's antara being synonymous with the former (ib. 343, 26; 350, 42—55). H 409 f. gives the names of the fourteen Manus recognised later, as well as those of the four Sāvarṇas (cf. VP. 3, 2); but all this is really out of the epic range. Prācetasa Manu gets his name from the fact that all the Pracetasas were born of Prācīnabarhis, great-grandson of Aṅga, son of Manu (1, 75, 4 f.; 13, 147, 24); as such he is a Prajāpati. Prajāpati himself is differentiated from Brahman (12, 108, 25 f.), but often is identical with the creator, and in plural form becomes secondary creators, which also include Aryaman and his sons, called Pradeśas as lords and creators (12, 208, 1 f.; ib. 10; ib. 269, 21, etc.), that is, another father of the race (Aryaman as race-name). Instead of fourteen, seven Manus are recognised in 13, 14, 397; 18, 73 (as Śiva-worshippers). Manu is reckoned the eighth sage after the seven mental sons of Brahman, who together constitute the group of pravṛtti or active saints as apposed to the nivṛtti or Yoga-devoted saints (Sana, Sanatsujāta, etc.; 12, 336, 44 f.; 341, 35 and 69).[1] In the holy G-verses (6, 43, 2 f.; spurious), Manu must be Gāyatrī (the holy Gs are G-āyatrī, G-ītā, G-aṅgā, and G-ovinda). In 3, 221, 4, Manu is a name of Agni, but this, like the identification of Manu and the Sun (3, 3, 56), is of no mythological importance. For Kāla and Kāma as creative powers, see § 31 and § 105 f.; for Dyaus and Pṛthivī as Father and Mother, see § 34 and § 35. Post-epical forms of the creation-myths will be found in H 11279—12277 (= 3, 7 f.).

§ 143. **Viṣṇu.** — He is youngest son of Aditi and Kaśyapa (§ 37). Philosophy recognises him (apart from Kṛṣṇa) as lord and ruler of all, creator of all (14, 43, 13; 44, 16). This means more than do his common titles devadeva, lokasvāmin, devadeveśa, viśveśvara, since these are born by other gods who are also titularly, "god of gods", etc. As most fundamental in Viṣṇu appears to be his sun-ship as bird, suparṇa, who goes on high, awakening earth, and having a thousand rays or flames (pra-

[1]) On the ethical distinction, see Dr. Otto Strauss, Ethische Probleme aus dem Mahābhārata (1912).

jāgara ūrdhvaga, sahasrārcis, sahasrāṃśu), the golden germ, hiraṇyagarbha, vasuretas, suvarṇavarṇa, having the seven steeds of the sun and his disc, saptavāhana, cakrin, who courses through air, vihāyasagati, etc., and is identified with the sun as ravi, sūrya, savitṛ, arka, āditya, bhrājiṣṇu (epithets of Viṣṇu). He has fire-names as well, and again the sun in his eye (agni, saṃvartaka, vahni, anala, dīpamūrti, and ravilocana). Many of his titles (e. g. Vaikuṇṭha) come from Indra ("Vāsudeva" appears to revert to this origin) and are again borrowed by Śiva. Lists of his titles as names are given, one shorter (6, 65, 61 f.; R 6, 120 = G 102), though not early, one of a "thousand names" (13, 149, 12 f.), presumably a later compilation of honorific appellations. Here are found "hair-names" of solar (Indric?) origin, harikeśava, hariśmaśru (cf., however, H 4337 and 13, 149, 82, trilokeśaḥ Keśavaḥ Keśihā Hariḥ); "the rays of sun and moon are called hairs" (7, 202, 134). As sun he is govinda, gopati, and goptṛ (also of Sūrya), and is represented by Garuḍa, first as his sign and then, Suparṇavāhana, as his vehicle (1, 33, 16; 13, 149, 51; R 6, 59, 127), probably as the (peacock) sun-bird (§ 12); later is his goose-car (R 7, 37, pra. 5, 93). The early texts represent him as going by himself (he is the "divinity of motion" in general as the three-stride-god; cf. 14, 42, 25) or, Sūrya-like, born by steeds. Then he has Garuḍa as his sign, Suparṇaketu, Garuḍadhvaja, which lasts into the period when Garuḍa is his vehicle (H 2491, 2707; cf. 6823). It is not unlikely that Viṣṇu's name itself means bird (first as the productive spirit).[1]) Perhaps Madhusūdana also (cf. RV. 9, 67, 9) implies that Viṣṇu is the ripening sun (interpreted as slayer of Madhu).[2])

§ 144. Viṣṇu is Mādhava and Kusumākara (and Mārgaśīrṣa), the Madhu-month as the spring-time or first (as well as best) month of the year (6, 34, 35; 13, 149, 31). As sun too he is Aśvaśirā Hariḥ (Hayaśiras, 12, 340, 59, etc.), for which reason, as the sun-horse rising from the sea, he identifies himself with Uccaiḥśravas, the loud-noised sea (6, 34, 27), as it

---

[1]) Compare Johansson, Solfågeln i Indien (The Vedic Soma-robbing eagle as Viṣṇu = bird = creative spirit).

[2]) This was written before the appearance of JRAS. Jan. 1913, but it may stand despite Mr. Macnicol's explanation of these epithets as peculiarly Kṛṣṇa's, for Madhusūdana is an epithet of Rāma as well as of Kṛṣṇa (in both epics), i. e. it is originally epithet of Viṣṇu. Govinda is govidāṃ patiḥ and gopatiḥ in the same passage (13, 149, 33 and 66) and probably the poets felt little or no difference between Govinda and Gopati; but the latter is an epithet common to Viṣṇu, Śiva, Varuṇa, and Sūrya, and cannot help to determine the nature of Kṛṣṇa as a vegetarian god (see below note to § 153). Viṣṇu is the first All-god recognised in the epic, but this is not wholly as a pu sto for Kṛṣṇa. In Kṛṣṇa's own laud Viṣṇu is chief of Ādityas, as Śaṅkara is of Rudras (Gītā 10, 21 and 23; cf. the appropriation of this passage by Śiva in 13, 14, 322). But in pure philosophy, where Viṣṇu stands alone, as in the passage cited above from the Anugītā, Viṣṇu, brahmamayo mahān, is the beginning of the world, lord, īśvara, of all spiritual beings, than who is no being higher (14, 43, 13 f.). It is not necessary to derive Viṣṇu's greatness from Indra (with Jacobi) nor to develop the epic triad (not really epic as triad) from Agni, Vāyu, and Sūrya (with Weber Ind. Str. 2, 226), as if Viṣṇu reached his supremacy through amalgamation with Indra = Vāyu (Omina und Portenta, p. 338). Viṣṇu is first a philosopher's god, i. e. a. priestly god, representing the active yet kindly sun as source of all, and one with the divine light, the best possible god to personify the Bhagavān nityaḥ (5, 42, 21, i. e. brahma) and at the same time to absorb the local bucolic divinities, Balarāma, Rāma, Kṛṣṇa, who were never less than demigod chieftains. It must not be forgotten that long before either epic the idea of the All-god as real being and as personified God was a commonplace. This God-idea was expressed variously, either as "Deva Nārāyaṇa, self of all" (14, 25, 17) or under the image of a god well-known, Viṣṇu or Śiva-Rudra, the latter representing to the priests Agni bhūtapati (cf. 14, 43, 6 f.).

is said: "Here (out of the sea) rises the sun with the head of a horse, filling the world made beautiful (by him), and causing it to be filled with voices" (5, 99, 5). In this form he slew demons and it is characteristic that Aśvagrīva, Hayagrīva, Rocamāna, indicates a demoniac as well as a divine form (1, 65, 23 f.; R 4, 42, 26). So the Mare's Head is at once a demoniac and divine form of fire, identified as such with the sun (§ 38), though as it is in water yet above the surface, it was probably a volcano (cf. R 5, 55, 14). Less usual is the identification of Viṣṇu with the light of the moon, which occurs only as part of his identification, quâ All-god, with many other gods (also as "physician", bhiṣak; Dhanvantari is a form of Viṣṇu, 13, 149, 43 f.). Fire, sun, and Viṣṇu combine to make the "horrible form", ghorā tanuḥ, of Śiva, as opposed to the "gentle lunar form" of that god (7, 202, 108 and 142). The names of the sacred apes, ("sun-faced", Hari, Dadhimukha, etc.), may be due to the fact that they represent the sun-ape, Kapi, Kapīndra, Vṛṣākapi, all names of Viṣṇu (R 6, 73, 59; 12, 343, 89; also of the Sun, etc. 3, 3, 61), later taken by Śiva (7, 202, 136). The king of apes was born of a tear of Viṣṇu (R 7, 37, pra. 1, 7 f.), but this a late passage and elsewhere the same father of Vālin and Sugrīva is son of Prajāpati (R 6, 67, 59). Indra passes over to Viṣṇu many of his titles and also his heroic deeds. Viṣṇu becomes the typical fighter for the gods (7, 14, 49; ib. 21, 37, etc.); though still united with Indra, as with the sun, to typify power (1, 88, 9). He is Vāsavānuja, Indra's junior by birth, and traces remain of his inferiority, as when he is Upendra, and Indra is Mahendra (3, 3, 41). But the later epic, while it cannot omit the derogatory title Upendra ("under Indra"), yet defiantly calls him Atīndra ("over Indra"), as it preserves his birth and then denies that he is born (agraja, aja, ayonija, 13, 149, 24, 108, etc.). In 13, 149, 29, Viṣṇu is "the world's first-born", Jagadādija (in PW as of Śiva!); but pūrvaja and ādija do not necessarily imply more than ayonija and anādi, existing from the beginning; though Viṣṇu in human form, as Devakīnandana, is of course both ātmayoniḥ svayaṃjātaḥ and really Haladharānuja, the unborn god yet younger born brother of Balarāma (2, 22, 36; 13, 149, 94 f.). Viṣṇu in the later epic is called quite rightly Indrakarman, "having Indra's deeds" (R 6, 120, 18; 13, 149, 97), not only as Kṛṣṇa but as independent slayer of demons (5, 10, 43); to whom the gods appeal for help (3, 103, 1 f.). He "looks after the gods" (3, 249, 26); he is their savior, gati (7, 4, 4). He even takes Indra's form on occasion (12, 64, 13 f.). For Indra Viṣṇu charges the bolt to kill the demon and is appealed to for purification, being hymned as Mahādeva (often of Śiva), who with three strides overpassed the three worlds (5, 10, 10 f.). But it is he also who makes Indra the overseer of the gods (ib. 7), and in other ways Viṣṇu is superior, being seldom sundered from the All-Soul Viṣṇu, who is the Who and What (kaḥ kim) of the universe. A few passages still make him inferior to Brahman (§ 137) as to Indra, but the epic in general is an apologia for Viṣṇu as Nārāyaṇa and All-god, either incorporate in Kṛṣṇa or as an independent superior god; retaining the old traditions of him as the bearer of discus and stepper over three worlds, but subordinating this to his identification with Kṛṣṇa. Viṣṇu is "created by Śiva" (Mahādeva) in 13, 14, 4, etc., in passages where Śiva is the All-soul and creator of Brahman, Viṣṇu, Indra, and the rest. All such passages are late epic (see Śiva).

§ 145. Appearance and weapons of Viṣṇu: Though the god is anirdeśyavapus, "one whose form cannot be described",[1]) yet efforts are made to describe him. Thus he is "four-armed" (R 6, 120, 15); he has four fangs, four forms, caturmūrti, -rūpa, four lights, caturbhānu, four souls, four presentations, vyūha, knows the four Vedas, and is caturasra(?); or he has eight or ten arms or is "many armed" and "many-fanged"; he is one-footed or three-footed, has one horn or several horns, many heads, a thousand; also a thousand eyes and feet. He has seven tongues or a hundred. The sacred three gives him the titles tripada, tridhātu, tridhāman, trisāman, triyuga. He is red-eyed, has eyes as large as a lotus (-leaf), aravindākṣa, jalajalocana, etc.; his color is varied, anekavarṇa; he is white and black and yellow and red, but especially yellow (śukla, kṛṣṇa, babhru, rohita, hari). For the glory of the greatness of the god he is described as having many members, faces, bellies, thighs, eyes, and so on, and in conformity therewith he is a "great eater". The epithets "having eyes (mouths, faces) on all sides" are derived from older tradition ("red-eyed" may be due to this or to the boar-avatar, 3, 142, 46). In general, it must be understood that the monstrous appearance is for grandeur; for Viṣṇu is fair, beautiful, lovely (svakṣa, sundara, peśala, śubhāṅga, sudarśana, sumukha, svāsya, etc.). It is as the embodiment of space with four or ten directions that he is called four and eight and even ten-armed (13, 147, 3 and 32). He has a hundred curly locks, śatāvarta, and shares with Śiva among others the title śikhaṇḍin; he is padmanābha; from his lotus-navel came Brahman (3, 203, 12f., as Govinda), jalajakusumayoni (8, 90, 24). Out of the lotus which sprang from his forehead came Śrī and became wife of Dharma (12, 59, 131), hence Śrī kamalālayā; who, with lotus in hand, is engraved on Kubera's car (R 5, 7, 14); padmahastā is auspicious. Viṣṇu wears the kaustubhaṃ maṇiratnam (R 1, 45, 26), the pearl which rose from ocean as maṇir divyaḥ (1, 18, 36) or maṇiratnam (5, 102, 12, etc.); then the diadem "of solar glory", which gives him the epithet kirīṭin. These he wears and clothes of yellow silk (kirīṭakaustubhadhara, pītakauśeyavāsas, 3, 203, 18), as he sits on the coils of the world-serpent, nāgabhoga; but he is usually addressed as one ornamented especially with the pearl of dazzling light, lasatkaustubhabhūṣaṇa (as voc., 3, 263, 13). He is Mukunda (13, 149, 68), perhaps as being himself the jewel. Kirīṭin is an Indra-epithet and not peculiar to gods. On his ringlets, Viṣṇu wears garlands, sragvin, of wild-flowers, vanamālin; he also wears jewelled ear-rings, kuṇḍalin, and arm-bands made of shining gold rubbed with sandal-paste, rucirāṅgada, candanāṅgadin, kanakāṅgadin. On his breast is the quatrefoil called Śrīvatsa (R 6, 120, 27), caused by Śiva's trident or by the wet hand of Bharadvāja (12, 343, 132 and cf. § 125). Hṛṣīkeśa and Śrīvatsāṅka apply to Viṣṇu and Kṛṣṇa; the former epithet being the name the Munis give to Keśava (6, 67, 21); also the Garuḍa worshippers of Viṣṇu are all marked with the Śrīvatsa (5, 101, 5). Mandodarī says that Rāma is the supreme creator-god who wears on his breast the Śrīvatsa, as he bears conch, discus and club (R 6, 114, 1 f.), which with bow and sword are the arms of Viṣṇu. A later passage says that Viṣṇu got his ear-rings from the ancestor of Bali whose prison-

[1]) 13, 149, 83. The descriptive epithets are found for the most part in this section, also H 2201 f., 12, 285, 77; 6, 35, 10 f., etc. Sahasrākṣa is Indra's own epithet. Many of the others, "lotus-eyed, all-faced, hari", etc., are solar epithets; some also belong to Śiva ("one-footed, hundred-tongued, thousand-formed"), while "seven-tongued" belongs to Agni.

door Viṣṇu now guards (R 7, 23, 1, 1f.). Viṣṇu's "horns" may be ornaments or remainders of his animal forms. He is ekaśṛṅgin, unicorn (3, 142, 29) as the boar, while as a bull he has two or several horns (naikaśṛṅga). The bull is his form as the sun, which is called a bull (goputra = son of Sun); but in general this beast is typical of virile strength. So Viṣṇu is "the bull, fond of bulls, with a bull-like belly, having eyes and form and the acts of a bull", as he is gohita, vṛṣapriya, etc., and of course gopati and goptṛ (13, 149, 41, 76, etc.). RG 6, 102, 17 gives him two "Veda-horns" (v. l. a thousand, ṛksāmaśṛṅgo for sahasraśṛṅgo). Besides conch, discus, bow, and club, Viṣṇu bears the sword Nandaka. The discus is a fiery wheel with a thousand spokes, borne in his right hand, and made by the All-maker for use against demons of darkness (13, 149, 120; R 6, 74, 70, etc.). It is the sun: yāvad āvartate cakram, "as far as the sun shines" (R 6, 131, 11). Kṛṣṇa uses the disc as a boomerang (1, 228, 10f.); it is Sudarśanam (6, 59, 91), "fair to see" (as name), by Śivaism interpreted as "hard for any one except Śiva to see", and made his gift to Viṣṇu! (13, 14, 79); it is of course an auspicious sign to have a discus-mark on the arm (1, 74, 4) and the dung of cattle is auspicious from its shape (§ 9). His usual arms give Viṣṇu the title Śaṅkhacakragadādhara (3, 189, 40, etc.). His bow is of horn (R 6, 120, 16; śārṅgadhanvan, 13, 149, 120); as "breaker of the axe" he is called in late description sudhanvā khaṇḍaparaśuḥ (ib. 74, explained by 12, 343, 117), and as Balarāma he is called Halāyudha (rathāṅgapāṇi = cakradhara). Nārāyaṇa has all these titles, as Viṣṇu, with whom, even to the halo or nimbus about the head, he is identical. Both have the web-sign jālapāda, -bhuj, of the foot of the goose. Nārāyaṇa is mystically in the disc of the sun and cleansed souls enter the sun-door into him, thence pass into Aniruddha, and there, becoming pure mind, go to Pradyumna, and so pass into Saṅkarṣaṇa (Jīva,) and then into Kṣetrajña (Vāsudeva; 12, 345, 13f.). It will not be necessary to go into further details of these speculations of theology; they really lie apart from mythology. As archer-sun and nimbus-god, jaṭāmaṇḍaladhārin, Viṣṇu is a warrior, darpahan, surārihan, durārihan, durga, durjaya, duratikrama; his chariot is wind or Garuḍa, he is borne by seven steeds; his fighting-titles come in part from Indra (dhanaṃjaya, puraṃdara, janārdana); he is "fond of fighting" and conquers all, to become kind, refuge of all, savior of the world (samitiṃjaya, also of Yama; trailokyanātha, jagannātha, etc., cf. 3, 49, 20 and in the list 13, 149, 76, 84, 86). He first promulgated the law of battle (12, 64, 21, says Indra!). Though he is the conqueror of innumerable demons he is known particularly as slayer of Keśin and Bhaga and Kālanemi; as hero he is Tāraḥ śūraḥ Śauriḥ; Śūraseno Yaduśreṣṭhaḥ (list 13, 149, 37 and R 6, 120, 17, as battle leader, and list 50, 82, 88). As warrior he carries his club (not goad) in his left hand because he needs the right for his chief weapon, the discus; other weapons he carries "in his other arms". His horn, pāñcajanya, he blows himself (R 7, 7, 9); his bow becomes the property of heroes (R 3, 12, 33f. etc.). Further description, like the epithet All-soul (a title also of the sun, 3, 3, 27; 189, 41) is philosophic ("formless, multiformed womb of all, all-enjoyer", etc.) and may be passed over; only gaṇeśvara, lord of hosts, may be mentioned, to emphasise the fact that the epic comes before Gaṇeśa is invented. Only the late introduction (1, 1, 74f.) acknowledges Gaṇeśa, though the idea of him is common enough (3, 65, 23, pūjā vighnakartṝṇām). Even the introduction has not stereotyped his name, which appears as Gaṇeśāna as well as Gaṇeśa. Gaṇeśvara is title of Viṣṇu alone in 13, 149, 79; but Gaṇeśvaravināyakāḥ (ib. 150, 25) are also recognised. Vināyakas are malevolent demons grouped with the leaders of the lords of divine hosts.[1]) Viṣṇu is however really identified with many gods. Thus he is Parameṣṭhin, Svayaṃbhū, Kāla, Dharma, Prajāpati, Viśvakarman, Arka, Agni, Vasu, Varuṇa, Tvaṣṭṛ, Śiva, Dhaneśvara, Skanda, Vācaspati, the Jyotir-Āditya (as distinguished from Āditya), etc. He is niyantā niyamo Yamaḥ (ib. 105); Vāyu, Dakṣa, Indra and Mahendra, Soma, Kāmadeva (and kāmahan), Dhātṛ, Vidhātṛ, Parjanya, Manu, Marīci, Tāra, Śaśabindu, Vyāsa, Jahnu, Kumbha, Nahuṣa, Sunda, etc. As Śiva he is Bhagahan and Nandin; he is star-clusters, Dhruva, Punarvasu, etc. He is at the same time creator. Thus he creates Brahman from his navel, Rudra from his ire and forehead, the Rudras from his right side, the Ādityas from his left side, the Vasus from his front and the (Aśvin) pair, Nāsatya and Dasra, from his back. The Prajāpatis, Seven Seers, four classes of Pitṛs, Śrī, Sarasvatī, Dhruva, etc., are of him or in him (matsthān paśya, 12, 340, 50f.). Daṇḍa as form of Viṣṇu is described as a Rākṣasa (12, 121, 14f.; 122, 24). As All-god, Dyaus is his head, earth his feet, water his sweat, and the stars are his hair-pits (3, 189, 4f.). Elsewhere the Aśvins are his ears, the moon and sun, his eyes; Brahman, his heart; Sarasvatī, his tongue (6, 65, 61; R 6, 120, 9 and 25). As heavenly light and orderer of time he is Ṛtadhāman (R 6, 120, 8; 12, 343, 69).

§ 146. As is evident from the preceding, Viṣṇu is not especially preserver, but as the All he is also destroyer, not only of grief and sin, śokanāśana, pāpanāśana, but as destroyer, antaka, of living things, svāpana, who puts the world to sleep, the viśātana and saṃhartṛ (3, 189, 4). As Avatar he saves; as wakener and maker, he creates; as Rudra, death, etc., he destroys. Thus it is he who as the Mare's Head destroys the world, a curious rôle for a preserver. In fact, like all All-gods, Viṣṇu has all functions. That he is especially the "divinity of gods" is too much to say, though it is said (unmetrically in S 1, 95, 7: devānāṃ daivataṃ Viṣṇur, viprāṇām agnir brahma ca). As such "he is called Vaikuṇṭha by the gods, while the Vedas call him Viṣṇu" (ib. 6, 8, 22), or, according to the Northern text, "men call him Viṣṇu". Both texts give him a local habitation north of the Sea of Milk; there he rides in the car of eight wheels (elements, 6, 8, 15). All texts have the story of his three strides, as Vikramin, Trivikrama (also Vikrama and Krama), as the son of Kaśyapa and Aditi in dwarf form (hence Govinda as "earth-finder", 12, 207, 26). This and other Avatars are to be distinguished from the four forms, caturmūrtidhara, as Keśava, Saṃkarṣaṇa, Pradyumna, and Aniruddha (12, 340, 102) or (7, 29, 26f.) one form is that of a saint practicing austerity on earth; one (as sun) "watches the world as it does good and evil"; one is active in the world of men; and one sleeps a thousand years. In R 6, 120, 26 night and day are the falling and rising,

[1]) This shows that Yājñavalkya is later than the epics and that a good deal of the stuff offered as epic text in the printed "Southern" version is late addition, plastered on to the epic, just as chapters always have been added (cf. S 12, 68, 46, where Maheśvara-Gaṇeśa causes the massacre of Saudāsa's army at Benares). Gaṇeśa is a title of Śiva (3, 39, 79 and R 7, 23, pra. 4, 34), but, though both passages are late for epic texts, neither implies Gaṇeśa as god. Compare (below) Kṛṣṇa as remover of difficulty. See on Gaṇeśa in Mbh. M. Winternitz in WZKM. 14, 51 (1900); JRAS. 1898, pp. 147, 380 and 631f., who shows that Gaṇeśa is not in the Southern Grantha recension.

respectively, of Viṣṇu's eyelids. It is said that his Avatars are "to exterminate evil", and so he "is born in the houses of good men" (3, 189, 27 f.), as if animal Avatars were excluded. One of his four forms here lasts a thousand times the four ages (ib. 40). Among the forms given by his titles, he is the lotus and the tree, especially the Nyagrodha, Udumbara, and Aśvattha. As bird, he is the goose and "fair-winged" (Suparṇa); as animal, the mahoraga bhujagottama (Śeṣa), the great snake and boar, mahāvarāha, the bull, the lion, śarabha, vyāla, and narasiṃhavapus. As boar perhaps he is trikakud. These real Avatars are indifferently mingled with his form as "teacher of Kapila", as Dāmodara (list, 53; cf. 3, 49, 22), etc. Jahnu and Pṛthu and Śasabindu (and Gupta?) may be incarnations. Vaikuṇṭha, Vaikhāna, Suyāmuna are uncertain titles, as is Śipiviṣṭa (3, 102, 19 f.)[1]. Pṛthu is a true incarnation (12, 59, 128 f.). Viṣṇu is twelvefold as being all the twelve Ādityas born of Aditi, who, however, is said elsewhere to have born him seven times (12, 43, 6; 47, 38, Kṛṣna Viṣṇu). Only here and in the later list of names is Viṣṇu especially Vājasana (12, 43, 9, Vājasani = Vājasana in 13, 149, 98). RB 7, 23, 4, 44 has v.l. In Śānti he is tricakṣuḥ, trikakup, tridhāmā, tridivāc cyutaḥ (Avatar), Kapila, others already cited, and dundubhi, gabhastinemi, Ṛbhu, Vibhu, svadhā, svāhā (etc., one hundred names in S). The title Mahādridhṛt probably refers to bearing the earth as tortoise (may be as Kṛṣṇa). Adhokṣaja, "born under the axle", must refer to the late legend of Pūtanā as told in H 9087 (cf. 13, 14, 69 and 12, 343, 83, where it is explained as upholder of earth!). Native etymologies are of little value or obvious. According to them Viṣṇu is bull as Dharma; Hari, because he receives a share of the sacrifice (hare bhāgam) and because it is his best color; Govinda (= gopendra), because he "found earth"; Kṛṣṇa, because he ploughs and is dark; Vaikuṇṭha, because Vāyu helps him to make earth; Viriñca, because this is the Kāpila name of Prajāpati; Kapila, as the sun; Dharmaja, born of Dharma, etc.

The most surprising and historically important fact in the various lauds of Viṣṇu as All-god is that he is nowhere called by the sacrosanct formula of the Vedānta. He is wise, knowing, blest, true, joy, etc., but he is not even said to be possessed of cit, still less is he designated as being saccidānanda in the phrase of the later Upaniṣads and Vedānta, though he is the supreme philosophical principle, pañcaviṃśatimo Viṣṇuḥ (12, 303, 38), as Nārāyaṇa, highest soul (302, 96) and highest knowledge, jñānam uttamam, buddhiḥ, sattvam (R 6, 120, 17), and siddhārtha (list, 24 f.). This is not because the Sāṅkhya theologians controlled the text, but because the Vedānta shibboleth was unknown when the Viṣṇuite passages even of Śānti were composed.

§ 147. The wife of Viṣṇu is Lakṣmī or Śrī (R 1, 77, 30; sometimes the two are distinct), who rose from ocean clothed in white and for whom gods and demons contended (1, 18, 35 f.). She is Fortune, as happiness and wealth; as Kṛṣṇa's wife she is Rukmiṇī (1, 61, 44; 67, 156), mother of Pradyumna. Lakṣmī is sister of Dhātṛ and Vidhātṛ and mother of the sky-steeds (1, 66, 50). It is a late epic trait to make her exclusively Viṣṇu's (she is also Dharma's wife). In the pseudo-epic often and occasionally earlier she discourses on religion (13, 82, 3 f.; she does not love excessive virtue, 5, 39, 62 f.; 13, 11, 6 f. tells whom she lives with). Often

[1]) On Śipiviṣṭa see Johansson, Solfågeln i Indien, p. 12; but too KZ. 46, 34.

the conception is but half-personal, "Śrī beautifies Viṣṇu" (R 2, 118, 20, etc.). "Fortune (Lakṣmī) favors those who keep the seventh day (sixth or seventh, 3, 3, 64); Ill-fortune comes to the lazy man" (alakṣmīr āviśaty enam alasam, 3, 32, 42, etc.); Lakṣmī is luck in 5, 125, 5f. She is padmālayā, padmahastā, etc. (4, 14, 16, etc.). As Supreme God, Viṣṇu himself is but a form (cf. Viṣṇutvam upajagmivān, 5, 13, 12 = R 7, 104, 9 and ib. 85, 18). Even his anger is a boon, since those killed by him are absorbed into him (R 7, 37, pra. 2, 20f.), the final word on this topic. Another late trait is his "holy dodeka-syllable name", otherwise Purāṇic (VP 1, 6, 39), only in S 12, 336, 34f., where an Apsaras (disguised as Piśācī) "baptises in the holy twelve-syllable name (śuddhaṃ nāma dvādaśākṣaram) of Hari". Viṣṇu's paramaṃ padam is interpreted as a place not inaccessible to Śāṇḍilī and Garuḍa (5, 113, 9f.), often locally defined, though sometimes as brahma (6, 32, 11); otherwise as paraṃ sthānam (seventh or highest world), reflected in Tīrthas called Viṣṇupadas. One is in the North, where Viṣṇu strode out (on the Ganges, 5, 111, 21); so a Viṣṇupada is where Aṅga sacrificed (S 7, 57, 11). A Tīrtha called Viṣṇoḥ sthānam, where "Hari is ever present" (3, 83, 10), results to bathers in attaining Viṣṇu's world; it is in Kurukṣetra, where Viṣṇu became boar, Vārāha Tīrtha (ib. 83, 18), though he actually raised earth at Lokoddhāra Tīrtha (ib. 45). A Dwarf-Tīrtha (ib. 84, 130) and a Tortoise-Tīrtha (ib. 120) are also known, as is a Śālagrāma Viṣṇu (ib. 124), which implies the place on the river Gaṇḍakī where Viṣṇu's holy stone is found, but not the present use of the stone, which is unknown to the epics (but Nīl. so interprets svarṇanābha at 5, 40, 10). On the Punjab or "Kashmir" Viṣṇupada, cf. 3, 130, 8; R 2, 68, 19 (the heavenly, R 4, 37, 17). It may be where Prahlāda and Viṣṇu showed their strength with Skanda's spear (12, 328, 17), in the North. The reading jātidharma in S makes Viṣṇu an upholder of caste (12, 63, 9). He does not accept offerings of brandy, fish, honey, meat, distilled liquor, or rice mixed with sesame; such offerings are not Vedic but have been introduced by rascals from greed and lust. Rice-cakes only should be offered to Viṣṇu, whom alone the Brahman-priests acknowledge in all sacrifices, and flowers with rice-milk cakes (12, 266, 9f.). "The people who are debased as eaters of meat and blood live in Yugandhara, Bhūtilaka, Acyutacchala, and Bāhlīka (Vāhīka), all four districts being in the West, where the people are opposed to Hari (Haribāhyās tu Vāhīkā, na smaranti Hariṃ kvacit) and care only for this-world-salvation, aihalaukikamokṣa. Viṣṇu, however, is the Devayānapatha (as the sun is Pitṛyānapatha), and salvation is from him" (S 12, 336, 53, with interpolation). This indication that the West was opposed to the Kṛṣṇa-Viṣṇu cult (here ordained) may be set beside the statement that the Dānavas "abandoned Viṣṇu as god of gods, hating him and censuring the praise of him" (nindanti stavanaṃ Viṣṇos tasya nityadviṣo janāḥ (S 12, 235, 75f.), as they too "eat meat and cook the offerings made to the gods for themselves, and abandon shrines and praises".[1])

§ 148. **Avatars of Viṣṇu.** — Those of the boar (§ 137), tortoise (§ 140), and fish (§ 142) have already been described.[2]) The difference

[1]) On the geographical-religious aspect, see Pargiter, JRAS. 1908, 309f.; Grierson, ib. 1908, p. 602f.; Keith, p. 831f.

[2]) The tortoise upholds Mandara in 1, 18, 10; in R 1, 45 pra. 11, and VP. 1, 9, 86, the tortoise is Viṣṇu; see § 13.

between an Avatar and incorporation as in Pṛthu, etc., is primarily that the god descends expressly to save the world in the Avatar; in other descents the motive may be personal. All the gods descend in "parts" (1, 2, 93) as human forms, avataraṇas, partial incarnations of divine essence. The boar, tortoise and fish Avatars become those of Viṣṇu (in the epic) only gradually. The epic has no systematic account of the Avatars and even in Hariv. the list is not that of the later ten. In H 5861 f., for example, an account of the god's great acts is given and among them are six of the usual four Avatars together with later deeds (conquest of tree-demons, etc.; cf. H 3451). The boy-form here appears distinct from the Devakīnandana form. Here too the "eight-arm form" is a later manifestation. The later epic has ten Avatars but not always as the same. In short, the theory of Avatars is still developing in the epic and since, after the epic, it continued till the epic ten became twenty or more, it may be said that the epic itself represents only a stage in the belief, where the factors were still not fixed. Pre-epic is the idea that a creator-god appears in animal form, Prajāpati as boar and tortoise. The epic in the deluge-story first makes the grampus Brahman and then substitutes Viṣṇu. In S, Buddha is an Avatar. The bhūmer bhārāvataraṇam (a repeated phrase) is an application of descent in active meaning; it is applied to the Avatar of the god to lower or remove the weight or burden of earth (cf. 12, 340, 101, etc.). A good short account of the Avatars occurs in 3, 102, 21 f.: Nārāyaṇa, as a boar, of old raised earth; as a man-lion, slew Hiraṇyakaśipu; as a dwarf, banished Bali and killed Jambha (both Asuras) for interfering with sacrifice; "and Nārāyaṇa performed other deeds the number of which is unknown". The two thousand verses, H 12278—14390, contain the fullest detailed account of the early incarnations.

§ 149. The Boar-Avatar. Earth burdened with creatures, incapable of dying in the perfect (Kṛta) age, appeals to Viṣṇu, who becomes a "unicorn boar" and with his tusk or horn raises her a hundred leagues, which distance she had sunk into Pātāla. This causes excitement among the gods, till Brahman explains that the boar is the eternal spirit Viṣṇu, Suparṇa (Nārāyaṇa but not necessarily Kṛṣṇa here, 3, 142, 29 f.). In 1, 21, 12, Viṣṇu is the boar-form of Govinda (= gāṃ vindat); identity with Kṛṣṇa emphasised in 12, 209, 7 f. (earth is rasātalagatā, 26); but earth's distress is due here not to surplus population but to infidels who "being fools do not recognise Viṣṇu" as Kṛṣṇa. Instructive is the fact that the gods also do not recognise that Kṛṣṇa is Viṣṇu (ib. 32); Brahman has to tell them, who in R 2, 110, 3 is himself the boar.[1]) In consequence of this Avatar, any boar rising out of water with earth on his head must be worshipped as representing Viṣṇu; just as a dwarf priest or disc-shaped cow-dung represents him, and a bali should be offered to the dung (13, 126, 3 f.; here Kṛṣṇa's brother, born of Nārāyaṇa's white hair, is also cited as sermoniser). The boar-form is that of a monstrous beast ten by one hundred leagues in size, having one tusk and red eyes (3, 272, 55); in this account earth is submerged by a flood, not by sinners nor by numbers. In H 12340 the "weight" is that of Viṣṇu's own energy.

§ 150. The Man-lion incarnation also is described in the same Vana passage. It is not often alluded to in the epic but becomes a favorite in

[1]) RG. 2, 119, 3 says that Brahman the boar is "Viṣṇu", a later version.

Hariv. and the Purāṇas. Hiraṇyakaśipu, slain by the man-lion, becomes Śiśupāla, as Kālanemi becomes Kaṃsa (1, 67, 5 f.). The Avatar is as old as the later Up. and Taitt. Ār. 10, 1, 7; but that may not be very old. Viṣṇu is Nṛsiṃha or Purāṇasiṃha (? R 7, 7, 52). The former means of itself only a "lion(-hearted) man", as it refers to such a hero (9, 53, 23), or "male lion" (3, 146, 53). The god, as man-lion, "makes half his body human and half leonine" (3, 272, 56) and with his claws tears to pieces Hiraṇyakaśipu, the infidel. He does not leap forth from a pillar as later (see H 2275 and 12707 = H 3, 43, 1 f.). Here Viṣṇu = Kṛṣṇa = god of gods, original spirit, absolute god. Hiraṇyakaśipu represents Śivaism. "Virtuous Prahlāda" is a Viṣṇuite.

§ 151. As Kṛṣṇa Govinda also, in the same account, Viṣṇu becomes a dwarf (3, 272, 31 and 69 f.). After a thousand years of parturition (sign of divinity), Aditi bears Viṣṇu as dwarf to overthrow Bali, usurper of Indra's power. Accompanied by Bṛhaspati, the dwarf, bālarūpadhṛt, vāmana, goes to Bali and asks for three paces of land, which being granted the god covers all with three paces, gives back his realm to Indra, and binds and sends below earth Bali, who still reigns there, wherefore the universe is now Viṣṇu's (vaiṣṇavam). Vālmīki refers often to this Avatar (e. g. R 3, 61, 24; R 6, 56, 38), besides describing it in full (ib. 1, 29), but adds nothing of importance. Neither epic has the Purāṇic account of Uśanas's interference in behalf of Bali (for v. l. cf. OST. 4, p. 132 f.). Cf. 12, 340, 79 f.; H 12900 f.

§ 152. Among the seven original Avatars (if this is the meaning of the statement above that Viṣṇu was reincarnated seven times)[1]), the preceding forms of boar and tortoise, man-lion and dwarf, were probably foremost. The three remaining may have been the fish, Rāma, and Kṛṣṇa. But there are no Avatar lists till the later epic, and by that time Rāma Jāmadagnya, instead of being a Śivaite foe of Viṣṇu, is a form or Avatar of the god, just as Buddha becomes an Avatar. This older Rāma descends from Bhṛgu and is son of Jamadagni and Reṇukā, hence called Bhārgava, Jāmadagnya, Kauśika, and from his weapon (obtained from Śiva) he is Paraśu-Rāma. For details see § 125. He lived in the Tretā age and, according to one account, into that period between this and the next age when Rāma Dāśarathi lived, with whom he fought. In 3, 99, 55 f., the All-godship of Rāma Dāśarathi overcomes him in a shooting match, and the apocalypse reveals the god, as in the case of Arjuna and Kṛṣṇa. Yet in 12, 207, Rāma Jāmadagnya exalts Govinda as Viṣṇu, source of all. Vālmīki joins him in the laud, as do Śiva's brother-in-law, Asita Devala, Vyāsa, etc. The younger Rāma (Dāśarathi) is regarded as a prādurbhāva (Avatar) in R 1, 76, 17, but as "one half" of Viṣṇu (R 1, 18, 10), his three brothers being respectively one quarter and one eighth each, which leaves no quarter for the sky, as arranged ib. 15, 16 f. (a late passage). In R 2, 110, 2, he is called lokanātha, but this is not more than a royal title; and Rāma in the real poem is not Viṣṇu but "like Viṣṇu", "like the sun", and like other superior powers with which he is not identified (R 2, 2, 44 f.). R 5, 35, 15 f. describes him as "four-fanged", etc., but as human. In the Jaṭāyus-episode, a clumsy interpolation in honor of Rāma, it is said that he killed often Daityas and Dānavas, as implying divinity, and in R

[1]) Perhaps it refers to the (unepic) legend that Kṛṣṇa was the seventh (eighth) son of Devakī (VP. 5, 1, 74; cf. the Jain legend Antaguḍa-Dāsuo).

4, 17, 8, he secures salvation (as a god) for the one he slays. He is "not his own master" (R 2, 105, 15). His Viṣṇu-form is fully recognised only in Bāla and Uttara (R 7, 27, 14 f.), although he is more than an ordinary man throughout.[1]) The Mbh., on introducing the Rāma-story, calls him Viṣṇu (3, 151, 7). He reigned ten thousand and ten hundred years at Ayodhyā (12, 29, 61, etc.). The Droṇa knows him well as a king of old who defeated Khara and Rāvaṇa (7, 107, 28; 109, 4); also Indrajit's contest with Lakṣmaṇa (ib. 108, 13) is noticed; and in 2, 76, 5 and 3, 85, 65 the episode of the golden deer and crossing the Ganges are referred to, but in no passage except 3, 99, 35 f. and 151, 7 is he the god Viṣṇu. Instead, in 3, 25, 8 f., he is merely "like Indra in power". Most of the allusions occur in one group of Droṇa (parv. 106—109; cf. 106, 17), and it is clear that in neither epic was he at first more than a local royal hero-god, who has the divinity of such but no more. The third Rāma is mythologically of greater importance. According to 1, 197, 33, Bala-Rāma (Baladeva) is as much Avatar as is his brother Kṛṣṇa, both representing hairs of Nārāyaṇa. He is a rustic god called Lāṅgalin, "ploughman"; or Saṃkarṣaṇa, his weapon being the ploughshare, whence Halāyudha (9, 47, 26; 49, 16) Deva; Pralambahan too, as slayer of the demon whose death was also attributed to Kṛṣṇa. Formal identification of Baladeva and Kṛṣṇa as forms of Viṣṇu, and of Baladeva with Śeṣa Nāga, is made in 13, 147, 54 f., where Halī Bala iti khyātaḥ bears the plough, as Kṛṣṇa the discus. His head is wreathed with snakes, his standard is a palm, tṛṇendra, with three heads, but he also carries a club; he is crowned with wild flowers and white-haired (3, 119, 4; 7, 11, 31; 13, 147, 54 f.). His palm-sign indicates his love of wine; when described in full, he is half drunk (1, 219, 7). He stands at the left of Keśava, as Arjuna on the right (5, 131, 8). Later his sons, Niśaṭha and Ulmuka, are well-known, who are mentioned (2, 34, 16) in the epic, but not as his sons by Revatī. After a drunken orgy the Nāga of the world comes out of his mouth and he dies (16, 4, 13 f.). Though usually a mere appendage of his younger brother, he appears to have had some battles of his own. He fought in the eighteen-day battle with king Haṃsa. He is as devoted to wine as his brother is to women (1, 220, 20, kṣībaḥ . . vanamālī nīlavāsā madotsiktaḥ). Such debauchery in no wise detracts from his divinity, however, any more than the tricks of Kṛṣṇa and cowardice of Rāma injure their godhead. But in the beginning both Rāma Dāśarathi and Kṛṣṇa are blamed as heroes for the outrageous behavior of which they are guilty (cf. R 3, 2, 22; ib. 4, 18, 20 f.), while Baladeva's drunkenness is an essential part of his character. Like Indra he gets drunk as a lord as a matter of course.

[1]) R 5, 51, 39 f. has a mixture of Ślokas and Triṣṭubhs. In the first, Rāma is "like Viṣṇu"; in the second, he is lokatrayanāyaka, against whom Brahman and Śiva are powerless. This seems to be an admission of divinity and on a par with R 5, 28, prakṣipta after 17, where Rāma is Viṣṇu, as in RG 6, 40, 46. But Sundara is an embellished book and in general, though space will not permit discussion of all passages (R 5, 31, 44, e. g., has Rāma as Jagatipati in a Puṣpitāgra not in the other text), Rāma is developing into a form of Viṣṇu, but the early epic does not know him as such. Rāma in R 6, 129 is not Viṣṇu, which is the chief point of ib. 120 (=B 117), and when heard surprises Rāma. R 6, 120, which identifies Rāma with Viṣṇu, is late. In R 7, 17, 35, Rāma is Viṣṇu and Sītā is Lakṣmī. On a possible ultimate identification of Rāma Dāśarathi and Bala-Rāma, see Jacobi, Das Rāmāyaṇa, p. 135. Professor Jacobi regards Rāma (in both forms) as a local Indra, and Viṣṇu as grown great through absorption of Indra's attributes (ib. p. 137 f.).

§ 153. Kṛṣṇa Devakīnandana (who is Vāsudeva) and Devakīmātṛ (7, 18, 5), whose nephew Abhimanyu is Viṣṇoḥ svasur nandakaraḥ (7, 49, 1), is the "god without end, unborn, born in the house of Yadu, and is called Kṛṣṇa (Yadukṣaye Viṣṇuḥ Kṛṣṇe'ti), bearer of conch, discus, and mace, who wears the Śrīvatsa and clothes of yellow silk" (3, 272, 71 f.). Even as slayer of Jarāsandha he is called Viṣṇu (2, 24, 34), as in Gītā 11, 30 (cf. 18, 75). Such is in short the position of Kṛṣṇa in nine tenths of the great epic and even the later Rām. recognises Vāsudeva as a form of Viṣṇu (7, 23, pra. 1, 43 f.). While Rāma becomes Viṣṇu only in late additions to the little epic, Kṛṣṇa as Viṣṇu permeates the great epic. This is not to deny that his divinity is questioned. Jarāsandha questions it, but as a Śivaite, and Śiva-worship, before it admits the identity of Kṛṣṇa with Nārāyaṇa (3, 40, 2), questions it; even 12, 281, 19 f. will not admit complete identity (see below). Yet even when one says that he fears Kṛṣṇa less than he fears Yudhiṣṭhira (5, 22, 34) it is admitted in the same breath that he is the eternal god (ib. 33, sanātano Vṛṣṇi-vīraś ca Viṣṇuḥ). The Kurus are old Śivaites (cf. IS. 1, 206) and they join with Jarāsandha in not admitting the divinity of Kṛṣṇa as Nārāyaṇa Viṣṇu, as they deny that Arjuna is Nara, who is revealed (as thus incorporate, 1, 228, 18) to Indra by a heavenly voice (cf. 3, 47, 10 f.; and the equations at 1, 67, 151; 199, 6). Nārāyaṇa is of old the supreme spirit (so still in H 35 f.), as Brahman, and Viṣṇu is first identified with him (R 1, 16, 1); then Kṛṣṇa is identified with Viṣṇu (Mādhava, as in the Khāṇḍava scene, 1, 213, 5 f.), and finally Arjuna is identified with Kṛṣṇa Janārdana in exactly the same words as those used to identify Viṣṇu and Śiva: "Who hateth (loveth) thee hateth me . . there is no difference between us" (3, 12, 45 f.; 12, 343, 133). Yet Nara is son of Indra and less than Nārāyaṇa (1, 67, 110 f.; 5, 96, 40), and so Arjuna is less than his "charioteer Nārāyaṇa" Kṛṣṇa, 8, 62, 1), and when the identity of the two is asserted, sattvam ekaṃ dvidhā kṛtam (5, 49, 20), it comes as something new, not even Bṛhaspati, Uśanas, gods, or seers having known it; but Nārada has to reveal it (ib. 22). Nārada is the revealer of this secret in general (Nara-Nārāyaṇau devau kathitau Nāradena me, 8, 96, 28), even to Arjuna's brother (cf. 12, 347, 19; 344, 13 f.; and 335, 8 f., where Nara, Nārāyaṇa, Hari, and "self-existent Kṛṣṇa" are four lokapāla forms of "Dharma's son Nārāyaṇa"; cf. 7, 201, 57). The Pāñcarātras simply intensify the cult introduced by Nārada (12, 340, 110 f.). So the Harigītās and Nārāyaṇagītam (12, 61, 13; 347, 11) are later imitations of the Bhagavadgītā.[1]) Arjuna acts as demiurge, for "Viṣṇu is not to be waked for a trifle", as Indra explains to Lomaśa (3, 47, 22), apropos of who should destroy the Nivātakavaca demons. He who, as Viṣṇu, is the All-soul, "becomes dearer" as the man-god, as Śiva himself (3, 84, 19 f.) prophesies. As such, however, Kṛṣṇa is still the god from whose mouth the world arises, and Viṣṇu's title saptārcis (cf. the seven suns, 3, 88, 65 f.), as the devouring fire, is also that of Keśava Kṛṣṇa (3, 82, 99). Yet even when the sleep of Viṣṇu is explained (ib. 188, 141; 189, 4 f.), it is only at the end that Mārkaṇḍeya adds: "Now I remember; this supreme god is your relative here, called Govinda and Janārdana; the All-god it is who

[1]) Compare Sir George Grierson, IA. 1909, on the Nārāyaṇas and Bhāgavatas and the same writer's article on Bhakti-mārga in Hastings Encyclopedia of Religion and Ethics. See also Bhandarkar's work cited p. 231, note 2.

has been born as Krsṇa" (ib. 189, 52). The Nārāyaṇas must have been original opponents of the Kṛṣṇa-cult, for they are represented as sworn antagonists of Kṛṣṇa Govinda, though they are Gopālas (7, 18, 31; ib. 19, 7). It is these Gopas whom Arjuna rejects, choosing Nārāyaṇa instead (5, 7, 18 f.). This must indicate that Nārāyaṇa was not Kṛṣṇa and that Kṛṣṇa's divine aspirations were opposed by an older Vāsudeva's followers (they are called Vāsudevasya anugāḥ; here they number only four thousand, 7, 27, 11). Nārāyaṇa did not at first imply Kṛṣṇa. Thus Viṣṇu Nārāyaṇa leads the timid gods to ask Brahman's help in re Dadhīca (3, 100, 13) without a hint of Kṛṣṇa; as Nārāyaṇa the god is invoked to uproot Mandara (1, 18, 4 f.); as the same god becomes a girl and seduces the demons to lose ambrosia (1, 18, 45), cuts off Rāhu's head (1, 19, 3), etc., Nārāyaṇa like Balarāma is the white god; Kṛṣṇa is the black, and the identification of Asita Devala (Black Devala) with Kṛṣṇa is in contrast to the slower and not complete identity of Arjuna, the "white", with Kṛṣṇa (8, 76, 35 f.). R 7, 53, 20 f. recognises Vāsudeva as Nārāyaṇa and in Mbh. 1, 218, 4 f., Mādhava Vārṣṇeya is the same god (festival scene). In R he rescues Nṛga from the lizard-form and generally "relieves burdens in the Kali age". The epic seldom distinguishes between Vāsudeva and Kṛṣṇa.

§ 154. Krsṇa as man is son of Vasudeva called Anakadundubhi, son of Śūra. son of (Sūra) Citraratha, son of Uśaṅgu, son of Vṛjinīvat, son of Krostr, son of Yadu (descendant of Manu) His mother was Devakī, daughter of Devaka, whose brother Ugrasena, king of the Bhojas, was deposed by his son Kaṃsa. His elder brother, by Rohinī, was Balarāma Kṛṣṇa's wives were 16000 in number; one was Rukmiṇī, whom Kṛṣṇa won from Siśupāla (2, 45, 15), and who became mother of Pradyumna (5, 48, 70 f.). The legend of H 9181 f., which relates that Pradyumna was adopted by Māyādevī, wife of Śambara, as Rati, and was incorporate Kāmadeva is not found in the epic, though Kṛṣṇa is creative Love (Kāmadeva, Dhātu, 13, 149, 18 and 83). Pradyumna is regarded as Sanatkumāra (1, 67, 152). His son was Aniruddha, loved by Uṣā, daughter of Bāṇa, the Śivaite (Purāṇic additions make Kṛṣṇa, Balarāma, and Pradyumna fight to recover him when carried to Śoṇitapura). Vajra, son of Aniruddha, by Uṣā (?), became king of Yādavas when Kṛṣṇa died (1, 111, 1, 13, 147, 23 f.; 16, 3, 4 f.; 4, 21 f.; 7, 10 f.). Kṛṣṇa as a child kills his cousin Kaṃsa (13, 148, 57), but this is later than 2, 14, and 7, 10 f., where Kṛṣṇa and Balarāma, when grown, kill Kaṃsa and Sunāman, his brother, king of the Śūrasenas, because of the alliance of Kaṃsa with Jarāsandha, his father-inlaw (2, 14, 31 f.), whose daughters, Asti and Prāpti, Kaṃsa married (2, 19, 22). In 7, 10—11, Kṛṣṇa appears as earthly hero but with supernatural power, conquering Varuṇa and Pañcajana, the Daitya of Pātāla, and Indra (to get the Pārijāta tree) and riding Garuḍa (as Viṣṇu), but not as the supreme being (he worships Durvāsas), though as Vāsudeva recognised as "father of all". The motive for slaying Kaṃsa given in 5, 128, 37 f., is that Kaṃsa was usurper, jīvataḥ pituḥ; it is said here that Kṛṣṇa reinstated his uncle Ugrasena (son of Āhuka). Kṛṣṇa is Arjuna's cousin, mātuleya, as son of Śūra's grandson, since this Śūrasena king of Mathurā was father of Kuntī (2, 22, 25; Śauri ib. 45, 39). Each cousin is essential to the other (2, 20, 3 and 14), since working together they are invincible. but neither is so without the other (na Śauriḥ Pāṇḍavaṃ vinā nā 'jeyo 'sti). They are known as the "two Kṛṣṇas" (both are triyugau, 3, 86, 5 f.; cf. 5, 69, 3; 12, 43, 6), as in 1, 227, 20. But Krsna receives invulnerability and other boons as gifts of the gods (5, 48, 86). The later epic makes Arjuna one thousandth part of the (divine) Kṛṣṇa (as śakti, S 7, 202, 60). Vārṣṇeya, however, is not savyasācin. Interpolations in regard to the wonders accomplished by Krsna are common (e. g. S. 2, 23). Rukmiṇī (S Rugmiṇī) is Kṛṣṇa's favorite wife who had seven special wives (cf. H 6579 f.) By her he lay when Kṛṣṇā invoked him to save her from Durvāsas's crew, and he performed a miracle for her. Eating a bit of rice from the magic dish of the Sun he made those unbelievers believe that they had feasted well. Though here Kṛṣṇa, Vāsudeva, All-soul", he says, "May Hari be pleased with this" as if not Hari himself (3, 263, 18 f.). During the epic war Krsna acts as charioteer for Arjuna, standing at his right. He transforms a weapon into a garland (7, 19, 18 f.); makes the sun seem to set (ib. 146, 68, a trick not redounding to his credit); and cures wounds, as part of his business as charioteer (kuśalo hy aśvakarmaṇi, 7, 100, 14). He has his own charioteer, Dāruka, the club Kaumodakī, the sword Nandaka, four steeds called Balāhaka, Meghapuṣpa, Śaibya, and Sugrīva, and a conch called Pāñcajanya (4, 45, 19 f.; 5, 131, 10; 10, 13, 3 f.; cf. 7, 147, 47), which he got from Pañcajana when he overcame that Daitya, flung Saubha into ocean, slew Keśin, Cāṇūra, Hayagrīva, Pūtanā, Ariṣṭa, Dhenuka, Pralamba, Naraka, Jambha, Pīṭha, Muru, Ogha, and Nagnajit (Gāndhāra), a mixture of myth and history (?); Kaṃsa is added (7, 11, 3 f.; cf. 5, 130, 47; S 2, 53, 16; S 7, 11, 3). As fighter he is blamed for ignoble conduct (5, 160, 55, māyā and indrajāla; 9, 61, 38, anāryeṇa jihmamārgeṇa). The acts of the man suggest, as do his gifts from the gods, that he was a man and this view has to be repudiated. "Foolish is he who says that Vāsudeva is only a man" (as his cousin says he is, 5, 160, 52; 6, 65, 40; 66, 19; 12, 47, 32); whereas, the devout believer says, it was he who as boar raised earth, he who destroys as Rudra with the phallic sign, etc. (12, 47, 56 f.); but he offers sacrifice to Śiva (7, 79, 4). Besides the slaughter of demons he killed Pāṇḍya, overcame the Kaliṅgas, and burned Benares (5, 48, 75 f., often referred to), and his family of sons are well-known warriors (Cārudeṣṇa, etc.; Āhuka here as his "father" 2, 14, 56 f.). S adds Kālayavana and Muṣṭika to the demons he slays (7, 11, 4 and 2, 22, 28; S here, as often, draws from H). Marks of humanity rather than divinity are his cow-boy manners in Magadhā (2, 21, 26 f.); his ignorance (in battle he cannot tell where Arjuna is, 7, 19, 21); his unreasonable rage and broken promise (6, 59, 88 f.); his worship of Umā and Śiva, from whom he gets his thousands of wives (2, 14, 64; 13, 15, 7 f.); his power "received from the gods", because he killed Naraka and recovered Aditi's ear-rings (5, 48, 80 f.), whereby "he won from the demon the bow of Viṣṇu" (in 5, 158, 8 he gets his wives from Naraka; his club and discus he gets from Varuṇa and Pāvaka, and only after getting them does he feel able to fight demons, 1, 225, 23 f.); his own admission that he was "unable at any time to perform a divine act", but he would do what he could as a man, puruṣakārataḥ, that is, he could not interfere with the will of the gods; and his susequent admission that he would have been unable to kill Karna if Karna had not thrown away Indra's spear (7, 180, 6 and 17; rebuked for his behavior, Krsna justifies himself by saying that neither Arjuna nor Kṛṣṇa himself with his discus could have slain Karṇa armed with Indra's spear). He is at most only a "half-quarter" of Viṣṇu (12, 281, 62, turīyārdha). He is repeatedly denounced not only as a deceitful person but as a low person, cowherd and coward (cf. Bhojasya puruṣa, 2, 44, 26; 9, 60, 26, etc.; S 2, 24, 5, matvā devaṃ gopa iti); he is weak and despairing because his kin plague him (cf. 12, 81, 7 and his flight from Mathurā, "because he was afraid", 2, 14, 48 f.). Of his amorousness the epic says little, but it alludes to his revels (1, 219 and 222); probably the lover-god was not compatible with the heroic side and not yet developed. That he who as a child could uphold a mountain and could steal Indra's Pārijāta tree (7, 11, 3 f.), could not overcome a hero because that hero carried Indra's spear, are views still less compatible. The first is evidently the later teaching, which leads to Kṛṣṇa being in the end the Sarveśvareśvareśeśa and Iśeśeśvareśāna, "lord of the lord of the lord of lords" (a meaningless hyperbole, 7, 149, 24). Recognition of his child-divinity is explicit but not common. The dwarf-form is that of the child (śiśur bhūtvā) Kṛṣṇa, who then "even as boy", bāla (3, 12, 26 and 43), did great acts. The particulars given in 2, 41, 4 f., are that as a child he slew a bird (fiend); then he kicked over a car, ate a great deal and for seven days upheld Govardhana, besides slaying Aśva and Vṛṣabha; but only the slaying of the bird (Pūtanā) is expressly ascribed here to his childhood. There is no great stress laid on the child-god. Like the lover-god the child-god develops later. It is as human warrior that he is lauded in 3, 12, 29 f. (destroying Mauravas, Nisunda and Naraka, making safe the road to Prāgjyotiṣa, killing Śiśupala, Krātha, etc. and as conquering the Greek Kaserumat). In 7, 11, 2 f., as a boy in the cowherd's family (Nanda), he slew (Keśin) Hayarāja and with his hands slew the "bull Dānava". Then follow the other demons slain, not in boyhood, Pralamba, Naraka, Jambha, Pīṭha, Mura, as in Vana (cited), with Kaṃsa's death added.[1])

The S text of Sabhā, absorbing the Hariv., identifies K. with Brahman and Rudra (41, 27), tells how Kṛṣṇa resurrected the son of "Sāndīpini" (sic) after the boy was drowned and eaten by a fish (S, 2, 54; cf. H 4906 f.), etc. The pseudo-epic, completing the divinity of Kṛṣṇa, unites Śiva with Kṛṣṇa. Thus in 13, 139, 16 f., fire comes out of Kṛṣṇa's mouth and burns hills and trees; he looks and they are restored. It is his soul, energising as fire to get a son. This soul of fire is told by Brahman that half of Śiva's energy will be born as the desired son (ib. 35; at ib. 140, 34 Śiva similarly burns and restores with a look Himavat, his father-in-law). Doubtless both tales reflect the Kapila story, as Vāsudeva is Kapila and Kapila

[1]) After Weber's essay on Kṛṣṇa's birthday (noticed only in the pseudo-epic, see § 155), nothing of importance appeared on Kṛṣṇa till in 1907—8 arose a discussion between Messers Kennedy and Keith as to the date of the cult of the Child-Kṛṣṇa. Kennedy distinguishes several Kṛṣṇas and attributes the Child to the Gujars, due to Christian influence. The perfected cult may have been influenced from this source but the divine child, as shown above, is explicitly recognised several times in the epic (prior to the pseudo-epic) and must be as old as the Christian era. Keith regards Kṛṣṇa as a vegetation god rather than a sun-god, but admits Viṣṇu as early sun-god identified with Vāsudeva. Kennedy regards Kṛṣṇa, a "monsoon sun-god slaying the Asura Kaṃsa", as distinct from the local Dvārakā god. See JRAS. 1907, p. 951 f.; ib. 1908, p. 169 f.; ib. 505 f.; ib. p. 847. See also above, § 143, note. No weight is to be laid on the equation Kṛṣṇa = Christos, for Kṛṣṇa was a god before Christ was born; the only question is whether he was as much of a god when the epic began as when it ended. Probably all the Kṛṣṇas (pace Kennedy) are one, but the early epic knew him rather as a man-god than as God. By the end of the pseudo-epic, even Vyāsa Kṛṣṇa was incarnate Logos (buddhi), an emanation of Nārāyaṇa, "born of a virgin", kānīnagarbha; also "born of the word of God in Brahman's seventh creation" (12, 350, 4, 38, 51). But this is the last word of the Bhāgavatas and not early epic.

with a look consumes the Sāgaras, who become grasshoppers (3, 47, 19; 106, 7 f.; S 107, 30). Śiva exalts Kṛṣṇa as Kālāgni (3, 272, 29 f.).

The worship of Kṛṣṇa Vāsudeva appears to have been hampered by a (Bengal) rival called Pauṇḍraka Vāsudeva, who imitated the insignia of Kṛṣṇa and was regarded by the latter as a "false god". He supported Jārasandha (2, 30, 22; cf. ib. 14, 19 f.; 1, 186, 12). See § 153.

§ 155. The worship of Kṛṣṇa (apart from laudation) is rather recommended than practiced in the epic, where only the late parts recognise his holy day. In 13, 14, 290, Śiva is said to be pleased with Kṛṣṇa's eighth day, Kṛṣṇāṣṭamirata, but the twelfth day of each month he is to be revered by a different name (ib. 109, 3 f., 15 f.), beginning in the month Mārgaśīrṣa with Keśava, and continuing with the names Nārāyaṇa, Mādhava, Govinda, Viṣṇu, Madhusūdana, Trivikrama, Vāmana, Śrīdhara, Hṛṣīkeśa, Padmanābha, Dāmodara. Who worships him thus on the twelfth of each month gets memory of former births, jātismaratvam, and gold; but he who worships him daily gets his nature and other rewards. The cult is one of harmless offerings. Viṣṇu himself, who receives sacrifice (3, 255, 10 f.), as Kṛṣṇa or otherwise, inculcates what appears to be a brand-new idea, that sacrifice should not be bloody; the god himself is the sacrifice, he demands only flowers and cakes (12, 269, 26; 277, 32 f. = Dh. Pada, 202; cf. 264, 36 f.). Kṛṣṇa's (shrine at?) Purī is recognised "in the hollow of the sea" (6, 66, 41), as made by him, but this may be Dvārakā (so N.; not in Bengal). Otherwise Dvārakā and Mathurā are his places but only Dvāravatī is puṇyā (holy, 3, 88, 24). His age is ādau Kaliyugasya, (though the absence of animal sacrifice is a sure mark of the Kṛta age, 12, 341, 82 f.), or more particularly between Dvāpara and Kali (6, 66, 40). As Kṛṣṇa represents the four ages and their qualities, he represents not only right but wrong, adharma, and as such he becomes the demon Bali (13, 159, 10 f. ib. 16 = 12, 285, 26), as Śiva becomes the eclipse-demon. As Nārāyaṇa Puruṣottama he lived thousands of years as an ascetic worshipping the supreme god Parāyaṇa Deva, but as the same time conquered Indradyumna, Kaserumat, Bhoja Śālva, Gopati, and Tālaketu, and took Dvārakā (3, 12, 32 f.).

§ 156. Other Avatars are mentioned either as incidents in Viṣṇu's great deeds or formally in a list. In H 5861 f., without mentioning the word Avatar, the poet describes the acts of the god: He raised earth as boar and slew Hiraṇyākṣa; as man-lion, he killed Hiraṇyakaśipu; as dwarf, bound Bali; as Rāma Jāmadagnya, between Tretā and Dvāpara, he cut off the thousand arms of Kārtavīrya; as Dāśarathi, killed Rāvaṇa; in the Kṛta age he killed Kālanemi, with eight arms (in Tārakāmaya war); he killed demons under all forms, viśvarūpo Viṣṇuḥ; as a child, he slew forest-demons, Pralamba, Ariṣṭa, Dhenuka; as cowherd, he slew Pūtanā (śakuni), Keśin, Yamala and Arjuna (the pair), and Kuvalayāpīḍa (Kaṃsa's elephant), Cāṇūra, Muṣṭika, and Kaṃsa. Lists also occur first in the pseudo-epic. In 12, 340, 77 f. with additions in S (348, 2 f.), a list like that just cited, with Kālayavana, Muru, Pīṭha, etc. as victims of Kṛṣṇa. Then follows a formal list of Avatars: Haṃsa, tortoise, fish, boar, man-lion, dwarf, two Rāmas, Kṛṣṇa, Kalki (ib. 104 and 16, 4, 13 Śeṣa might be mentioned). The S text at 12, 348, 2, has: Matsyaḥ kūrmo varāhaś ca narasiṃho 'tha vāmanaḥ, Rāmo Rāmaś ca Rāmaś ca Buddhaḥ Kalkī 'ti te daśa, as preliminary to the list above, which is quite different (it anticipates the story of Nṛga, 13, 6, 38 and the story of Uṣā).

After explaining how Kṛṣṇa held up the mountain for seven nights while Indra rained, S (vs. 41 f.) describes the Buddha and Kalki incarnations: "At the beginning of the Kali age, leaning against a kingly tree, clothed in yellow, shorn, and having white teeth, as Buddha, son of Śuddhodana, I shall confuse men; and when I become Buddha, slaves will make use of the pure; all men will become yellow-gowned Buddhas, and priests will neither study nor sacrifice; offerings to fire and respect for Gurus will vanish; sons will not obey parents . . Śruti and Smṛti will be forgotten, owing to men's indulgence toward deceitful rules; till, at the end of this Kali age, a green-yellow (haripiṅgala, epithet of the Śivaite Durvāsas in 13, 160, 14) Brāhmaṇa will appear, called Kalki, son of Viṣṇuyaśas, a Yājñavalkya Purohita. He will come as a warrior-priest riding on a horse, haya, with other priests as (warrior-)companions, to destroy barbarians and heretics". In 3, 190, 93, Kalki himself is named Viṣṇuyaśas (cf. H 2367) and is a priestly warrior, born at Sambhala-grāma (cf. 3, 191, 5 and Vāyu P. 58, 78, Mlecchatvaṃ hanti); a late addition to the epic based on Vāyu P. (cf. 3, 191, 16, Vāyuproktam). S 2, 50, 45 also makes Viṣṇuyaśas the name of Kalki (Kalkin). Cf. H 2368, Yājñavalkyapuraḥsara, "follower of Yājñavalkya" (or of his works). According to 12, 342, 24 f., Viṣṇu worships Rudra Śiva as himself, born of his wrath, as Brahman was born of his grace: "Rudra and Nārāyaṇa are one being in two forms . . Viṣṇu adores none save himself". This is what is recognised in H 10662 f. Rudra is not Avatar but identical. "The mūrti is one, the gods are three, Rudra, Viṣṇu, Pitāmaha" (not epical).

The whole list of twenty-two Avatars (Bhāg. Pur. 2, 7) contains many prādurbhāvas which appear as titles in the epic, such as Puruṣa, Nārada, Kapila, Pṛthu, Ṛṣabha, Yajña, Dhanvantari. The serpent seems to be an Avatar in 12, 350, 35: "I take the form of the earth-upholding serpent; the form of boar, lion, dwarf, and man" (Vyāsa is Avatar of Nārāyaṇa here). Other titles of late but instructive form in the lists at 12, 339, 40 f. are: Cāturmahārājika, Tuṣita (and Mahātuṣita, Buddhistic); Saptamahābhāga, Mahāyāmya (= Citragupta), Pāñcarātrika and Pañcakālakartṛpati, (Indra's) ākhaṇḍala, harihaya; haṃsa, mahāhaṃsa, hayaśiras, vaḍavāmukha (as Avatars, cf. 12, 300, 2 f. with 5, 36, 1 f.). Viṣṇu is here ascetic with water-pot, vedī, etc. (12, 339, 4 f., a late addition). Ātreya is here ascetic but soon becomes an Avatar. In H 2225 to 2374 the ten Avatars are lotus (cf. 12, 343, 76), boar, man-lion, dwarf, Datta (= Dattātreya), two Rāmas, Keśava, Vyāsa, and Kalki. These are pravṛttis or prādurbhāvas (cf. 1, 63, 99). As All-god, Viṣṇu is Rudro bahuśirāḥ (13, 149, 26), but as the "one in many" (eko Viṣṇur mahad bhūtam, pṛthag bhūtāny anekaśaḥ (ib. 140). The Rām. recognises the tortoise and boar incarnations as well as that of Rāma, though only in the later Bāla and Uttara with interpolated passages elsewhere (Buddha is mentioned, but not as Avatar, in the interpolated R 2, 109, 34; the dwarf, 1, 29; the tortoise, 1, 45, pra. 11).[1]) For Viṣṇu and Brahman, see § 137.

[1]) See Muir, Original Sanskrit Texts, 4, 175 f. and 266 f.; 441 f.; Jacobi, Das Rāmāyaṇa, p. 65. In H 10660 f. the three gods who have one form are androgynous, ardhanārīśvarāḥ. Rudra is of the nature of fire; Viṣṇu, of the moon (agnimaya, somātmaka), these two powers composing the world (8, 34, 49, agnīṣomau jagat kṛtsnam). Pitāmaha is ignored here after the introductory and perfunctory recognition of him as one of the three. The laud is given to Hari-Harau, "with Brahman", but the last is really left out in favor of the "two highest" who are one, (etau paramau devau) as creators, preservers, destroyers (eka eva dvidhābhūtaḥ).

As brother of Durgā (§ 161) Viṣṇu shares with her the peculiarity of appearing with either two, four, or eight arms (§ 145), while Śiva has either two, four, six, ten, or eighteen arms (13, 14, 250; 14, 8, 30). Varāhamihira (BS. 58, 31 f.) speaks only of Viṣṇu and Durgā as having four or eight arms.

§ 157. **Śiva.** — In Rām., Śiva as Śaṃkara and Rudra is god of the North (R 6, 74, 59 f.), but he is not regarded as higher than other Devas (R 6, 59, 132; Rāvaṇa is kṣeptā Śaṃkarasya, R 6, 114, 49), except as destroyer, yugānte, in his special rôle as Hara (R 3, 65, 2; ib. 24, 26, Rudra Pinākin, etc.). As Maheśvara he has a wonder-tree on Himavat, near where Kubera became yellow-eyed from seeing him (R 4, 37, 28; ib. 7, 13, 22 f.). Rāma is likened to Bhava, as Sītā to Giriputrī (R 6, 75, 35 f. etc.). Śiva is called Mahādeva and Śambhu (ekādaśātmaka, R 4, 43, 59), Tryambaka (R 6, 43, 6). He is Amareśa, lord of Bhūts (ib. 59, 9), smiter of Tripura, burner of Kāma (ib. 1, 23, 13), father of Skanda (ib. 36, 7 f.); his chief notable deeds are to take the world-destroying poison, destroy Dakṣa's sacrifice (R 1, 66, 9 f.), and receive the falling Ganges (R 1, 43, 26). The Uttara exalts him more but puts him under Viṣṇu (steps on Rāvaṇa, 7, 16 and 16, 27). He carries a rosary (Hara Gaṇeśa, 7, 23, pra. 4, 29).[1] He is ṣaḍardhanayana and Mahādeva, "great god with three eyes" (R 6, 120, 3). In R 1, 45, pra. 5 f., it is Hari who gets Hara to drink the poison. See § 163.

The Mbh. also allows Kṛṣṇa and Arjuna to bow to and receive boons from Śiva and Umā (eight boons from the god of eight principles and forms (1, 123, 44; 3, 39, 70; 13, 15, 7 f.; ib. 16, 34 and 54, two octads, tanus and prakṛtis). In the scheme of creation, Skanda bears no relation to Śiva, who is ignored; it is Brahman here who is īśa and śambhu; the Rudras are sons of Sthāṇu, who is then himself one of the eleven (1, 64, 45 and 66, 1 f.). Mahādeva is a title of Viṣṇu (3, 84, 147, etc.). Hara is name of a demon (1, 67, 23); Rudra and Mahākāla are, however, recognised in 1, 65, 21, as the god Bāṇa followed. Śiva is called Nīlakaṇṭha because he drank the poison at Brahman's bidding (1, 18, 42; but see below). Brahman creates Śiva; Śiva is Brahman's son (references above in § 138). The later epic exalts Śiva, and here he becomes creator of Brahman (13, 14, 4). Śiva is known as Rudra, Īśa, Śambhu, Devadeva, Deveśa, Mahādeva, Bhagavat (as are other gods). Generally, however, Mahādeva and Śambhu mean Śiva, who is called Kapardin from his hair and

[1]) Compare akṣa in 12, 38, 23, the rosary worn by (the friend of Duryodhana) Cārvāka, a Rākṣasa disguised as a Śivaite priest (on the Cārvāka, see Pizzagalli, Nāstika, Cārvāka e Lokāyatika). The Kurus are Śiva-worshippers, though Duryodhana performs the Vaiṣṇava-sacrifice (3, 255, 10 f.). References to Rudra-Śiva as a great god are not uncommon in the Rām., but the force of the number of these is dissipated by the reflection that most of the references are to Rudra as battle-god and are introduced as similes. They are frequent enough to show that Rudra was generally recognised as a fearsome god, but they do not indicate that he was regarded as supreme. The few passages referring to the Śivaite rosary are all late. The passage above and one in 12, 285, 100 are in late lauds and the epithet used here, akṣamālin, is found again in another similar laud at 7, 201, 69. The early epic has no allusion to a rosary. In 3, 112, 5, the Ṛṣyaśṛṅga episode is late (cf. R 1, 9—19; and Lüders, Nachrichten der K. Gesell. d. Wissensch. zu Göttingen, Philol-hist. Kl. 1897 and 1901). Akṣamālā as wife of Vasiṣṭha in Manu is not epic. Perhaps in 13, 104, 84, the kāñcanīyā mālā (na sā duṣyati karhicit) may be a rosary (compare on this subject, Leumann, Aupapātika, p. 72, and the same writer's "Rosaries mentioned in Indian Literature", p. 888). Akṣasūtra, Rudrākṣa, Japamāla, Gaṇettiyā are not epic terms and as akṣamālā appears in A. V. Pariśiṣṭa, 43, 4, 11, this would seem to be the first word used for the rosary. RG 6, 82, 84 is late. Śiva akṣapriya, 12, 285, 47, is "fond of dice"; cf. akṣaiḥ pramattaḥ, 1, 197, 15.

Pinākin from his bow, Triśūlin and Trinetra (Tryakṣa) from his trident and eyes; and generally these epithets are names only of him. But other grandiose names are the epithets of other gods. Maheśvara is Indra in 1, 211, 23, where Śiva becomes four-faced through staring at Tilottamā; and in 1, 227, 29 Tridaśānāṃ maheśvaraḥ is also Indra. Of his four faces (explained otherwise here) the pseudo-epic calls his southern face destructive (13, 141, 1 f.; he also has four forms). He has a hundred tongues, a thousand feet, etc. Three-eyed monsters are not uncommon and, till Kṛṣṇa improved his appearance, Śiśupāla had three eyes and four arms (image of Śiva, 2, 43, 1). Śiva's third eye is like a sun on his brow (Virūpākṣa, 12, 343, 25; 13, 140, 34). Śiva has Rākṣasa characteristics also as kumbhakarṇa, śaṅkukarṇa, gokarṇa, etc. (3, 84, 157; 173, 44; 12, 285, 75 and 83). As husband of Umā, he is Umāpati. She is Mahādevī Haimavatī identified with Pārvatī as he is Mahādeva Giriśa, Girika, etc., as god of the mountains. A festival to him as mountain-god is given in the spring-month Vaiśākha (lasts 34 days; he is Mahādeva, S 1, 241, 69 f.; B suppresses the title, apparently because Kṛṣṇa was the worshipper). In the South, his fane at Gokarṇa was known as holy (both epics; gokarṇa as epithet). Theological animus has varied the recipients of Tīrtha honors. For example, B at 3, 84, 129 has Maheśvara and Vṛṣadhvaja, but S has Vaṭeśvara and then Keśava as those honored. Most of Śiva's titles are clear but Tryambaka, interpreted as "having three eyes" or "lord of three worlds" (H 7589), is doubtful. Śiva is Ambikābhartṛ only in late passages. Possibly "having three rivers", as Ganges is and Umā may be river; or, as in parvatas Tryambakaḥ in v. l. at R 7, 46, 20 (cf. RG 4, 44, 46), ambaka = śṛṅga (Triśṛṅga, cf. Triśīrṣa), the "three-peaked mountain" being originally the god itself (triyambaka is metrical, S 2, 23, 36). If amba = pupilla, the "three-eyed" meaning would agree with tradition. No three "mothers" are known[1]), but this may be derived from the Rudra-Agni conception (Agni has three mothers in RV. 3, 56, 5?). Of doubtful meaning also is Hiṇḍuka in 12, 285, 139. As carried on a bull, Śiva is Vṛṣavāhana (Bhava Giriśa, 1, 197, 21). As ascetic god he is skull-wreathed (14, 8, 29), worshipped by asceticism (1, 169, 8), and called virajo nīrajo 'maraḥ (13, 17, 148; but nīra-ja = moon), "passionless". A hekatomb of human victims are prepared for him as Śaṃkara Paśupati (2, 22, 11; ib. 15, 23). His festival in 1, 143, 3 f., is also a Paśupati utsava, calling forth a great samāja of worshippers (ib. 145, 34; the date would be about the beginning of March).

§ 158. Although the latest parts of the epic (before the final chapters of Śānti) are devoted to Śiva-worship, as if it rose in a new form to oppose the exaggerated Nārāyaṇa-Kṛṣṇa cult, yet the passages in the earlier books (cf. above and 7, 79, 4, where Arjuna offers the "regular nightly offering" to Tryambaka) may indicate that there was not at first much antagonism between the sects. Śiva is the Kuru-maker, lives with Kurus, 13, 17, 107. Each party believes in the supreme greatness of his own god, but neither decries the other openly. As Devadeva, Rudra gives Arjuna

[1]) The simplest explanation of Tryambaka may be that Śiva has not three mothers but three Mother-goddesses (Gaurī, Kālī, Umā), who are called Ambikās, each originally an Ambā or Mother. These Mothers are known as a group of attendants and comprise such forms (names) as Māgadhī, showing a local cult, Bhadrakālī (independent of Kālī = Bhadrakālī, but originally the same), Vetālajaninī, Bhaganandā (sexual), Bhāvinī (= mother), etc. The list, as attendants of Skanda, is given in 9, 46, 3 f. Vetālas next appear in H 14533; as mātṛ, 9542; graha, 9562; Vetālī is Durgā, 10240.

his own raudram astram (3, 167, 47f.; 173, 42f.), and has a pretended struggle to test the knight. Śiva is here "snake-wearer, club-bearer, of many forms, his ensign the bull, trident in hand; he has three heads (nine eyes), six arms, flame-(red) hair, is clothed in snakes"; but at the same time is conventionally trinetra, three-eyed (elsewhere he has "a thousand eyes"). Both passages call him by his ancient name Śarva. Arjuna worships him, building him an altar, when the flowers thereon appear on the god's head, who is described as "lord of all gods, blue-necked, destroyer of Dakṣa's sacrifice", etc., and, finally, as "Viṣṇu in form of Śiva, Śiva in form of Viṣṇu", or Harirudra, a dualism antecedent to trinitarianism (3, 39, 76). He is "lord of weal, pure helper, guardian of the bow, great lord of all beings, lord of hosts, gaṇeśa, destroyer of impurity, a user of māyā (illusion), bull-marked, of eleven forms, ekādaśatanu, and of eight, aṣṭamūrti" (3, 49, 4; ib. 8). He hides in holes (13, 17, 61); is Guha and Rāhu; wears garlands, sports with Umā in the grove north of Meru, unseen save by Siddhas (6, 6, 24f.). In 10, 6, 3f., Aśvatthāman is estopped from murder by the vision of a gigantic being, bright as the sun or moon, clothed in tiger-skins, with snakes as armbands, with terrible fangs and thousands of eyes. This was Kṛṣṇa as god. Then the knight invoked the aid of the "god of gods, husband of Umā, decked with skulls, called Kapardin, Hara, Rudra, Bhaganetrahara". As "the mighty boon-giver, white-necked, living in crematoria, having all forms, whose club is a post, smiter of Tripura, blue-necked, red-haired, who is fond of courtiers, leader of ghosts, dear to Gaurī, overseer of treasure, father of Kumāra, clothed in space, wearer of the moon" (etc., epithets already noted; 10, 7, 11), as "Brahman and as Śakra", Śiva appears (as does Umā), surrounded with his Bhūts, "over-short and over-long", deformed in all ways. What is lacking here and above is almost more important than what is supplied, viz., all reference to Śiva as the phallic god, such as he is described in later passages. The Pāriṣadas are the manifold forms of him they worship and are sexually deformed, bṛhacchephāṇḍapiṇḍikāḥ (10, 7, 39), as they are "huge-bellied", etc., but in the description of the god the Liṅga attributes are lacking. The Mahāpāriṣadas of Rudra are described again in 9, 45, 104f., as long-necked (etc.) linguists with pendent bellies, etc., pralambodaramehanāḥ (ib. 97), five-tufted, three-tufted, cock-faced, etc., attendants of Śiva's son Skanda (their faces are those of animals). It is as destructive rather than reproductive energy that Śiva is famed; hence "slayer of animals", and the battle-ground of death is his playground (7, 19, 35; cf. ākrīḍam iva Rudrasya purā 'bhyardayataḥ paśūn). His fists are like Śakra's bolts; he blazes in glory as he burns Tripura (3, 39, 56; 7, 156, 135). As god of procreation he grants the boon of a son and is worshipped expressly for this purpose by Drupada (5, 188, 3; cf. 7, 144, 15f.; 1, 110, 9). A distinction is made between Śiva and Rudra. Śiva created Brahman and Viṣṇu from his right and left side, (respectively, for purposes of creation and preservation), and he created Rudra as Kāla (13, 14, 347f.); hence Rudra is usually his devastating form; it is Rudra who makes the demoniac arms of Rākṣasas (the eight-wheeled bolt, 7, 175, 96). Rudrāṇī with Ṣaṣṭhī (Gaurī?) also separate the female powers of the two (2, 11, 41). Mystically Rudra is Agni (q. v. and cf. 13, 85, 88f.). Rudra is born when crime is committed, like a portentous storm of wind (12, 73, 17f.; 341, 37, as one of eleven Rudras; cf. ib. 285, 19). A later passage than that cited above first introduces Śiva as a phallic god, where, as Rudra, the god "discarded his Liṅga" (10, 17, 22). In 12, 47, 80 (as Kṛṣṇa) and 166, 25f., he appears with four arms, three eyes, black, yellow, and the third sunlike, and mahāliṅga (ib. 48). So in 13, 17, 77, Śiva, identified with Nandīśvara, Nandin, Nandana, is four-faced and mahāliṅga, cāruliṅga, liṅgādhyakṣa, and ib. 46, ūrdhvaretas, ūrdhvaliṅga. Another late passage, which gives him a rosary (7, 201, 69f.; cf. 12, 285, 100) and makes him the All-god and god of a thousand eyes, arms, legs, and heads, says that he creates in Liṅga-form (7, 201, 93 and 96); by his divine Liṅga the worlds are increased; it is worshipped by gods, seers, Gandharvas, and Apsarasas; and Maheśvara rejoices when his heavenly Liṅga is revered; he is Sthāṇu because sthitaliṅga (ib. 202, 124f. and 133): "He who always reveres the Liṅga obtains great happiness" (ib. 140). That this long passage is a late addition to Droṇa[1]) may easily be shown. It contains a reference to the "two bodies" (cf. 13, 162, 3f.), has the sthiraliṅga of 13, 162, 11, and the late dhūrjaṭi (7, 202, 129), etc. The "two bodies" in themselves are the dve tanū called ghorā and śivā or saumyā, fire, lightning, and sun being the first body, and stars, water, and moon the second. Droṇa replaces vidyut with Viṣṇu as one form of the horrible body, as stars ("heavenly lights") interchange with virtue as a kind form (on Śiva's invention of Death, see 12, 258; he is lightning, and sun and moon). Śiva has two lauds (cf. 12, 285, 71), one giving him a thousand and the other a thousand and eight titles (13, 17, 130 as tala or foundation), both marked by late Purāṇic elements (Manvantaras, Lokāloka worlds, tanmātras created by Śiva, recognition of the Kṛṣṇāṣṭamī; cf. 13, 14, 211, etc.). Kṛṣṇa here worships Śiva (to get his son Sāmba by Jāmbavatī). Śiva's ornaments are Nāgas, worn as ear-rings and girdle; his clothes are of snake-skin; his arms are club, bow (snake), sword, axe, and trident; also the discus (from Viṣṇu), 13, 14, 154f.; cf. ib. 160, 1f. The crescent-moon is on his brow, ib. 253.

§ 159. The pseudo-epic describes in detail Śiva and his many great acts. He inspired sundry authors, "makers of books and Sūtras"; even Sāvarṇi was made a granthakṛt. He made Indra king of Devas at Benares, and promised Nārada the post of musician to himself, the "naked ash-strewn god" (digvāsā bhasmaguṇṭhitaḥ, 13, 14, 101f.; 105). As (above) he has four arms (instead of six), so he has six faces instead of four; he is seen and not seen (dṛśyate 'dṛśyate cā 'pi, negative verb); naked he sports with daughters and wives of saints; has a huge śepha; sometimes rides a white elephant with red ears and four tusks; he is "beyond the reach of logical argument"; his worshipper needs no logic but should be willing to become worm or bird or beast at his wish. He

[1]) On the source of Liṅga-worship, see Stevenson in JRAS., 8, 330; Lassen, Indian Antiquities, 1, 524; and the discussion in OST. 4, 406f. There is no evidence that Liṅga-worship was adopted by Brahmanic priests in early days. As creative god, however, nothing was more natural than for Rudra-Śiva even as representing Agni bhūtādi to exhibit himself in this form. The usual theory (Muir agrees with the authors cited above) is that the savage cult of wild tribes as śiśna-worshippers lent phallicism to Brahmanism, but I do not know of any wild tribes that were distinguished by the use of this emblem in the epic, whereas Śiva was a god invoked for procreative purposes and both he and Kubera are not without priapine elements likely to become symbolised among a people never very shy of sexual matters. It may be that the usual theory is right but it lacks confirmation. At any rate the Liṅga is late in its appearance in literature; it certainly is not an early epic trait. Śiva is Vāmadeva, 17, 14, 71; H 14842.

is half male and half female. He is the best god, because other gods worship his Liṅga. All creatures bear the male or female sign, hence all are Śiva's creatures. If they were Viṣṇu's or Brahman's or Indra's, they would be marked with discus, lotus, or thunderbolt! But the universe is all male and female, pulliṅga and strīliṅga, dve tanū, belonging to Śiva or Devī, who is the female part of Śiva. He gives Vāsudeva "sixteen and eight" boons; around him stand eleven hundred Rudras and seven Manus; but he is above the seven winds and seven fires; his forms are "diseases and sorrows and vices", for he embraces all. His forms are three, tanavas tisraḥ, Kāla, Puruṣa, Brahman, with the overman, adhipuruṣa, as fourth. His eight forms are water, fire, priest, sun, moon, space, earth and wind; he is the eight elements, seven worlds, seven seers, the all, the kāṣṭhā and kalā, and the five ways of salvation (ib. 16, 65, cf. Kaṭh. Up. 3, 11). Probably mahāṅga in 13, 17, 83 f., where new titles are found, is one with mahāliṅga. He is here maker of Vedas, tridaśa and dvādaśa, higher than grammar, etc. etc. His fondness for dancing and music is dwelt upon, nṛtyapriyo nityanarto nartakaḥ sarvalālasaḥ (ib. 50), mahānṛtya (117); he is leonine, and a tiger (vyāghro vyāghreśvaranāmā Kaliṅgarūpaḥ, refers to an image in Kaliṅga, N.); he here has mules as his steeds; ten golden arms; carries ten weapons; is gajahan (at Benares, ib. 48). As creator he is identified with Viśvakarman in 12, 285, 59, but as one who sacrificed (cf. 269, 21, of Prajāpati) in the great universal sacrifice (of ŚB. 13, 7, 1, 14) after his birth from earth.

§ 160. Śiva's weapons are Pāśupata or Brahmaśiras, with which he killed demons and will destroy the world (given to Arjuna!); the Pināka, a club or bow (explained 13, 14, 256, as bow) made of serpents (cf. Ājagava, 3, 126, 34; 7, 145, 94); the trident called Vijaya, etc. The bull is his usual vehicle and Devī Umā rides with him. It is driven by Kāla and was given Śiva by Brahman, also by Dakṣa. The early epic, in distinction from the fantastic account of the pseudo-epic, recognises Śiva as an ascetic god granting boons chiefly as reward of asceticism and famous for a few great acts. He destroyed Tripura, the three cities of demons, hence Tripurāntakara, etc. He slew many demons but especially Andhaka (9, 17, 48, etc., sometimes confused with Antaka). He knocked out Bhaga's eyes and burned Kāma (12, 190, 10) and destroyed Dakṣa's sacrifice. He received Ganges as she fell from the sky (6, 6, 31). His vehicle in going to attack Tripura is drawn by a thousand lions (3, 231, 29). On destroying Dakṣa's sacrifice, because not invited, Śiva shot the sacrifice, that fled as a deer, broke Savitṛ's arms, kicked out Pūṣan's teeth, and destroyed Bhaga's eyes, paralysing all the gods who failed to honor him (cf. 10, 18). He was assisted by Umā as Bhadrakālī, and by Vīrabhadra, and other (Raumya) spirits born of Śiva's hair-pits (12, 285, 34 f.). His wrath produced Jvara, Fever (12, 284, 47). Another account (13, 77, 20 f.) makes Śiva annoyed with Dakṣa for creating cows, but he accepts the bull from him. Śiva is type of the Yogins who have the "eightfold lordship", and imparts this as a boon to Jaigīṣavya at Benares; but also he represents arts and literature, imparting the sixty-four divisions of Kalājñāna to Garga (other boons also recorded here, 13, 18, 2 f., won by repeating the god's 1008 names). He is the inspirer of artists (etc., sarvaśilpapravartaka, 12, 285, 148). For his relation to Brahman, see § 138.

Historically, the most important facts are his identity with Viṣṇu, but at the same time the absence of trinitarian interpretation, except in one late passage (3, 272, 47) as three avasthāḥ of Prajāpati (cf. H 10662); the virtual absence of Gaṇeśa (§ 145; cf. 3, 39, 79 as epithet of Śiva); the rare mention of the rosary (3, 112, 5, Ṛṣyaśṛṅga, late; cf. § 157); and the late references to Liṅga (above). Also the late form Pārvatī (below). Not unimportant too is the fact that Śiva appears as patron of arts and literature only in the later epic. S 12, 122 makes Śiva the author of all literature. As teacher Śiva is found in 2, 78, 15. His "law-treatise" called Vaiśālākṣa from his epithet is referred to (12, 58, 2; 59, 82). Only in H 14841 is he Kaṇāda.

§ 161. Umā, wife of Śiva, is known as Pārvatī (her modern name) only in a few late passages (R 1, 36, 21, Śailasutā Pārvatī, in an added vs.; R 7, 13, 23 has the parallel Rudrāṇī; Mbh. 3, 231, 49; 7, 80, 40; 9, 45, 53; 10, 7, 46). Her birth as "daughter of Himavat", whence this name, is recognised everywhere. Hariv. and Purāṇas call her Pārvatī repeatedly (H also Tryakṣapatnī, vs. 10000). Common are synonyms, Giriputrī, Girirājaputrī, Śailarājaputrī, Nagarājaputrī, Girijā, Nagakanyā, Girīśā, Parvatarājakanyā (R 3, 16, 43; Mbh. S 1, 172, 28; 1, 187, 4). Her old name is Umā (Kena 25, Umā Haimavatī, etc.; in Up. no Pārvatī occurs before the late Haṃsa). R 6, 60, 11 has Umā; RG 5, 89, 7, Umāsahāyo deveśaḥ (not in the Bombay text; all other Umā passages in R cited in PW. lacking in this text except for the first book); Mbh. 3, 37, 33, "Hrī, Śrī, Kīrti, Dyuti, Puṣṭi, Umā, Lakṣmī, and Sarasvatī protect thee"; 9, 45, 13; ib. 46, 49. H 946, derives U-mā from "don't", as her mother Menā thus addressed her (then called Aparṇā) for being austere. Śiva is Umādhava, Umāpati, Umāsahāya (1, 215, 21; 3, 38, 32, etc.). Devī and Maheśvarī usually refer to her (5, 111, 9, etc.). Viśākha reveres her as Girivarātmajā Śailaputrī (9, 44, 39). She lectures on the duties of good women (13, 146, 33 f.), being called here Surakāryakarī and Lokasaṃtānakāriṇī, "doer of the gods' work", "peopling earth" (ib. 11). As Pārvatī she is accompanied by Gaurī and other inferior female divinities (3, 231, 48). She is younger sister of Ganges, whence Śiva received Ganges on his head and held her there a hundred thousand years (6, 6, 31; see § 4). As Gaurī she is sister of Vāsudeva and in this form inhabits the southern mountains. She is called Bhadrakālī and Mahākālī, Maheśvarī, and Durgā, Great Death, Great Sleep (Mahānidrā), and has, as female part of Śiva, his characteristics, being cruel and kind; as slayer she is Kaiṭabhanāśinī, Mahiṣāsṛkpriyā (rejoicing in the blood of the demons she slays, 6, 23, 8). The Durgāstotra gives her family relations, Nandagopakulodbhavā, Gopendrasyānujā, Kātyāyanī, Kauśikī; she is also Śākambharī (corn-mother). As Sāvitrī Vedamātṛ, she usurps the place of older goddesses. She lives not only in Himavat but all over the land, in deserts and under earth, and conquers as war-goddess (6, 23, 8 f.). But she is unknown as Durgā except in H and two late hymns, 4, 6, 1 f.; and 6, 23, 2 f., where she is Bhuvaneśvarī, Yaśodāgarbhasambhūtā, Vāsudevasya bhaginī and lives in Vindhya. She is fond of drink and flesh and her name Durgā is a lucus a non, because she saves from durga, difficulty (4, 6, 20). Her sign is a peacock's tail; she wears diadem and snakes, with the usual jewels. She has four arms and faces (also two arms), and carries bow, discus, noose, and other weapons, as well as lotus, bell, and dish. She saves from robbers and death and is the "pure woman on earth". As Khaḍgakheṭadhāriṇī, she carries sword and shield (late words). Added to the arms above, this makes her eight-armed (so N.), though said to be caturbhujā. She is the "pure lightener of burdens", identified with Fame, Beauty, Success, Patience, Modesty, and Wisdom (common abstractions) and with Saṃtati and Mati (the former new) as with Twilight, Dawn, Night, Sleep, Lustre (Jyotsnā), Grace, Endurance, and Pity. She is addressed as Mandaravāsinī Kumārī (cf. Comorin), Kālī Kāpālī (kapilā kṛṣṇapiṅgalā, 6, 23, 4); she is caṇḍī and caṇḍā (ib. 5), feminines of Śiva's and Skanda's epithets. The great difference between the two lauds (both awkward insets) is that, in Virāṭa, Durgā is the sister of Kṛṣṇa and wife of Nārāyaṇa and is invoked as if she had nothing to do with Śiva; while in Bhīṣma she is identified with Umā (see later, H 3268 f.). Durgā is also Jātavedasī, and Kālī was originally a flame-name (Muṇḍ. Up. 1, 2, 4). In these lauds, Mahākālī, synonym of Bhadrakālī Durgā, is elsewhere Pārvatī or Devī; but Mahādevī may also be Lakṣmī (wife of Viṣṇu), as in 13, 62, 6. She may be meant in the Tīrthas called Kanyā and Anaraka (3, 83, 112; 84, 136, Kanyāsaṃvedya, sacred to the Virgin, as in Kanyāśrama, ib. 83, 189). The later epic adds a Kanyākūpa and -hrada (13, 25, 19 and 53). Here too belongs the cult of Kokāmukhā (ib. 52) for this means Durgā (6, 23, 8, "wolf-faced, loving loud laughter, fond of battles"). Devī's popularity, Maheśvarī, is largely due to her being interpreted as goddess of desire, a Venus (14, 43, 15, Bhagadevānuyātānāṃ māheśvarī mahādevī Pārvatī hi sā). Durgā is a late adoption of Viṣṇuism; originally a goddess worshipped by savages (Śavaras, Barbaras, Pulindas, H 3274). In H 10235 she is called (Gautamī) "Sister of Indra and Viṣṇu". The identity of Gaurī and Durgā is not obvious. Gaurī is at first wife of Varuṇa (q. v.). But in 3, 84; 151, she is the great goddess of the mountain-peak, Mahādevī. At 3, 84, 97, for the well-known phrase, "Go to Gayā or sacrifice with a horse", S has Gaurīṃ vā varayet kanyām (S 82, 96, repeated S 85, 10). Gaurī accompanies Pārvatī (3, 231, 48), who is Umā and rides with Paśupati Mahādeva; in whose train are "Gaurī, Vidyā, .. Sāvitrī", who "walk behind Pārvatī", as the Vijaya weapon walks incorporate here and Rudra's spear (paṭṭiśa). S 2, 9, 7, also makes Gaurī wife of Varuṇa and in 13, 146, 10, the word means earth. Gaurīśa is Śiva (14, 8, 30), who is here identified with Anaṅga, Kṛṣṇa, etc. (as in H 10658). In R 5, 49, 11 and R 7, 25, 2, the minister Nikumbha may be connected with the Caitya Nikumbhilā (ib. 6, 84, 13) which in turn gets its name from "dancing Nikumbhilā" (R 5, 24, 47, with brandy-offerings), whom Indrajit should revere (cf. R 6, 87, 30). The goddess revered is Bhadrakālī (R 6, 85, 11 f.), and "dancing Nikumbhilā" means dancing the goddess (worshipping her).

§ 162. Umā is a "pitiful goddess" and, for example, persuades Śiva to imitate Rāma and restore Jambuka (Śambuka) to life (12, 153, 114, Śiva weeps); though Śiva himself is really kind, and especially in the later epic appears as the holy comforter. Thus to comfort Vyāsa for the death of his son Śuka, Rudra-Śiva gives the father "a shadow like his son and never leaving him", which only the bereaved father may see (chāyā anapagā sadā, a shadow-soul, 12, 334, 38); so Gālava, going to his widowed mother, by grace of Maheśvara saw his father alive again (a vision, 13, 18, 58). The moral of his grace is that "even after committing all crimes, men by mental worship of Śiva are freed from sin" (ib. 65 f.). As a child in the lap of Umā, he who is "lord of all mothers", paralyses Indra (7, 202, 85). Śiva in female form causes a female condition in his neighbourhood, which converts Ila into Ilā (R 7, 87, 12); it is his northern form which sports with Umā (13, 141, 1 f.). According to 12, 343, 25 f.,

Śiva's neck was made blue because Uśanas's snaky locks bit him, or because Nārāyaṇa throttled him (ib. 115), and his third eye (whence "Virūpākṣa") was caused by Dakṣa's austerity; but in 13, 140, 34, Umā covers his two eyes in sport, whereat a third eye breaks out on his forehead (H 7592 explains the blue neck from Indra's axe smiting him). A name of Gaurī is Ambikā, and Ambikā lokadhātrī, that is the world-upholding female principle, is a late title of Śiva. Umā appears as a female forester in company with Śiva as mountaineer (3, 39); he is her darling, Gaurīhṛdayavallabha (10, 7, 8). It was her jealousy which roused Śiva to destroy Dakṣa's sacrifice. Maheśvara himself says that it is the custom to exclude him from sacrifice and seems to be indifferent, till Umā rouses him (12, 284—285; Mahādeva here is only one of eleven Rudras and only Dadhīci worships him). Śiva himself is called Gaura (7, 80, 39) as he sits with Pārvatī and hosts of Bhūts, with matted locks and trident in hand, while music and dancing and noise of song and laughter and shouting are going on around them, and is extolled as Ambikābhartṛ (ib. 59). The two, Śiva and Umā, become visible only at the end of every Yuga (3, 130, 14) and may be propitiated in Kashmir at the lake Vātikaṣaṇḍa (or -khaṇḍa). The account of Jarāsandha and the flinging of the mace (99 leagues from Girivraja to Gadāvasāna near Mathurā) show that Śivaism flourished in the North (Kashmir) and East (Benares, Magadha) as opposed to Kṛṣṇaism (Mathurā to Surat). The story how Rudra got Umā away from Bhṛgu is told in 12, 343, 62 (here too the saint's curse on Himavat). Their marriage is told in 13, 84, 71, where Umā curses the gods for trying to keep Rudra from her (see also § 24). Dialogues between the spouses are reported in 13, 140, 2f.; 12, 236, 29f. In the latter in S, Umā is told by Śiva that he is enjoyer and she enjoyed, he soul and she body, he the real thing and she the śakti, and nature as śakti is the universe (he is eightfold in form, and with eight connections, aṣṭamūrti, aṣṭasaṃdhivibhūṣita). Oddly enough, it is as "son of Brahman" that Śiva, śrīkaṇṭha, proclaims his Pāśupata religion (12, 350, 67).

All these forms of Umā (= Amma, the great mother-goddess) go back to the primitive and universal cult of the mother-goddess (cf. Aditi), who in popular mythology appears as Kālamma and as Ellamma, that is as destructive or as kind. Although Kālī (as śyāmā) shows that the popular etymology connects Kālī with "black", it is probable that the goddess in this form is related rather to Kali, the genius of destruction. Her appellation Bhadrakālī (epic above, and Manu, 3, 89) euphemises the name (Cāmuṇḍā is a later name, not epic). Her modern cult represents her with four or eight hands. The cult of the disease-goddess in the epic is expanded in modern times into a definite cult of Māri-amma as "destructive" (Śītalā, etc.) sickness (a goddess). The connection of Paraśu-Rāma with the Śiva-cult is maintained to the present day, the temples of Kālī having a special shrine to this Rāma, owing to the legend that his wife Reṇukā was revived by her head being placed on the body of a Pariah woman. The goddess Ellamma (= sarvāmba) is recognised as the "goddess with the head of Reṇukā", while Paraśu-Rāma adores Ambikā (Ellamma).[1]

[1] Compare Gustav Oppert, Zeitschrift für Ethnologie, 1905, p. 726f. Oppert derives Umā from ammā (Original Inhabitants of India, p. 421). It is interesting to note that Ellamma in modern mythology becomes the mother of the Trimūrti, hatching out the three gods as a hen. The part played by serpents in her worship connects her with the Nāgas. See Oppert (Ztschr. für Ethn. 1905, p. 729). The local forms become in the

§ 163. Skanda belongs to Śiva through a doubtful sonship but more through his characteristics. He reverts in his earlier form to respectable antiquity and the fact that the Gītā recognises him as chief of army-leaders, when Śaṅkara is only chief of Rudras (6, 34, 23 f.), together with his identification with Sanatkumāra in Chānd. Up. 7, 26, 2, seems to show that he is not an intruded deification of Alexander. He is not mentioned enough in the early epic to indicate that he is important, but, as is the case with Durgā, when exploited he is lauded *ad nauseam*. This too looks as if he were not a late addition to the epic but a god rapidly increasing in importance, as the epic expanded, or more particularly as the Śiva-cult expanded. The reason is indeed obvious. Śiva had no use for Viṣṇu and Indra; he needed a new battle-leader of the gods, and for this chose Kumāra (Skanda), son of Agni, and made him at once his own son and leader of the gods in battle. The genealogy (1, 66, 23 f.) makes Kumāra son of Agni, and Agni is called (2, 31, 44) both Kumārasū and Rudragarbha. As mothered by the Kṛttikās he is (R 3, 12, 20) Kārttikeya (Pāvaki). His forms as brothers or sons are Śākha, Viśākha (= Skanda in 3, 232, 7) and Naigameya (1, 66, 24; "Pṛṣṭhaja" is a fourth, traditional error); but the later epic makes Skandaviśākha a title of Śiva and Viśākha interchanges with Skanda (epithet of Śiva, 13, 17, 72). Whose son Skanda was, is debated in the epic itself: "Some explain him as son of Pitāmaha, Sanatkumāra, eldest born of Brahman (so 12, 37, 12); some say he is son of Maheśvara; some say he is son of Agni (Vibhāvasu); some say he is son of Umā; some say he is son of the Kṛttikās (Pleiades); some say he is son of Ganges" (9, 46, 98 f.). In the laud of Śiva, 13, 14, Skanda appears "like Agni", beside Umā, riding on a peacock and holding a bell and javelin (vs. 378). Exclusively his are the epithets Guha, Kumāra, Kārttikeya, Pāvaki, Mahāsena, except as Viṣṇu or Śiva appropriate them. He is son of Agni and son of Ganges, as the former is associated with the Kṛttikās and the latter with Rudra. He is Guha as a mysterious being (*sarvaguhyamaya*, 1, 137, 13). Śiva is Guha in 13, 17, 150.

Still another tradition makes Skanda the son of Revatī (3, 232, 6, *Svāheyo Revatīsutaḥ*), i. e. selects the special wives of Agni and of Kāma, as Agni, to be his mothers. Rohītaka, "a pleasant land, rich in cattle and corn and beloved by Kārttikeya" (2, 32, 4) is inhabited by the Mad-Peacock folk, Mattamayūrakas, and lies in the West, perhaps a Maurya realm (conquered by Karṇa, 3, 254, 20). The peacock is the god's invariable emblem. Skanda's birth from the Kṛttikās is explained in R 1, 37, 28 (*ṣaḍānana*, the "six-faced" god). Rām. knows also the tale of his piercing Mt. Krauñca (R 4, 43, 26 and R 6, 67, 19, as Guha). He is here Śikhigata, "riding a peacock" (R 6, 69, 30) and is armed with javelin (called Kārttikeya in R 4, 8, 22 and RG 4, 44, 72; Skanda invoked in *maṅgala*, R 2, 25, 11). His birth-place, Śaravaṇa, is where Ila became a woman (R 7, 63, 14 and 87, 10, Mahāsena as Subrahmaṇya, Schol.).

§ 164. Skanda's birth is narrated at length in 9, 43—46. Maheśvara's energy being dissipated fell on fire but merely enhanced Agni's power, who flung it as seed into Ganges. She in turn cast it upon Himavat, "adored by the immortals", and the six Kṛttikās nursed the child, who developed six mouths to suck them. He lay on a *śarastamba* of gold

end all manifestations of Umā, just as the follower of Śiva called Vīrabhadra (12, 285, 34) is only a local genius raised eventually to be a form of Śiva with four, sixteen, or two thousand hands (ib.), and as Khāṇḍoba is now a form of Śiva (ib. p. 724).

(the mountain then became golden). Apsarasas danced about the child and the gods adored it, as Bṛhaspati performed the birth-rites. Fourfold Veda and Dhanur-Veda and Music attended him. He approached Rudra (Śiva, deveśa, pinākin) in the form of Skanda; Umā, daughter of Girivara (Himavat), as Viśākha; Agni, as Śākha (vāyumūrti, in wind-form); Ganges, as Naigameya (thus caturmūrti, 9, 44, 37). His birth-place is old (Pāṇ. 6, 3, 16, śareja = śaraja must refer to this). It becomes a proper name of the place, and is often alluded to, 6, 122, 3; 11, 23, 18, etc. Brahman bestowed leadership over the gods' army upon Skanda and he was installed on the Sarasvatī (9, 44, 49; consecration, ib. 45, 1 f.). He was like fire, ascetic, and endowed with Yoga power, also fair as the moon (ib. 44, 17 f.). His attendants resemble those of Śiva, malformed animal-headed sprites and the seven hosts of Mothers, fiends of varied vindictiveness. Several Tīrthas celebrate him (3, 83, 165; 84, 145; 85, 60). Allusions to Kārttikeya as senāpati are common (5, 165, 7; 6, 50, 33, etc.). His six faces, ṣaṇmukha, ṣaḍvaktra, ṣaḍānana, are transferred (epithet) to Śiva but seem to be original with Skanda as Kārttikeya. His birth was due primarily to the need of leader in the Tārakāmaya war, where he crushed the gods opposed, as he slew demons, even Mahiṣa, who was slain by other gods also but assigned to Skanda (8, 5, 57; cf. 7, 166, 16, Mahiṣaṃ ṣaṇmukho yathā). He is twelve-armed (12, 122, 32). His peacock is his battle-emblem. Karṇa's son Vṛṣasena (a Maurya name) has as standard a peacock which stood "as if about to crow, like that of Skanda" (7, 105, 17). He is known as disperser of the Āsurī pṛtanā, either as Kārttikeya, Pāvaki, Mahāsena, or Skanda (7, 159, 43; 9, 6, 20 f.). The later epic relates that when challenged to raise his spear Prahlāda failed; only Viṣṇu could move it; none could brandish it (12, 328, 8 f.). Gifts at his birth were given by the gods: Garuḍa gave him the peacock; Aruṇa, a fiery cock; the Moon, a sheep; Rākṣasas, a boar and buffalo; Agni, a goat, etc. So he grew up and killed Tāraka (13, 86, 11 f.; ṣaḍānana, dviṣaḍakṣa, dvādaśabhuja, ib. 86, 18 f.). His names are derived from the circumstances of his birth (ib. 86, 14, skannatvāt Skandatāṃ prāpto guhāvāsād Guho 'bhavat). He lives where Sarasvatī appears at Plakṣarāja (or under such a tree, 9, 43, 49). On the relation between Skanda and Agni (§ 49 f.) see 13, 84, 78 f., where Rudra's seed falling on Agni produces Kāma, Love as form of eternal Will: sanātano hi saṃkalpaḥ Kāma ity abhidhīyate (ib. 85, 11). As Kumāra is a form of Agni and Agni is the "leaper", plavaṃga, the name Skanda, if not from the leaping goat (below), may have originated from the leaping (skand) of his "son". Cf. 2, 31, 44, where Fire is invoked as plavaṃgaḥ .. Kumārasūḥ. In H 9814 f., Skanda protects Bāṇa, who is "friend of Rudra and Skanda". Compare 1, 65, 20, Bāṇa as follower of Rudra. But in 9, 46, 90, Skanda kills Bāṇa (yet see p. 48).

§ 165. Skanda not only slew Tāraka, Mahiṣa, Tripāda, Hradodara, and Bāṇa (son of Bali), but he pierced Mt. Krauñca and split it with the dart given him by Agni (9, 46, 84; but ib. 44, given by Indra), because Bāṇa had sought refuge in that mountain. All were destroyed by the lightning flashes of the great javelin (a śaktyastra "very bright and noisy, adorned with bells") and by the noises and yawnings (jṛmbhamāṇābhiḥ) of Skanda's infernal hosts. Skanda made himself multiform. In this account Skanda is throughout the son of Agni and nothing is said of his leading one division of the army of Śiva, as in Vana, where Śiva says to him, "Guard thou the seventh Māruta-skandha" (3, 231, 55 f.). The latter passage contains his formal titles, many being Śiva's, such as Amogha, Bhūteśa, Caṇḍa, Anāmaya, Kāmajit. The rest are complimentary, "hero, glorious, swift, pure, ascetic, fair, good"; he is "dear" and "fond of Viśvāmitra and Vāsudeva"; Mayūraketu, "peacock-bannered", etc. Indra cannot kill him. As child he is śiśu, bālakrīḍanakapriya, lalita; Mātṛvatsala, as darling of the wild Mothers. None of the fifty odd epithts assign him sonship in Śiva, only making him son of Gaṅgā and Agni's wives and of Agni; but this is probably due to the passage being a laud of Agni. He is called here Ṣaṣṭhīpriya; and his play with the cock, his possession of conch and bow, his "six" hands and six faces are mentioned 3, 225, 25 f. He is not called Subrahmaṇya in any epic passage (a Southern epithet), but, like Viṣṇu, he is Brahmaṇya, Brahmeśaya, Brahmavit, and Brahmaja; as fire too he is "six-flamed", ṣaḍarcis; also he has a thousand members, heads, faces, arms, and feet (S by v. l. makes him hold ten javelins, daśaśaktidhārin); he is identified with Svāhā and Svadhā (ib. 232, 10 f.). His attendants are war-imps in 9, 45, but disease-demons, grahas, in 3, 230, 26 f. They include Pūtanā and other foes of children and of men, nightmares, fevers, etc., personified, also tree-spirits, nurses of Skanda, who are kind; but some are horrible and eat human flesh (S 3, 231, 16 f., Vṛkṣakā nāma; B Vṛddhikā). They are distributed over gods, Manes, and Saints, as Devagrahas, etc., as well as Rākṣasagrahas, Paiśācagrahas, Yakṣagrahas. Skanda here is called Kṛttikāsuta and son of Rudra, and his wife is Devasenā, sister of Daityasenā, ravished by Keśin. In defence of Devasenā, Indra wounded Keśin. Her mother was sister of Indra's mother, a daughter of Dakṣa. Indra sought a husband for Devasenā and, when Skanda was born and had conquered the world in six days, presented her to the youthful god. Bṛhaspati married them and she is his queen and has various names, Ṣaṣṭhī, Lakṣmī, Āsā, Sukhapradā, Sinīvālī, Kuhū, Sadvṛtti, Aparājitā. Śrīpañcamī is the blessed fifth day on which Śrī in person blessed him, and the sixth day also is his great day, mahātithi, because he then accomplished his aim (3, 229, 52). The account of his birth here gives a description of his six faces, one of which was that of a goat (see also Agni). Viśvāmitra first "accepted him" and performed for him the thirteen auspicious rites and instituted his worship (on the fifth day of the bright fortnight of the Kṛttikās' month). Agni, as a goat-faced naigameya, soothed and amused him. Seven Mothers guarded him, Kākī, Halimā, Mālinī, Bṛṃhitā, Āryā, Palālā, Vaimitrā (v. l. in S). Clear is here the posteriority of his relationship to Śiva: Rudrasūnuṃ tataḥ prāhur Guham, "after this they called Guha the son of Rudra" (3, 229, 28). The Vana account is mystical and late in many ways. The javelin here becomes a potency, śakti; the imps of war becomes diseases; the Mothers take the place in number as in nurture of the original mothers. Disease-demons and dog-shaped imps afflicting children are not new, but their assignment to Skanda marks a late phase. Skanda is a composite god. First there is Agni Kumāra the "ever youthful", with whom first Skanda was formally identified. On the other hand, as son of Agni, Skanda was identified with all burnings (fevers) and other afflictions. The god who represented fire and affliction was naturally associated with the troops of afflicting beings grouped about Śiva and so became "son of Śiva", the more readily as the "hidden" god of mystery was naturally associated with the hidden places of the mountains (Guha and guhya; cf. Kubera). The "holiest night" is Kārttikī (3, 182, 16). As the association of six-faced Skanda with the six mother-stars seems as old a trait as any, it may be well to derive the name Kārttikeya from the stars themselves, who are the divinity of the Sword (War) and regents directly of war, as well as those who govern the month when war begins (3, 230, 11, S has śakaṭākāram for saptaśīrṣam; cf. 12, 166, 82), as it sometimes does (2, 23, 29). Viśākha may derive from the fever-time beginning with the month Vaiśākha, but Śākha (unless from Viśākha) is not clear and Naigameya is not necessarily (naigameṣa) a sheep-head form. These names like Chāgavaktra come from a time when different imps were regarded as sons of the great "leaper", who eventually, as identical with Śiva, becomes "creator of gods", etc. (3, 231, 111; 232, 14f.). After Skanda's birth, the gods feared and opposed him; but then the Mothers suckled him and Agni being kind, śiva, protected him (3, 226, 26). Possible Agni as śiva may have furthered the fatherhood of Śiva, but the general agreement in nature between the fiery burning spirit of fever, love, and wounds and Śiva's own original nature had more to do with it. The native explanation of his forms is that when Indra's bolt touched Skanda, another spirit Viśākha arose from its 'entering' viśana (3, 227, 17), and that in the same way all the child-seizers (sicknesses) as Kumārakas are Skanda's children. Owing to their power over children all who desire offspring revere Svāhā as Umā and Śiva as Agni as the "goat-faced" (C 3, 14391 has Rudram Agnim; B and S have Rudram Agnimukham). Here the Chāgamukha is some "goat" form spirit identified with Skanda, who may himself be a leaping goat in his first form, obviously as goat a good genius of children (and their production), Bhadraśākha, which is called the sixth form of the god. As the goat is the animal sacred to Prajāpati as Agni, it is, so to speak, the sanctified form of the productive spirit whether as god or as demoniac power.

The attendants given by the various gods to Skanda (Jvalanasūnu and Agniputra) are mentioned in 9, 45, 30f.: Yama gave him Unmātha and Pramātha; Sūrya gave Subhrāja and Bhāsvara; Soma gave Maṇi and Sumaṇi; Agni gave Jvālājihva and Jyotis; Aṃśa gave Parigha, Vaṭa, Bhīma, Dahati, and Dahana; Vāsava, Utkrośa and Satkara or (v. l.) Pañcaka; Viṣṇu gave Cakra, Vikramaka, and Caṅkrama; the Aśvins, Vardhana and Nandhana; Dhātṛ gave five, Kunda, Kusuma, Kumuda, Ḍambara, Āḍambara; Tvaṣṭṛ gave Cakra and Anucakra (meghacakrau);[1] Mitra gave Suvrata and Satyasandha; Vidhātṛ gave Suprabha and Śubhakarman; Pūṣan gave Pāṇītaka and Kālika (or Pāṇika); Vāyu gave Bala and Atibala; Varuṇa gave Yama and Atiyama; Himavat gave Suvarcas and Ativarcas; Meru gave Kāñcana, Meghamālin, Sthira, and Atisthira; Vindhya gave Ucchṛṅga and Atiśṛṅga; Samudra gave Saṃgraha and Vigraha; Pārvatī gave Unmāda, Śaṅkukarṇa, and Puṣpadanta; Vāsuki gave two (Nāgas), Jaya and Mahājaya.[2] The Sādhyas, Rudras, Vasus, Pitṛs, Sāgaras, rivers and mountains also gave "armed overseers of the army", characteristic names of them being Kṛṣṇa, Upakṛṣṇaka, Nanda, Upanandaka, Dvādaśabhuja, Bāṇa, Meṣa, Dvādaśākṣa, Hari, Caturdaṃṣṭra, Kaliṅga, Siddhārtha, Svastika, Gāyana, Vaitālin, Kathaka, Vātika, Yajñavāha, Devayājin, Somapa, Manmathakara, Jambuka, Śambūka, and Jambūka, representing devotees, de-

[1]) S has vakrānuvakrau meṣavakrau.

[2]) S, for nāgau Jvalanasūnave has Gaṅgā-Jvalanasūnave (Vāsuki is pannageśvaraḥ); ib. 24, Brahman gives four (Nandisena, etc.).

formities, arts, and abstractions, for the most part. Kṛṣṇa and Hari as servants of Skanda betray the sectarian. Miñjika and Miñjikā form a pair of spirits begotten by Rudra and worshipped by those desiring wealth or health (3, 231, 10—15).[1])

§ 166. The union of the three highest gods into a trinity forms no part of epic belief. As said above (§ 160), the trinitarian doctrine is recognised only in one late epic passage; others do not really imply it and the aim of the later epic poets is to equalise Kṛṣṇa-Viṣṇu and Śiva as two aspects of God rather than to establish a trinity or reconcile militant factions. In fact, there seems to be no special antagonism between the two beliefs. Militant powers opposed to each other appear to hold different faiths and Śiva-worshippers scorn the claims of Kṛṣṇa to be regarded as God, but only because the claim is presented by Pāṇḍus as an excuse for political preferment. Theological animus, lacking political aims, appears to be in abeyance. The ancient catholicity of Indian thought is maintained in the epics. Both Viṣṇu and Śiva are recognised as chief gods; both eventually represent God. But the epic, cultivating a godling as Viṣṇu, naturally gave first place to Viṣṇu, and it is for this reason that the Śiva-cult appears in its extreme form (Śiva as God) as a later (literary) addition; for the passages exalting Śiva as All-God, the appendage of Śiva-worship, cult of Durgā, Gaurī, Skanda, etc., are clearly later than the passages thus exalting Kṛṣṇa-Viṣṇu, till the latest additions of all, such as the last chapters of Śānti and the interpolations in the S text, which, so to speak, again offset the Śiva-cult with the final word of the Bhāgavatas.[2])

[1]) Rudra's seed is here cast upon the mountain and produces this pair, also on the Lohitoda (Red Sea?), on sunbeams, earth, and trees, thus productive of five kinds of demons, especially worshipped, as children of Śiva and apparently also servants of Skanda, with arkapuṣpas (Calotropis gigantea, used in the Śatarudriya, ŚB. 9, 1, 1, 4, to revere Śiva).

[2]) In WZKM. 23, 151 f., and ib. 25, 355 f., Dr. Jarl Charpentier argues that the first Rudra-Śiva worshippers are to be identified with the Vrātyas, whose initiation into the orthodox cult forms a well-known Vedic ceremony. In Charpentier's opinion, they worshipped Rudra-Śiva with horrible rites and are the ancestors of the later Śivaite sects. Of this origin, which does not perhaps accord very well with the esteem in which the god was held even in Vedic literature, the epic shows no cognisance. To the Mbh. the vrātyas are simply outlawed sinners and the Rudra-Śiva worshippers are aristocrats, kings of the East as well as Kurus. On the form of Viṣṇu and Śiva cults, as also the later theology of the Great Epic, see now Sir R. G. Bhandarkar's Vaiṣṇavism, Śaivism and Minor Religious Systems, 1913 (III Bd. 6 Heft of this series). Bhandarkar shows that Vāsudeva was originally a proper name, not, as in the epic, a patronymic.

Index.

(The numbers refer to the pages.)

Additions and Corrections.

P. 5, l. 3 for wife read sister. — P. 7, l. 17 for Vṛkṣikā read Vṛkṣakā. — P. 10, l. 22 for Śaṇḍilī read Śāṇḍilī. — P. 33, l. 28 for Sudhāvatas read Sudhāvantas. — P. 56, l. 6 from below for Dhanvantari read Dhanvantara (sic.). — P. 64, l. 19 for emplasised read emphasised. — P. 64, note, last line, for devatvaṃ read devas tvaṃ. — P. 66, l. 2 from below for a witness of the world" read „witness of the world". — P. 85, l. 17 from below add In 3, 281, 7, the mouse-destroying hawk that becomes a golden bird in the sky resembles Apollo and his rat. — P. 92, middle, add With this Candravrata cf. BS. Ch. CV. — P. 92, l. 2 from below for father read „father". — P. 100, l. 11 for Dṛṣṭadyumna read Dhṛṣṭadyumna. — P. 100, l. 30 for Subhā read Śubhā. — P. 104, l. 41 und 44 for Dṛṣṭadyumna read Dhṛṣṭadyumna. — P. 106, l. 7 delete no. — P. 107, l. 10 from below for § 32 read § 37. — P. 111, l. 3 for Vama's read Yama's. — P. 114, l. 9 for Dhamarāja read Dharmarāja. — P. 121, l. 3 for Roḥinī read Rohiṇī. — P. 125, l. 1 for slew read defeated. — P. 127, l. 4 add H 8925. — P. 128, l. 13 from below for six read (six). — P. 132, last line, for son of Vairocana read son of Virocana. — P. 134, l. 5 for 8 f. read 8 b. — P. 135, last line, after references to H, add by Madhu and Hiraṇyākṣa. — P. 145, l. 32 for on Yakṣas read or Yakṣas. — P. 147, last line, add Revanta as chief Guhyaka is not epic. — P. 153, l. 23 from below for Bṛhatvan read Bṛhaddhan. — P. 156, l. 7 from below for Urmilā read Ūrmilā. — P. 157, l. 14 from below for fonnds read founds. — P. 160, in the list of Apsarasas, after Anūkā add (H). — ibid. for Varananā read Varānanā. — P. 172, l. 5 for „like immortals read „like immortals". — P. 174, l. 15 from below for Cāksuṣa read Cākṣuṣa. — P. 177, l. 14 for seven some, in read seven, some in. — ibid. l. 22 for R 59 read R 7, 59. — P. 180, l. 7 add C, Śataparvā, B and S, -parvan. — P. 183, l. 13 from below for 18 read 4 and for his read this. — P. 199, l. 10 for Danāyu read Danāyus. — ibid. l. 33 for Nanda read Nandā. — P. 200, l. 7 for Aruṇā read Aruṇa. — ibid. l. 16 for Īrāvatī read Irāvatī. — P. 203, note 2, l. 7 for § 153 read § 154. — P. 211, l. 23 add On the antiquity of the Dwarf-Avatar, cf. Macdonell, JRAS., 1895, p. 168 f. Charpentier explains Śipiviṣṭa as hairy dwarf. — P. 213, l. 5 from below for 3, 88 read 3, 188. — P. 216, l. 27 add Rādhā is unknown to the epic. — P. 222, end of l. 29 delete 1 f.

ABBREVIATIONS.

AB. = Aitareya Brāhmaṇa.
Āp. = Āpastamba.
AV. = Atharva-Veda.
B = Bombay edition of Mahābhārata.
Bṛh. Up. = Bṛhadāraṇyaka-Upaniṣad.
C = Calcutta edition of Mahābhārata.
GDS. = Gautama Dharmaśāstra.
H = Harivaṃśa.
Hit. = Hitopadeśa.
IS. = Indische Studien.
JAOS. = Journal of the American Oriental Society.
JRAS. = Journal of the Royal Asiatic Society.
M = Manu.
Muṇḍ. = Muṇḍaka-Upaniṣad.
OST. = Original Sanskrit Texts.
Praś. = Praśna-Upaniṣad.
PW. = Petersburger Wörterbuch.
R = Rāmāyaṇa, Text of Krishnacharya.
RB = Rāmāyaṇa, Bombay edition.
RG = Rāmāyaṇa, Text of Gorresio.
RV. = Rig-Veda.
S = South Indian (Kumbakonam) edition of the Mahābhārata.
ŚB. = Śatapatha-Brāhmaṇa.
SBE. = Sacred Books of the East.
ŚGS. = Śāṅkhāyana Gṛhyasūtra.
TS. = Taittirīya-Saṃhitā.
VP. = Viṣṇu-Purāṇa.
VS. = Vājasaneya-Saṃhitā.
WZKM. = Wiener Zeitschrift für die Kunde des Morgenlandes.
ZDMG. = Zeitschrift der Deutschen Morgenländischen Gesellschaft.

N.B. Figures without prefixed abbreviation refer to the Bombay edition of the Mahābhārata, designated at times, to avoid confusion, by B or Mbh. R's numbers, except in a few passages, coincide exactly or very nearly with those of RB (called C by Jacobi).

CONTENTS.